(Continued on back endsheets)

German Writers in the Age of Goethe, 1789-1832

Dictionary of Literary Biography • Volume Ninety

German Writers in the Age of Goethe, 1789-1832

Edited by
James Hardin
University of South Carolina

and
Christoph E. Schweitzer
University of North Carolina, Chapel Hill

A Bruccoli Clark Layman Book
Gale Research Inc.
Detroit, New York, Fort Lauderdale, London

Manufactured by Braun-Brumfield
Ann Arbor, Michigan
Printed in the United States of America

Copyright © 1989
Gale Research Inc.
835 Penobscot Bldg.
Detroit, MI 48226-4094

**Library of Congress Cataloging-in-
Publication Data**

German writers in the age of Goethe, 1789-1832/edited
by James Hardin and Christoph Schweitzer.
  p. cm. – (Dictionary of literary biography; v. 90)
"A Bruccoli Clark Layman book."
ISBN 0-8103-4568-4
  1. German literature–18th century–Bio-bibliography. 2.
German literature–19th century–Bio-bibliography. 3. Au-
thors, German–18th century–Biography–Dictionaries. 4.
Authors; German–19th century–Biography–Dictionaries.
I. Hardin, James N. II. Schweitzer, Christoph E., 1922-
III. Series.
PT311.G47   1989
830.9'006–dc20

[B]   89-23646

                                                       CIP

Contents

Plan of the Series

... Almost the most prodigious asset of a country, and perhaps its most precious possession, is its native literary product—when that product is fine and noble and enduring.

Mark Twain*

The advisory board, the editors, and the publisher of the *Dictionary of Literary Biography* are joined in endorsing Mark Twain's declaration. The literature of a nation provides an inexhaustible resource of permanent worth. We intend to make literature and its creators better understood and more accessible to students and the reading public, while satisfying the standards of teachers and scholars.

To meet these requirements, *literary biography* has been construed in terms of the author's achievement. The most important thing about a writer is his writing. Accordingly, the entries in *DLB* are career biographies, tracing the development of the author's canon and the evolution of his reputation.

The purpose of *DLB* is not only to provide reliable information in a convenient format but also to place the figures in the larger perspective of literary history and to offer appraisals of their accomplishments by qualified scholars.

The publication plan for *DLB* resulted from two years of preparation. The project was proposed to Bruccoli Clark by Frederick G. Ruffner, president of the Gale Research Company, in November 1975. After specimen entries were prepared and typeset, an advisory board was formed to refine the entry format and develop the series rationale. In meetings held during 1976, the publisher, series editors, and advisory board approved the scheme for a comprehensive biographical dictionary of persons who contributed to North American literature. Editorial work on the first volume began in January 1977, and it was published in 1978. In order to make *DLB* more than a reference tool and to compile volumes that individually have claim to status as lit-

erary history, it was decided to organize volumes by topic, period, or genre. Each of these freestanding volumes provides a biographical-bibliographical guide and overview for a particular area of literature. We are convinced that this organization—as opposed to a single alphabet method—constitutes a valuable innovation in the presentation of reference material. The volume plan necessarily requires many decisions for the placement and treatment of authors who might properly be included in two or three volumes. In some instances a major figure will be included in separate volumes, but with different entries emphasizing the aspect of his career appropriate to each volume. Ernest Hemingway, for example, is represented in *American Writers in Paris, 1920-1939* by an entry focusing on his expatriate apprenticeship; he is also in *American Novelists, 1910-1945* with an entry surveying his entire career. Each volume includes a cumulative index of subject authors and articles. Comprehensive indexes to the entire series are planned.

With volume ten in 1982 it was decided to enlarge the scope of *DLB*. By the end of 1986 twenty-one volumes treating British literature had been published, and volumes for Commonwealth and Modern European literature were in progress. The series has been further augmented by the *DLB Yearbooks* (since 1981) which update published entries and add new entries to keep the *DLB* current with contemporary activity. There have also been *DLB Documentary Series* volumes which provide biographical and critical source materials for figures whose work is judged to have particular interest for students. One of these companion volumes is entirely devoted to Tennessee Williams.

We define literature as the *intellectual commerce of a nation:* not merely as belles lettres but as that ample and complex process by which ideas are generated, shaped, and transmitted. *DLB* entries are not limited to "creative writers" but extend to other figures who in their time and in their way influenced the mind of a people. Thus the series encompasses historians, journalists, publishers, and screenwriters. By this means readers of *DLB* may be aided to perceive litera-

*From an unpublished section of Mark Twain's autobiography, copyright © by the Mark Twain Company.

ture not as cult scripture in the keeping of intellectual high priests but firmly positioned at the center of a nation's life.

DLB includes the major writers appropriate to each volume and those standing in the ranks immediately behind them. Scholarly and critical counsel has been sought in deciding which minor figures to include and how full their entries should be. Wherever possible, useful references are made to figures who do not warrant separate entries.

Each *DLB* volume has a volume editor responsible for planning the volume, selecting the figures for inclusion, and assigning the entries. Volume editors are also responsible for preparing, where appropriate, appendices surveying the major periodicals and literary and intellectual movements for their volumes, as well as lists of further readings. Work on the series as a whole is coordinated at the Bruccoli Clark Layman editorial center in Columbia, South Carolina, where the editorial staff is responsible for accuracy of the published volumes.

One feature that distinguishes *DLB* is the illustration policy—its concern with the iconography of literature. Just as an author is influenced by his surroundings, so is the reader's understanding of the author enhanced by a knowledge of his environment. Therefore *DLB* volumes include not only drawings, paintings, and photographs of authors, often depicting them at various stages in their careers, but also illustrations of their families and places where they lived. Title pages are regularly reproduced in facsimile along with dust jackets for modern authors. The dust jackets are a special feature of *DLB* because they often document better than anything else the way in which an author's work was perceived in its own time. Specimens of the writers' manuscripts are included when feasible.

Samuel Johnson rightly decreed that "The chief glory of every people arises from its authors." The purpose of the *Dictionary of Literary Biography* is to compile literary history in the surest way available to us—by accurate and comprehensive treatment of the lives and work of those who contributed to it.

The *DLB* Advisory Board

Foreword

DLB 90: The Age of Goethe: 1789-1832 includes articles on forty-seven German writers whose first printed work appeared in or after 1789. *DLB 94: The Age of Goethe: 1750-1789* will treat literary figures whose first work appeared before 1789. The editors are acutely aware of the fact that any attempt to place writers in presumed literary "periods" is as problematic as it is arbitrary. Nonetheless, the preparation of reference books demands lines of demarcation, and in this volume, as in the previous six *DLB* volumes on German and Austrian literature, we have seen fit to use a historical event—the French Revolution—as that most significant break between the ancien régime and the modern age. After much deliberation on the matter of the title for these volumes, we decided that "The Age of Goethe" was, with whatever inadequacies, the most appropriate description of the unprecedented German cultural efflorescence from the Sturm und Drang through Romanticism.

As in previous volumes we have made a conscious effort not only to include writers who appear in virtually every literary history—writers of unquestioned literary significance, those who are notable for their influence on contemporary writers and the broad public, and lesser talents who are especially typical of a given movement or tendency—but also unjustly neglected writers who may have received little attention either in English, or, in some cases, in German literary histories. We have also included influential cultural figures who are not known primarily as writers, such as Alexander von Humboldt.

The contributors to this volume have attempted to look at the authors with fresh eyes, to reexamine their place in the literary canon, to examine the works themselves rather than the secondary literature about them. They have also devoted special attention to the matter of the primary bibliography of each author, as in some cases it was discovered that no reliable bibliography of any kind existed. The primary bibliography at the beginning of each entry lists all first editions of the author's books in chronological order. When English translations of a work exist, the first American or British editions are listed together with the original work. The primary bibliography also lists selected periodical publications and translations into German, forewords, contributions to collections, and books edited by the author. As a result of our stress on the bibliographical aspect of each author's literary production, even the specialist will find information in some entries that was previously unavailable in English or German reference works.

The editors and contributors have attempted to present the articles in a way that will be understandable and useful. Assuming that many readers will have little or no knowledge of German, contributors have included translations of all German titles and quotations. German terms not readily understandable to a native speaker of English are also translated. Important secondary literature in both English and German is listed at the end of each entry. The locations of the letters and other papers (the *Nachlaß* to use the more specific German term) have been provided in all cases when available. The editors are grateful to the contributors and to the publisher for their efforts to provide interesting illustrations for the contributions.

James Hardin
Christoph E. Schweitzer

Acknowledgments

This book was produced by Bruccoli Clark Layman, Inc. Karen L. Rood is senior editor for the *Dictionary of Literary Biography* series. Philip B. Dematteis was the in-house editor.

Production coordinator is James W. Hipp. Systems manager is Charles D. Brower. Photography editor is Susan Todd. Layout and graphics supervisor is Penney L. Haughton. Copyediting supervisor is Bill Adams. Typesetting supervisor is Kathleen M. Flanagan. Laura Ingram, and Michael D. Senecal are editorial associates. The production staff includes Rowena Betts, Anne L. M. Bowman, Joseph M. Bruccoli, Teresa Chaney, Patricia Coate, Allison Deal, Holly Deal, Charles Lee Egleston, Sarah A. Estes, Susan C. Heath, David Marshall James, Kathy S. Merlette, Laura Garren Moore, Sheri Beckett Neal, and Jack Turner. Jean W. Ross is permissions editor.

Walter W. Ross and Jennifer Toth did the library research with the assistance of the reference staff at the Thomas Cooper Library of the University of South Carolina: Lisa Antley, Daniel Boice, Faye Chadwell, Cathy Eckman, Gary Geer, Cathie Gottlieb, David L. Haggard, Jens Holley, Jackie Kinder, Marcia Martin, Jean Rhyne, Beverly Steele, Ellen Tillett, Carol Tobin, and Virginia Weathers.

The editors express special thanks to the Goethe Institut of Chicago and the Goethe Institute of San Francisco for their assistance in securing illustrations.

Dictionary of Literary Biography • Volume Ninety

German Writers in the Age of Goethe, 1789-1832

Dictionary of Literary Biography

Ernst Moritz Arndt
(26 December 1769-29 January 1860)

Jürgen E. Schlunk
West Virginia University

SELECTED BOOKS: *Ein menschliches Wort über die Freiheit der alten Republiken* (Greifswald: Eckhardt, 1800);

Bruchstücke aus einer Reise von Baireuth bis Wien im Sommer 1789 (Leipzig: Gräff, 1801);

Bruchstücke aus einer Reise durch einen Theil Italiens im Herbst und Winter 1789 und 1799, 2 volumes (Leipzig: Gräff, 1801);

Bruchstücke einer Reise durch Frankreich im Frühling und Sommer 1799, 3 volumes (Leipzig: Gräff, 1802-1803); edited by Wolfgang Gerlach as *Pariser Sommer 1799* (Munich: Hugendubel, 1982);

Versuch einer Geschichte der Leibeigenschaft in Pommern und Rügen: Nebst einer Einleitung in die alte teutsche Leibeigenschaft (Berlin: Realschulbuchhandlung, 1803);

Germanien und Europa (Altona: Hammerich, 1803);

Gedichte (Greifswald: Eckhardt, 1803);

Der Storch und seine Familie: Eine Tragödie in drei Aufzügen. Nebst einer Zugabe (Leipzig: Gräff, 1803 [dated 1804]);

Ideen über die höchste historische Ansicht der Sprache, entwickelt in einer Rede, am hohen Geburtsfeste unsers allerdurchlauchtigsten, großmächtigsten Königs und Herrn Gustav IV. Adolfs, am 1sten November 1804 (Greifswald: Eckhardt, 1804);

Ernst Moritz Arndts Reisen durch einen Theil Teutschlands, Ungarns, Italiens und Frankreichs in den Jahren 1798 und 1799, 4 volumes (Leipzig: Gräff, 1804)—comprises *Bruchstücke aus einer Reise von Baireuth bis Wien im Sommer 1789*, *Bruchstücke aus einer Reise durch einen Theil Italiens im Herbst und Winter 1789 und 1799*,

Ernst Moritz Arndt

Bruchstücke einer Reise durch Frankreich im Frühling und Sommer 1799;

Fragmente über Menschenbildung, 2 volumes (Altona: Hammerich, 1805);

Ernst Moritz Arndt's Reise durch Schweden im Jahr 1804, 4 volumes (Berlin: Lange, 1806);

Geist der Zeit, volume 1 (Altona: Hammerich, 1806); excerpts translated by Peter Will as *Arndt's Spirit of the Times: Being the work for the publication of which the unfortunate Palm, of Erlangen, was sacrificed by Napoleon, the destroyer; containing historical and political sketches, with prognostics, relative to Spain & Portugal, Russia, Turkey, Austria, France and Bonaparte* (London: Thiselton, 1808); volume 2, anonymous (Stockholm: Sohm, 1809); volume 3, anonymous (London: Boosey, 1813; Berlin: Realschulbuchhandlung, 1814 [dated 1813]); volume 4, anonymous (Berlin: Reimer, 1818);

Der Nordische Kontrolleur, anonymous, 2 volumes (Stockholm: Lindh, 1808-1809);

Einleitung zu historischen Karakterschilderungen (Berlin: Realschulbuchhandlung, 1810);

Der Bauernstand, politisch betrachtet: Nach Anleitung des Königlich Preußischen Edikts vom 9. Oktober 1807. Mit einer Beilage, anonymous (Berlin: Schmidt, 1810);

Gedichte (Greifswald: Eckhardt, 1811);

Die Glocke der Stunde in drei Zügen (St. Petersburg: Iversen, 1812; revised edition, Königsberg: Nicolovius, 1813; revised edition, Leipzig: Rein, 1813; revised, 1814);

Kurzer Katechismus für teutsche Soldaten, nebst einem Anhang von Liedern, anonymous (St. Petersburg, 1812); revised as *Katechismus für den teutschen Kriegs- und Wehrmann, worin gelehrt wird, wie ein christlicher Wehrmann seyn und mit Gott in den Streit gehen soll* (Reichenbach: Hayn, 1813; revised edition, Cologne: Rommerskirchen, 1815);

Historisches Taschenbuch für das Jahr 1813 (St. Petersburg: Lissner, 1812); republished as *Historisches Taschenbuch für das Jahr 1814* (Königsberg: Nicolovius, 1814);

An die Preußen (Königsberg: Nicolovius, 1813);

Ueber den kriegerischen Geist der Böhmen, so wie er sich in verschiedenen Epochen wirksam bewiesen hat: Ein Beitrag zur Kriegsgeschichte der Nation, anonymous (Prague: Enders, 1813);

Aufruf an die Deutschen zum gemeinschaftlichen Kampfe gegen die Franzosen (Königsberg: Degen, 1813);

Was bedeutet Landsturm und Landwehr?, anonymous (Königsberg: Nicolovius, 1813); republished as *Was bedeutet Landsturm und Landwehr?: Nebst einer Aufforderung an teutsche Jünglinge und Männer zum Kampfe für Teutschlands Frei-*

heit von Justus Gruner Kaiserl. Rußischer Etats-Rath (Leipzig: Rein, 1813); revised as *Was bedeutet Landsturm und Landwehr?: Nebst einer Mahnung an deutsche Männer und Jünglinge in Preussens rheinischen Landen* (Cologne: Rommerskirchen, 1815);

Fünf Lieder für deutsche Soldaten (Berlin: Realschulbuchhandlung, 1813);

Zwei Worte über die Entstehung und Bestimmung der Teutschen Legion, anonymous (Königsberg: Nicolovius, 1813);

Das preußische Volk und Heer im Jahr 1813 (Leipzig: Fleischer, 1813);

Lieder für Teutsche im Jahr der Freiheit 1813 (Leipzig: Fleischer, 1813);

Ueber Volkshaß und über den Gebrauch einer fremden Sprache (Leipzig: Fleischer, 1813);

Entwurf der Erziehung und Unterweisung eines Fürsten (Berlin: Realschulbuchhandlung, 1813);

Auf Scharnhorsts Tod (Berlin: Realschulbuchhandlung, 1813);

Ueber das Verhältniß Englands und Frankreichs zu Europa (Leipzig: Fleischer, 1813);

Der Rhein, Teutschlands Strom, aber nicht Teutschlands Gränze (Leipzig: Rein, 1813);

Grundlinien einer teutschen Kriegsordnung (Leipzig: Fleischer, 1813); republished as *Bilder kriegerischer Spiele und Vorübungen* (Bonn: Weber, 1848);

Kurze und wahrhaftige Erzählung von Napoleon Bonapartens verderblichen Anschlägen, von seinen Kriegen in Spanien und Rußland, von der Zerstörung seiner Heeresmacht, und von der Bedeutung des gegenwärtigen teutschen Krieges: Ein Büchlein dem teutschen Volke zum Trost und zur Ermahnung gestellt, anonymous (Leipzig: Fleischer, 1813; revised edition, Frankfurt am Main: Körner, 1814);

Der heilige Kampf der Deutschen: Mit chronologischer Angabe aller Schlachten vom 27. Aug. 1812 bis zur Schlacht bei Hanau den 30. Octob. 1813, anonymous (Frankfurt am Main: Körner, 1814);

Lob teutscher Helden (Frankfurt am Main: Körner, 1814; enlarged edition, Cologne: Rommerskirchen, 1815);

Ueber Sitte, Mode und Kleidertracht: Ein Wort aus der Zeit (Frankfurt am Main: Körner, 1814);

Ueber künftige ständische Verfassungen in Teutschland (Frankfurt am Main: Körner, 1814);

Noch ein Wort über die Franzosen und über uns (Leipzig: Rein, 1814);

Friedrich August, König von Sachsen, und sein Volk, im Jahr 1813, anonymous (Frankfurt am Main: Eichenberg, 1814);

Ein Wort über die Feier der Leipziger Schlacht (Frankfurt am Main: Eichenberg, 1814);

Entwurf einer teutschen Gesellschaft (Frankfurt am Main: Eichenberg, 1814);

Die Regenten und die Regierten: Dem Congresse zu Wien gewidmet, anonymous (N.p., 1814);

Beherzigungen vor dem Wiener Kongreß, as X.Y.Z. (Frankfurt am Main: Eichenberg, 1814);

Ansichten und Aussichten der Teutschen Geschichte: Erster Theil (Leipzig: Rein, 1814);

Fantasien für ein künftiges Teutschland, as E. von S. (Frankfurt am Main: Eichenberg, 1815);

Blick aus der Zeit auf die Zeit (Frankfurt am Main: Eichenberg, 1815 [dated 1814]);

Ueber den Bauernstand und über seine Stellvertretung im Staate (Berlin: Realschulbuchhandlung, 1815);

Das Wort von 1814 und das Wort von 1815 über die Franzosen (Frankfurt am Main: Eichenberg, 1815);

Ueber Preußens Rheinische Mark und über Bundesfestungen (Frankfurt am Main: Eichenberg, 1815);

Der Wächter: Eine Zeitschrift in zwanglosen Heften, 3 volumes (Cologne: Rommerskirchen, 1815-1816);

Zum Neuen Jahre 1816 (Cologne: Rommerskirchen, 1816);

Geschichte der Veränderung der bäuerlichen und herrschaftlichen Verhältnisse in dem vormaligen Schwedischen Pommern und Rügen vom Jahr 1806 bis zum Jahr 1816 durch E. M. Arndt als ein Anhang zu dessen im Jahr 1803 erschienenem Versuch einer Geschichte der Leibeigenschaft in Pommern und Rügen (Berlin: Reimer, 1817);

Prinz Victor von Neuwied: Eine deutsche Mähr (Neuwied: Lichtfers, 1817);

Urtheil über Friedrich den Großen (Berlin: Flittner, 1818);

Gedichte, 2 volumes (Frankfurt am Main: Eichenberg, 1818; revised and enlarged edition, Leipzig: Weidmann, 1840);

Mährchen und Jugenderinnerungen, volume 1 (Berlin: Realschulbuchhandlung, 1818; revised edition, Berlin: Reimer, 1842); volume 2 (Berlin: Reimer, 1843); selections from volume 1 translated by Anna Dabis as *Fairy Tales from the Isle of Rügen* (London: Nutt, 1896);

Von dem Wort und dem Kirchenliede nebst geistlichen Liedern (Bonn: Weber, 1818 [dated 1819]);

Erinnerungen aus Schweden: Eine Weihnachtsgabe (Berlin: Realschulbuchhandlung, 1818);

Briefe an Psychidion, oder: Ueber weibliche Erziehung (Altona: Hammerich, 1819);

Ein Wort über die Pflegung und Erhaltung der Forsten und der Bauern im Sinne einer höheren, d.h. menschlichen Gesetzgebung (Schleswig: Königliches Taubstummen-Institut, 1820);

Ein abgenöthigtes Wort aus seiner Sache, zur Beurtheilung derselben (Altenburg & Leipzig: Verlag des literarischen Comptoirs, 1821);

Nebenstunden (Leipzig: Hartknoch, 1826);

Christliches und Türkisches (Stuttgart: Franckh, 1828);

Die Frage über die Niederlande und die Rheinlande (Leipzig: Weidmann, 1831);

Mehrere Ueberschriften, nebst einer Zugabe zum Wendtschen Musenalmanach für 1832 (Leipzig: Weidmann, 1831);

Belgien und was daran hängt (Leipzig: Weidmann, 1834);

Schwedische Geschichten unter Gustav dem Dritten, vorzüglich aber unter Gustav dem Vierten Adolf (Leipzig: Weidmann, 1839);

Erinnerungen aus dem äußeren Leben (Leipzig: Weidmann, 1840); translated, with abridgments and additions, by John Robert Seeley as *The Life and Adventures of Ernst Moritz Arndt, the Singer of the German Fatherland: Compiled from the German* (London: Seeley, Jackson & Halliday, 1879; Boston: Roberts, 1879);

Versuch in vergleichender Völkergeschichte (Leipzig: Weidmann, 1843);

Wanderungen aus und um Godesberg (Bonn: Weber, 1844); revised as *Rhein- und Ahr-Wanderungen* (Bonn: Weber, 1846); edited by Hermann Kochs as *Wanderungen rund um Bonn ins Rheinische Land* (Cologne: Bachem, 1978);

Die Rheinischen ritterbürtigen Autonomen (Leipzig: Weidmann, 1844);

Ernst Moritz Arndts Schriften für und an seine lieben Deutschen: Zum ersten Mal gesammelt und durch Neues vermehrt, volumes 1-3 (Leipzig: Weidmann, 1845); volume 4 (Berlin: Weidmann, 1855);

Nothgedrungener Bericht aus seinem Leben und aus und mit Urkunden der demagogischen und antidemagogischen Umtriebe, 2 volumes (Leipzig: Weidmann, 1847);

Das verjüngte, oder vielmehr das zu verjüngende Deutschland: Ein Büchlein für den lieben Bürgers- und Bauersmann (Bonn: Marcus, 1848);

Polenlärm und Polenbegeisterung (Berlin: Hofmann, 1848);

Reden und Glossen (Leipzig: Weidmann, 1848);

Blätter der Erinnerung meistens um und aus der Paulskirche in Frankfurt (Leipzig: Weidmann, 1849);

Anklage einer Majestätsbeleidigung des großen dänischen Volkes aus dem Jahre 1845, begangen von E. M. Arndt (Leipzig: Weidmann, 1851);

Pro Populo germanico (Berlin: Reimer, 1854);

Geistliche Lieder (Berlin: Weidmann, 1855);

Vom nordischen Hausbau und Hausgeist: Ein Schreiben an Herrn Geheimen Justiz-Rath Michelsen (Jena: Frommann, 1857);

Meine Wanderungen und Wandelungen mit dem Reichsfreiherrn Heinrich Karl Friedrich von Stein (Berlin: Weidmann, 1858); edited by Rolf Weber as *Ernst Moritz Arndt: Erinnerungen 1769-1815* (Berlin: Verlag der Nation, 1985);

Kriegslied gegen die Wälschen vom Jahre 1840, jetzt brauchbar (Lahr: Schauenburg, 1859);

Gedichte: Vollständige Sammlung, mit der Handschrift des Dichters aus seinem neunzigsten Jahre (Berlin: Weidmann, 1860);

Spät erblüht! Aufgefundene Gedichte, edited by A. von Freydorf (Leipzig: Knaur, 1888);

Ernst Moritz Arndts Werke: Erste einheitliche Ausgabe seiner Hauptschriften, edited by Hugo Rösch, Heinrich Benno Meisner, and Ludwig Freytag, 6 volumes (Leipzig: Pfau, 1892-1895); enlarged as *Ernst Moritz Arndts ausgewählte Werke*, 14 volumes (Leipzig: Pfau/Magdeburg: Magdeburger Verlags-Anstalt, 1902-1909);

Ausgewählte Werke, edited by Meisner and Robert Geerds, 4 volumes (Leipzig: Hesse, 1908);

Arndts Werke, edited by August Leffson and Wilhelm Steffens, 4 volumes (Berlin, Leipzig, Vienna & Stuttgart: Bong, 1912).

OTHER: Karl Hoffmann and others, eds., *Des Teutschen Volkes feuriger Dank- und Ehrentempel oder Beschreibung wie das aus zwanzigjähriger französischer Sklaverei durch Fürsten-Eintracht und Volkskraft gerettete Teutsche Volk die Tage der entscheidenden Völker- und Rettungsschlacht bei Leipzig am 18. und 19. Oktober 1814 zum erstenmale gefeiert hat*, preface by Arndt (Offenbach: Brede, 1815);

Jahrbuch der Preußischen Rhein-Universität, edited by Arndt and August Wilhelm von Schlegel, 3 volumes (Bonn: Weber, 1819);

Sechs Stimmen über geheime Gesellschaften und Freimaurerei, contribution by Arndt (Solothurn: Typographische Gesellschaft, 1824);

Christian Gottfried Aßmann, *Das Leben eines evangelischen Predigers*, edited by Arndt (Berlin: Dümmler, 1834);

Morelly, *Grundgesetz der Natur von Diderot, nebst einer Zugabe von E. M. Arndt*, translated, with commentary, by Arndt (Leipzig: Weidmann, 1846); republished as *Gesetzbuch der natürlichen Gesellschaft, oder der wahre Geist ihrer Gesetze zu jeder Zeit übersehen oder verkannt*, edited by Werner Krauss (Berlin: Deutsche Akademie der Wissenschaften zu Berlin, 1964);

Johann Friedrich Ferdinand Delbrück, *Das Volkslied, Was ist des Deutschen Vaterland?: Würdigung desselben*, contribution by Arndt (Bonn: Marcus, 1846);

Friedrich Heinrich Jens Reiche, *Holsteins Rechte in Schleswig*, foreword by Arndt (Frankfurt am Main: Sauerländer, 1858);

Christian Georg Schütz, *Eine malerische Rheinreise: Von Köln nach Mainz*, text by Arndt (Cologne: Bachem, 1977).

PERIODICAL PUBLICATION: "Hoffnungsrede vom Jahr 1810 (Für den 7. October bestimmt, den Geburtstag des Königs von Schweden, doch nicht gehalten)," *Deutsche Vierteljahrsschrift*, 3 (1847): 281-322.

Ernst Moritz Arndt was a patriot who rallied Prussia against Napoleon's westward expansion; he was also a passionate fighter for German national unity. His historical and political writings form the core of his literary output, but he was also an inspired poet and a competent educator. Major sources of strength throughout his long life were his reliance on the wisdom of nature, iron discipline, strong Lutheran convictions, and burning love for the nascent German nation. Convinced that rationalism, which had culminated in the anarchy of the French Revolution, would undermine the political willpower of his beloved Germans, he saw it as his life's mission to awaken them from their slumber, to mobilize their patriotic feelings against Napoleon, and to work toward the creation of a nation. To these ends he resurrected values such as national pride, religious faith, loyalty, and obedience, which had been discounted in a rationalistic age. Arndt developed conservative nationalistic positions that were later misused by the monarchists of the Wilhelminian era and even more during the Third Reich.

The second of eight children, Arndt was born on 26 December 1769 in Schoritz on the isle of Rügen in the Baltic Sea, then a dependency of Sweden, to Ludwig Nikolaus Arndt and Friederike Wilhelmine Schumacher Arndt. Although his father had risen rapidly from serf to farm manager, the impressionable youth became intimately familiar with the impoverished existence of sharecropping farmers and was to devote his first major historical work, *Versuch einer Geschichte der Leibeigenschaft in Pommern und Rügen* (Prolegomena to a History of Serfdom in Pomerania and Rügen, 1803), to the fight for abolition of serfdom. Proud of his lowly birth, he made it his principle to support the rights of the politically powerless.

After private instruction at home, Arndt attended school in Stralsund, the capital of Swedish Pomerania, from 1787 to 1789. He studied theology at the University of Greifswald and the University of Jena between 1793 and 1795, but he found the prospect of a theological career stifling. He was attracted to reality and contemporary issues rather than to abstract thought, a preference that distinguishes him from the Romantics of his generation. Hungry for real life, Arndt embarked on a series of travels, often on foot, that kept him in touch with the people and provided him with the extraordinary knowledge of human nature that is evidenced in *Ernst Moritz Arndts Reisen durch einen Theil Teutschlands, Ungarns, Italiens und Frankreichs in den Jahren 1798 und 1799* (Ernst Moritz Arndt's Travels through Parts of Germany, Hungary, Italy, and France in 1798 and 1799, [1804]). He was not only highly receptive to each country's atmosphere but was also a careful observer with a keen interest in facts. His descriptions of this important historical period are still valuable.

In 1800 he became a private lecturer in history and philology at the University of Greifswald. The following year he married Charlotte Quistorp, who died shortly after the birth of their son, Karl Treu, in 1801. With his *Fragmente über Menschenbildung* (Some Thoughts on Human Education, 1805) Arndt entered the pedagogical debate that had been revived by the eminent educator and social reformer Johann Heinrich Pestalozzi. Regarding the education of young children, Arndt's trust in nature made him reject any rigid system, and he defended fantasy against rationality. For young adults, however, he recommended firm guidance and increased attention from teachers and parents as appropriate methods to raise a

superior future generation. Arndt discussed the education of girls in *Briefe an Psychidion, oder: Ueber weibliche Erziehung* (Letters to Psychidion, or: On Educating Women, 1819).

With the stupendously successful part 1 of *Geist der Zeit* (Spirit of the Times, 1806; excerpts translated as *Arndt's Spirit of the Times: Being the work for the publication of which the unfortunate Palm, of Erlangen, was sacrificed by Napoleon, the destroyer; containing historical and political sketches, with prognostics, relative to Spain & Portugal, Russia, Turkey, Austria, France and Bonaparte*, 1808)–three more parts followed in 1809, 1813, and 1818– Arndt found himself the spokesman for the budding national movement in Germany. Since the Austrian defeat at Marengo he had harbored no illusions concerning Napoleon's expansionist intentions and considered him the incarnation of absolute evil; eventually Arndt came to hate everything French. When Kaiser Franz II laid down his crown in 1806, a thousand years of the "Holy Roman Empire of the German Nation" had ended. Arndt scathingly criticized not only Germany's external enemies but even more its own citizens for their lack of resolve. To him, simple values such as love, fantasy, innocence, and a religiousness based on life's abundance were the best antidotes to a debilitating rationalism; a successful German quest for national identity required the rejection of widely cherished attainments of the Enlightenment. Arndt's position was not popular in most of Germany's states, which were heavily dependent on France. Arndt attacked the spiritual leaders of German society–the theologians, poets, critics, and philosophers–as well as the petty princes, whom he considered the true stumbling block to a united defense effort: "Ihr [Fürsten] schreiet in eurer Not zur deutschen Nation, ihr gebärdet euch, als wenn ihr an eine solche glaubtet. Verbrecher an ihr, ihr habt sie nie geglaubt, sie nie geliebt noch gekannt! Daß keine mehr da ist . . . es ist euer Werk" (You [princes] are crying out in despair for the German nation; you behave as if you believed in her. You traitors, neither have you ever believed in her nor loved and known her! That she no longer exists . . . is your doing). Hoping that a renewed Prussia might rise from the ashes of destruction, Arndt glorified war and appealed to the patriotism of the common people.

With the publication of his outspoken *Geist der Zeit* Arndt also made enemies among his Napoleon-admiring colleagues and soon found himself isolated. When Napoleon's troops ad-

The Prussian statesman Karl Freiherr vom und zum Stein,
who employed Arndt as his personal secretary and propagan-
dist (painting by Johann Christoph Rincklake, 1804)

vanced after their victories at Jena and Auer-
städt, Arndt escaped to Stockholm where he
found employment as a translator. He also edited
a new government-sponsored journal, *Der Nordische Kontrolleur* (The Nordic Controller), which
propagated anti-Napoleonic sentiments, and
wrote the second volume of *Geist der Zeit*, activities that could easily provoke revenge from the
French and their informers. When Swedish officers conspired and imprisoned their king for his
militant stance against Napoleon, Arndt could
not feel safe any longer and left Sweden under a
false name. In October of 1809 he arrived in
Trantow where he lived in hiding with relatives.
From there he ventured in disguise to Berlin,
where in December his publisher Georg Reimer
first introduced him to members of the Prussian
resistance—among them August Wilhelm Gneisenau, who had held the city of Kolberg against
the French in 1807, and Gerhard von Scharnhorst. This encounter made him consider himself
a Prussian. His previous criticism of Prussia's policy of neutrality gave way to the realization that
Prussia alone had the historical background and

political might to make itself the spearhead of German resistance against foreign domination. He
briefly returned to his former position at the University of Greifswald, but after some of his Franco-
phile colleagues prevented him from delivering
his "Hoffnungsrede vom Jahr 1810" (Speech of
Hope from the Year 1810), he tendered his resignation. Again he left for Trantow, but when the
French advanced to Pomerania, Arndt fled across
the frozen Peene river to Prussia, in which he
now placed all his hope. From Berlin he traveled
to Breslau where once again he met with Prussian patriots, including Gebhard von Blücher. In
Prague in June of 1812 Arndt received an invitation to travel to St. Petersburg to become Karl
Freiherr vom und zum Stein's personal secretary
and propagandist for the Prussian cause. Stein
had perceived the magic appeal of Arndt's literary style and his potential for reawakening Germany. The years 1812 to 1815 represent the
most productive and heroic period in Arndt's
life. He admired the Russians' willingness to
make sacrifices and considered their religious enthusiasm against Napoleon's rapacity a model for
the Germans. He proclaimed national unity to be
the religion of his time.

Arndt's rousing *Kurzer Katechismus für
teutsche Soldaten* (Brief Catechism for German Soldiers, 1812) called upon every soldier to resist
Napoleon—even against his own sovereign if the
latter surrendered the flag of the fatherland.
This advice was directed against the Confederation of the Rhine—the alliance of sixteen German
princes under French protectorate that had enabled Napoleon to consolidate his power over Central Europe—which was dissolved after the Battle
of Leipzig in October of 1813. But Arndt was
not satisfied with Napoleon's retreat beyond the
Rhine: against the prevailing sentiment he insisted on pursuing Napoleon further, effectively
arguing his point in the pamphlet *Der Rhein,
Teutschlands Strom, aber nicht Teutschlands Gränze*
(The Rhine, Germany's River, but Not Germany's Border, 1813).

After Napoleon's final defeat Arndt wanted
to maintain the momentum and consolidate the
political gains but learned that the Junkers were
not about to share their power by passing the
promised constitution. Though immensely popular, Arndt found himself treated as a criminal.
His continued agitation against the forces of restoration put him on a collision course with the authorities. Searching for peace in his private life,
in September 1817 he married Nanna Schleier-

macher, half sister of the Berlin theologian Friedrich Schleiermacher; she bore him seven children. In 1818 he was offered a professorship at the newly founded Bonn University but was suspended two years later. In the fourth volume of *Geist der Zeit* he had claimed democratic freedom and national unity as inalienable human rights, doctrines that made him suspect as a teacher and brought a warning from the Prussian king, Frederick William III. The assassination of the dramatist and Russian spy August von Kotzebue in 1819 by Karl Ludwig Sand, member of a radical student fraternity, created a climate of hysteria among the aristocratic monarchists and served as a pretext for squelching the opposition movement. Arndt became one of the first victims.

To be prohibited from teaching for the following twenty years was the severest of punishments for a man whose productivity depended on dialogue. As Arndt put it in *Erinnerungen aus dem äußeren Leben* (Memories from the Exterior Life, 1840; partially translated as *The Life and Adventures of Ernst Moritz Arndt, the Singer of the German Fatherland*, 1879): "Ich bin so geboren, daß ich sprechen und reden muß, damit meine Gefühle und Gedanken sich ordnen; ich bedarf der umrollenden und gegeneinander Funken schlagenden Kieselsteine des Gesprächs und der Rede, damit mein bißchen Geist aus mir herauskomme. Die Sperrung meines Katheders war für die Universität wohl kein Verlust, aber für mich ein Unglück . . ." (I was born a person who needs to speak and talk so that my feelings and thoughts become focused; for my limited intellect to come forth, I need conversation and dialogue which, like struck flintstones, generate sparks. The termination of my professorship may not have been a loss to the university, but for me it was a misfortune . . .). The humiliation continued even after Arndt had been suspended from his teaching position. Accused of demagoguery in February of 1821, he had to defend himself in daily hearings conducted by court-baron Pape until the summer of the following year, and the Prussian minister of police, Wittgenstein, used Arndt's case to test the limits of his personal authority: "Entweder Arndt nicht Professor oder ich nicht Minister!" (Either Arndt not a professor or I not a minister!). Growing impatient with the protracted investigation, Arndt finally began his counterattack, which led to an end of the proceedings, but not until 1826 was he informed of the official sentence, a repetition of his suspension from teaching for political reasons. Although his literary output during this period was diminished, it still demonstrates considerable diversity: it includes poems, fairy tales, philological and theological treatises, translations, biographical and historical pieces, and, naturally, political pamphlets. Even in his greatest isolation Arndt never ceased to comment on major political developments. His religion prevented him from becoming so embittered as to lose sight of his ultimate goal, and Luther's words "Und wenn die Welt voll Teufel wär . . ." (Though hordes of devils fill the land . . .) most concisely sum up Arndt's defiance during this difficult period. Adversity in fact intensified his faith and made him turn away from his earlier pantheist belief in the powers of nature toward active Protestantism. To him, Christianity demanded a secular commitment, and he accepted this demand in the face of deep distress: after his favorite son's death in 1834 he did not turn his back on the world. With his straightforward and undogmatic faith, equally removed from pietism and from spiritualism, he felt kin to virile religions that encouraged involvement with the world.

Arndt's forced hiatus ended in 1840 when he was allowed to return to his teaching post and was promptly elected president of the university. With the revolts of 1848 Arndt found himself again at the center of turbulent developments. But this time he exerted a moderating influence, directing his energies both against the anarchistic demands of the republican wing, which wanted to destroy what he considered an organically grown aristocratic power structure, and against the budding Marxist Communists, whose "Gleichmacherei" (egalitarianism) he loathed. Arndt's vision for Germany's future was the establishment of a constitutional monarchy under the Prussian king with a parliament representing all social classes. In the Prussian work ethic and strict morality he saw the guarantee for progress and economic growth.

In 1848 Arndt joined the National Assembly at Frankfurt as its oldest delegate. He received thanks and admiration for his efforts on behalf of German unity and warned the assembly against prematurely dismantling the current power structures. He resigned from the parliament in 1849 when Frederick William IV rejected the imperial crown, thus postponing indefinitely Arndt's hope for German unity. Although disappointed, he never gave up his belief that it was Prussia's eventual destiny to unite the German states. The final words of *Geist der Zeit* reflect his optimism: "Denn wenn ihr glaubet und bekennet, daß das Vaterland ein glorreiches, freies, unvergängliches Deutschland sein soll . . . so wird der Glaube die neue Zeit gebären . . ." (For if you believe and testify that the fatherland shall be a glorious, free, immortal Germany . . . then faith shall give birth to the new era . . .).

The year 1854 brought the publication of *Pro Populo germanico* (For the German Nation), a continuation of his *Geist der Zeit*. Remarkable for its clear-sighted analysis of a time no longer truly Arndt's own, the book exposes many problems of the dawning industrial age. Still putting his trust in Prussia, Arndt attacks the Junkers for their self-serving opportunism and lack of political will and independence. The sudden rise of Napoleon III and the Crimean War led him to warn against the "russischen Satan" (Russian Satan) and the "österreichische Blindschleiche" (Austrian blindworm). His nostalgic dreams of a Pan-Germanic Reich including the Scandinavian countries and the Netherlands were later eagerly exploited by the Nazis.

Of lasting impact, finally, was *Meine Wanderungen und Wandelungen mit dem Reichsfreiherrn Heinrich Karl Friedrich von Stein* (Excursions and Exchanges with Freiherr Heinrich Karl Friedrich von Stein, 1858), Arndt's lively account of the years he spent with Stein during the Wars of Liberation. No other contemporary source provides equally vivid and subtle character portraits of Stein and other Prussian patriots such as Blücher, Scharnhorst, or Gneisenau. A best-seller in its own time, the book has often been reprinted. Arndt's sympathetic picture of Stein is an expression of his hope that a prominent political figure might appear who could complete the unfinished task of making Germany a nation. When Arndt died in Bonn on 29 January 1860, the fulfillment of this hope was but a decade away.

A detached assessment of Arndt's literary accomplishments is difficult. His concern with the events of the day has overshadowed his accomplishments as a poet. Written in response to rapidly changing political realities, the poems greatly vary in quality; yet in diversity, spontaneity, and vitality they surpass those of other political poets such as Friedrich Rückert or Theodor Körner. Like Luther's church chorales, most address the collective spirit and aim for an emotional effect. A comprehensive evaluation of his lyrical output is still lacking. Hellmut Diwald has noted that Arndt's writing was not so much rooted in a balanced picture of the world as determined by politi-

cal events and by his passionate desire to change the course of history through his writings; his propagandistic intentions frequently distorted his judgment. An example is Arndt's intense hatred of the French, a tool for rousing German patriotism. Outside the historical context, such passionate hatred remains incomprehensible. Whereas East German critics have eagerly embraced Arndt to the extent that he fits their political ideology, West German critics have generally been more cautious; they have found it difficult to overcome their own ambivalence toward a nationalism that has had such tragic political consequences since Arndt's day. Although a critical edition of his works is still lacking, the most obvious testimony to Arndt's continued topicality are the two excellent bibliographies, the critical edition of his letters, and the handful of thoughtful studies which have come out since his two-hundredth birthday in 1969. This controversial figure continues to inspire the German imagination.

Letters:

Briefe an Freunde (Altona: Hammerich, 1810);

Aus Arndts Briefen, edited by Fritz Jonas, in *Preußische Jahrbücher*, 34 (1874): 589-620;

Ernst Moritz Arndt's Briefe an eine Freundin, edited by Eduard Langenberg (Berlin: Schleiermacher, 1878); revised edition, edited by Erich Gülzow (Stuttgart & Berlin: Cotta, 1928);

Briefe an Johanna Motherby, von Wilhelm von Humboldt und Ernst Moritz Arndt, edited by Heinrich Meisner (Leipzig: Brockhaus, 1893);

Ernst Moritz Arndt: Ein Lebensbild in Briefen, edited by Meisner and Robert Geerds (Berlin: Reimer, 1898);

Heimatbriefe Ernst Moritz Arndts: Aus dem Besitz und unter Mitw. von Josef Loevenich, edited by Gülzow (Greifswald: Abel, 1919);

Ernst Moritz Arndts Briefe aus Schweden an einen Stralsunder Freund, edited by Gülzow (Stralsund: Königliche Regierungs-Buchdruckerei, 1926);

Ernst Moritz Arndt: Briefe, edited by Albrecht Dühr, 3 volumes (Darmstadt: Wissenschaftliche Buchgesellschaft, 1972-1975).

Bibliographies:

Gerhard Loh, *Arndt Bibliographie: Verzeichnis der Schriften von und über Ernst Moritz Arndt* (Berlin: Deutscher Verlag der Wissenschaften, 1969);

Karl Heinz Schäfer and Josef Schawe, *Ernst Moritz Arndt: Ein bibliographisches Handbuch 1769-1969* (Bonn: Röhrscheid, 1971).

Biographies:

Heinrich Meisner, *Ernst Moritz Arndts Leben und Schaffen* (Leipzig: Hesse, 1909);

Ernst Müsebeck, *Ernst Moritz Arndt: Ein Lebensbild. Der junge Arndt. 1769-1815* (Gotha: Perthes, 1914);

Johannes Paul, *Ernst Moritz Arndt* (Göttingen, Zurich & Frankfurt am Main: Musterschmidt, 1971);

Gustav Sichelschmidt, *Ernst Moritz Arndt* (Berlin: Stapp, 1981).

References:

Otto Friedrich Bollnow, *Die Pädagogik der deutschen Romantik: Von Arndt bis Fröbel* (Stuttgart: Kohlhammer, 1952);

Paul Breitenkamp, *Künder deutscher Einheit: Das Leben Ernst Moritz Arndts* (Berlin: Haude & Spener, 1939);

Hellmut Diwald, *Ernst Moritz Arndt: Das Entstehen des deutschen Nationalbewußtseins* (Munich: Carl Friedrich von Siemens-Stiftung, 1970);

Gustav Erdmann, *Ernst Moritz Arndt: Freiheitssänger und Patriot. Zum 100. Todestag am 29. Januar 1960* (Putbus, Rügen: Cummerow & Jokiel, 1960);

L. F. Gengler, "Ernst Moritz Arndt: Ein Wegbereiter des Dritten Reiches," *Der Altherrenbund*, no. 2 (1939/1940): 101-102;

Friedrich Gundolf, *Hutten; Klopstock; Arndt: Drei Reden* (Heidelberg: Weiss, 1924);

Ingrid Hruby, *Imago Mundi: Eine Studie zur Bildungslehre Ernst Moritz Arndts* (Frankfurt am Main & Bern: Lang, 1981);

F. Oswald (pseudonym of Friedrich Engels), "Ernst Moritz Arndt," *Telegraph für Deutschland*, no. 2-5 (January 1841): 5-7; 11-12; 13-15; 18-20; reprinted in *Meisterwerke deutscher Literaturkritik II*, edited by Hans Mayer (Berlin: Rütten & Loening, 1956), pp. 239-254;

Günther Ott, *Ernst Moritz Arndt: Religion, Christentum und Kirche in der Entwicklung des deutschen Publizisten und Patrioten* (Bonn: Röhrscheid, 1966);

Hermann Pakull, ed., *Ernst Moritz Arndt und Wir: Nationalpolitische Weckrufe und Wegweisungen* (Langensalza, Berlin & Leipzig: Beltz, 1939);

Carl Petersen and Paul Hermann Ruth, eds., *Ernst Moritz Arndt: Deutsche Volkswerdung. Sein politisches Vermächtnis an die Gegenwart* (Breslau: Hirt, 1934);

Robert Piloty, *Ernst Moritz Arndt: Seine Bedeutung für die deutsche Gegenwart* (Würzburg: Perschmann, 1914);

Alfred G. Pundt, *Arndt and the Nationalist Awakening in Germany* (New York: Columbia University Press, 1935);

Paul Hermann Ruth, *Arndt und die Geschichte: Ein Beitrag zur Arndtforschung und zur Problemgeschichte des Historismus vornehmlich bis zum Ende der Befreiungskriege* (Munich & Berlin: Oldenbourg, 1930);

Karl Heinz Schäfer, *Ernst Moritz Arndt als politischer Publizist: Studien zu Publizistik, Pressepolitik und kollektivem Bewußtsein im frühen 19. Jahrhundert* (Bonn: Röhrscheid, 1974);

Johannes Schildhauer, Walter Stark, and Hildegard Schacht, eds., *1769-1969: Ernst Moritz Arndt. Festschrift zum 200. Geburtstag*, special issue of *Wissenschaftliche Zeitschrift der Ernst-Moritz-Arndt-Universität Greifswald: Gesellschafts- und Sprachwissenschaftliche Reihe*, 18, no. 1/2 (1969);

Ernst Weber, "Ernst Moritz Arndt: Versuch einer Neubewertung am Beispiel seiner *Reise durch Schweden* und seines Berichts über die Lappen," *Trajekt*, 2 (1982): 148-172;

Günther Wiegand, *Zum deutschen Rußlandinteresse im 19. Jahrhundert: E. M. Arndt und Varnhagen von Ense* (Stuttgart: Klett, 1967);

Uno Willers, *Ernst Moritz Arndt och hans svenska förbindelser: Studier i svensk-pommersk historiografi och svensk opinionsbildning* (Stockholm: Geber, 1945);

Richard Wolfram, *Ernst Moritz Arndt und Schweden: Zur Geschichte der deutschen Nordsehnsucht* (Weimar: Duncker, 1933; reprinted, Hildesheim: Gerstenberg, 1978).

Papers:

Ernst Moritz Arndt's papers are at the Akademie der Wissenschaften der DDR, Berlin, and the Stadtarchiv Bonn. The Akademie holds six boxes of biographical materials, manuscripts for three volumes of poetry, and the voluminous manuscript for *Schwedische Geschichten unter Gustav dem Dritten, vorzüglich aber unter Gustav dem Vierten Adolf.* The Stadtarchiv Bonn has thirty-nine boxes of poems, letters, and newspaper clippings. Three smaller collections of Arndt papers are at the Staatsbibliothek Preußischer Kulturbesitz, West Berlin; the Universitätsbibliothek Bonn; and the Deutsche Staatsbibliothek, East Berlin.

Achim von Arnim
(26 January 1781-21 January 1831)

Bernd Fischer
Ohio State University

BOOKS: *Versuch einer Theorie der elektrischen Erscheinungen* (Halle: Gebauer, 1799);

Hollin's Liebeleben: Roman, anonymous (Göttingen: Dieterich, 1802);

Ariel's Offenbarungen: Roman. Erstes Buch (Göttingen: Dieterich, 1804);

Kriegslieder: Erste Sammlung, anonymous (Göttingen, 1806);

Der Wintergarten: Novellen (Berlin: Realschulbuchhandlung, 1809);

Armuth, Reichthum, Schuld und Buße der Gräfin Dolores: Eine wahre Geschichte zur lehrreichen Unterhaltung armer Fräulein aufgeschrieben. Mit Melodien, 2 volumes (Berlin: Realschulbuchhandlung, 1810);

Nachtfeier nach der Einholung der hohen Leiche Ihrer Majestät der Königin: Eine Kantate, music by G. A. Schneider (Berlin: Gedruckt zum Besten der Armen, 1810; revised edition, Berlin: Realschulbuchhandlung, 1810);

Halle und Jerusalem: Studentenspiel und Pilgerabenteuer (Heidelberg: Mohr & Zimmer, 1811);

Stiftungslied der deutschen Tisch-Gesellschaft am Krönungstage, dem 18ten Januar 1811 (Berlin: Petsch, 1811);

Isabella von Aegypten, Kaiser Karl des Fünften erste Jugendliebe: Eine Erzählung; Melück Maria Blainville, die Hausprophetin aus Arabien: Eine Anekdote; Die drei liebreichen Schwestern und der glückliche Färber: Ein Sittengemälde; Angelika, die Genueserin, und Cosmus, der Seilspringer: Eine Novelle. Nebst einem Musikblatte (Berlin: Realschulbuchhandlung, 1812); "Isabella von Aegypten" condensed and translated by Carl F. Schreiber as "Isabella of Egypt," in *Fiction and Fantasy of German Romance: Selections from the German Romantic Authors, 1790-1830*, edited by Frederick E. Pierce (New York & London: Oxford University Press, 1927), pp. 171-243;

Schaubühne: Erster Band (Berlin: Realschulbuchhandlung, 1813)–comprises *Jann's erster Dienst: Posse; Der Auerhahn: Dramatische Geschichte; Das Frühlingsfest: Nachspiel; Mißver-*

Achim von Arnim *(engraving by H. Meyer; Bildarchiv der Österreichischen Nationalbibliothek, Vienna)*

ständnisse: Lustspiel; Die Befreiung von Wesel: Schauspiel; Das Loch: Schattenspiel; Hanrei und Maria: Pickelheringsspiel; Der wunderthätige Stein: Hanswurstspiel; Jemand und Niemand: Trauerspiel; Die Appelmänner: Puppenspiel;

Die Kronenwächter, erster Band: Berthold's erstes und zweites Leben. Ein Roman (Berlin: Maurer, 1817);

Die Gleichen: Schauspiel (Berlin: Maurer, 1819);

Landhausleben: Erzählungen. Erster Band (Leipzig: Hartmann, 1826)–comprises "Metamorphosen der Gesellschaft," "Holländische Liebhabereien," "Rembrandt's Versteigerung," "Wunder über Wunder," "Marino Caboga,"

"Schlußbericht, wie diese Handschrift dem Marchese überreicht wurde";

Sechs Erzählungen: Nachlaß von L. Achim von Arnim, edited by Friedrich Wilhelm Gubitz (Berlin & Königsberg: Vereins-Buchhandlung, 1835)—comprises "Frau von Saverne," "Die Einquartierung im Pfarrhause," "Die Weihnachts-Ausstellung," "Juvenis," "Fürst Ganzgott und Sänger Halbgott," "Der tolle Invalide auf dem Fort Ratonneau"; "Der tolle Invalide auf dem Fort Ratonneaü translated by William Metcalfe as "The Mad Veteran of Fort Ratonneau," in *The Blue Flower*, edited by Hermann Kesten (New York: Roy, 1946), pp. 318-335; translated by Helene Scher as "The Mad Invalid of Fort Ratonneau," in *Four Romantic Tales from Nineteenth Century German* (New York: Ungar, 1975), pp. 59-84;

Ludwig Achim's von Arnim sämmtliche Werke, edited by Wilhelm Grimm, 19 volumes (volumes 1-3, 5-8, Berlin: Veit (volume 4 never published); volumes 9-12, Grünberg & Leipzig: Levysohn; volume 13, Charlottenburg: Bauer; volumes 14-20, Berlin: Arnim, 1839-1848); revised edition, edited by Bettina von Arnim and Karl August Varnhagen von Ense, 22 volumes (Berlin: Von Arnim's Verlag, 1853-1856; revised, 21 volumes, 1857; reprinted, Hildesheim & New York: Olms, 1982);

Gedichte (Weimar: Kuhn, 1856);

Ludwig Achim von Arnim: Unbekannte Aufsätze und Gedichte. Mit einem Anhang von Clemens Brentano, edited by Ludwig Geiger (Berlin: Paetel, 1892);

Werke: Kritisch durchgesehene und erläuterte Ausgabe, edited by Julie Dohmke (Leipzig & Vienna: Bibliographisches Institut, 1892);

Arnims Werke: Auswahl, edited by Monty Jacobs, 4 volumes (Berlin, Leipzig, Vienna & Stuttgart: Bong, 1908);

Achim von Arnims Werke, edited by Reinhold Steig, 3 volumes (Leipzig: Insel, 1911);

Arnims Werke: Kritisch durchgesehene und erläuterte Ausgabe, edited by Alfred Schier (Leipzig: Bibliographisches Institut, 1925);

Dramen von Clemens Brentano und Achim von Arnim, edited by Paul Kluckhohn (Leipzig: Reclam, 1938);

Dramen von Ludwig Achim von Arnim und Joseph Freiherrn von Eichendorff, edited by Kluckhohn (Leipzig: Reclam, 1938);

Sämtliche Romane und Erzählungen, edited by Walther Migge, 3 volumes (Munich: Hanser, 1962-1965);

Gedichte von Ludwig Achim von Arnim, edited by Herbert R. Liedke and Alfred Anger (Tübingen: Niemeyer, 1976);

Die Erzählungen und Romane, edited by Hans-Georg Werner, 4 volumes (Leipzig: Insel, 1981-1984).

OTHER: "Aloys und Rose," in *Französische Miscellen*, volume 3 (Tübingen: Cotta, 1803), pp. 1-18, 74-94;

Des Knaben Wunderhorn: Alte deutsche Lieder, edited by Arnim and Clemens Brentano, 3 volumes (Heidelberg: Mohr & Zimmer, 1805 [dated 1806]-1808); selections translated by Margarete Münsterberg as "The Boy's Magic Horn," in *The German Classics of the Nineteenth and Twentieth Centuries*, edited by Kuno Francke and W. G. Howard, volume 5 (New York: German Publishing Society, 1913), pp. 163-169;

Tröst-Einsamkeit: Alte und neue Sagen und Wahrsagungen, Geschichten und Gedichte, edited by Arnim (Heidelberg: Mohr & Zimmer, 1808);

Predigten des alten Herrn Magister Mathesius über die Historien von des ehrwürdigen, in Gott seligen, theuren Manns Gottes, Doktor Martin Luthers Anfang, Lehre, Leben und Sterben: Mit einer Vorrede, edited by Arnim (Berlin: Maurer, 1817);

Christopher Marlowe, *Doktor Faustus*, translated by Wilhelm Müller, foreword by Arnim (Berlin: Maurer, 1818).

PERIODICAL PUBLICATIONS: "Was soll geschehen im Glücke: Ein unveröffentlichter Aufsatz Achim von Arnims," edited by Jörn Göres, *Jahrbuch der Deutschen Schillergesellschaft*, 5 (1961): 196-221;

"Unveröffentlichte Prosaentwürfe zur Zeitkritik Achim von Arnims um 1810," edited by Hermann F. Weiss, *Jahrbuch des Freien Deutschen Hochstifts* (1977): 251-291.

In his critical account of the Romantic movement (1836) Heinrich Heine calls Achim von Arnim a great poet and one of the most original minds of German Romanticism; he concedes, however, that Arnim has remained relatively unknown to the general public, and that even the praise of men of letters is reserved. As far as the latter are concerned, Heine suspects that Arnim was too much of a Protestant for his Catholic friends, while the Protestants thought that he was a clandestine Catholic. But why did the German public neglect an author whose writings were primarily directed toward their concerns? Heine suggests that the one thing that this poet lacks is precisely what the public looks for in books: life. The public demands that a writer sympathize with their everyday passions and that he excite their emotions, either pleasantly or painfully. Arnim fails to satisfy this need, and therefore Heine calls him a poet of death. This conclusion seems puzzling, since Arnim relied on the traditions of German popular art: the grotesque, the fantastic, the comic, the satiric, and the sentimental. But Heine's argument points out that Arnim's writings, with the exception of some of his poems, have little emotional involvement, sentimental identification, or adventurous suspense. Instead, rational principles and interests are hidden in his grotesque and fantastic settings and plots. Not satisfied with merely telling a good story, Arnim searches for allegories that will reveal historical laws.

Arnim has always been best known for *Des Knaben Wunderhorn* (excerpts translated as "The Boy's Magic Horn," 1913), a three-volume collection of folk songs and poems from various centuries which he edited with the poet Clemens Brentano from 1805 to 1808. The purpose of this venture, as Arnim explains in the afterword to the first volume, was to revitalize popular culture. For Arnim, these historical documents mirrored a tradition of cultural and social unity which Germany should strive to regain. Upon publication of the first volume, however, Arnim and Brentano's editorial principles came under attack: the collection appeared unstructured and hastily compiled; the editors, moreover, had shown no hesitation in adding romantic pathos to the allegedly orally transmitted songs and poems; as much as one-sixth of the first volume stemmed from the editors' own hands. Nevertheless, Arnim's aims were sanctioned by the success of the book among both the general public and the cultural elite. He succeeded in making a substantial amount of German folk art available not only to future poets and composers but also to the common people. To promote further his sociopolitical goal of repopularizing German folk art and its underlying social structures, Arnim founded the short-lived *Zeitung für Einsiedler* (Journal for Hermits; republished in book form as *Tröst-Einsamkeit* [Solace of Solitude, 1808]) in

1808 and retold many folktales in his first novella collection, *Der Wintergarten* (The Conservatory, 1809).

In recent years Arnim has gained increased renown as one of the most imaginative prose writers of the late Romantic movement. At the same time his reputation as a conservative Prussian aristocrat–attributed to him by nationalistic German scholars–has undergone substantial revision. Arnim's literary work and aesthetic thought are not fully comprehensible without consideration of his political involvement during the turbulent years of the Napoleonic occupation of Prussia from 1806 to 1813.

Carl Joachim Friedrich Ludwig Achim von Arnim was born in Berlin on 26 January 1781 to Joachim Erdmann von Arnim, a Prussian diplomat, and Amalie Caroline von Labes von Arnim. His mother died three weeks after his birth, and Arnim and his brother were raised by their grandmother, Caroline Marianne Elisabeth Daum von Labes. Educated in the enlightened atmosphere of the Joachimsthaler Gymnasium in Berlin, Arnim studied law and science at the universities of Halle and Göttingen from 1798 to 1801. With the publication of *Versuch einer Theorie der elektrischen Erscheinungen* (Attempt at a Theory of Electrical Phenomena, 1799) Arnim established a reputation as a gifted young scientist, and in rapid succession he published essays and reviews on magnetism, galvanism, and electricity. The obligatory European tour from 1801 to 1804 and acquaintance with Ludwig Tieck, Goethe, and Brentano, however, led the young aristocrat to turn to poetry. Skeptical of the ability of science to formulate the universal laws governing life processes by rational means, Arnim looked instead to the whimsical realm of artistic imagination in such early works as *Hollin's Liebeleben* (Hollin's Love Life, 1802), "Aloys und Rose" (1803), and *Ariel's Offenbarungen* (Ariel's Revelations, 1804). All three works radically break with the constraints of contemporary genre, interweaving fiction, drama, and poetry.

The shock of the Prussian defeats at Jena and Auerstedt on 14 October 1806 moved the young poet to participate in Prussia's political life. Arnim shared the opinion of the reformer Karl Freiherr vom Stein that a fundamental change in its political, military, and economic structures had to take place if Prussia were to liberate itself from French occupation. Arnim's many utopian ideas for reform, ranging from prostitution laws to a new education system, also find ex-

Sketches by Arnim of a title-page vignette for Des Knaben Wunderhorn *(Universitätsbibliothek Heidelberg)*

pression in his literary works. In 1811, as a forum for the various political factions, Arnim founded the Christlich-Deutsche Tischgesellschaft (Christian-German Round Table), which has often been misinterpreted by historians as pursuing ultrareactionary goals. In an essay that was rediscovered in the 1960s, "Was soll geschehen im Glücke (What Should Be Done in Fortunate Times, 1961), Arnim discusses the French Revolution: while he welcomed its goals, he disagreed with the violent form the revolution had taken and suggested that Prussia follow an evolutionary course of social transformation. At the same time he warned against changes which would serve only the interests of the merchant class and result in social unrest. Social strife such as he claimed to have observed in England stood in opposition to his utopian vision of a unified and harmonious society, which in Arnim's view could be attained by replacing the aristocracy based on birth with one based on merit. During the wars of liberation from Napoleonic occupation Arnim attempted to join the Prussian army, but he only served as a battalion captain of the Berlin veteran reserve. To Arnim's dismay, however, the Prussian king disbanded the reserve on 17 July 1813, before it was ever engaged in battle.

Partly due to his disappointment over restorative tendencies in the Prussian reform politics, Arnim and his wife, Bettina–Clemens Brentano's sister, whom Arnim had married on 11 March 1811–left the Prussian capital in 1814 for his family's estate in Wiepersdorf, forty miles south of the city. Bettina, however, could not reconcile herself to country life, and in 1817 she returned to Berlin with their four (of an eventual seven) children.

Arnim's first novel, *Armuth, Reichthum, Schuld und Buße der Gräfin Dolores* (Poverty, Wealth, Guilt and Repentance of the Duchess Dolores, 1810), constitutes a counterpart to Friedrich Schlegel's *Lucinde* (1799; translated as *Lucinda*, 1913) and Goethe's *Die Wahlverwandschaften* (1809; translated as *Elective Affinities*, 1927). The struggle between old and new in this didactic novel is symbolized by the marriage of the ill-suited couple Karl and Dolores. Karl, who occupies a stout medieval castle, stands for an enlightened and progressive aristocracy whose values are rooted in tradition; Dolores, who grew up in an extravagantly modern palace–which, however, already shows signs of decay–represents the self-centered and opportunistic modern age. Typically, Arnim does not present a character study but a panorama of thoughts on reform and historical interpretation mediated through complex symbols. The tensions between the couple are reflected on various narrative levels and through inserted stories, poems, ballads, essays, and dramatic dialogues as Arnim attempts to involve the reader in the search for ethical principles which could remedy the superficial modern thirst for pleasure.

Arnim's penchant for experimentation with form is also apparent in his dramatic works. The first half of *Halle und Jerusalem* (1811), for example, consists of a loose adaptation of Andreas Gryphius's baroque play *Cardenio und Celinde* (1657), while in the second half the dramatis personae are sent on a mystical journey to Jerusalem. The two realms are linked by the legendary figure of the Wandering Jew, Ahasver. *Schaubühne* (Stage, 1813) is a collection of experimental dramatic works, including adaptations of folk drama such as puppet and shadow plays.

Arnim's lyrical endeavors remained oriented toward a revitalization and imitation of folk songs. For a short time he worked closely with the German composers Johann Friedrich Reichardt and Louise Reichardt. It is, however, fair to say that Arnim's poetry lacks the lyrical qualities of that of his friends Brentano and Eichendorff, who have become the dominant representatives of German late Romantic poetry. It is in fiction that Arnim's talent comes to full light.

His best-known works appeared in a novella collection in 1812. The Grimm brothers were among the first to point out a chief characteristic of Arnim's narrative style: a seemingly arbitrary intertwining of fantastic motifs taken from legends and fairy tales with historical figures such as the Holy Roman Emperor Charles V. In these "Bilder im Rahmen der Geschichte" (pictures within the frame of history), as he calls his technique, Arnim attempts to capture the essential laws governing the historical eras he depicts. He is not so much concerned with the typical romantic yearning for a lost Golden Age as with analyzing the reasons behind the great epochs of upheaval and the collapse of outmoded orders. In "Isabella von Aegypten" (translated as "Isabella of Egypt," 1927), the first novella in the collection, Arnim interweaves the biography of Charles V with the magical and mythical figures of the gypsy princess Isabella, the golem, the mandrake root that is transformed into the treasure-finding dwarf Cornelius, and the soldier Bärnhäuter (Bearskin). Through these fantastic configurations he tries to convey the reasons for the collapse of the Hapsburg dynasty. The allegory signifies historical shifts in social and political structures. Charles's empire is shown to be jeopardized by the disruption of his personal relations, as represented by his obsession with the golem's sexuality. The social hierarchy of the feudal empire collapses when Charles appoints Cornelius as finance minister, since the latter's inexhaustible financial resources permit Charles to establish an absolutistic rule. The figure of Bärnhäuter foreshadows the dehumanizing consequences of alienated labor.

The second fundamental upheaval in European history, the French Revolution, is treated in the second story, "Melück Maria Blainville, die Hausprophetin aus Arabien" (Melück Maria Blainville, the House Prophetess from Arabia). Arnim portrays the revolution as a reaction to the corruption of the French aristocracy, which had lost its legitimacy as the ruling class. The fantastic elements in the narrative (Melück's magic powers) reveal the parasitic nature of the aristocracy and question its favorite art form, the classical drama–specifically, Racine's *Phèdre* (1677).

The third novella, "Die drei liebreichen Schwestern und der glückliche Färber" (The Three Lovely Sisters and the Happy Dyer), focuses on the difference between the economic success of Amsterdam and the economic backwardness of Prussia during the reign of Frederick William I. Arnim uses another fantastic figure, an alchemist, to unmask the principles of capitalist economy.

During the years in Wiepersdorf Arnim produced many socially critical and moralistic narratives which go far beyond the Romantic paradigm and treat such topics as religious politics, war, the battle of the sexes, national prejudices, and the relationship of art, politics, and history. Published in 1826, *Landhausleben* (Life at the Country Manor) combines satires, parodies, ironic idyllic treatises, and witty but moralistic accounts of social life. With "Der tolle Invalide auf dem Fort Ratonneau" (1835; translated as "The Mad Veteran of Fort Ratonneau, 1946) Arnim was one of the first to move toward the realistic style which would dominate German prose writing for the remainder of the nineteenth century.

Arnim considered the historical novel *Die Kronenwächter* (The Guardians of the Crown) his major work. The first volume appeared in 1817, and fragments of the second part were published posthumously by Bettina in his collected works (1853-1856). In the introduction Arnim presents his view of the relationship between literature and history: all ages possess laws which govern historical processes; these laws are inaccessible to those who live under them. The poetic imagination of subsequent generations, however, may succeed in divining fragments of the laws of earlier times. This insight can be used as a basis for the creation of a new historical myth which will aid understanding of the past, present, and future. Arnim's principle, to which he gives the paradoxical title "getäuschte Täuschung" (deceived deception) and which was later adopted by the French surrealists, holds that the poet is conscious of the fictitious nature of his writing, that is, of his deception. If the poet allows the creative process to be directed by the prerational associations of his fantasy, however, his poetic deception is itself deceived by a poetic truth which is a reflection of the eternal laws underlying all history. The poet, therefore, is less an autonomous creator of an ironic world (as in early romantic aesthetics) than a voice of an eternal poetry springing from life itself.

Die Kronenwächter centers around the decay of the German empire in the sixteenth century. Unbeknownst to him, Berthold, the main protagonist of the first part of the novel, has been chosen by the secret society of the crown's guardians to help prepare the way for the return of the Hohenstaufen dynasty. But instead of using the treasure he discovers to refurbish Barbarossa's decrepit castle, Berthold establishes a textile factory in one wing of the ruins. The profits from the factory soon make him wealthy, and he is elected mayor of Waiblingen. On his political journey Berthold is seduced by a desire for power which ultimately leads to ill-guided military ventures and problems in his private life. The novel investigates the role art and culture could have played in overcoming the century's social unrest. Anton, the second protagonist in the novel, is an artist. He, too, has been secretly chosen to serve the crown, and his life has been magically connected to Berthold's through the supernatural powers of the alchemist Dr. Faust. Politics without art and art without politics, according to Arnim, constitute the flaws in the culture of the sixteenth century (and, for that matter, of the nineteenth). The German crown, symbolizing Arnim's utopian concept of a harmonic society, can only be regained through cultural rejuvenation. The political activities of the crown's guardians are not legitimate, since their ultrareactionary position is anachronistic and `dangerous: they strive to recreate a utopia which they no longer understand. In this sense the novel may also be viewed as a comment on reactionary tendencies during the Prussian restoration.

Arnim's attempts to combine popular culture, art, and politics into a utopian concept of harmonious historical evolution seem to have been too experimental to have had the effect upon his contemporaries that he hoped for. His interest in reforming the political, scientific, and cultural life of his time is also manifested in his letters and in essays published in the leading journals of the day.

Arnim died at Wiepersdorf on 21 January 1831 of a stroke. He left behind an enormous oeuvre, whose literary merit has not yet been fully assessed.

Letters:

Achim von Arnim und die ihm nahe standen, edited by Reinhold Steig, 3 volumes (Stuttgart: Cotta, 1894-1913);

Achim und Bettina in ihren Briefen: Briefwechsel Achim von Arnim und Bettina Brentano, edited by Werner Vordtriede, 2 volumes (Frankfurt am Main: Suhrkamp, 1961);

"Exzerpte Achim von Arnims zu unveröffentlichten Briefen," edited by Roswitha Burwick, *Jahrbuch des Freien Deutschen Hochstifts* (1978): 298-395;

"Unveröffentlichte Briefe Achim von Arnims nebst anderen Lebenszeugnissen," edited by Hermann F. Weiss, *Literaturwissenschaftliches Jahrbuch*, 21 (1980): 89-169; 22 (1981): 71-154;

Arnims Briefe an Savigny: 1803-1831, edited by Heinz Härtl (Weimar: Böhlau, 1982);

Unbekannte Briefe von und an Achim von Arnim aus der Sammlung Varnhagen und anderen Beständen, edited by Weiss (Berlin: Duncker & Humblot, 1986).

Bibliographies:

Otto Mallon, *Arnim-Bibliographie* (Berlin: Fraenkel, 1925; reprinted, Hildesheim: Olms, 1965);

Ulfert Ricklefs, *Arnims lyrisches Werk: Register der Handschriften und Drucke* (Tübingen: Niemeyer, 1980).

Biographies:

Helene M. Kastinger Riley, *Ludwig Achim von Arnims Jugend- und Reisejahre: Ein Beitrag zur Biographie mit unbekannten Briefzeugnissen* (Bonn: Bouvier, 1978);

Riley, *Achim von Arnim in Selbstzeugnissen und Bilddokumenten* (Reinbek: Rowohlt, 1979).

References:

Herma Becker, *Achim von Arnim in den wissenschaftlichen und politischen Strömungen seiner Zeit* (Berlin & Leipzig: Rothschild, 1912);

Roswitha Burwick, "Achim von Arnim: Physiker und Poet," *Literaturwissenschaftliches Jahrbuch*, 26 (1985): 121-150;

Bernd Fischer, "Interpretation als Geschichtsschreibung: Zur poetischen Imagination Achim von Arnims," *Etudes Germaniques* (1988): 179-194;

Fischer, *Literatur und Politik: Die 'Novellensammlung von 1812' und das 'Landhausleben' von Achim von Arnim* (Bern & Frankfurt am Main: Lang, 1983);

Hans Vilmar Geppert, *Achim von Arnims Romanfragment "Die Kronenwächter"* (Tübingen: Niemeyer, 1979);

Heinrich Heine, *Die Romantische Schule* (Hamburg: Hoffmann & Campe, 1836);

Roland Hoermann, *Achim von Arnim* (Boston: Twayne, 1984);

Volker Hoffmann, "Die Arnim-Forschung 1945-1972," *Deutsche Vierteljahresschrift*, special issue (1973): 270-342;

Jürgen Knaack, *Achim von Arnim–Nicht nur Poet* (Darmstadt: Thesen, 1976);

Herbert R. Liedke, *Literary Criticism and Romantic Theory in the Works of Achim von Arnim* (New York: Columbia University Press, 1937);

Renate Moering, *Die offene Romanform von Arnims "Gräfin Dolores"* (Heidelberg: Winter, 1978);

Wolfdietrich Rasch, "Achim von Arnims Erzählkunst," *Der Deutschunterricht*, 7 (1955): 38-55;

Helene M. Kastinger Riley, "Arnims Nationaltrauerspiel 'Friedrichs Jugend': Eine dramatische Darstellung des Fluchtversuchs Friedrichs des Großen," *Jahrbuch des Freien Deutschen Hochstifts* (1976): 189-210;

Riley, *Idee und Gestaltung: Das konfigurative Strukturprinzip bei Ludwig Achim von Arnim* (Bern & Frankfurt am Main: Lang, 1977);

Thomas Sternberg, *Die Lyrik Achim von Arnims* (Bonn: Bouvier, 1983);

Hermann F. Weiss, "Achim von Arnims 'Metamorphosen der Gesellschaft,' " *Zeitschrift für deutsche Philologie*, 91 (1972): 234-251;

Hans-Georg Werner, "Zur Wirkungsfunktion des Phantastischen in Erzählungen Ludwig Achim von Arnims," *Weimarer Beiträge*, 25 (1979): 22-40;

Aimé Wilhelm, *Studien zu den Quellen und Motiven von Achim von Arnims "Kronenwächtern"* (Winterthur: Keller, 1955).

Papers:

Achim von Arnim's papers are principally held by the Freies Deutsches Hochstift, Frankfurt am Main, and the Goethe-Schiller-Museum, Weimar.

Bettina von Arnim

(4 April 1785-20 January 1859)

Helene M. Kastinger Riley
Clemson University

BOOKS: *Goethe's Briefwechsel mit einem Kinde: Seinem Denkmal,* anonymous, 3 volumes (Berlin: Dümmler, 1835); translated by Arnim and Mrs. Austin as *Goethe's Correspondence with a Child: For His Monument* (3 volumes, Berlin: Trowitzsch, 1837-1838; London: Longman, Orme, Brown, Green & Longmans, 1837-1839; 2 volumes, Lowell, Mass.: Bixby, 1841);

Die Günderode: Den Studenten, anonymous (Grünberg & Leipzig: Levysohn, 1840); partially translated by Margaret Fuller Ossoli as *Günderode* (Boston: Peabody, 1842); translation completed by Minna Wesselhoeft as *Correspondence of Fräulein Günderode and Bettina von Arnim* (Boston: Burnham, 1861);

Dédié à Spontini (Leipzig: Breitkopf & Härtel, 1843);

Dies Buch gehört dem König, anonymous, 2 volumes (Berlin: Schroeder, 1843);

Clemens Brentano's Frühlingskranz aus Jugendbriefen ihm geflochten, wie er selbst schriftlich verlangte (Charlottenburg: Bauer, 1844; reprinted, Leipzig: Reclam, 1974);

Ilius Pamphilius und die Ambrosia, 2 volumes (Leipzig & Berlin: Volckmar, 1847-1848);

An die aufgelös'te Preußische National-Versammlung: Stimmen aus Paris, as St. Albin (Paris: Massue / Berlin: Reuter & Stargardt, 1848); republished as *Polenbroschüre,* edited by Ursula Püschel (Berlin: Henschel, 1954);

Gespräche mit Daemonen (Berlin: Arnim, 1852);

Sämmtliche Schriften, 11 volumes (Berlin: Arnim, 1853); republished, 10 volumes (1857);

Bettina von Arnims sämtliche Werke, edited by Waldemar Oehlke, 7 volumes (Berlin: Propyläen, 1920-1922);

Das Leben der Hochgräfin Gritta von Rattenzuhausbeiuns, by Arnim and Gisela von Arnim, edited by Otto Mallon (Berlin: Fraenkel, 1926);

Bettina von Arnim und die Polen, edited by Jürgen Kuczynski and Ruth Krenn (Berlin: Aufbau, 1949);

Bettina Brentano in 1809, before her marriage to Achim von Arnim (etching by Ludwig Grimm)

Werke und Briefe, edited by Gustav Konrad and Joachim Müller, 4 volumes (Cologne: Bartmann, 1959-1963).

OTHER: Achim von Arnim, "Der Kaiser flieht vertrieben," music by Bettina von Arnim, in Achim von Arnim's *Armuth, Reichthum, Schuld und Buße der Gräfin Dolores,* volume 2 (Berlin: Realschulbuchhandlung, 1810), p. 389;

Ludwig Achim's von Arnim sämmtliche Werke, edited by Arnim, Wilhelm Grimm, and Karl August Varnhagen von Ense, 22 volumes (Berlin: Arnim, 1853-1856); revised, 21 volumes (1857); reprinted (Hildesheim & New York: Olms, 1982).

PERIODICAL PUBLICATIONS: "Seelied," *Zeitung für Einsiedler*, 1, no. 12 (1808): 96; "Bettina von Arnims Armenbuch," edited by Werner Vordtriede, *Jahrbuch des Freien Deutschen Hochstifts* (1962): 379-518.

Bettina von Arnim was a multitalented, spirited woman who participated in the cultural, social, economic, and political revolutions of her lifetime, recorded them in her documentary-style fictional works, and was an outspoken advocate of the disadvantaged. Like her contemporaries Goethe, E. T. A. Hoffmann, and Princess Marie Amalia, she was gifted in several of the arts: she sketched, composed songs, and designed a monument to Goethe. Her personality intrigued many and left none who knew her untouched. She was perceived by some as an enfant terrible, by others as an embodiment of the Undine, Sibyl, Psyche, or Goethe's Mignon figures. She has provided inspiration for many other writers.

Catarina Elisabetha Ludovica Magdalena Brentano, who called herself "Bettine" (but the name is frequently spelled "Bettina"), was one of twenty children of the prosperous Italian-born Frankfurt merchant Peter Anton Brentano and the seventh of his marriage to Maximiliane von La Roche. Bettina's life was molded by the literary background of her family: her grandmother Sophie von La Roche was a successful and well-known writer and a friend of Christoph Martin Wieland and Goethe. Bettina's mother charmed Goethe and found herself remembered in his *Die Leiden des jungen Werthers* (1774; translated as *The Sorrows of Werther*, 1779); Bettina returned the favor in her novel *Goethe's Briefwechsel mit einem Kinde* (1835; translated as *Goethe's Correspondence with a Child*, 1837-1838). Her brother Clemens was one of the foremost writers of the Romantic movement. After her mother's death in 1793 Brentano and her sisters were sent to the Ursuline convent in Fritzlar; after her father's death in 1797 she and her sisters Lulu and Meline were raised by her grandmother La Roche in Offenbach. Thus she barely knew her brother Clemens until 1801. They developed a close relationship, which she commemorated in *Clemens Brentano's Frühlingskranz* (Clemens Brentano's Spring Garland, 1844) after his death. The poet Caroline von Günderrode became a friend whom she later honored in her epistolary novel *Die Günderode* (1840; translated as *Correspondence of Fräulein Günderode and Bettina von Arnim*, 1861). On 11 March 1811 she married Clemens's closest friend, Ludwig

Achim von Arnim, who had become famous as the coeditor of the folk-song collection *Des Knaben Wunderhorn* (1805-1808; selections translated as "The Boy's Magic Horn," 1913). They had four sons and three daughters, of whom Friedmund, Kühnemund, Maximiliane, Armgardt, and Gisela were gifted writers. Achim and Bettina were genuinely fond of each other, although after 1817 Achim spent most of his time managing his estate in Wiepersdorf while Bettina, preferring the intellectual and social life of Berlin, lived in the city with their children. After her husband's death in 1831 Arnim embarked on her own literary career. Although she had published minor items earlier, such as "Seelied" (Lake Song, 1808) in number 12 of Achim's *Zeitung für Einsiedler*, and had composed songs such as "Der Kaiser flieht vertrieben" (The Emperor Is Driven Out), published in Achim's novel *Armuth, Reichthum, Schuld und Buße der Gräfin Dolores* (Poverty, Wealth, Guilt and Repentance of the Duchess Dolores, 1810), her full potential was reached only after her duties as a wife and mother had ceased. Her writing became politically and socially engaged in *Dies Buch gehört dem König* (This Book Belongs to the King, 1843), *An die aufgelös'te Preußische National-Versammlung* (To the Dissolved Prussian National Assembly, 1848), *Gespräche mit Daemonen* (Conversations with Demons, 1852), and "Armenbuch" (Book of the Poor, 1962). She crusaded against capital punishment, worked with the sick in the cholera epidemic of 1831, and defended the rights of Jews. With her daughters Gisela and Armgardt she coauthored several fairy tales, and with Wilhelm Grimm's help she published Achim's *Sämmtliche Werke* (Collected Works, 1853-1956).

Bettina von Arnim lived different roles at different stages of her life, to each of which she devoted herself completely: child, friend, sister, musician, wife and mother, protector of the arts, defender of the poor, and political activist. Each of these roles she commemorated in literary fashion, so that her written legacy constitutes an autobiography. The image of the child surfaces in her first book, *Goethe's Briefwechsel mit einem Kinde*, which immediately established her as a writer. In Romantic writing the symbol of the child frequently connotes the innocent, as yet unbroken, relationship of mankind with God in the beginning of time. For the impressionable Bettina, whose childhood lacked parenting, the revered poet laureate Goethe took on divine status. She visited his aged mother and spent hours writing down the anecdotes she told about her beloved son. "Seelig ist der Leib, der Dich getragen hat" (blessed is the womb that bore you), she wrote to Goethe in December 1807, drawing the parallel to Christ's mother. In June 1806 she had found a large number of letters and a poem Goethe had sent to her grandmother, in which he had spoken lovingly of her mother. With a letter of introduction from Wieland–"Sophiens Schwester, Maximilianens Tochter, Sophien La Roches Enkelin wünscht dich zu sehen" (Sophie's sister, Maximiliane's daughter, Sophie La Roche's granddaughter wishes to see you)–she met Goethe on 23 April 1807. The letters she wrote Goethe after this meeting are full of devotional symbolism, describing the lost child turning like a sunflower to its God. The fifty-seven-year-old Goethe was flattered, and before Christmas she received from him two sonnets containing some of her own phrases. "Ich ... fand mich darinn in Göttlichem Glanz wiedergebohren, und zum erstenmal glaubte ich an meine Seeligkeit" (I ... found myself reborn in [the sonnets], and for the first time I believed in my salvation), she wrote. It would not have mattered, even if she had known, that the originals went to Minchen Herzlieb, and that Goethe wrote similar sonnets with Silvie von Ziegesar in mind. It also did not matter that after a public confrontation between Bettina and Goethe's jealous wife in 1811 Goethe avoided all further contact with what he termed the crazy Arnims. He had acknowledged his creative kinship with her, and she knew that she would live on in his work as her mother and grandmother had before her.

Her first major creative work was her literary monument to Goethe (her Goethe monument in stone was begun in 1847 by Karl Steinhäuser and erected in 1853 in Weimar). The first two parts of *Goethe's Briefwechsel mit einem Kinde* contain transformed, edited, and supplemented versions of Arnim's correspondence with Goethe and his mother and describe the events, dreams, and thoughts of her daily life. The documentary base deluded many readers about the fictional character of the book. The third part of the work, titled "Tagebuch" (Diary), is a continuation of the "correspondence" begun on the day Goethe died.

The book was a literary sensation. Between its publication and April 1838 it was reviewed more than eighty times. Some, including Clemens, objected to the eroticized passages, such as the one where the (twenty-two-year-old) child sits on Goethe's lap, or the one where Goethe asks her to open her blouse to cool off. Others, recognizing the fictionalization, objected to her "lies."

The technique of using documentary material for the creation of a work of fiction remained Arnim's method for her other epistolary novels, particularly *Die Günderode* and *Clemens Brentano's Frühlingskranz*. If the Goethe book constitutes a monument to childhood in its various symbolic forms, then *Die Günderode* does the same for friendship and *Clemens Brentano's Frühlingskranz* for brotherhood. Arnim explores different kinds of love–for a parent figure, a friend, or a brother–and creates idealized relationships in which confidences, thoughts, and philosophies are exchanged. Interspersed among these memories and dreams are passages from letters and poems actually written and received. In this manner a pleasing and plausible whole is formed which differs substantially from the original correspondence. *Ilius Pamphilius und die Ambrosia* (1847-1848) displays a similar technique, but with a role reversal from the Goethe book: Arnim is the mature, influential adviser attempting to inspire Philipp Nathusius, the adoring younger man aspiring to be a writer. It is based on the correspondence of Nathusius (Pamphilius) with Arnim (Ambrosia) and was originally to have contained letters of Julius Döring (Ilius). The letters contain eroticism, but Arnim is cast as the motherly friend and benefactor which, in fact, she was.

Arnim's musical talent has not yet been sufficiently explored by scholars. She admired Ludwig van Beethoven's music, visited him in Vienna in 1810, and tried to bring Beethoven and Goethe together (the two met in Teplitz in July 1812). The book in which she preserved her musicianship, the song collection *Dédié à Spontini* (1843), contains seven of her compositions to texts by Achim von Arnim and Goethe. The collection includes only a few of the many songs she composed.

Her motherhood phase is commemorated in the fairy tales. Here, too, much research needs to be done to clarify the extent of Arnim's share in her collaborative efforts with her daughters. The fairy-tale "novel" *Das Leben der Hochgräfin Gritta von Rattenzuhausbeiuns* (The Life of the High Duchess Gritta von Rattenzuhausbeiuns, 1926) appears to be chiefly Bettina's work with Gisela's participation; other works of Gisela's may also have had Bettina's help.

After the Goethe book, the so-called Königsbuch (King's Book)—comprising *Dies Buch gehört dem König* and *Gespräche mit Daemonen*—created another sensation. Bettina was accused of being a communist because of her constant intercessions on behalf of the poor and the politically persecuted. She also supported the Hungarian and Polish uprisings and even lobbied to free H. L. Tschech, who attempted to assassinate King Friedrich Wilhelm IV on 26 July 1844; but she was not interested in political dogma or strategy. She saw poverty, censorship, and abuse all around her and, like Achim von Arnim, believed in a constitutional monarchy with a free press and substantial popular freedoms. The "Königsbuch" was intended to advise "den schlafenden König" (the sleeping king, as she called him) of the needs of his people and to inspire him to remedy abuses by his officials. This "advice" was couched in Bettina's usual poetic and visionary language, which lent itself to misinterpretation. Disappointed by the king's inaction after publication of *Dies Buch gehört dem König*, she became more specific in *Gespräche mit Daemonen*, describing the horrors of the prisons and documenting the abysmal living conditions of the poor. But the king, it was said, was like Hamlet: always talking, never doing anything.

At the height of her social and political engagement she collected statistics, pauper lists, and other materials for her "Armenbuch," which was never completed. The revolt of the poor, which she had prophesied, began with the uprising of the Silesian weavers on 4-6 June 1844. It was brutally crushed by the military, and Arnim was accused of inciting the proletariat. Knowing that publication of her book would not be permitted, she deferred work on it. Werner Vordtriede edited and published the extant materials in 1962.

Arnim's final years were devoted to the edition and publication of the collected works of her husband. In October 1854, while visiting her daughter Maximiliane in Bonn, she suffered a stroke that left her partially paralyzed, deaf, and unable to speak. It was a devastating fate for someone so active and articulate. After a slow recovery she was able to return to Berlin in December 1855 to the care of her children. She died on 20 January 1859 and was buried at her husband's side in the family grave at Wiepersdorf.

Letters:

Aus dem Nachlaß Varnhagens von Ense: Briefe von Stä-

Bettina von Arnim in 1838, with a model of her monument to Goethe (etching by Ludwig Grimm; Verwaltung der Staatlichen Schlößer und Gärten Hessen, Bad Homburg)

gemann, Metternich, Heine und Bettina von Arnim nebst Briefen, Anmerkungen und Notizen von Varnhagen von Ense, edited by Ludmilla Assing (Leipzig: Brockhaus, 1865);

Aus dem Nachlaß des Fürsten Pückler-Muskau: Briefwechsel und Tagebücher, edited by Assing, volume 1 (Hamburg: Hoffmann & Campe, 1873; reprinted, Bern: Lang, 1971);

Briefe Goethes an Sophie von La Roche und Bettina Brentano nebst dichterischen Beilagen, edited by Gustav von Loeper (Berlin: Hertz, 1879);

"Bettina von Arnim und Kanzler von Müller," in *Goethe und die Romantik: Briefe mit Erläuterungen*, part 2, volume 14, edited by C. Schüddekopf and O. Walzel (Weimar: Goethe-Gesellschaft, 1899);

Bettine von Arnim und Friedrich Wilhelm IV: Ungedruckte Briefe und Aktenstücke, edited by Ludwig Geiger (Frankfurt am Main: Rütten & Loening, 1902);

"Bettina von Arnim und ihr Briefwechsel mit Pauline Steinhäuser," edited by Karl Obser, *Neue Heidelberger Jahrbücher*, 12 (1903): 85-137;

"Aus Bettina von Arnims Briefwechsel," edited by Otto Pfülf, *Stimmen aus Maria-Laach*, 64 (1903): 437-454, 564-573; 65 (1903): 74-88;

Frauenbriefe von und an Hermann Fürsten Pückler-Muskau, edited by Heinrich Conrad (Munich & Leipzig: Müller, 1912);

Achim von Arnim und die ihm nahe standen, edited by Reinhold Steig, volume 2 (Stuttgart: Cotta, 1913);

"Bettina von Arnims Briefwechsel mit Hortense Cornu," edited by Otto Mallon, *Neue Quellen zur Geistesgeschichte des 18. und 19. Jahrhunderts* (1926): 398-408;

"Zehn ungedruckte Briefe von Bettina von Arnim und Achim von Arnim an Ludwig Emil Grimm," edited by Raimond Pissin, *Preußische Jahrbücher*, 240 (1935): 109-127;

Aus den Schätzen der Universitäts-Bibliothek zu Greifswald: Bettina von Arnim und Rudolf Baier. Unveröffentlichte Briefe und Tagebuchaufzeichnungen, edited by Kurt Gassen (Greifswald: Bamberg, 1937);

Die Andacht zum Menschenbild: Unbekannte Briefe von Bettina Brentano, edited by Wilhelm Schellberg and Friedrich Fuchs (Jena, 1942; reprinted, Bern: Lang, 1970);

Gertrud Meyer-Hepner, "Briefe und Konzepte aus den Jahren 1849-1852," *Sinn und Form*, 5, no. 1 (1953): 38-64; no. 3/4: 27-58;

"Der edelste Geist seiner Zeit: Ein bisher unveröffentlichter Brief Bettina von Arnims," *Neue literarische Welt*, 4 (25 January 1953): 16;

Bettina von Arnim in ihrem Verhältnis zu Staat und Politik: Mit einem Anhang ungedruckter Briefe (Weimar: Böhlau, 1959);

Achim und Bettina in ihren Briefen: Briefwechsel Achim von Arnim und Bettina Brentano, edited by Werner Vordtriede, 2 volumes (Frankfurt am Main: Suhrkamp, 1961);

"Bettina von Arnims Briefe an Julius Döring," edited by Vordtriede, *Jahrbuch des Freien Deutschen Hochstifts* (1963): 341-488;

"Jacob und Wilhelm Grimms Brief vom 9. Mai 1816 an Bettina von Arnim," *Jahrbuch der Sammlung Kippenberg*, new series 1 (1963): 163-168;

Karl-Heinz Hahn, " '. . . denn Du bist mir Vater und Bruder und Sohn': Bettina von Arnim im Briefwechsel mit ihren Söhnen," *Wissen-

schaftliche Zeitschrift der Friedrich-Schiller-Universität Jena*, 20, no. 3 (1971): 485-489;

Der Briefwechsel zwischen Bettine Brentano und Max Prokop von Freyberg, edited by Sibylle von Steinsdorff (Berlin & New York: De Gruyter, 1972);

"Briefe Friedrich Carl von Savignys an Bettina Brentano," edited by Heinz Härtl, *Wissenschaftliche Zeitschrift der Martin-Luther-Universität Halle-Wittenberg*, 28 (1979): 105-128;

Frauke Meyer-Gosau, " 'Liebe Freundin, es ist nicht weit her mit all den wirren Worten': Ein vertraulicher Brief der Caroline Schlegel-Schelling an Bettina von Arnim," *Alternative*, 143/144 (1982): 82-88;

Der Briefwechsel Bettine von Arnims mit den Brüdern Grimm 1838-1841, edited by Hartwig Schultz (Frankfurt am Main: Insel, 1985).

Bibliographies:

Otto Mallon, "Bibliographische Bemerkungen zu Bettina von Arnims Sämtlichen Werken," *Zeitschrift für deutsche Philologie*, 56 (1931): 446-465;

Mallon, "Bettina-Bibliographie," *Imprimatur*, 4 (1933): 141-156;

Gisela Brinker-Gabler and others, *Lexikon deutschsprachiger Schriftstellerinnen 1800-1945* (Munich: Beck, 1986), pp. 16-21.

Biographies:

Fritz Bergemann, ed., *Bettinas Leben und Briefwechsel mit Goethe: Auf Grund des von Reinhold Steig bearbeiteten handschriftlichen Nachlasses* (Leipzig: Insel, 1927);

Herbert Levin-Derwein, ed., *Die Geschwister Brentano in Dokumenten ihres Lebens* (Berlin: Fischer, 1927);

Arthur Helps and Elizabeth Jane Howard, *Bettina: A Portrait* (London: Chatto & Windus, 1957).

References:

Conrad Alberti, *Bettina von Arnim: Ein Erinnerungsblatt zu ihrem 100. Geburtstag* (Leipzig: Wigand, 1885);

Hans von Arnim, *Bettina von Arnim* (Berlin: Haude & Spener, 1963);

Elfriede Bansa, "Bettina von Arnims Verhältnis zur Kunst," Ph.D. dissertation, University of Frankfurt am Main, 1938;

Konstanze Bäumer, *"Bettine, Psyche, Mignon": Bettina von Arnim und Goethe* (Stuttgart: Heinz, 1986);

Adolf Beck, "Christoph Theodor Schwab über Bettina von Arnim: Ein briefliches Porträt 1849/1850," *Jahrbuch des Freien Deutschen Hochstifts* (1964): 366-378;

Hilde Beck, "Die Bedeutung der Natur in dem Lebensgefühl der Bettina von Arnim," Ph.D. dissertation, University of Frankfurt am Main, 1950;

Barbara Becker-Cantarino, "Priesterin und Lichtbringerin: Zur Ideologie des weiblichen Charakters in der Frühromantik," in *Die Frau als Heldin und Autorin*, edited by Wolfgang Paulsen (Bonn: Francke, 1979);

David Bellos, "Balzac and Goethe's Bettina," in *Proceedings of the 9th Congress of the Int. Comp. Lit. Association* (Innsbruck: Institut für Sprachwissenschaft der Universität Innsbruck, 1980), pp. 359-364;

Richard Benz, *Bettina schaut, erlebt, verkündet: Weibliches Wissen, Wesen, Wirken in ihrem Wort* (Munich: Piper, 1935);

Fritz Bergemann, "Neues von und über Bettina," *Jahrbuch der Sammlung Kippenberg*, 2 (1922): 285-328;

Wilhelm Berger, *Berühmte Frauen: Bettina von Arnim, Henriette Sontag, George Sand* (Berlin & Leipzig: Verlag der Frauen-Rundschau, n.d.);

Paul Beyer, "Bettinas Arbeit an 'Goethes Briefwechsel mit einem Kinde,'" in *Von deutscher Sprache und Art*, edited by Max Preitz (Frankfurt am Main: Diesterweg, 1925);

Alois Bihler, "Beethoven und 'das Kind,'" *Die Gartenlaube*, 20 (1870): 314-315;

Kurt Böttcher and Johann Mittenzwei, *Dichter als Maler* (Stuttgart: Kohlhammer, 1980), pp. 89-91;

Moritz Carrière, "Bettina von Arnim," in his *Lebensbilder: Gesammelte Werke*, volume 12 (Leipzig: Brockhaus, 1890);

Gordon A. Craig, "Romance and Reality: Bettina von Arnim and Bismarck," in his *The End of Prussia* (Madison & London: University of Wisconsin Press, 1984);

Georg Daumer, *Bettina: Gedichte aus Goethes Briefwechsel mit einem Kinde. Nebst erläuternden und vergleichenden Anmerkungen* (Nuremberg: Bauer & Raspe, 1837);

Gisela Dischner, *Bettina von Arnim: Eine weibliche Sozialbiographie aus dem 19. Jahrhundert* (Berlin: Wagenbach, 1977);

Ingeborg Drewitz, "Bettina von Arnim Portrait," *Anstöße*, 27 (1980): 48-52;

Drewitz, *Bettina von Arnim: Romantik–Revolution–Utopie* (Munich: Heyne, 1979);

Drewitz, "'Kühne Vorrednerin' der Emanzipation," *Zitty*, 7 (28 March 1985): 65;

Karl Escher, *Bettinens Weg zu Goethe* (Berlin: Runge, 1922);

Curt von Faber du Faur, "Goethe und Bettina von Arnim: Ein neuer Fund," *PMLA*, 75 (1960): 216-230;

Oscar Fambach, "Eine Brieffälschung der Bettina von Arnim als Nachklang des Beethoven-Jahres," *Deutsche Vierteljahrsschrift*, 45 (1971): 773-778;

Elke Frederiksen, "Die Frau als Autorin zur Zeit der Romantik," in *Gestaltet und gestaltend: Frauen in der deutschen Literatur*, edited by Marianne Burkhard (Amsterdam: Rodopi, 1980);

Wilhelm Frels, "Bettina von Arnims Königsbuch," Ph.D. dissertation, University of Rostock, 1912;

Leberecht Fromm, *Ruchlosigkeit der Schrift: "Dies Buch gehört dem König." Ein unterthäniger Fingerzeig gewagt von Leberecht Fromm* (Zwickau: Ullmann, 1926);

Ludwig Geiger, "Bettina von Arnim: Mitarbeiterin an einem historischen Werk," *Euphorion*, 9 (1902): 122-130;

Marjanne Elaine Goozé, "Bettina von Arnim, the Writer," Ph.D. dissertation, University of California at Berkeley, 1984;

Guido Görres, "Bettina von Arnim und Clemens Brentano," *Historisch-politische Blätter für das katholische Deutschland*, 15 (1845): 481-500, 732-746, 806-820;

Gertrud Grambow, "Bettinas Weltbild," Ph.D. dissertation, University of Berlin, 1941;

Hermann Grimm, "Bettinas letzter Besuch bei Goethe," *Deutsche Rundschau*, 87 (1896): 35-46;

Grimm, "Goethe, Minna Herzlieb und Bettina Brentano," *Preußische Jahrbücher*, 30 (1872): 591-603;

Herbert Günther, *Künstlerische Doppelbegabungen* (Munich: Heimeran, 1960);

Heinz Härtl, ed., *Bettina von Arnim: Eine Chronik: Daten und Zitate zu Leben und Werk* (Weimar: Schöpfel, 1984);

Hermann Hesse, "Goethe und Bettina," in his *Betrachtungen* (Berlin: Fischer, 1928), pp. 212-223;

Jochen Hieber, "Genauigkeit und Seele: Eine bemerkenswerte Ausstellung über Bettina von Arnim," *Frankfurter Allgemeine Zeitung*, 25 April 1985, p. 25;

Anneliese Hopfe, "Formen und Bereiche schöpferischen Verstehens bei Bettina von Arnim," Ph.D. dissertation, University of Munich, 1953;

Hans Wilhelm Kelling, "The Idolatry of Poetic Genius in 'Goethes Briefwechsel mit einem Kinde," *Publications of the English Goethe Society*, new series 39 (1969): 16-30;

Petra Kipphoff, "Außer aller Ordnung: Ausstellungen in Kassel, Frankfurt und Marburg: Bettina von Arnim und die drei Brüder Grimm," *Die Zeit*, 7 June 1985;

Friedrich Kittler, "Writing into the Wind, Bettina," translated by Marilyn Wyatt, *Glyph*, 7 (1980): 32-69;

Gustav Konrad, "Bettina von Arnim," in *Deutsche Dichter der Romantik*, edited by Benno von Wiese (Munich: Schmidt, 1971), pp. 310-340;

Paul Kühn, *Die Frauen um Goethe: Weimarer Interieurs* (Leipzig: Klinkhardt & Biermann, 1912);

Peter Küpper, "Bettina Brentano—1936," *Euphorion*, 61 (1967): 175-186;

Marianne Langewiesche, "Bettine Brentano, die erste Sozialistin," *Veröffentlichung der Evangelischen Akademie Tutzing: Jahrbuch 15* (1965/1966): 236-248;

Albert Leitzmann, "Beethoven und Bettina: Mit Benutzung ungedruckten Materials," *Deutsche Revue*, 43, no. 1 (1918): 109-119;

Heinrich Lilienfein, *Bettina: Dichtung und Wahrheit ihres Lebens* (Munich: Bruckmann, 1949);

Gabriele Lindner, " 'Natürlich geht das nächste Leben heute an': Wortmeldung zu Christa Wolfs Brief über die Bettine," *Weimarer Beiträge*, 28 (1982): 166-171;

Anneliese Löffler, "Eine Frau als Zeuge ihrer Zeit. Zum 200. Geburtstag der Bettina von Arnim," *Berliner Zeitung*, 4 April 1984, p. 7;

Gertrud Mander, *Bettina von Arnim* (Berlin: Stapp, 1982);

Doris Maurer, " 'Ich bedarf, daß ich meine Freiheit behalte': Bettina von Arnim—Zum 200. Geburtstag der Schriftstellerin," *General-Anzeiger* (Bonn), 30 March 1985;

Sylvia McCullar, " 'Ideal' versus 'Real': Womanhood as Portrayed in the Literature and Correspondence of Early Romanticism," Ph.D. dissertation, Rice University, 1979;

Gertrud Meyer-Hepner, "Bettina in Ost und West," *Neue deutsche Literatur*, 7, no. 1 (1959): 152-154;

Meyer-Hepner, "Das Bettina von Arnim-Archiv," *Sinn und Form*, 6, no. 1 (1954): 594-611;

Meyer-Hepner, "Die Differenz: Nach Bettinas Tod," *Neue deutsche Literatur*, 12, no. 3 (1964): 188-190;

Meyer-Hepner, "Ein fälschlich Bettina zugeschriebener Aufsatz," *Zeitschrift für deutsche Literaturgeschichte*, 6 (1960): 132-134;

Meyer-Hepner, *Der Magistratsprozeß der Bettina von Arnim* (Weimar: Arion, 1960);

Meyer-Hepner, "Neues über Bettina," *Neue deutsche Literatur*, 7, no. 1 (1950): 148-151;

Meyer-Hepner, "Richtigstellende Kritik: Zu einem Bettina Aufsatz," *Jahrbuch der Goethe-Gesellschaft*, new series 22 (1960): 237-239;

Werner Milch, *Bettine und Marianne* (Zurich: Artemis, 1947);

Milch, "Goethe und die Brentano," in his *Kleine Schriften zur Literatur- und Geistesgeschichte* (Heidelberg & Darmstadt: Schneider, 1957), pp. 145-155;

Milch, *Die junge Bettine 1785-1811*, edited by Peter Küpper (Heidelberg: Stiehm, 1968);

Renate Möhrmann, *Die andere Frau: Emanzipationsansätze deutscher Schriftstellerinnen im Vorfeld der Achtundvierziger-Revolution* (Stuttgart: Metzler, 1977);

Möhrmann, ed., *Frauenemanzipation im deutschen Vormärz: Texte und Dokumente* (Stuttgart: Reclam, 1980);

Elisabeth Moltmann-Wendel, "Bettina von Arnim und Schleiermacher," *Evangelische Theologie*, 31 (1971): 395-414;

Roman Nahrebecky, "Bettina von Arnim," in his *Wackenroder, Tieck, E. T. A. Hoffmann, Bettina von Arnim: Ihre Beziehung zur Musik und zum musikalischen Erlebnis* (Bonn: Bouvier, 1979), pp. 195-219;

Helge Nyssen, "Zur Soziologie der Romantik und des vormarxistischen Sozialismus in Deutschland: Bettina von Arnims soziale Ideen," Ph.D. dissertation, University of Heidelberg, 1950;

Waldemar Oehlke, *Bettina von Arnims Briefromane* (Berlin: Mayer & Müller, 1905);

Alfons Pausch, *Steuerromantik: Rund um Bettina von Arnims Hundesteuerprozeß* (Cologne: Schmidt, 1978);

Christoph Perels, ed., *Bettina von Arnim Ausstellungskatalog* (Frankfurt am Main: Goethe-Museum, 1985);

Julius Petersen, "Frau Rat und Bettina," in his *Aus der Goethezeit* (Leipzig: Quelle & Meyer, 1932);

Ernst-Ullrich Pinkert, " 'Goethes Briefwechsel mit einem Kinde' und das Ende der Kunstperiode," in his *Freiheit, die Brecht meinte: Aufsätze zur deutschen Literatur* (Aalborg: Universitetsforlag, 1980), pp. 47-59;

Ursula Püschel, "Bettinas Zorn," *Neue deutsche Literatur*, 10, no. 1 (1962): 151-153;

Püschel, *Bettina von Arnims Polenbroschüre* (Berlin: Henschel, 1954);

Püschel, "Bettina von Arnims politische Schriften," Ph.D. dissertation, Humboldt University, 1965;

Püschel, "Weibliches und Unweibliches der Bettina von Arnim," in her *Mit allen Sinnen: Frauen in der Literatur* (Halle & Leipzig: Mitteldeutscher Verlag, 1980), pp. 48-82;

Frieda Margarete Reuschle, *An der Grenze einer neuen Welt: Bettina von Arnims Botschaft vom freien Geist* (Stuttgart: Urachhaus, 1977);

Romain Rolland, *Goethe and Beethoven*, translated by G. A. Pfister and E. S. Kemp (New York & London: Blom, 1968), pp. 161-187, 199-202;

Wilhelm Schoof, "Berlin und die Brüder Grimm: Bettinas Wirken für die Berufung nach Berlin," *Zeitschrift des Vereins für die Geschichte Berlins*, 2 (1940): 49-62;

Schoof, "Goethe und Bettina Brentano: Zu Bettinas 100. Todestag," *Jahrbuch der Goethe-Gesellschaft*, new series 20 (1958): 213-224;

L. Secci, "Per un nuovo 'Gesamtbild' die Bettina von Arnim Brentano," *Studi germanici*, new series 6, no. 3 (1968): 139-176;

Ina Seidel, *Bettina* (Stuttgart: Cotta, 1944);

Adolf Stahr, *Bettina und ihr Königsbuch* (Hamburg: Verlags-Comptoir, 1844);

Reinhold Steig, "Bettina," *Deutsche Rundschau*, 72 (1892): 262-274;

Steig, "Christiane von Goethe und Bettina Brentano: Mit ungedruckten Briefen," *Jahrbuch der Goethe-Gesellschaft*, 3 (1916): 135-163;

Steig, "Drei Märchen von Bettina Brentano," *Westermanns Monatshefte*, 113 (1912): 554-558;

Selma Steinmetz, "Bettina Brentano: Persönlichkeit, Künstlertum und Gedankenwelt," Ph.D. dissertation, University of Vienna, 1931;

Helene Stöcker, "Bettina von Arnim," *Die neue Generation*, 25 (1929): 99-105;

Karl Hans Strobl, *Bettina von Arnim* (Bielefeld: Velhagen & Klasing, 1926);

Alev Tekinay, "Zum Orient-Bild Bettina von Arnims und der jungen Romantik," *Arcadia*, 16 (1981): 47-49;

Werner Vordtriede, "Der Berliner Saint-Simonismus," *Heine Jahrbuch*, 14 (1975): 93-110;

Vordtriede, "Bettina und Goethe in Teplitz," *Jahrbuch des Freien Deutschen Hochstifts* (1964): 343-365;

Vordtriede, "Bettinas englisches Wagnis," *Euphorion*, 51 (1957): 271-294;

Annalisa Wagner, "Bettina von Arnim und die preußische Zensur," *Jahrbuch für Brandenburgische Landesgeschichte*, 21 (1970): 100-128;

Karl J. Walde, "Goethes Briefwechsel mit einem Kinde und seine Beurteilung in der Literaturgeschichte," Ph.D. dissertation, University of Freiburg, 1942;

Edith Waldstein, "Bettina von Arnim and the Literary Salon," Ph.D. dissertation, Washington University, 1982;

Hans-Georg Werner, "Zur literarhistorischen Eigenart der Polenbroschüre Bettina von Arnims," *Germanica Wratislaviensia*, 34 (1978): 79-92;

Th. Wiedemann, "Leopold von Ranke und Bettina von Arnim," *Deutsche Revue*, 20, no. 2 (1895): 56-81;

Christa Wolf, " 'Kultur ist, was gelebt wird,' " *Alternative*, 143/144 (1982): 118-127;

Wolf, " 'Nun ja! Das nächste Leben geht aber heute an': Ein Brief über die Bettine," *Sinn und Form*, 32, no. 2 (1980): 392-419;

Hilde Wyss, *Bettina von Arnims Stellung zwischen der Romantik und dem jungen Deutschland* (Bern & Leipzig: Haupt, 1935);

Maria Zimmermann, "Bettina von Arnim als Dichterin," Ph.D. dissertation, University of Basel, 1958.

Papers:

Collections of Bettina von Arnim's letters and manuscripts are held by the Goethe-Museum, Frankfurt am Main; Goethe und Schiller-Archiv, Weimar; Deutsche Staatsbibliothek, Berlin; Stadt- und Universitätsbibliothek, Frankfurt am Main; and the Pierpont Morgan Library, New York.

Bonaventura

Andreas Mielke
Skidmore College

BOOK: *Nachtwachen* (Penig: Dienemann, 1804 [dated 1805]).

Editions: *Nachtwachen von Bonaventura*, edited by Alfred Meissner (Lindau & Leipzig: Ludwig, 1877);

Nachtwachen, von Bonaventura, edited by Hermann Michel (Berlin: Behr, 1904);

Die Nachtwachen von Bonaventura, edited by Franz Schultz (Leipzig: Insel, 1909);

Clemens Brentano: Nachtwachen, von Bonaventura, edited by Erich Frank (Heidelberg: Winter, 1912);

Nachtwachen, von Bonaventura, nach Rahel Varnhagens Exemplar mit einem Nachwort, edited by Raimund Steinert (Weimar: Kiepenheuer, 1915);

Nachtwachen, edited by Jørgen Hendriksen (Copenhagen: Gyldendal, 1943);

Nachtwachen. Im Anhang: Des Teufels Taschenbuch, edited by Wolfgang Paulsen (Stuttgart: Reclam, 1964);

Die Nachtwachen des Bonaventura–The Night Watches of Bonaventura, edited and translated by Gerald Gillespie (Austin: University of Texas Press, 1971; Edinburgh: University Press, 1972);

August Klingemann: Nachtwachen von Bonaventura, edited by Jost Schillemeit (Frankfurt am Main: Insel, 1974).

PERIODICAL PUBLICATIONS: "Prolog des Hanswurstes zu einer Tragödie: Der Mensch," *Zeitung für die elegante Welt*, 21 July 1804, columns 691-694;

"Einleitung: Des Teufels Taschenbuch," *Zeitung für die elegante Welt*, 26 March 1805, columns 294-296.

Title page for the first book publication of Bonaventura's novel

The most controversial book of the Age of Goethe is the satirical-nihilistic *Nachtwachen* (1804; translated as *The Night Watches of Bonaventura*, 1971) by the pseudonymous author Bonaventura. It appeared at a turning point in the history of German literature and philosophy, shortly after the young Romantics had left Jena and between the death of Immanuel Kant in 1804 (referred to in the text) and that of Friedrich Schiller in 1805. Chapter 8 of this Romantic–or anti-Romantic–"novel" appeared in Karl Spazier's respectable *Zeitung für die elegante Welt* on 21 July 1804; the book was published at the end of the year (dated 1805) by the parochial publishing house F. Dienemann as number seven in a series of new, mostly trivial, original novels. Bonaventura's only other text, the "Einleitung" (Introduction) to "Des Teufels Taschenbuch" (The Devil's Almanac), appeared in the *Zeitung für die elegante Welt* on 26 March 1805. Beyond the facts connected to these publications, nothing about Bonaventura is known.

Early evaluations of the *Nachtwachen* oscillated between praise and rejection, much as they do today. Johannes Paul Friedrich Richter (Jean Paul) recommended it as "eine treffliche Nachahmung" (an excellent imitation) of his own "Des Luftschiffers Giannozzo Seebuch" (The Airship Pilot Giannozzo's Logbook), a satirical-nihilistic appendix to the first volume of his novel *Titan* (1801), and suggested the Idealist philosopher Friedrich Wilhelm Joseph Schelling as the author; in 1802 Schelling had published a few poems under the popular pseudonym Bonaventura in an almanac edited by Friedrich Schlegel and Ludwig Tieck. The only known contemporary review speaks simply of humoristisch-satyrische Bruchstücke" (humoristic-satirical fragments) and "gelegentliche Herzensergießungen" (occasional outpourings of the heart). One of Schelling's students, the church historian Ernst von Lasaulx, found the work more frightening than what he called the "Faustische Poesie" (Faustian poesy) of Goethe or Byron. Questioned by Lasaulx, Schelling refused to talk about the book. An opponent of Schelling, Karl August Varnhagen von Ense, considered the book a "sin" of the young philosopher, labeling it "unreif, willkürlich, unorganisch, ebenso talentvoll, aufblitzend und versprechend, auch an Keckheit fehlt es nicht" (immature, arbitrary, inorganic, likewise talented, flashing and promising, and not without daring). In 1870 Rudolf Haym praised the work as one of the "geistreichsten Produktionen der Romantik" (most ingenious products of Romanticism) and said that it was probably not by Schelling.

Ever since, doubts and suggestions about the identity of the author along with various reevaluations have characterized the Bonaventura discussion. Some fifteen names have been mentioned so far, among them famous ones such as Clemens Brentano, E. T. A. Hoffmann, and Jean Paul, and less celebrated ones such as Friedrich Wetzel and August Klingemann. Bonaventura was probably male, although Caroline Schlegel-Schelling and Sophie Mereau-Brentano have been suggested as possible collaborators. His publications in the *Zeitung für die elegante Welt* and by the Dienemann publishing house connect him with Saxony. The actual places of his origin or literary activity are unknown, but Bamberg, Erfurt, and Braunschweig have been suggested as models for the setting of the vigils.

Satirical asides directed at writers and philosophers in Weimar and Jena indicate a person with inside knowledge; most interpretations, however, presuppose an outsider. His extensive reading and references to pre-Romantic ethical discussions make it safe to assume that he was probably not very young. He drew easily from all sorts of texts, ancient and modern, sublime and trivial. Bonaventura has been called Protestant since his protagonist refers to "andre ehrliche protestantische Schriftsteller" (other honest Protestant writers), and several critical references to Catholicism are included in the novel. These considerations are, of course, not conclusive: the author Bonaventura ought not to be confused with his creation, the protagonist and narrator of the *Nachtwachen*, the foundling, apprentice, satirist, prisoner, minstrel, inmate of an insane asylum, puppeteer, and night watchman Kreuzgang. Tensions have been observed even between narrator and narrated self.

The seemingly chaotic book is divided into sixteen chapters, called "Nachtwachen," somewhat resembling the structure of the chapters in the five books of Juvenal. They are not arranged in a chronological order corresponding to the watches of the night. The table of contents gives one to four subtitles for each chapter. One can observe, according to Jeffrey L. Sammons, five "successive circles, each moving from satire to nihilism." The contents of the chapters overlap, with main motifs being reflected in subsections determined by the shifting moods of the narrator. Occasional anachronisms suggest a hasty or sloppy hand. The kaleidoscopic technique, resembling Friedrich Schlegel's concept of the "arabesque," continues a tradition found in novels by Schlegel, Brentano, and Richter. Connecting leitmotivs are those of death and dying, illusion and delusion, art and nature, truth and appearance, and laughter. The Gothic atmosphere often resembles that of Edward Young's *Night Thoughts* (1742-1746). The subtext frequently indicates a radically ironic or humorous attitude.

Besides the chronological narrative of his encounters with a variety of people, Kreuzgang relates his own fragmentary memoirs. Metaphysical questions lurk behind this biography, even in seemingly straightforward satirical diatribes. The main question is: what is man? As in many Romantic texts, he learns about his origin only in the end: according to his mother, a Gypsy, he is the son of an alchemist and was conceived in the presence of the devil, who offered to be the child's "Pate" (godfather). Thus, Kreuzgang is a thoroughly unreliable narrator.

In the first chapter, titled "Der sterbende Freigeist" (The Dying Free Spirit) in the table of contents, the watchman mentions Voltaire's death; this reference connects the scene with the eighteenth-century discussion of atheism and fanaticism, a somewhat dated topic were it not for its (unmentioned) relevance to contemporary events in Jena, where the Idealist philosopher Johann Gottlob Fichte was being accused of atheism. This referential method can be observed throughout the *Nachtwachen*. During a burlesque encounter between the watchman and the devil (the priest wearing a mask), for instance, the important contemporary discussion of body and soul is introduced simply by mentioning the name of the popular Viennese phrenologist Dr. Franz Josef Gall.

Legal and ethical problems are frequently addressed. In the subchapter "Rede des steinernen Crispinus über das Kapitel de adulteriis" (Speech of the Stone Crispinus on the Chapter *de adulteriis*—the title refers to the cobbler-saint who stole for the poor) the watchman, hiding in the marketplace, overhears two adulterous lovers (Caroline Böhmer-Schlegel and Schelling?) arrange a date and witnesses the poetic Don Juan's rejection of "Moral völlig, dem Geiste der neuesten Theorien gemäss" (morality completely, according to the spirit of the newest theories). The watchman exposes the couple to the cuckolded husband (August Wilhelm Schlegel?), a cold lawyer who mechanically signs death sentences to please his wife, a lover of crime stories. All three have to listen to the watchman's biting defense of Justice.

Chapter 4 supplies background information both on Kreuzgang and on the literature favored by the adulterous wife. First, the bored narrator introduces new subtopics: two descriptions of woodcuts with mystical signs from the cabala and the third chapter of a family album written by his foster father, a cobbler. References to the two most famous German shoemakers, the poet Hans Sachs and the mystic Jakob Böhme, who had just been rediscovered by the Romantics, indicate Bonaventura's talent for literary satire. He attacks Romantic hubris, as he also does in the Introduction to "Des Teufels Taschenbuch" with a reference to Schlegel's concept of universality.

These biographical readings are interrupted by the appearance of a man who tries to stab himself but cannot proceed. (Contemporary discussions had established that the ability to commit suicide differentiates man from beast.) The watchman associates the theatrical scene with plays of Shakespeare and Aristophanes and stops short of recommending suicide for trivial German playwrights such as August von Kotzebue. The visitor tells his "Leben eines Wahnsinnigen als Marionettenspiel" (Life of a Madman as a Marionette Play) in another form of theater, the commedia dell'arte, accompanied by a Mozart symphony executed by bad village musicians (with possible but disputed references to several contemporaries). Kreuzgang retells this story in the form of a Spanish novella, a popular Romantic genre. The story echoes a tale known through Dante and Klingemann and points to a moral of biblical proportions: the slayer of his brother cannot escape his guilt and must wander about like the Eternal Jew. Kreuzgang mocks the cheap and fashionable bloody tales for ladies and easily tops them with a fundamental and universal counterexample.

In the chapter "Weltgericht" (The Judgment of the World) the watchman plays a practical joke on the town by announcing the arrival of the world's end. In an address to his fellow citizens he gives the most radical condemnation of the social and political system of his time and its representatives: brothers, princes, loan sharks, warriors, murderers, capitalists, thieves, civil servants, jurists, theologians, philosophers, fools, and so on. The powers that be silence the critic by taking his horn away, thus reducing him to a modern man, a voiceless employee mechanically punching time clocks—just invented by Samuel Day, as a footnote explains.

Kreuzgang's biography can be read as a parody of the Bildungsroman, yet the questions raised are increasingly more ontological than personal. A satirical broadsheet, "Leichenrede am Geburtstage eines Kindes" (Funeral Sermon on the Birthday of a Child), provides "comfort" by discrediting life in general. More biographical is a pasquinade in which Kreuzgang insults a man of standing; the incident leads to Kreuzgang's arrest, then to a new career as a "Bänkelsänger (wandering minstrel). He bases his sophisticated defense on contemporary theories of the aesthetic autonomy of the artist and on A. D. Weber's writings on the new idea that the law has nothing to do with morality.

In the chapter "Des Dichters Himmelfahrt" (The Poet's Ascension) a poor poet achieves a state of sublimity by hanging himself. A speech to the deceased is followed by the poet's bitter "Absagebrief an das Leben" (Rejection Letter to Life) and excerpts from his "Prologue des Hanswurstes zu der Tragödie: der Mensch" (The Clown's Prologue to the Tragedy: Man). The latter includes notes on the puppet in Goethe's *Der*

Triumph der Empfindsamkeit (Triumph of Sensitivity, 1787) and on Erasmus Darwin's *The Temple of Nature* (1803), in which apes and humans are connected in a proto-theory of evolution. (A critical report on Darwin's book had appeared in Kotzebue's journal *Der Freimüthige* of 2 March 1804; Bonaventura's satire parallels Kotzebue's mockery of such a theory.)

The discussion of evolution is followed by a powerful presentation of creationism by God himself–or rather, by an inmate in the insane asylum who believes himself to be God. He offers a thorough condemnation of man in his "Monolog des wahnsinnigen Weltschöpfers" (Monologue of the Insane Creator of the World). The inmate has "ebensogut sein konsequentes System wie Fichte und nimmt es im Grunde mit dem Menschen noch geringer als dieser" (his consistent system just as well as Fichte and basically has an even smaller opinion of man than the latter). Fichte is not the only victim of Bonaventura's satire: several inmates, representing various ideologies, are also attacked. Portraying himself as the wise fool, the narrator concludes that human wisdom is a cover hiding an incomprehensible God.

This incomprehensibility is illustrated in the five subchapters of chapter 10, especially in "Die Winternacht" (The Winter Night) and "Der Traum der Liebe" (The Dream of Love), in which life and death in nature are shown to be juxtaposed. These facts of nature are sad, to be sure; the acts of men, by contrast, are tragic: a nun is buried alive after giving birth.

In chapter 11–sometimes thought to have been written by a different author–the nun's lover, a formerly blind man, becomes the new narrator and delivers a fragmented autobiography. He tells of his love for the orphan girl his mother had adopted and promised to give to heaven should he ever see, his healing, and the simultaneous loss of his beloved. The chapter ends with the desperate cry: "Ich ertrage all das Licht und die Liebe nicht länger" (I cannot suffer all that light and love any longer).

The pettiness of the following chapter creates an embarrassing contrast. It is a clear criticism of the contemporary literary business, in which imitators lacking substantial identities wear Gotthold Lessing's "unsterbliche Perücke" (immortal wig) or claim to possess Kant's nose, Goethe's eyes, Lessing's forehead, Schiller's mouth, or the behinds of "mehrerer berühmter Männer" (several famous men). The ultimate irony occurs when the watchman offers an "Apologie des Lebens" (Apology of Life) to another imitator, a seemingly suicidal man who turns out to be a rehearsing comedian with no intention of killing himself.

On a mountaintop Kreuzgang creates an enthusiastic dithyramb on spring, only to realize the alienated position of man as the "Gedankenstrich" (hyphen) after the book of nature, "Der Titel ohne das Buch" (The Title without the Book). Rejecting the classicists' antiquity cult, Kreuzgang mocks their small artificial museum in the grand museum of nature, their "Invalidenhaus der Götter" (Infirmary of Gods). The spiteful narrator encourages the art lover to kiss the "Hintere der Venus" (Behind of Venus) and be done with antiquity.

The imitation of Shakespearean characters also leads nowhere. Back in the insane asylum, the narrator identifies with Hamlet, offers a text to the moon for sensible souls and one, which he claims to reject, to love. Nevertheless, he engages in an epistolary exchange with the inmate "Ophelia." After the discourse, and the intercourse following it, Ophelia gives birth to a stillborn child and dies. For the first time, the narrator sheds a tear; consequently, he is expelled from the asylum. A second tear is shed when Kreuzgang loses his favorite marionette, the clown, to German peasants close to the French border who are directing their revolutionary attack against these "Holzköpfe" (blockheads). This episode is less a reference to Johann Christoph Gottsched's infamous 1737 ban of the clown from the German stage than a critique of revolutionary activities directed at figureheads and not at the system.

In the final chapter, the Hogarthian "Schwanzstück" (Tail-piece; Hogarth's etching is subtitled "The Bathos"), Kreuzgang reports various dreams of immortality before he meets his parents. While his mother digs up the corpse of his alchemist father, the watchman observes a man (Novalis?) who is following his deceased beloved to the churchyard, claiming to be able to see the dead underground (a footnote cites Karl Philipp Moritz's *Magazin zur Erfahrungsseelenkunde*, a periodical devoted to empirical psychology). In an attempt at cynical materialism, Kreuzgang addresses a worm and once again associates himself with Hamlet. Finally, in an emotionally charged, iconoclastic Sturm und Drang (Storm-and-Stress) gesture, he rips apart his dead father's praying hands. Significantly, with the destruction of the symbolically religious gesture, the corpse disintegrates into "Nichts" (nothing), the lover at the

Portrait by Hugo Burath of Ernst August Friedrich Klingemann, thought by some to be the author of Nachtwachen *(Horst Flieg,* Literarischer Vampirismus: Klingemanns "Nachtwachen von Bonaventura" *[1985])*

other grave embraces nothing, and the echo resounds nothing.

The majority of readers have interpreted this threefold final "Nichts" as nihilistic, viewing the work as an "expression of existential despair" or as "illustrations of a deeper catastrophe of being." Yet it is the dubious character Kreuzgang who does not find an answer to his mercilessly radical questions; it is from *his* point of view that all of the figures, including himself, suffer from illusion and fall prey to deception. An ambiguous narrator who deceives and is deceived can hardly be taken as proof of his creator's nihilism; at most, the *Nachtwachen* represents experimental, or, according to Dieter Arendt, "poetischen Nihilismus" (poetic nihilism).

Other readers have focused on the satirical aspects, wondering why a "nihilist" would bother to write a book and to announce another one in the "Einleitung" to "Des Teufels Taschenbuch."

In addition, they have found throughout the book hints pointing to Bonaventura as a moralist. Bonaventura is an exceedingly playful writer, possibly the most powerful humorist of his time, hovering between morality and play, humanism and nihilism, laughter and agony, triviality and existential despair. The multitude of writers suggested as authors of the *Nachtwachen*, and its philosophical relationships to the works of writers such as Richter, Heinrich von Kleist, Georg Büchner, Fyodor Dostoyevski, Henrik Ibsen, and Samuel Beckett, indicate the depth of the book.

References:

Dieter Arendt, *Der "poetische Nihilismus" in der Romantik: Studien zum Verhältnis von Dichtung und Wirklichkeit in der Frühromantik* (Tübingen: Niemeyer, 1972);

Erich Wilhelm Werner Arendt, "Die Gestalt der Mutter in den 'Nachtwachen' von Bonaventura," Ph.D. dissertation, Queen's University, 1982;

John Ole Askedal, "Bonaventuras *Nachtwachen*— en kilde til Henrik Ibsens *Peer Gynt*," *Edda*, 5 (1983): 299-304;

Thomas F. Barry, "Madness and the Disoriented Self in Bonaventura's *Nightwatches*," *Journal of the Midwest Modern Language Association*, 19 (1986): 50-58;

Klaus Bartenschläger, "Bonaventuras Shakespeare: Zur Bedeutung Shakespeares für die Nachtwachen," in *Grossbritannien und Deutschland 53: Festschrift für John W. P. Bourke*, edited by Ortwin Kuhn (Munich: Goldmann, 1974), pp. 347-371;

Hubert Beckers, *Schelling's Geistesentwicklung in ihrem inneren Zusammenhang: Festschrift zu Friedrich Wilhelm Joseph Schelling's hundertjährigem Geburtstag am 27. Januar 1875* (Munich: Verlag der k. b. Akademie, 1875), pp. 72-73, 90-101;

Eduard Berend, "Der Typus des Humoristen," in *Die Ernte: Abhandlungen zur Literaturwissenschaft: Festschrift für Franz Muncker zu seinem 70. Geburtstage*, edited by Fritz Strich and Hans Borchardt (Halle: Niemeyer, 1926), pp. 93-115;

Rudolf Böttger, "Eine bisher unerkannte Satire auf Goethe und Frau von Stein," *Zeitschrift für deutsche Philologie*, 94 (1975): 256-264;

Richard Brinkmann, *Nachtwachen von Bonaventura: Kehrseite der Frühromantik* (Pfullingen: Neske, 1966);

Neil Brough and R. J. Kavanagh, "Kreuzgangs Precursors: Some Notes on the *Nachtwachen des Bonaventura*," *German Life & Letters*, new series 39 (1985-1986): 173-192;

Norman Malcolm Brown, "Critical Studies of Bonaventura's *Nachtwachen*," Ph.D. dissertation, Stanford University, 1971;

Kathy Brzović, "*Nachtwachen* von Bonaventura: A Critique of Order," *Monatshefte*, 76 (1984): 380-395;

Hans-Dietrich Dahnke, "Friedrich Gottlob Wetzel: Die 'Nachtwachen von Bonaventura,'" in *Romantik: Erläuterungen zur deutschen Literatur*, edited by the "Kollektiv für Literaturgeschichte" under the direction of Kurt Böttcher (Berlin: Volk und Wissen, 1967), pp. 222-228;

Paul Davies, "Why Mozart in the *Nachtwachen?*," *Forum for Modern Language Studies*, 23 (1987): 265-273;

Steffen Dietzsch, "Schelling als Verfasser der 'Nachtwachen' des Bonaventura? Eine Replik," *Deutsche Zeitschrift für Philosophie*, 33, no. 4 (1985): 352-355;

Erich Eckertz, "Nachtwachen von Bonaventura: Ein Spiel mit Schelling und Goethe gegen die Schlegels von Caroline," *Zeitschrift für Bücherfreunde*, 9 (1905-1906): 234-249;

Ellis Finger, "Bonaventura Through Kreuzgang: *Nachtwachen* as Autobiography," *German Quarterly*, 53, no. 3 (1980): 282-297;

Reinhard Finke, "Anonymität und satirisches Konzept in Bonaventuras 'Nachtwachen,'" in *Wege der Literaturwissenschaft*, edited by Jutta Kolkenbrock-Netz, Gerhard Plumpe, and Hans Joachim Schrimpf (Bonn: Bouvier, 1985), pp. 100-105;

Horst Fleig, *Literarischer Vampirismus: Klingemanns "Nachtwachen von Bonaventura"* (Tübingen: Niemeyer, 1985);

Erich Frank, "Clemens Brentano: Der Verfasser der Nachtwachen von Bonaventura," *Germanisch-Romanische Monatsschrift*, 4 (1912): 417-440;

Gerald Gillespie, "Bonaventura's Romantic Agony: Prevision of an Art of Existential Despair," *Modern Language Notes*, 85 (1970): 697-726;

Gillespie, "Kreuzgang in the role of Crispin: Commedia dell'arte transformation in *Die Nachtwachen*," in *Herkommen und Erneuerung: Essays für Oskar Seidlin*, edited by Gillespie and Edgar Lohner (Tübingen: Niemeyer, 1976), pp. 185-200;

Gillespie, "Night-Piece and *Tail-Piece:* Bonaventura's Relation to Hogarth," *Arcadia*, 8 (1973): 284-295;

Sigrid Gölz, "Die Formen der Unmittelbarkeit in den *Nachtwachen von Bonaventura*," Ph.D. dissertation, University of Frankfurt am Main, 1955;

Arseni Gulyga, "Schelling als Verfasser der 'Nachtwachen' des Bonaventura," *Deutsche Zeitschrift für Philosophie*, 32, no. 11 (1984): 1027-1036;

Friedrich Gundolf, "Über Clemens Brentano," *Zeitschrift für Deutschkunde*, 42 (1928): 1-17, 97-115;

Ruth Haag, "Noch einmal: Der Verfasser der *Nachtwachen von Bonaventura*," *Euphorion*, 81, no. 1 (1987): 286-297;

Karl-Heinz Habersetzer, "Bonaventura aus Prag und der Verfasser der *Nachtwachen*," *Euphorion*, 77 (1983): 470-482;

Rudolf Haym, *Die Romantische Schule: Ein Beitrag zur Geschichte des deutschen Geistes* (Berlin: Gaertner, 1870), p. 636;

Franz Heiduk, "Bonaventuras 'Nachtwachen': Erste Bemerkungen zum Ort der Handlung und zur Frage nach dem Verfasser," *Aurora*, 42 (1982): 143-165;

Walter Hinderer, "'Dieses Schwanzstück der Schöpfung': Büchner's *Dantons Tod* und die *Nachtwachen* des Bonaventura," *Georg Büchner Jahrbuch*, 2 (1982): 316-342;

Gerhard Hoffmeister, "Bonaventura: *Nachtwachen* (1804/05)," in *Romane und Erzählungen der deutschen Romantik: Neue Interpretationen*, edited by Paul Michael Lützeler (Stuttgart: Reclam, 1981), pp. 194-212;

Rosemarie Hunter-Lougheed, "Humanität in den *Nachtwachen* von Bonaventura," in *Proceedings: Pacific Northwest Conference on Foreign Languages 24* (Corvallis: Oregon State University Press, 1973), pp. 270-275;

Hunter-Lougheed, "Der Mann in Kants Schuhen und Lessings Perücke: Eine unbekannte Quelle zu den 'Nachtwachen von Bonaventura,'" *Aurora*, 40 (1980): 147-151;

Hunter-Lougheed, *Die Nachtwachen von Bonaventura: Ein Frühwerk E. T. A. Hoffmanns?* (Heidelberg: Winter, 1985);

Hunter-Lougheed, "*Nachtwachen von Bonaventura* und *Tristram Shandy*," *Canadian Review of Comparative Literature*, 1 (1974): 218-234;

Hunter-Lougheed, "*Des Teufels Taschenbuch* von 'Bonaventura'?," *Neophilologus*, 65 (1981): 589-593;

Linde Katritzky, "Georg Christoph Lichtenberg, F. R. S.," *Notes and Records of the Royal Society of London*, 39 (September 1984): 41-49;

R. J. Kavanagh, "Bonaventura Unmasked–Again?," *German Life & Letters*, new series 40 (1986 / 1987): 97-116;

Wolfgang Kayser, *Das Groteske in Malerei und Dichtung* (Reinbek: Rowohlt, 1960);

Alfons K. Knauth, "Luckys und Bonaventuras unglückliche Weltansichten: Ein Vergleich von Beckets *En attendant Godot* mit den *Nachtwachen* von Bonaventura," *Romanistisches Jahrbuch*, 26 (1975): 147-169;

Peter Kohl, *Der freie Spielraum im Nichts: Eine kritische Betrachtung der "Nachtwachen" von Bonaventura* (Frankfurt am Main, Bern & New York: Lang, 1986);

Werner Kohlschmidt, "Das Hamlet-Motiv in den *Nachtwachen* des Bonaventura," in *German Studies Presented to Walter Horace Bruford* (London: Harrap, 1962), pp. 163-175;

Kohlschmidt, "Nihilismus der Romantik," *Neue Schweizer Rundschau*, new series 21 (1953): 466-482;

Kohlschmidt, "Zwischen Moralismus und Spiel: Der Anonymus der *Nachtwachen des Bonaventura* und sein Werk," in *Miscellanea di studi in onore di Bonaventura Tecchi*, II, edited by Paolo Chiarini and others (Rome: Edizioni dell'Ateneo, 1969), pp. 367-378;

Heinrich Köster, "Das Phänomen des Lächerlichen in der Dichtung um 1800 (Jean Paul, E. T. A. Hoffmann, Bonaventura)," Ph.D. dissertation, University of Freiburg, 1956;

Peter Küpper, "Unfromme Vigilien: Bonaventuras *Nachtwachen*," in *Festschrift für Richard Alewyn*, edited by Herbert Singer and Benno von Wiese (Cologne: Böhlau, 1967), pp. 309-327;

Johann Leopoldseder, *Groteske Welt: Ein Beitrag zur Entwicklungsgeschichte des Nachtstücks in der Romantik* (Bonn: Bouvier, 1973);

Fernand Lion, "Les 'veilles' de Bonaventura," in *Le Romantisme allemand*, edited and translated by Albert Beguin (Liguge & Vienne, France: Cahiers de Sud, 1949), pp. 367-376;

Franz Loquai, "Der Nachtwächter im Irrenhaus: Zum Thema des Wahnsinns in den *Nachtwachen von Bonaventura*," *Internationales Archiv für Sozialgeschichte der deutschen Literatur*, 12 (1987): 134-155;

Rudolf Majut, *Lebensbühne und Marionette: Ein Beitrag zur seelengeschichtlichen Entwicklung von*

der Genie-Zeit bis zum Biedermeier (Berlin: Ebering, 1931);

Alfred Meissner, "Schelling als Dichter," in *Mosaik 2* (Berlin: Paetel, 1886), pp. 17-31;

Ernst Erich Metzner, Review of *Bonaventura: Der Verfasser der Nachtwachen* by Jost Schillemeit, *Aurora*, 34 (1974): 96-100;

Karl-Heinz Meyer, "Johann Karl Wezel und die 'Nachtwachen von Bonaventura,' " *Neues aus der Wezel-Forschung*, 2 (1984): 62-86;

Richard M. Meyer, "Nachtwachen von Bonaventura," *Euphorion*, 10 (1903): 578-588;

Andreas Mielke, "Bonaventuras *Nachtwachen* als 'treffliche Nachahmung' Richters," *Zeitschrift für deutsche Philologie*, 104 (1985): 520-542;

Mielke, "Überlegungen zu 'Des Teufels Taschenbuch' von Bonaventura und Schlegels Begriff der 'diabolischen Dichtkunst,' " *Aurora*, 39 (1979): 197-205;

Mielke, *Zeitgenosse Bonaventura* (Stuttgart: Akademischer Verlag Heinz, 1984);

Joachim Müller, "Die Nachtwachen des Bonaventura," *Neue Jahrbücher für Deutsche Wissenschaft*, 12 (1936): 433-444;

R. Russell Neuswanger, "Investigation of Some Central Motifs in *Die Nachtwachen des Bonaventura*," Ph.D. dissertation, Ohio State University, 1970;

Neuswanger, "On Laughter in Bonaventura's 'Nachtwachen,' " *German Life & Letters*, 30, no. 1 (1976): 15-24;

Wolfgang Paulsen, "Bonaventuras *Nachtwachen* im literarischen Raum: Sprache und Struktur," *Jahrbuch der deutschen Schillergesellschaft*, 9 (1965): 447-510;

Hertha Perez, "Betrachtungen zu den 'Nachtwachen' von Bonaventura," in *Ansichten zur deutschen Klassik*, edited by Helmut Brandt and Manfred Beyer (Berlin & Weimar: Aufbau, 1981), pp. 365-381, 446;

Walter Pfannkuche, *Idealismus und Nihilismus in den "Nachtwachen" von Bonaventura* (Frankfurt am Main & Bern: Lang, 1983);

Wolfgang Pfeiffer-Belli, "Antiromantische Streitschriften und Pasquille (1798-1804)," *Euphorion*, 26 (1925): 602-630;

Rado Pribic, *Bonaventura's "Nachtwachen" and Dostoevsky's "Notes from the Underground"* (Munich: Sagner, 1974);

Pribic, "Kreuzgang: The Alienated Hero of the *Nachtwachen*," *Acta Germanica*, 17 (1984): 21-28;

Paul F. Proskauer, "The Phenomenon of Alienation in the Work of Karl Philipp Moritz, Wilhelm Heinrich Wackenroder and in 'Nachtwachen' von Bonaventura," Ph.D. dissertation, Columbia University, 1966;

Wolfgang Pross, "Jean Paul und der Autor der *Nachtwachen*: Eine Hypothese," *Aurora*, 34 (1974): 65-74;

Eleonore Rapp, *Die Marionette in der deutschen Dichtung vom Sturm und Drang bis zur Romantik* (Leipzig: Lehmann & Schüppel, 1924);

Walter Rehm, "Experimentum suae medietatis," *Jahrbuch des Freien deutschen Hochstifts* (1940): 237-336;

Review of *Nachtwachen*, *Neue Leipziger Literaturzeitung*, 25 August 1805, columns 1734-1735;

Mary-Neal Richerson, "Satirical and nihilistic elements in Bonaventura's *Nachtwachen*," Ph.D. dissertation, Pennsylvania State University, 1976;

Max Rouché, "Bonaventure ne serait-il pas Jean Paul Richter lui-même?," *Études Germaniques*, 24 (1969): 329-445;

Jeffrey L. Sammons, "In Search of Bonaventura: The *Nachtwachen* Riddle 1965-1985," *Germanic Review*, 61, no. 2 (1986): 50-56;

Sammons, *The Nachtwachen von Bonaventura: A Structural Interpretation* (The Hague: Mouton, 1965);

Jost Schillemeit, *Bonaventura: Der Verfasser der "Nachtwachen"* (Munich: Beck, 1973);

Jörg Schönert, "Fragen ohne Antwort: Zur Krise der literarischen Aufklärung im Roman des späten 18. Jahrhunderts: Wezels *Belphegor*, Klingers *Faust* und die *Nachtwachen von Bonaventura*," *Jahrbuch der deutschen Schillergesellschaft*, 14 (1970): 183-229;

Franz Schultz, "Gundolf und die *Nachtwachen von Bonaventura*," *Euphorion*, 29 (1928): 234-239;

Schultz, *Der Verfasser der Nachtwachen von Bonaventura: Untersuchungen zur deutschen Romantik* (Berlin: Weidmann, 1909);

Dorothee Sölle-Nipperdey, *Untersuchungen zur Struktur der Nachtwachen von Bonaventura* (Göttingen: Vandenhoeck & Ruprecht, 1959);

Joachim Stachow, "Studien zu den *Nachtwachen von Bonaventura* mit besonderer Berücksichti-

gung des Marionettenproblems," Ph.D. dissertation, University of Hamburg, 1957;

Gerhard Steiner and others, "Echo zur Wezel-Bonaventura-Hypothese und zu Johann Karl Wezel und die 'Nachtwachen von Bonaventura,'" *Neues aus der Wezel-Forschung*, 2 (1984): 1-22;

Remigius Stölzle, *Ernst von Lasaulx (1805-61): Ein Lebensbild* (Münster: Aschendorff, 1904), p. 29;

Rita Terras, "Juvenal und die satirische Struktur der *Nachtwachen* von Bonaventura," *German Quarterly*, 52, no. 1 (1979): 18-31;

J. Thiele, "Untersuchungen zur Frage des Autors der *Nachtwachen von Bonaventura* mit Hilfe einfacher Textcharakteristiken," *Grundlagenstudien aus Kybernetik und Geisteswissenschaft*, 4 (1963): 36-44;

Karl August Varnhagen von Ense, *Aus dem Nachlaß Varnhagen's von Ense: Tagebücher von K. A. Varnhagen von Ense*, edited by L. Assing, volume 2 (Leipzig: Brockhaus, 1861), p. 206;

Kurt Wais, "Shakespeare und die neueren Erzähler, von Bonaventura und Manzoni bis Laforgue und Joyce," in *Shakespeare: Seine Welt–Unsere Welt*, edited by Gerhard Müller-Schwefe (Tübingen: Niemeyer, 1964), pp. 97-133;

Dieter Wickmann, *Eine mathematisch-statistische Methode zur Untersuchung der Verfasserfrage literarischer Texte: Durchgeführt am Beispiel der "Nachtwachen von Bonaventura" mit Hilfe der Wortartübergänge* (Cologne & Opladen: Westdeutscher Verlag, 1969);

Wickmann, "On Disputed Authorship, Statistically," in *Association for Literary and Linguistic Computing: Bulletin* (London: Association for Literary and Linguistic Computing, 1976), pp. 32-41;

Wickmann, "Zum Bonaventura-Problem: Eine mathematisch-statistische Überprüfung der Klingemann-Hypothese," *Zeitschrift für Literaturwissenschaft und Linguistik*, 4, no. 16 (1975): 13-29.

Ludwig Börne

(6 May 1786-12 February 1837)

James Hardin
University of South Carolina

BOOKS: *Freimütige Bemerkungen über die neue Stät-
tigkeits- und Schutzordnung für die Judenschaft
in Frankfurt am Main* (N.p., 1808);
Der ewige Jude (N.p., 1821);
Denkrede auf Jean Paul (Frankfurt am Main [ac-
tually Erfurt], 1826);
*Einige Worte über die angekündigten Jahrbücher für wis-
senschaftliche Kritik, herausgegeben von der Socie-
tät für wissenschaftliche Kritik zu Berlin* (Heidelberg: Winter, 1827);
Hamlet, von Shakespeare (Hamburg: Hoffmann &
Campe, 1829);
Gesammelte Schriften, 8 volumes (Hamburg: Hoff-
mann & Campe, 1829-1834); enlarged edi-
tion, 5 volumes (Stuttgart: Brodhag, 1840);
Briefe aus Paris: 1830 bis 1831, 2 volumes (Ham-
burg: Hoffmann & Campe, 1832);
*Mitteilungen aus dem Gebiete der Länder- und Völker-
kunde von Ludwig Börne* (Offenbach: Brunet,
1832);
Briefe aus Paris: 1831 bis 1832, 2 volumes (Paris:
Brunet, 1833);
Briefe aus Paris: 1832 bis 1834, 2 volumes (Paris:
Brunet, 1834);
Gesammelte Schriften, 17 volumes (Hamburg: Hoff-
mann & Campe, 1835-1847);
Menzel der Franzosenfresser (Paris: Barrois, 1837;
New York: Radde, 1844);
*Ludwig Börne's Urtheil über H. Heine: Ungedruckte
Stellen aus den Pariser Briefen* (Frankfurt am
Main: Sauerländer, 1840);
Fragments politiques et littéraires, edited by Louis
Marie de Lahaye, vicomte de Cormenin
(Paris: Pagnerre, 1842);
Nachgelassene Schriften, 6 volumes (Mannheim: Bas-
sermann, 1844-1850);
Französische Schriften, edited by Cormenin, trans-
lated by E. Weller (Bern: Jenni, 1847);
Gesammelte Schriften: Neue vollständige Ausgabe, 12
volumes (Hamburg: Hoffmann & Campe,
1861-1862);
Gesammelte Schriften: Vollständige Ausgabe, 12 vol-
umes (Vienna: Tendler, 1868);

*Ludwig Börne (portrait by M. Oppenheim, 1827-1828; Hel-
mut Bock,* Ludwig Börne *[1962])*

*Börnes Werke: Historisch-kritische Ausgabe in zwölf
Bänden*, edited by Ludwig Geiger, Joseph
Dresch, Rudolf Fürst, Erwin Kalischer, Al-
fred Klaar, Alfred Stern, and Leon Zeitlin
(Berlin, Leipzig, Vienna & Stuttgart: Bong,
1912-1913; only volumes 1-3, 6-7, and 9 ap-
peared);
*Études sur l'histoire et les hommes de la Révolution fran-
çaise inédites*, edited by Joseph Dresch (Lyon:
I. A. C., 1952);
Werke, edited by Helmut Bock and Walter Dietze
(Weimar: Volksverlag, 1959);
Ludwig Börne: Schriften zur deutschen Literatur, ed-
ited by Dietze (Leipzig: Reclam, 1960);

Sämtliche Schriften, revised and edited by Inge and Peter Rippmann, 5 volumes (Düsseldorf & Darmstadt: Melzer, 1964-1968);

Menzel der Franzosenfresser und andere Schriften, edited by Walter Hinderer (Frankfurt am Main: Insel, 1969);

Briefe aus Paris, edited by Alfred Estermann (Frankfurt am Main: Insel, 1986).

OTHER: *Die Wage: Eine Zeitschrift für Bürgerleben, Wissenschaft und Kunst,* edited by Börne, 2 volumes (Frankfurt am Main: Hermann, 1818-1820);

Zeitung der freien Stadt Frankfurt, edited by Börne (Frankfurt am Main, 1819);

Zeitschwingen oder Des deutschen Volkes fliegende Blätter, edited by Börne (Frankfurt am Main: Wilmanns, 1819);

B. Reinwald, ed., *Die Spende: Eine Auswahl von Aphorismen, Epigrammen, Anekdoten, Bemerkungen usw.,* foreword by Börne (Offenbach, 1823);

Worte des Glaubens von Abbé de Lammenais, translated by Börne (Paris: Herisau, 1834);

"Goethe as a Patriot," translated by James D. Haas, in his *Gleanings from Germany* (London: Hodson, 1839), pp. 381-382.

Ludwig Börne wrote no novels or plays and was rather more a critic and journalist than poet. Yet his influence on writers of his generation and his unshakable belief that a writer's duty is to attempt to influence history and to ameliorate social injustice have secured him a prominent place in the history of German literature of the Restoration period. Börne's liberal views in a time of reaction brought him into frequent conflict with the authorities; he therefore spent a large part of his life in Paris, which for him was the center of the civilized world. In many respects his life and outlook resemble that of his better-known contemporary and sometime friend, Heinrich Heine, with whom he shared the burdens and indignities of discrimination against Jews.

Börne was born Juda Löw Baruch in Frankfurt am Main on 6 May 1786 (as he claimed, though other records give later dates in the same month) to Jakob Baruch, a banker, and Julie Baruch. He was brought up in the ghetto at a time when virtually every aspect of the life of Jewish inhabitants of Frankfurt was regulated by the city government; for instance, only fourteen Jewish marriages were allowed in a given year. His earliest experiences of anti-Semitism made an indelible impression on him, sensitizing him to the worth of freedom and justice and strengthening his determination to work for them in his writings. Baruch was raised in the strict Orthodox Talmudic tradition, but he also received from a private tutor instruction informed by the spirit of the Enlightenment.

In 1800 he was sent to study in Gießen, and in 1802 he went to Berlin to embark on a medical curriculum. His accommodations were in the house of his mentor, Marcus Herz, a respected doctor and philosopher and friend of the late playwright and critic Gotthold Ephraim Lessing. But Herz died in 1803, and Baruch's interest in medicine and the sciences, already waning under the influence of the lively cultural atmosphere of Berlin and contact with such prominent intellectuals as Wilhelm von Humboldt and Friedrich Schlegel, began to be replaced by an interest in literature and philosophy. At about the same time he fell in love with Herz's widow, the beautiful thirty-eight-year-old Henriette. She was horrified to learn of his attraction, assumed the role of a motherly friend, and informed Baruch's father about the situation. The latter arranged to have his son sent to Halle to continue his studies.

In 1804 Baruch registered as a student of medicine in Halle; but he did not like the city, was not in good health, and apparently made little progress in his medical studies. In 1807 he moved to Heidelberg, where, under the more liberal laws of the Rhine States established by Napoleon, Jews had free choice of profession. He studied law for a year there, then briefly in Gießen. In 1808 he received his doctorate in philosophy and returned to Frankfurt. In the same year he wrote the essay *Freimütige Bemerkungen über die neue Stättigkeits- und Schutzordnung für die Judenschaft in Frankfurt am Main* (Candid Remarks on the New City and Protective Ordinance for the Jewish Community in Frankfurt am Main), an early indication of the political trend of his thought: although the 1807 statute provides the Frankfurt Jews considerable relief from the restrictive laws of the past, he says, it does not approach the ideal of providing equality to Jew and gentile. The caustic wit of the essay foreshadows the tone of his later work. Baruch's position as a Jew in German society sharpened his perception of injustices to the underprivileged in general; for him the touchstone of a nation's humanitarianism was its treatment of its Jewish population.

In 1811 Baruch entered the police administration in Frankfurt. In 1815, after the defeat of

German Snail-Coach), published in *Die Wage* in 1821, which compared the German people's progress toward enlightenment to the slow progress of a stagecoach, revealed his talent as humorist, satirist, and stylist.

No abstract theoretician of art, Börne wrote from a practical standpoint that measured the value of literature in its applicability to current problems and abuses. The demand of the day, in his view, was political engagement, not withdrawal to the aestheticism of the ivory tower: the drama should have to do with improvement of the lot of the people, and the foremost dramatist of the time did not fulfill that requirement. The dramatist should treat significant contemporary themes, should make significant figures the protagonists of his plays, and should avoid the artificial. And yet drama should represent a heightened reality, a world that is more dignified than dreary everyday life. While he had high regard for the plays of the Austrian Franz Grillparzer, he vigorously attacked the celebrated playwrights August Wilhelm Iffland and August von Kotzebue, whose facile but superficial works were long the rage both in Germany and abroad. One of his pet peeves was the voguish Schicksalstragödie (fate tragedy), a type of play that shows fate as all-powerful and people as driven to commit crimes, seemingly against their will, and his scathing review of Ernst Christoph Houwald's absurd verse play *Der Leuchtturm* (The Lighthouse, 1821) is considered a masterpiece.

For the plays of Friedrich Schiller and Johann Wolfgang von Goethe, Börne had few words of praise. Schiller's *Don Carlos* (1787) was nothing more than "ein schönes vergoldetes Lehrbuch über Seelenkunde und Staatskunst" (a beautiful gilded guidebook to psychology and diplomacy); "Nichts geschieht, wenig wird empfunden, am meisten wird gedacht" (Nothing happens, little is felt, one mostly thinks). For Börne, Schiller was no longer timely because his works did not touch on the political and human needs of the present and therefore had done as little for the German people as had the works of Goethe.

Goethe was his special target: in Börne's view Goethe was selfish and unfeeling, an egotistical aesthete and aristocrat who warmed himself in the light of his own carefully chosen words and was cold to human suffering. In 1830 Börne wrote: "Seit ich fühle, habe ich Goethe gehaßt, seit ich denke, weiß ich warum" (Since the time I could feel I've hated Goethe, and since the time I

Jeanette Wohl, Börne's friend and his collaborator on several essays (portrait by L. Allemand; Helmut Bock, Ludwig Börne *[1962])*

Napoleon, the Congress of Vienna rescinded the liberal laws governing Jews, and he was removed from the bureaucracy because of his religion. In early 1817 he met Jeanette Wohl, a divorcée three years his senior, who recognized his abilities, built his self-confidence, and prodded him to live up to the promise of his talent. Baruch decided to change his name and religion so that he would have the freedom to pursue his plan to found and edit what would today be called a literary-cultural-political magazine, and on 5 June 1818 he was baptized by a Lutheran minister as Carl Ludwig Börne. The next month the first issue of Börne's *Die Wage: Zeitschrift für Bürgerleben, Wissenschaft und Kunst* (The Scale: Newspaper for Civic Life, Science, and Art) appeared. It was this periodical, edited by Börne until 1821, that established his fame. *Die Wage* was especially noteworthy for its biting theater reviews, which later appeared as the first volume of his *Gesammelte Schriften* (Collected Writings, 1829-1834) under the title *Dramaturgische Blätter* (Notes on the Drama). Not since the time of Lessing had such penetrating criticism of the theater been written. And pieces such as "Monographie der deutschen Postschnecke" (Monograph on the could think I know why). Yet Börne prized earlier works of Goethe, especially *Götz von Berlichingen* (1773), *Die Leiden des jungen Werthers* (1774; translated as *The Sorrows of Werther*, 1779), and *Egmont* (1788), and esteemed Goethe as a great poet. But Goethe's failure to use his immense influence to oppose political reaction in Germany made him the object of Börne's hatred. Goethe "hätte ein Herkules sein können, sein Vaterland von großem Unrate zu befreien" (could have been a Hercules who could have freed his fatherland of great piles of rubbish), but he was silent and therefore was a handmaiden to political reaction and repression. In contrast to his attacks on Schiller and Goethe, Börne lauded the romantic novels of Jean Paul (Johann Paul Friedrich Richter). In his *Denkrede auf Jean Paul* (Memorial Oration to Jean Paul, 1826) Börne praised the writer more for his high moral character than for his artistic achievement: "Er war der Dichter der Niedergebornen, er war der Sänger der Armen, und wo Betrübte weinten, da vernahm man die süßen Töne seiner Harfe" (He was the poet of the lowly, the singer of the poor, and wherever grieving ones wept one heard the sweet tones of his harp). Jean Paul was the people's poet, Goethe the court poet.

In 1819 Börne became editor of the *Zeitung der freien Stadt Frankfurt* (Newspaper of the Free City of Frankfurt). Much hindered by the repressive censorship of the time, he made his first trip to Paris in October 1819. On 22 March 1820, after his return to Frankfurt in November 1819, he was arrested on suspicion of distributing revolutionary pamphlets. After two weeks his innocence was established, and he was released.

His reputation had grown so that the publisher of Goethe's and Schiller's works, Johann Friedrich Cotta, hired Börne to write pieces in Paris for Cotta's *Morgenblatt* from 1822 to 1824. Even the Austrian statesman Prince von Metternich attempted to lure this supremely talented writer to Vienna to lend his abilities as a publicist to the cause of the Holy Alliance. Until 1830 Börne lived in Frankfurt, Munich, Stuttgart, Paris, and Hanover. In 1827 he became friends with Heine in Frankfurt, and in 1828 he traveled to Berlin via Weimar (where he did not see Goethe) and found himself something of a celebrated figure. He visited Henriette Herz daily while in Berlin. That year the Heidelberg publisher Julius Campe agreed to publish Börne's collected works. Börne wrote a few additional critical essays and prepared the works for publication, assisted by Jeanette Wohl, with whom he lived in Hanover until the spring of 1829.

During this period he had several bouts of illness. While taking a cure in Soden in 1830 he heard the news of the July Revolution in France and went to Paris full of enthusiasm for the new regime, only to be disappointed by the actual course of events. In Paris he wrote the *Briefe aus Paris* (Letters from Paris, 1832-1834), published as volumes 9-14 of his *Gesammelte Schriften*. These immensely influential essays treat the theme of freedom for France, Germany, and Poland. The style of the letters–energetic, vigorous, owing much to Luther's Bible, simple but rich in metaphor and simile, and appealing more to the emotions than to the intellect–made them unique in their time and influential throughout the century. The letters were praised by liberals but damned by conservatives as insane outbursts or pieces of demagogy. Their intent was to influence events in Germany and to interpret recent historical and cultural phenomena in the light of Börne's hard-won insights as a liberal and a Jew. In the seventy-eighth letter Börne speaks of the short-lived reign under Napoleon of equality for Jews in Frankfurt: "In dem Kriege, den sie den *Befreiungskrieg* genannt, der aber nichts befreit als unsere Fürsten von den Banden, in welche die große, mächtige und erhabene Leidenschaft eines Helden ihre kleinen schwachen und verächtlichen Leidenschaften geschmiedet, haben auch wir die Waffen geführt. Ehe der Kampf begann, genossen wir in Frankfurt, wie überall in Deutschland, wo französische Gesetzgebung herrschte, gleiche Rechte mit unsern christlichen Brüdern.... Die nämlichen Bürger tranken herzlich aus einem Glase mit uns, die noch den Tag vorher uns mit Verachtung angesehen oder mit Haß den Blick von uns gewendet. Denn das ist der Segen des Rechts, wenn es mit Macht gepaart, daß es wie durch einen Zauber die Neigungen der Menschen umwandelt: Mißtrauen in Vertrauen, Torheit in Vernunft, Haß in Liebe" (In the war, which they called the *War of Liberation*, which however liberated nothing but our princes from the shackles forged for their petty, weak, and contemptible passions by the great, powerful, and sublime passion of a hero, we too bore arms. Before the battle began we enjoyed in Frankfurt, as in all of Germany under French law, equal rights with our Christian brothers.... The same citizens drank heartily from the same glass with us, those very citizens who the day before had looked at us with contempt or had turned away from us in hatred. For that is the blessing of the law, when it is paired with authority, that it transforms as if by magic the inclinations of men: suspicion into trust, foolishness into reason, hate into love).

In 1832, ignoring the possibility of arrest, he traveled to Frankfurt, then spent several weeks with Wohl and her fiancé Salomon Strauss in Baden-Baden. He then traveled to Freiburg and Switzerland, returning to Paris in November.

In 1833 Wohl and her husband moved in with Börne in Paris. By this time Börne was gradually withdrawing from the political fray, and also from the many social contacts he had maintained with such care over the years. His friendship with Heine had been broken for some time; Heine, who had been living in Paris since 1831, was, Börne charged in his 109th letter, artistically vain, an opportunist, politically fickle, and a spiritual coward. He linked Heine with Goethe in his presumed glorification of the beautiful over the real.

Börne took up the cudgels for freedom one last time in a confrontation with German reaction in *Menzel der Franzosenfresser* (Menzel the Devourer of Frenchmen, 1837), published as volume 15 of his *Gesammelte Schriften*. Wolfgang Menzel, an influential and unscrupulous journalist and chauvinist, published attacks on the German liberal wing of writers represented primarily by Heine, Börne, and the writers of Junges Deutschland (Young Germany)–Karl Gutzkow, Heinrich Laube, Ludolf Wienbarg, Theodor Mundt, Ferdinand Gustav Kühne, and Ernst Adolf Willkomm. His polemics against the liberals had their effect in the German parliament, and the Young Germans were banned partly as a result of his efforts. Börne's masterwork attacked the mindless chauvinism of Menzel and all those who used patriotism as a pretext for repression, and it argued that love of one's country must be balanced by humanitarianism. As in his earlier writings, Börne expressed his love for Germany, "das gebildetste, geistreichste, tüchtigste und tugendhafteste Volk der Welt" (the most cultivated, intelligent, industrious, and virtuous people in the world), which had been reduced to slavery because of the lack of a free press, of public courts of justice, of juries, and of other institutions enjoyed by civilized peoples. Börne's language in his last work is biting and bitter, his attitude toward Menzel one of utter contempt. One can discern quite clearly the influence of the Bible on his vigorous style. He observes that

Menzel refers slightingly to Börne's Jewish origins and traces Börne's attacks on German reaction to Jewish resentment. Menzel had written of Börne: "In Frankfurt am Main, wo der große Goethe als Patrizierkind aufgehätschelt wurde, kam ein kleines kränkliches Kind zur Welt, der Jude Baruch. Schon den Knaben verspotteten die Christenkinder" (In Frankfurt am Main, where the great Goethe was lovingly brought up as a young patrician, a small, sickly child came into the world, the Jew Baruch. The Christian children made fun of him even as a boy). Börne responds: "Das wäre alles sehr schön, wenn es nur wahr wäre; ja es würde mich freuen, wenn es wahr wäre; aber so ist es nicht. Nie glomm auch nur ein Funke des Hasses gegen die christliche Welt in meiner Brust; denn ob ich zwar die Verfolgung der Juden lange schmerzlich an mir selbst gefühlt und immer mit Erbitterung verdammt, so erkannte ich doch gleich darin nur eine Form des Aristokratismus, nur eine Äußerung des angebornen menschlichen Hochmuts.... Nie habe ich mich für erlittene Schmach ... zu rächen gedacht. Und wie hätte ich es auch vermocht seit den Jahren, da ich durch die Schrift zu wirken gesucht? Hätte ich tausend Dolche und tausend Gifte und tausend Flüche und das Herz eines Teufels, sie alle zu gebrauchen, –was könnte ich meinen alten Feinden denn noch antun? Sind sie jetzt nicht meine Glaubensgenossen und Leidensbrüder? Ist nicht Deutschland der Ghetto Europas? Tragen nicht alle Deutschen einen gelben Lappen am Hute?" (That would all be very nice if it were only true; in fact I would be glad if it were true; but that's not the way it is. There was never even a spark of hatred toward the Christian world in my breast; for although I have long experienced at first hand the persecution of the Jews and have always bitterly condemned it, I immediately recognized in it only a form of aristocracy, only an expression of innate human arrogance.... I have never considered ... avenging myself for any shame I have experienced. And how could I have done so in the years since I have attempted to influence matters through my writing? If I had a thousand daggers and a thousand vials of poison and a thousand curses and the heart of a devil to make use of them all, –what could I in fact do to my old enemies? Are they not now my fellow believers and brothers in suffering? Is not Germany the ghetto of Europe? Do not all Germans wear a yellow rag on their hats?).

Börne died of influenza on 12 February 1837 and was buried in the Père Lachaise cemetery. German papers of all parties printed obituaries that lamented the loss of a man of great intelligence and noble character. Heine remarked that Börne seemed "wirklich jetzt von den Deutschen kanonisirt zu werden" (really to have been canonized by the Germans).

Letters:

Briefe des jungen Börne an Henriette Herz (Leipzig: Brockhaus, 1861);

Börne und Treitschke: Offenes Sendschreiben über die Juden, von Löb Baruch (Dr. Ludwig Börne) an den deutschen Reichstagsabgeordneten und Heidelberger Professor Dr. Heinrich Gotthard von Treitschke (Berlin: Verlag von Stein's Literarischem Büreau, 1880);

Briefwechsel des jungen Börne und der Henriette Herz, edited by Ludwig Geiger (Oldenburg & Leipzig: Schwartz, 1905);

Ludwig Börnes Berliner Briefe 1828: Nach den Originalen mit Einleitung und Anmerkungen, edited by Geiger (Berlin: Fontane, 1905).

Biographies:

Karl Gutzkow, *Börnes Leben* (Hamburg: Hoffmann & Campe, 1840);

Heinrich Heine, *Ludwig Börne: Eine Denkschrift* (Hamburg: Hoffmann & Campe, 1840);

Karl Grün, *Ludwig Börne*, in Börne's *Gesammelte Schriften*, volume 12 (Vienna: Tendler, 1868), pp. 113-174;

Conrad Alberti, *Ludwig Börne: Eine biographisch-literarische Studie* (Leipzig: Wigand, 1886);

Michael Holzmann, *Ludwig Börne: Sein Leben und Wirken nach den Quellen dargestellt* (Berlin: Oppenheim, 1888);

Georg Brandes, *Ludwig Börne und Heinrich Heine: Zwei literarische Charakterbilder* (Leipzig: Barsdorf, 1896);

Ludwig Marcuse, *Revolutionär und Patriot: Das Leben Ludwig Börnes* (Leipzig: List, 1929); republished as *Börne–Aus der Frühzeit der deutschen Demokratie* (Rothenburg ob der Tauber: Peter, 1968);

Helmut Bock, *Ludwig Börne: Vom Gettojuden zum Nationalschriftsteller* (Berlin: Rütten & Loening, 1962);

Inge Rippmann, *Börne-Index: Historisch-biographische Materialien zu Ludwig Börnes Schriften und Briefen*, 2 volumes (Berlin & New York: De Gruyter, 1985).

References:

Alfred Estermann and others, *Ludwig Börne 1786-1837* (Frankfurt am Main: Buchhändler-Vereinigung, 1986);

Walter Hinderer, "Ludwig Börne, der Apostel der Freiheit," in his *Über deutsche Literatur und Rede* (Munich: Fink, 1981), pp. 126-153;

Wolfgang Labuhn, *Literatur und Öffentlichkeit im Vormärz: Das Beispiel Ludwig Börne* (Königstein: Athenäum, 1980);

Labuhn, "Die Ludwig-Börne-Forschung seit 1945," *Zeitschrift für deutsche Philologie*, 96 (1977): 264-286;

Norbert Oellers, "Ludwig Börne," in *Deutsche Dichter des 19. Jahrhunderts*, edited by Benno von Wiese (Berlin: Schmidt, 1979), pp. 155-180;

Oellers, "Die zerstrittenen Dioskuren: Aspekte der Auseinandersetzung Heines mit Börne," *Zeitschrift für deutsche Philologie*, 91 (1972): 66-90;

Helmut Richter, "Ludwig Börne 1987: Anmerkungen zu Stand und Perspektiven der Forschung nach zwei Gedenkjahren," *Weimarer Beiträge*, 33 (1987): 2066-2081;

Inge Rippmann, "Ludwig Börne," in *Literatur Lexikon: Autoren und Werke deutscher Sprache*, edited by Walther Killy, volume 2 (Gütersloh: Bertelsmann, 1989), pp. 83-86;

Rippmann and Labuhn, eds., *"Die Kunst—eine Tochter der Zeit": Neue Studien zu Ludwig Börne* (Bielefeld: Aisthesis, 1988).

Papers:

Ludwig Börne's papers are in the Börne Archive of the Stadt- und Universitätsbibliothek, Frankfurt am Main.

Clemens Brentano

(9 September 1778-28 July 1842)

John Francis Fetzer
University of California, Davis

SELECTED BOOKS: *Ehe Du scheidest, Freund Büschler, auch eine Thräne von Deinem Brentano* (Frankfurt am Main: Privately printed, 1795);

Satiren und poetische Spiele Erstes Bändchen: Gustav Wasa, as Maria (Leipzig: Rein, 1800);

Godwi oder Das steinerne Bild der Mutter: Ein verwilderter Roman, as Maria, 2 volumes (Bremen: Wilmans, 1801-1802);

Die lustigen Musikanten: Singspiel (Frankfurt am Main: Körner 1803);

Ponce de Leon: Ein Lustspiel (Göttingen: Dieterich, 1804);

Entweder wunderbare Geschichte von BOGS dem Uhrmacher, wie er zwar das menschliche Leben längst verlassen, nun aber doch, nach vielen musikalischen Leiden zu Wasser und zu Lande, in die bürgerliche Schützengesellschaft aufgenommen zu werden Hoffnung hat, oder Die über die Ufer der badischen Wochenschrift als Beilage ausgetretene Konzert-Anzeige, by Brentano and Joseph von Görres (Heidelberg: Mohr & Zimmer, 1807);

Universitati Litterariae: Kantate auf den 15. Oktober 1810 (Berlin: Hitzig, 1810);

Der Philister vor, in und nach der Geschichte: Scherzhafte Abhandlung, anonymous (Berlin, 1811);

Rheinübergang; Kriegsrundgesang (Vienna, 1814);

Die Gründung Prags: Ein historisches-romantisches Drama (Pest: Hartleben, 1815);

Das Lied vom Korporal (Berlin, 1815);

Viktoria und ihre Geschwister mit fliegenden Fahnen und brennender Lunte: Ein klingendes Spiel (Berlin: Maurer, 1817);

Das Mosel-Eisgangs-Lied von einer wunderbaren erhaltenen Familie und einem traurig untergegangenen Mägdlein in dem Dorfe Lay bei Coblenz, am 10. Februar 1830 (Coblenz, 1830);

Die Barmherzigen Schwestern in bezug auf Armen- und Krankenpflege: Nebst einem Bericht über das Bürgerhospital in Coblenz und erläuternden Beilagen (Coblenz: Hölscher, 1831);

Das bittere Leiden unsers Herrn Jesu Christi: Nach den Betrachtungen der gottseligen Anna Katharina Emmerich, Augustinerin des Klosters Agne-

Clemens Brentano, circa 1835 (oil painting by Emilie Linder, Abtei St. Bonifaz, Munich)

tenberg zu Dülmen (Sulzbach: Seidel, 1833); translated anonymously as *The Passion of Our Lord Jesus Christ According to the Revelations of Anne Catharina Emmerich* (Clyde, Mo: Benedictine Convent, 1914);

Gockel, Hinkel, und Gackeleia: Märchen, wiedererzählt (Frankfurt am Main: Schmerber, 1838); translated by C. W. Heckethorn as *The Wondrous Tale of Cocky, Clucky, and Cackle* (London: Hogg, 1889); translated by Doris Orgel as *The Tale of Gockel, Hinkel & Gackeliah* (New York: Random House, 1961);

Geschichte vom braven Kasperl und dem schönen Annerl (Berlin: Vereins-Buchhandlung, 1838); translated by T. W. Appell as *Honor; or, The Story of the Brave Caspar and the Fair Annerl*

(London: Chapman, 1847); translated by Helene Scher as "The Story of Honest Casper and Fair Annie," in *Four Romantic Tales* (New York: Ungar, 1975), pp. 21-57;

Legende von der heiligen Marina: Ein Gedicht (Munich: Cotta, 1841);

Rotkehlchens, Liebseelchens Ermordung und Begräbniß (Zurich: Veith, 1843);

Die mehreren Wehmüller und ungarischen Nationalgesichter: Erzählung (Berlin: Vereins-Buchhandlung, 1843); includes "Das Pickenick des Katers Mores," translated by Jane B. Greene as "The Picnic of Mores the Cat," in *German Stories and Tales*, edited by Robert Pick (New York: Washington Square Press, 1955), pp. 213-219;

Die Märchen des Clemens Brentano: Zum Besten der Armen nach dem letzten Willen des Verfassers, edited by Guido Görres, 2 volumes (Stuttgart & Tübingen: Cotta, 1846-1847);

Leben der heil. Jungfrau Maria: Nach den Betrachtungen der gottseligen Anna Katharina Emmerich (Munich: Literarisch-artistische Anstalt, 1852);

Gesammelte Schriften, edited by Christian Brentano, 9 volumes (Frankfurt am Main: Sauerländer, 1852-1855); comprises volume 1: *Geistliche Lieder;* volume 2: *Weltliche Gedichte;* volume 3: *Romanzen vom Rosenkranz;* volume 4: *Der kleinen Schriften erster Theil* ("Aus der Chronika eines fahrenden Schülers," "Blätter aus dem Tagebuch der Ahnfrau," "Geschichte vom braven Kasperl und dem schönen Annerl," "Die mehreren Wehmüller und ungarischen Nationalgesichter," "Die drei Nüsse," "Lebensumriß der Anna Katharina Emmerich," "Bilder und Gespräche aus Paris," "Vermischte Aufsätze," "Von dem Leben und Sterben der Grafen Gaston Phöbus von Foix und von dem traurigen Tode seines Kindes Gaston"); volume 5: *Der kleinen Schriften zweiter Theil* ("Gockel, Hinkel, und Gackeleia," "Die Rose: Ein Mährchen," "Fragment aus Godwi," "Wunderbare Geschichte von BOGS dem Uhrmacher," "Der Philister vor, in und nach der Geschichte," "Geschichte und Ursprung des ersten Bärenhäuters"); volume 6: *Die Gründung Prags: Ein historisch-romantisches Drama;* volume 7: *Comödien (Ponce de Leon; Die lustigen Musikanten; Viktoria und ihre Geschwister; Am Rhein, Am Rhein!)*; volumes 8-9: *Gesammelte Briefe;*

Gedichte von Clemens Brentano: In neuer Auswahl, edited by Christian Brentano (Frankfurt am Main: Sauerländer, 1854);

Das Leben unseres Herrn und Heilandes Jesu Christi, edited by Karl E. Schmöger, 3 volumes (Regensburg: Pustet, 1858-1860);

Das Leben der gottseligen Anna Katharina Emmerich, edited by Schmöger, 2 volumes (Freiburg im Breisgau: Herder, 1867-1870); translated by Helen Ram as *Life of Anna Catharina Emmerich* (London: Quarterly Series, 1885);

Das arme Leben und bittere Leiden unseres Herrn Jesu Christi und seiner heiligsten Mutter Maria, nebst den Geheimnissen des alten Bundes, edited by Schmöger (Regensburg: Pustet, 1881); translated as *The Life of Our Lord and Saviour Jesus Christ; Combined with the Bitter Passion, and The Life of Mary: From the Revelations of Anna Catharina Emmerick as Recorded in the Journals of Clemens Brentano* (Fresno, Cal.: Academy Library Guild, 1954);

Valeria oder Vaterlist: Ein Lustspiel in fünf Aufzügen edited by Reinhold Steig (Berlin: Behr, 1901);

Sämtliche Werke, edited by Heinz Amelung, Victor Michels, Julius Petersen, August Sauer, Erich Schmidt, Franz Schultz, Reinhold Steig, and Carl Schüddekopf, 9 volumes (Munich & Leipzig: Müller, 1909-1917)– includes, in volume 9, *Aloys und Imelde*, edited by Agnes Harnack;

Romanzen vom Rosenkranz: Unter erstmaliger Benutzung des gesamten handschriftlichen Materials, edited by Alphons M. von Steinle (Trier: Petrus, 1912);

Die Schachtel mit der Friedenspuppe, edited by Josef Körner (Vienna: Strache, 1922);

Gockel und Hinkel: In der Urfassung zum erstenmal nach der Handschrift des Dichters veröffentlicht, edited by Karl Viëtor (Frankfurt am Main: Gieschen, 1923);

Die Chronika des fahrenden Schülers: Urfassung, edited by Joseph Lefftz (Leipzig: Wolkenwanderer-Verlag, 1923);

Clemens Brentanos Romanfragment "Der schiffbrüchige Galeerensklave vom Todten Meer," edited by Walter Rehm (Berlin: Akademie-Verlag, 1949);

Anna Katharina Emmerich: Der Gotteskreis, edited by Anton Brieger (Munich: Manz, 1960);

Werke, edited by Friedhelm Kemp, 4 volumes (Munich: Hanser, 1963);

Sämtliche Werke und Briefe, edited by Jürgen Behrens, Wolfgang Frühwald, and Detlev Lüders, 6 volumes (Stuttgart: Kohlhammer, 1975-1980).

Editions in English: *Fairy Tales from Brentano*, translated by Kate Freiligrath Kroeker (London: Unwin, 1884 [dated 1885]; New York: Armstrong, 1886)–comprises "Dear-my-soul" ("Das Märchen von den Märchen oder Liebseelchen"), "The Story of Sir Skip-and-a-jump" ("Das Märchen von dem Baron von Hüpfenstich"), "The Story of Ninny Noddy" ("Das Märchen vom Dilldapp"), "The Story of Wakkemhard and of His Five Sons" ("Das Märchen von dem Schulmeister Klopfstock und seinen fünf Söhnen");

New Fairy Tales from Brentano, translated by Kroeker (New York: Armstrong, 1888; London: Unwin, 1888)–comprises "Gockel, Hinkel, and Gackeleia," "Frisky Wisky" ("Das Märchen von dem Witzenspitzel"), "Myrtle Maiden" ("Das Märchen von dem Myrthenfräulein"), "Brokerina," "Old Father Rhine and the Miller" ("Das Märchen von dem Rhein und dem Müller Radlauf");

Schoolmaster Whackwell's Wonderful Sons: A Fairy Tale, translated by Doris Orgel (New York: Random House, 1962).

OTHER: "Die Rose," in *Memnon*, edited by August Klingemann (Leipzig: Rein, 1800), pp. 143-175;

"Der Sänger," in *Kalathiskos*, edited by Sophie Mereau (Berlin: Fröhlich, 1801), pp. 151-224;

Spanische und italienische Novellen, edited by Brentano and Sophie Brentano, probably translated by Brentano, 2 volumes (Penig: Dienemann, 1804-1806);

Des Knaben Wunderhorn: Alte deutsche Lieder, edited by Brentano and Achim von Arnim, 3 volumes (Heidelberg: Mohr & Zimmer, 1805 [dated 1806-1808]); selections translated by Margarete Münsterberg as "The Boy's Magic Horn," in *The German Classics of the Nineteenth and Twentieth Centuries*, edited by Kuno Francke and W. G. Howard, volume 5 (New York: German Publications Society, 1913), pp. 163-169;

Jörg Wickram, *Der Goldfaden: Eine schöne alte Geschichte wieder herausgegeben*, edited by Brentano (Heidelberg: Mohr & Zimmer, 1809);

Friedrich Spee, *Trutz Nachtigall, ein geistlich poetisches Lustwäldlein . . . Durch den ehrwürdigen Pater Friedrich Spee, Priester der Gesellschaft Jesu: Wörtlich treue Ausgabe vermehrt mit den Liedern aus dem güldenen Tugendbuch desselben*

Dichters, edited by Brentano (Berlin: Dümmler, 1817);

"Die drei Nüsse" and "Die mehreren Wehmüller und ungarischen Nationalgesichter," in *Der Gesellschafter oder Blätter für Geist und Herz*, edited by F. W. Gubitz, volume 1 (Berlin: Maurer, 1817), pp. 521-534, 625-671;

"Geschichte vom braven Kasperl und dem schönen Annerl," in *Gaben der Milde*, edited by Gubitz, volume 2 (Berlin, 1817), pp. 7-81;

"Aus der Chronika eines fahrenden Schülers," in *Die Sängerfahrt*, edited by Friedrich Förster (Berlin: Maurer, 1818), pp. 234-258;

Fenelon's Leben, aus dem Französischen des Ritters von Ramsay übersetzt und mit einigen Anmerkungen und Beilagen begleitet, foreword by Brentano (Coblenz: Hölscher, 1826);

Spee, *Goldnes Tugendbuch*, edited by Brentano, 2 volumes (Coblenz: Hölscher, 1829);

"Am Rhein schweb' ich her und hin," in *Clemens Brentano's Frühlingskranz aus Jugendbriefen ihm geflochten, wie er selbst schriftlich verlangte*, by Bettina von Arnim, volume 1 (Charlottenburg: Bauer, 1844), pp. 261-263.

PERIODICAL PUBLICATIONS: "Geschichte vom Ursprung des ersten Bärenhäuters," *Zeitung für Einsiedler*, 1 (1808): 169-198;

"Der arme Raimondin: Ein unbekanntes Fragment," edited by Friedrich Fuchs, *Die neue Rundschau*, 55 (1944): 107-117.

Clemens Brentano is not only a decisive figure in the history of German Romanticism but also a force with which to be reckoned on the modern German literary scene. Brentano began as a writer of catholic purview and became a Catholic writer with a somewhat narrow, parochial perspective. Before his much-heralded reversion in 1817 to the faith of his ancestors he wrote novellas, fairy tales, an innovative novel, comedies, tragedies, festival plays, the first third of a monumental dramatic trilogy chronicling Czech history in mythic-symbolic form, a host of dramatic fragments, and a long, fragmentary verse romance (in the mold of the *Divine Comedy* but with Faustian overtones) dealing with the redemption of a family from a hereditary curse originating in biblical times. But it is primarily as a craftsman of lyric verse–of lilting, hauntingly musical quality during his early years and a more complex, hermetic character later in his life–that Brentano etched his name indelibly on the mind of the German reading public. In the last decades of his career, however, he carved out a niche for himself as the amanuensis for a stigmatized nun, Anna Katharina Emmerich. He recorded her visions of the life of Christ in what purported to be objective fashion but proved upon closer inspection to bear Brentano's usual idiosyncratic stamp. Nevertheless, these texts reached perhaps the widest readership of all his writings and have, by far, stirred the greatest controversies over the course of the last century.

The four decades of Brentano's creative career extended from the heyday of Romanticism to the incipient stages of realism, while his personality embraced a spectrum of traits from crass sensualism to pious asceticism. About the only consistency to be found in Brentano seems to be his inconsistency. The result is a writer of extreme complexity who longs for simplicity; a poet who idealizes the past in a modern, often avant-garde idiom; an author whom some consider an iconoclastic revolutionary moving toward a revitalized future but others see as an anachronistic reactionary clinging to icons from the dead past.

Clemens Maria Wenzeslaus Brentano was born in Ehrenbreiten on 9 September 1778 to a well-to-do Frankfurt merchant of Italian ancestry, Peter Anton Brentano, and the aesthetically minded Maximiliane Euphrosine von La Roche Brentano, whose mother, Sophie von La Roche, had been a pioneer among feminist writers in Germany. Among Brentano's siblings was his sister, Bettina, who married Ludwig Achim von Arnim in 1811. In her youth Bettina gave the impression of being a kind of multitalented will-o'-the-wisp personality, but after the death of her husband in 1831 she became a writer of note and a staunch defender of social causes.

After some schooling on the secondary level Brentano matriculated at the University of Bonn in 1794; received some short-lived exposure to the business world, which he bungled; went to the University of Halle in 1797; and finally arrived in Jena in 1798 to study medicine. Jena was then the hotbed of an innovative literary trend called Romanticism, and in the next few years some of the leading figures of Romanticism–such as Ludwig Tieck, August Wilhelm Schlegel, and Friedrich Schlegel–congregated there. Jena provided fertile soil and intellectual stimulus for Brentano's literary creativity. Early in his career Brentano joined ranks with those who defended the Romantic approach against the attacks of the more conservative practitioners of literature. One of his first published works, the satire *Gustav*

Wasa (1800), ridicules the standard trappings and stereotyped stage techniques of a pedestrian writer, the playwright August von Kotzebue, whom the Romantics felt was anathema to their cause.

Brentano not only reacted defensively to the broadsides of the antiromantic faction; he also proceeded offensively, producing with his two-volume novel *Godwi oder Das steinerne Bild der Mutter: Ein verwilderter Roman* (Godwi; or, The Stone Statue of the Mother: A Novel Grown Wild, 1801-1802) a kind of counterstatement to Goethe's "classical" Bildungsroman, *Wilhelm Meisters Lehrjahre* (1795-1796; translated as *Wilhelm Meister's Apprenticeship*, 1824). Brentano's partly epistolary, partly expository work indulges in considerable play with the fictional conventions of the age, such as delayed revelation of identity to sustain an aura of mystery or Romantic "confusion." Godwi runs the erotic gamut in the course of his seemingly aimless wanderings, experiencing in succession a relationship with a mature woman of the world; maternal affection, projected into the statue of his deceased mother, Marie; the idealized amorous soulmates Joduno and Otilie; and finally a reluctant prostitute, Violette, whose transfigured memory and intrinsically laudable nature are celebrated in a stone monument and described in a series of sonnets. Godwi's odyssey from the statue of his mother to Violette's monument lacks the kind of teleological thrust found in *Wilhelm Meisters Lehrjahre*. The literal meaning of Goethe's protagonist's name suggests that he is destined to "master" the course of his development; on the other hand, "Godwi" is derived, according to the author, from the expression "Gott, wie dumm" (God, how stupid). His "development" is not linear but labyrinthine.

The amorous confusion to which Godwi is exposed reflects, to some degree, the emotional upheavals to which the young Brentano was subject during his hectic courtship of Sophie Mereau, whose divorce from the university librarian and professor of jurisprudence was pending. During periods of alienation from Sophie, Brentano meandered through Germany, making the acquaintance of a variety of young ladies–including Minna Reichenbach, who rejected his marriage proposal, in Altenburg. But it was Sophie who dominated his thoughts, and they were married on 11 December 1803.

During these times of turmoil Brentano wrote two works for the stage. *Die lustigen*

Musikanten (The Merry Minstrels, 1803), the libretto for an operetta that was set to music in 1805 by E. T. A. Hoffmann for a Warsaw performance, deals with a band of wandering street singers whose wretched physical conditions and deteriorating mental states are in ironic contrast to the boisterous music they are compelled to perform to survive. The concept of "singing through a veil of tears" which comes to the fore here is one which Brentano was to repeat throughout his life, especially when his heart was breaking and he concealed his grief behind a cascade of lovely verbal music. *Ponce de Leon* (1804), on the other hand, is a comedy of intrigue in which costumes and disguises are used to conceal identities, and the language the characters speak is so ambiguous that confusion and chaos result. But in the "all's well that ends well" finale, made possible by the clever machinations of a well-meaning father-figure aided by some deus ex machina tactics, the proper mates find each other. *Ponce de Leon* falls short of the mark of true comedy because most of the humor resides in acrobatics of language rather than in the situations or characters. This verbal ballast proved too heavy a burden when the work was performed, even after it was revised for a Vienna production under the title *Valeria oder Vaterlist* (Valeria or Paternal Deception, 1901) in 1814, and it proved a theatrical failure.

The three years of Brentano's first marriage were marred by discord and tragedy. The poet seemed happiest when he was separated from his wife, traveling to visit his friend Achim von Arnim, for instance; proximity to Sophie bred conflict. The three children of the couple died in early infancy, and Sophie herself succumbed after the birth of the last offspring on 31 October 1806. While Brentano began during this period several projects which bore fruit only much later, it was primarily a time for collecting and editing the writings of others rather than for original work. The most sensational and controversial of these efforts was a three-volume set of folk songs which appeared from 1805 to 1808 under the title *Des Knaben Wunderhorn* (The Boy's Magic Horn). The editorial practices of Brentano and Arnim were, in the eyes of trained philologists and the practitioners of verbatim transcription of source materials, highly suspect; the editors sought to transmit the spirit rather than the letter of the texts. In spite of this philological license, however, the anthology was to be a major

influence on poets and musicians for more than a century.

After assisting Sophie in editing the two-volume *Spanische und italienische Novellen* (Spanish and Italian Novellas, 1804-1806), Brentano published in 1809 an adaptation of Jörg Wickram's romance *Der Goldfaden* (The Golden Thread, 1557). Avid interest in the literature of Germany's past and attempts to rescue neglected masterpieces were characteristic of German Romanticism in its second phase (the geographic center of which was no longer Jena but Heidelberg) and became a feature in the short-lived journal *Zeitung für Einsiedler* (News for Hermits) founded by Arnim and Brentano in 1808. Brentano contributed to this journal an adaptation of the "Geschichte vom Ursprung des ersten Bärenhäuters" (Tale of the Origin of the First Sluggard).

In part, at least, the love of the Romantics for the literary achievements of the German past had patriotic–even chauvinistic–roots. The German states had been under the yoke of Napoleon since the demise of the Holy Roman Empire in 1806, and one means to fan the francophobic fires and to rally support for ouster of the foreign invader was the appeal to German cultural roots and past accomplishments. Later, during the Wars of Liberation from 1813 to 1815, Brentano composed a verbose patriotic stage extravaganza, *Viktoria und ihre Geschwister mit fliegenden Fahnen und brennender Lunte* (Victoria and Her Siblings with Flying Colors and Burning Fuse, 1817); its performance, however, was banned by the censor.

The flow of lyric poetry seldom ebbed throughout Brentano's life, even during times of emotional stress such as his hasty and ill-conceived marriage to Auguste Bußmann in 1807, which led from bizarre "hide and seek" escapades on both sides to a two-month separation and finally to a bitter divorce in 1812. Such periods of strife, however, were not conducive to the production of original works of larger scope. Thus, no major writings were published by Brentano from 1808 until 1814. Two shorter satiric works of more than passing interest did appear, however. The first, written jointly with Joseph von Görres, bears the fantastic, playfully baroque title *Entweder wunderbare Geschichte von BOGS dem Uhrmacher, wie er zwar das menschliche Leben längst verlassen, nun aber doch, nach vielen musikalischen Leiden zu Wasser und zu Lande, in die bürgerliche Schützengesellschaft aufgenommen zu werden Hoffnung hat, oder Die über die Ufer der badischen*

Wochenschrift als Beilage ausgetretene Konzert-Anzeige (Either the Strange Story of BOGS, the Watchmaker, How He, to Be Sure, Has Long Ago Departed from Human Existence, but Who, However, Now Has Hope of Being Admitted to the Civic Gun Club after Much Suffering at Sea and on Land; or, The Concert Advertisement Which, as a Supplement, Has Overflowed the Banks of the Baden Weekly, 1807). This account pokes fun at a watchmaker who, to gain entry into a strictly philistine organization–a gun club–must document how he is able to withstand the powerful effect which music can exert on the imagination of the listener. In describing his "resistance" to various musical stimuli at a concert, he creates the most extravagant phantasmagoria conceivable, thereby proving himself particularly vulnerable to music's fantastically eidetic force. The second satire, *Der Philister vor, in und nach der Geschichte* (The Philistine in Pre-, Present-, and Post-History, 1811), which Brentano read aloud to the exclusive Christian-German Dinner Society of Berlin in 1811, had existed in a less elaborate version dating from 1799; it thus attests to the writer's persistent aversion to the "philistine," the avowed enemy of all activities and attitudes which transcend carefully circumscribed, calculable, and practical considerations.

Brentano's journey to Bohemia in 1811 for the purpose of assuming management of the family estate Bukowan proved a fiasco in practical terms but provided the catalyst for new creative activity as the poet gained insights into, and inspiration from, the history and mythology of the Czech people. In addition his brief amorous encounter with a Prague actress, Auguste Brede, also buoyed his sagging emotional spirits at the time when his marriage to Auguste Bußmann was staggering toward its terminal stage. One outgrowth of these experiences was an attempt at a second novel, "Der schiffbrüchige Galeerensklave vom Todten Meer" (The Shipwrecked Galley Slave from the Dead Sea); the extant fragments of this provocative, puzzling work were published in 1949. Initial allusions to the comet of 1811 with its flickering, fiery orbit across the heavens seem to symbolize the meanderings of Brentano himself. In the later sections a cavalierlike German poet wandering from Rome to Naples who comes across a "lost" young woman of dubious moral quality named Perdita, and, by contrast, also meets the charming actress Topina d'Avorio, with whose voice he becomes enamored, has biographical ties to the author. A second work from

this period is the unwieldy fatalistic drama *Aloys und Imelde* (Aloys and Imelde, 1912), which is set against the background of religious wars in the Pyrenees and portrays the misfortunes of the titular lovers stemming from the animosity between their families. This play reveals many of the dramatic weaknesses to which Brentano fell victim–aside from an overall lack of stringent dramatic development, one notes a plethora of subsidiary plots–due to his overactive "fantasy," which he denounced in his declining years: "wir hatten nichts genährt als die Phantasie, und sie hatte uns teils wieder aufgefressen" ("We had nurtured nothing but fantasy, and it had, in part, consumed us").

In 1812, while still in Bohemia, Brentano began work on the first of a planned trilogy of dramas dealing with the mythical past of the Czech people, *Die Gründung Prags* (The Founding of Prague); this "historisch–romantisches Drama" (historical–romantic drama) was published in 1815. Although by then Brentano had spent the years 1813-1814 in Vienna writing perceptive theatrical reviews for several journals, revising his comedy *Ponce de Leon* for stage production, and completing the sprawling patriotic pageant *Viktoria und ihre Geschwister*, he never evinced in his own creations a sense for true theatrical effectiveness or dramatic economy. This lack is nowhere more evident than in *Die Gründung Prags*, in which an elaborate mythic superstructure (necessitating a footnote apparatus) is obscured by the music and lyric components. The larger forces in the play, however, are clearly drawn: the dark, heathen idols of the mythical past are about to cede precedence to the radiant deity of the Christian faith; the enemies of the incipient Bohemian state both from without (invading Slavic tribes) and within (recalcitrant warrior women opposed to those female factions who seek peace) must be overcome for the new era to begin; finally, the struggle between men and women for dominance in society must be resolved. All of the conflicts seem to be on the path to resolution when the divinely ordained leader of the new state, Libussa, the daughter of the mythical King Krokus, takes the peasant Primislaus as her husband, and the bridal pair proceeds triumphantly toward the newly founded capital of Prague (the name of which Brentano, adhering to an erroneous philological derivation, interprets to mean "threshold").

Brentano's move from Vienna to Berlin in 1814 was followed by changes in his attitudes and life-style which were to have wide-reaching im-

Pencil sketch of Brentano by Wilhelm Hensel, 1819
(Staatliche Museen Preußischer Kulturbesitz,
Nationalgalerie, Berlin)

plications for the remainder of his career. First, there appeared in his correspondence signs of a growing fear of the loss of poetic inspiration as well as skepticism with regard to the ability of language to articulate essentials. Second, in Berlin Brentano came into contact with a Catholic revival movement which had originated in Bavaria and began a reexamination of his religious orientation. Third, it was in Berlin that he met Luise Hensel in 1816. She was not only a fellow poet and a love interest but also an individual in the throes of a religious crisis.

Brentano's artistic and religious crises are evident most strongly in his lyric poetry; on the other hand, from 1815 to 1817 some of his best, but also his most unusual, short fiction appeared in print. The novella *Die Schachtel mit der Friedenspuppe* (The Chest with the Doll of Peace), published in the Vienna paper *Friedensblätter* in 1815 (in book form, 1922), deals with the dire consequences of substituting the corpse of a dead child for the true family heir in order to deprive the latter of his rightful inheritance. The chest used to transport the body has a long history of macabre affiliations and therefore resembles a familiar requisite of the popular "fate tragedies" of the time: some object, such as a knife, linked to a series of deaths. Elements of a detective story or murder mystery surface in "Die drei Nüsse" (The Three Nuts), published in the Berlin paper *Der Gesellschafter* in 1817 (and in volume 4 of Brentano's collected works, 1852-1855), in which a homicide committed out of jealousy is allied with the themes of incest and the potentially deleterious effects of beauty.

The year 1817 brought the publication of two other stories. "Geschichte vom braven Kasperl und dem schönen Annerl" (translated as *Honor; or, The Story of the Brave Caspar and the Fair Annerl*, 1847), published in the anthology *Gaben der Milde* (Charitable Gifts) and in book form in 1838, is a somber tale about suicide and murder, both acts stemming from an exaggerated sense of honor. Concern for his good name leads Kasperl to take his life when he discovers that members of his family are thieves, while his former lover Annerl is hanged for infanticide. The father of Annerl's illegitimate child, a member of the nobility who had used drugs and magical means to gain his way with her, confesses his guilt too late to save her from the scaffold. But his act does persuade the reigning duke, who is involved in a clandestine affair which compromises the honor of the nobleman's sister, to marry the lady. A monument is erected at the gravesite of Kasperl and Annerl, allegorically celebrating true and false honor. This "honorable" burial vindicates the efforts of the eighty-year-old woman who, in recounting the fate of the lovers, reveals a deepseated, fervid piety characteristic of simple peasants who have only their religious faith to which to cling.

The second narrative, *Die mehreren Wehmüller und ungarischen Nationalgesichter* (The Numerous Wehmüllers and Hungarian National Countenances), published in *Der Gesellschafter* (and in book form in 1843), consists of a frame story treating the problem of Wehmüller's "double" and three tales related to each other and to the account of Wehmüller by both content and form. In the frame the reader learns that the painter Wehmüller has evolved a successful artistic technique now being counterfeited by an imposter; the trio of subsidiary fantastic narratives–"Das Pickenick des Katers Mores" (translated as "The Picnic of Mores the Cat," 1955), "Devilliers Erzählung von den Hexen auf dem Austerfelsen" (Devillier's Story of the Witches on Oyster Rock), "Baciochis Erzählung vom wilden Jäger" (Baciochi's Story of the Cursed Huntsman)— are correlated with events in the frame and reflect the structural principle of doubling, a major principle of the later Romantics.

The Wehmüller and Kasperl stories, appearing in the same year, reflect two facets of Brentano's creative wellsprings which went hand in hand from this time until the end of his life: unbridled imagination and religious devotion. To a certain extent these components had been prefigured in earlier works such as the fragmentary lyric cycle *Romanzen vom Rosenkranz* (Romances of the Rosary), begun in 1803, abandoned in 1812, and published in 1912, in which a hereditary curse placed on a family in biblical times is expiated in the Middle Ages by three "rose" sisters (Rosadora, Rosarosa, and Rosablanka) and their three brothers. These siblings overcome necromancer Apo and his Mephistophelean cohort Moles, who subject them to perils ranging from threats of physical harm to enticement to incest. Had Brentano been able to complete the epic, the rose sisters would have brought redemption to their family through the power of pure love.

A somewhat different blend of the spirit of medieval religiosity and poetic fantasy prevails in *Die Chronika des fahrenden Schülers* (The Chronicle of the Traveling Student, 1923), written from 1803 to 1810 and published in an abridged and revised adaptation, "Aus der Chronika eines fahrenden Schülers" (Excerpts from the Chronicle of a Traveling Student), in 1818. In the early version of the work Johannes, a student and scribe, recounts with simple, childlike piety the life of his mother, the lovely Els, then reads aloud a parable titled "Von dem trauerigen Untergang zeitlicher Liebe" (Concerning the Sorrowful Downfall of Temporal Love). In this story a handsome youth, the son of a siren and a simple fisherman, uses his poetic gifts to garble the enticing song of the "Perlengeist" (Pearl Spirit), whose sweet sounds have lured unsuspecting lovers to their deaths on a rocky crag. But in the course of recording the seductive songs of the Pearl Spirit, which he intends to neutralize, the handsome youth falls victim to arrogance, a cardinal sin and an attitude detrimental to religious humility and pious devotion. The images of the poet-singer as both victor over the forces of temptation and as victim of the temptations of his own art reflect the precarious balance of those elements of religiosity and fantasy which

constantly vied for dominance in Brentano, especially after his reversion to the Catholic faith.

A similar clash between the quest for a simple piety and the disruptive impulse to allow imagination free rein can be detected in Brentano's ventures into the fairy tale. Two major groups, the "Rheinmärchen" (Fairy Tales of the Rhine) and the "Italienische Märchen" (Italian Fairy Tales), eventually emerged, and even though portions of each appeared during Brentano's lifetime (on one occasion against the author's expressed wishes), it was only upon their posthumous publication in two volumes (1846-1847) that their full scope could be assessed. Both collections have at their core the theme of the restoration of an original state of happy, childlike innocence after infractions have brought about the forfeiture of that condition of naive bliss. The frame tale of the Rhine group has as its hero the miller Radlauf, an ingenuous lad who wins the hand of a princess, only to lose her when she and her playmates, as a consequence of the machinations of corrupt courtiers, are drawn into the Rhine River by the magical tone of a pied piper. Father Rhine demands that for each child released a fairy tale be told. The first series of stories deals with Radlauf's mythical ancestors: each successive male progenitor married a woman linked with one of the four elements; every one of the husbands, being prodded by natural inquisitiveness, posed the forbidden question concerning his spouse's origin and was punished. This punishment entails confinement to a state of suspended animation until they find redemption and release through a later member of the line—Radlauf—who does not fall prey to the same temptation. The tales are overladen with fantastic verbal acrobatics and fascinating minor figures and episodes, details which interrupt the overall narrative progression. Perhaps because of the repetitive nature of the central plot, however, Brentano felt that such extraneous elements might be aesthetically warranted.

In the principal story from the Italian fairy tales, *Gockel, Hinkel, und Gackeleia* (translated as *The Wondrous Tale of Cocky, Clucky, and Cackle*, 1889), enlarged and published separately in 1838, another prohibition is violated when Gackeleia, the daughter of Gockel and Hinkel, having been forbidden to play with dolls because of prior disobedience, is enticed to do so by three Jewish seal engravers (Brentano, like several of his romantic contemporaries, was not free of anti-Semitic stereotypes). In return for Solomon's magic wishing ring, which had been bequeathed to the Gockel family by its pet rooster, the trio offers Gackeleia an enchanting dancing doll, labeling the beautifully handcrafted artifact a "Schöne Kunstfigur" (lovely figurine) rather than a "Puppe" (doll). This subterfuge enables Gackeleia to cling to the letter of the interdiction while circumventing its spirit. The forfeiture of the ring, however, brings a loss of wealth and prosperity to the Gockel clan; but by helping a white mouse princess—the moving force behind the dancing figurine—return to her homeland, Gackeleia atones for her infraction and is rewarded when the grateful rodents regain the ring for her. With this ring Gackeleia is able to restore her family to its previous happy state, and in a grand finale the power of the ring is invoked to turn adults back into children. This ending has obvious religious overtones, recalling the biblical injunction that only those who "become as little children" can enter the kingdom of heaven. The impossible dream of regained innocence was also an ideal of those romantic writers who felt that the burden of conscience might be alleviated in this fashion. But along the path to this goal Brentano paradoxically indulges in such sophisticated games of fantasy, ironic asides, and word play that he seems to undermine the very ideal of childlike naiveté which he has set out to recapture.

In 1817 Brentano auctioned off the secular holdings in his library and publicly confessed the Catholic faith. His work from that time on is set in a predominantly religious framework. His six-year vigil at the bedside of a stigmatized nun, Anna Katharina Emmerich, resulted in his recording her vision of Christ's life (in some cases Brentano actually inspired them by reading excerpts from mystical tracts and other religious writings to her). The decade following her death in 1824 was one of intense devotion to Catholic causes and charity work including an 1829 edition of the lyrics of the seventeenth-century Catholic poet Friedrich von Spee, who was instrumental in ending witch burning; a history of the charitable work of the Sisters of Mercy in 1831; and a trilogy on the life of Christ derived from Emmerich's visionary ramblings. The aim of the latter work was, perhaps, to counteract the demythologizing of Jesus that had begun to appear in the early nineteenth century.

The burden of organizing the vast array of notes of the Emmerich visions proved too much for Brentano, however, and he was only able to supervise the publication of *Das bittere Leiden unsers*

Herrn Jesu Christi: Nach den Betrachtungen der gottseligen Anna Katharina Emmerich (1833; translated as *The Passion of Our Lord Jesus Christ According to the Revelations of Anna Catharina Emmerich*, 1914), and to prepare the material for the remaining two parts of the undertaking: the life of the Virgin Mary and the story of Jesus' years of apprenticeship. Brentano's behavior toward the stigmatic was sometimes bizarre—his fetish for her wounds and his nocturnal exhumation of her body for example—but his transcriptions of her visions have enjoyed wide popularity.

That the post-1817 Brentano was not solely the instrument of Catholic propaganda that Heine, among others, accused him of being can be attested by his detailed reworking of his fairy tales as well as by his continued production of love lyrics and occasional poems in the service of humanitarian causes such as relief for the flood victims of the Mosel disaster of 1831. Brentano's gift for song persisted from his earliest to his latest poems, in spite of his occasional strong invectives against lyric poetry, which almost always lies, or his accusations of a sinful, sensuous allure inherent in the verbal medium.

The very title of the 1802 poem "Am Rhein schweb' ich her und hin" (I float up and down upon the Rhine, 1844), in which the speaker travels to an anticipated yet dreaded rendezvous with his beloved, is indicative of a situation on which Brentano's oeuvre thrives: the sense of a hovering suspension or tension between conflicting emotions. This tension is indicated by several other contrary pairs from the first to the last stanza and is expressed most effectively by the chiasmus: "O wähnend Lieben, Liebeswahn" (O imagining love, love imaginary). Brentano's narrator, having experienced the full spectrum of love "Vom blauen Kelch zum goldenen Saum" (from the blue calyx to its golden fringe) is prepared for a life-or-death commitment to this azure bed of love: "Vergifte mich, umdüfte mich" (Poison me, encircle me with fragrance). The text concludes in a limbo of uncertainty. Like many of Brentano's lyrics, this poem has been transmitted in several divergent forms; a somewhat less authoritative rendering closes with the speaker, now clearly identified as a boatman on the Rhine, being driven by the wind into the eddy at Bingen, suggesting a tragic outcome.

During the years of emotional agitation in the wake of his divorce from Auguste, Brentano produced a cluster of poems in which the speaker openly cavorts with women of highly dubious reputations. In "Die Welt war mir zuwider" (The world was repulsive to me), in volume 2 of Brentano's collected writings (1852), the speaker pursues a prostitute for two years through the streets of the city like a man possessed: "Ich lebt' und starb in dir, in dir!/O lieb Mädel, wie schlecht bist du!" (I lived and died in you, in you! /O dear girl, how evil you are!). The last of these lines, which serves as an ostinato refrain throughout all eleven stanzas of the poem, contains another of those paradoxical oxymora found in the previous verses, but the implications here are unique: the vile nature of the female constitutes an irresistible force of attraction, even unto death itself; death at her hands has made his life worth living. In radical verses which give voice to a perverse form of erotic fascination, one also senses elements of that romantic agony to which Brentano fell prey and for which no remedy seemed forthcoming except to search for new bondings on either the personal level or in religious affiliations which were likewise closely allied with specific women.

The latter situation prevailed in his last amorous liaison, that with the Swiss painter Emilie Linder, whom he met in 1833 and who rejected his marriage proposal in 1834. From this period comes a large group of love lyrics which recapitulates themes and motifs Brentano had used in his poetry before. In some cases entire poems written originally for a former love are simply recast to suit the circumstances with Emilie. The concept of the siren, for instance, which had manifested itself in Brentano's poetry from the outset, is present in the Linder lyrics also. The ambivalence associated with the siren figure as an embodiment of both attraction and destruction, of a love-giving yet death-dealing force, is evident in these lines from 1834 (in volume 2 of Brentano's collected writings): "Und als sie so gesungen/Ein bißchen süß gegaukelt,/Und sich herum geschwungen/Geschlungen und geschaukelt/Rief sie: 'Gut' Nacht, mein Brüderchen/Addio! schreib, mach Liederchen'" (And when she had sung thus,/Sweetly flitted about a bit,/And writhed, twisted and rocked around/She cried: "Good night, little brother/Good bye! Write, create little songs").

The romantic agony of being wedged between desire and disdain, commitment and contempt is transferred here to another mode favored by Brentano to cope with such a situation: romantic irony. The allure of the siren's gyrations is as enticing as it ever had been, but her

words, couched in mocking diminutives and inferring a neutralized relationship (Brüderchen), dismissing the liaison with a foreign phrase of farewell and a trite piece of advice (mach Liederchen), are countered by the speaker in the closing stanza with a string of taunting diminutives of his own: "mein Gebieterchen" (my little mistress), and so on. The torment resulting from a relationship is, in a sense, relativized and rendered harmless by being kept in a state of unresolved suspense. Her advice to the poet to "create little songs" from such great spiritual anguish–romantic irony at it most acrid–is taken to heart by him in his equally ironic response. When Brentano could gain proper aesthetic distance from the object of his affections, he was capable of lyric lines which give adequate expression to the romanticist's dilemma of unresolved existential tension, as opposed to the harmonious resolution which his contemporaries of the more "classical" persuasion exhibited. The following couplet might serve as an example of the Romantic brand of eternal duality in response to the "closure" of classical vintage. These haunting verses run through much of Brentano's writings during the 1830s like a signature leitmotif, one which subsumes both romantic agony and irony into a unique synthesis:

> O Stern und Blume, Geist und Kleid,
> Lieb', Leid und Zeit und Ewigkeit.
> (O star and flower, spirit and garment,
> Love, sorrow and time and eternity.)

Brentano spent his declining years alienated from society and in ill health. He felt himself at odds with the pragmatically oriented world of the 1840s, and his works found little resonance in an audience which sought utilitarian values in all things. Brentano became a Romantic anachronism in a realistic milieu, and thus he could speak of his poetry in 1841 as "nur ein Musizieren in der Luft" (merely a music-making in the air). When he died in 1842 from a combination of edema and heart trouble, the contemporary world took little note of his passing; it was left to posterity to discover that Clemens Brentano was not merely a romantic renegade or a proselytizer for Catholicism, but rather a poet "for all seasons."

Letters:
Clemens Brentano: Briefe, edited by Friedrich Seebaß, 2 volumes (Nuremberg: Carl, 1951);

Clemens Brentano: Briefe an Emilie Linder, edited by Wolfgang Frühwald (Bad Homburg & Zurich: Gehlen, 1970);

Clemens Brentano, edited by Werner Vordtriede and Gabriele Bartenschlager (Munich: Heimeran, 1970);

Clemens Brentano, Philipp Otto Runge: Briefwechsel, edited by Konrad Feilchenfeldt (Frankfurt am Main: Insel, 1974).

Bibliographies:

Otto Mallon, *Brentano-Bibliographie* (Berlin: 1926; reprinted, Hildesheim: Olms, 1965);

Hazel Walldorf, *Clemens Brentano: A Bibliography to Supplement Mallon 1926* (Johannesburg: University of Witwatergrand, 1971).

Biography:

Johannes B. Diel and Wilhelm Kreiten, *Clemens Brentano: Ein Lebensbild nach gedruckten und ungedruckten Quellen*, 2 volumes (Freiburg im Breisgau: Herder, 1877-1878).

References:

Eric A. Blackall, "Anxiety of the Spirit: Brentano and Arnim," in his *The Novels of the German Romantics* (Ithaca, N.Y.: Cornell University Press, 1983), pp. 173-208;

Paul Böckmann, "Die romantische Poesie Brentanos und ihre Grundlagen bei Friedrich Schlegel und Tieck: Ein Beitrag zur Entwicklung der Formensprache der deutschen Romantik," *Jahrbuch des Freien Deutschen Hochstifts* (1934-1935): 56-176;

Claude David, "Clemens Brentano," in *Die deutsche Romantik: Poetik, Formen und Motive*, edited by Hans Steffen (Göttingen: Vandenhoeck & Ruprecht, 1967), pp. 159-179;

Hans Magnus Enzensberger, *Brentanos Poetik* (Munich: Hanser, 1961);

Konrad Feilchenfeldt, "Brentano-Forschung in der Sicht der Auslandsgermanistik," *Göttingsche Gelehrte Anzeigen*, 236 (1985): 95-113;

John F. Fetzer, *Clemens Brentano* (Boston: Hall, 1981);

Fetzer, "Old and New Directions in Clemens Brentano Research 1931-1968)," *Literaturwissenschaftliches Jahrbuch*, 11 (1970): 87-119; 12 (1971): 113-203;

Fetzer, "Recent Trends in Clemens Brentano Research: 1968-1970," *Literaturwissenschaftliches Jahrbuch*, 13 (1970): 217-232;

Fetzer, *Romantic Orpheus: Profiles of Clemens Brentano* (Berkeley: University of California Press, 1974);

Wolfgang Frühwald, "Clemens Brentano," in *Deutsche Dichter der Romantik*, edited by Benno von Wiese (Berlin: Schmidt, 1971), pp. 280-309;

Frühwald, *Das Spätwerk Clemens Brentanos (1815-1842): Romantik im Zeitalter der Metternich'schen Restauration* (Tübingen: Niemeyer, 1977);

Frühwald, "Stationen der Brentano-Forschung: 1924-1972," *Deutsche Vierteljahrsschrift für Literaturwissenschaft und Geistesgeschichte*, 47, special issue: "Forschungsreferate" (1973): 182-269;

Lawrence Frye, "The Art of Narrating a Rooster Hero in Brentano's *Das Märchen von Gockel und Hinkel*," *Euphorion*, 72 (1978): 400-420;

Bernhard Gajek, "Die Brentano-Literatur 1973-1978," *Euphorion*, 72 (1978): 439-502;

Gajek, *Homo poeta: Zur Kontinuität der Problematik bei Clemens Brentano* (Frankfurt am Main: Athenäum, 1971);

René Guignard, *Un poète romantique allemand: Clemens Brentano* (Paris: Presses Universitaires, 1933);

Ian Hilton, "Clemens Brentano," in *German Men of Letters*, volume 5, edited by Alex Natan (London: Wolff, 1969), pp. 51-74;

Werner Hoffmann, *Clemens Brentano: Leben und Werk* (Bern & Munich: Francke, 1966);

Glyn Tegai Hughes, "Brentano," in his *Romantic German Literature* (New York: Holmes & Meier, 1979), pp. 81-89;

Alan Menhennet, "Clemens Brentano," in his *The Romantic Movement* (London: Croom Helm, 1981), pp. 81-94, 201-206;

Walter Müller-Seidel, "Brentanos naive und sentimentalische Poesie," *Jahrbuch der deutschen Schillergesellschaft*, 18 (1974): 441-465;

Wolfgang Pfeiffer-Belli, *Clemens Brentano: Ein romantisches Dichterleben* (Freiburg im Breisgau: Herder, 1947);

Helene M. K. Riley, *Clemens Brentano* (Stuttgart: Metzler, 1985);

Oskar Seidlin, "Prag: Deutsch-romantisch und Habsburg-Wienerisch," in *Austriaca: Beiträge zur österreichischen Literatur. Festschrift für Heinz Politzer*, edited by Winfried Kudszus and Hinrich Seeba (Tübingen: Niemeyer, 1975), pp. 201-229;

Seidlin, "Wirklich nur eine schöne Kunstfigur? Zu Brentanos Gockel-Märchen," in *Texte und*

Kontexte: Studien zur deutschen und vergleichenden Literaturwissenschaft. Festschrift für Norbert Fuerst, edited by Manfred Durzak, Eberhard Reichmann, and Ulrich Weisstein (Bern: Francke, 1973), pp. 235-248;

Elisabeth Stopp, "Brentano's 'O Stern und Blume': Its Poetic and Emblematic Context," *Modern Language Review,* 67 (1972): 95-117;

Erika Tunner, *Clemens Brentano (1778-1842): Imagination et sentiment religieux,* 2 volumes (Lille: University of Lille, 1977);

Ralph Tymms, "Clemens Brentano," in his *German Romantic Literature* (London: Methuen, 1955) pp. 207-264.

Papers:

The major holding of unpublished material by Clemens Brentano is at the Freies Deutsches Hochstift, Frankfurt am Main, Federal Republic of Germany.

Adelbert von Chamisso

(30 January 1781-21 August 1838)

Helene M. Kastinger Riley
Clemson University

BOOKS: *Peter Schlemihl's wundersame Geschichte,* edited by Friedrich de la Motte Fouqué (Nuremberg: Schrag, 1814); translated by John Bowring as *Peter Schlemihl* (London: Whittaker, 1823; Boston: Wells & Lilly, 1824); German version revised and enlarged (Berlin: Schrag, 1827);

De animalibus quibusdam e classe Vermium Linnaeana in circumnavigatione terrae auspicante comite N. Romanzoff duce Ottone de Kotzebue annis 1815. 1816. 1817. 1818. peracta observatis (Berlin: Dümmler, 1819);

Bemerkungen und Ansichten auf einer Entdeckungs-Reise, unternommen in den Jahren 1815-1818 auf Kosten Sr. Erlaucht des Herrn Reichs-Kanzlers Grafen Romanzoff, auf dem Schiffe Rurick, unter dem Befehle des Lieutenants der Russisch-Kaiserlichen Marine Otto von Kotzebue, published as volume 3 of Otto von Kotzebue's *Entdeckungsreise in die Süd-See und nach der Berings-Straße zur Erforschung einer nördlichen Durchfahrt in den Jahren 1815-1818* (Weimar: Hoffmann, 1821); translated by H. E. Lloyd as *Remarks and Opinions of the Naturalist of the Expedition,* published as volume 2 of Kotzebue's *A Voyage of Discovery into the South Sea and Bering's Straits, for the Purpose of Exploring a North-east Passage, Undertaken*

Adelbert von Chamisso

in the Years 1815-1818, at the Expense of His Highness . . . Count Romanzoff, in the Ship Ru-

rick, under the Command of the Lieutenant in the Russian Imperial Navy, Otto von Kotzebue (London: Longman, Hurst, Rees, Orme & Brown, 1821);

Uebersicht der nutzbarsten und der schädlichsten Gewächse, welche wild oder angebaut in Norddeutschland vorkommen: Nebst Ansichten von der Pflanzenkunde und dem Pflanzenreiche (Berlin: Dümmler, 1827);

Gedichte (Leipzig: Weidmann, 1831)–includes "Frauen-Liebe und Leben," translated by Frank V. McDonald as *Woman's Love and Life: A Cycle of Song* (Cambridge, Mass., 1881);

Werke, 3 volumes (Leipzig: Weidmann, 1836-1839)–comprises volume 1: *Reise um die Welt, mit der Romanzoffischen Entdeckungs-Expedition in den Jahren 1815-18, auf der Brigg Rurik, Kapitain Otto von Kotzebue*; translated by Henry Kratz as *A Voyage around the World with the Romanzov Exploring Expedition in the Years 1815-1818 in the Brig "Rurik," Captain Otto von Kotzebue* (Honolulu: University of Hawaii Press, 1986); volume 2: *Gedichte; Adelberts Fabel; Peter Schlemihl*; volume 3: *Leben und Briefe von Adelbert von Chamisso*, edited by Julius Eduard Hitzig;

Ueber die Hawaiische Sprache: Versuch einer Grammatik der Sprache der Sandwich-Inseln (Leipzig: Weidmann, 1837);

Zwei Gedichte (ein altes und ein neues): Zum Besten der alten Waschfrau (Berlin: Sittenfeld, 1838);

Fortunati Glückseckel und Wunschhütlein: Ein Spiel, edited by E. F. Koßmann (Stuttgart: Göschen, 1895).

OTHER: *Musenalmanach auf das Jahr 1804*, edited by Chamisso and Karl August Varnhagen von Ense (Leipzig: Schmidt, 1804)–includes *Faust*, translated by Henry Phillips, Jr., as *Faust: A Dramatic Sketch* (Philadelphia: Privately printed, 1881);

Musenalmanach auf das Jahr 1805, edited by Chamisso and Varnhagen von Ense (Berlin: Frölich, 1805);

Musenalmanach auf das Jahr 1806, edited by Chamisso and Varnhagen von Ense (Berlin: Frölich, 1806);

"Adelberts Fabel," in *Erzählungen und Spiele*, edited by Varnhagen von Ense and Wilhelm Neumann (Hamburg: Schmidt, 1807);

Deutscher Musenalmanach für das Jahr 1833, edited by Chamisso and Gustav Schwab (Leipzig: Weidmann, 1833);

Deutscher Musenalmanach für das Jahr 1834, edited by Chamisso and Schwab (Leipzig: Weidmann, 1834);

Deutscher Musenalmanach für das Jahr 1835, edited by Chamisso and Schwab (Leipzig: Weidmann, 1835);

Deutscher Musenalmanach für das Jahr 1836, edited by Chamisso and Schwab (Leipzig: Weidmann, 1836);

Deutscher Musenalmanach für das Jahr 1837, edited by Chamisso (Leipzig: Weidmann, 1837);

Deutscher Musenalmanach für das Jahr 1838, edited by Chamisso (Leipzig: Weidmann, 1838);

Pierre J. de Béranger, *Bérangers Lieder*, translated and adapted by Chamisso and Franz Gaudy (Leipzig: Weidmann, 1838);

Deutscher Musenalmanach für das Jahr 1839, edited by Chamisso and Gaudy (Leipzig: Weidmann, 1839).

Adelbert von Chamisso is known as one of the German Romantics chiefly for his first major work, the novella *Peter Schlemihl's wundersame Geschichte* (Peter Schlemihl's Marvelous History, 1814; translated as *Peter Schlemihl*, 1823), which was widely translated and made him internationally famous. A gentleman scientist like Achim von Arnim and Novalis, Chamisso remained curiously detached from the mainstream Romantics; instead, he chose his close friends predominantly from a circle of intellectuals such as Julius Eduard Hitzig and Karl August Varnhagen von Ense. Consequently, he has remained a somewhat shadowy figure in literary histories. Chamisso's work is generally placed in the late Romantic period or that of early realism. The incomparable humor in his poetry and prose varies from innocent mirth to macabre irony. Other poems depict social inequities with stark realism. He was a master in the use of the older lyrical forms of terza rima and alliteration. His botanical, zoological, and linguistic writings and his travelogues have barely received attention in literary circles.

Chamisso was born on the family estate of Boncourt in the French province of Champagne on 30 January 1781 to Louis Marie and Marie Anne Gargam Chamisso and christened Louis Charles Adelaide Chamisso de Boncourt. During the French Revolution the estate was destroyed and the family stripped of their possessions. Chamisso's parents fled France in 1790 with Chamisso and his siblings and began a search for asylum that led them to Liège, The Hague,

Düsseldorf, Würzburg, and Bayreuth before they finally settled in Berlin in 1796.

During his early years in exile Chamisso's future seemed anything but promising. He made and sold flowers while the family debated whether he should become a carpenter. After the family settled in Berlin he became a decorator of porcelain wares, while his brothers Hippolyt and Carl attained some renown as painters of miniatures. In 1796 Chamisso had the good fortune to be selected as attendant to Queen Friederike Luise. He received a private tutor and was permitted to attend the French gymnasium, an excellent secondary school, where he was educated in the humanistic tradition. His papers on military topics found favor with Friedrich Wilhelm III, and in 1798 Chamisso was commissioned as ensign to a regiment stationed in Berlin. He was promoted to lieutenant in 1801 and remained in Berlin when his family returned to France in the same year.

Chamisso became increasingly disenchanted with Prussian military life and, as a Frenchman in the German forces, felt isolated. After an 1802 visit to France, where he found his father ill and his family estranged from him, he sought contact with literary intellectuals in Berlin. Hitzig became his friend for life. With Hitzig, Varnhagen von Ense, the theologian Franz Theremin, Wilhelm Neumann, and David Ferdinand Koreff he founded the "Nordsternbund" (North Star Alliance), whose members included Friedrich de la Motte Fouqué, August Ferdinand Bernhardi, and the publisher G. Reimer. This liberal literary circle began meeting in 1803 on the occasion of August Wilhelm Schlegel's lectures in Berlin. Its policy of admitting Jews for membership separated the Nordsternbund from more conservative literary circles such as the "Christlich-deutsche Tischgesellschaft" (Christian-German Table Society), founded in 1811, which counted among its members Clemens Brentano, Achim von Arnim, Heinrich von Kleist, Johann Gottlieb Fichte, Friedrich Karl von Savigny, and some of the most influential individuals of the time. Although Chamisso was a member of this group as well, and Fichte maintained contact with the Nordsternbund, ideological differences between the two literary groups account at least in part for Chamisso's distance from the mainstream Romantics.

A first attempt at literary independence came in 1804 with the one-act play *Faust* (translated, 1881). The terms *Wille* (the will to do some-

thing) and *wollen* (to want to do something) and the limitations of free choice appear again prominently in "Adelberts Fabel" (Adelbert's Story, 1807), in *Peter Schlemihl's wundersame Geschichte*, and elsewhere. *Faust* legitimized Chamisso as a poet in his circle of friends and led to his becoming coeditor with Varnhagen von Ense of a Musenalmanach (poetry annual). The volume for 1804 was introduced by Chamisso's poem "Die jungen Dichter" (The Young Poets), which characterizes the group's enthusiasm and youthful expectations and also displays Chamisso's skillful use of terza rima and enjambment:

> Wir Namenlosen: Kronen zu erstreiten,
> Muß das Unendliche der Mann erzielen.
> Wir ringen aufwärts, und den goldnen Saiten
> Entbeben leise Töne schon; es spielen
> Apollons Strahlen leuchtend um die Leier,
> Und mächtig in dem regen Busen fühlen
> Auflodern wir der künft'gen Lieder Feuer.

(We who are without name: to win a crown, man must reach the infinite. We strive upward, and already the golden strings softly reverberate; Apollo's rays play gleaming in the lyre, and powerfully we feel the fire of future songs flare in the swelling bosom.)

The *Musenalmanach* for 1804 contains poems by Chamisso, Varnhagen von Ense, Neumann, Hitzig, Theremin, and Robert Levin; the volumes for 1805 and 1806 also contain poems by Fichte, Koreff, Bernhardi, Karl von Raumer, and Caroline de la Motte Fouqué.

Chamisso's regiment left Berlin in October 1805 and arrived at Hameln in April 1806; its task was to resist Napoleon's forces, requiring Chamisso to fight his countrymen. Twice he requested to be discharged, but his requests were denied. On 21 November the fortress of Hameln surrendered without a fight in the aftermath of the Prussian defeats of Jena and Auerstedt.

While stationed at Hameln Chamisso wrote "Adelberts Fabel," a short, distinctly Romantic tale reminiscent of Novalis's "Atlantismärchen" (Fairy Tale of Atlantis) in his novel *Heinrich von Ofterdingen* (1802). Adelbert awakens to find himself frozen in ice in a wintry landscape. Years go by without a change in Adelbert's lonely and helpless condition. "Er dachte: man muß die Notwendigkeit männlich ertragen, und murren gegen das Verhängte ist töricht. Gibt es einmal Gott, daß es Tauwetter werde, so erlang' ich vielleicht wohl einmal noch meine Freiheit wieder"

(He thought: necessity must be borne bravely, and to grumble over one's destiny is foolish. If it were God's will to send a thaw, perhaps someday I might regain my freedom). Necessity is a fetter that restrains every human being from time to time, and Chamisso had ample experience with it: political forces, poverty, linguistic limitations, and military rules had all curtailed his personal and intellectual freedom. The hope for an act of God is tantamount to resignation. In "Adelberts Fabel" divine intervention comes in the form of an engraving in a ring given to him by a spirit. Like the apprentices in Novalis's *Die Lehrlinge zu Sais* (The Novices of Sais, 1802), Adelbert spends much time deciphering the hieroglyphics of divine knowledge and advice. Eventually he recognizes that it is only his own will that can change his situation: "Ich will's! rief er mit Macht aus und sprang im Zorn auf, und die Bande des Eises, die ihn gehalten, waren zerschellt worden" (I will it! he cried out forcefully and sprang up in anger, and the bonds of ice that held him were shattered). The remainder of the tale describes Adelbert's travels through allegorical landscapes until he awakens from his dream, facing the rising sun. This compact story is, despite its obvious indebtedness to Novalis, a jewel of Romantic writing. The circular form cleverly depicts the tenet that life is a dream and the dream is life. The key to personal freedom and mastery of one's destiny lies in unlocking the mysteries of the unconscious, in deciphering the "hieroglyphics" or symbols (in the tale, Greek letters) provided by dreams or life.

After Hameln's surrender Chamisso was free to travel, but his formal discharge from the service did not occur until January 1808. Between 1806 and 1812 he traveled repeatedly from Germany to France and Switzerland, searching for a suitable position and an aim in life. In Paris he met the Romantic poet Ludwig Uhland and Mme. de Staël (Anne Louise Germaine Necker Staël-Holstein). Chamisso spent the summer of 1810 with Mme. de Staël and her literary circle of friends at her castle, Chaumont on the Loire, followed her to Blois, and stayed with her during her exile in Coppet, Switzerland, in 1811-1812. He collected old French folk songs, studied English and Spanish, and collected botanical specimens on an excursion to the Mont Blanc region. The majesty of the mountains had an overwhelming effect on him; Chamisso recalls the mood at the beginning of the tenth chapter of *Peter Schlemihl's wundersame Geschichte:* "Ich fiel in

stummer Andacht auf meine Kniee und vergoß Tränen des Dankes, denn klar stand plötzlich meine Zukunft vor meiner Seele. Durch frühe Schuld von der menschlichen Gesellschaft ausgeschlossen, ward ich zum Ersatz an die Natur, die ich stets geliebt, gewiesen, die Erde mir zu einem reichen Garten gegeben, das Studium zur Richtung und Kraft meines Lebens, zu seinem Ziel die Wissenschaft" (I fell to my knees in mute devotion and shed tears of gratitude, for my future suddenly was clear to me. Cut off from human society by a youthful guilt, I had by way of compensation been thrown back on nature, which I had always loved. The earth had been given me as a rich garden; study was to be the direction and strength of my life, with science as its goal).

In the fall of 1812 Chamisso enrolled at the University of Berlin as a medical student. The Napoleonic wars interrupted his studies in 1813, and he retreated to a friend's estate in Kunersdorf to continue his botanical work. There he wrote *Peter Schlemihl's wundersame Geschichte*, ostensibly to entertain Hitzig's children. It became his most successful work and assured his place in the history of literature.

In a moment of monetary need Peter Schlemihl trades his shadow for a leather pouch with a never-ending supply of gold coins. The donor of the pouch is a servile, "shadowy" little man dressed in gray who takes Peter's shadow and disappears for a year. During this time Peter learns to regret his hasty bargain. He is soon wealthy beyond belief, a respected citizen, and celebrated for his inexhaustible generosity; but he is ostracized and feared as soon as people realize that he has no shadow. Thus Peter shows himself only at night, on rainy days, or indoors and fears the light of day. The connection of the bargain with sin and guilt, the curtailment of personal freedom, and the denial of love–his fiancée leaves him when he cannot refute the rumor that he has no shadow–are major themes. As has been noted by many critics, there are symbolic parallels between Peter and his creator: the expulsion from home and country, the financial need, the "shadowy" existence in exile. After the year is over Peter wants his shadow back, but now the little gray man shows his true colors: only if Peter signs in blood the promise of his soul will he be reunited with his shadow and become whole again. The temptation to acquiesce to this new bargain is almost irresistible, and Peter's tormentor becomes a constant, teasing companion. Chamisso shows that life's choices are rarely made in complete freedom; necessity always influences one's decisions in an endless string of compromises, and unforeseen occurrences often replace planned actions. Chamisso's philosophy is summarized in a passage which has been translated in a variety of ways because of its ambiguous syntax: "Ich habe erstlich die Notwendigkeit verehren lernen, und was ist mehr, als die getane Tat, das geschehene Ereignis, ihr Eigentum! Dann hab' ich auch diese Notwendigkeit als eine weise Fügung verehren lernen, die durch das gesamte große Getriebe weht, darin wir bloß als mitwirkende, getriebene, treibende Räder eingreifen" (First I learned to honor necessity and–what is more–the deed which has been done, the event that has occurred as the property of necessity! Then I also learned to revere this necessity as a wise providence which drifts through the entire great mechanism in which we engage merely as contributing, driven, and driving gears).

The story ends happily: Peter withstands temptation and reconciles himself to the loss of his shadow. With his last pennies he acquires a pair of used shoes which turn out to be seven-league boots. He is now able to travel to the ends of the earth collecting botanical and zoological specimens and charting unknown territories. He has found his life's vocation in scientific inquiry. The last lines of *Peter Schlemihl's wundersame Geschichte* are prophetic of Chamisso's own destiny: "Ich habe die Geographie vom Innern von Afrika und von den nördlichen Polarländern, vom Innern von Asien und von seinen östlichen Küsten festgesetzt. Meine *Historia stirpium plantarum utriusque orbis* steht da als ein großes Fragment der *Flora universalis terrae* und als ein Glied meines *Systema naturae*. . . . Ich arbeite jetzt fleißig an meiner Fauna. Ich werde Sorge tragen, daß vor meinem Tode meine Manuskripte bei der Berliner Universität niedergelegt werden" (I have established the geography of the interior of Africa and of the northern polar regions, of the interior of Asia and of its eastern coasts. My *History of the Stems of Plants of Both Worlds* stands as a large fragment of the *Flora of the Entire Earth* and as a part of my *System of Nature*. . . . I am now working diligently at my fauna. I shall see to it that before my death my manuscripts are deposited with the University of Berlin).

The novella's charming simplicity of style, humorous and ironic elements, and novel theme contributed to its success, which at first came slowly. In 1817 it was adapted as a "Zau-berposse" (magic comedy) for Viennese audiences; in 1822 it appeared in French translation; and in 1824 the caricaturist George Cruikshank popularized the characters in England. Hugo von Hoffmannsthal's *Die Frau ohne Schatten* (The Woman without a Shadow, 1919) is thematically indebted to the novella.

After the war Chamisso returned to his studies. In July 1815 an unforeseen opportunity presented itself: through the efforts of his friend Hitzig he was appointed naturalist on a three-year Russian expedition to the South Seas and to the northern Pacific in search of a "Northeast Passage" aboard the *Rurik*, commanded by Otto von Kotzebue, son of the playwright August von Kotzebue. Kotzebue wrote an account of the voyage, published in 1821, to which he appended Chamisso's *Bemerkungen und Ansichten auf einer Entdeckungs-Reise* (Comments and Views on a Journey of Discovery; translated as *Remarks and Opinions of the Naturalist of the Expedition*, 1821) as a separate volume. Chamisso was not happy with this edition. Nevertheless, he waited some fifteen years to write his own account, *Reise um die Welt* (translated as *A Voyage around the World*, 1986), which he published in his collected works in 1836. In the preface Chamisso explains his dissatisfaction with the 1821 edition by Kotzebue: his findings had been distorted, severely edited, and made incomprehensible. Worse, Eschscholtz's opinions on coral reefs had been juxtaposed in such a manner that they were confused with Chamisso's own; yet he had considered his refutation of Eschscholtz's theories to be one of the chief merits of his work.

Reise um die Welt is as much a critical commentary on European society and a collection of trivia as it is a travelogue; for instance, Chamisso notes with considerable pride of discovery that the fourth stanza of Goethe's "Die Braut von Korinth" (The Bride of Corinth, 1798) has one verse foot too many. Chamisso's style is tedious, but his depiction of the cultures, flora, and fauna of the islands and of the petty behavior in the small "civilized" world aboard ship makes his narrative interesting. His geological observations on the formation of coral reefs and his scientific descriptions and classifications of vegetation in the Americas have earned the respect of scientists.

The journey also ended his years of wandering and indecision. Upon his return to Berlin he donated his rich collection of natural curiosities to the museum, and in 1819 he received an honorary doctorate from the University of Berlin and a

*Drawing of Chamisso by E. T. A. Hoffmann, 1805
(Bildarchiv der Österreichischen Nationalbibliothek, Vienna)*

position as curator in the Berlin Museum Botanial Gardens. In the same year he married Hitzig's eighteen-year-old foster daughter, Antonie Piaste, with whom he had several children and appears to have lived happily until her death in 1837. Although he made a few relatively short trips–to Greifswald and the island of Rügen for barometric observations in 1823, to the Harz region in 1824, to Paris in 1825–Chamisso's traveling days were essentially over. He wrote a botanical textbook and established school herbaria at the request of the Prussian Ministry of Education. In 1824 he completed a book on useful and harmful plants, which was published three years later. At the suggestion of Alexander von Humboldt, Chamisso was made a member of the Berlin Academy of Sciences in 1835. His analysis of the language of the Hawaiian islands was published in 1837.

His talent as a lyric poet flourished in these later years and received impetus through the "Mittwochsgesellschaft" (Midweek Society), a literary circle founded by Hitzig in 1824 that met on Wednesdays; but Chamisso still considered his lit-

erary work merely a pastime and kept most of his lyric poems in a "poetisches Hausbuch" (poetic housekeeping book) locked away in his desk. It was chiefly Hitzig who promoted the publication of Chamisso's literary endeavors and who later edited his collected works. For one of the Wednesday meetings Chamisso wrote the comedy *Die Wunderkur* (The Magic Cure, 1824), which derides mesmerism. It was performed at the Royal Theater in Potsdam on 9 May 1825 and repeated in Berlin on 15 May, both times with the famous actor Ludwig Devrient in the role of Count Maximilian zur Sonnenburg; both times it was unsuccessful. The comedy *Der Wunder-Doktor* (The Quack, 1828), a prose adaptation of a comedy by Molière, was to be performed at the Königstädter Theater but was returned to the author in 1830. An unfinished play Chamisso had written in 1806 was published in 1895 by E. F. Koßmann as *Fortunati Glückseckel und Wunschhütlein* (Fortunatus's Money Bag and Wishing Cap).

Some of Chamisso's poems were published in well-known literary journals and magazines, such as the *Morgenblatt, Der Gesellschafter*, the *Taschenbuch der Liebe und Freundschaft gewidmet*, and the *Berliner Musen-Almanach*. Chamisso also included a selection of his lyric poems and ballads in the second edition of *Peter Schlemihl's wundersame Geschichte* (1827). Between 1827 and 1832 he wrote more than a hundred song cycles, ballads, and poems. "Frauen-Liebe und Leben" (1831; translated as *Woman's Love and Life*, 1881) was set to music by Robert Schumann. These poems became some of the best loved of Chamisso's works, and suddenly he found himself recognized as one of Germany's foremost lyric poets.

"Der Klapperstorch" (The Stork) is of interest because of its swift changes in form and style. The poem takes its title from the nursery tale that the stork delivers babies, and the first segment is written in couplets and addressed to children: in nursery-rhyme language the arrival of a sibling is explained. In the second segment the scene shifts to the new mother's bedside, and with the change in perspective there is a change in rhyme and meter. The mother's smile through her tears introduces a didactic element: love lives by pain, life lives by love. The last part probes the father-son relationship, again with a shift in meter: the father attempts to soothe the screaming infant with a song. With another surprise turnabout in the second stanza of this segment, introduced with the statement "Als so ich schrie, wie du nun schreist" (When I screamed like you are now screaming), it becomes clear that the narrator is retelling the story of his own birth at the birth of his son. To symbolize the transference of security, wealth, and honor to the newborn, the narrator explains, his father's family crest and sword were placed in his cradle. The legacy was meant for eternity, but times changed and the inheritance literally went up in smoke. The moral of the story is contained in the last two verses: life's gifts cannot be bestowed by well-meaning forebears; everyone is what he makes of himself. In the small space of one page the poem takes the reader through the experiences and feelings of three generations and points out the cyclical nature of life. The poem is so emotionally effective because it touches on the reader's most personal experiences with honesty, simplicity, and truth.

"Die alte Waschfrau" (The Old Washwoman) can be considered an extension of the last verses in "Der Klapperstorch," which insist on personal accountability. Rather than encompassing generations, this poem recounts the life of one individual. Chamisso has frequently been referred to as a writer who prepared the way for the social, political, and literary activism of the authors of "Junges Deutschland" (Young Germany)–Heinrich Heine, Karl Gutzkow, Heinrich Laube, Ludolf Wienbarg, Theodor Mundt, Ludwig Börne, Ferdinand Gustav Kühne, and Ernst Adolf Willkomm. Poems such as "Die alte Waschfrau" do focus on the plight of the lower classes and attest to Chamisso's social consciousness, but they do not overtly accuse or advocate radical social change: Chamisso believes in "necessity."

The poem consists of six stanzas in iambic meter, five of which depict the course of the woman's life; the last stanza gives the conclusions the narrator draws from her example. In the first stanza some key facts about the laundress are presented with almost visual clarity; it is a "personal" introduction to the reader, beginning with the phrase "du siehst" (you see): "Du siehst geschäftig bei dem Linnen/Die Alte dort in weißem Haar,/Die rüstigste der Wäscherinnen / Im sechsundsiebenzigsten Jahr" (You see busy at the linen/The old woman there with white hair / The hale-and-hearty laundress/In her seventy-sixth year). She has always earned her bread by the sweat of her brow, has worked honestly with hard discipline and untiring diligence in the time span accorded to her by God. The key words

that describe her character, *Ehre* (honor), *Zucht* (discipline), *Fleiß* (assiduity), are repeated in different contexts in subsequent strophes. The picture Chamisso presents is that of a woman who has done all she could do, yet in her old age she has nothing but her continued stamina to provide for her. The second stanza describes "des Weibes Los" (the lot or destiny of womanhood). In her younger years she loved, hoped, and married, but there was no lack of sorrows. The repetition of the phrase "sie hat" (she did) again emphasizes her diligence in all things: "Sie hat den kranken Mann gepflegt,/Sie hat drei Kinder ihm geboren,/Sie hat ihn in das Grab gelegt /Und Glaub' und Hoffnung nicht verloren" (She did nurse her sick husband/She did bear him three children/She did lay him in the grave /And faith and hope never lost). Love, faith, and hope–the three theological virtues–are the strengths of her character. These virtues are combined with a sunny disposition as she begins the formidable task of raising her children alone. Chamisso repeats the key words of the first stanza–*Zucht, Ehre, Fleiß*–in the third and adds to them *Ordnung* (orderliness). Having raised her children and sent them off with a blessing to fend for themselves, she is portrayed at the conclusion of the third stanza with a visual image that refers back to the beginning: "So stand sie nun allein und alt, / Ihr war ihr heitrer Mut geblieben" (So she stands now alone and old/To her remains her good-naturedness). Again, key words and phrases such as *allein* (alone), *alt* (old), *heitrer Mut* (good-naturedness) provide structural unity and thematic cohesiveness within the strophe and a connection to earlier segments.

The woman, having finished her duties as wife and mother, now looks to her future. This future is her death, and she prepares for it with all the diligence, discipline, and steadfast work with which she has approached all of life's tasks. Her main concern is a proper burial in a presentable "Sterbehemd" (burial shirt), for which she has no money. She saves to buy flax, then spends the nights spinning yarn from it for the weaver. From the linen he weaves she sews a garment for her burial. Her industriousness, her patience in overcoming seemingly insurmountable obstacles to obtain even the most basic needs, her pride in procuring them without requesting charity are the dominant features of her character. The funeral garment is her first and last jewel, the treasure for which she has saved. The very difficulty with which she obtained it, the denials she has suffered, make this garment dear to her. Chamisso changes from the past to the present tense in this stanza: in her view she now has riches that she did not have before and that secure her future. On Sundays she puts on her linen gown to go to church, putting it back in its place of honor afterward–"Bis sie darin zur Ruh' sie legen" (Until they put her to rest in it).

In the final stanza the narrator shifts the focus from the woman to himself. She is an exemplary figure, a yardstick by which to measure his own success in life. This strophe's sentences are kept in the subjunctive, indicating unfulfilled wishes on the narrator's part: that he could look back on his life as this woman could, that he had known how to drink from the cup of life as she had, that he could gain the same pleasure from his own shroud at the end of his days. The narrator's didactic closing statement points out that a successful life is not measured in worldly goods and riches; neither is it found in an existence without trials and tribulations. Want and poverty, sorrow and loneliness were all part of the woman's life, yet they did not diminish her spirits. It is not the luck of the cards which destiny deals that determines happiness. Instead, success depends on attitude: how one plays the hand and what one makes of what one has.

One of the characteristics of Romantic writing is the simultaneity of jest and seriousness. Chamisso's unique contribution to this style is the subtlety of timing with which he effects the change from solemnity to irony. Unlike other Romantics, he favors a succession rather than a mixture of these emotions and frequently startles the reader with a funny "punch line" after presenting a tale of woe. A good example of this technique is the poem "Das ist's eben" (That's It, Exactly), written in 1838. This phrase functions not only as the title but also as the refrain and the punch line, and it is the sudden shift in meaning that gives the poem its startling conclusion. The somber mood is set in the first strophe with the funeral procession of a king. The black casket, black horses, stately golden carriage with crown and sword, and the solemnly lowered flag constitute a show of might even in death, unsurpassed in splendor: "Das ist's eben, das ist's eben" that makes the crowd rejoice. In the second stanza the narrator notices a poor old woman who is beside herself with grief, wringing her hands in despair. Strange that at every funeral some rejoice and others mourn: "Das ist's eben, das ist's eben" what is so alarming. In the last strophe the narrator tries

to console the woman: not all is lost; even though the father is dead, the son remains; he will be like the father, everything will stay the same. "Das ist's," she cries, "das ist's eben" what is causing my grief!

Another form of irony is used in "Roland ein Roßkamm" (Roland, a Horse Trader), in which Chamisso discusses metaphorically the decline of contemporary literature. Roland has a mare for sale. She is a superb animal: her neck, bone structure, and limbs are flawless, and Roland repeats the phrase "Sieh' her, die vortreffliche Stute,/Du kaufst sie, das sag' ich dir!/ Mein Ohm, der mächtige Kaiser,/Besitzt kein schöneres Tier" (Observe the splendid mare,/I tell you, you'll buy her!/My uncle, the powerful emperor,/Owns no animal more beautiful). There is only one problem: the mare is dead. Roland contends that this condition is not a flaw: it is inherent in the nature of such animals to die, and that fact is no reason not to sell it. Chamisso uses the parable to illustrate his contention that a poem may have a perfect structure and beautiful words and phrases and yet be lacking in inspiration; its beauty is lifeless: "Ist musterhaft auch geschrieben/Und regelrecht das Gedichte,/Wir kaufen die tote Stute,/Wir lesen die Verse doch nicht" (Even though the poem is written perfectly/And according to rule,/We do not buy the dead mare,/We do not read the verse).

Chamisso's use of irony in this poem differs from his use of it in "Das ist's eben." In the latter the reader is led to believe up to the last verse that the old woman genuinely mourns the death of her sovereign; the punch line then destroys this illusion while at the same time opening the poem to an entirely different interpretation as a critical comment on a political system. The creation of an illusion, the deliberate destruction of it, and the subsequent reconstruction on a higher plane has come to be known as "Romantic irony." In "Roland ein Roßkamm" Chamisso uses Socratic irony: the reader is immediately told that the mare is not alive; there is no suspense or illusion. Instead, Chamisso uses the imagery of a beautiful but dead horse in a didactic fashion to illustrate the message of the sententious last stanza.

Many of Chamisso's poems contain gruesome subjects, and he frequently gives them a humorous twist. In "Die Sterbende" (The Dying Woman) a young woman confesses on her deathbed that she has betrayed her husband, only to find out that she is dying of the poison he has given her. In "Ein Lied von der Weibertreue" (A Song of Women's Fidelity) a young widow, who swore to follow her husband in death, quickly finds a new lover and saves him by substituting her husband's body for that of her lover on the gallows. Less humorous but not less macabre is "Die Giftmischerin" (The Poisoner), in which a woman confesses to sending her husband, brothers, father, and three children to their deaths and faces the hangman without guilt.

Chamisso's first collection of poems was published in 1831. In 1833 he became coeditor of the *Deutscher Musenalmanach* with his friend Gustav Schwab. He continued in this position until his death, despite deteriorating health and the withdrawal of Schwab over the issue of Heine's portrait on the 1837 volume. The last few years of Chamisso's life were also devoted to additions to his journal of his Pacific voyage, his grammar of the Hawaiian language, and a translation of Pierre J. de Béranger's poetry with his friend Franz Gaudy (1838). After the death of his wife in May 1837 Chamisso returned to writing poetry. His lung ailment suddenly worsened, and he died on 21 August 1838.

Letters:
Aus Chamissos Frühzeit: Ungedruckte Briefe nebst Studien, edited by Ludwig Geiger (Berlin, 1905);
Adelbert von Chamisso und Helmina von Chézy: Bruchstücke ihres Briefwechsels, edited by Julius Petersen and Helmuth Rogge (Berlin: Literaturarchiv-Gesellschaft, 1923).

Bibliographies:
Philipp Rath, *Bibliotheca Schlemihliana: Ein Verzeichnis der Ausgaben und Übersetzungen des Peter Schlemihl* (Berlin, 1919);
Günther Schmid, *Chamisso als Naturforscher: Eine Bibliographie* (Leipzig, 1942).

Biography:
Peter Lahnstein, *Adelbert von Chamisso: Der Preuße aus Frankreich* (Munich: List, 1984).

References:
Dorothea von Chamisso and Friedrich Karl Timmler, eds., *Chamissos Berliner Zeit* (Berlin: Presse- und Informationsamt, 1982);
Werner Feudel, "Chamisso als Mittler zwischen französischer und deutscher Literatur," *Weimarer Beiträge*, 32 (1986): 753-765;

Gonthier-Louis Fink, "*Peter Schlemihl* et la tradition du conte romantique," *Recherches germaniques*, 12 (1982): 24-54;
Winfried Freund, "Verfallene Schlösser: Ein gesellschaftliches Motiv bei Kleist, E. T. A. Hoffmann, Uhland und Chamisso," *Diskussion Deutsch*, 11, no. 54 (1980): 361-369;
Freund, ed., *Adelbert von Chamisso: Peter Schlemihl. Geld und Geist. Ein bürgerlicher Bewußtseinsspiegel* (Paderborn: Schöningh, 1980);
Klaus F. Gille, "Der Schatten des Peter Schlemihl," *Deutschunterricht*, 39, no. 1 (1987): 74-83;
Volker Hoffmann, "Künstlerbezeugung durch Metamorphose: Naturpoesie aus den Ruinen der Zivilisation. Zu Adelbert von Chamissos Gedicht 'Das Schloß,'" in *Gedichte und Interpretationen*, edited by Günter Häntzschel, volume 4 (Stuttgart: Reclam, 1983), pp. 58-68;
Arthur Hübscher, "Schopenhauer und Chamisso," *Schopenhauer-Jahrbuch*, 39 (1958): 176-178;
Friedrich Kittler, "Romantik–Psychoanalyse–Film: Eine Doppelgängergeschichte," in *Eingebildete Texte*, edited by Jochen Hörisch and Georg Christoph Tholen (Munich: Fink, 1985), pp. 118-135;
Wolfgang Koeppen, "Chamisso und Peter Schlemihl," in *Die elenden Skribenten*, edited by Marcel Reich-Ranicki (Frankfurt am Main: Suhrkamp, 1981), pp. 25-35;
Albert Peter Kroner, "Adelbert von Chamisso," in *Deutsche Dichter der Romantik*, edited by Benno von Wiese (Berlin: Schmidt, 1983), pp. 439-458;
Kroner, "Adelbert von Chamisso, sein Verhältnis zur Romantik, Biedermeier und romantischem Erbe," Ph.D. dissertation, University of Erlangen, 1941;
Alice Kuzniar, "'Spurlos.... verschwunden': 'Peter Schlemihl' und sein Schatten als der verschobene Signifikant," *Aurora*, 45 (1985): 189-204;
Ilse Langner, "Adelbert von Chamisso: Zu seinem 200. Geburtstag," *Neue deutsche Hefte*, 28 (1981): 100-116;
Thomas Mann, "Chamisso," in his *Adel des Geistes* (Stockholm: Bermann-Fischer, 1945);
Peter von Matt, "Sisyphos in preußischer Uniform," in *Frankfurter Anthologie*, edited by Reich-Ranicki, volume 7 (Frankfurt am Main: Insel, 1983), pp. 73-76;

Norbert Miller, "Chamissos Schweigen und die Krise der Berliner Romantik," *Aurora*, 39 (1979): 101-119;

Brian Murdoch, "Poetry, Satire and Slave-Ships: Some Parallels to Heine's 'Sklavenschiff,'" *Forum for Modern Language Studies*, 15 (1979): 323-335;

Wolfgang Neubauer, "Zum Schatten-Problem bei Adelbert von Chamisso oder zur Nicht-Interpretierbarkeit von 'Peter Schlemihls wundersamer Geschichte,'" *Literatur für Leser*, 1 (1986): 24-34;

Marko Pavlyshyn, "Gold, Guilt and Scholarship: Adelbert von Chamisso's *Peter Schlemihl*," *German Quarterly*, 55, no. 1 (1982): 49-63;

René-Marc Pille, "David Ferdinand Koreff: Sechs ungedruckte Briefe an Chamisso. Zeugnisse einer erloschenen Freundschaft," *Zeitschrift für Germanistik*, 8, no. 1 (1987): 171-178;

Ernst Rose, "Chamissos 'Klage der Nonne,'" in *Blick nach Osten*, edited by Ingrid Schuster (Bern: Lang, 1981), pp. 133-144;

Hans Schneider, "Chamissos Balladentechnik," Ph.D. dissertation, University of Breslau, 1917;

Gerhard Schulz, "Erfahrene Welt: Berichte deutscher Weltreisender am Übergang vom 18. ins 19. Jahrhundert," in *Antipodische Aufklärungen: Festschrift für Leslie Bodi*, edited by Walter Veit (Bern: Lang, 1987), pp. 439-456;

Jürgen Schwann, *Vom Faust zum Peter Schlemihl: Kohärenz und Kontinuität im Werk Adelbert von Chamissos* (Tübingen: Narr, 1984);

Egon Schwarz, "Naturbegriff und Weltanschauung: Deutsche Forschungsreisende im 19. Jahrhundert," in *Natur und Natürlichkeit*, edited by Reinhold Grimm and Jost Hermand (Königstein: Athenäum, 1981), pp. 19-36;

K.-D. Seemann, "Adelbert von Chamissos Beziehungen zur russischen Literatur," *Zeitschrift für slavische Philologie*, 31 (1963/1964): 97-123;

Waldemar Ties, "Adelbert von Chamissos Verskunst, mit einer Einleitung zur Chamisso-Forschung," Ph.D. dissertation, University of Frankfurt am Main, 1953;

Christian Velder, "Das Verhältnis Adelbert von Chamissos zu Weltbürgertum und Weltliteratur," Ph.D. dissertation, University of Berlin, 1955;

Dagmar Walach, "Adelbert von Chamisso: *Peter Schlemihls wundersame Geschichte (1814)*," in *Romane und Erzählungen der deutschen Romantik*, edited by Paul Michael Lützeler (Stuttgart: Reclam, 1981), pp. 285-301.

Papers:
Adelbert von Chamisso's papers are in the Deutsche Staatsbibliothek, East Berlin.

Joseph Freiherr von Eichendorff

(10 March 1788-26 November 1857)

Liselotte M. Davis
Yale University

BOOKS: *Ahnung und Gegenwart: Ein Roman* (Nuremberg: Schrag, 1815);

Krieg den Philistern! Dramatisches Mährchen in fünf Abentheuern (Berlin: Dümmler, 1824);

Aus dem Leben eines Taugenichts und Das Marmorbild: Zwei Novellen nebst einem Anhange von Liedern und Romanzen (Berlin: Vereinsbuchhandlung, 1826); "Aus dem Leben eines Taugenichts" translated by Charles Godfrey Leland as *Memoirs of a Good-for-Nothing* (New York: Leypoldt & Holt, 1866); translated by Bayard Quincy Morgan as *Memoirs of a Good-for-Nothing* (London: Calder, 1955; New York: Ungar, 1955); "Das Marmorbild" translated by F. E. Pierce as "The Marble Statue," in *Fiction and Fantasy of German Romance: Selections from German Romantic Authors*, edited by Pierce and C. F. Schreiber (New York: Oxford University Press, 1927);

Ezelin von Romano: Trauerspiel in fünf Aufzügen (Königsberg: Bornträger, 1828);

Meierbeths Glück und Ende: Tragödie mit Gesang und Tanz (Berlin: Vereinsbuchhandlung, 1828);

Der letzte Held von Marienburg: Trauerspiel (Königsberg: Bornträger, 1830);

Die Freier: Lustspiel in drei Aufzügen (Stuttgart: Brodhag, 1833);

Viel Lärmen um Nichts, von Joseph Freiherrn von Eichendorff; und: Die mehreren Wehmüller und ungarischen Nationalgesichter, von Clemens Brentano, edited by F. W. Gubitz (Berlin: Vereinsbuchhandlung, 1833);

Dichter und ihre Gesellen: Novelle (Berlin: Duncker & Humblot, 1834);

Gedichte (Berlin: Duncker & Humblot, 1837; revised and enlarged edition, Berlin: Simion, 1843);

Joseph Freiherrn von Eichendorff's Werke, 4 volumes (Berlin: Simion, 1841);

Die Wiederherstellung des Schlosses der deutschen Ordensritter zu Marienburg: Mit einem Grundriß der alten Marienburg (Königsberg & Berlin: Duncker, 1844);

Joseph Freiherr von Eichendorff in 1832 (lithograph from a portrait by Franz Kugler, courtesy of the Prussian Picture Archive, West Berlin)

Ueber die ethische und religiöse Bedeutung der neueren romantischen Poesie in Deutschland (Leipzig: Liebeskind, 1847);

Neue Gedichte (Berlin: Simion, 1847);

Die Geheimnisse des christlichen Alterthums (Hamburg: Hoffmann, 1847);

Der deutsche Roman des achtzehnten Jahrhunderts in seinem Verhältnis zum Christenthum (Leipzig: Brockhaus, 1851);

Julian (Leipzig: Günther, 1853);

Zur Geschichte des Dramas (Leipzig: Brockhaus, 1854);

Robert und Guiscard (Leipzig: Voigt & Günther, 1855);

Geschichte der poetischen Literatur Deutschlands, 2 volumes (Paderborn: Schöningh, 1857);

Lucius (Leipzig: Voigt & Günther, 1857);

Sämmtliche Werke, 6 volumes (Leipzig: Voigt & Günther, 1863-1864);

Vermischte Schriften, 5 volumes (Paderborn: Schöningh, 1866-1867);

Gedichte aus dem Nachlasse, edited by Heinrich Meisner (Leipzig: Amelang, 1888);

Eichendorffs Werke: Kritisch durchgesehene und erläuterte Ausgabe, edited by Richard Dietze (Leipzig & Vienna: Bibliographisches Institut, 1891);

Das Incognito: Ein Puppenspiel. Mit Fragmenten und Entwürfen anderer Dichtungen nach den Handschriften, edited by Konrad Weichberger (Oppeln: Maske, 1901);

Joseph und Wilhelm Eichendorffs Jugendgedichte: Vermehrt durch ungedruckte Gedichte aus dem handschriftlichen Nachlaß, edited by R. Pissin (Berlin: Frensdorff, 1906);

Ungedruckte Dichtungen Eichendorffs: Ein Beitrag zur Würdigung des romantischen Dramatikers, edited by Friedrich Castelle (Münster: Aschendorff, 1906)—comprises *Hermann und Thusnelda*, *Wider Willen*;

Aus dem Nachlaß des Freiherrn Joseph von Eichendorff Briefe und Dichtungen: Im Auftrag seines Enkels, Karl Freiherrn von Eichendorff, edited by Wilhelm Kosch (Cologne: Bachem, 1906);

Fahrten und Wanderungen, 1802-1814: Nach ungedruckten Tagebuchaufzeichnungen mit Erläuterungen, by Eichendorff and Wilhelm von Eichendorff, edited by Alfons Nowack (Oppeln: Verlag des oberschlesischen Geschichtsvereins, 1907);

Lubowitzer Tagebuchblätter Joseph von Eichendorffs: Mit Erläuterungen, edited by Nowack (Groß-Strehlitz: Wilpert, 1907);

Sämtliche Werke des Freiherrn Joseph von Eichendorff: Historisch-kritische Ausgabe, edited by Kosch, Philipp August Becker, and August Sauer, 25 volumes published (Regensburg: Habbel, 1908-1939, 1950-   );

Neue Gesamtausgabe der Werke und Schriften, edited by Gerhart Baumann and Siegfried Grosse, 4 volumes (Stuttgart: Cotta, 1957-1958);

Eichendorffs Werke in 6 Bänden, edited by Wolfgang Frühwald and Brigitte Schillbach, 6 volumes (Frankfurt am Main: Deutscher Klassiker Verlag, 1987);

Edition in English: *The Happy Wanderer and Other Poems*, translated by Marjorie Rossy (Boston: Badger, 1925).

OTHER: "Das Schloß Dürande," in *Urania: Taschenbuch für das Jahr 1837* (Leipzig: Brockhaus, 1837);

"Die Entführung," in *Urania: Taschenbuch für das Jahr 1839* (Leipzig: Brockhaus, 1839);

Juan Manuel, *Der Graf Lucanor*, translated by Eichendorff (Berlin: Simion, 1840);

"Die Glücksritter," in *Rheinisches Jahrbuch für Kunst und Poesie*, edited by Ferdinand Freiligrath and Karl Simrock (Cologne: DuMont-Schauburg, 1841);

Pedro Calderón de la Barca, *Geistliche Schauspiele*, translated by Eichendorff, 2 volumes (Stuttgart & Tübingen: Cotta, 1846, 1853);

Lebrecht Dreves, *Gedichte*, edited by Eichendorff (Berlin: Duncker, 1849).

PERIODICAL PUBLICATIONS: "Die geistliche Poesie in Deutschland," *Historisch-politische Blätter*, 20 (1847): 449-468;

"Kapitel von meiner Geburt," edited by Herbert Pöhlein, *Aurora*, 1 (1929);

"Unstern," edited by Pöhlein, *Aurora*, 3 (1933).

    Joseph Freiherr von Eichendorff is considered one of Germany's foremost lyric poets of the Romantic period. His works give expression to quintessential traits of this literary movement. Mention of Eichendorff's poetry immediately brings to mind the song of the lark as it ascends into a beautiful summer sunrise, and the song of the nightingale filling a lush summer night with its song of beauty and love. It also brings to mind the romance of the poet's wanderings through large forests with their "Waldeinsamkeit" (wooded seclusion), as well as the many-faceted symbols for the demonic forces of nature found in his work, their modes of expression bordering both on folk song and fairy tale. It brings to mind, finally, his story "Aus dem Leben eines Taugenichts" (1826; translated as *Memoirs of a Good-for-Nothing*, 1866), which became a classic during his lifetime. Eichendorff's other prose works, however, received scant notice at the time of their appearance, which may be the reason for his dissatisfaction with his standing in the German "Dichterwald" (grove of poets). More recent explications of his works have found new avenues of approach, while criticizing those of previous decades as superficial.

Like Goethe in *Dichtung und Wahrheit* (Poetry and Truth, 1811-1814; translated as *Memoirs of Goethe*, 1824), Eichendorff in his autobiographical writings emphasized that the constellations were extremely favorable just before his birth: "Jupiter und Venus blinkten freundlich auf die weissen Dächer, der Mond stand im Zeichen der Jungfrau und mußte jeden Augenblick kulminieren" (Jupiter and Venus were blinking kindly upon the white rooftops, the moon stood in the sign of Virgo and would be culminating any minute). Whereas Goethe settled on a definitive "truth" about his birth, Eichendorff offers two different fictions: in "Kapitel von meiner Geburt" (Chapter of My Birth, 1929) the physician fell asleep in the coach sent to fetch him, while in "Unstern" (Misfortune; published in his collected works, 1933) it was because of a miscued firing of the celebratory cannon that Eichendorff missed the culmination by one and a half minutes. The result was the same in both versions: the author would never have a chance at true fortune and greatness. "Eine lumpige Spanne Zeit! Und doch holt sie keiner wieder ein, das Glück ist einmal im Vorsprung, er im Nachtrab" (Such a miserably small span of time! And yet there is no catching up with it again, fortune has the advantage, he [the poet] brings up the rear).

Missed chances are frequently to be found in Eichendorff's life as well as in his work. He was born on 10 March 1788, the second child and second son of Adolf Freiherr von Eichendorff and Karoline Freiin von Eichendorff (née von Kloch), members of the landed gentry of Upper Silesia. His birthplace, the ancestral castle of Lubowitz, appears again and again in his poetry and prose. Only three of the family's six children survived: Eichendorff; his older brother Wilhelm; and his younger sister Luise, in her later years a close friend of Adalbert Stifter. Eichendorff shared his growing-up years with his brother, who was only eighteen months older than he: schooling by a private tutor, the Reverend Bernhard Heinke; and friendship and high jinks with Paul Ciupke, the chaplain whom Eichendorff immortalized in his novel *Ahnung und Gegenwart* (Presentiment and the Present, 1815) in the figure of Viktor. The boys spent three years in Breslau, where they attended the Matthias Gymnasium and lived at the St. Joseph's Seminary. There Eichendorff was introduced to music; learned to play several instruments (he was particularly fond of the violin); and frequented the theater, where he became acquainted with the dramas of Lessing, Schiller, and Goethe and was impressed by Mozart's *Die Zauberflöte* (The Magic Flute). He took part in dramatic productions at his school, where he was often given ladies' roles because of his slender build and good looks. Gender role reversals occur in almost all of Eichendorff's novels— mostly in the form of young ladies dressing as men, but also in the form of young men being mistaken for young ladies.

In 1805 Eichendorff and his brother enrolled at the University of Halle, where they saw Goethe attending the anatomy lectures of Franz Joseph Fall; they also saw him at a performance of his play *Götz von Berlichingen mit der eisernen Hand* (1773; translated as *Goetz von Berlichingen with the Iron Hand*, 1837) in Lauchstädt, a nearby spa with an excellent theater. After Napoleon shut down the university in 1807, they continued their studies at Heidelberg, where they were influenced by Joseph Görres and joined the literary circle of the count of Loeben (who wrote under the pseudonym Isidorus Orientalis). At this time Eichendorff published his first poems in the *Zeitschrift für Wissenschaft und Kunst* under the pseudonym "Florens," a name given to him by the Loeben group. His first larger effort centered on a collection of Silesian fairy tales which was never published. During the Heidelberg years the brothers journeyed on foot and by coach to Hamburg, via the Harz mountains and the Lüneburg Heath; Eichendorff was overawed by his first view of the sea in Travemünde.

After the conclusion of their studies the brothers went on a Bildungsreise (educational trip) to Paris, then returned to Lubowitz via Vienna. While trying to help his father with the failing family estates Eichendorff found his own lyrical style, which was greatly influenced by Clemens Brentano and Achim von Arnim's *Des Knaben Wunderhorn* (The Boy's Magic Horn, 1805-1808). His poems no longer had the imitative content and style he had absorbed from the Loeben circle. On a trip to Berlin in November 1809 the brothers visited Loeben and made the acquaintance of Arnim, Brentano, Adam Müller, and Heinrich von Kleist; their lack of funds was obvious to Brentano. Eichendorff's biographer Paul Stöcklein has noted that Eichendorff was lucky in his friendships—he met and often kept in close contact with most of the important literary and public figures of his time; but he was unlucky in making the personal connections necessary to better his position. After returning to Lubowitz the brothers, realizing that the family's time on the estate was running out, went to Vienna to take the bar examinations necessary for entry into the civil service; Eichendorff passed with highest honors. While in Vienna he made friends with Friedrich and Dorothea Schlegel and the latter's son, the Romantic painter Philipp Veit.

Eichendorff's first and longest novel, *Ahnung und Gegenwart*, was beginning to take shape. Dorothea Schlegel read the manuscript and probably suggested the title, and both Schlegels encouraged Eichendorff in his work. The novel was completed by October 1812. Eichendorff dropped the pseudonym "Florens" for the first time, allowing the novel to appear under his own name. It was not widely noticed at first, and later its reception was mixed: after initial cautious approbation, the judgment of the late nineteenth century was that the novel was "uncooked pap." Modern critics see in it a criticism of Eichendorff's epoch and its intellectual elite, and also an embodiment of Friedrich Schlegel's theory of the novel. "Romantic boredom"–of the suffering of Eichendorff and his contemporaries because of their "narrow times" and their "narrow lives" and the necessity to create alternate worlds of fiction–is also seen as a reason for the writing of *Ahnung und Gegenwart.*

On the outbreak of the War of Liberation against Napoleon in March 1813 Eichendorff volunteered for service in the Lützow Freikorps. In 1815 he was made secretary of the High Military Command in Berlin, and in July he entered Paris with General Blücher. On 7 April 1815 Eichendorff married Aloysia (Luise) von Larisch against the wishes of his mother, who would have liked a more affluent daughter-in-law. The Eichendorffs had five children: Hermann in 1815, Rudolf in 1817, Therese in 1819, Agnes in 1821 (she died the same year), and Anna Hedwig in 1830 (she died in 1832). In 1816 Eichendorff became an intern for the royal government in Breslau, where, after passing his state examinations in Berlin, he continued as assistant judge. He was employed without salary for half a year at the Cultural Ministry in Berlin; then in 1821 he was given the office of Catholic church and school superintendent in Danzig. Later that year he was named government councillor. In 1824 he was transferred to Königsberg, where he disliked the situation intensely and tried to be transferred or to obtain a position elsewhere. In 1831 he rejoined the Cultural Ministry in Berlin, and in 1841 he was promoted to the position of coun-

cillor to the government. Always in frail health, Eichendorff contracted a lung ailment in 1843. He asked for an early retirement, which was granted in 1844. He died on 26 November 1857 at the house of his daughter Therese, where he had lived for the past two years and where his wife had died two years before him.

Although *Ahnung und Gegenwart* cannot be called an autobiographical novel, there are long stretches which correspond to Eichendorff's own life, and many figures are modeled after his friends and relatives. At the outset of the story the protagonist, Friedrich, goes into the world after his university years. He falls in love with Rosa, whose brother Florentin becomes his lifelong friend. Friedrich is a poet, and there are many other poets in *Ahnung und Gegenwart*. The poetic figures are contrasted with the average philistine citizen: "Das Leben der meisten ist eine immerwährende Geschäftsreise vom Buttermarkt zum Käsemarkt, des Leben der Poetischen dagegen ein freies, unendliches Reisen nach dem Himmelreich" (The lives of most people are a continuous business trip between the butter market and the cheese market [here Eichendorff is quoting Brentano], the lives of the poets on the other hand a bold, infinite trip up to the heavens). Eichendorff makes distinctions among the poets, however. Leontin, modeled after Eichendorff's brother, Wilhelm, is poetical, but he is not a poet. He expresses his feelings about life in poems and songs, but he never bothers to write them down and forgets them after having given spontaneous expression to them. Faber, on the other hand, writes for the sake of writing. Leontin and Faber, in the broad sense both poets, can therefore not speak to each other, and they end up in "egoistischen Monologen" (egotistical monologues). Leontin eventually decides to migrate to America with his sweetheart, Julie. He wants to wipe his Old World slate clean and begin a new life "in dem noch unberührten Waldesgrün eines anderen Weltteils" (in the as yet untouched greenery of a different continent).

The first of the novel's three books is set in the country, on the estate of Herr v. A., who is based on Eichendorff's father; the estate, modeled after Lubowitz, is a place where everything is harmonious and makes sense but where a young person longs for the action of the big world. A chaplain in a nearby village, Viktor, with his various histrionics, brings much-needed relief from the inherent tensions. The aunt who runs the household is modeled after

Eichendorff's mother, and the picture is not altogether flattering. The city of the second book is full of diversions, but in the end it alienates Friedrich. The third book sends the protagonist and his friends into war, from which they come back chastened; the historical background here is the Tyrolean uprising against the French in 1809. Friedrich, whose poetic energies have begun to concentrate on religion, decides to enter a monastery and dedicate his life to God.

Eichendorff's most famous work is "Aus dem Leben eines Taugenichts," of which more than eighty editions are extant. It has been translated into English many times, as well as into Dutch, French, Swedish, Italian, and Japanese. The number of explications of the story, positive as well as negative, is endless. The novella is the story of a "Sonntagskind" (Sunday's Child), a young man who seems to have been born under a lucky star. Since he does not want to work, his father throws him out of the house; the young man goes out into the world accompanied only by his violin, feeling wonderfully free. He hitches a ride on the back of a coach belonging to two lovely ladies, and his sense of freedom increases as he watches the landscape rushing by. He becomes a toll collector at the castle in Vienna where the ladies live and settles down with the former collector's pipe and morning jacket. In the garden he raises beautiful flowers and leaves a special bouquet of them for the younger of the two ladies, with whom he has fallen in love. But the older lady receives the flowers by mistake, and the young man comes to believe erroneously that the younger lady is about to marry someone else. He decides to travel again; this time he goes to the country of every German poet's dreams, Italy, and ends up in Rome. Thus he leaves the castle misunderstanding the situation, and this state of affairs persists until the end of the novella: the young man is forever "erstaunt, verwirrt, verblüfft, erschrocken, ratlos" (astonished, bewildered, amazed, startled, at a loss). After many adventures and much confusion in Rome, he returns to the castle in Vienna. The beautiful young "countess" turns out to be the butler's niece and as much in love with the young man as he is with her. Even though he has never read a novel, he realizes that he has been part of one. The story does not end with the typical "und wenn sie nicht gestorben sind, dann leben sie heute noch" (and if they have not died, they are living to this day) of the fairy tale but with an equally formulaic and optimistic "und es war

Eichendorff in later years (Deutsche National-Litteratur, volume 146 [Stuttgart: Union Deutsche Verlagsgesellschaft, n.d.])

alles, alles gut" (and everything, everything was well). Interwoven into the story are some of the best known of Eichendorff's poems: "Wem Gott will rechte Gunst erweisen" (Whom God wants to show real favor), "Wohin ich geh und schaue" (Wherever I go and look), "Schweigt der Menschen laute Lust" (When men's loud joy is silent), and "Wer in die Fremde will wandern" (He who wants to go out into the world).

Inexplicable premonitions and secrets not yet known make up the plot of "Das Marmorbild" (1826; translated as "The Marble Statue," 1927), which was published together with "Aus dem Leben eines Taugenichts." The young nobleman Florio one evening comes upon a marble statue of Venus in an old park in Lucca; the statue's strange allure is heightened by its mirror image in a pond. When Florio tries to return in the daytime he loses his way, wanders into another park, and finds a young lady, playing a lute and singing a sonnet, who resembles the statue. Florio finds himself enamored of this demonic figure. After having at first pushed aside young Bianca's love for him, Florio is finally able to withstand the heathen sensuality connected to the statue and to reciprocate Bianca's pure, maidenly feelings.

The basic quest motif of *Ahnung und Gegenwart*–to finish his education after proper schooling a young hero goes out into the world and meets other men in similar situations (thus gaining new friends) and young ladies (thus falling in love)–recurs in Eichendorff's second novel, *Dichter und ihre Gesellen* (Poets and their Companions, 1834). Count Victor of Hohenstein, a well-known and revered poet, travels through Germany and Italy as "Lothario," first tenor in the theatrical troupe of Mr. Sorti, hoping to gain valuable experiences along the way. He distances himself from the theater world when he comes to the conclusion that "ich will selber so verliebt sein wie Romeo, so tapfer wie Götz, so tiefsinnig wie Don Quixote" (I myself want to be as much in love as Romeo, as brave as Götz, as meditative as Don Quixote). He falls in love with the exotic Juanna; after she drowns, Victor decides to become a priest. Another poet, Fortunat, and his friend Walter are luckier: Fortunat wins the hand of Fiametta, the daughter of the Marchese A., and is able to buy back the family estate for her; Walter marries Florentine and becomes the owner of a small estate. Florentine's brother Otto, who believes himself to be a poet even though Victor counsels against such an assumption, goes even further in denouncing philistine life than Friedrich did when he calls out: " 'Lieber Schweine hüten als so zeitlebens auf der Treckschute gemeiner Glückseligkeit vom Buttermarkt zum Käsemarkt fahren' " ("I'd rather be a swineherd than go from butter market to cheese market on the barge of common happiness all my life"). He goes to Rome and marries his sweetheart, Annidi, who does not remain true to him. Otto returns to Germany and dies when he sees his home in front of him again. *Dichter und ihre Gesellen* is even more diversely and colorfully peopled than *Ahnung und Gegenwart*, and its structure is even more loose and open.

"Das Schloß Dürande" (The Castle of Dürande, 1837) is set in Provence. The young forester Renald realizes that his sister Gabriele has a secret lover, whom he recognizes as the count of Dürande. The latter removes himself to Paris; Gabriele flees from the nunnery where Renald has put her. Renald goes in search of her; she has been near her beloved, disguised as a gardener. Both men die in a duel, and the castle is burned to the ground.

In "Eine Meerfahrt" (An Ocean Voyage), written in 1855-1856 and published posthu-mously in Eichendorff's *Sämmtliche Werke* (Collected Works) in 1864, there is an even more exotic quest. A ship sets sail under the command of Captain Alvarez on an expedition to find gold. Except for Don Antonio, a poor student and poetic soul who seeks adventure, the crew is out for material gains. After they have some hair-raising adventures on an island with natives led by a supernaturally beautiful princess, they find a hermit who gives them his gold. The crew returns with the gold; Antonio has found his love in Alma, a simple island girl.

In the 1840s and 1850s Eichendorff's main focus was on literary criticism, mostly work he was commissioned to do by journals such as the *Historisch-politische Blätter*. As Dietmar Kunisch has pointed out, there was an "allmählicher Wandel in Eichendorffs Gesamtwerk zu einem verstärkt wirklichkeits- und zeitbezogenen Schrifttum" (gradual change in Eichendorff's output to a writing ever more strongly connected to reality and to his own time). Eichendorff evaluated literary periods as well as the individual authors from an ethical and religious point of view. According to Eichendorff, Christoph Wieland was the first to free poetics of religion and morals; Ludwig Tieck had a secretly demoralizing irony; Novalis adhered to a certain pantheism; in Ludwig Uhland he saw an open return to Protestantism; Heinrich von Kleist's was a poetics of hatred; Adelbert von Chamisso was indifferent in religious matters. No one seemed to escape Eichendorff's harsh judgment, except possibly Arnim, whose work is said to be, "even though he was and has remained of the Protestant faith, much more Catholic in content than that of most of his catholicizing colleagues."

Eichendorff kept a diary from the age of ten until he returned home from the war in 1815, and from a close reading of his diary fragments one can arrive at a reevaluation of his development. The early entries show nothing of the sentiments connected with "Heimat" (home), "Waldeinsamkeit," or "Wanderschaft" (wandering). The young Eichendorff saw things with clear and somewhat mocking eyes. He had a quite different attitude toward the lark, for example, a bird which was so laden with symbolism in his later work. In his childhood he simply caught larks to eat; at one point in the diary he exults at having caught twenty-three in a single day! Only after becoming familiar with an accepted Romantic vocabulary could Eichendorff articulate his feelings. In distinction to Goethe, who expressed a *knowledge* of nature, Eichendorff became a master at expressing a *feeling* for nature.

Eichendorff wrote hundreds of poems, many of which have been set to music by composers such as Franz Schubert, Felix Mendelssohn, Robert Schumann, Hugo Wolf, and Richard Strauss. The appeal of Eichendorff's poetry, which has not diminished with time, lies in a perfect union of content and form, embellished by the musicality of his language. Eichendorff, more than any other poet, was responsible for the discovery that such a musicality existed. That he was aware of its existence can be seen in the often-quoted four-line poem "Wünschelrute" (Divining Rod):

> Schläft ein Lied in allen Dingen,
> Die da träumen fort und fort,
> Und die Welt fängt an zu singen,
> Triffst du nur das Zauberwort.
>
> (There sleeps a song in all objects
> Which are dreaming on and on,
> And the world begins to sing,
> If only you hit the magic word.)

Biographies:

Hans Brandenburg, *Joseph von Eichendorff: Sein Leben und sein Werk* (Munich: Beck, 1922);

Hermann von Eichendorff, *Joseph Freiherr von Eichendorff: Sein Leben und seine Schriften*, revised by Karl Freiherr von Eichendorff and Wilhelm Kosch (Leipzig: Amelang, 1923);

Willibald Köhler, *Joseph von Eichendorff* (Augsburg: Oberschlesischer Heimatverlag, 1957);

Paul Stöcklein and Inge Feuchtmayer, eds., *Der Dichter des Taugenichts: Eichendorffs Welt und Leben. Geschildert von ihm selbst und von Zeitgenossen* (Munich: Süddeutscher Verlag, 1957).

References:

Richard Alewyn, *Probleme und Gestalten* (Frankfurt am Main: Insel, 1974);

Otto Friedrich Bollnow, "Das romantische Weltbild bei Eichendorff," in his *Unruhe und Geborgenheit im Weltbild neuerer Dichter*, third edition (Stuttgart: Kohlhammer, 1953), pp. 227-259;

Alexander von Bormann, "Philister und Taugenichts: Zur Tragweite des romantischen Antikapitalismus," *Aurora*, 30 (1970): 94-112;

R. H. Farquarson, "Poets, Poetry, and Life in Eichendorff's *Ahnung und Gegenwart*," *Seminar*, 17 (February 1981): 17-34;

Wolfgang Frühwald, "Der Philister als Dilettant: Zu den satirischen Texten Joseph von Eichendorffs," *Aurora*, 36 (1976): 7-26;

G. Guder, "Joseph von Eichendorff and Reality," *Modern Language Notes*, 39 (1958): 89-95;

Amala M. Hanke, *Spatiotemporal Consciousness in English and German Romanticism: A Comparative Study of Novalis, Blake, Wordsworth, and Eichendorff* (Bern & Frankfurt am Main: Lang, 1981);

Ansgar Hillach and Klaus-Dieter Krabiel, eds., *Eichendorff-Kommentar zu den Dichtungen* (Munich: Winkler, 1971);

Marie Luise Kaschnitz, *Florens—Eichendorffs Jugend* (Düsseldorf: Claassen, 1984);

Dietmar Kunisch, "Joseph von Eichendorff: Fragmentarische Autobiographie," Ph.D. dissertation, University of Munich, 1985;

Josef Kunz, *Eichendorff: Höhepunkt und Krise der Spätromantik* (Darmstadt: Wissenschaftliche Buchgesellschaft, 1967);

Eberhard Lämmert, "Eichendorffs Wandel unter den Deutschen: Überlegungen zur Wirkungsgeschichte seiner Dichtung," in *Die deutsche Romantik: Poetik, Formen und Motive*, edited by Hans Steffen (Göttingen: Vandenhoeck & Ruprecht, 1967), pp. 219-252;

L. McGlashan, "A Goethe Reminiscence in Eichendorff," *Monatshefte*, 51 (1959): 177-182;

Wolfgang Nehring, "Eichendorff und der Leser," *Aurora*, 37 (1977): 51-65;

Günter and Irmgard Niggl, eds., *Joseph von Eichendorff im Urteil seiner Zeit*, 2 volumes (Stuttgart: Kohlhammer, 1975);

Wolfgang Paulsen, *Eichendorff und sein Taugenichts* (Bern: Francke, 1976);

Brigitte Peucker, *Lyric Descent in the German Romantic Tradition* (New Haven: Yale University Press, 1986);

Lothar Pikulik, *Romantik als Ungenügen an der Normalität: Am Beispiel Tiecks, Hoffmanns, Eichendorffs* (Frankfurt am Main: Suhrkamp, 1979);

Lawrence Richard Radner, "The Instrument, the Musician, the Song: An Introduction to Eichendorff's Symbolism," *Monatshefte*, 56 (1964): 236-248;

Walther Rehm, "Prinz Rokoko im alten Garten: Eine Eichendorffstudie," in his *Späte Studien* (Bern: Francke, 1964), pp. 122-214;

Detlev W. Schumann, "Betrachtungen über zwei Eichendorffsche Novellen, 'Das Schloss Dürande'–'Die Entführung,'" *Jahrbuch der deutschen Schillergesellschaft*, 18 (1974): 466-481;

Egon Schwarz, "Ein Beitrag zur allegorischen Deutung von Eichendorffs Novelle 'Das Marmorbild,'" *Monatshefte für deutschen Unterricht*, 48 (1956): 215-220;

Egon Schwarz, *Joseph von Eichendorff* (New York: Twayne, 1972);

Peter Paul Schwarz, *Aurora: Zur romantischen Zeitstruktur bei Eichendorff* (Bad Homburg, Berlin & Zurich: Gehlen, 1970);

Oskar Seidlin, *Versuche über Eichendorff* (Göttingen: Vandenhoeck & Ruprecht, 1965);

William D. Sims-Gunzenhauser, "The Treacherous Forest of Symbols: Duality and Anti-self-consciousness in Eichendorff and Baudelaire," *Comparative Literature Studies*, 17 (September 1980): 305-315;

Paul Stöcklein, *Joseph von Eichendorff in Selbstzeugnissen und Bilddokumenten* (Reinbek: Rowohlt, 1963);

Stöcklein, ed., *Eichendorff heute: Stimmen der Forschung mit einer Bibliographie* (Darmstadt: Wissenschaftliche Buchgesellschaft, 1966);

E. Stopp, "The Metaphor of *Death* in Eichendorff," *Oxford German Studies*, 4 (1969): 67-89;

Günter Strenzke, "Die Problematik der Langeweile bei Joseph von Eichendorff," Ph.D. dissertation, University of Hamburg, 1973;

Reinhard H. Thum, "Cliché and Stereotype: An Examination of the Lyric Landscape in Eichendorff's Poetry," *Philological Quarterly*, 62 (Fall 1983): 435-457;

Franz Uhlendorff, "Eichendorff, der Freiheitsgedanke und die Freiheitsbewegung," *Aurora*, 16 (1956): 35-44;

Martin Wettstein, *Die Prosasprache Joseph von Eichendorffs–Form und Sinn* (Zurich & Munich: Artemis, 1975);

Benno von Wiese, ed., *Deutsche Dichter der Romantik: Ihr Leben und Werk* (Berlin: Schmidt, 1971), pp. 416-441;

Joachim Wolff, "Romantic Variations of Pygmalion Motifs by Hoffmann, Eichendorff, and Edgar Allan Poe," *German Life and Letters*, new series 33 (October 1979): 53-60;

Vladimir Zernin, "The Abyss in Eichendorff: A Contribution to a Study of the Poet's Symbolism," *German Quarterly*, 35 (May 1962): 280-291.

Johann Gottlieb Fichte
(19 May 1762-29 January 1814)

Martin Donougho
University of South Carolina

SELECTED BOOKS: *Versuch einer Critik aller Offenbarung,* anonymous (Königsberg: Hartung,
1792; revised, 1793); translated by Garrett
Green as *Attempt at a Critique of All Revelation*
(Cambridge & New York: Cambridge University Press, 1978);
*Zurückforderung der Denkfreiheit von den Fürsten Eu-
ropens, die sie bisher unterdrückten: Eine Rede,*
anonymous (Danzig, 1793);
*Beitrag zur Berichtigung der Urtheile des Publikums
über die französische Revolution: Erster Theil.
Zur Beurtheilung ihrer Rechtmäßigkeit,* anony-
mous, 2 volumes (Danzig, 1793);
*Ueber die Würde des Menschen, beym Schlusse
seiner philosophischen Vorlesungen gesprochen*
(Jena[?], 1794); translated by Daniel Brea-
zeale as "Concerning Human Dignity," in
Fichte: Early Philosophical Writings, edited by
Breazeale (Ithaca, N.Y.: Cornell University
Press, 1988), pp. 83-86;
*Ueber den Begriff der Wissenschaftslehre oder der soge-
nannten Philosophie, als Einladungsschrift zu sei-
nen Vorlesungen über diese Wissenschaft* (Jena:
Industrie-Comptoirs, 1794; revised edition,
Jena & Leipzig: Gabler, 1798); translated by
Breazeale as "Concerning the Concept of
the *Wissenschaftslehre* or, of So-called 'Philosophy,'" in *Fichte: Early Philosophical Writings,*
pp. 94-135;
*Grundlage der gesammten Wissenschaftslehre als Hand-
schrift für seine Zuhörer* (Leipzig: Gabler,
1794; revised, 1802); translated by A. E.
Kroeger as *The Science of Knowledge* (Philadelphia: Lippincott, 1868); edited and translated by Peter Heath and John Lachs as *Foundations of the Entire Science of Knowledge (Wissenschaftslehre), with the First and Second Introductions* (New York: Appleton-Century-
Crofts, 1970; Cambridge: Cambridge University Press, 1982);
Einige Vorlesungen über die Bestimmung des Gelehrten
(Jena & Leipzig: Gabler, 1794); translated
by William Smith as *The Vocation of the Scholar* (London: Chapman, 1847); translated by

Johann Gottlieb Fichte (Bibliothèque Nationale, Paris)

Breazeale as "Some Lectures Concerning
the Scholar's Vocation," in *Fichte: Early Philosophical Writings,* pp. 144-184;
*Grundriß des Eigenthümlichen der Wissenschaftslehre
in Rüksicht auf das theoretische Vermögen als
Handschrift für seine Zuhörer* (Jena & Leipzig: Gabler, 1795; revised, 1802); translated
by Breazeale as "Outline of the Distinctive
Character of the *Wissenschaftslehre* with Respect to the Theoretical Faculty," in *Fichte:
Early Philosophical Writings,* pp. 233-306;
*Grundlage des Naturrechts nach Prinzipien der Wissen-
schaftslehre,* 2 volumes (Jena & Leipzig: Gabler, 1796-1797); translated by Kroeger as
Science of Rights (Philadelphia: Lippincott,
1869; London: Trübner, 1889); excerpts

70

translated by H. S. Reiss & P. Brown as "The Foundations of Natural Law according to the Principles of the Theory of Science," in *The Political Thought of the German Romantics 1793-1815*, edited by Reiss (Oxford: Oxford University Press, 1955), pp. 44-86;

Das System der Sittenlehre nach den Principien der Wissenschaftslehre (Jena & Leipzig: Gabler, 1798); translated by Kroeger as *The Science of Ethics as Based on the Science of Knowledge*, edited by W. T. Harris (London: Kegan Paul, Trench, Trübner, 1897);

Appellation an das Publikum über die durch ein Kurf. Sächs. Confiscationsrescript ihm beigemessen atheistischen Aeusserungen: Eine Schrift, die man erst zu lesen bittet, ehe man sie confisciert (Jena & Leipzig: Gabler / Tübingen: Cotta, 1799);

Die Bestimmung des Menschen (Berlin: Voss, 1800); translated by Mrs. Percy Sinnett as *The Destination of Man* (London: Chapman, 1846); translated by Smith as *The Vocation of Man* (London: Chapman, 1848; Chicago: Open Court, 1906); translated by Peter Preuss as *The Vocation of Man* (Indianapolis: Hackett, 1987);

Der geschlossne Handelstaat: Ein philosophischer Entwurf als Anhang zur Rechtslehre, und Probe einer künftig zu liefernden Politik (Tübingen: Cotta, 1800); excerpt translated by Reiss as "The Closed Commercial State," in *The Political Thought of the German Romantics*, pp. 86-102;

Sonnenklarer Bericht an das grössere Publikum über das eigentliche Wesen der neuesten Philosophie: Ein Versuch, die Leser zum Verstehen zu zwingen (Berlin: Realschulbuchhandlung, 1801); translated by John Botterman & William Rasch as "A Crystal Clear Report to the General Public Concerning the Actual Essence of the Newest Philosophy: An Attempt to Force the Reader to Understand," in *Philosophy of German Idealism*, edited by Ernst Behler (New York: Continuum, 1987), pp. 39-115;

Antwortschreiben an Herrn Professor Reinhold, auf dessen im ersten Hefte der Beiträge zur leichtern Übersicht des Zustandes der Philosophie beim Anfange des 19ten Jahrhunderts . . . (Hamburg, bei Perthes, 1801) befindliches Sendschreiben an den erstern (Tübingen: Cotta, 1801);

Friedrich Nicolai's Leben und sonderbare Meinungen: Ein Beitrag zur Litterar-Geschichte des vergangenen und zur Pädagogik des angehenden Jahrhunderts (Tübingen: Cotta, 1801);

Die Grundzüge des gegenwärtigen Zeitalters (Berlin: Realschulbuchhandlung, 1806); translated by Smith as *The Characteristics of the Present Age* (London: Chapman, 1847);

Ueber das Wesen des Gelehrten, und seine Erscheinungen im Gebiete der Freiheit: In öffentlichen Vorlesungen, gehalten zu Erlangen, im Sommer-Halbjahre 1805 (Berlin: Himburgische Buchhandlung, 1806); translated by Smith as *On the Nature of the Scholar, and Its Manifestations* (London: Chapman, 1845);

Die Anweisung zum seeligen Leben, oder auch Religionslehre (Berlin: Realschulbuchhandlung, 1806); translated by Smith as *The Way towards the Blessed Life; or, The Doctrine of Religion* (London: Chapman, 1849);

Reden an die deutsche Nation (Berlin: Realschulbuchhandlung, 1808); translated by R. F. Jones and G. H. Turnbull as *Addresses to the German Nation* (Chicago & London: Open Court, 1923);

Die Wissenschaftslehre, in ihrem allgemeinen Umrisse dargestellt (Berlin: Hitzig, 1810); translated by Walter E. Wright as "The Science of Knowledge in Its General Outline," *Idealistic Studies*, 6, no. 2 (1976): 106-117;

Ueber die einzig mögliche Störung der akademischen Freiheit: Eine Rede beim Antritte seines Rektorats an der Universität zu Berlin den 19ten Oktober 1811 gehalten (Berlin: Wittich, 1812); excerpts translated by Turnbull as "Concerning the Only Possible Disturbance of Academic Freedom," in his *The Educational Theory of J. G. Fichte* (London: Hodder & Stoughton, 1926), pp. 262-265;

Über die Bestimmung des Gelehrten: Erste Vorlesung (Berlin: Safeldsche Buchhandlung, 1812);

Über den Begriff des wahrhaften Krieges in Bezug auf den Krieg im Jahre 1813: Ein Entwurf für den Vortrag, mit einer Rede verwandten Inhalts herausgegeben (Tübingen: Cotta, 1815);

Deducirter Plan einer zu Berlin errichtenden höhern Lehranstalt (Stuttgart & Tübingen: Cotta, 1817); translated by Turnbull as "Deduced Scheme for an Academy to Be Established in Berlin," in *The Educational Theory of J. G. Fichte*, pp. 170-259;

Die Tatsachen des Bewußtseyns: Vorlesungen, gehalten an der Universität zu Berlin im Winterhalbjahr 1810-11 (Stuttgart & Tübingen: Cotta, 1817); translated by Kroeger as "Facts of Consciousness," *Journal of Speculative Philosophy*, 5 (1871): 53-60, 130-143, 226-231, 338-349; 6 (1872): 42-52, 120-125, 332-340; 7

(1873): 36-42; 17 (1883): 130-141, 263-296; 18 (1884): 47-71, 152-161;

Die Staatslehre, oder Über das Verhältniß des Urstaates zum Vernunftreiche in Vorträge gehalten im Sommer 1813 auf der Universität zu Berlin (Berlin: Reimer, 1820); excerpt translated by Turnbull as "The Theory of the State; or, The Relationship of the Primitive State to the Kingdom of Reason," in *The Educational Theory of J. G. Fichte*, pp. 265-283; excerpt from section 3 translated by Reiss as "Comments on the Theory of the State," in *The Political Thought of the German Romantics 1793-1815*, pp. 118-124;

Nachgelassene Werke, edited by Immanuel Hermann Fichte, 3 volumes (Bonn: Marcus, 1834-1835)–includes, in volume 3, "Ascetik als Anhang zur Moral," pp. 119-144, translated by Kroeger as "Asceticism, or Practical Moral Culture," in *The Science of Ethics as Based on the Science of Knowledge*, pp. 379-399; "Der Patriotismus und sein Gegenteil: Patriotische Dialogen vom Jahre 1807," selections translated by Turnbull as "Patriotism and Its Opposite," in *The Educational Theory of J. G. Fichte*, pp. 160-170;

Sämmtliche Werke, edited by Immanuel Hermann Fichte, 8 volumes (Berlin: Veit, 1845-1846)–includes, in volume 2, "Darstellung der Wissenschaftslehre: Aus dem Jahre 1801," translated by Kroeger as *New Exposition of the Science of Knowledge* (London: Trübner, 1869); in volume 5, "Rückerinnerung, Antworten, Fragen," excerpt translated by Kroeger as "The Religious Significance of the Science of Knowledge," in *The Science of Knowledge*, pp. 339-377; in volume 8, "Bericht über den Begriff der Wissenschaftslehre und die bisherigen Schicksale derselben. (Geschrieben im Jahre 1806)," translated by Kroeger as "Fichte's Criticism of Schelling," *Journal of Speculative Philosophy*, 12 (1878): 160-170, 316-326; 14 (1879): 225-244;

Werke, edited by Fritz Medicus, 6 volumes (Leipzig: Eckardt, 1908-1912);

Machiavell, nebst einem Briefe Carls von Clausewitz an Fichte, edited by Hans Schulz (Leipzig: Meiner, 1918);

Philosophie der Maurerei, edited by Wilhelm Flitner (Leipzig: Meiner, 1923); translated by Roscoe Pound as "The Philosophy of Masonry: Letters to Constant," *Masonic Papers*, 2, no. 2 (1945): 26-65;

Ueber den Unterschied des Geistes und des Buchstabens in der Philosophie: Drei akademische Vorlesungen (1794), edited by Siegfried Berger (Leipzig: Meiner, 1924); translated by Breazeale as "Concerning the Difference between the Spirit and the Letter within Philosophy," in *Fichte: Early Philosophical Writings*, pp. 192-215;

Nachgelassene Schriften, edited by Hans Jacob, 2 volumes (Berlin: Juncker & Dünnhaupt, 1937);

Johann Gottlieb Fichte: Gesamtausgabe der Bayerischen Akademie der Wissenschaften, edited by Reinhard Lauth and Hans Gliwitzky, 21 volumes to date (Stuttgart & Bad Cannstatt: Fromann-Holzboog, 1962-);

Erste Wissenschaftslehre von 1804: Aus dem Nachlaß, edited by Gliwitzky (Stuttgart: Kohlhammer, 1969);

Von den Pflichten der Gelehrten: Jenaer Vorlesungen 1794 / 95, edited by Lauth, Jacob, and P. K. Schneider (Hamburg: Meiner, 1971);

Wissenschaftslehre 1805, edited by Gliwitzky (Hamburg: Meiner, 1982);

Prinzipien der Gottes-, Sitten- und Rechtslehre (1805), edited by Lauth (Hamburg: Meiner, 1986).

PERIODICAL PUBLICATIONS: "Aenesidemus, oder über die Fundamente der von dem Hrn. Prof. Reinhold in Jena gelieferten Elementar-Philosophie. Nebst einer Vertheidigung des Skeptizismus gegen die Anmässungen der Vernunftkritik. 1792," *Allgemeine Literatur-Zeitung*, 47-49 (February 1794): columns 369-374, 377-383, 385-389; translated by George di Giovanni as "Review of *Aenesidemus*," in *Between Kant and Hegel: Texts in the Development of Post-Kantian Idealism*, edited by di Giovanni and H. S. Harris (Albany: State University of New York Press, 1985), pp. 136-157;

"Ueber Belebung und Erhöhung des reinen Interesse für Wahrheit," *Die Horen*, 1, no. 4 (1795): 79-93;

"Versuch einer neuen Darstellung der Wissenschaftslehre," *Philosophisches Journal einer Gesellschaft Teutscher Gelehrten*, 15, no. 1 (1797): 1-49; 17, no. 1 (1797): 1-20; excerpt translated by John Lachs as "First Introduction," in *Science of Knowledge*, edited and translated by Lachs and Peter Heath (New York: Appleton-Century-Crofts, 1970; Cambridge: Cambridge University Press), pp. 3-28;

"Zweite Einleitung in die Wissenschaftslehre für Leser, die schon ein philosophisches System haben," *Philosophisches Journal,* 5, no. 4 (1797): 319-378; 6, no. 1 (1797): 1-43; translated by Heath as "Second Introduction," in *Science of Knowledge,* pp. 29-85;

"Ueber den Grund unsers Glaubens an eine göttliche Weltregierung," *Philosophisches Journal,* 7, no. 1 (1798): 1-20; translated by Paul Edwards as "On the Foundation of Our Belief in a Divine Government of the Universe," in *Nineteenth Century Philosophy,* edited by Patrick Gardiner (New York: Free Press, 1969), pp. 19-26;

"Ueber Geist und Buchstab in der Philosophie: In einer Reihe von Briefen," *Philosophisches Journal,* 9, no. 3 (1799): 199-232; 9, no. 4 (1799): 291-305; translated by Elizabeth Rubenstein as "On the Spirit and the Letter in Philosophy in a Series of Letters," in *German Aesthetic and Literary Criticism: Kant, Fichte, Schelling, Schopenhauer, Hegel,* edited by David Simpson (Cambridge: Cambridge University Press, 1984), pp. 74-93.

"Die Französische Revolution, Fichtes Wissenschaftslehre, und Goethes Meister sind die größten Tendenzen des Zeitalters" (The French Revolution, Fichte's *Wissenschaftslehre,* and Goethe's *Wilhelm Meister* are the three greatest tendencies of the age), wrote Friedrich Schlegel in 1798. Even if one takes this comment in context (Schlegel called his time "the age of tendencies") and with a pinch of aphoristic salt, it serves to indicate how important philosophy could seem, in its strategic place between political and poetic revolutions. The French had, after all, only changed the world: the important thing, however, was to *interpret* it. The aphorism serves, moreover, to bring out the prestige enjoyed by Fichte's system—or, rather, attempts at system—with Romantic poets and literary theorists, among them Novalis, Friedrich Hölderlin, and the Schlegel brothers.

Johann Gottlieb Fichte was significant not just with respect to literary culture but also in philosophy, education, and emergent German nationalism. He was, after Karl Leonhard Reinhold, the first to try to systematize Immanuel Kant's suggestion that the world be measured against the constitutive power of the transcendental ego. He formulated an educational philosophy that combined private scholarship with a public calling, and as rector of the newly founded University of Berlin—the first modern university—he was the very embodiment of ethical (if autocratic) idealism. Finally, he articulated a potent and high-minded

patriotism in his celebrated *Reden an die deutsche Nation* (1808; translated as *Addresses to the German Nation,* 1923). He was, then, a philosopher for his times, whether these times are taken as revolutionary or as Napoleonic.

Fichte published works both of technical philosophy and of "popular philosophy." After 1800 he tended to publish only the latter; although he continued to lecture on the Wissenschaftslehre (science of knowledge), he came to feel that a written format allowed too much distortion by hostile readers—distortion that continues to this day. Fichte was—and is—too easily portrayed as a subjective idealist, reducing everything and everyone to his own ego. "Und das läßt *Madame* Fichte so hin?" (And *Madame* Fichte doesn't mind?), Heinrich Heine imagines people protesting, then rightly counters that the Fichtean ego is not individual—that is, Fichte himself—but universal, a "Welt-Ich" (world-ego). It is only since the 1960s that a fairer picture of the philosopher has emerged with the inauguration of a critical edition of his works and publication of much previously unknown material.

Fichte was born in 1762 in the small town of Rammenau near Bischofswerda in Saxony to Christian and Johanna Dorothea Schurich Fichte. His paternal ancestors were linen weavers and traders, and Fichte inherited their strong, stocky physique; his pride and impetuosity, on the other hand, stemmed from his mother. Sponsorship enabled the precocious youth to attend the foundation school of Schulpforta, near Naumberg, from 1774 to 1780; there he found relief from the narrow curriculum in the ideas of Gotthold Ephraim Lessing and Spinoza, both of whom left a deep impression on his thought. Obedient to his mother's wish that he become a pastor, Fichte studied theology at Jena in 1780-1781 and at Leipzig from 1781 to 1784. Financial hardship forced him to take a succession of family tutorships near Leipzig from 1784 to 1788. He was in Zurich in 1788 and 1789, where he met the well-known physiognomist Johann Kaspar Lavater as well as a local official, Hermann Rahn, whose daughter Johanna Maria he married in 1793. They had a son, Immanuel Hermann. From Zurich he moved to tutorships in Warsaw and Danzig.

Tutoring was a job for which Fichte's volatile temperament was not at all suited. In the event, he was saved by becoming famous. Having immersed himself in Kant's transcendental idealism, in 1791 Fichte sent Kant a manuscript (with the dedication "Dem Philosoph" [To the philoso-

Drawing of Fichte by Bury (Staatsbibliothek Berlin, Bildarchiv Handke)

pher]) treating religion from a Kantian standpoint; it argued that philosophy demands a place for religious belief and feeling, that faith in the moral law entails faith in God, and that God is revealed through the operation of moral reason. Approving of what he had read of the work, Kant recommended it to his own publishers. When it came out in 1792 with the title *Versuch einer Critik aller Offenbarung* (translated as *Attempt at a Critique of All Revelation,* 1978), by some oversight without the author's name, it was promptly taken to be by Kant himself. Kant soon corrected this impression. In 1793 Fichte was invited to fill the chair at Jena recently vacated by Reinhold, one of Kant's first disciples (whose interpretation of Kant Fichte was to criticize in the brief but important review of "Aenesidemus").

It was at Jena that Fichte developed first his concept of Wissenschaftslehre, as well as an application of its principles to ethical, political, and religious matters. The term *Wissenschaftslehre* poses some difficulty for the translator. More than philosophy—the mere search for wisdom—more

too than Kantian "Kritik" (critique)—that is, the testing of claims to know—it asserts nothing less than knowledge of the true ground of experience. Fichte's thinking contains two main elements: an urge toward system, on the one hand, and an activist epistemology (theory of knowledge) which confers an ethical tinge to even the most abstract speculation, on the other. It is central to what he called *Idealismus* (idealism) (as opposed to *Dogmatismus* [dogmatism]) that theory itself receives a practical justification. The sort of philosophy one chooses depends, he held, on the sort of person one is. And one must choose, with no ulterior justification for one's choice. Yet if one's philosophy derives from one's practical stance, conversely, its moral dynamism can be grasped only from within the system. Fichte advised Madame de Staël that in order to understand his ethics she would need to understand his metaphysics.

Fichte's philosophical activity was always centered on the classroom: his thinking is by nature expository and pedagogical. He was a gifted and powerful speaker; his works often show their oral basis, the best of them having a clarity and directness rare in such complex philosophizing. He taught that it was the scholar's duty to teach as well as to publish—although he had his doubts in regard to publishing and was dismayed that writing had been corrupted by special interests and journalistic fashions. He became more and more suspicious of publication, of the letter as opposed to the spirit, as can be seen in his essay "Über Geist und Buchstab in der Philosophie" (1794; translated as "On the Spirit and the Letter in Philosophy in a Series of Letters," 1984), written for Friedrich Schiller's monthly *Die Horen.* Schiller rejected the article, apparently because he detected a parody of his own "Briefe über die ästhetische Erziehung des Menschen" (translated as "On the Aesthetic Education of Mankind," 1967); the rejection led to a permanent break in their relations.

Besides the activist tendency in Fichte's theory, the other main element is its reflexive basis. This element—described by Dieter Henrich as "Fichtes ursprüngliche Einsicht" (Fichte's original insight) into the self-constitution of systemic thought—captured the imagination of the young Romantics. The reflexive element pervades both the theoretical and practical aspects of Fichte's system. It can be observed, for example, in the three basic principles of his theory: the ego posits itself; the ego then posits a nonego; finally, the ego posits itself as limited by the nonego. But how is the ego to find this theoretical self-grounding via subjective activity confirmed in fact? Theory thus devolves into practical deed, for which the world becomes not so much an object of knowledge as, in a famous phrase, "das versinnlichte Materiale unser Pflichte" (the sensuous material of our duty). Fichte explores the reach of self-constitution into the moral realm in *Das System der Sittenlehre nach den Principien der Wissenschaftslehre* (1798; translated as *The Science of Ethics as Based on the Science of Knowledge*, 1897) and into the intersubjective realm of rights in *Grundlage des Naturrechts nach Prinzipien der Wissenschaftslehre* (1796-1797; translated as *Science of Rights*, 1869).

Fichte's attempts to close the circle of reflection—to see the ego seeing itself in the practical realm—repeat conclusions the early Romantics had already drawn from the 1794 system. Fichte was led, just as they had been, to treat reflection ironically and to suggest that knowledge was but a "Bild" (image), mere "Schein" (semblance), a limit beyond which cognition cannot penetrate. As he puts it in *Die Bestimmung des Menschen* (1800; translated as *The Destination of Man*, 1846): "Alle Realität verwandelt sich in einen wunderbaren Traum. . . . Das *Anschauen* ist der Traum; das *Denken* . . . ist der Traum von jenem Traum" (All reality is transformed into a wonderful dream. . . . *Intuition* is the dream; *thought* . . . the dream of that dream). Yet Fichte was not a Romantic, if the term includes an acceptance of the "dream": he did not, for example, ironize the world, as Friedrich Schlegel sought to do. Instead, he was led to meditate on the unbridgeable gulf between knowledge and a being that he increasingly conceived of as the Absolute or God.

Fichte's tenure at Jena came to an abrupt end with the notorious "Atheismusstreit" (Atheism Controversy). He had already made trouble by daring to criticize student fraternities, which resulted in his house being stoned. But the immediate cause of the controversy was an innocent enough arrangement by Fichte to teach his class on Sundays, following which there appeared an anonymous pamphlet accusing him of heretical opinions. The charge may have been partly motivated by Fichte's Jacobin reputation; but it also had some basis in his tendency to express religious belief in terms of moral conviction, as if the divine order were no more than the moral order and God were neither personal nor providential in nature. Characteristically, Fichte mishandled both the public accusation and the subsequent governmental pressure. His clumsy offer of resignation was, to his surprise, accepted. In 1799 he left for Berlin.

Over the next few years Fichte lectured in Berlin and in Erlangen. He also published several books drawn from his lectures, including *Die Bestimmung des Menschen, Die Grundzüge des gegenwärtigen Zeitalters* (1806; translated as *The Characteristics of the Present Age*, 1847), *Ueber das Wesen des Gelehrten, und seine Erscheinungen im Gebiete der Freiheit* (1806; translated as *On the Nature of the Scholar, and Its Manifestations*, 1845), and *Die Anweisung zum seeligen Leben, oder auch Religionslehre* (1806; translated as *The Way towards the Blessed Life; or, The Doctrine of Religion*, 1849). *Die Bestimmung des Menschen*, a popular work, was intended as an indirect answer to the charge of atheism, arguing that skepticism and philosophical knowledge must each in turn give way to a faith that is at once moral and religious. Its earnest tone only alienated Fichte from the Romantic circles within which he had initially moved in Berlin, drawing an especially sharp review from Friedrich Schleiermacher. *Die Grundzüge des gegenwärtigen Zeitalters*, which greatly influenced Thomas Carlyle's *Sartor Resartus* (1833-1834), presents Fichte's philosophy of history in its most developed form. He locates his own age midway between an Enlightenment liberation from dogmatism and the threat of licentiousness or lack of principle. The book contains Fichte's most extended discussion of artistic and literary culture, to which he applies a Romantic aesthetic of self-expression.

Between December 1807 and March 1808, in the wake of Napoleon's defeat of the German states, Fichte delivered to enormous popular acclaim a series of speeches that were published in 1808 as *Reden an die deutsche Nation*. Their exalted moral tone—even the title echoes Luther—and their technical language no doubt hid from the occupying forces their actual intent: to lay out the path by which Germans might recover a sense of moral purpose and institute an education for nationhood. Most notable are its detailed educational recommendations, on which Johann Heinrich Pestalozzi's ideas are especially influential. But the factor that accounts for the work's celebrated reception is its nationalistic call to unity. It has gone through more than fifty editions in German alone, carrying a special resonance during times of national defeat. It should be stressed, however, that Fichte's ideal is an ethical hero, not some proto-fascist leader.

Reden an die deutsche Nation proved to be Fichte's last major work. He continued his teaching and was active in the founding of the University of Berlin, though his plan for its constitution was rejected in favor of Schleiermacher's more liberal ideas. He became dean of the philosophical faculty at its opening in 1810 and first rector of the university in 1811; by all accounts he was a somewhat autocratic administrator. He lent his considerable vocal support to the Wars of Liberation. In December 1813 his wife contracted typhus while tending wounded soldiers in a hospital; Fichte caught the disease from her and died on 29 January 1814. His grave is next to Hegel's in the cemetery of the Dorotheenkirche. His epitaph aptly sums up the various sides of this "popular," public philosopher, being at once prophetic, ethical, pedagogic, and political. The text, from Daniel 12:3, was usually interpreted as a prefiguring of the Roman imperium, but the Napoleonic yoke could just as easily be read in: "Die Lehrer aber werden leuchten wie des Himmels Glanz, und die, so viel zur Gerechtigkeit weisen, wie die Sterne immer und ewiglich" (And they that be wise shall shine as the brightness of the firmament, and they that turn many to righteousness as the stars that shine forever and ever).

Letters:

J. G. Fichte Briefwechsel, edited by Hans Schulz, 2 volumes (Leipzig: Haessel, 1925; reprinted, Hildesheim: Olms, 1967).

Bibliographies:

Hans Michael Baumgartner and Wilhelm G. Jacobs, eds., *Johann Gottlieb Fichte–Bibliographie* (Stuttgart & Bad Cannstatt: Fromann-Holzboog, 1968);

Daniel Breazeale, "English Translations of Fichte, Schelling, and Hegel: An Annotated Bibliography," *Idealistic Studies,* 6 (September 1976): 279-297.

Biographies:

Immanuel Hermann Fichte, ed., *Fichtes Leben und literarischer Briefwechsel* (Sulzbach: Seidel, 1830-1831);

"Fichtes Leben," translated by William Smith as "Memoir of Fichte," in his *On the Nature of the Scholar and Its Manifestations* (London: Chapman, 1845), pp. 1-115;

Robert Adamson, *Fichte* (Edinburgh & London: Blackwood, 1881);

Fritz Medicus, *Fichtes Leben,* second edition (Leipzig: Meiner, 1922);

Erich Fuchs, ed., *Johann Gottlieb Fichte im Gespräch: Berichte der Zeitgenossen,* 3 volumes (Stuttgart & Bad Cannstatt: Fromann-Holzboog, 1981).

References:

Frederick C. Beiser, *The Fate of Reason: German Philosophy from Kant to Fichte* (Cambridge, Mass.: Harvard University Press, 1987);

Walter Benjamin, *Der Begriff der Kunstkritik in der deutschen Romantik,* edited by H. Schweppenhauser (Frankfurt am Main: Suhrkamp, 1973), pp. 14-29;

Bernard Bourgeois, *L'idéalisme de Fichte* (Paris: Presses Universitaires de France, 1968);

Daniel Breazeale, "Fichte's Aenesidemus Review and the Transformation of German Idealism," *Review of Metaphysics,* 34 (March 1981): 545-568;

Ulrich Claesges, *Geschichte des Selbstbewußtseins: Der Ursprung des spekulativen Problems in Fichtes Wissenschaftslehre von 1794-95* (The Hague: Nijhoff, 1974);

Frederick Copleston, *A History of Philosophy,* volume 7: *Fichte to Nietzsche* (London: Burns & Oates, 1963), pp. 32-93;

H. C. Engelbrecht, *Johann Gottlieb Fichte: A Study of His Political Writings, with Special Reference to His Nationalism* (New York: Columbia University Press, 1933);

Patrick Gardiner, "Fichte and German Idealism," in *Idealism, Past and Present,* edited by Godfrey Vesey (Cambridge: Cambridge University Press, 1982);

Helmut Girndt, "Forschungen zu Fichte seit Beginn und im Umkreis der kritischen Edition seiner Werke 1962," *Zeitschrift für philosophische Forschung,* 38, no. 1 (1984): 100-110;

Martial Gueroult, *Études sur Fichte* (New York & Hildesheim: Olms, 1974);

Gueroult, *L'évolution et la structure de la Doctrine de la Science chez Fichte* (New York & Hildesheim: Olms, 1973);

Heinz Heimsoeth, *Fichte* (Munich: Reinhardt, 1923);

Dieter Henrich, "Fichtes ursprüngliche Einsicht," in *Subjektivität und Metaphysik,* edited by Henrich and Hans Wagner (Frankfurt am Main: Klostermann, 1960), pp. 188-232; translated by David Lachterman as "Fichte's Original Insight," in *Contemporary German Philosophy*

(University Park: Pennsylvania State University Press, 1982), pp. 15-52;

T. P. Hohler, *Imagination and Reflection: Intersubjectivity in Fichte's Grundlage of 1794* (The Hague: Nijhoff, 1982);

Wilhelm G. Jacobs, *Johann Gottlieb Fichte* (Hamburg: Rowohlt, 1984);

Wolfgang Janke, *Fichte: Sein und Reflexion—Grundlage der kritischen Vernunft* (Berlin: De Gruyter, 1970);

G. A. Kelly, *Idealism, Politics and History: Sources of Hegelian Thought* (Cambridge: Cambridge University Press, 1969), pp. 181-285;

Richard Kroner, *Von Kant bis Hegel,* volume 1 (Tübingen: Mohr, 1921), pp. 303-612;

Kroner, "The Year 1800 in the Development of German Idealism," *Review of Metaphysics,* 1 (June 1948): 1-31;

John Lachs, "Fichte's Idealism," *American Philosophical Quarterly,* 9 (October 1972): 311-318;

Emil Lask, *Fichtes Idealismus und die Geschichte* (Tübingen: Mohr, 1902);

Reinhard Lauth, "The Transcendental Philosophy of the Munich School," *Idealistic Studies,* 11, no. 1 (1981): 8-40;

Xavier Léon, *Fichte et son temps,* 2 volumes (Paris: Colin, 1922-1924);

Alexis Philonenko, *La liberté humaine dans la philosophie de Fichte* (Paris: Vrin, 1966);

Philonenko, *L'oeuvre de Fichte* (Paris: Vrin, 1984);

Philonenko, *Théorie et praxis dans la pensée morale et politique de Kant et de Fichte en 1793* (Paris: Vrin, 1968);

Philosophical Forum, special double issue, "Fichte and Contemporary Philosophy," 19 (Winter-Spring 1987-1988);

Tom Rockmore, *Fichte, Marx, and the German Philosophical Tradition* (Carbondale: Southern Illinois University Press, 1980);

John Sallis, "Fichte and the Problem of System," *Man and World,* 9 (February 1976): 75-90;

Heinz Schuffenhauer, *Johann Gottlieb Fichte: Bildbiographie* (Cologne: Pahl-Rugenstein, 1985);

George Seidel, *Activity and Ground: Fichte, Schelling, and Hegel* (Hildesheim & New York: Olms, 1976), pp. 41-87;

Ludwig Siep, *Hegels Fichtekritik und die Wissenschaftslehre von 1804* (Freiberg: Alber, 1970);

Margaret Storrs, *The Relation of Carlyle to Kant and Fichte* (Folcroft, Pa.: Folcroft Library Editions, 1970);

Stefan Summerer, *Wirkliche Sittlichkeit und ästhetische Illusion: Die Fichterezeption in den Fragmenten und Aufzeichnungen F. Schlegels und Hardenbergs* (Bonn: Bouvier, 1974);

G. H. Turnbull, *The Educational Theory of J. G. Fichte* (London: Hodder & Stoughton, 1926);

Hans J. Verweyen, "New Perspectives on J. G. Fichte," *Idealistic Studies,* 6 (May 1976): 118-159;

Joachim Widman, *Johann Gottlieb Fichte: Einführung in seine Philosophie* (Berlin & New York: De Gruyter, 1982).

Papers:

The largest collection of Fichte manuscripts and letters is in the Staatsbibliothek Preußischer Kulturbesitz, West Berlin. Most of the remainder is in the possession of the Fichte family.

Caroline de la Motte Fouqué

(7 October 1774-21 July 1831)

Erich P. Hofacker, Jr.
University of Michigan

BOOKS: *Drei Mährchen*, as Serena (Berlin: Wittich, 1806)–comprises "Die Blumen," "Der Vogel," "Die Thränen";

Rodrich: Ein Roman in zwei Theilen, anonymous (volume 1, Berlin: Hitzig, 1806; volume 2, Berlin: Dümmler, 1807);

Die Frau des Falkensteins: Ein Roman von der Verfasserin des Rodrich, anonymous, 2 volumes (Berlin: Hitzig, 1810);

Kleine Erzählungen von der Verfasserin des Rodrich, der Frau des Falkensteins, anonymous (Berlin: Hitzig, 1811)–comprises "Arnold und Marie," "Das Seegestade," "Der Rosengarten," "Der Hochzeit-Abend," "Das Fräulein vom Thurme," "Der Ring von Savoien," "Keusche Minne";

Briefe über Zweck und Richtung weiblicher Bildung (Berlin: Dümmler, 1811);

Magie der Natur: Eine Revolutions-Geschichte (Berlin: Hitzig, 1812);

Briefe über die griechische Mythologie für Frauen (Berlin: Dümmler, 1812);

Ruf an die deutschen Frauen (Berlin: Dümmler, 1812);

Der Spanier und der Freiwillige in Paris: Eine Geschichte aus dem heiligen Kriege (Berlin: Nikolai, 1814);

Feodora: Ein Roman, 3 volumes (Leipzig: Fleischer, 1814);

Über deutsche Geselligkeit, in Antwort auf das Urtheil der Frau von Staël (Berlin: Wittich, 1814);

Edmunds Wege und Irrwege: Ein Roman aus der nächsten Vergangenheit, 3 volumes (Leipzig: Fleischer, 1815);

Das Heldenmädchen aus der Vendée: Ein Roman (Leipzig: Fleischer, 1816);

Neue Erzählungen (Berlin: Dümmler, 1817)–comprises "Die unsichtbaren Schlingen"; "Die Verwünschung," translated by N. Stenhouse as *The Curse: A Tale* (Edinburgh: Privately printed, 1825); "Der Waldbrunnen: Eine Sage"; "Der Cypressenkranz"; "Der Abtrünnige"; "Bilder aus dem Leben der Kaiserin

Caroline de la Motte Fouqué (Dr. C. C. von Pfuel, Bonn)

Eudoxia"; "Der heilige Athanasius"; "Treu bis zum Tode";

Die früheste Geschichte der Welt: Ein Geschenk für Kinder (Leipzig: Fleischer, 1818);

Frauenliebe: Ein Roman, 3 volumes (Nuremberg: Schrag, 1818);

Blumenstrauß gewunden aus den neuesten Romanen und Erzählungen von Friedrich und Caroline de la Motte Fouqué (Reutlingen: Mäcken, 1818)–includes "Der Delphin," "Der Scharffenstein";

Fragmente aus dem Leben der heutigen Welt (Berlin: Schlesinger, 1820);

Lodoiska und ihre Tochter: Ein Roman, 3 volumes (Leipzig: Fleischer, 1820);

Ida: Ein Roman, 3 volumes (Berlin: Schlesinger, 1820);

Kleine Romane und Erzählungen; Neue Sammlung, 2 volumes (Jena: Schmidt, 1820)–comprises in volume 1, "Die Fahrt im Walde," "Der Ragusaner," "Das goldene Schloß," "Die Richter," "Der Klostergarten," "Die Nonne von Moret"; in volume 2, "Die eine Liebe," "Alphonsine," "Der nächtliche Gast," "Laura," "Dornen und Blüthen des Lebens," "Bruchstücke aus den Papieren des Lord B.," "Der Gasthof";

Heinrich und Marie: Ein Roman, 3 volumes (Jena: Schmidt, 1821);

Die blinde Führerin: Ein Roman (Berlin: Schlesinger, 1821);

Briefe über Berlin im Winter 1821 (Berlin: Schlesinger, 1822);

Vergangenheit und Gegenwart; Ein Roman in einer Sammlung von Briefen (Berlin: Schlesinger, 1822);

Die Herzogin von Montmorency: Ein Roman (Leipzig: Hartmann, 1822);

Die Vertriebenen: Eine Novelle aus der Zeit der Königin Elisabeth von England, 3 volumes (Leipzig: Hartmann, 1823); translated by George Soane as *The Outcasts: A Romance*, 2 volumes (London: Printed for G. and W. G. Whittaker, 1824);

Reiseerinnerungen, by Fouqué and Friedrich de la Motte Fouqué, 2 volumes (Dresden: Arnoldi, 1823);

Neueste gesammelte Erzählungen, 2 volumes (Berlin: Schlesinger, 1824)–comprises in volume 1, "Der Zweikampf," "Die Familie Aslingen," "Die drei Wanderer," "Der Mönch am Bache"; in volume 2, "Der letzte der Paläologen," "Der Meierhof zu Southwark," "Ottilie," "Das Wahrzeichen," "Der Maltheser";

Die beiden Freunde: Ein Roman, 3 volumes (Berlin: Schlesinger, 1824);

Bodo von Hohenried: Ein Roman neuerer Zeit, 3 volumes (Berlin: Schlesinger, 1825);

Aurelio: Eine Novelle (Berlin: Schüppel, 1825);

Die Frauen in der großen Welt: Bildungsbuch beim Eintritt in das gesellige Leben (Berlin: Schlesinger, 1826);

Valerie, Die Sinnesänderung, und Der Weihnachtsbaum: Drei Erzählungen (Berlin: Herbig, 1827);

Resignation, 2 volumes (Frankfurt am Main: Wilmans, 1829);

Geschichte der Moden, vom Jahre 1785 bis 1829, als Beitrag zur Geschichte der Zeit (Stuttgart & Tübingen: Cotta, 1830);

Memoiren einer Ungenannten, anonymous (Stuttgart & Tübingen: Cotta, 1831);

Der Schreibtisch oder alte und neue Zeit: Ein nachgelassenes Werk (Cologne: Bachem, 1833).

Edition in English: *The Physician of Marseilles, The Revolutionists, Etc.: Four Tales from the German*, translated anonymously (London: Burns, 1845)–comprises "Sophie Ariele; or, The Physician of Marseilles," "The Christmas Tree," "The Revolutionists," "Valerie."

OTHER: "Perlen," "Edelsteine," in *Musenalmanach auf das Jahr 1806*, edited by Adelbert von Chamisso and Karl August Varnhagen von Ense (Berlin: Fröhlich, 1806);

Für müßige Stunden: Vierteljahresschrift, edited by Fouqué, Friedrich de la Motte Fouqué, and others, 7 volumes (volumes 1-2, Hildburghausen: Comptoir für Literatur; volumes 3-7, Jena: Schmid, 1816-1821).

PERIODICAL PUBLICATION: "Das schwarze Zeichen," *Mitternachtsblatt für gebildete Stände* (June 1827).

Caroline de la Motte Fouqué was the most successful woman writer of her time in Germany, publishing over one hundred works in twenty-five years. Among these works were twenty novels, sixty novellas or short stories, and twenty-one nonfiction pieces on cultural history for women. She also worked with her husband in editorial ventures.

Caroline Philippine von Briest was born on 7 October 1774 at Schloß Nennhausen, a mansion on an island in the Havel River in western Brandenburg, to Friedrich Wilhelm August and Caroline von Zinnow von Briest. The cultural tone at Nennhausen was set by her father, a politically active country gentleman with a good education along philosophical lines. Her early schooling was in the hands of a French governess with spiritual and intellectual interests. Caroline's childhood recollections contrasted the old-fashioned simple black or gray attire of her serious governess with the elaborate dress and elegant coiffure of her worldly stepmother, Friederike von Luck, whom her father married in 1804 after the death of his first wife. For Caroline, the two women stood for the contradictory traits of her own complex nature. Her education was continued by the young philosopher August Ludwig Hülsen. The progressive thinking of the elder Briest was reflected in his selection of clothing for his daughter: he designed free-flowing, natural attire and left her hair to hang in long curls, unpowdered, freeing her of the discomfort of adult fashions often forced upon the children of her day.

As a young woman, Caroline von Briest had an open mind and a sophistication beyond her years. She was tall, with a beautiful figure; it was said that in facial features she resembled the Apollo Belvedere; and she had an imposing air which commanded respect. In 1789, at the age of fifteen, she married Friedrich Ehrenreich Adolph Ludwig von Rochow, a young military officer from a neighboring estate, and moved with him to Potsdam. She was quite happy at first, enjoying a full schedule of social events in nearby Berlin; but the relationship deteriorated as her husband's immoderation in drinking and gambling increased. She bore two sons, Gustav Adolph in 1792 and Theodor Heinrich in 1795. Shortly after the birth of her second son Count Karl von Lehndorff, the largest landholder in East Prussia, declared in the Officers' Club that no woman is virtuous and wagered that he could seduce Caroline von Rochow, whose reputation was then untarnished. That he was successful in his attempt was confirmed by the birth, sometime in the late 1790s, of their daughter Klara. (A certain disregard of social convention was not uncommon in the last decade of the eighteenth century, when the commonsense attitude of the Age of Reason was giving way to the emotionalism of Romanticism.)

In 1799 the bitterness, disappointment, and humiliation of her failed marriage forced Caroline von Rochow to return home. Before their divorce become final, Rochow committed suicide over gambling debts. Compared to Berlin and the festivities at the royal court, her estate was a secluded, quiet country retreat, but it was by no means a lonely hermitage. Visitors were always present, some remaining for weeks. With the arrival of Friedrich Baron de la Motte Fouqué, a young officer and poet, the literati were more frequently seen at Nennhausen. Caroline herself dominated the scene by her brilliance and lively personality. After her marriage to Fouqué on 9 January 1803, the estate became a meeting place for philosophers and writers of the Romantic school, including Hülsen, the brothers August Wilhelm and Friedrich Schlegel, Adelbert von Chamisso, Ludwig Tieck, Clemens Brentano,

Jean Paul, Johann Gottlieb Fichte, the Stolbergs, Hermann von Pückler-Muskau, Karl August Varnhagen von Ense, Joseph Freiherr von Eichendorff, and E. T. A. Hoffmann.

Through the readings and discussions of these young writers Caroline Fouqué acquired an enthusiasm for Romanticism, with its ideals, emotional intensity, and loyalty to the past. With the encouragement of her husband, she began to write. Her first attempts at poetry appeared anonymously in 1806 in the *Musenalmanach* (Almanac of the Muses), edited by Chamisso and Varnhagen von Ense. Negative reviews, however, led her to turn to prose. The year 1806 also saw the publication of *Drei Mährchen* (Three Fairy Tales) under her pen name, Serena. The first of these stories, "Die Blumen" (The Flowers), shows her propensity to inject Romantic and fairy-tale elements into a realistic world: in a Romeo-and-Juliet story set in Spain, strange, unseen forces rule the hero's destiny. The atmosphere and motifs of "Der Vogel" (The Bird) are characteristically Romantic: a Turkish sultan's daughter is in love only with her own beauty until she comes close to nature. Indecipherable, dreamlike fantasies fill "Die Thränen" (The Tears).

Having maintained friendships among the nobility in Berlin and at the Prussian court, Fouqué spent several months each year in the city while her husband remained at Nennhausen. She expressed a lifelong preference and veneration for the high nobility, who figure prominently in most of her works. Her first novel, *Rodrich* (1806-1807), begins with the hero's entrance into a capital city. (Only seldom does Fouqué name the city of royal residence or the sovereign, who is usually a duke.) Romantic symbolism is employed against this realistic background: four brothers and sisters representing the four natural elements (earth, water, air, and fire) meet for the first time under circumstances of hatred or love. The novel bears a striking resemblance to E. T. A. Hoffmann's *Die Elixire des Teufels* (The Elixir of the Devil, 1815-1816).

Fouqué's early writing shows a strong Romantic influence in style (interpolated verses; brilliant imagery; the melting and fusion of colors; enigmatic, figurative language; frequent symbolism) and motif (the hero or heroine often suffers mental confusion or is simply unstable; an abundance of ancestral guilt is accompanied by fateful curses and the appearance of apparitions; characters are guided by superstition, prophecy, and gloomy foreboding). Her later, starkly realistic works are incongruously embellished with scattered Romantic motifs.

Die Frau des Falkensteins (The Lady of Castle Falkenstein, 1810) was begun in 1807, but Fouqué's poor health delayed its completion until 1810. The focus is on the nobility and its lifestyle. At her mother's deathbed Luise reluctantly marries the overly serious and somewhat inhibited Julius, to whom she has been betrothed since childhood. On the way to the gloomy castle Falkenstein he informs her of the imminent arrival of his friend Fernando, whose reputation as a charming Don Juan has preceded him. The moment they meet, Luise knows that her fate is sealed. In due course Julius dies, and she finds the strength to send Fernando away. In the ensuing years Luise is tempted each time Fernando appears; finally he is shot in a duel, dies in her arms, and is buried next to Julius. Many years of untroubled, pious, and useful life follow, and Luise dies at peace with herself. In part the novel appears to be Fouqué's attempt to overcome troublesome recollections of her unhappy first marriage. Her correspondence indicates that she herself is Luise and the engaging Fernando is Count von Lehndorff, to whom she sent a long (and unanswered) letter with a copy of the novel. Friedrich Fouqué appears as a young officer and poet; her publisher and members of her literary circle are depicted as well, occasionally in uncomplimentary characterizations. Luise, who ultimately develops and grows through her experience, becomes the antithetical Romantic heroine. Her eventual practice of self-restraint is a requisite for a life "nach der Natur" (according to nature). Goethe's works strongly influenced Fouqué's thinking, and his emphasis on perseverance and properly considered decisions is reflected in the law-and-order tone of her work: salvation is to be found only in the performance of one's duty in an orderly world.

"Das Fräulein vom Thurme" (The Girl in the Tower, 1811) tells of Klare, a nobleman's daughter whose unpardonable sin is her "unedle" (ignoble) love for a man beneath her station. She is punished by being walled up and left to perish in a small tower room, while her lover dies imprisoned in the cellar. Centuries later war and the ancestral curse provoked by Klare's act have taken their toll. Kunigunde, the sole surviving member of the now-impoverished noble family, chooses to live in the tower, the only part of the castle that still stands, rather than accept a forester who has expressed a romantic interest in

her. Kunigunde's rejection of the commoner makes amends for Klare's disdain of family honor. The curse is lifted, and the forester is revealed to be an aristocrat in disguise and thus worthy of her love.

On the surface, *Magie der Natur* (Magic of Nature, 1812) deals with the French Revolution, but the author's main concern is the limits prescribed by the laws of man and nature. The revolution is viewed as a misguided attempt to destroy a form of society which has evolved through the centuries. Fouqué is also concerned about the Romantic interest in "mesmerism" or hypnotism: she fears that hypnotism may release uncontrollable forces. Because of a supposed "Magnetismus im Menschen" (human magnetism) analogous to animal magnetism, it was believed that a room in which a person is hypnotized might become magnetized, with the result that persons entering later could "see" the former occupant. This phenomenon, in Fouqué's view, amounts to lifting the veil shielding nature's secrets; people should see no more than the human eye is naturally capable of seeing. When man oversteps the bounds, he causes more confusion than clarification. It is probable that Goethe's *Die Wahlverwandtschaften* (Elective Affinities, 1809) influenced this work; like Goethe, Fouqué felt that man should stand in awe of the mysteries of the world and should not attempt to unravel them. Goethe read the novel because of his interest in mesmerism and sent the author an approving letter.

In *Briefe über Zweck und Richtung weiblicher Bildung* (Letters Concerning the Purpose and Direction of Women's Education, 1811) Fouqué asserts that piety serves as the foundation of education; she warns women against aspiring to fame in the arts and recommends that they cultivate their artistic talents merely as social graces. In *Briefe über die griechische Mythologie für Frauen* (Letters for Women Concerning Greek Mythology, 1812) she holds that the power of the human intellect is insufficient to gain insight into the essence of mythology. True religion is the sole guide in the search for the meaning of myths, for the purpose of mythological research is to recognize God in His eternal revelation. The volume covers the various stages in the development of humanity and relates them to the history of mythology.

In 1813 Fouqué's husband and sons answered the Prussian call to arms. Since Fouqué had witnessed the French pillage of the countryside after Prussia's defeat at Jena in 1806 and had even been compelled to quarter French soldiers at Nennhausen, she responded with patriotic fervor. Her *Ruf an die deutschen Frauen* (Summons to the German Women, 1812) is a plea for full support in the nation's effort to regain its freedom and honor. She deplores changes in the German national character resulting from French influence. For the sake of their children, German women should guard their traditions of language, dress, and "einfache edle Haltung" (simple noble bearing).

Fouqué rose strongly to the defense of the German character and customs against the negative characterizations of Mme de Staël's *De l'Allemagne* (On Germany, 1813). In *Über deutsche Geselligkeit, in Antwort auf das Urtheil der Frau von Staël* (On German Social Life, in Reply to the Opinion of Mme de Staël, 1814) she reminds the Swiss critic that present conditions in Germany are manifestations of "eine zeitweilige Krankheit" (a temporary illness). She is particularly indignant over caricatures of her countrymen as mentally stunted, boring, pedantic, weak creatures and calls upon women not to lose sight of the genuine greatness of the German people.

The first novel in which Fouqué expresses her disenchantment with the times is *Feodora* (1814), a work of character development. The heroine fears that the new, freer spirit now prevailing will undermine old habits of discipline and obedience to authority. Though it is difficult for her to believe that this new direction is the will of God, Feodora consoles herself with the faith that the world moves according to an eternal law of progress, of which even backward steps are an integral part. Fouqué's correspondence reveals that the three central female characters of this novel represent aspects of her own personality: the first strictly upholds law and order; the second is frank, impetuous, imprudent, and overly passionate; the third is her ideal self-image, a loving woman in whose nature law and order are inherent.

Das Heldenmädchen aus der Vendée (The Heroic Girl of the Vendée Nobility, 1816) is one of Fouqué's best historical novels. The facts of the French Revolution are recorded in realistic detail, although often in Romantic trappings, and her characterizations of historical figures, such as Robespierre, are accurate and well executed. The admirable character of the Vendée as they struggle against the revolutionaries illustrates Fouqué's conception of the nobility as the natural link between the common people and their ruler. The Vendée are exemplary in their piety: they sing

only hymns, say the rosary regularly, and pray before battle. As she inspires the troops, the "Heldenmädchen" reminds one of Joan of Arc. She falls in the battle that destroys the Vendée army and dies with one arm around the crucifix, convinced that the honor of France and the Vendée has been saved. In general, Fouqué's historical novels are better written than the others and contain plots that are relatively simple, straightforward, and fast moving.

"Der Delphin" (The Dolphin, 1818) tells of a pious German knight who is cuckolded by a member of an old aristocratic family; atonement comes generations later in the Dolphin Inn, which was once the castle of the wronged knight. The style of writing here is reminiscent of Hoffmann: both weird and realistic events are described in meticulous detail against a vague and obscure background. Hoffmann himself probably served as the model for the fantastic and enigmatic painter and conductor Gottmund, whose body disappears at his death. "Der Waldbrunnen" (The Forest Well, 1817) opens with a realistic depiction of the noise and confusion of carriage traffic as bored individuals, on their way to yet another elegant social function, busily exercise the gallantries of high society; but the story soon turns into a fairy tale of a wicked water sprite who has bewitched a young nobleman on the eve of his engagement to a princess. This work is one of Fouqué's unsuccessful attempts to integrate reality and fantasy.

Ida (1820) recounts the experiences of "eine schöne Seele" (a beautiful soul) who, despite the temptations of court life, follows the dictates of conscience and leads an existence above reproach. In a confusion of identities a young prince falls in love with Ida, the lady-in-waiting to the older, overbearing, and stout princess whom he is to marry purely for reasons of state. Ida, goodness personified, is horrified that the prince might break his word and therefore places their relationship on a high spiritual plane, with union and bliss scheduled for the world beyond. The work is of interest chiefly for its social satire of the shallow café society, including that at the fashionable resort of Carlsbad.

In "Die drei Wanderer" (The Three Wanderers, 1824) she gives voice to her first serious criticism of the nobility, whom she describes as a crude mixture of conceit and usury on the one hand and defiant hatred and craftiness on the other. This condition has brought about a deterioration in noblesse oblige, the traditional ideal of honorable conduct associated with the station of an aristocrat.

The admonition of "Das schwarze Zeichen" (The Black Sign, 1827) recalls *Magie der Natur* fifteen years earlier: do not attempt to break down the barriers between this life and the next; cling to the true faith and guard against skepticism. A highly emotional and mystically inclined girl is exceedingly devoted to her brother and cannot face the prospect of separation by death: she wishes to remain in contact with him if one of them should die. The brother dies but returns in spirit form, imploring her to repent of her sins. When she refuses to accept objects moving on her desk as proof of his presence, he grasps her wrist, leaving a black mark as if the skin were charred by a band of red-hot iron. For good measure, his fingerprints are burned into the desk top. Convinced, his sister awaits their reunion in heaven.

Fouqué's *Geschichte der Moden, vom Jahre 1785 bis 1829, als Beitrag zur Geschichte der Zeit* (History of Fashion, from 1785 to 1829, as a Contribution to the History of the Age) appeared in installments in 1829-1830 in the popular *Morgenblatt* and was published separately in 1830. Her last publication was the anonymous novel *Memoiren einer Ungenannten* (Memoirs of a Woman without a Name, 1831), an account of the tribulations of a noblewoman who flees to Spain after the battle of Jena in 1806 to escape the experience of Prussia's subjugation and occupation by French forces.

In her later years Fouqué was forced to increase her production to compensate for the financial losses resulting from the steep decline in Friedrich Fouqué's popularity; the quality of her work suffered accordingly. She continued to spend months at a time among the nobility in Berlin. When at Nennhausen she often communicated her dire financial straits in letters to "Princess Wilhelm"–Princess Marianne von Hess-

en-Homburg, wife of Prince Wilhelm, brother of the king–but assistance was seldom forthcoming. After a winter of illness in Berlin Fouqué returned to her family estate to recuperate. Unable to regain her strength, she died in her sleep on 21 July 1831 at the age of fifty-six.

Letters:

Albertine, Baronin de la Motte Fouqué, ed., *Briefe an Friedrich, Baron de la Motte Fouqué* (Berlin: W. Adolf, 1848).

References:

Ludmilla Assing, ed., *Briefwechsel zwischen Varnhagen und Rahel: Aus dem Nachlaß Varnhagens von Ense*, 6 volumes (Leipzig: Brockhaus, 1874-1875);

Richard Benz, *Märchen-Dichtung der Romantiker* (Jena: Diederichs, 1926);

Rudolf Herd, "Der Kapellmeister Gottmund im Delphin der Karoline de la Motte Fouqué, eine Verkörperung E. T. A. Hoffmanns," *Mitteilungen der E. T. A. Hoffmann Gesellschaft*, 10 (1963): 27-32;

Vera Prill, *Caroline de la Motte Fouqué* (Berlin: Eberring, 1933);

Caroline von Rochow and Marie de la Motte Fouqué, *Vom Leben am preussischen Hofe 1815-1852*, revised by Luise von der Marwitz (Berlin: Mittler, 1908);

Arno Schmidt, *Fouqué und einige seiner Zeitgenossen* (Karlsruhe: Stahlberg, 1958);

Jean T. Wilde, *The Romantic Realist: Caroline de la Motte Fouqué* (New York: Bookman Associates, 1955).

Papers:

Papers of Caroline de la Motte Fouqué are in the Goethe and Schiller Archives in Weimar, the Deutsche Staatsbibliothek in East Berlin, and the Bayerische Staatsbibliothek in Munich.

Friedrich de la Motte Fouqué
(12 February 1777-23 January 1843)

Erich P. Hofacker, Jr.
University of Michigan

BOOKS: *Dramatische Spiele,* as Pellegrin, edited by August Wilhelm Schlegel (Berlin: Unger, 1804)—comprises *Liebe und Streit; Streit und Liebe; Aquilin; Des heiligen Johannis Nepomuceni Märtyrer-Tod; Rübezahl; Die Minnesinger;*

Romanzen vom Thale Ronceval, anonymous (Berlin: Realschulbuchhandlung, 1805);

Zwei Schauspiele von Pellegrin (Berlin: Lange, 1805)—comprises *Der Falke, Das Reh;*

Die Zwerge: Ein dramatisches Spiel, as Pellegrin (Berlin: Quien, 1805);

Historie vom edlen Ritter Galmy und einer schönen Herzogin aus Bretagne, as Pellegrin, 2 volumes (Berlin: Himburg, 1806);

Schillers Todtenfeier: Ein Prolog, by Fouqué, as Pellegrin, and August Ferdinand Bernhardi (Berlin: Himburg, 1806);

Alwin: Ein Roman in zwei Bänden, as Pellegrin, 2 volumes (Berlin: Braunes, 1808);

Gespräch zweier Preußischen Edelleute über den Adel (Berlin: Hitzig, 1808);

Sigurd, der Schlangentödter: Ein Heldenspiel in sechs Abentheuern (Berlin: Hitzig, 1808);

Der Held des Nordens: Drei Heldenspiele, 3 volumes (Berlin: Hitzig, 1810)—comprises volume 1, *Sigurd, der Schlangentödter;* volume 2, *Sigurds Rache;* volume 3, *Aslauga;*

Das Galgenmännlein (Berlin: Hitzig, 1810); translated anonymously as "The Bottle-Imp," in *Popular Tales and Romances of the Northern Nations,* volume 1 (London: Printed for W. Simpkin & R. Marshall, 1823); translated by Thomas Tracy as "The Vial-Genie and Mad Farthing," in his *Miniature Romances from the German, with Other Profusions of Light Literature* (Boston: Little, Brown, 1841);

Eginhard und Emma: Ein Schauspiel in drei Aufzügen (Nuremberg: Schrag, 1811);

Der Todesbund: Ein Roman (Halle: Schimmelpfennig, 1811);

Vaterländische Schauspiele (Berlin: Hitzig, 1811)—comprises *Waldemar der Pilger, Markgraf von Brandenburg: Trauerspiel in fünf Aufzügen; Die*

Friedrich de la Motte Fouqué, drawing by W. Hensel (Bildarchiv der Österreichischen Nationalbibliothek)

Ritter und die Bauern: Schauspiel in vier Aufzügen;

Undine: Eine Erzählung (Berlin: Hitzig, 1811; New York: Radde, 1846; London: Allan, 1860); translated by George Soane as *Undine: A Romance* (London: Printed for W. Simpkin & R. Marshall, 1818); translated by Tracy as "Undine," in *Undine, and Sintram and His Companions* (New York: Wiley & Putnam, 1845);

Über den sogenannten falschen Waldemar (Berlin: Hitzig, 1811);

Der Zauberring: Ein Ritterroman, 3 volumes (Nuremberg: Schrag, 1812); translated by A. L. L. as *The Magic Ring; or, Ingratitude Punished:*

An Eastern Tale (London: Printed for J. Evers, 1812); translated anonymously as *The Magic Ring: A Knightly Romance* (London & New York: Routledge, 1876);

Die beiden Hauptleute (Berlin: Hitzig, 1812); translated anonymously as *The Two Captains: A Romance* (London: Lumley, 1846);

Aslaugas Ritter und Alpha und Jucunde (Berlin: Hitzig, 1813); "Aslaugas Ritter" translated by Thomas Carlyle as "Aslauga's Knight," in his *German Romance: Specimens of Its Chief Authors, with Biographical and Critical Notices* (Edinburgh & London: Tait, 1827);

Gedichte vor und während dem Kriege 1813: Als Manuskript für Freunde (Berlin: Hitzig, 1813);

Alboin der Langobardenkönig: Ein Heldenspiel in sechs Abentheuern (Leipzig: Weygand, 1813);

Dramatische Dichtungen für Deutsche: Mit Musik (Berlin: Hitzig, 1813)—comprises *Alf und Yngwi: Trauerspiel; Die Irmensäul: Trauerspiel; Die Runenschrift: Altsächsisches Schauspiel; Die Heimkehr des großen Kurfürsten: Dramatisches Gedicht; Die Familie Hallersee: Trauerspiel aus der Zeit des siebenjährigen Krieges;*

Corona: Ein Rittergedicht in drei Büchern (Stuttgart & Tübingen: Cotta, 1814);

Kleine Romane, 6 volumes (Berlin: Hitzig, 1814-1819);

Auch ein Wort über die neueste Zeit: Nebst einigen Beilagen, anonymous (Berlin: Dümmler, 1815);

Jahrbüchlein Deutscher Gedichte auf 1815, by Fouqué, H. Löst, and others (Berlin & Stettin: Nicola, 1815);

Sintram und seine Gefährten: Eine nordische Erzählung nach Albrecht Dürer (Vienna: Haas, 1815; London: Allan, 1860; New York: Holt, 1884); translated by J. C. Hare as *Sintram and His Companions: A Romance* (London: Ollier/Edinburgh: Blackwood, 1820); translated anonymously as *Sintram and His Companions* (New York: Allen, 1869);

An Christian Grafen zu Stolberg: Zum 15. Oktober 1815 (N.p., 1815);

Tassilo: Vorspiel (Berlin: Duncker & Humblot, 1815);

Die Fahrten Thiodolfs des Isländers: Ein Ritterroman, 2 volumes (Hamburg: Campe, 1815); translated anonymously as *Thiodolf, the Icelander* (London: Burns, 1845); translated anonymously as "Thiodolf the Icelander," in *Thiodolf the Icelander, and Aslauga's Knight* (New York: Wiley & Putnam, 1845);

Die Pilgerfahrt: Ein Trauerspiel in fünf Aufzügen, edited by Franz Horn (Nuremberg: Schrag, 1816);

Sängerliebe: Eine provenzalische Sage in drei Büchern (Stuttgart & Tübingen: Cotta, 1816); translated by Soane as *Minstrel-love* (London: Printed for W. Simpkin & R. Marshall, 1821);

Karls des Großen Geburt und Jugendjahre: Ein Ritterlied, edited by Horn (Nuremberg: Schrag, 1816);

Kindermärchen, by Fouqué, Karl Wilhelm Contessa, and E. T. A. Hoffmann, 2 volumes (Berlin: Realschulbuchhandlung, 1816-1817);

Reidmar und Diona: Ein Roman (Vienna: Haas, 1816);

Gedichte, 5 volumes (Stuttgart & Tübingen: Cotta, 1816-1827);

Die zwei Brüder: Trauerspiel in vier Aufzügen, mit einem Vorspiel (Stuttgart & Tübingen: Cotta, 1817);

Die wunderbaren Begebenheiten des Grafen Alethes von Lindenstein: Ein Roman, 2 volumes (Leipzig: Fleischer, 1817);

Abendunterhaltungen zu gemüthlicher Erheiterung des Geistes, by Fouqué, Heinrich Daniel Zschokke, and others (Vienna: Gerold, 1817);

Liebesrache: Ein Trauerspiel in drei Aufzügen (Leipzig: Fleischer, 1817);

Heldenspiele (Stuttgart & Tübingen: Cotta, 1818);

Blumenstrauss: Gewunden aus den neuesten Romanen und Erzählungen, by Fouqué and Caroline de la Motte Fouqué (Reutlingen: Mäcken, 1818);

Altsächsischer Bildersaal, 4 volumes (Nuremberg: Schrag, 1818-1820)—comprises volume 1, *Herrmann: Ein Heldenspiel in vier Abentheuern* (1818); volume 2, *Welleda und Ganna: Eine altdeutsche Geschichte* (1818); volume 3, *Schön Irsa und ihre weiße Kuh: Ein Mährchen* (1818); volume 4, *Die vier Brüder von der Weserburg: Eine altdeutsche Geschichte* (1820);

Romantische Dichtungen, by Fouqué, Johann Peter Hebel, Justinus Kerner, and others (Karlsruhe: Braun, 1818);

Jäger und Jägerlieder: Ein kriegerisches Idyll (Hamburg: Perthes & Bessner, 1818);

Etwas über den deutschen Adel, über Rittersinn und Militärehre in Briefen, by Fouqué and Friedrich Perthes (Hamburg: Perthes & Besser, 1819);

Gefühle, Bilder und Ansichten: Sammlung kleiner prosaischer Schriften, 2 volumes (Leipzig: Fleischer, 1819);

Hieronymus von Stauf: Trauerspiel in fünf Aufzügen (Berlin: Schlesinger, 1819);

Der Mord August's von Kotzebue: Freundes Ruf an Deutschlands Jugend (Berlin: Maurer, 1819);

Der Leibeigene: Schauspiel in fünf Aufzügen (Berlin: Schlesinger, 1820);

Wahrheit und Lüge: Eine Reihe politisch-militärischer Betrachtungen in Bezug auf den Vendeekrieg, nach dem Werke: "Memoires de Madame la Marquise de Laroche Jaquelin, écrites par elle-même" (Leipzig: Knobloch, 1820);

Bertrand du Guesclin: Ein historisches Rittergedicht in vier Büchern mit erläuternden Anmerkungen, 3 volumes (Leipzig: Fleischer, 1821);

Der Verfolgte: Eine Rittersage, 3 volumes (Berlin: Schlesinger, 1821);

Betrachtungen über Türken, Griechen und Türkenkrieg (Berlin: Maurer, 1822);

Ritter Elidouc: Eine altbretannische Sage, 3 volumes (Leipzig: Hartmann, 1822); translated anonymously as *Sir Elidoc: An Old Breton Legend* (London: Mozley & Masters, 1849);

Wilde Liebe: Ein Ritterroman, 2 volumes (Leipzig: Hartmann, 1823); translated anonymously as *Wild Love: A Romance* (Philadelphia: Ferrett, 1845);

Don Carlos, Infant von Spanien: Ein Trauerspiel. Mit einer Zueignung an Friedrich von Schiller (Danzig: Alberti, 1823);

Feierlieder eines Preußen im Herbste 1823: Seiner königlichen Hoheit mit dem Kronprinzen von Preußen allerunterthänigst (Berlin: Herbig, 1823);

Geistliche Lieder: Erstes Bändchen. Missions-Lieder (Leipzig: Tauchnitz, 1823);

Reiseerinnerungen, by Fouqué and Caroline de la Motte Fouqué, 2 volumes (Dresden: Arnoldi, 1823);

Die Fahrt in die neue Welt, by Fouqué, and *Das Grab der Mutter*, by Alexis dem Wanderer (Quedlinburg & Leipzig: Basse, 1824);

Lebensbeschreibung des königlich preußischen Generals der Infanterie Heinrich August Baron de la Motte Fouqué: Verfaßt von seinem Enkel (Berlin: Schüppel, 1824);

Der Refugié oder Heimath und Fremde: Ein Roman aus der neuern Zeit, 3 volumes (Gotha & Erfurt: Hennings, 1824);

Sophie Ariele: Eine Novelle (Berlin: Schüppel, 1825);

Die Saga von dem Gunlaugur, genannt Drachenzunge und Rafn dem Skalden: Eine Islandskunde des elften Jahrhunderts (Vienna: Pichler, 1826);

Geschichte der Jungfrau von Orleans, nach authentischen Urkunden und dem französischen Werke des Herrn Le Brun de Charmettes, 2 volumes (Berlin: Schlesinger, 1826);

Erdmann und Fiammetta: Novelle (Berlin: Schlesinger, 1826);

Erhörung: Sechs Psalme (Berlin: Published by the author, 1827);

Mandragora: Eine Novelle (Berlin: Sander, 1827);

Ernst Friedrich Wilhelm Philipp von Rüchel, Königlich Preußischer General der Infanterie: Militärische Biographie, 2 volumes (Berlin: Maurer, 1828);

Der Sängerkrieg auf der Wartburg: Ein Dichterspiel (Berlin: Herbig, 1828);

Moritz Gottlieb Saphir und Berlin, by Fouqué, F. W. Gubitz, and Willibald Alexis (Berlin: Cosmar & Krause, 1828);

Der Mensch des Südens und der Mensch des Nordens: Sendschreiben in Bezug auf das gleichnamige Werk des Herrn von Bonstettin an den Freiherrn Alexander von Humboldt (Berlin: Vereinsbuchhandlung, 1829);

Fata Morgana: Novelle (Stuttgart: Hoffmann, 1830);

Jakob Böhme: Ein biographischer Denkstein (Greiz: Henning, 1831);

Sendschreiben an den Verfasser der Betrachtungen über die neuesten Begebenheiten in Deutschland (Berlin, Posen & Bromberg: Mittler, 1831);

Von der Liebes-Lehre (Hamburg: Perthes, 1837);

Der Geheimrath: Erzählung (Wernigerode: Thiele, 1838);

Goethe und einer seiner Bewunderer: Ein Stück Lebensgeschichte (Berlin: Duncker, 1840);

Lebensgeschichte des Baron Friedrich de la Motte Fouqué: Aufgezeichnet durch ihn selbst (Halle: Schwetschke, 1840);

Preußische Trauersprüche und Huldigungsgrüße für das Jahr 1840 (Halle: Anton, 1840);

Ausgewählte Werke: Ausgabe letzter Hand, 12 volumes (Halle: Schwetschke, 1841-1873);

Denkschrift über Friedrich Wilhelm III, König von Preußen: Eine biographische Mittheilung (Nordhausen & Leipzig: Schmidt, 1842);

Der Pappenheimer Kürassier: Scenen aus der Zeit des dreißigjährigen Krieges (Nordhausen & Leipzig: Schmidt, 1842);

Novellen-Mappe, by Fouqué, Gubitz, and others (Berlin: Vereinsbuchhandlung, 1843);

Abfall und Buße oder Die Seelenspiegel: Ein Roman aus der Grenzscheide des XVIII. und XIX. Jahrhunderts, 2 volumes (Berlin: Enslin, 1844);

Violina: A Romance, translated anonymously (New York: Ferret, 1845);

Joseph und seine Geige; Kaiser Karls V. Angriff auf Algier; Zwei Novellen (Potsdam: Horvath, 1845);

Fouqué's Works, 6 volumes (London: Burns, 1845-1846)–comprises volume 1, *The Four Seasons;* volume 2, *Romantic Fiction;* volume 3, *Wild Love, and Other Tales;* volume 4, *Thiodolf the Icelander;* volume 5, *Minstrel Love;* volume 6, *The Magic Ring;*

Geistliche Gedichte, edited by Albertine de la Motte Fouqué (Berlin: Adolf, 1846);

Christlicher Liederschatz zur Erbauung von Jung und Alt: Gesammelt aus dem nachgelassenen Tagebuche des Verfassers, edited by Albertine de la Motte Fouqué (Berlin: Kastner, 1862);

Fouqué's Werke: Auswahl in drei Teilen, edited by Walther Ziesemer, 3 volumes (Berlin: Bong, 1908);

Belisar, edited by Christoph F. Lorenz (Frankfurt am Main & New York: Lang, 1985).

OTHER: *Taschenbuch für Freunde der Poesie des Südens,* edited by Fouqué, 2 volumes (Berlin: Hitzig, 1809);

Die Jahreszeiten: Eine Vierteljahresschrift für romantische Dichtungen, edited by Fouqué, 4 volumes (Berlin: Hitzig, 1811-1814);

Die Musen: Eine norddeutsche Zeitschrift, edited by Fouqué and Wilhelm Neumann, 3 volumes (volume 1, Berlin: Salfeld, 1812; volumes 2-3, Berlin: Hitzig, 1813-1814);

Taschenbuch der Sagen und Legenden, edited by Fouqué and Amalie von Helwig, 2 volumes (Berlin: Realschulbuchhandlung, 1812-1817);

Adelbert von Chamisso, *Peter Schlemihl's wundersame Geschichte,* edited by Fouqué (Nuremberg: Schrag, 1814);

Joseph Freiherr von Eichendorff, *Ahnung und Gegenwart: Ein Roman,* foreword by Fouqué (Nuremberg: Schrag, 1815);

Für müßige Stunden: Vierteljahresschrift, edited by Fouqué, Caroline de la Motte Fouqué, and others, 4 volumes (volumes 1-2, Hildburghausen: Comptoir für Literatur, 1816-1817; volumes 3-4, Jena: Schmidt, 1819-1820);

Carl Heinrich Ludwig von Wangenheim, *Familienleben: Ein moralisches Unterhaltungsbuch für Mädchen von reiferem Alter,* foreword by Fouqué, 2 volumes (Halle & Berlin: Hallisches Waisenhaus, 1817);

"Paul Pommer: Scenen aus dem Leben eines preußischen Invaliden," in *Gaben der Milde,*

edited by F. W. Gubitz, volume 1 (Berlin, 1817), pp. 1-46;

Wunderbuch, edited by Fouqué and Friedrich Laun, 3 volumes (Leipzig: Göschen, 1817);

August Fresenius, *Hinterlassene Schriften: Erster Band,* edited by Fouqué (Frankfurt am Main: Körner, 1818);

Aus der Geisterwelt: Geschichten, Sagen und Dichtungen, edited by Fouqué and Laun, 2 volumes (Erfurt: Keyser, 1818);

Samuel Christian Pape, *Gedichte,* foreword by Fouqué (Tübingen: Osiander, 1821);

Christoph E. L. Blochmann, *Gertha von Stalimene,* foreword by Fouqué (Danzig, 1822);

Thomas Moore, *Lalla Rukh, oder Die mongolische Prinzessin: Romantische Dichtung. Aus dem Englischen in den Sylbenmaaßen des Originals übersetzt,* translated by Fouqué (Berlin: Schlesinger, 1822);

Pique-Dame: Berichte aus dem Irrenhause, in Briefen. Nach dem Schwedischen, translated by Fouqué (Berlin: Rücker, 1825);

Bernhard Severin Ingemann, *Tasso's Befreiung: Ein dramatisches Gedicht. Aus dem Dänischen,* translated by H. Gardthausen, introduction by Fouqué (Leipzig: Tauchnitz, 1826);

E. T. A. Hoffmann, *Wanderlieder,* foreword by Fouqué (Greiz: Henning, 1828);

Alessandro Manzoni, *Der fünfte May: Ode auf Napoleons Tod. In der italienischen Urschrift nebst Uebersetzungen,* translated by Fouqué, Johann Wolfgang von Goethe, and others (Berlin: Maurer, 1828);

Jean Baptiste Rousseau, *Spiele der Muse: Zweite, stark vermehrte Ausgabe,* foreword by Fouqué (Frankfurt am Main: Brönner, 1829);

Berlinische Blätter für deutsche Frauen: Eine Wochenschrift, edited by Fouqué, 12 volumes (Berlin: Maurer, 1829-1830);

Friedrich Tietz, *Erzählungen und Phantasiestücke,* foreword by Fouqué (Leipzig: Böhme, 1834);

Ingemann, *Drei Erzählungen: Aus dem Dänischen,* translated by Fouqué (Halle: Kümmel, 1837);

Zeitung für den deutschen Adel, edited by Fouqué and L. von Alvensleben, 3 volumes (Leipzig: Franke, 1840-1842);

Hans Christian Andersen, *Bilderbuch ohne Bilder: Aus dem Dänischen,* translated by Fouqué (Berlin: Besser, 1842).

The name Friedrich Baron de la Motte Fouqué rose like a comet on the literary horizon of the early nineteenth century but faded as suddenly as it had appeared. Beginning in 1810 all segments of German society, from the aristocracy to the working class, were captivated by Fouqué's romantic fantasies. The Austrian dramatist Franz Grillparzer ranked Fouqué next to the "Altmeister Goethe" himself, and the Romantic poet Joseph Freiherr von Eichendorff concluded a long poem, "An Fouqué," with the line, "Wir wollen bei dir bleiben bis zum Tode" (We intend to remain true to you till death).

Friedrich Heinrich Karl Baron de la Motte Fouqué was descended from the family of Folko von Montfaucon, a member of the Huguenot aristocracy who left Normandy with the renewed persecution of the Protestants resulting from the revocation of the Edict of Nantes by King Louis XIV in 1685. His great-grandfather, Karl de la Motte Fouqué, fled to Holland, where he married the refugee Susanne de Robillard. Soon widowed, Susanne Fouqué moved to Celle in Lower Saxony with her three young sons. The second oldest, Fouqué's grandfather Henry Auguste, entered military service, became a court favorite, rose to the rank of general, and was, at his death, one of the closest friends of King Friedrich II. Fouqué revered his grandfather, who died three years before his birth, because he shared the older man's basic values: allegiance to Prussia (*Preußentum*), pride in the aristocracy, and a fervent desire for a military career. In 1824 he published a glorified biography of Henry Auguste.

Fouqué was born in Brandenburg on 12 February 1777, the son of Heinrich August Karl Fouqué, a member of the landed gentry, and Marie Louise von Schlegell. A dreamy child with an active imagination, he was inclined to take long walks in the parklands of his father's estates, to visit ruined castles, and to spend hours reading. From 1780 until 1787 his family lived in the manor house Sacrow on an island of a lake formed by the Havel River, a tributary of the Elbe. During a protracted illness, the boy passed time with richly illustrated books on chivalric and religious themes. His writings reflect impressions from the books he encountered in childhood, particularly in the strong visual quality of the episodes depicted in his dramas and novels. From 1788 until 1794 young Fouqué was educated by A. L. Hülsen, a writer of the early Romantic period and a friend of the philosophers Johann Gottlieb Fichte and Friedrich Ernst Daniel Schleiermacher. To Hülsen he owed his advances in the knowledge of English and the Scandinavian languages as well as his growing interest in literature. He avidly read the popular works of the day—for example, Leonhard Wächter's seven-volume *Sagen der Vorzeit* (Legends of Olden Times, 1787-1798)—but under the tutelage of Hülsen, Fouqué was also introduced to the Greek classics, to Shakespeare, and to Norse mythology. A favorite work was *Lieder Sineds des Barden,* or Songs of Sined, the Bard, a German translation, by the Austrian Jesuit Michael Denis, of the so-called Ossianic poems, which purportedly had been translated from the Gaelic by James Macpherson. This volume awakened Fouqué's interest in Germanic-Norse myth and helped shape his image of the Middle Ages as a time of legendary rather than historical events. The young Fouqué's outlook was also conditioned by his confrontation with death, especially by his viewing of the body of his godfather, King Friedrich II, who died 16 August 1786, and by the death of his mother on 27 November 1788. He developed his own peculiar melancholy and pessimistic view of the world; the presence of death permeated his works. The extensive and dense forests in the vicinity of Sacrow stimulated his boyish imagination and led him to view the world and the enigma of human existence as a maze, variously represented in his works by the metaphors "der Wald der Welt" (the world as a forest) and "das dunkel Thal des Irrens" (the dark valley of perplexity).

As a young military officer of the Weimar Dragoons, Fouqué served as a cornet or standard bearer. In 1798 he met and married Marianne von Schubaert, the daughter of his military commander. However, neither married life nor the routine of a military camp proved fulfilling. So deep was his dissatisfaction with life in the Prussian army that he considered joining the forces of Napoleon! After a divorce from his first wife, he married Caroline von Rochow, a widow with literary ambitions. Released from military service, Fouqué and Caroline lived on her family's estate, Nennhausen, near Rathenow, until the early 1830s. He became acquainted with many German writers and visited Goethe on several occasions. Nennhausen became a center of literary society, and the Fouqués entertained frequent guests. Contemporaries described Fouqué as a man of unprepossessing exterior, short stature, and weak physical constitution. Caroline Fouqué, by contrast, was statuesque and attractive. Although Fouqué's public statements told of his happiness in this marriage, he seems to have had many moments of insecurity, intensified perhaps by his knowledge of

Title page for the first edition of the first part of Fouqué's trilogy Der Held des Nordens

Caroline's infidelity in her first marriage (one of her children from that period had not been fathered by her husband). In his works the motif of the man between two women occurs repeatedly. One woman is typically lucid and pure, the other demonic, a possible reflection of Fouqué's perception of a dual nature in Caroline.

Around the turn of the century the author's life took a decisive turn when he met August Wilhelm Schlegel, who became both his friend and his teacher. Stimulated by Schlegel, Fouqué began an intensive study of medieval texts and acquired a thorough grounding in the Nordic languages and mythology. His interest in Nordic tradition is later reflected in his free paraphrase of an old Icelandic legend, *Die Saga von dem Gunlaugur, genannt Drachenzunge und Rafn dem Skalden* (The Saga of Gunlaugur, called Tongue of the Dragon and Warrior by the Poet, 1826), which he dedicated to the scholars of the Icelandic Literary Society. In the year of his remarriage, 1803, Fouqué's first works began to appear

under the pseudonym Pellegrin in Friedrich Schlegel's journal *Europa*. During the next four years he wrote *Der gehörnte Siegfried in der Schmiede* (The Horny-skinned or Invulnerable Siegfried at the Forge, 1803), which was the first dramatic treatment of the Siegfried legend since Hans Sachs's *Der hürnen Sewfried* (The Horny-skinned Siegfried), written in 1557. He also attempted allegorical plays influenced by Cervantes and Calderón and a versified version of Jörg Wickram's *Goldfaden* (Golden Thread).

Fouqué achieved his literary breakthrough in 1808 with the chivalric romance *Alwin*, published under the name Pellegrin. The historical period during which the romance is set is hazy and imprecise but reminiscent of the Thirty Years' War. Fouqué tells a story of vague dreams of heroism, chivalric deeds, and the experience of love. Though the novel has a happy ending, it is pervaded by the melancholy tone which characterizes Fouqué's works. Behind the altered names, historical figures as well as persons from

Fouqué's life are easily recognized: his wives, Marianne and Caroline; a religious mystic, Jakob Böhme; Napoleon; Friedrich Nicolai, a contemporary novelist and popular philosopher; and even a literary critic who once gave him a bad review. Caroline Fouqué's counterpart, Mathilde, is of special biographical interest. She is portrayed as proud and domineering, ambitious but also flighty, worldly but also superficial. *Alwin* received a warm public reception.

In 1807 Fouqué had begun to work on *Die wunderbaren Begebenheiten des Grafen Alethes von Lindenstein* (The Wondrous Experiences of Alethes von Lindenstein, 1817), another novel of chivalry with a melancholy tone. Although the novel seems vaguely to be set in the time of the Thirty Years' War, it also exhibits the influence of contemporary historical events, such as the Prussian defeat by Napoleon in 1806 and the subsequent French occupation. After completing three of the four parts Fouqué laid the work aside until 1816. By this time Fouqué had undergone a religious catharsis through the study of Böhme's works. He now considered his earlier writing to reflect a questionable morality, and the solution he had planned for the fourth part appeared to him to contain "einen allzusündigen Flecken" (a too-sinful blemish). The antiseptic tone of the last volume is noticeably different from that of its predecessors.

The years 1810 to 1813 saw a rapid increase in the author's productivity and the growth of his reputation. The trilogy *Der Held des Nordens* (The Hero of the North, 1810), based on Icelandic legends and written in alternating iambic and short alliterative lines, includes the dramas *Sigurd, der Schlangentödter* (Siegfried the Dragon Killer), *Sigurds Rache* (Siegfried's Revenge), and *Aslauga*. Although this trilogy, like other works of the period, was not well suited for the stage, it did serve as one of Richard Wagner's sources for *Der Ring des Nibelungen* (1876).

Der Todesbund (The Bond of Death), published in 1811, is a short novel set in Scotland, incorporating sinister legends, and pervaded by Fouqué's gloomy tone. In 1810 Fouqué had written *Das Galgenmännlein* (Little Men of the Gallows), a story that was admired by E. T. A. Hoffmann. It is a Faustian tale of little black devils imprisoned in bottles who serve their owners for a period of time. At his death each owner owes his soul in exchange, unless he has sold his devil for a sum less than what he paid. *Galgenmännlein* is characteristic of a series of ghost stories and uncanny tales that Fouqué was writing during the period.

Undine (1811; translated as *Undine: A Romance,* 1818) is an idyllic fairy tale of a sprightly water nymph raised by a poor fisherman and his wife. Through marriage to the handsome knight Huldbrand, Undine receives a human soul. Though she is all her husband could desire, he proves too weak to withstand the charms of the elegant and crafty Bertalda. The consequences are tragic for all. *Undine* was received with enthusiasm. Fouqué called it "die Liebesblüte," the love flowering of his poetic muse. Goethe, Heinrich Heine, and Sir Walter Scott spoke of its charm; Wagner read it to family members gathered around him on the evening before his death. According to Fouqué's biographer, Arno Schmidt, Edgar Allan Poe called *Undine* the "finest possible example of the purely ideal.... With each note of the lyre is heard an august and soul-exalting echo. In every glimpse of beauty we catch visions of a far more ethereal beauty beyond." In his enthusiasm Poe declared that "for one Fouqué there are fifty Molières." Fouqué wrote the libretto for E. T. A. Hoffmann's opera *Undine,* which was presented at the Royal Theater in Berlin in 1816, and in 1845 Albert Lortzing composed a romantic opera on Fouqué's theme.

The author published several literary journals and contributed to a dozen others. *Undine* appeared in the initial issue of *Die Jahreszeiten,* a periodical restricted to his own work which ran from 1811 to 1814. Writers of note, including Johann Gottlieb Fichte, Ludwig Uhland, Friedrich Rückert, and Joseph Görres, contributed to *Die Musen* (1812-1814). In 1811 Fouqué wrote to his frequent correspondent Adelbert von Chamisso with great enthusiasm for a new major novel which would present in panoramic display the heroic deeds of Germanic, Franconian, Spanish, and Italian knights interacting with kings and knights of the northern seas, as well as with Amazons and Moors. The setting and tone of the completed three-volume work, *Der Zauberring* (1812; translated as *The Magic Ring, or, Ingratitude Punished: An Eastern Tale,* 1812), are similar to those of *Alethes von Lindenstein,* the novel Fouqué began in 1807 but did not complete until 1817. In both works the reader enters a labyrinthine world on whose edges chaos lies waiting. In Fouqué's *Wald der Welt* his figures lose their way as predicaments and dilemmas entangle them inextricably. Mired in guilt, the heroes hesitate until they are no longer exercising self-will but merely reacting to circumstances. Feeling pursued by fate, they flee to take refuge in a monastery or hermitage. In the portion of *Alethes von Lindenstein* written in 1807, the hero clearly is at fault for his failure to perform great deeds. Count Alethes has not progressed beyond the reading of heroic tales, an activity that he substitutes for action in the field. The third part of the novel finds him sitting at home, an easily bored married man, his dreams of glory out of reach. Although Fouqué may not have intended to allude here to his own dependency as a married man working comfortably at his wife's estate, a recurrent situation in his books is that of a guilt-ridden hero who assigns at least partial blame for his failure to a woman. Human failure is another important theme in Fouqué's works. The promise of eternal bliss in the world beyond serves as a counterweight to the almost universal earthly failures of his characters. Death does not appear senseless and horrifying but as a means of transition to another existence.

After Napoleon's retreat from Moscow in the winter of 1812, the Prussian army seized the opportunity to attack and defeat the decimated Grand Army. Ten years after his release from active service, Fouqué entered the military (as did Caroline Fouqué's sons and her father) as a "freiwilliger Jäger zu Pferd," or cavalryman. He fought in the battles at Lützen, Dresden, Kulm, and Leipzig and was released the following year with the rank of major. In the years between the Prussian defeat by Napoleon at Jena in 1806 and final victory at Leipzig in 1813, much of the German public had sought to bolster national self-esteem with literary fantasies of Germanic heroes, and it was during these years that Fouqué's works were popular. As the national mood started to change to one of confidence, Fouqué's reputation began to decline. He continued to write in the same vein, immersed in a long-abandoned social order. His heroes were aristocratic knights; common citizens were portrayed as honorable but dull and often comic characters. Consistently he appeared to favor the reestablishment of a social order rejected centuries before. Negative criticism of Fouqué's works far outweighed the positive, as the author was scolded for his exaggerated and irrational fixation on the Middle Ages and the aristocratic ideals of honor, privilege, heroic deeds, knighthood, and fatherland.

According to Caroline Fouqué, he never understood the reasons for his declining popularity. After his return from military service, Fouqué resumed his attempts to publish literary journals with *Für müßige Stunden* (For Idle Hours), which ran from 1816 to 1820. So few and unreliable were the contributors to this inferior journal that Fouqué found it necessary to turn the management of the last three issues over to his wife, who published her novel *Heinrich und Marie* in serialized form. Fouqué mustered the courage to establish one more journal, destined to be the very last one published by a German Romantic. *Berlinische Blätter für deutsche Frauen* (1829-1930) was a weekly whose purpose was to publish manuscripts by women as "worthy entertainment" for women in rural areas. A tally at the end of its forty-eight-issue lifespan found only five women among twenty-five contributors. *Das Frauentaschenbuch* (The Women's Reader), edited by Fouqué from 1815 to 1821, attracted many well-known literati: Hoffmann, Uhland, Eichendorff, and Rückert.

Fouqué's last works to attract attention were the four volumes of his *Altsächsischer Bildersaal* (Old Saxon Picture Gallery, 1818-1820), which depicted Lower Saxony of ages past in the hope of strengthening the spirit of nationalism in German youth. In volume 1, *Herrmann*, Fouqué offers a dramatic treatment of the victory of Arminius, also known as Herrmann der Cherusker, over the Romans in the Battle of the Teutoburg Forest in the year 9 A.D. Volume 2, the novel *Welleda und Ganna*, is also set in Germanic tribal times, Fouqué's favorite historical period, in the area of the Weser River, a region the author knew in his youth. The third volume comprises the fairy tale *Schön Irsa und ihre weiße Kuh* (Beautiful Irsa and her White Cow), and the final work in the series is the novel *Die vier Brüder von der Weserburg* (The Four Brothers of the Weser Fortress), about four brothers, each of whom went his separate way among the Germanic tribes. The discontinuance of the *Altsächsischer Bildersaal*, dictated by declining sales, signaled the end of Fouqué's literary fame, although he continued writing until his death. His reputation had been severely damaged by his memorial *Der Mord August's von Kotzebue: Freundes Ruf an Deutschlands Jugend* (The Murder of August von Kotzebue: A Friend's Call to Germany), published in 1819. Intended as a warning to German youth to cool revolutionary fervor in the wake of the stabbing of the playwright August von Kotzebue by a politically motivated student, the essay branded Fouqué as a hopeless reactionary whose worldview was completely out of step with the times. Eichendorff and other Romantics deserted him, and his subsequent novels–*Der Verfolgte* (The Man Pursued, 1821), *Ritter Elidouc* (The Knight Elidouc, 1822), *Wilde Liebe* (Impetuous Love, 1823), *Der Refugié oder Heimath und Fremde* (The Refugee or My Homeland and in Foreign Lands, 1824), *Mandragora* (1827), and *Abfall und Buße* (Desertion and Penitence, 1844)–met with little public response.

Caroline Fouqué's letters tell of the despairing mood of her husband in the 1820s and of his increasing emotional instability and loss of contact with reality. Caroline died in 1831. Fouqué stayed on at Nennhausen, where he wrote his own version of Wolfram von Eschenbach's thirteenth-century epic *Parzival*. This monumental verse epic of six books, which is still in manuscript, is considered the best of Fouqué's chivalric romances and, of all his works, second only to *Undine*.

It was Fouqué's good fortune to find emotional support in a third marriage. In 1833 he wed Albertine Tode, a teacher and minor writer thirty years his junior, losing his widower's right to remain at the estate. The couple moved to Halle an der Saale, where Albertine bore him two sons and he eked out an existence writing (most of the manuscripts from this period remain unpublished) and lecturing on history and current events. After the succession to the throne of Friedrich Wilhelm IV of Prussia, Fouqué was summoned to Berlin in 1841 and given financial support. There he died of a heart attack on 23 January 1843.

Letters:

Briefe an Friedrich Baron de la Motte Fouqué von Chamisso, Chezy, Collin, u.a., edited by Albertine Baronin de la Motte Fouqué (Berlin: W. Adolf, 1848);

Otto Güntter, "Fouqué's Briefe an Uhland," *Schwäbischer Schillerverein. Rechenschaftsbericht,* 21 (1916/1917): 37-59;

Max Ewert and Felix Hasselberg, "Aus dem Briefwechsel von Fouqué und W. Alexis," *Willibald-Alexis-Bund Jahrbuch 1928* (1929): 1-19.

Biography:

Arno Schmidt, *Fouqué und einige seiner Zeitgenossen* (Karlsruhe: Stahlberg, 1958; revised and en-

larged edition, Frankfurt: Zweitausendeins, 1977).

References:

W. Walker Chambers, "Die Dramen von Friedrich de la Motte Fouqué," *Maske und Kothurn,* 10 (1964): 521-531;

J. Douglas Clayton, " 'Spaer Dame,' 'Pique-Dame,' and 'Pikovaia dama': A German Source for Pushkin?," *Germano-Slavica*, no. 4 (1974);

David Bonnell Green, "Keats and La Motte Fouqué's 'Undine,' " *Delaware Notes,* 27 (1954): 33-48;

Ulrich Groenke, "Fouqué und die isländische Literaturgesellschaft," *Island-Berichte,* 20, no. 2 (1979): 94-101;

Carl Gross, "Fouqué's Frauentaschenbuch," Ph.D. dissertation, University of Münster, 1925;

Erich Hagemeister, "Friedrich Baron de la Motte Fouqué als Dramatiker," Ph.D. dissertation, University of Greifswald, 1905;

Julius Haupt, *Die Elementargeister bei Fouqué* (Leipzig: Immermann, 1923);

Max Kammerer, *Der Held des Nordens von Friedrich Baron de la Motte Fouqué und seine Stellung in der deutschen Literatur* (Rostock, 1909);

Theodor Krämer, "Das romantische Ritterepos bei Fouqué," Ph.D. dissertation, University of Münster, 1913;

Volker Klotz, "Friedrich de la Motte Fouqué," in *Das europäische Kunstmärchen,* edited by Klotz (Stuttgart: Metzler, 1985), pp. 162-173;

Laurente LeSage, "Die Einheit von Fouqués Undine. An unpublished essay in German by Jean Giroudoux," *Romanic Review,* 42 (1951): 122-134;

W. J. Lillyman, "Fouqué's 'Undine,' " *Studies in Romanticism,* 10, no. 2 (1971): 94-104;

Edward Marnin, "Some Patriotic Novels and Tales by La Motte Fouqué," *Seminar,* 11 (1975): 141-156;

Frank Rainer Max, "E. T. A. Hoffmann parodiert Fouqué. Ein bislang unentdecktes Fouqué-Zitat in der 'Prinzessin Brambilla,' " *Zeitschrift für deutsche Philologie* (Sonderheft E. T. A. Hoffmann), 10 (1976): 156-159;

Max, "Fouqué's *Parcival:* Romantische Renovation eines poetischen MA," *MA-Rezeption,* 2 (1982): 541-555;

Max, *Der "Wald der Welt:" Das Werk Fouqués* (Bonn: Bouvier, 1980);

Erika Mayer, "Die Nibelungen bei Fouqué und Wagner," Ph.D. dissertation, University of Vienna, 1948;

Alfred R. Neumann, "La Motte Fouqué, the Unmusical Musician," *Modern Language Quarterly,* 15 (1954): 259-272;

Ursula Rautenberg, "Parzivals Bildungs– und Entwicklungsstufen: Zu Friedrich de la Motte Fouqués 'Parcival,' " *MA-Rezeption,* 2 (1982): 557-572;

Karl Schindler, "Fouqués *Die Familie Hallersee* als Schlüsseldrama der Familie Eichendorff ?," *Aurora,* 38 (1978): 122-126;

Jürgen Schläder, *Undine auf dem Musiktheater* (Bonn: Verlag für systematische Musikwissenschaft, 1979);

Joachim Schwabe, *Friedrich Baron de la Motte Fouqué als Herausgeber literarischer Zeitschriften der Romantik* (Breslau: Priebatsch, 1937);

Elisabeth Christa Seibicke, *Friedrich Baron de la Motte Fouqué: Krise und Verfall der Spätromantik im Spiegel seiner historisierenden Ritterromane* (Munich: tuduv-Verlagsgesellschaft, 1985);

Iris Sells, "Stevenson und La Motte Fouqué: 'The Bottle Imp,' " *Revue de littérature comparée,* 28 (1954): 334-343.

Papers:

The papers of Friedrich de la Motte Fouqué are at the Staatsbibliothek Preußischer Kulturbesitz, West Berlin, and at the Deutsches Literaturarchiv at the Schiller-Nationalmuseum, Marbach am Neckar.

Joseph Görres

(25 January 1776-29 January 1848)

Richard Littlejohns
University of Birmingham

SELECTED BOOKS: *Der allgemeine Friede, ein Ideal* (Coblenz, 1798);

Resultate meiner Sendung nach Paris im Brumaire des achten Jahres (Coblenz & Andernach: Lassaulx, 1800);

Aphorismen über die Kunst als Einleitung zu Aphorismen über Organonomie, Physik, Psychologie und Anthropologie (Coblenz: Lassaulx, 1802);

Aphorismen über die Organonomie (Coblenz: Lassaulx, 1803);

Glauben und Wissen (Munich: Scherer, 1805);

Die teutschen Volksbücher: Nähere Würdigung der schönen Historien-, Wetter- und Arzneybüchlein, welche theils innerer Werth theils Zufall, Jahrhunderte hindurch bis auf unsere Zeit erhalten hat (Heidelberg: Mohr & Zimmer, 1807);

Entweder wunderbare Geschichte von BOGS der Uhrmacher, wie er zwar das menschliche Leben längst verlassen, nun aber doch, nach vielen musikalischen Leiden zu Wasser und zu Lande, in die bürgerliche Schützengesellschaft aufgenommen zu werden Hoffnung hat, oder Die über die Ufer der badischen Wochenschrift als Beilage ausgetretene Konzert-Anzeige, by Görres and Clemens Brentano (Heidelberg: Mohr & Zimmer, 1807);

Schriftproben von Peter Hammer (Heidelberg: Mohr & Zimmer, 1808);

Mythengeschichte der asiatischen Welt, 2 volumes (Heidelberg: Mohr & Zimmer, 1810; reprinted, New York: Arno Press, 1978);

Teutschland und die Revolution (Coblenz: Hölscher, 1819); translated by John Black as *Germany and the Revolution* (London: Longman, Hurst, Rees, Orme & Brown, 1820);

Europa und die Revolution (Stuttgart: Metzler, 1821);

Emanuel Swedenborg, seine Visionen und sein Verhältniß zur Kirche (Strasbourg, Mainz & Speyer: Expedition des Katholiken, 1827);

Die Christliche Mystik, 4 volumes (Regensburg & Landshut: Manz, 1836-1842); translated and edited by H. Austin as *The Stigmata: A History of Various Cases* (London: Richardson, 1883);

Joseph Görres (lithograph by Schöniger after Setlegast)

Athanasius (Regensburg: Manz, 1838);

Kirche und Staat nach Ablauf der Cölner Irrung (Weissenburg: Meyer, 1842);

Die Wallfahrt nach Trier (Regensburg: Manz, 1845);

Gesammelte Schriften, edited by Marie Görres and Franz Binder, 9 volumes (Munich: Literarisch-artistische Anstalt, 1854-1874);

Ausgewählte Werke und Briefe, edited by Wilhelm Schellberg, 2 volumes (Kempten & Munich: Kösel, 1911);

Gesammelte Schriften, edited by Schellberg, Adolph Dyroff, Leo Just, and Heribert Raab, 15 volumes and 1 supplement to date (volumes 1, 3, 6-11, 13, Cologne: Gilde, 1926-1929; volumes 2, 4, 12, 15, 16, Cologne: Bachem, 1932-1958; volume 14 and supplement, Paderborn: Schöningh, 1985-1987 [volume 5 never published]);

Ausgewählte Werke, edited by Wolfgang Frühwald, 2 volumes (Freiburg im Breisgau: Herder, 1978);

Joseph Görres: Ein Leben für Freiheit und Recht. Auswahl aus seinem Werk, edited by Raab (Paderborn: Schöningh, 1978).

OTHER: *Das rothe Blatt: Eine Dekadenschrift*, edited by Görres, 2 volumes (Coblenz: Lassaulx, 1798);

A. F. de Fourcroy, *Synoptische Tabellen der Chemie*, translated by Görres (Andernach: Herold, 1802);

"Wachstum der Historie," in *Studien*, edited by Karl Daub and Friedrich Creuzer (Frankfurt am Main & Heidelberg: Mohr & Zimmer, 1808);

Lohengrin: Ein altteutsches Gedicht. Nach der Abschrift des Vaticanischen Manuscriptes von F. Gloekle, edited by Görres (Heidelberg: Mohr & Zimmer, 1813);

Der Rheinische Merkur, edited by Görres, 3 volumes (Coblenz: Heriot, 1814-1816);

Altteutsche Volks- und Meisterlieder aus den Handschriften der Heidelberger Bibliothek, edited by Görres (Frankfurt am Main: Wilmans, 1817);

Das Heldenbuch von Iran aus dem Schah Nameh des Firdussi, translated by Görres, 2 volumes (Berlin: Reimer, 1820);

Altteutsche Zeit und Kunst, edited by Görres, E. von Groote, and others (Frankfurt am Main: Körner, 1822);

Henricus Suso, *Leben und Schriften: Nach ältesten Handschriften und Drucken*, edited by M. Diepenbrock, introduction by Görres (Regensburg: Pustet, 1829);

L. von Bornstedt, *Legende von der hl. Jungfrau und Märtyrerin St. Katharina*, foreword by Görres (Munich: Deiters, 1838);

P. G. J. Lechleitner, *Von dem Urgrunde und letzten Zwecke aller Dinge*, translated by C. Sommerer, foreword by Görres (Regensburg: Manz, 1839);

L. Clarus, *Darstellung der spanischen Literatur im Mittelalter*, foreword by Görres (Mainz & Kirchheim: Schott & Thielmann, 1846).

Johann Joseph Görres (von Görres after his ennoblement in Bavaria in 1839), an eloquent but erratic political writer, a visionary and a polemicist, a patriot and a religious propagandist, an autodidact and polymath, assumed an important

role in German literature during the years 1804 to 1811, and especially from 1806 to 1808, when he was lecturing at Heidelberg University. At this time, researching the origins of myth and enthusiastically publishing and editing older German literature, he collaborated with the Heidelberg Romantics Achim von Arnim and Clemens Brentano and associated briefly with the poet Joseph von Eichendorff.

Born in Coblenz in 1776 to Moriz Görres, a timber dealer, and Helena Theresia Mazza Görres, Joseph Görres was inspired throughout his life by affection for his native Rhineland, and in later years he reverted to the traditional Catholicism of this area of Germany. Equally influential, on the other hand, were the libertarian ideas of the Enlightenment which he encountered at school: a belief in natural justice and an insistence on moral order in political relationships were to remain constants in the kaleidoscope of his changing ideological positions. It was natural, therefore, that his youthful idealism led him in his teens to reject both the power of the Catholic church and the absolutism of the German princes and to support the ideals of the French Revolution, embracing the political thought of Jean-Jacques Rousseau and the Marquis de Condorcet. In one of his first published works, *Der allgemeine Friede, ein Ideal* (General Peace, an Ideal, 1798), a reaction to the debate initiated by Immanuel Kant in his 1795 treatise *Zum ewigen Frieden* (On Eternal Peace) as to the best means of securing stability in war-torn Europe, Görres declared fervently that the solution was for every state to adopt a republican constitution on the French pattern. For some time he had also been active in circles agitating for an independent Rhenish republic, comprising the German territories on the west bank of the Rhine and under the protection of revolutionary France, and in 1798 he set up two short-lived journals, *Das rothe Blatt* and *Der Rübezahl*, as vehicles for both his regional patriotism and his sympathies with the French republic.

Characteristically, however, Görres also used these publications to express his growing resentment over the autocratic rule of the French authorities in the Rhineland, and late in 1799 he joined a delegation which was sent from Coblenz to Paris in order to present grievances and explore the possibility of replacing the French occupation by full union with France. Their arrival coincided with Napoleon's seizure of power on 18 Brumaire, and Görres concluded, as he explained on his return in *Resultate meiner Sendung nach Paris im Brumaire des achten Jahres* (Conclusions of My Mission to Paris in Brumaire of the Eighth Year, 1800), that the French Revolution had failed. The example of France proved, he argued in this essay, that his own generation had no hope of political liberation because a democratic form of government could not be sustained at the present stage of human development.

Following this disillusionment, Görres withdrew from political activity and settled into a period of private study, earning his livelihood as a schoolmaster in Coblenz. In 1801 he married Katharina von Lassaulx, who bore him three children: Sophie; Guido, later an editor and writer; and Marie, who after her father's death edited his collected works, including his letters. Görres's intellectual interests moved away from politics to science, medicine, philosophy, and the arts. In *Aphorismen über die Kunst* (Aphorisms on Art, 1802), which in spite of its title contains wide-ranging philosophical observations, his historical optimism was replaced by Romantic nostalgia for a lost ideal state in the past. At the same time his discovery of the speculative Naturphilosophie (nature philosophy) of Friedrich Wilhelm Joseph von Schelling caused him to adopt a pervasive organic approach in his thought, which in turn led to an emphasis on continuity and tradition in history and in society. Such views found expression in his *Aphorismen über die Organonomie* (Aphorisms on Organonomy, 1803), in *Glauben und Wissen* (Faith and Knowledge, 1805), and particularly in the essay "Wachstum der Historie" (Growth of History, 1808), in which he drew attention to the process of historical evolution, to the emergence of the present from the past. During these outwardly tranquil years in Coblenz, Görres also began the study of medieval German literature and in 1804 began contributing reviews and mainly literary essays to the *Allgemeine Literatur-Zeitung* in Jena and to the journal *Aurora*. In 1806, having built a reputation with these writings and feeling frustrated under the French regime in the Rhineland, he obtained permission to give courses of lectures on a casual basis at the University of Heidelberg.

Görres arrived in Heidelberg at a propitious moment, for in 1802 it had come under the control of the state of Baden, and the university was enjoying a period of regeneration. Friedrich Creuzer, an authority on myth in general and on German legends in particular, had been appointed professor of classical philology in 1805,

and the Romantic poet Brentano had taken up residence in Heidelberg in 1804, accompanied by his wife, the poet Sophie Mereau; his literary collaborator, Arnim; and their subsequent publisher, Johann Georg Zimmer. With these writers Görres formed the group known as the Heidelberg Romantics; indeed, Brentano may have been instrumental in bringing Görres to Heidelberg, for Brentano came from Ehrenbreitstein near Coblenz and had been acquainted with Görres since their school days. Görres, who had never attended a university, at once created a stir in Heidelberg by lecturing on a bewildering range of subjects, including physiology, psychology, physics, philosophy, and aesthetics, and by his exposition of esoteric ideas in a grandiose poetic style.

The Romantic writers in Germany were at this time developing an intense interest in the origins of German literature, and particularly in the vestiges of a folk culture which the rationalistic and cosmopolitan literary establishment of the eighteenth century had sought to suppress. Thus in 1805 Arnim and Brentano had published the first volume of *Des Knaben Wunderhorn* (The Boy's Magic Hunting Horn, 1805), a collection of German folk songs assembled mainly from oral sources. Such activities were bound to appeal to Görres's new sense of tradition and to his regional patriotism. In 1807 Görres published *Die teutschen Volksbücher* (The German Chapbooks), in which he provided summaries of several popular works, including the tales surrounding such figures as Fortunatus, Herzog Ernst, Till Eulenspiegel, and Faust. In some cases Görres added bibliographical information, but his real purpose in publishing this material was not scholarly but, as usual, polemical and covertly political, as is clear from his preface. He interprets the popular legends as the vigorous and authentic products of a culture not yet corrupted by intellect. The value of the chapbooks, he maintains, is that they reflect the true spirit of the German people, which has been obscured or deformed by modern civilization and foreign influences. The nation must "zurückkehren in sich selbst, zu dem was ihr Eigenstes und Würdigstes ist, wegstoßend und preisgebend das Verkehrte; damit sie nicht gänzlich zerbreche in dem feindseligen Andrang der Zeit" (revert to itself, to that which is its most distinctive and estimable, rejecting and abandoning the distorted; so that it does not entirely disintegrate under the hostile onslaught of the age). The last phrase betrays the political import of

*Death mask of Görres (Die Deutsche Romantiker, edited by
Gerhard Stengel [Salzburg & Stuttgart: Bergland, n.d.])*

these remarks, for it refers to the French occupation of Germany and the defeat of Prussia in 1806; the plea for a regeneration of national cultural identity is itself a gesture of political nationalism. This connection is implied, too, in Görres's review in the *Heidelbergische Jahrbücher* in 1809 of the folk songs in the second volume of *Des Knaben Wunderhorn*, in which he argues that individuals (and by implication nations) who preserve these lyrical memories in their consciousness will survive the greatest calamities, while those lacking this "innere Resonanz" (inner resonance), as he calls it, will be doomed to subjugation.

In 1807 Görres also delivered a notable series of lectures in praise of Philip P. Otto Runge's four symbolical drawings entitled *Die Tageszeiten* (The Times of Day). Arguing again in terms of Romantic "nature philosophy," which postulated metaphysical energies in the phenomena of nature, Görres developed a free but imaginative Christian reading of these sketches and thus influenced the young poet Eichendorff, who attended these lectures and was also invited to discussions at Görres's home in Heidelberg. Görres's

audacious and unorthodox ideas gained him a circle of admiring students; his enthusiasm for speculative natural science and his assertion of the value of primitive culture, however, contributed in no small measure to the bitter literary feud which he and his fellow Romantics waged with the rationalist and classicistic party in Heidelberg, in particular with Johann Heinrich Voß, whose reputation rested on his translations from Homer. Görres again proved himself adept at journalistic controversy and invective. With Brentano he composed the satire *BOGS der Uhrmacher* (BOGS the Watchmaker, 1807), the name in the title being assembled from the first and last letters of the two authors' surnames. This work tells the ironic story of Bogs's attempts to enter a philistine society which has expelled all those of a poetic disposition. The 1808 volume *Schriftproben von Peter Hammer* (Specimens of Writing by Peter Hammer), which Görres published pseudonymously, is in similar satirical vein, except that his targets here extend beyond the academic and literary pedantry of literati like Voß to encompass the general mediocrity of the age, the pusillanimity of the German princes, and the injustice of French rule.

Görres was by this time contributing not only to the *Heidelbergische Jahrbücher* but also to the *Zeitung für Einsiedler* (Journal for Hermits), which Arnim published briefly in 1808. The title of the latter periodical reflected its rejection of conventional modern culture, its primary concern being the publication of texts from the earliest phases of German literature. Görres's principal contribution was an essay on the Nibelungen legend and the various forms in which it had been recorded. His interest in such matters continued after his departure from Heidelberg and is reflected in two volumes he edited, *Lohengrin* (1813) and *Altteutsche Volks- und Meisterlieder* (Old German Folk and Master Songs, 1817). His lectures on the oriental origins of myth and its connection with religion formed the basis of his voluminous and erudite *Mythengeschichte der asiatischen Welt* (History of Myths of the Asiatic World, 1810). In 1820 he translated the epic poem *Shah Nama* by the tenth-century Persian poet Firdausi.

Görres was unable to obtain a permanent professorship in Heidelberg, and in autumn 1808 he returned to the teaching post in Coblenz which had been held for him. Political and particularly patriotic journalism was again his dominating concern for the next decade. From 1814 to 1816 he wrote and published the newspaper *Der*

Rheinische Merkur, initially demanding the liberation of Germany from the French, then after the defeat of Napoleon criticizing the illiberal and bureaucratic nature of the monarchist regimes which had been restored in Germany. In *Der Rheinische Merkur* Görres's lifelong flair for polemical and campaigning journalism reached a peak, and it was this publication which made his name throughout Germany. The Rhineland had come under Prussian control at the Congress of Vienna, and Görres's wrath after 1815 was directed not only against the failure of the German princes to grant democratic constitutions but specifically against Prussian (and therefore Protestant) domination. He advocated a strong monarchy, in accordance with his belief in organic historical continuity, but also parliamentary institutions and civil rights, a combination which earned him the dislike of both liberals and conservatives. *Der Rheinische Merkur* was banned in 1816, and three years later Görres fell foul of the Prussian authorities with his essays "Kotzebue und was ihn gemordet" (Kotzebue and What Murdered Him), published in Ludwig Börne's periodical *Die Wage* in 1819, and *Teutschland und die Revolution* (1819; translated as *Germany and the Revolution*, 1820). While Görres condemned the assassination of the playwright August von Kotzebue by a radical student, he maintained that in reality the underlying cause of the murder lay in the oppressive political circumstances in Germany. Forewarned of his impending arrest, Görres fled to Strasbourg and remained there, with a brief interlude in Aarau, Switzerland, until 1827. In Switzerland he wrote *Europa und die Revolution* (1821), in which he assessed the effect of revolutionary change on Europe and declared it cataclysmic and destructive.

Görres's ideological position underwent a further mutation. His hostility to the Catholic church as a young man had been based on its support for political absolutism, but when reforming Catholic movements began to emerge in Europe and at the same time the state seemed to be oppressing the church, the way was open for his return to Catholicism. In 1824 he took up the editorship of the journal *Der Katholik*, denouncing pedantic rationalism and insisting on the independence of the church from the state. His work on the journal led in turn to his appointment in 1827 as professor of history and literary history at the University of Munich in Catholic Bavaria, where he remained at the center of a propagandizing conservative and Christian circle until his

death in 1848. There he collaborated with Franz Baader and contributed extensively to the journal *Eos* and to the *Historisch-politische Blätter*, arguing against liberalism and for the traditions of the church. From 1836 to 1842 he published his four-volume *Christliche Mystik* (Christian Mysticism; translated as *The Stigmata: A History of Various Cases*, 1883); he regarded this monumental work as his crowning achievement, but obscurity of thought and language has condemned it to neglect. The arrest of the archbishop of Cologne in 1838 provoked Görres to write *Athanasius* (1838), in which he again insisted on the independence of the church, a theme to which he returned in *Kirche und Staat nach Ablauf der Cölner Irrung* (Church and State after the End of the Cologne Aberration, 1842). His last important publication, *Die Wallfahrt nach Trier* (The Pilgrimage to the Holy Relic in Trier, 1845), makes it clear that his religious views do not amount to unsubtle Catholic propaganda; he sees the contemporary mass pilgrimage to the holy relic in Trier both as an assertion of Catholic faith in the face of state oppression and as the ecumenical unification of Protestants and Catholics in a triumphant religious revival.

Görres was at all times an impassioned and imaginative writer; his rhetoric frequently ran away with him, leading to a florid, associative, and complex style in which the reader is carried along (and sometimes flounders) in torrents of metaphors. It has been argued by Franz Schultz and by Oskar F. Walzel that this rhetorical extravagance conditions and even distorts his arguments. Faced with the contradictions of Görres's changing political views, it is tempting to conclude that he was motivated fundamentally by negative opposition to all existing authority, to whatever prevailing institutions he encountered; the publisher Friedrich Perthes once said of him, "Görres weiß gewiß nicht, was er will. In ihm ist etwas Positives, aber seine Zeit und sein Land und seine Stadt haben ihm eine leidenschaftliche, nicht würdige Opposition eingepflanzt" (It is certain that Görres does not know what he wants. There is something positive in him but his age and his country and his town have implanted in him a passionate, unseemly opposition). It would be fairer to say that he denounced any form of arbitrary or, in his view, illegitimate power. His activity as a writer stretched over a long period of unparalleled political and philosophical change, and he reflected all the intellectual turmoil of his age. Other German Romantics who lived on well into the nineteenth century–Ludwig Tieck, for example, and particularly Friedrich Schlegel–underwent a similar evolution from enthusiasm for republican ideals to conservatism and religious orthodoxy. It was Görres's fate that his outspoken, pugnacious nature and his involvement in political journalism highlighted this apparent inconsistency.

Letters:

Familienbriefe, edited by Marie Görres, volume 7 of Görres's *Gesammelte Schriften*, and *Freundesbriefe*, edited by Franz Binder, volumes 8 and 9 of *Gesammelte Schriften* (Munich: Literarisch-artistische Anstalt, 1858, 1874);

"Joseph von Görres' Briefe an Achim von Arnim," edited by Reinhold Steig, *Neue Heidelberger Jahrbücher*, 10 (1900) and 19 (1916);

Briefe von Joseph von Görres an Friedrich Christoph Perthes (1811-1827), edited by Wilhelm Schellberg (Cologne: Görres-Gesellschaft, 1913);

Briefe an seine Braut und Familie, edited by Robert Stein (Mönchen-Gladbach: Volksvereins-Verlag, 1926).

Biographies:

Johann Nepomuk Sepp, *Görres und seine Zeitgenossen 1776-1848* (Nördlingen: Beck, 1877);

Wilhelm Schellberg, *Joseph von Görres* (Mönchen-Gladbach, 1913; second edition, Cologne: Gilde, 1926);

Heribert Raab, "Joseph Görres," in *Deutsche Dichter der Romantik*, edited by Benno von Wiese (Berlin: Schmidt, 1971); enlarged in *Joseph Görres: Ein Leben für Freiheit und Recht*, edited by Raab (Paderborn: Schöningh, 1978).

References:

Martin Berger, *Görres als politischer Publizist* (Bonn & Leipzig: Schroeder, 1921);

Georg Bürke, *Vom Mythos zur Mystik: Joseph von Görres' mystische Lehre und die romantische Naturphilosophie* (Einsiedeln: Johannes, 1958);

Reinhardt Habel, *Joseph Görres: Studien über den Zusammenhang von Natur, Geschichte und Mythos*

in seinen Schriften (Wiesbaden: Steiner, 1960);

Karl Hoeber, ed., *Görres-Festschrift: Aufsätze und Abhandlungen zum 150. Geburtstag von Joseph Görres* (Cologne: Bachem, 1926);

Leo Just, "Görres in Heidelberg," *Historisches Jahrbuch*, 74 (1955): 416-431;

Georg Kallen, *Joseph Görres und der deutsche Idealismus* (Münster: Aschendorffsche Verlagsbuchhandlung, 1926); republished in Kallen's *Probleme der Rechtsordnung in Geschichte und Theorie* (Cologne & Graz: Böhlau, 1965);

Herbert Levin, *Die Heidelberger Romantik* (Munich: Parcus, 1922);

Lothar Pikulik, "Die sogenannte Heidelberger Romantik: Tendenzen, Grenzen, Widersprüche. Mit einem Epilog über das Nachleben der Romantik heute," in *Heidelberg im säkularen Umbruch. Traditionsbewußtsein und Kulturpolitik um 1800*, edited by Friedrich Strack (Stuttgart: Klett-Cotta, 1987);

Heribert Raab, "Görres und die Revolution," in *Deutscher Katholizismus und Revolution im frühen 19. Jahrhundert*, edited by Anton Rauscher (Paderborn: Schöningh, 1975), pp. 51-80;

Roman Reisse, *Die weltanschauliche Entwicklung des jungen Joseph Görres (1776-1806)* (Breslau: Müller & Seiffert, 1926);

Franz Schultz, *Joseph Görres als Herausgeber, Literarhistoriker, Kritiker im Zusammenhang mit der jüngeren Romantik* (Berlin: Mayer & Müller, 1902; republished, New York & London: Johnson Reprint Corporation, 1967);

László Tarnói, *Joseph Görres zwischen Revolution und Romantik* (Budapest: Lórand-Eötrös-Universität, 1970);

Oskar F. Walzel, "Görres' Stil und seine Ideenwelt," *Euphorion*, 10 (1903): 792-809.

Papers:

Some letters and material connected with Görres's contributions to the *Historisch-politische Blätter* are in the Staatsbibliothek in Munich. There is a Görres-Archiv at the Stadtbibliothek in Coblenz.

Jacob Grimm

(4 January 1785-20 September 1863)

Ruth B. Bottigheimer
State University of New York at Stony Brook

BOOKS: *Über den altdeutschen Meistergesang* (Göttingen: Dieterichs, 1811);

Kinder- und Hausmärchen, by Grimm and Wilhelm Grimm, 2 volumes (Berlin: Realschulbuchhandlung, 1812-1815; revised and enlarged seven times, Reimer, 1819-1857); translated by Edgar Taylor as *German Popular Stories, Translated from the Kinder und Haus Marchen*, 2 volumes (London: Baldwyn, 1823-1826);

Irmenstraße und Irmensäule: Eine mythologische Abhandlung (Vienna: Mayer, 1815);

Deutsche Sagen, by Grimm and Wilhelm Grimm, 2 volumes (Berlin: Nicolai, 1816-1818); edited and translated by Donald Ward as *The German Legends of the Brothers Grimm*, 2 volumes (Philadelphia: Institute for the Study of Human Issues, 1981);

Deutsche Grammatik, 4 volumes (Göttingen: Dieterich, 1819-1837);

Zur Recension der Deutschen Grammatik (Cassel: Bohne, 1826);

Deutsche Rechtsalterthümer (Göttingen: Dieterich, 1828);

Hymnorum veteris ecclesiae XXVI interpretatio Theodisca nunc primum edita (Göttingen: Dieterich, 1830);

Reinhart Fuchs (Berlin: Reimer, 1834);

Deutsche Mythologie (Göttingen: Dieterich, 1835); translated by James Steven Stallybrass as *Teutonic Mythology*, 4 volumes (London: Bell, 1883-1888);

Jacob Grimm über seine Entlassung (Basel: Schweighauser, 1838);

Sendschreiben an Karl Lachmann über Reinhart Fuchs (Leipzig: Weidmann, 1840);

Frau Aventiure klopft an Beneckes Thür (Berlin: Besser, 1842);

Über zwei entdeckte Gedichte aus der Zeit des deutschen Heidenthums (Berlin: Akademie, 1842);

Deutsche Grenzalterthümer (Berlin: Druckerei der Königlichen Akademie der Wissenschaften, 1844);

Über Diphthonge nach weggefallnen Consonanten (Berlin: Akademie der Wissenschaften, 1845);

Jacob Grimm (etching by Ludwig Emil Grimm, 1815)

Der Fundevogel: Ein Märlein (Munich: Kaiser, 1845);

Über Iornandes und die Geten: Eine in der Akademie der Wissenschaften am 5. März 1846 von Jacob Grimm gehaltene Vorlesung (Berlin: Akademie der Wissenschaften, 1846);

Geschichte der deutschen Sprache, 2 volumes (Leipzig: Weidmann, 1848);

Über Marcellus Burdigalensis (Berlin: Dümmler, 1849);

Das Wort des Besitzes: Eine linguistische Abhandlung (Berlin: Akademie der Wissenschaften, 1850);

Rede auf Lachmann, gehalten in der öffentlichen Sitzung der Akademie der Wissenschaften am 3.

Juli 1851 (Berlin: Druckerei der Königlichen Akademie der Wissenschaften, 1851);

Über den Liebesgott: Gelesen in der Akademie am 6. Januar 1851 (Berlin: Königliche Akademie der Wissenschaften, 1851);

Über den Ursprung der Sprache (Berlin: Königliche Akademie der Wissenschaften, 1851);

Über Frauennamen aus Blumen (Berlin: Dümmler, 1852);

Deutsches Wörterbuch, by Grimm, Wilhelm Grimm, and others, 32 volumes (Leipzig: Hirzel, 1854-1961);

Über die Namen des Donners (Berlin: Dümmler, 1855);

Über die Marcellischen Formeln, by Grimm and A. Pictet (Berlin: Dümmler, 1855);

Über den Personenwechsel in der Rede (Berlin: Dümmler, 1856);

Über einige Fälle der Attraction (Berlin: Dümmler, 1858);

Von Vertretung männlicher durch weibliche Namensformen (Berlin: Dümmler, 1858);

Über Schule, Universität, Academie (Berlin: Dümmler, 1859);

Über das Verbrennen der Leichen: Eine in der Academie der Wissenschaften am 29. November 1849 von Jacob Grimm gehaltene Vorlesung (Berlin: Dümmler, 1859);

Rede auf Schiller, gehalten in der feierlichen Sitzung der Königl. Akademie der Wissenschaften, am 10. November 1859 (Berlin: Dümmler, 1859);

Rede auf Wilhelm Grimm; und Rede über das Alter, edited by Herman Grimm (Berlin: Harrwitz & Gossman, 1863);

Kleinere Schriften, edited by Karl Victor Müllenhoff and Eduard Ippel, 8 volumes (Berlin: Dümmler, 1864-1890).

OTHER: *Die beiden ältesten deutschen Gedichte aus dem achten Jahrhundert: Das Lied von Hildebrand und Hadubrand und das Weißenbrunner Gebet*, edited by Grimm and Wilhelm Grimm (Cassel: Thurneissen, 1812);

Altdeutsche Wälder, edited by Grimm and Wilhelm Grimm, 3 volumes (volume 1, Cassel: Thurneissen, 1813; volumes 2-3, Frankfurt am Main: Körner, 1815-1816);

Lieder der alten Edda, edited by Grimm and Wilhelm Grimm (Berlin: Realschulbuchhandlung, 1815);

Hartmann von Aue, *Der arme Heinrich: Aus der Straßburgischen und Vatikanischen Handschrift*, edited by Grimm and Wilhelm Grimm (Berlin: Realschulbuchhandlung, 1815);

Silva de romances viejos, edited by Grimm (Berlin: Mayer, 1815);

Wuk Stephanovitsch, *Kleine serbische Grammatik*, translated, with a foreword, by Grimm (Leipzig & Berlin: Reimer, 1824);

C. Croker, *Irische Elfenmärchen*, translated by Grimm and Wilhelm Grimm (Leipzig: Fleischer, 1826);

Taciti Germania edidit et quae ad res Germanorum pertinere videntur e reliquo Tacitino opere excerpsit, edited by Grimm (Göttingen: Dieterich, 1835);

Lateinische Gedichte des X. und XI. Jahrhunderts, edited by Grimm and Andreas Schmeller (Göttingen: Dieterich, 1838);

Andreas und Elene, edited by Grimm (Cassel: Fischer, 1840);

Weisthümer, edited by Grimm and others, 7 volumes (Göttingen: Dieterich, 1840-1878);

Gedichte des Mittelalters auf König Friedrich I., den Staufer, und aus seiner, sowie der nächstfolgenden Zeit, edited by Grimm (Berlin: Besser, 1844);

Emil Franz Rössler, ed., *Das altprager Stadtrecht aus dem XIV. Jahrhunderts, nach den vorhandenen Handschriften*, foreword by Grimm (Prague: Calve, 1845);

J. Merkel, *Lex salica*, foreword by Grimm (Berlin: Hertz, 1850).

No single individual in German letters did as much to form the way Germans thought about their past as did Jacob Grimm. His research among medieval manuscripts laid the foundations for subsequent research in folklore and custom, law, literature, linguistics, and mythology; his historical grammar of the German language illuminated the roots and internal structure of the German language and its interconnections within larger linguistic groupings; and the historical dictionary of the German language undertaken with his brother Wilhelm was at the time an organizational masterpiece and remains the standard work on the historical development and usage of the German language.

Jacob Grimm was born in Hanau on 4 January 1785 to Philipp Wilhelm Grimm, a German official, and Dorothea Zimmer Grimm. The Grimm family was descended from Reformed (Zwinglian Protestant) forebears, many of whom had served as pastors in Hanau and Steinau. Politically and officially allied with the count of Hanau, the Grimms were the leading family in the administrative seat in Steinau. On the paternal side the

Grimm family came principally from Hanau at the southern reach of Hesse-Cassel, on the maternal side from the northern end in Cassel itself.

Grimm's early childhood years in Steinau were secure and full of delight. Philipp Grimm's death in 1796, however, declassed his wife and children overnight. The five brothers, one sister, mother, and aunt had to leave their commodious house and move into modest quarters. The town school provided an inadequate education, and in 1798 Grimm and his brother Wilhelm were sent to the Cassel lyceum to prepare for university admission. Both brothers spent virtually all their time studying, so much so that Jacob remarked uncharacteristically in later years that a little leisure would have done them good. Supported by their mother's sister, Henriette Philippine Zimmer, lady-in-waiting to the electoral princess, Jacob and Wilhelm lived in a room rented from the court cook. Despite his neediness, Jacob was passed over for stipends which were awarded to the sons of wealthy Hessian noble families. An awareness of social injustice was awakened in Grimm that remained with him throughout his life.

At the age of seventeen Jacob Grimm went to Marburg to study law, a subject which his family hoped would lead to a secure position later in life. Beginning in the winter semester 1802-1803 he took every course offered by the expert in Roman law, Friedrich Karl von Savigny. Until Savigny left the university in the summer of 1804, Grimm was also a frequent visitor in his home. It was there that Grimm first took into his hands Johann Jakob Bodmer's edition of the songs of the German minnesingers, which, he later reflected, symbolized for him the direction his adult scholarly life was to take.

Without taking his final examinations and thus not receiving his degree, Grimm left for Paris in January 1805 to assist Savigny with his research. He spent the late winter, spring, and summer of 1805 in Paris working in libraries and archives, returning in September 1805 to Cassel. After applying unsuccessfully for library positions, he finally found work in the secretariat of the War Office beginning in early 1806. Grimm spent nearly a year in this capacity, until the French occupation of Cassel altered the nature of his work.

Under French rule the War Office became the Commission for Army Provisioning, and Grimm's facility in French made him useful to the French occupiers. Hoping to find a more com-patible position in the Cassel library, he resigned, but he spent nearly a year without regular employment or salary. In July 1808 Grimm was offered the position of librarian for King Jérôme Bonaparte's private library at Wilhelmshöhe (at the time renamed Napoleonshöhe), in the newly established Kingdom of Westphalia. With minimal duties and generous pay Grimm had ample time to pursue his own project: collecting tales which Achim von Arnim and Clemens Brentano published in their journal, *Zeitung für Einsiedler*, or which eventually found their way into the two-volume *Kinder- und Hausmärchen* (Children's and Household Tales, 1812-1815; translated as *German Popular Stories*, 1823-1826; generally known as *Grimm's Fairy Tales*). In February 1809 Grimm took a position with the Council of State and received a raise in salary, which lightened his burden as the sole supporter of his younger brothers and sister.

His continuing archival research resulted in polemics against contemporary literary worthies–Bernhard Docen, Friedrich von der Hagen, and Johann Gustav Büsching–and in the publication in 1811 of his first book, *Über den altdeutschen Meistergesang* (Of Medieval German Mastersong), in which he expounded his thesis that both Minne- and Meistergesang exemplified the artistic use of language. This was a theme that also informed the first volume of the *Kinder- und Hausmärchen* (1812), to which Grimm contributed both tales and scholarly notes. The early years of Grimm's career were characterized by close collaboration with his brother Wilhelm. In addition to the *Kinder- und Hausmärchen* the two worked together in editing *Das Lied von Hildebrand und Hadubrand und das Weißenbrunner Gebet* (The Lay of Hildebrand and Hadubrand and the Weissenbrunn Prayer, 1812) and produced the journal *Altdeutsche Wälder* (Old German Forests), which appeared in three volumes in 1813, 1815, and 1816. In these politically turbulent years Jacob and Wilhelm Grimm formulated basic positions on issues central to the development of a German medieval literary canon: the nature and relationship of Middle High German to modern German, the use of alliteration as a poetic device in the *Hildebrandslied*, and the importance of folk literature as art.

By 1813 the French had suffered several defeats, and French rule was clearly coming to an end in Cassel. French authorities ordered the most valuable books in Cassel's libraries packed up and shipped to France, but Jacob Grimm used his position to sequester and save valuable manuscripts dealing with Hessian history. The return of the electoral prince Wilhelm I at the end of 1813 led to great public joy and to Grimm's being named legation secretary for Hessian diplomats dispatched to France. He set off in January 1814 and arrived in Paris in April, visiting every library in his path. Once in Paris he assisted in reclaiming Hessian books and paintings that had been carried off the previous year. From October 1814 to June 1815 Grimm served at the Congress of Vienna, using the opportunity to learn the basics of Slavic languages and to cofound the Wollzeiler Society. This society promulgated the Circular of 1815, well-known among folklorists for calling for the preservation of folk songs and rhymes, folk tales and fairy tales, jests, puppet theater, customs, superstitions, and proverbs.

Returning home from Vienna in the summer of 1815, Grimm was quickly sent to Paris by Prussian authorities to reclaim additional manuscripts that had been looted by the departing French. He remained in Paris busy with these duties until December 1815. Despite his official duties he continued his extensive scholarship, editing the *Silva de romances viejos* (Forest of Ancient Ballads) for publication in 1815 and writing the introductory remarks in a Spanish which mixed seventeenth- and nineteenth-century vocabulary and usage. It was a bold undertaking, and Grimm's contemporaries were greatly impressed with his linguistic skills.

In April 1816 Jacob Grimm was appointed to the electoral library in Cassel as a librarian. In succeeding years Jacob's scholarly reputation grew throughout both Germany and Europe. In addition to numerous honorary and corresponding memberships in learned societies, he was offered a professorship at Bonn. But he preferred to remain in his Hessian homeland, where he hoped for and expected advancement and preferment. Overworked and underpaid, Grimm became frustrated when he was not promoted. Although he and Wilhelm continued to collaborate in later years, their translation of *Irische Elfenmärchen* (Irish Folktales) in 1826 effectively marked the end of their career as the "Brüder Grimm," for despite the fact that this designation appeared on the title page of their most famous publication, the *Kinder- und Hausmärchen*, it was Wilhelm who principally guided the editing of the fairy tales in volume 2 (1815) and in subsequent editions, while Jacob turned in other directions. The brothers, however, had established

themselves as scholars of international importance; in 1819 Marburg University awarded each of them an honorary doctorate. Jacob Grimm received degrees from Berlin in 1828 and Breslau in 1829.

The years from 1816 to 1829 saw the foundations laid for two trailblazing undertakings by Grimm, a historical grammar of the German language and a study of German law and custom. With his librarianship Grimm was well situated to work on both projects, and he drew on an ever-increasing network of colleagues and acquaintances for raw material. The first volume of the *Deutsche Grammatik* dealt with inflection and appeared in 1819. The second volume appeared in 1826 and treated regular sound shifts; the third volume followed in 1831 and dealt with gender; and the fourth, which was published in 1837, described and analyzed the syntax of simple sentences. The fifth volume, still in the planning stage in 1857, was to examine the syntax of complex sentences but was never completed. Grimm's comprehensive study of German law, *Deutsche Rechtsalterthümer* (German Legal Antiquities), appeared in 1828 and quickly became a model for similar undertakings in France and the Netherlands. His intention was to ferret out evidence of law as it penetrated people's lives; thus the volume may be seen as historical juridical folklore.

Finally realizing that he would never earn a living wage in Hesse, Grimm accepted a combination librarianship and professorship at Göttingen in 1830 at the age of forty-five. Although Grimm had many devoted admirers, he was not a successful university lecturer. Indeed, the historian Heinrich von Treitschke reported that Grimm's lectures were almost impossible to follow. During his entire life he preferred learning to teaching, and he chose cloistered retirement over the university podium whenever possible. Despite the double duties of librarian and professor during his Göttingen years (1830-1837), after an initial hiatus (1831-1834) he continued to collect material which resulted in a broad range of studies dealing with the medieval and ancient Germanic past, including a long essay on the animal tales which had coalesced around the trickster figure Reinhart Fuchs (1834) and, in 1835, the monumental *Deutsche Mythologie* (translated as *Teutonic Mythology*, 1883-1888).

Grimm's interest in religion and mythology fit into an established and well-trodden path in early-nineteenth-century scholarship, concerned with the question of origins in general and with

Pencil drawing of Grimm by Ludwig Emil Grimm, dated 23 September 1858 (by permission of the Historisches Museum Hanau)

the origins of religion in particular. Because of widespread lay interest in the subject *Deutsche Mythologie* met wide public acclaim. Unlike other scholarly studies of myth, Grimm's *Deutsche Mythologie* excluded Nordic mythology and searched for patterns of belief which remained embedded in German language and custom.

All over Germany, as in Europe as a whole, political events were simmering in the 1830s, as revolutionary fervor was repressed by conservative forces. In Hannover, where Göttingen was located, a relatively liberal constitution had been instituted in 1833 by Wilhelm IV. Ernst August II ascended the Hannoverian throne in June 1837, and, wishing to abrogate the constitution, he unilaterally declared it invalid. However, like other citizens of Hannover, the faculty at Göttingen had sworn allegiance to the Constitution of 1833, and Grimm and six other professors—including Wilhelm Grimm—protested vigorously. All of the Göttingen Seven, as they came to be known, immediately lost their positions; Grimm and two others were banished on three days' notice.

Grimm returned to Cassel, where he lived with his younger brother Ludwig Emil, without income or position but sharing in funds from a Germany-wide subscription in support of the Göttingen Seven. Within months he published a

justification of his actions protesting the suspension of the Hannoverian Constitution, but nonetheless—or perhaps because of his outspoken self-defense—he remained without employment for the next three years. In this period Grimm collaborated with the Bavarian scholar Andreas Schmeller on an 1838 edition of Latin poems of the tenth and eleventh centuries. At the same time he laid the foundation for the enduring monument, the thirty-two-volume *Deutsches Wörterbuch* (German Dictionary), by Grimm, Wilhelm Grimm, and others. Unlike contemporary dictionaries, the *Deutsches Wörterbuch* described historical usage rather than prescribing acceptable speech. Like other projects Grimm undertook, it grew over several years as examples poured in. The first complete volume appeared in 1854. Jacob composed copy for entries beginning with *A*, *B*, *C*, *E*, and *F*, reaching the entry for *Frucht* (fruit) when death overtook him. The dictionary occupied scholars for well over a century; the final volume appeared in 1961, and soon thereafter a new edition was begun.

For years Grimm had hoped for a call to Berlin, the center of power for the emerging German nation. The death of the conservative Prussian monarch Friedrich Wilhelm III in 1840 and the accession to the throne of his more liberal son, Friedrich Wilhelm IV, who was well-disposed to the Grimms as the result of Bettina von Arnim's intervention, resulted in an invitation for Jacob and Wilhelm to become members of the Academy of Sciences in Berlin. Although membership in the Academy carried with it the privilege of lecturing at the university, Jacob restricted his occasional lectures to the Academy itself.

Many projects both major and minor came to fruition during the twenty-three years that Grimm spent in Berlin. First to appear was the *Weisthümer* (Legal Tradition), edited by Grimm and comprising descriptions of old legal practices, judicial precedents, and common-law judgments. The first two volumes were published in 1840, the third volume in 1842, and the fourth volume in 1863, the year of his death. The *Weisthümer*, completed by others in 1878, eventually ran to seven volumes. Grimm thought these traditions represented constituted evidence of a Germanic system of peasant justice, but they actually embodied the law of the lord. His two-volume *Geschichte der deutschen Sprache* (History of the German Language) appeared in 1848, with a second edition in 1853; a second edition of his

Deutsche Rechtsalterthümer appeared in 1854; and subsequent editions of his *Deutsche Mythologie* were published in 1844 and 1854.

The move to Berlin reunited both Jacob and Wilhelm Grimm with many former acquaintances: Savigny, who had been in Berlin since 1810, Bettina von Arnim, Karl Lachmann, and Hartwig Gregor von Meusebach. Receptions, open houses, and concerts in the company of kings, dukes, ministers, and ambassadors, along with suppers with academic and family friends, claimed much of Jacob Grimm's time.

Until his appointment to the Academy of Sciences, Grimm's life had been a financial roller coaster with long lows–the first following his father's death, later as an underpaid librarian in Cassel, and finally as an unemployed professor in a peculiar homeland exile–punctuated by brief highs as an employee of King Jérôme and as a professor at Göttingen. In Berlin Grimm was assured an ample income and, at fifty-six, was a revered national figure. When the new king created the Orden pour le mérite in 1842, Jacob was one of only thirty members from all of the Germanies chosen for the honor.

Grimm was president of the conferences of Germanists in Frankfurt am Main in 1846 and in Lübeck in 1847. In May 1848 Grimm was elected to the Frankfurt Parliament, whose main aims were national unity and the establishment of constitutional government. Grimm sat unaligned with any party, neither on the left nor on the right but in the central gangway facing the speaker's platform. His stature as a national political symbol underscored his calls for national unity. Because the Prussian government understood his position as confirmation of their leadership within Germany, Grimm escaped censure, although others who attended the parliament subsequently suffered for their political activity and rhetoric.

Grimm's career and the image of the man have been interpreted in response to the need of nationalistically minded historians and literary critics to reformulate the past to suit the needs of the present. It has long been asserted, for example, that Grimm's early devotion to Friedrich Carl von Savigny continued throughout Grimm's life. In fact, Grimm's friendship with Savigny underwent considerable change during the sixty years of their acquaintance. The alterations can best be seen by comparing Grimm's reverential account of Savigny's influence on him in his 1830 autobiography (in volume 1, *Kleinere Schriften*

[Minor Works], 1864) with his biting address "Das Wort des Besitzes" (Words for "Property"), given in 1850 on the fiftieth anniversary of Savigny's earning his doctorate.

In terms of his Germanness, Grimm has been variously hailed as a defender of freedom, as the founder of the study of Germanics, and as a great patriot. He was all of these things, but any appraisal of his thought in these areas seems full of contradictions. He remained devoted to the person of his monarch but often disapproved of the monarch's actions. He conceived of language both as an expression of national unity and as a unifying force. Grimm distinguished his own work from that of his contemporary Karl Lachmann when he asserted that Lachmann investigated literary works for the sake of the words which constituted them, whereas he himself studied works for the sake of the facts the words conveyed.

Because Grimm became a hallowed national figure in the later nineteenth century, his person came to incorporate a variety of exemplary virtues, including unceasing diligence. The volume of Grimm's published work has led his biographers to describe his intellectual labors in Herculean terms. There is no doubt about his unremitting work habits, to which Grimm himself repeatedly alluded, but it is also true that his accomplishments grew out of a fortunate choice of topics as well as out of his ability to inspire people to collaborate in his scholarly efforts. One example may stand for many: in collecting the raw material for his monumental *Weisthümer* Grimm was assisted first by Joseph von Laßberg, then by J. K. V. Bluntschli, Ernst Dronke, and Rudolf Schröder. Grimm's scholarly work captured the imagination of nineteenth-century Europeans because it meshed neatly with the German need for a national history and with the European hunger for folk expression. His collaborators were many, including people of leisure in remote corners of central Europe who contributed citations and excerpts to Grimm's formidable and growing caches of information on law, language, and custom. Grimm organized vast quantities of material, composed learned forewords and accompanying texts, and published the resulting scholarship, but he rarely publicly acknowledged the considerable assistance he received.

Like his oeuvre, Grimm's physical constitution has come to be thought of as superhuman and has often been cited as one of the factors enabling him to be so prolific in his work. His health was certainly more robust than Wilhelm's, but as letters between the brothers demonstrate, Jacob was frequently subject to illnesses and indispositions. Jacob clearly benefited from sharing a household with Wilhelm. Jacob remained unmarried, and Wilhelm–or his wife Dorothea and their daughter Auguste–managed most aspects of daily life.

The Napoleonic occupation of the Germanies set the course of Jacob Grimm's life, and he often expressed the thought that in the dark days of Germany's humiliation by Napoleonic France he had sought consolation in the study of indigenous literary antiquities. At a time when the Holy Roman Empire had been abolished, the Germanies were an area divided in terms of religion into Protestant and Catholic and politically into a crazy quilt of bishoprics, principalities, dukedoms, free cities, and kingdoms. Nonetheless, Grimm spoke of Germany as a fatherland united by a common language. From the beginning of his scholarly life, Grimm asserted the indivisibility of language and the folk and the correlation of language with political boundaries. This perception dominated both his private and public rhetoric throughout his career, beginning in 1812 with *Das Lied von Hildebrand und Hadubrand* and ending with Grimm's calls for incorporating Schleswig-Holstein into Prussia on the grounds that its language was German, not Danish.

Grimm's belief in the centrality of the German language culminated in his greatest creation, the *Deutsches Wörterbuch*, which described German usage from the time of Charlemagne to that of Goethe. In the foreword to the dictionary he addressed all Germans, including those who had emigrated to other lands: "Deutsche geliebte landsleute, welches reichs, welches glaubens ihr seiet, tretet ein in die euch allen aufgethane halle eurer angestammten, uralten sprache, lernet und heiliget sie und haltet an ihr! ... auch zu euch, ihr ausgewanderten Deutschen, über das salzige meer gelangen wird das buch ..." (Beloved German countrymen, of whatever realm, of whatever belief you may be, enter here into the halls of your ancient language, learn it and sanctify it and maintain it! ... this book will also reach those of you who have emigrated beyond the salty seas ...). Taken together with his radical assertions that whoever spoke German belonged to the German folk and that the Germanic people would never accept foreigners, Grimm's identification of people with the language they spoke subsequently became the basis for a patriotically in-

spired oversimplification. For him it had been a lifelong guiding principle.

Letters:

Briefwechsel zwischen Jacob Grimm und Friedrich David Graeter aus den Jahren 1810-1813, edited by Hermann Fischer (Heilbronn: Henninger, 1877);

Freundesbriefe von Wilhelm und Jacob Grimm: Mit Anmerkungen, edited by Alexander Reifferscheid (Heilbronn: Henninger, 1878);

Briefwechsel zwischen Jacob und Wilhelm Grimm aus der Jugendzeit, edited by Herman Grimm and Gustav Hinrichs (Weimar: Böhlau, 1881);

Briefe an Hendrik Willem Tydeman: Mit einem Anhange und Anmerkungen, edited by Reifferscheid (Heilbronn: Henninger, 1883);

Briefwechsel zwischen Jacob und Wilhelm Grimm, Dahlmann und Gervinus, edited by Eduard Ippel, 2 volumes (Berlin: Dümmler, 1885-1886);

Briefwechsel der Gebrüder Grimm mit nordischen Gelehrten, edited by Ernst Schmidt (Berlin: Dümmler, 1885);

Briefwechsel von Jakob Grimm und Hoffmann von Fallersleben mit Hendrik van Wyn: Nebst anderen Briefen zur deutschen Literatur, edited by Karl Theodor Gaedertz (Bremen: Müller, 1888);

Briefe der Brüder Jacob und Wilhelm Grimm an Georg Friedrich Benecke aus den Jahren 1808-1829, edited by Wilhelm Müller (Göttingen: Vandenhoeck & Ruprecht, 1889);

Briefe der Brüder Grimm an Paul Wigand, edited by Edmund Stengel (Marburg: Elwert, 1910);

Briefwechsel der Brüder Jacob und Wilhelm Grimm mit Karl Lachmann, edited by Albert Leitzmann, 2 volumes (Jena: Frommann, 1927);

Briefwechsel zwischen Jacob Grimm und Karl Goedeke, edited by Johannes Bolte (Berlin: Weidmann, 1927);

Briefe der Brüder Grimm, edited by Leitzmann and Hans Gürtler (Jena: Frommann, 1928);

Briefe der Brüder Grimm an Savigny: Aus dem Savignyschen Nachlaß, edited by Wilhelm Schoof and Ingeborg Schnack (Berlin: Schmidt, 1953).

Bibliography:

Ludwig Denecke, "Bibliographie der Briefe von und an Wilhelm und Jacob Grimm: Mit einer Einführung," *Aurora: Jahrbuch der Eichendorff-Gesellschaft*, 43 (1983): 169-277.

Biographies:

Wilhelm Schoof, *Jacob Grimm: Aus seinem Leben*

(Bonn: Dümmler, 1961);

Schoof, *Die Brüder Grimm in Berlin* (Berlin: Haude & Spener, 1964);

Ruth Michaelis-Jena, *The Brothers Grimm* (London: Routledge & Kegan Paul, 1970);

Murray B. Peppard, *Paths through the Forest: A Biography of the Brothers Grimm* (New York: Holt, Rinehart & Winston, 1971);

Hermann Gerstner, *Brüder Grimm* (Reinbek: Rowohlt, 1973);

Ludwig Denecke and Karl Schulte Kemminghausen, *Die Brüder Grimm in Bildern ihrer Zeit* (Cassel: Röth, 1980);

Hans-Bernd Harder and Ekkehard Kaufmann, eds., *Die Brüder Grimm in ihrer amtlichen und politischen Tätigkeit* (Cassel: Weber & Weidemeyer, 1985);

Dieter Hennig and Bernhard Lauer, ed., *Die Brüder Grimm: Dokumente ihres Lebens und Wirkens* (Cassel: Weber & Weidemeyer, 1985);

Gabriele Seitz, *Die Brüder Grimm: Leben–Werk–Zeit* (Munich: Winkler, 1985).

References:

Ludwig Denecke, *Jacob Grimm und sein Bruder Wilhelm* (Stuttgart: Metzler, 1971);

Gunhild Ginschel, *Der junge Jacob Grimm 1805-1819* (Berlin: Deutsche Akademie der Wissenschaften, 1967);

Ulrich Wyss, *Die wilde Philologie: Jacob Grimm und der Historismus* (Munich: Beck, 1979).

Papers:

The Verwaltung der staatlichen Schlösser und Gärten Hessen, Bad Homburg, has drawings by the young Jacob Grimm; the library of Humboldt University, East Berlin, has a large part of the Grimms' personal library; the Staatsbibliothek Preußischer Kulturbesitz, West Berlin, has personal copies of Jacob Grimm's publications and those of others with extensive marginal notes, memorabilia, copies of journal publications, diaries, lecture notes, letters, and published and unpublished manuscripts; the Brüder Grimm-Archiv, Cassel, has editions of the *Kinder- und Hausmärchen*, personal copies with marginal notations, and related secondary literature; the Brüder Grimm-Museum, Cassel, has editions of the *Kinder- und Hausmärchen* and personal effects; the Murhard Library, Cassel, has Grimm's lecture notes for the summer semester of 1836; the Bodmer Library, Geneva, has the 1810 Ölenberg manuscript of the *Kinder- und Hausmärchen*; the Niederhessisches Staatsarchiv und Universitätsbibliothek, Göttingen, has Grimm's lecture notes for the summer semester of 1834 and the winter semester of 1835-1836.

Wilhelm Grimm

(24 February 1786-16 December 1859)

Ruth B. Bottigheimer

State University of New York at Stony Brook

BOOKS: *Kinder- und Hausmärchen,* by Grimm and Jacob Grimm (2 volumes, Berlin: Realschulbuchhandlung, 1812-1815; revised and enlarged seven times, 1819-1857); translated by Edgar Taylor as *German Popular Stories, Translated from the Kinder und Haus Marchen,* 2 volumes (London: Baldwyn, 1823-1826);

Deutsche Sagen, by Grimm and Jacob Grimm, 2 volumes (Berlin: Nicolai, 1816-1818); edited and translated by Donald Ward as *The German Legends of the Brothers Grimm,* 2 volumes (Philadelphia: Institute for the Study of Human Issues, 1981);

Über deutsche Runen (Göttingen: Dieterich, 1821);

Zur Literatur der Runen: Nebst Mittheilung runischer Alphabete und gothischer Fragmente aus Handschriften (Vienna: Gerold, 1828);

Bruchstücke aus einem Gedichte von Assundin (Lemgo, 1829);

Die deutsche Heldensage (Göttingen: Dieterich, 1829);

De Hildebrando antiquissimi carminis teutonici fragmentum edidit (Göttingen: Published by the author, 1830);

Die Sage vom Ursprung der Christusbilder (Berlin: Königliche Akademie der Wissenschaften, 1843);

Exhortatio ad plebem christianam Glossae Cassellanae: Über die Bedeutung der deutschen Fingernamen. Gelesen in der Königlichen Akademie der Wissenschaften am 24. April 1845 und 12. November 1846 (Berlin: Königliche Akademie der Wissenschaften, 1848);

Über Freidank: Zwei Nachträge. Gelesen in der Königlichen Akademie der Wissenschaften am 15. März 1849 (Berlin: Königliche Akademie der Wissenschaften, 1850);

Altdeutsche Gespräche: Nachtrag (Berlin: Königliche Akademie der Wissenschaften, 1851);

Zur Geschichte des Reims: Gelesen in der Königlichen Akademie der Wissenschaften, am 7. März 1850 (Berlin: Königliche Akademie der Wissenschaften, 1852);

Wilhelm Grimm (drawing by Ludwig Emil Grimm, 1837; by permission of the Brüder Grimm Museum)

Deutsches Wörterbuch, by Grimm, Jacob Grimm, and others, 32 volumes (Leipzig: Hirzel, 1854-1961);

Nachtrag zu den Casseler Glossen (Berlin: Dümmler, 1855);

Thierfabeln bei den Meistersängern (Berlin: Dümmler, 1855);

Die Sage von Polyphem (Berlin: Dümmler, 1857);

Kleinere Schriften, edited by Gustav Hinrichs, 4 volumes (volumes 1-3, Berlin: Dümmler; volume 4, Gütersloh: Bertelsmann, 1881-1887).

OTHER: *Altdänische Heldenlieder, Balladen und Märchen,* translated by Grimm (Heidelberg: Mohr & Zimmer, 1811); translated anonymously as *Old Danish Ballads* (London: Hope, 1856);

Die beiden ältesten deutschen Gedichte aus dem achten Jahrhundert: Das Lied von Hildebrand und Hadubrand und das Weißenbrunner Gebet, edited by Grimm and Jacob Grimm (Cassel: Thurneissen, 1812);

Drei altschottische Lieder im Original und Übersetzung aus zwei neuen Sammlungen: Nebst einem Sendschreiben an Herrn Professor F. D. Gräter, edited and translated by Grimm (Heidelberg: Mohr & Zimmer, 1813);

Altdeutsche Wälder, edited by Grimm and Jacob Grimm, 3 volumes (volume 1, Cassel: Thurneissen, 1813; volumes 2-3, Frankfurt am Main: Körner, 1815-1816);

Lieder der alten Edda: Band I, edited by Grimm and Jacob Grimm (Berlin: Realschulbuchhandlung, 1815);

Hartmann von Aue, *Der arme Heinrich: Aus der Straßburgischen und Vatikanischen Handschrift*, edited by Grimm and Jacob Grimm (Berlin: Realschulbuchhandlung, 1815);

C. Croker, *Irische Elfenmärchen*, translated by Grimm and Jacob Grimm (Leipzig: Fleischer, 1826);

Grâve Ruodolf: Ein altdeutsches Gedicht, edited by Grimm (Göttingen: Dieterich, 1828);

Vrîdankes Bescheidenheit, edited by Grimm (Göttingen: Dieterich, 1834);

Der Rosengarten, edited by Grimm (Göttingen: Dieterich, 1836);

Konrad, der Pfaffe, *Ruolandes liet*, edited by Grimm (Göttingen: Dieterich, 1838);

Ludwig Achim's von Arnim sämmtliche Werke, edited by Grimm, 19 volumes (volumes 1-3, 5-8, Berlin: Veit; volumes 9-12, Grünberg & Leipzig: Levysohn; volume 13, Charlottenburg: Bauer; volumes 14-20, Berlin: Arnim, 1839-1848);

Wernher vom Niederrhein, edited by Grimm (Göttingen: Dieterich, 1839);

Konrads von Würzburg Goldene Schmiede, edited by Grimm (Berlin: Klemann, 1840);

Konrads von Würzburg Silvester, edited by Grimm (Göttingen: Dieterich, 1841);

Athis und Prophilias: Mit Nachtrag, edited by Grimm, 2 volumes (Berlin & Göttingen: Dieterich, 1846-1852);

Altdeutsche Gespräche: Mit Nachtrag, edited by Grimm, 2 volumes (Göttingen: Dieterich, 1851-1852);

Bruchstücke aus einem unbekannten Gedicht vom Rosengarten, edited by Grimm (Berlin: Dümmler, 1860).

Wilhelm Grimm's lasting contribution to German life and letters was the *Kinder- und Hausmärchen* (Children's and Household Tales, 1812-1815; translated as *German Popular Stories*, 1823-1826; generally known as *Grimm's Fairy Tales*), to which both contemporaries and subsequent generations turned to find sources of German folk identity. Although both Wilhelm Grimm and his brother Jacob were initially responsible for assembling the raw material for the collection, it was Wilhelm who, especially in the later editions, shaped the narratives' content and style. An accomplished storyteller, Wilhelm Grimm imbued the tales with a straightforward, spare style. Because it was widely believed that the collection exhibited a sure grasp of the historical German folk spirit, the *Kinder- und Hausmärchen* found favor in many quarters. Within a few years of its first publication it had been translated into several European languages, and in both content and style it significantly influenced folk tale collections in other countries.

Born in Hanau on 24 February 1786 to Philipp Wilhelm and Dorothea Zimmer Grimm, Wilhelm Grimm spent idyllic childhood years in Steinau, where his father was a German official. After Philipp Grimm's death in 1796, Wilhelm studied at the Cassel lyceum from 1798 until 1803. During this period he began to suffer from the ill health that would plague him intermittently for the rest of his life. Nonetheless, Grimm's schoolboy diligence gave his teachers grounds to expect that he would one day become a distinguished scholar. Grimm studied law at Marburg from 1803 to 1806, passing his final examinations (pro advocatura) in 1806. From his legal studies, and especially from the lectures of Friedrich Carl von Savigny, to whom he was deeply devoted, he gained insight into the value of the historical method for his subsequent literary studies.

Grimm devoted the first years of his scholarly life to the transcription and translation of ancient manuscripts and to writing articles and book reviews for a variety of journals, including Achim von Arnim and Clemens Brentano's *Zeitung für Einsiedler*, to which he contributed in 1808. Because German journals paid honoraria for scholarly writing, Grimm was able to contribute to his family's support. His first published book was a translation titled *Altdänische*

Heldenlieder, Balladen und Märchen (1811; translated into English as *Old Danish Ballads*, 1856). Its occasional imperfections were counterbalanced by the volume's effectiveness in acquainting German readers with the folk literature of another nation.

Since the early 1800s Wilhelm and Jacob Grimm had been collecting tales from their friends and acquaintances in Cassel. Their efforts were given further impetus after Napoleon installed his brother Jérôme as King of Westphalia, an act which accentuated France's humiliating occupation of German territory and fostered deeply nationalistic sentiment. Published in 1812 as the *Kinder- und Hausmärchen* with eighty-four tales and several fragments, the first volume of the collection reflected published sources and bourgeois taste. Nonetheless, the preface to volume one put forth the brothers' flawed conviction that the tales resulted from an unbroken oral folk tradition which had borne the stories unchanged from their earliest tellings to the present day. The second volume appeared in 1815 and incorporated a larger proportion of tales with folk provenance, a direction which Grimm followed in subsequent reworkings. Through the seven "Large Editions" meant for an adult readership, the collection slowly grew to a total of two hundred numbered tales and ten religious legends. Beginning in 1825, Grimm also put together ten "Small Editions" intended for children. Despite the scholarly acclaim accorded the *Kinder- und Hausmärchen* and the collection's ultimate success, initial sales were slow.

The tales represent many different genres, including magic tales, burlesques, tales of origins, morality tales, and literary fairy tales. Except for the fairy tales, they are generally brief and are told in a spare style with a set of formulaic adjectives such as *beautiful* and *ugly*, *good* and *evil*, *diligent* and *lazy*. The heroes and heroines suffer humiliation and hunger until their woes are relieved by magical intervention occasioned by evidence of their inherent virtues, such as compassion, piety, or bravery. The rewards are typically the acquisition of great wealth or power, often through marriage, although on occasion the protagonists receive assurance of an abundance of food for the rest of their lives.

Soon after publication of the *Kinder- und Hausmärchen*, individual tales from it were incorporated into readers' and children's annuals, though often in substantially edited and reworked form, so that specific tales circulated

much more widely than sales of the collection would suggest. In the first edition, scholarly notes demonstrating distribution patterns and variant forms of individual tales were appended to each volume; beginning with the second edition (1819-1822), Wilhelm Grimm put all the notes in a separate volume. Initially the Small Editions of the tales were illustrated by the Grimms' younger brother, Ludwig Emil, but over the years the *Kinder- und Hausmärchen* has attracted the efforts of hundreds of illustrators, both within Germany and beyond its borders.

Continuing his efforts to bring the ancient literature of other nations within the orbit of the German scholarly public, Grimm published a translation entitled *Drei altschottische Lieder* (Three Ancient Scottish Songs) in 1813. In the same year Wilhelm and Jacob Grimm initiated a short-lived journal, *Altdeutsche Wälder* (Old German Forests), which appeared in three volumes in 1813, 1815, and 1816. Here they published their own essays representing the entire range of their interests—mythology, literature, folklore, linguistics, and history—as well as documents they had unearthed in their archival research.

After the French were driven out of German territory in 1813 and Jacob Grimm was sent to Paris in 1814 as legation secretary for Hessian diplomats, Wilhelm Grimm was appointed assistant librarian in the electoral library in Cassel. He continued to transcribe and publish medieval manuscripts, thus contributing to the retrieval of Germany's medieval literary past—an effort in which many nineteenth-century scholars were active. His collaboration with Jacob on the two volumes of *Deutsche Sagen* (1816-1818; edited and translated as *The German Legends of the Brothers Grimm*, 1981) continued his work in reviving the German past, this time using mostly materials published from the sixteenth through the eighteenth centuries. Wilhelm Grimm's publications reaffirmed the cultural basis of the emerging German nation. During this same period Wilhelm also collaborated with Jacob in editing *Lieder der alten Edda* (Songs of the Ancient Edda), published in 1815.

In 1819 both Wilhelm and Jacob Grimm received honorary doctorates from Marburg University. In 1825 Wilhelm married Henriette Dorothea (Dortchen) Wild, with whom he had four children: Jacob, Herman Friedrich, Rudolf Georg Ludwig, and Auguste Luise Pauline Marie. In 1829 he resigned his position at the electoral library in Cassel, where his service had been

Wilhelm Grimm's study in Berlin (drawing by Michael Hofmann; by permission of the Germanisches Nationalmuseum, Nuremberg)

unappreciated and undercompensated, and accepted a call to a professorship at Göttingen. Jacob Grimm was appointed to a chair at Göttingen that same year.

At the beginning of his appointment in Göttingen in 1830, Wilhelm Grimm was married with one child and another on the way. His health was precarious, and his family's welfare was not secured should he fall ill or die. In 1835 he was appointed Ordentlicher Professor (full professor), which offered him financial security for the first time in his life. The Göttingen years were fruitful ones for Grimm, who published editions of *Vrîdankes Bescheidenheit* (Freidank's Wisdom) in 1834, *Der Rosengarten* (The Rose Garden) in 1836, and *Ruolandes liet* (The Song of Roland) in 1838. The third edition of *Kinder- und Hausmärchen* appeared in 1837. At the university his lectures covered some of the same material: *Bescheidenheit*, Walther von der Vogelweide, the *Nibelungenlied, Iwein*, and *Kudrun*.

When the Grimms first arrived in Göttingen they gloried in the freedom of expression they found, so different from the mute reserve that had been necessary in Cassel. Wilhelm spent much time with the historian Friedrich Christoph Dahlmann, who embodied the tradition of classic political liberalism in early nineteenth-century Germany. An admirer of the English constitution, Dahlmann was in the process of working out the basis for constitutional monarchy within the German context. In 1837 the Grimms, Dahlmann, and four other Göttingen professors clashed with the newly crowned king, Ernst August of Hannover, when they refused to acquiesce in his suspension of the Constitution of 1833, to which they had sworn fealty. The seven professors were summarily dismissed; Jacob Grimm was exiled from Göttingen on three days' notice; but Wilhelm was allowed to remain for several months for reasons of family and health.

Wilhelm Grimm wanted his and Jacob's participation in the protest against the king's abrogation of the constitution to be understood not politically but in terms of personal honor and ethics, a point which he made in his editorial amendments to Jacob's pamphlet *Jacob Grimm über seine Entlassung* (Jacob Grimm on His Dismissal, 1838). Both brothers were outraged by Ernst August's arbitrary exercise of power, and Wilhelm demonstrated his sense of solidarity with the protesters by rejecting overtures to be rehired at Göttingen unless such an offer were to include all seven protesters. That offer never materialized, and Wilhelm returned to Cassel, living with his wife, children, and Jacob for two years in the home of their youngest brother, Ludwig Emil Grimm.

In late 1840 when Friedrich Wilhelm IV acceded to the throne, Bettina von Arnim's efforts to secure the brothers positions at the Humboldt University in Berlin were successful. Berlin was a city growing by leaps and bounds, very different from the rolling Hessian countryside as well as from the placid atmosphere of Göttingen. Wilhelm Grimm, fifty-five years old when he arrived in Berlin in the spring of 1841, was regarded with affection by students and colleagues and had an active social life.

As a scholar Grimm was characterized by intensive rather than extensive labors. His work habits were conditioned by his poor health (he suffered from tachycardia, asthma, erysipelas, rheumatism, and myocarditis), which curtailed his ability in later life to travel to libraries and archives. He had fewer foreign languages at his command than Jacob did, and rather than working with the original language, he preferred to translate foreign texts into German, as he did in *Altdänische Heldenlieder, Balladen und Märchen, Drei altschottische Hische Lieder*, and *Irische Elfenmärchen* (Irish Folktales), an 1826 collaboration with his brother. Similarly, his many scholarly editions of medieval manuscripts involved faithful transcription and collation of variants. Grimm was a master of reworking and polishing, techniques perhaps most notable in successive editions of *Grimm's Fairy Tales*. The remainder of Wilhelm's scholarly oeuvre consists of critical editions, scholarly articles on Germanic philology, and his collaboration with Jacob on the monumental *Deutsches Wörterbuch* (German Dictionary), which eventually ran to thirty-two volumes, the first of which appeared in 1854. Throughout his life Grimm demonstrated a decidedly artistic bent. Repeated references to landscapes and paintings in his autobiography of 1839 (in *Kleinere Schriften* [Minor Writings], volume 1, 1881) mirror his scholarly concern for the visual arts, evident, for example, in his use of medieval paintings to support philological argument.

In order to appreciate Grimm's worldview, it is essential to understand the religious divisions which existed within Germany and the nature of the fragmented society in which Grimm grew up. When Landgrave Karl of Hesse invited Huguenots and Waldensians to Cassel and built a new city for them south of the city walls in the 1680s, his action united a significant French Calvinist presence with an already existing German Reformed, or Zwinglian Protestant, group of Swiss theological origin. It also made Hesse-Cassel one of the relatively few German states with a Reformed monarch ruling a subject population, a large proportion of whom were Reformed, while most others were Lutheran. The Grimms, who came from a long line of Reformed pastors, were acutely aware of their heritage: as young children in Hanau they learned religion and reading from the catechism that had belonged to their great-grandfather, who was a Reformed pastor; in Steinau they attended the Reformed school and continued their study of religion from the Reformed school preceptor; they also learned to despise Lutherans, whom they mocked as "Dickköpfe" (blockheads). In embracing German folk culture, however, they came into contact with Lutheran Protestantism. Without ever overtly describing the sea change that must have taken place in his awareness of his own religious identity, Grimm incorporated into *Kinder- und Hausmärchen* values of the Lutheran culture that had been defined for him as alien when he was a child.

One of the earliest assessments of Grimm's character came from his maternal grandfather, Johann Hermann Zimmer, who described the twelve-year-old boy as extremely self-confident. Jacob Grimm once declared that Wilhelm was his alter ego. Through his family and friendships Wilhelm supplied the sociable half of the scholar's personality, while Jacob remained a solitary figure, pursuing his research and writing. Wilhelm Grimm came to intellectual maturity in the early years of the nineteenth century with an acute sense of a heroic German past which contrasted starkly with Germany's divided and subjugated present. This perception kindled a lifelong interest in Germanic philology and in reviving and securing traditional national culture. By studying Germany's past, Grimm believed, one might be able to reconstitute and restore to the present an endurng sense of wholeness.

Letters:
Freundesbriefe von Wilhelm und Jacob Grimm: Mit An-

merkungen, edited by Alexander Reiffer-scheid (Heilbronn: Henninger, 1878);

Briefwechsel zwischen Jacob und Wilhelm Grimm aus der Jugendzeit, edited by Herman Grimm and Gustav Hinrichs (Weimar: Böhlau, 1881);

Briefwechsel der Gebrüder Grimm mit nordischen Gelehrten, edited by Ernst Schmidt (Berlin: Dümmler, 1885);

Briefwechsel zwischen Jacob und Wilhelm Grimm, Dahlmann und Gervinus, edited by Eduard Ippel, 2 volumes (Berlin: Dümmler, 1885-1886);

Briefe der Brüder Jacob und Wilhelm Grimm an Georg Friedrich Benecke aus den Jahren 1808-1829, edited by Wilhelm Müller (Göttingen: Vandenhoeck & Ruprecht, 1889);

Briefe der Brüder Grimm an Paul Wigand, edited by Edmund Stengel (Marburg: Elwert, 1910);

Briefwechsel der Brüder Jacob und Wilhelm Grimm mit Karl Lachmann, edited by Albert Leitzmann, 2 volumes (Jena: Frommann, 1927);

Briefe der Brüder Grimm, edited by Leitzmann and Hans Gürtler (Jena: Frommann, 1928);

Briefwechsel zwischen Jenny von Droste-Hülshoff und Wilhelm Grimm, edited by K. Schulte (Münster: Aschendorff, 1929);

Briefe der Brüder Grimm an Savigny: Aus dem Savignyschen Nachlaß, edited by Wilhelm Schoof and Ingeborg Schnack (Berlin: Schmidt, 1953).

Bibliography:

Ludwig Denecke, "Bibliographie der Briefe von und an Wilhelm und Jacob Grimm: Mit einer Einführung," *Aurora: Jahrbuch der Eichendorff-Gesellschaft*, 43 (1983): 169-227.

Biographies:

Wilhelm Schoof, *Wilhelm Grimm: Aus seinem Leben* (Bonn: Dümmler, 1960);

Schoof, *Die Brüder Grimm in Berlin* (Berlin: Hande & Spener, 1964);

Ruth Michaelis-Jena, *The Brothers Grimm* (London: Routledge & Kegan Paul, 1970);

Ludwig Denecke, *Jacob Grimm und sein Bruder Wilhelm* (Stuttgart: Metzler, 1971);

Murray B. Peppard, *Paths through the Forest: A Biography of the Brothers Grimm* (New York: Holt, Rinehart & Winston, 1971);

Hermann Gerstner, *Brüder Grimm* (Reinbek: Rowohlt, 1973);

Gabriele Seitz, *Die Brüder Grimm: Leben–Werk–Zeit* (Munich: Winkler, 1985);

Hans-Bernd Harder and Ekkehard Kauffmann, eds., *Die Brüder Grimm in iher Zeit* (Cassel: Röth, 1985);

Dieter Hennig and Bernhard Lauer, eds., *Die Brüder Grimm: Dokumente ihres Lebens und Wirkens* (Cassel: Weber & Weidemeyer, 1985).

References:

Ruth B. Bottigheimer, *Grimms' Bad Girls and Bold Boys: The Moral and Social Vision of the Tales* (New Haven & London: Yale University Press, 1987);

James M. McGlathery, ed., *The Brothers Grimm and the Folktale* (Urbana: University of Illinois Press, 1988);

Maria M. Tatar, *The Hard Facts of the Grimms' Fairy Tales* (Princeton: Princeton University Press, 1987);

Jack Zipes, *The Brothers Grimm* (London: Routledge, 1988).

Papers:

The library of the Humboldt University, East Berlin, has a large part of the Grimms' personal library; the Brüder Grimm-Archiv, Cassel, has editions of the *Kinder- und Hausmärchen*, personal copies with marginal notations, and related secondary literature; the Brüder Grimm-Museum, Cassel, has editions of the *Kinder- und Hausmärchen* and personal effects; the Staatsbibliothek Preußischer Kulturbesitz, West Berlin, has personal copies of Wilhelm Grimm's publications and those of others with extensive marginal notes, memorabilia, copies of journal publications, diaries, lecture notes, letters, and published and unpublished manuscripts; Grimm's lecture notes for the summer semester of 1836 are in the Germanisches Nationalmuseum, Nuremberg.

Caroline von Günderrode

(11 February 1780-26 July 1806)

Helene M. Kastinger Riley
Clemson University

BOOKS: *Gedichte und Phantasien*, as Tian (Hamburg & Frankfurt am Main: Hermann, 1804);

Poetische Fragmente, as Tian (Frankfurt am Main: Wilmans, 1805)–includes *Hildgund*; *Piedro*; *Die Pilger*; *Mahomed, der Prophet von Mekka*;

Gesammelte Dichtungen: Zum ersten Male vollständig herausgegeben, edited by Friedrich Götz (Mannheim: Götz, 1857);

Briefe und Dichtungen, by Günderrode and Friedrich Creuzer, edited by E. Rohde (Heidelberg: Winter, 1896);

Melete, as Ion, edited by Leopold Hirschberg (Berlin: Harrwitz, 1906);

Gesammelte Werke, edited by Hirschberg, 3 volumes (Berlin: Goldschmidt-Gabrielli, 1920-1922);

Dichtungen, edited by Ludwig V. Pigenot (Munich: Bruckmann, 1922);

Gesammelte Dichtungen, edited by Elisabeth Salomon (Munich: Drei Masken, 1923);

Günderode, edited by Friedhelm Kemp (Lorch: Bürger, 1947);

Ein apokalyptisches Fragment: Gedichte und Prosa, edited by Herbert Blank (Stuttgart: Freies Geistesleben, 1960);

Der Schatten eines Traumes: Gedichte, Prosa, Briefe, Zeugnisse von Zeitgenossen, edited by Christa Wolf (Darmstadt: Luchterhand, 1979).

OTHER: *Udohla, in zwei Acten: Von Tian; Magie und Schicksal, in drei Acten: Von Demselben*, in *Studien*, edited by Carl Daub and Friedrich Creuzer, volume 1 (Frankfurt am Main & Heidelberg: Mohr & Zimmer, 1805), pp. 363-401, 403-461;

"Geschichte eines Braminen: Von Tian," in *Herbsttage*, edited by Sophie von La Roche (Leipzig: Gräf, 1805);

Nikator: Eine dramatische Skizze von Tian, in *Taschenbuch für das Jahr 1806: Der Liebe und Freundschaft gewidmet* (Frankfurt am Main: Wilmans, 1806), pp. 85-120.

Caroline von Günderrode (print by C. Lang, by permission of the Schiller-Nationalmuseum)

Caroline von Günderrode was born in Karlsruhe on 11 February 1780. The oldest of the six children of Hector and Louise von Drachstädt von Günderrode, she spent her early years in Hanau. After her father's death she was sent in 1797 to Frankfurt am Main, to the Cronstetter-Hynspergische Stift for unmarried gentlewomen, where the house rules were altered to permit her entry as a woman younger than thirty years of age. Although the institution was not restrictive, Günderrode felt isolated and suffered under the limitations imposed on women at that time: she yearned for more education, more freedom of movement, more opportunity to associate with individuals who had interests similar to hers. On 11 August 1801 she wrote to her friend Gunda Brentano that she perceived her ignorance as the most intolerable contradiction in her life: possessing an inquisitive mind without the opportunity to satisfy it. She took private lessons from the theologian C. W. J. Mosche, read extensively, and took copious notes on historical, geographical, and philosophical works, studied Latin, metrics, physics, chemistry, oriental and Indian mythology, and read Friedrich Wilhelm Joseph von Schelling, August Wilhelm von Schlegel, and Friedrich Schleiermacher. The search for knowledge and truth is a constant topic in her poems, prose, and dramatic works.

Having the wish but not the opportunity for intellectual exchange with her peers was not the only contradiction in Günderrode's life. There were others. Tall in stature, shy and feminine in manner, she yearned for the physically active life permitted only to men. In an 1801 letter to Brentano, she wrote: "Schon oft hatte ich den unweiblichen Wunsch mich in ein wildes Schlachtgetümmel zu werfen, zu sterben, Warum ward ich kein Mann! ich habe keinen Sinn für weibliche Tugenden, für Weiberglückseeligkeit. Nur das wilde Grose, Glänzende gefällt mir. Es ist ein unseliges aber unverbesserliches Mißverhältnis in meiner Seele . . . denn ich bin ein Weib, und habe Begierden wie ein Mann, ohne Männerkraft. Darum bin ich so wechselnd, und so uneins mit mir" (Often I have had the unfeminine wish to throw myself into the midst of a wild battle, to die. Why was I not born a man! I have no sense for feminine virtues, women's joys. Only the wild and grand, the splendid pleases me. It is an accursed but incorrigible incongruity of my soul . . . for I am a woman and have desires like a man without the strength. Therefore I am so changeable and so at odds with myself).

Günderrode's one-act play *Hildgund* (1805) has a protagonist that embodies her feminine ideal. With her fiancé, Walther of Aquitania, Hildgund, the princess of Burgundy, escapes the court of Attila, King of the Huns, taking along Attila's armor and sword–the symbols of his might. When her father praises the gods for the return of his daughter, Hildgund replies that she has saved herself: "Der Gott, der mich befreit, wohnt in dem eig'nen Herzen" (The god who liberated me lives in my own heart).

The joys of reunion are, however, short-lived: under the threat of war Attila demands Hildgund's return. In the reaction of the three men to the situation Günderrode shows the vulnerability of women in a supposedly protective society. Hildgund's father is willing to barter his daughter for peace; Attila is willing to repudiate his wife, Ospiru, if Hildgund will marry him. Hildgund, who does not value a quiet life, vows to kill Attila herself. This unfeminine attitude puzzles Walther, who breaks their engagement. Before she embarks on her mission to rid the world of Attila, Hildgund ponders why men enjoy the freedom to guide their own lives while women are bound by want and custom:

> Wie herrlich ist der Mann, sein Schicksal bildet er,
> Nur eigener Kräfte Maß ist sein Gesetz am Ziele,
> Des Weibes Schicksal, ach! ruht nicht in eig'ner Hand!
> Bald folget sie der Noth, bald strenger Sitte Wille

> (How excellent is the man, his destiny he molds,
> The measure of his strengths alone limits his goal in th' end,
> The woman's destiny, alas! rests not in her own hand!
> Either she follows need, or what strict custom holds).

The figure of Hildgund closely parallels the warriorlike Brünhild of the *Nibelungenlied* and the avenging Kriemhild of *Die Klage*. While Günderrode's other plays–*Nikator* (1806), *Udohla* (1805), *Mahomed* (1805), *Magie und Schicksal* (1805)–have male protagonists, the woman's need for more freedom of action is a dominant theme.

In her life Günderrode perhaps suffered most because she was excluded from intellectual and social contact with men of talent who were suspicious of her ambition. Christa Wolf explains the problem in the introductory essay to her 1979 edition of Günderrode's work, *Der Schatten eines Traumes* (The Shadow of a Dream). These were irreconcilable incongruities in 1800: to be a wife and poet, to be a woman loved by a man and to publish one's own creative works. According to Wolf, "Drei Männer haben in ihrem Leben eine Rolle gespielt: Savigny, Clemens Brentano, Friedrich Creuzer–drei Varianten der gleichen Erfahrung: Was sie begehrt, ist unmöglich" (Three men played a role in her life: Savigny, Clemens Brentano, Friedrich Creuzer–three variations on the same experience: what she wants is impossible). The jurist Friedrich Karl von Savigny bantered with her for a time, then went on to marry Gunda Brentano. Clemens Brentano, who had encouraged the marriage between his sister and Savigny, was himself enamored of Günderrode. He had asked her why she wanted her work published. Günderrode replied on 10 June 1804: "immer . . . lebendig ist die Sehnsucht in mir, mein Leben in einer bleibenden Form auszusprechen, in einer Gestalt die würdig sei, zu den Vortrefflichsten hinzutreten, sie zu grüßen und Gemeinschaft mit ihnen zu haben. Ja, nach dieser Gemeinschaft hat mir stets gelüstet, dies ist die Kirche nach der mein Geist stets wallfahrtet auf Erden" (Always . . . alive in me is the yearning to express my life in a lasting form, in a manner worthy of standing beside the most splendid ones, to greet them and have communion with them. Indeed, I have always coveted this communion, this is the church to which my spirit ever sojourns here on earth). Brentano did not comprehend this yearning in a woman; he failed to understand it in his own wife.

Günderrode's relationship with Creuzer, a married philologist in Heidelberg, created a scandal. There was talk of divorce, a suicide pact, a ménage à trois. Creuzer was her adviser on literary matters. Günderrode gave him the manuscript for a volume of verse, and together they decided on the title *Melete*. Creuzer arranged for its publication under the pseudonym Ion by the Heidelberg publisher Mohr and Zimmer.

The volume comprises some of Günderrode's best poems, including "Die eine Klage" (The One Lament). The poem follows the contemporary Romantic style. With its deceptive simplicity and ease of rhythm and rhyme it differs from many of her other lyrics, which have philosophical or classical subjects and more complex forms. The topic is the uniqueness of each individual and experience and the irreplaceable void caused by loss:

> Wer die tiefste aller Wunden
> Hat in Geist und Sinn empfunden
> Bittrer Trennung Schmerz;
> Wer geliebt was er verlohren,
> Lassen muß was er erkohren,
> Das geliebte Herz;
>
> . . . .
>
> Wer so ganz in Herz und Sinnen
> Konnt' ein Wesen liebgewinnen
> O! den tröstet's nicht
> Daß für Freuden, die verlohren,
> Neue werden neu gebohren:
> Jene sind's doch nicht.
> Das geliebte, süße Leben,
> Dieses Nehmen und dies Geben,

> Wort und Sinn und Blick,
> Dieses Suchen und dies Finden,
> Dieses Denken und Empfinden
> Giebt kein Gott zurück

> (He who has felt the deepest of all
> wounds in mind and heart:
> the bitter call to part;
> he who loved what's lost, elected
> to relinquish the selected
> beloved heart;
>
> . . . .
>
> He who with earnest heart and mind
> a dear soul so had cherished,
> O, he can never comfort find
> in thoughts that for the perished
> pleasures new ones are born:
> if those remain forlorn.
> The beloved one, sweet living,
> O this taking and this giving,
> Word and touch and glances binding,
> And this searching and this finding,
> for which thought and feeling yearns,
> No divinity returns).

As early as 29 August 1801 Günderrode had written Gunda Brentano of her wish to die and of how impossible it seemed to continue living: "Der alte Wunsch einen Heldentod zu sterben ergrif mich mit großer Heftigkeit; unleidlich war es mir noch zu leben . . ." (The old wish for a heroic death gripped me with great force; it was intolerable to me to go on living . . .). On 26 July 1806 she died her "heroic death" on the banks of the Rhine River. Having carefully written her own epitaph (a slightly edited version of an Indian verse she had found in Johann Gottfried Herder's work), she stepped to the edge of the river, filled her shawl with rocks, and stabbed herself twice in the heart with a dagger.

The bizarre manner of her death caused a sensation. Her affair with Creuzer was immediately assumed to be the cause of her despair, and until well into the twentieth century her amorous life was the major topic of inquiries into her work. In the light of Günderrode's suicide Creuzer felt severely compromised by the love poems in *Melete*, which was already being printed. He ordered the publisher to stop the process and to destroy any portions in print. According to Christa Wolf, Günderrode died a second death. The existence of the work remained unknown until a single copy was found in Burg Neuburg, consisting in part of printed pages, in part of manuscript material. Excerpts from the work appeared in 1896, and an edition of four hundred copies was published by Leopold Hirschberg in 1906.

Günderrode's best work is found among her poems, for which Goethe expressed admiration in a letter of 28 April 1804. She experimented with many forms and subjects, from Romantic folk songs to ballads and sonnets, from love lyrics to philosophical poems in Friedrich von Schiller's manner and classical verse in hexameter. Because of her versatility, critics have failed in attempts to classify her as belonging to either the Romantic or classical school. The rich variety of formal means she employed can perhaps best be sampled in her love poems "Hochroth" (Crimson), "Die Liebe" (Love), and "An Eusebio" (To Eusebio), the Romantic "An Clemens" (To Clemens), "Ist alles stumm und leer" (Everything Is Mute and Empty), and "Einstens lebt ich süßes Leben" (Once I Lived a Sweet Life), and the classicistic "Ariadne auf Naxos" (Ariadne on Naxos), "An Melete" (To Melete), and "Orphisches Lied" (Orphic Song). Günderrode also favored topics inspired by exotic lands to which she yearned to travel. "Die Malabrischen Witwen" (The Malabar Widows), for example, celebrates the Indian custom of reuniting living wives with their deceased husbands in a ritual burial by fire, and "Der Nil" (The Nile) presents a personification of the river Nile in a semantically daring description of a fertility ritual. Among her philosophical poems, the best are "Der Adept" (The Expert) and "Des Wanderers Niederfahrt" (The Wanderer's Descent), both treating the Faustian motif of the search for ultimate truth and knowledge.

Günderrode's prose is limited to the philosophical questions that occupied German poets intensely at the time. In "Die Manen" (The Manes) she discusses the effects which the accomplishments of a great individual can have beyond the grave. In the form of a dialogue between Teacher and Pupil, the apprentice learns that history communicates a spiritual understanding between the living and the deceased. Some of Schiller's poems ("Das Götterbild zu Sais" [The Idol of Sais], "Resignation") and Novalis's *Die Lehrlinge zu Sais* (The Novices of Sais, 1802) employ similar topics and methods. "Ein apokalyptisches Fragment" (An Apocalyptic Fragment) is a vivid, step-by-step description of the soul's mystical union with its surroundings in a Spinozistic merger of "Eins und Alles" (one and all). Günderrode was one of few women writers of her time who wrote drama. Of the two short

prose dramas *Immortalita* (an Orphic descent-and-rescue story) and *Mora*, the latter is more innovative. As her lover Mora has chosen Frothal, King of Scandinavia, over his rival, Karmor. Frothal clothes her in his armor on a hunting trip: "Nimm die Waffen der Könige Scandinaviens, daß du glänzest im Stahle der Helden" (Take the weapons of the Scandinavian kings so you will glisten in the steel of the heroes). When she meets Karmor in this disguise, he assumes that she is Frothal and challenges her to a duel. After some hesitation, Mora accepts the dare: "mich dürstet nach Kampf, mein Muth jauchzt der Gefahr entgegen, komm!" (I thirst for battle, my courage rejoices in danger, come!), she declares and dies in the battle, another of Günderrode's heroic women.

Günderrode's heroic female protagonists share the knowledge that death is not final but is "ein chemischer Prozeß, eine Scheidung der Kräfte, aber kein Vernichter" (a chemical process, a separation of the powers, but not a destroyer) and a lofty spirit whose sense of justice always causes them to choose the noble but difficult means of resolving a conflict rather than accepting a compromise. Clearly, Günderrode also refused to suffer the indignities to which an imperfect, sometimes petty society subjected her. In 1840, Bettina von Arnim, who popularized the spelling of Günderrode's name with one *r*, commemorated the friend of her youth with a book titled *Die Günderode*. In 1979 Christa Wolf revived interest in this versatile writer with her edition of Günderrode's works and with the novel *Kein Ort, nirgends* (translated as *No Place on Earth*, 1982), in which Wolf portrays Günderrode and her contemporary Heinrich von Kleist as they meet at an 1804 tea party in the small town of Winkel on the Rhine.

Letters:

R. Dittenberger, "Karoline von Günderode: Briefe an Daub," *Westermanns Illustrierte Deutsche Monatshefte*, 79 (December 1895): 352-357;

Friedrich Creuzer und Karoline von Günderode: Briefe und Dichtungen, edited by Erwin Rohde (Heidelberg: Winter, 1896), pp. 124-142;

Die Liebe der Günderode: Friedrich Creuzers Briefe an Karoline von Günderode, edited by Karl Preisendanz (Munich: Piper, 1912);

P. Pattloch, "Unbekannte Briefe der Günderode an Friedrich Creuzer," *Hochland*, 35, 1 (1937 / 1938): 50-59;

Walther Rehm, "Eim unbekannter Brief der Günderode an Friedrich Creuzer," *Deutsche Vierteljahrsschrift*, 24 (1950): 387-388;

Max Preitz, "Karoline von Günderrode in ihrer Umwelt: I. Briefe von Lisette und Gottfried Nees von Esenbeck, Karoline von Günderrode, Friedrich Creuzer, Clemens Brentano und Susanne von Heyden," *Jahrbuch des Freien Deutschen Hochstifts* (1962): 208-306;

Preitz, "Karoline von Günderrode in ihrer Umwelt: II. Karoline von Günderrodes Briefwechsel mit Friedrich Karl und Gunda von Savigny," *Jahrbuch des Freien Deutschen Hochstifts* (1964): 185-235;

Frauenbriefe der Romantik, edited by Katja Behrens (Frankfurt am Main: Insel, 1981), pp. 9-60.

Biographies:

Ludwig Geiger, *Karoline von Günderode und ihre Freunde* (Stuttgart: Deutsche Verlags-Anstalt, 1895);

Ernst Jeep, *Karoline von Günderode: Mittheilungen über ihr Leben und Dichten* (Wolfenbüttel: Zwissler, 1895);

Karl Groos, *Friedrich Creuzer und Karoline von Günderode: Mitteilung über deren Verhältnis* (Heidelberg: Universitätsbuchhandlung, 1895).

References:

Bettina von Arnim, *Die Günderode: Den Studenten* (Grünberg & Leipzig: Levysohn, 1840); translated by Margaret Fuller as *Günderode* (Boston: Peabody, 1842); translation completed by Minna Wesselhoeft as *Correspondence of Fräulein Günderode and Bettina von Arnim* (Boston: Burnham, 1861);

O. Berdrow, "Eine Priesterin der Romantik," *Die Frau*, 2 (1894 / 1895): 681-688;

Geneviève Bianquis, *Caroline de Günderode* (Paris: Alcan, 1910);

M. Brion, "Caroline von Günderode," *L'Allemagne romantique*, 1 (1962): 299-343;

Roswitha Burwick, "Liebe und Tod in Leben und Werk der Günderode," *German Studies Review*, 3 (1980): 207-223;

Max Büsing, *Die Reihenfolge der Gedichte Karolinens von Günderrode* (Berlin: Ebering, 1903);

Gisela Dischner, "Die Günderrode," *Bettina von Arnim: Eine weibliche Sozialbiographie aus dem 19. Jahrhundert* (Berlin: Wagenbach, 1977), pp. 61-143;

A. Fleckenstein, "Karoline von Günderode," *Hochland*, 37 (1939 / 1940);

Karl Foldenauer, "Karoline von Günderrode (1780-1806)," in *Kostbarkeiten*, edited by Beatrice Steiner (Karlsruhe: Scheffelbund, 1981), pp. 81-111;

F. Hetmann, *Drei Frauen zum Beispiel: Die Lebensgeschichte der Simone Weil, Isabel Burton und Karoline von Günderode* (Weinheim: Beltz & Gelberg, 1980);

Otto Heuschele, *Karoline von Günderode* (Halle, 1932);

Doris Hopp and Max Preitz, "Karoline von Günderrode in ihrer Umwelt: III. Karoline von Günderrodes Studienbuch," *Jahrbuch des Freien Deutschen Hochstifts* (1975): 223-323;

Waltraud Howeg, "Karoline von Günderode und Hölderlin," Ph.D. dissertation, University of Halle, 1953;

A. Kelletat, " 'Die Gestalt der männlichen Göttin.' J. Bobrowskis Widmung an Karoline von Günderode," in *Selbständigkeit und Hingabe: Frauen der Romantik*, edited by Wolfgang Böhme, 1980), pp. 51-61;

W. Kohlschmidt, "Ästhetische Existenz und Leidenschaft: Mythos und Wirklichkeit der Karoline von Günderode," *Zeitwende*, 51 (1980): 205-216;

Ursula Krechel, " 'Getaumelt in den Räumen des Äthers': Karoline von Günderode und Friedrich Creuzer," *Die schwarze Botin*, 16 (1980): 32-38;

Margarethe Mattheis, *Die Günderrode: Gestalt, Leben und Wirkung* (Berlin, 1934);

M. Peter, "Zwischen Klassik und Romantik: Karoline von Günderode," *Das goldene Tor*, 4 (1949): 465-473;

Erich Regen, *Die Dramen Karolinens von Günderode* (Berlin: Ebering, 1910);

Walther Rehm, "Über die Gedichte der Karoline von Günderode," in *Goethe-Kalender auf das Jahr 1942* (Frankfurt am Main: Goethe-Museum, 1941), pp. 93-121;

Helene M. Kastinger Riley, "Zwischen den Welten: Ambivalenz und Existentialproblematik im Werk Caroline von Günderrodes," in her *Die weibliche Muse* (Columbia, S.C.: Camden House, 1986), pp. 90-119;

Alex Tekinay, "Zum Orient-Bild Bettina von Arnims und der jüngeren Romantik," *Arcadia*, 16 (1981): 47-49;

Uta Treder, "Karoline von Günderode: Gedichte sind Balsam auf unfüllbares Leben," *Studi dell'Istituto Linguistico*, no. 3 (1980): 35-59;

E. Wallace, "Die Günderode und Bettina," *Castrum peregrini*, 12 (1953): 5-31;

Richard Wilhelm, *Die Günderode: Dichtung und Schicksal* (Frankfurt am Main: Societats Verlag, 1938);

Wilhelm, "Karoline von Günderode," *Genius*, 2 (1948 / 1951): 21-35;

Christa Wolf, *Kein Ort, nirgends* (Darmstadt: Luchterhand, 1979); translated by Jan Van Heurck as *No Place on Earth* (New York: Farrar, Straus & Giroux, 1982; London: Virago, 1983);

Wolf, "Kultur ist, was gelebt wird," *Alternative*, 25 (1982): 118-127.

Wilhelm Hauff
(29 November 1802-18 November 1827)

Erich P. Hofacker, Jr.
University of Michigan

BOOKS: *Der Mann im Mond oder Der Zug des Herzens ist des Schicksals Stimme,* as H. Clauren (Stuttgart: Franckh, 1825 [dated 1826]);

Lichtenstein: Romantische Sage aus der würtembergischen Geschichte, 3 volumes (Stuttgart: Franckh, 1826); translated anonymously as *The Banished: A Swabian Historical Tale,* edited by James Morier, 3 volumes (London: Colburn, 1839);

Maehrchenalmanach auf das Jahr 1826, für Söhne und Töchter gebildeter Stände (Stuttgart: Metzler, 1826);

Mittheilungen aus den Memoiren des Satan, 2 volumes (Stuttgart: Franckh, 1826-1827); excerpts translated anonymously as *Memoirs of Beelzebub* (New York: Taylor, 1846);

Controvers-Predigt über H. Clauren und den Mann im Monde, gehalten vor dem deutschen Publikum in der Herbstmesse 1827. Text: Ev. Matt. VIII. 31-32 (Stuttgart: Franckh, 1827);

Phantasien im Bremer Rathskeller: Ein Herbstgeschenk für Freunde des Weines (Stuttgart: Franckh, 1827); translated by E. Sadler and C. R. L. Fletcher as *The Wine-Ghosts of Bremen* (Oxford: Blackwell, 1889; New York: White & Allen, 1889);

Novellen, 3 volumes (Stuttgart: Franckh, 1828);

Phantasien und Skizzen (Stuttgart: Franckh, 1828);

Sämmtliche Schriften, edited by Gustav Schwab, 36 volumes (Stuttgart: Brodhag, 1830);

Wilhelm Hauff's Werke, edited by Adolf Stern, 4 volumes (Berlin: Grote, 1878);

Prosaische und poetische Werke, 12 volumes (Berlin: Hempel, 1879);

Werke, edited by Max Mendheim, 3 volumes (Leipzig: Bibliographisches Institut, 1891);

Wilhelm Hauffs Werke, edited by Felix Bobertag, 5 volumes (Stuttgart: Union, deutsche Verlagsgesellschaft, 1891-1892);

Sämtliche Werke, edited by Carl Georg von Maassen, 5 volumes (Munich & Berlin: Paetel, 1923);

Werke, edited by Hermann Engelhardt, 2 volumes (Stuttgart: Cotta, 1961-1962);

Wilhelm Hauff (oil painting by Karl Leybold; Wilhelm Hauff, Werke, edited by Bernhard Zeller, 1969)

Hauffs Werke, edited by Leopold Magon, 2 volumes (Weimar: Volksverlag, 1962);

Werke, edited by Bernhard Zeller, 2 volumes (Frankfurt am Main: Insel, 1969);

Sämtliche Werke, edited by Sibylle von Steinsdorff, 3 volumes (Darmstadt: Wissenschaftliche Buchgesellschaft, 1970);

Sämtliche Märchen, edited by Steinsdorff (Munich: Deutscher Taschenbuch Verlag, 1979);

Märchen, edited by Jürgen Jahn (Berlin & Weimar: Aufbau, 1982);

Sämtliche Märchen, edited by Hans-Heino Ewers (Stuttgart: Reclam, 1986).

Editions in English: *Select Popular Tales: From the German,* translated anonymously (London:

Burns, 1845)–comprises "The Caravan," "The Cold Heart," "The Sheik of Alexandria and His Slaves," "The Legend of the Hirschgulden," and "The Portrait of the Emperor";

The Caravan: A Collection of Popular Tales, translated by George Pays Quackenbos (New York: Appleton, 1850);

Arabian Days' Entertainments, translated by Herbert Pelham Curtis (Boston: Phillips, Sampson, 1858);

Little Mook, and Other Fairy Tales, translated by P. E. Pinkerton (New York: Putnam's, 1881); republished as *Longnose the Dwarf and Other Fairy Tales* (London: Swan Sonnenschein, 1903)–comprises "Longnose, the Dwarf," "The History of Little Mook," "The Caliph Turned Stork," "The Adventures of Said," "The Stone-Cold Heart," and "The Story of the Silver Florin";

Tales of the Caravan, Inn, and Palace, translated by Edward L. Stowell (Chicago: Jansen, McClurg, 1881)–comprises "The Caravan," "The Inn in the Spessart," "The Sheik's Palace," "The Dwarf Nosey," "Little Muck," "The Marble Heart," "The Caliph Stork," "The Story of Almansor," "The Rescue of Fatima," "The False Prince," "The Hirschgulden," "Said's Adventures," "The Cave of Steenfoll," "Abner the Jew," "The Young Englishman," and "The Amputated Hand."

OTHER: *Kriegs- und Volks-Lieder*, edited by Hauff (Stuttgart: Metzler, 1824);

"Die Sängerin," in *Frauentaschenbuch für das Jahr 1827*, edited by Georg Döring (Nuremberg: Schrag, 1826);

Maehrchenalmanach für Söhne und Töchter gebildeter Stände auf das Jahr 1827, edited by Hauff (Stuttgart: Franckh, 1827)–includes Hauff's "Der Scheihk von Alessandrien und seine Sclaven," "Der Zwerg Nase," and "Abner der Jude, der nichts gesehen hat";

Maehrchenalmanach für Söhne und Töchter gebildeter Stände auf das Jahr 1828, edited by Hauff (Stuttgart: Franckh, 1828)–includes tales by Hauff;

"Das Bild des Kaisers" and "Erklärung der Kupfer," in *Taschenbuch für Damen: Auf das Jahr 1828* (Stuttgart: Cotta, 1828).

PERIODICAL PUBLICATIONS: "Freie Stunden am Fenster" and "Der ästhetische Klub," *Der Eremit in Deutschland*, 1, no. 4 (1826);

"Die Bettlerin vom Pont des Arts," 50 installments, *Morgenblatt*, nos. 276-325, November-December 1826; translated anonymously as *The True Lover's Fortune; or, The Beggar of the Pont des Arts* (Boston: Munroe, 1843); translated anonymously as *Josephine; or, The Beggar-Girl of the Pont-des-Arts* (London: Clarke, 1844);

"Die belletristischen Zeitschriften in Deutschland," 2 installments, *Blätter für literarische Unterhaltung*, nos. 18-19 (20 and 22 January 1827);

"Urtheil der Engländer über deutsche Sitten und Literatur," 2 installments, *Morgenblatt*, nos. 22-23, 26-27 January 1827;

"Korrespondenz," 2 installments, *Berliner Conversations-Blatt für Poesie, Literatur und Kritik*, 1 (15 and 17 February 1827);

"Jud Süss," 24 installments, *Morgenblatt*, nos. 157-163, 165-170, 172-182, 2-31 July 1827; translated by "B. T." as *The Jew Suss: A Tale of Stutgard, in 1737* (Philadelphia: Moore, 1845).

Today Wilhelm Hauff is not considered a major writer. When he is remembered, it is principally for his romantic historical novel *Lichtenstein: Romantische Sage aus der würtembergischen Geschichte* (Lichtenstein: Romantic Saga from the History of Württemberg, 1826; translated as *The Banished: A Swabian Historical Tale*, 1839) and for the picturesque castle near Reutlingen in his native Württemberg that the novel inspired. He is also known for his Märchen (fairy tales), which have retained their charm as fascinating and realistic stories set in his own world. Hauff's talent lay in his versatility, his ability to perceive the interests and moods of the reading public. In a society that valued conformity, Hauff followed literary convention; he was a "Modedichter" (fashionable writer), and a gifted one. In light of the critical enthusiasm for Hauff's writing which persisted through the middle of the nineteenth century, it is not surprising that all of his works were included in Josef Kürschner's *Deutscher Literatur-Kalender*. Even in the middle of the twentieth century he had not been forgotten. In 1965 Ernst Bloch, a writer and philosopher concerned with the hopes and dreams of modern man, praised as an example of a lost art in his *Literary Essays* Hauff's "geradezu authochthone märchenbildende Phantasie . . . in einer von echter Märchenbildung doch längst entfernten Zeit" (his absolutely autochthonous imagination in creating fairy tales in an age which is now very far removed from the creation of genuine fairy tales). Hauff's works continue to be republished separately and in collections. Critics now consider him a precursor of two literary trends: unlike most others of his day, he tended to focus on society as a whole as well as on individuals; he also introduced strong elements of realism into his works. Both of these literary directions became significant later in the century.

Wilhelm Hauff was born in Stuttgart on 29 November 1802, the second child of a governmental official, August Friedrich Hauff, and his wife, Hedwig Wilhelmine Elsässer Hauff. Hauff had an older brother, Hermann, and two younger sisters, Marie and Sophie. In 1806 the family moved to Tübingen, where Hauff's father served as a secretary at the royal Württemberg court of appeals until his premature death in 1809. Hauff, his mother, and siblings then resided with the maternal grandparents. In his grandfather's library Hauff read the ancient and modern classics and also Scottish and English novels by Tobias Smollett, Henry Fielding, and Oliver Goldsmith. During his pre-university years in Tübingen he immersed himself in tales of knights and robbers by Christian August Vulpius, Christian Heinrich Spiess, Karl Gottlieb Cramer, and Friedrich de la Motte Fouqué.

Hauff prepared for theological study in Tübingen in a tuition-free course of study at a monastery in the small town of Blaubeuren (1817-1820). For the extroverted young man, the insular seclusion was a "Jammertal" (vale of tears). Later, at the Tübinger Stift, the renowned Protestant theological college of Georg Wilhelm Friedrich Hegel, Friedrich Wilhelm Joseph von Schelling, Friedrich Hölderlin, and Eduard Mörike, Hauff took an active part in student life. He became an unofficial member of the most radical student fraternity, the "Feuerreiter" who frequently "rode into the fire" of political controversy. He became the fraternity poet and composed humorous verse, satires, and patriotic hymns sung at the Waterloo-Feste commemorating Napoleon's defeat. A student trip down the Rhine marked Hauff's first crossing of the border of his native Swabia and brought memorable experiences which would be reflected in his literary works, particularly in *Mittheilungen aus den Memoiren des Satan* (1826-1827; excerpts translated as *Memoirs of Beelzebub*, 1846).

In January 1824 Hauff went to Nördlingen to answer charges lodged by the Central Investigative Commission of Mainz against his fraternity's activities. While he was there he became acquainted with his cousin Luise Hauff. After a brief correspondence they became engaged in April, although for financial reasons they did not marry for almost three years. Frequently reprimanded for tardiness and improper dress, Hauff nevertheless remained in good standing at the university and received his doctorate in theology in September 1824. While he was a student he edited *Kriegs- und Volks-Lieder* (War and Folk Songs, 1824), an anthology of poetry which included two of his own folk songs, "Reiters Morgengesang" (Morning Song of the Rider) and "Soldatenliebe" (Soldier's Love). He also outlined a novel, *Der Mann im Mond* (The Man in the Moon, 1825), and a novella published in *Memoiren des Satans*, "Der Fluch" (The Curse).

Even as a student of theology it was apparent to Hauff that he preferred a literary career to the profession of clergyman, and in October 1824 he became the Hauslehrer (tutor) with the family of Ernst Eugen, Freiherr von Hügel, the president of the Württemberg Ministry of War. The atmosphere in this aristocratic household was stimulating for Hauff. In contrast to the simple and spartan life at the Tübinger Stift, he found there an environment open to the world, the atmosphere of the elegant salon, with witty conversation and refined literary tastes. During the time he lived with Eugen's family, Hauff was able to plan and complete many works. The summer of 1825, spent with the family in the Guttenberg castle on the Neckar River, provided the background for his last and most contemporary novella, set in the post-Napoleonic era, "Das Bild des Kaisers" (published in *Taschenbuch für Damen* [Pocket Book for Ladies, 1828], and translated as "The Portrait of the Emperor," 1845).

Hauff borrowed themes and techniques from Fouqué, Ludwig Tieck, and, especially, from E. T. A. Hoffmann, whose sense of ironic fantasy was similar to his own. Still he maintained, "Ich gehöre allen, ich gehöre mir selbst, aber keiner Schule gehöre ich an. Ich fühle keinen Herrn und Meister über mir . . . als die ewigen Gesetze des Guten und Schönen, denen ich, wenn auch auf unvollkommene Weise nachzustreben suche" (I belong to everyone, I belong to myself but to no literary school. I owe allegiance to no lord and master . . . except the eternal laws of the good and beautiful for which I strive, though it be in an imperfect way). Hauff did not follow any specific aesthetic theories in his short literary career. His goal was to develop

Front cover of Hauff's Märchenalmanach auf das Jahr 1827, *etching after a drawing by D. Fohr* (Wilhelm Hauff Werke)

a sophisticated style; his works were considered modern because of his strong orientation toward contemporary society.

Hauff's first major work, *Mittheilungen aus den Memoiren des Satan,* was written in August of 1825. Published anonymously, and with links to the satiric novel of the eighteenth century, this work parodies the wave of memoir literature that, through eyewitness accounts and individual self-portraits, was creating a panorama of the age. The persona Hauff adopts is that of Satan's editor. In the long narrative with which the work begins, the editor describes his chance meeting with the devil, who entrusts him with the publication of his memoirs. Hauff's book achieves a satiric effect by the complete lack of unanimity in perspective: Satan describes what he has seen, only to face the criticism and contradiction of the editor, who undergoes self-criticism; Satan is followed by other narrators who are themselves in disagreement. Satan appears in many guises, now as a conceited world traveler, now as a student among students, now as a transparent mask for Hauff himself. Satan does not bear the traditional mark of the spirit of evil but rather is the voice of a general disillusionment with the world. Hauff's satire is not harsh or biting but playful: he observes society with amusement and from a distance. His touch is light and skillful when he

is concerned with the familiar; for example, when he ridicules doltish professors and pious Teutonic students whose patriotism reaches emotional excess when they agitate for revolution. But in this work Hauff's satire of the unfamiliar often becomes exaggerated and distorted to the point of humorless caricature.

In Hauff's day the novelist Karl Heun of Berlin, writing under the pen name H. Clauren, had in rapid succession produced some forty sentimental novels, best-sellers among the masses. As a twenty-year-old student Hauff had written the outline of such a novel. In 1825 his friend and publisher Friedrich Franckh and the literary critic Wolfgang Menzel encouraged him to complete *Der Mann im Monde* and to publish it under Heun's pseudonym. The novel appeared later that year, under the title *Der Mann im Mond oder Der Zug des Herzens ist des Schicksals Stimme* (The Man in the Moon or The Tug of the Heart Is the Voice of Fate). Only in the last three chapters does it become clear that Hauff was writing a parody. He thus provided himself a literary defense and, beyond that, broadened his public to include sophisticated readers who would understand the parody. Heun, as Clauren, published a disclaimer in 1826 concerning his authorship of *Mann im Mond*. Hauff's *Controvers-Predigt über H. Clauren und den Mann im Monde* (Sermon on Controversy over H. Clauren and *The Man in the Moon*, 1827) followed, wherein he called on Germany's great writers by name to become his partners in the struggle against the literary and moral desolation with which H. Clauren "das ganze Land bedroht" (is threatening the whole nation). The virtuosity of Hauff's parody had a long-lasting, if negative, effect: his novel endured throughout the nineteenth century as a model for German literary kitsch.

Hauff wrote at a rapid pace. He published his texts without revision and worked on several simultaneously. Thus, in 1825, in addition to his *Memoiren des Satan* and *Der Mann im Mond,* Hauff began to write the works that he included in his "Maerchenalmanache" (fairy-tale almanacs). In the first, published in 1826, he prefaced his tales with a vignette recounting how the fairy tale, the daughter of fantasy, had gone out of fashion and become "eine alte Jungfer," an old maid no longer accorded respect. Now, however, in the new clothes and jewels of the almanac, she has returned to find refuge among children, who are always receptive to images of the magical world. Hauff's fairy tales, more than any of his other works, have retained their vitality and are his most-often-republished works. His "Märchen" differ from others in that they are blended with tales of worldly adventure; the wondrous element of the traditional tale is transformed into the sensational, linking the story to the rational world and giving it the accent of bourgeois morality. Thus do they approach realistic narrative. The fairy tales in each almanac are connected to form a narrative cycle with which the frame story merges, making its characters a part of the central action.

For the first almanac, Hauff chose an oriental theme in line with the fashionable charm of the distant, adventurous, and exotic. The second, for the year 1827, joins the occidental with the oriental and introduces contemporary European events. In the final almanac, for 1828, mysterious and ghostly events take place in a German environment inhabited by aristocrats, craftsmen, and students. Middle-class morality pervades these stories) which have little in common with the fairy tales of German Romanticism. From the first almanac to the third, the tales evolve from true Märchen (with the intervention of the supernatural) to Erzählungen, narratives which remain on the solid ground of everyday experience. The latter contain little symbolism, good and evil human beings replace their enchanted counterparts, and the characters' decisions are based strictly on moral consciousness, as in the small-town social satire "Der Mensch als Affe" (Man, the Monkey). Characteristic of Hauff's secularization of fairy tales is the conclusion, "Bürgerglück löst Märchenglück ab" (solutions must now be found in society rather than in the land of make-believe). Most of Hauff's narratives end happily, but dependence upon possessions, reputation, or power proves fateful.

On 1 December 1825, a little more than a year after assuming his position with Freiherr von Hügel, Hauff sent his publisher the first twelve chapters of his historical novel *Lichtenstein*. In a letter of 14 December to his school friend Moriz Pfaff, Hauff indicated that he was working on his novel "con amore," to the exclusion of all else. In his student days, he told Pfaff, a measure of vanity and self-confidence had given him the inner strength to succeed as a writer despite the criticism of fellow students of theology. He was also planning submissions to five newspapers and periodicals which had requested literary contributions. His pace did not slow. By March 1826 the second volume of *Lichtenstein* was in press, and he was at work on pieces for various journals:

ten book reviews for the literary page of Johann Friedrich Cotta's *Morgenblatt*, a novella for a ladies' magazine, several humorous sketches for a journal, as well as the outline for volume 2 of *Memoiren des Satan*. His contributions were providing good remuneration. Correspondence with his brother-in-law Christian Friedrich Klaiber, professor of aesthetics at the gymnasium in Stuttgart, brought the advice to broaden his horizon by travel through France, Holland, and northern Germany. Hauff resigned his post with Freiherr von Hügel to travel from 1 May to 30 November 1826. Before his departure he received an attractive offer from Cotta to revive the recently suspended *Damen-Almanach*. On 18 April the third and last volume of his historical novel was published; his publisher sent him twenty bottles of wine and six of champagne.

Lichtenstein is a work of history and legend in the manner of Sir Walter Scott. Hauff, whose aspiration it was to become the German Scott, immersed himself in the novels of the Scottish author and in the life and times of the subject of his novel, Ulrich, Herzog von Württemberg (1487-1550). Unfortunately, writes Hauff in his introduction, German readers of Scott, James Fenimore Cooper, and Washington Irving have a better knowledge of the Scottish highlands, the sources of the Susquehanna, and the picturesque heights around Boston than they have of their own countryside, history, and lore. Determined to offer a fascinating "romantische Sage," or legend, Hauff combed encyclopedias and read the travelogue by Gustav Schwab, *Die Neckarseite der Schwäbischen Alb* (The Neckar River Side of the Swabian Alps, 1823), as well as a work by Schwab on Ulrich's son, Duke Christoph, including the author's somewhat questionable historical documentation. These volumes, rather than standard histories, were his principal sources; recent investigation has shown that the "historical" information in his footnotes is often incorrect.

Hauff justified his own "legendary" historical portrait on the basis of the great public interest in this figure from the "dunkle Anfänge," or dark beginnings of the state of Württemberg. The rule of the historical Duke Ulrich was bloody and capricious. Hauff made Ulrich a creator of peace and harmony and a religious reformer who had founded the Tübinger Stift. Hauff's desire was to give dignity to Württemberg after it had become a subject state of Napoleon in his 1805 attempt to split up and destroy the Holy Roman Empire. In *Lichtenstein*

Hauff's grave in the Hoppelau cemetery in Stuttgart (Wilhelm Hauff Werke)

Hauff imbued Ulrich with the qualities of an ideal king: honesty, fidelity, firmness, justice, and a readiness to struggle for the right. In Ulrich's situation he saw a sixteenth-century parallel to the recent time of Napoleonic control, and many of his characters were, as one critic put it, "Bürger in Ritterrüstung" (everyday nineteenth-century types decked out in chivalric armor). The ideal picture of Ulrich's achievements in the past reflected the political hopes and expectations of the post-Napoleonic present.

The fifteenth-century Lichtenstein fortress, which historical documents indicate was visited by Ulrich, figures prominently in the novel. Fifteen years after Hauff's death, *Lichtenstein* inspired the construction on that height of a picturesque castle, which remains a popular tourist attraction. Hauff's novel was well written and well received. According to Menzel, the reader progresses from page to page as if walking on soft grass, without encountering the sharp edges of metaphor, antithesis, and other figures of speech, just as the manner of Sir Walter Scott requires. Following Scott, chapters are headed by

verse mottos (from Ludwig Uhland, Friedrich von Schiller, Walther von der Vogelweide, Christoph Martin Wieland, and William Shakespeare).

On the whole Hauff's novellas are inferior to his "Märchen" and tend to be typical examples of this form in his day. In them he strives for the attraction of the unusual, and one of his frequent themes is the enigmatic course of fate. In "Othello" (1825) Hauff demonstrates an ability for psychological analysis in the story of the continuing puzzling effects of a curse resulting from an aristocrat's betrayal of his beloved many years before. Hauff also presents a psychological portrait in his "Die Bettlerin vom Pont des Arts" (1826; translated as *The True Lover's Fortune; or, the Beggar of the Pont des Arts*, 1843). Full of chance occurrences and complications, this unusual story of a family shows the influence of Ludwig Tieck in its settings on the Rhine River estates and in Stuttgart and Paris. (Hauff admired Tieck and had visited him in Dresden at the end of his European travels.) In "Jud Süss" (1827; translated as *The Jew Suss: A Tale of Stutgard, in 1737*, 1845) Hauff portrays a historical figure of seventeenth-century Württemberg, Joseph Süß-Oppenheimer, the much-hated and feared minister of finance, in his final days of power. The motif of the detrimental effect of money and possessions offered an opportunity for caricature, which the author avoided. Instead, his portrayal is enriched by psychological nuances so that, in spite of the dark side of the man's character, the reader becomes aware of a certain element of greatness. (Hauff's depiction is romantic by comparison with Lion Feuchtwanger's portrayal in his novel *Jud Süss*, published in 1918).

Stylistically, Hauff's best novella is *Phantasien im Bremer Ratskeller* (1827; translated as *The Wine-Ghosts of Bremen*, 1889), his last work published before his death. In this masterly tale he mixes fairy-tale atmosphere and historical reality in a nostalgic look at the past and, at the same time, a critical evaluation of the present. In the cellar restaurant of the town hall the spirits of long-deceased patrons appear and join the living. Their presence gives the author an opportunity to criticize the political status quo in a work considered by many to be his most mature and independent.

In December 1826 Hauff was back in Stuttgart after eight months of travel. In hand were a half dozen offers to serve as editor of newspapers and periodicals, and in January he became editor of Cotta's *Morgenblatt*. In February he married Luise Hauff and continued to work at an almost frantic pace, disregarding warnings that his many activities were taking a toll on his health. He went into the field to do research for a planned historical novel on the Tyrolean freedom fighter Andreas Hofer. In September he began to complain of lack of appetite and by October was suffering from "Nervenfieber" (nerve fever). Bloodletting did not help him, and his condition grew steadily worse, possibly developing into encephalitis. On 10 November Hauff's first child was born, and on the morning of the eighteenth he asked that chairs be brought into his room and that the "Compagnie," his group of friends from student days, be assembled. He died that afternoon at the age of twenty-four.

References:

Sabine Beckmann, *Wilhelm Hauffs Märchenalmanache als zyklische Kompositionen* (Bonn: Bouvier, 1976);

Klaus L. Berghahn, "Der Zug des Herzens ist des Schicksals Stimme: Beobachtungen zur Clauren-Hauff-Kontroverse," *Monatshefte*, 69 (1977): 58-65;

Barbara Inge Czygan, "Wilhelm Hauff: The Writer and his Work as Seen through his Correspondences," Ph.D. dissertation, University of Wisconsin-Madison, 1976;

J. F. Haussmann, "E. T. A. Hoffmanns Einfluß auf Wilhelm Hauff," *Journal of English and Germanic Philology*, 16 (1917): 53-66;

Jörg Hienger, "Die Domestizierung des Unheimlichen: Romantische Schauerphantastik und ihr Funktionswandel in den Märchenalmanachen Wilhelm Hauffs," *Fragmente*, 11 (1984): 30-43;

Otto Hinz, *Wilhelm Hauff mit Selbstzeugnissen und Bilddokumenten* (Hamburg: Rowohlt, 1989);

Hans Hofmann, *Wilhelm Hauff: Eine nach den Quellen bearbeitete Darstellung seines Werdegangs* (Frankfurt am Main: Diesterweg, 1902);

Dorothea Hollstein, "Dreimal 'Jud Süss': Zeugnisse 'schmählichster Barbarei.' Hauffs Novelle, Feuchtwangers Roman und Harlans Film in vergleichender Betrachtung," *Der Deutschunterricht* (Stuttgart), 37, no. 3 (1985): 42-54;

H. H. Houben, "Wer im Glashaus sitzt . . . Eine Schmutz- und Schundgeschichte," *Preussische Jahrbücher*, 231 (1933): 69-79;

Hans-Wolf Jäger, "Ein Schwabe in Bremen: Zu Wilhelm Hauffs *Phantasien im Bremer Ratskeller*," *Bremisches Jahrbuch*, 64 (1986): 150-157;

Günther Koch, "Clarens Einfluß auf Wilhelm Hauff," *Euphorion*, 4 (1897): 804-812;

Tilman Krömer, "Die Handschriften des Schiller-Nationalmuseums. Teil 8: Die Nachlässe Hauff-Kölle und Wilhelm Hauff," *Jahrbuch der deutschen Schillergesellschaft*, 9 (1965): 593-632;

Heinrich Löwenthal, "*Der Mann im Mond*," *Sinn und Form*, 4 (1952): 151-158;

Fritz Martini, "Wilhelm Hauff," in *Deutsche Dichter der Romantik*, edited by Benno von Wiese (Berlin: Schmidt, 1983), pp. 532-562;

Irmgard Otto, "Das Bild der Dichterpersönlichkeit Wilhelm Hauff und das Bild des Menschen in seinen Werken," Ph.D. dissertation, University of Munich, 1967;

Friedrich Pfäfflin, *Wilhelm Hauff: Der Verfasser des "Lichtenstein." Chronik seines Lebens und Werkes* (Stuttgart: Fleischhauer & Spohn, 1981);

Walter A. Reichart, "Washington Irving's Influence on German Literature," *Modern Language Review*, 52 (1957): 537-553;

Klaus Rek, "Autor und literarischer Markt: Zur Stellung Wilhelm Hauffs im literarischen Leben der 20er Jahre des 19. Jahrhunderts," Ph.D. dissertation, University of Leipzig, 1985;

Christoph E. Schweitzer, "Ein ungedruckter Brief Wilhelm Hauffs," *Germanic Review,* 48 (1973): 243-246;

Edwin Sommermeyer, *Wilhelm Hauffs "Memoiren des Satan," nebst einem Beitrag zur Beurteilung Goethes in den 20er Jahren des 19. Jahrhunderts* (Berlin: Ebering, 1932);

Eugen Teucher, "Sprachliche Vergleichung zweier literarischer Werke über den gleichen Gegenstand," *Sprachspiegel,* 35 (1979): 2-3;

Teucher, "Sprachlich-literarische Wanderungen in die Vergangenheit, 4: Die Welt der Hauff'-schen *Novellen,*" *Sprachspiegel,* 41 (1985): 79-81;

J. Wesley Thomas, "Paul Bunyan and Holländer Michel," *Journal of American Folklore,* 65 (1952): 305-306;

Garrett W. Thompson, "Wilhelm Hauff's Specific Relation to Walter Scott," *PMLA,* 26 (1911): 549-593;

Heinrich Tidemann, *Wilhelm Hauff in Bremen: Die Entstehung der "Phantasien im Bremer Ratskeller"* (Bremen: Schünemann, 1929).

Papers:

Wilhelm Hauff's papers are in the Deutsches Literatur-Archiv in the Schiller Nationalmuseum, Marbach, West Germany.

Johann Peter Hebel
(10 May 1760-22 September 1826)

John L. Hibberd
University of Bristol

BOOKS: *Etwas über die Bevestigung des Glaubens an die göttliche Wahrheit und Güte bey den Schicksalen unglücklicher Gottesverehrer und Menschenfreunde* (Karlsruhe: Macklot, 1795);

Allemannische Gedichte: Für Freunde ländlicher Natur und Sitten, anonymous (Karlsruhe: Macklot, 1803; revised as Hebel, 1805; enlarged edition, Aarau: Sauerländer, 1820); translated by Mrs. Alice Howland Goodwin as *Rhymes from the Rhineland* (Boston: Sherman, French, 1913);

Schatzkästlein des rheinischen Hausfreundes (Tübingen: Cotta, 1811); selections translated by Robert Pick in *German Stories and Tales* (New York: Knopf, 1954); selections translated by Clavia Goodman and Bayard Quincy Morgan in *Francesca and Other Stories* (Lexington, Ky.: Anvil Press, 1957);

Biblische Geschichten, für die Jugend bearbeitet, 2 volumes (Stuttgart & Tübingen: Cotta, 1824); translated by Emily Anderson as *Hebel's Bible Stories* (London: Barrie & Rockcliff, 1961);

Christlicher Katechismus: Aus den hinterlassenen Papieren herausgegeben (Karlsruhe: Müller, 1828);

J. P. Hebels sämmtliche Werke, 8 volumes (Karlsruhe: Müller, 1832-1834);

Aus Joh. Peter Hebel's ungedruckten Papieren: Nachträge zu seinen Werken, Beiträge zu seiner Charakteristik, edited by Georg Längin (Tauberbischofsheim: Land, 1882).

OTHER: *Der Rheinländische Hausfreund oder: Neuer Kalender auf das Schaltjahr 1808 mit lehrreichen Nachrichten und lustigen Erzählungen,* edited, with contributions, by Hebel (Karlsruhe: Verlag des großherzoglichen Gymnasiums, 1808);

Der Rheinländische Hausfreund oder: Neuer Kalender auf das Schaltjahr 1809 mit lehrreichen Nachrichten und lustigen Erzählungen, edited, with contributions, by Hebel (Karlsruhe: Verlag des großherzoglichen Gymnasiums, 1809);

Johann Peter Hebel in 1809 (painting by Philipp Jakob Becker)

Der Rheinländische Hausfreund oder: Neuer Kalender auf das Schaltjahr 1810 mit lehrreichen Nachrichten und lustigen Erzählungen, edited, with contributions, by Hebel (Karlsruhe: Verlag des großherzoglichen Gymnasiums, 1810);

Der Rheinländische Hausfreund oder: Neuer Kalender auf das Schaltjahr 1811 mit lehrreichen Nachrichten und lustigen Erzählungen, edited, with contributions, by Hebel (Karlsruhe: Verlag des großherzoglichen Gymnasiums, 1811);

Rheinischer Hausfreund oder: Allerley Neues zu Spaß und Ernst. Kalender auf 1813, edited, with contributions, by Hebel (Lahr & Pforzheim: Geiger & Katz, 1813);

Rheinischer Hausfreund oder: Allerley Neues zu Spaß und Ernst. Kalender auf 1814, edited, with contributions, by Hebel (Lahr & Pforzheim: Geiger & Katz, 1814);

Rheinischer Hausfreund oder: Allerley Neues zu Spaß und Ernst. Kalender auf 1815, edited, with contributions, by Hebel (Lahr & Pforzheim: Geiger & Katz, 1815);

Rheinischer Hausfreund oder: Allerley Neues zu Spaß und Ernst. Kalender auf 1819, edited, with contributions, by Hebel (Lahr & Pforzheim: Geiger & Katz, 1819).

Johann Peter Hebel, a schoolmaster and churchman, scarcely saw himself as a born poet or writer of genius and stood aside from German Classicism and Romanticism, the literary movements of his time. Yet Goethe's admiration for his *Allemannische Gedichte* (Alemannic Poems, 1803; translated as *Rhymes from the Rhineland,* 1913) as the product of an imagination delightfully uncorrupted by modern civilization set the seal on the reputation Hebel earned as Germany's greatest dialect poet. In the southwest corner of Germany, Switzerland, and Alsace, where Alemannic is spoken, he is treasured as Robert Burns is by the Scots. Yet any reader familiar with standard German has little difficulty in understanding and appreciating his poetry. Hebel won equal fame as a prose writer. His short tales in *Schatzkästlein des rheinischen Hausfreundes* (Treasury of the Rhinelanders' Family Friend, 1811) became popular classics throughout Germany and were well known in prerevolutionary Russia too. They proved eminently suitable as reading matter for the young. Unpretentious in style, they have tended to be passed over by literary scholars as unproblematic works for simple minds, scarcely needing detailed examination. Hebel's secure faith in God and humanity and his paternalism may now seem to belong firmly to the past. Yet the best of his tales are not easily forgotten. There is art in their simplicity, brevity, clarity, and concreteness and also a solid wisdom which has not failed to appeal to modern minds tired of complexity.

Hebel rose from humble origins. His father, Johann Jakob Hebel, trained as a weaver before leaving Germany to enter the service of a Swiss patrician who, as a major in the French army, took him as batman on his campaigns. Hebel's mother, Ursula Oertlin Hebel, came from German peasant stock and was a maid in Basel to the same Swiss family that employed her husband. Hebel was born in Basel on 10 May 1760, and his earliest years were divided between that Swiss town and his mother's village in the Wiese valley just across the Rhine in the margravate of Baden. His father and infant sister died in 1761, his pious mother in 1773. Her ambition for her son, and Hebel's own, was a career in the Lutheran church. His parents' employers had set aside money for his education. The orphan was sent to the leading school in Karlsruhe, the capital of Baden. He arrived there in 1774, after four days en route from the Wiese valley, sporting his first pair of shoes. In 1778 he progressed to Erlangen University to study theology. There he joined a dueling club, kept a dog as his constant companion, and was never seen without his pipe. In 1780 he qualified for the ministry but was not offered a parish. Then followed ten years as a poor teacher, once more in the countryside that he loved and knew best, first as tutor to a rural vicar's children, then in a school in the largest town in the Wiese valley (Lörrach, seventeen hundred inhabitants). There he met his lifelong friends, Tobias Günttert, his senior colleague in the school, the young clergyman Friedrich Wilhelm Hitzig, and Günttert's sister-in-law, Gustave Fecht. Why he did not marry Gustave Fecht later, when he could afford to do so remains a minor mystery. With Hitzig he indulged in a semiserious, semijocular cult of Proteus as the spirit of the perpetual mutability of the physical world. Hebel's Christian faith was profound but liberal. He could sympathize with the polytheism that sees nature full of spirits. For the rest of his life, during his long "exile" in Karlsruhe, he regarded these years in the Wiese valley and the mountains of the Black Forest as his happiest. For in 1791 he was appointed to teach in his old school in Karlsruhe, and as subdeacon he gave monthly sermons before the margrave's court.

It was in this provincial capital, which he instinctively regarded as a foreign place, that Hebel wrote his *Allemannische Gedichte.* By writing his poems in the local dialect he hoped to persuade others that the dialect was not a deformed version of standard German, but a language with its own merits and a distinguished pedigree. He noted that, according to linguistic experts of his time, it shared the name Alemannic with the language of the great medieval German poets, the Minnesänger. He succeeded in his aim of "ennobling" it, putting it to edifying purpose, revealing

Statue of Hebel in Lörrach, erected in 1910

its inherent "poetry," molding it into folk-song-like strophes, blank verse, and classical hexameters. The dialect gave a vigor and freshness to his poems and enabled him to escape the conventions of idyllic verse. Foremost among his models was Theocritus. But his collection is varied (nature poetry, songs, dialogues, a frightening ballad, and reflections on death), and his great inspiration was his own feeling for his homeland.

His loving imagination transfigured the landscape and its people, but in Hebel's verse the Wiese valley remains a real, localized area, no ideal Arcadia. Hebel anthropomorphizes all nature. The river Wiese becomes a Black Forest girl who falls into the arms of the handsome Rhine. He invents his own mythology. He writes as if with the mind of the region's peasant inhabitants. It is doubtful that many of them read the poems when they appeared in 1803, for they had never seen their dialect written down; but in the course of time some of his poems became as familiar to them as the Bible or their folk songs. Hebel found a public among educated Alemannic speakers–and among Germans from other

areas too, for whom he provided brief notes on grammar, vocabulary, and pronunciation.

He wished to nourish his readers' feeling for nature, their moral sense, and religious faith. He bent local superstitions (ghosts, will-o'-the-wisps) to fit an optimistic Christian framework. Because his convictions were so secure his didacticism was never aggressive and he could allow himself a playful tone and a sense of humor. In "Die Vergänglichkeit" (Sic transit), one of the greatest poems on mortality in any language, in which Hebel draws on his memories of his mother's death, a father tells his son, simply and soberly, that all men must age and die, but that those who act as conscience dictates will rise from the dead and be taken to the better homeland in the skies. Here we are far from the farce for which dialect was traditionally held to be the appropriate medium.

In the early 1800s it became clear that the Lutheran almanac which was published by Hebel's school needed a change of image. The rural population of Baden, its intended audience, would not buy it. Hebel suggested improvements and was told to take the task in hand. Already, from 1803 on, he had written pieces for it. Beginning in 1808 he edited and wrote most of *Der Rheinländische Hausfreund* (The Rhinelander's Family Friend). Hebel was responsible for the volume for the years from 1808 to 1811, 1813 to 1815, and again in 1819. (After 1813, the almanac was titled *Rheinischer Hausfreund* [Rhenish Family Friend].) He gave new life to this organ for the instruction and improvement of the people. His broad knowledge (he taught arts and sciences), his gift for clear and simple presentation of facts and arguments, and his familiarity with the mentality of the common man stood him in good stead. The almanac became a great success, even beyond the borders of Baden. Hebel assumed an intimacy with the reader to whom he presented riddles and mathematical problems, gave the last year's news, explained the workings of nature and the universe, and told of exemplary deeds, sensational events, catastrophes, and comic pranks. The heroes of his anecdotes range from Napoleon and the Emperor Joseph to the common soldier, servants, Jews, a ne'er-do-well, and a trio of good-natured rogues. Hebel acclaims fairness and generosity shown by those in positions of power or authority, but his sympathies lie with the little man. He deals with the intellectual and moral challenges of everyday life. He encourages his readers to think for themselves. The tales are mostly not of his invention, but such was his skill as a storyteller that he was able to transform even the most unpromising material and bring out its essential interest. He adopted a style close to ordinary speech. At the suggestion of the leading publisher, Johann Friedrich Cotta, many of these pieces were collected in one volume in 1811. Hebel revised them, removing traces of dialect but making certain to hold to his essential principle of variety–instruction mixed with entertainment. The collection has been republished in whole or part many times. Hebel's art of using a brief story to make a particular point to a particular public was emulated by Bertolt Brecht in his *Kalendergeschichten* (1948; translated as *Tales from the Calendar*, 1961). Hebel practiced the same art in rewriting for children selected stories from the Bible (*Biblische Geschichten*, 1824; translated as *Hebel's Bible Stories*, 1961). As he intended, they were used in Baden schools, until 1855 when his approach was judged to be too rational.

In 1808 Hebel had become headmaster of his school. By all accounts he was an outstanding teacher. His reputation as an excellent preacher and his administrative ability secured his steady advance within the church. In 1819 he became prelate in Baden, which was now, because of Napoleon, a grand duchy. The union of the two Protestant churches in Baden was accomplished under his direction. As a church leader he was a member of the upper house of the state Diet, where he cooperated with a liberal Catholic aristocrat in furthering state support for charitable institutions. He opposed the introduction of rigid censorship laws. He was the loyal servant of a relatively liberal state (serfdom was abolished in Baden in 1783, the Jews emancipated in 1809). He was no stuffed shirt: he enjoyed convivial evenings in a hostelry, lost his heart to an actress, and remained a somewhat eccentric bachelor who kept an owl and a frog as pets. He died 22 September 1826 on official duty, en route to conduct examinations in Heidelberg.

Hebel lived at a time of great historical events. He saw the Baden government leave Karlsruhe in 1793 under the threat of French invasion; the French revolutionary army retreat across the Rhine in 1796; Baden take sides with Napoleon; the end of the (German) Holy Roman Empire; the defeat of Napoleon; and the restoration of Germany. A powerless citizen of a powerless state, Hebel, with his eye on social cohesion and on eternal life, judged that it was proper to trust in God, do one's immediate duty, and bend a little with the wind when necessary. His political detachment has not recommended him to all modern critics, but the central challenge for admirers of his poems and stories remains (as Martin Heidegger recognized) that of describing and explaining their particular magic.

Letters:
Johann Peter Hebel's Briefe, edited by Wilhelm Zentner (Karlsruhe: Müller, 1938; enlarged, 2 volumes, 1957).

Biographies:
Wilhelm Altwegg, *Johann Peter Hebel* (Frauenfeld: Huber, 1935);

Wilhelm Zentner, *Johann Peter Hebel* (Karlsruhe: Müller, 1965);

Ulrich Däster, *Johann Peter Hebel in Selbstzeugnissen und Bilddokumenten* (Reinbek: Rowohlt, 1973).

References:
Walter Benjamin, "Zu J. P. Hebels 100. Geburtstag," in his *Gesammelte Schriften,* volume 2 (Frankfurt am Main: Suhrkamp, 1977);

Ernst Bloch, "Hebel, Gotthelf und bäurisches Tao," in his *Werke,* volume 9 (Frankfurt am Main: Suhrkamp, 1965);

Renate Böschenstein, *Idylle* (Stuttgart: Metzler, 1967);

Robert Feger, *Annäherung an einen Prälaten: Fragestellungen zu Leben und Werk von Johann Peter Hebel* (Lahr: Schauenburg, 1983);

Leonard Forster, "Johann Peter Hebel und 'Die Vergänglichkeit,'" *German Life and Letters,* new series 29 (October 1975): 59-71;

Martin Heidegger, *Hebel–der Hausfreund* (Pfullingen: Neske, 1957);

Theodore Heuss and others, *Über Johann Peter Hebel* (Tübingen: Wunderlich, 1964);

John L. Hibberd, "J. P. Hebel's 'Allemannische Gedichte' and the Idyllic Tradition," *Forum for Modern Language Studies,* 8 (July 1972): 243-260;

Georg Hirtsheifer, *Ordnung und Recht in der Dichtung Johann Peter Hebels* (Bonn: Bouvier, 1968);

Jan Knopf, *Geschichten zur Geschichte: Kritische Tradition des "Volkstümlichen" in den Kalendergeschichten Hebels und Brechts* (Stuttgart: Metzler, 1973);

Rolf Max Kully, *Johann Peter Hebel* (Stuttgart: Metzler, 1969);

Susi Löffler, *Johann Peter Hebel* (Frauenfeld: Huber, 1944);

Maria Lypp, " 'Der geneigte Leser versteht's': Zu J. P. Hebels Kalendergeschichten," *Euphorion*, 64 (December 1970): 385-398;

Charles Philip Magill, "Pure and Applied Art: A Note on Johann Peter Hebel," *German Life and Letters*, new series 10 (1956-1957): 183-188;

Robert Minder, "Hebel und die französische Heimatliteratur" and "Heidegger und Hebel," in his *Dichter in der Gesellschaft* (Frankfurt am Main: Suhrkamp, 1966);

Walter Muschg, "Gottfried Keller und Johann Peter Hebel," *Schweizer Monatshefte*, 20 (1940-1941);

Hans-Gerhart Oeftering, *Naturgefühl und Naturgestaltung bei den alemannischen Dichtern von Beat L. Muralt bis Jeremias Gotthelf: Mit Erstdruck des Hymnus 'Ekstase' von Johann Peter Hebel* (Berlin: Ebering, 1940);

Ludwig Rohner, *Kalendergeschichte und Kalender* (Wiesbaden: Athenaion, 1978);

Rohner, *Kommentarband zum Faksimiledruck der Jahrgänge 1808-15 und 1819 des "Rheinischen Hausfreunds" von Johann Peter Hebel* (Wiesbaden: Athenaion, 1981);

Hans Trümpy, "Volkstümliches und Literarisches bei J. P. Hebel," *Wirkendes Wort*, 20 (January-February 1970): 1-19;

Hanns Uhl, ed., *Hebeldank: Bekenntnis zum alemannischen Geist* (Freiburg im Breisgau: Rombach, 1964).

Papers:

Johann Peter Hebel's papers are in the Badische Landesbibliothek, Karlsruhe.

Georg Wilhelm Friedrich Hegel

(27 August 1770-14 November 1831)

Otto W. Johnston
University of Florida

BOOKS: *Vertrauliche Briefe über das vormalige staats-rechtliche Verhältnis des Waadtlandes zur Stadt Bern: Aus dem Franz. eines verstorbenen Schweizers* (Frankfurt am Main: Ostern, 1798);

Differenz des Fichte'schen und Schelling'schen Systems der Philosophie, in Beziehung auf Reinholds Beiträge zur leichteren Übersicht des Zustandes der Philosophie zu Anfang des neunzehnten Jahrhunderts (Jena: Akademische Buchhandlung, 1801); translated by H. S. Harris and Walter Cerf as *The Difference between Fichte's and Schelling's System of Philosophy* (Albany: State University of New York Press, 1977);

Dissertationi philosophicae de orbitis planetarum praemissae these . . . Publice defendet die XXVII. August a MDCCCI (Jena: Praeger, 1801);

System der Wissenschaft: 1. Theil. Die Phänomenologie des Geistes (Bamberg & Würzburg: Goebhardt, 1807); translated by J. B. Baillie as *The Phenomenology of Mind,* 2 volumes (London: Sonnenschein/New York: Macmillan, 1910; revised edition, 1 volume, London: Allen & Unwin/New York: Macmillan, 1931); translated by A. V. Miller as *Phenomenology of Spirit* (Oxford: Clarendon Press, 1977);

Wissenschaft der Logik, 3 volumes (Nuremberg: Schrag, 1812-1816)–comprises volume 1, *Die objektive Logik, 1: Die Lehre vom Sein;* volume 2, *Die objektive Logik, 2: Die Lehre vom Wesen;* volume 3, *Die Subjektive Logik oder die Lehre vom Begriff;* translated by W. H. Johnston and L. G. Struthers as *Hegel's Science of Logic,* 2 volumes (London: Allen & Unwin, 1929; New York: Macmillan, 1961);

Encyklopädie der philosophischen Wissenschaften im Grundrisse. Theil 1: Die Logik (Heidelberg: Oßwald, 1817; enlarged, 1827; revised, 1830); translated by Wallace as *The Logic of Hegel: Translated from the Encyclopaedia of the Philosophical Sciences* (Oxford: Clarendon Press, 1874);

Beurtheilung der im Druck erschienenen Verhandlungen der in der Versammlung der Landstände des

Georg Wilhelm Friedrich Hegel (etching by Bollinger after a painting by Xeller)

Königreichs Würtemberg in Jahre 1815 und 1816 (Heidelberg: Mohr, 1818);

Grundlinien der Philosophie des Rechts, oder Naturrecht und Staatswissenschaft im Grundrisse (Berlin: Nicolai, 1820); translated by S. W. Dyde as *Philosophy of Right* (London: Bell, 1896); translated by Jacob Loewenberg as "The Philosophy of Law," in *German Classics of the 19th and 20th Centuries,* edited by Kuno Francke and W. G. Howard, volume 7 (New York: German Publications Society, 1914); translated by T. M. Knox as *Hegel's Philoso-*

phy of Right (Oxford: Clarendon Press, 1942);

Oratio in sacris saecularibus tertiis traditae confessionis Augustanae ab Universitate regia Friderica Guilelma Berolinensi die XXV. m. Iunii a. MDCCCXXX rite peractis habita a Georgio Guilelmo Friderico Hegel (Berlin & Stettin: Nicolai, 1830);

Werke: Vollständige Ausgabe durch einen Verein von Freunden des Verewigten, edited by Philipp Marheineke and others, 23 volumes (Berlin & Leipzig: Duncker & Humblot, 1832-1887)–comprises volume 1, *Philosophische Abhandlungen,* edited by Karl Ludwig Michelet; volume 2, *Phänomenologie des Geistes,* edited by Johannes Schultz; volumes 3-5, *Wissenschaft der Logik,* edited by Leopold von Henning; volume 6, *Encyklopädie der philosophischen Wissenschaften im Grundrisse und zwar der Encyklopädie erster Teil, die Logik,* edited by Henning; volume 7, part 1, *Vorlesungen über die Naturphilosophie als der Encyklopädie zweiter Theil,* edited by Michelet; translated by Michael John Petry as *Hegel's Philosophy of Nature,* 3 volumes (London: Allen & Unwin/ New York: Humanities Press, 1970); volume 7, part 2, *Der Encyklopädie dritter Teil: Die Philosophie des Geistes,* edited by Ludwig Boumann; translated by William Wallace as *Hegel's Philosophy of Mind* (Oxford: Clarendon Press, 1894); volume 8, *Grundlinien der Philosophie des Rechts oder Naturrecht und Staatswissenschaft im Grundrisse,* edited by Eduard Gans; volume 9, *Vorlesungen über die Philosophie der Geschichte,* edited by Gans; translated by J. Sibree as *Lectures on the Philosophy of History* (London: Bohn, 1857); translation revised as *The Philosophy of History* (New York: Colonial Press, 1899); volume 10, *Vorlesungen über die Aesthetik,* edited by Heinrich Gustav Hotho, 3 volumes; translated by F. P. B. Osmaston as *The Philosophy of Fine Art,* 4 volumes (London: Bell, 1920; New York: Harcourt, 1921); volumes 11-12, *Vorlesungen über die Philosophie der Religion, nebst einer Schrift über die Beweise vom Dasein Gottes,* edited by Marheineke; translated by E. B. Speirs and J. Burdon Sanderson as *Lectures on the Philosophy of Religion: Together with a Work on the Proofs of the Existence of God,* 3 volumes (New York: Humanities Press, 1962); volumes 13-15, *Vorlesungen über die Geschichte der Philosophie,* edited by Michelet (1833-1836; revised, 1840-1844); translated

by Elizabeth S. Haldane and Frances H. Simson as *Lectures on the History of Philosophy,* 3 volumes (London: Kegan Paul, Trench, Trübner, 1892-1896; New York: Humanities Press, 1955); volumes 16-17, *Vermischte Schriften,* edited by Friedrich Förster and Ludwig Boumann; volume 18, *Philosophische Propädeutik,* edited by Karl Rosenkranz; volume 19, *Briefe von und an Hegel,* edited by Karl Hegel, 2 volumes;

Kritik der Verfassung Deutschlands: Aus dem handschriftlichen Nachlasse, edited by Georg Mollat (Cassel: Fischer, 1893);

Hegel-Nachlaß II: System der Sittlichkeit aus dem Nachlasse, edited by Mollat (Osterwieck: Zieckfeldt, 1893);

Das Leben Jesu: Harmonie der Evangelien nach eigener Übersetzung. Nach der ungedruckten Handschrift in ungekürzter Form, edited by Paul Roques (Jena: Diederichs, 1906);

Hegels theologische Jugendschriften nach den Handschriften der Kgl. Bibliothek in Berlin, edited by Herman Nohl (Tübingen: Mohr, 1907); translated by Knox as *Early Theological Writings* (Chicago: University of Chicago Press, 1948; London: Cambridge University Press, 1949);

Sämtliche Werke, edited by Georg Lasson, 24 volumes (Leipzig: Meiner, 1907-1940);

Hegels erstes System: Nach den Handschriften der Königlichen Bibliothek in Berlin im Auftrage der Heidelberger Akademie der Wissenschaften, edited by Hans Ehrenberg and Herbert Link (Heidelberg: Winter, 1915);

Sämtliche Werke: Jubiläumsausgabe. Auf Grund des von Ludwig Boumann, Friedrich Förster, Eduard Gans, Karl Hegel, Leopold von Henning, Heinrich Gustav Hotho, Philipp Marheineke, Karl Ludwig Michelet, Karl Rosenkranz und Johannes Schulze besorgten Originaldrucks im Faksimileverfahren, edited by Hermann Glockner, 26 volumes (Stuttgart: Frommann, 1927-1940);

Sämtliche Werke: Neue kritische Ausgabe, edited by Johannes Hoffmeister, 8 volumes (Hamburg: Meiner, 1952-1960);

Gesammelte Werke: In Verbindung mit der Deutschen Forschungsgemeinschaft herausgegeben von der Rheinisch-Westfälischen Akademie der Wissenschaften, 12 volumes to date (Hamburg: Meiner, 1968-);

Vorlesungen über Rechtsphilosophie, 1818-1831, edited by Karl-Heinz Ilting, 4 volumes (Stuttgart-Bad Cannstatt: Frommann-Holzboog, 1972-1974);

Vorlesungen über Platon 1825-1826: Unveröffentlicher Text, edited by Jean-Louis Vieillard-Baron (Frankfurt am Main: Ullstein, 1979).

OTHER: Hermann Friedrich Wilhelm Hinrichs, *Religion im inneren Verhältnis zur Wissenschaft,* foreword by Hegel (Heidelberg: Groos, 1822).

PERIODICAL PUBLICATIONS: "Glauben und Wissen: Die Reflexionsphilosophie der Subjektivität in der Vollständigkeit ihrer Formen als kantische, jacobische und fichtesche Philosophie," *Kritisches Journal der Philosophie,* 2, no. 1 (1802): 1-188;
"Über die wissenschaftlichen Behandlungsarten des Naturrechts, seine Stelle in der praktischen Philosophie und sein Verhältnis zu den positiven Rechtswissenschaften," 2 installments, *Kritisches Journal der Philosophie,* 2, no. 2 (1802): 1-88; no. 3 (1802): 1-34;
"Verhandlungen in der Versammlung der Landstände des Königreichs Württemberg im Jahre 1815 und 1816," 8 installments, *Heidelbergische Jahrbücher der Literatur,* 10, nos. 66, 67, 68, 73, 74, 75, 76, 77 (1817);
"Über die englische Reformbill," 4 installments, *Allgemeine preußische Staatszeitung,* nos. 115-118 (1831).

Georg Wilhelm Friedrich Hegel was the last of the great German Idealist philosophers. He perfected the dialectical method, which, in his philosophy, is not only a way of thinking but also the process by which reality evolves. The harmonious integration of the parts of reality into the whole is achieved in three stages: the thesis provokes an antithesis; out of the latter emerges a synthesis, representing a higher and more comprehensive level than the first two stages. Having developed by preserving some aspects of an existing circumstance and reacting against others, this higher synthesis becomes a new thesis which produces another antithesis, and the process begins anew. The human mind operates in the same manner: logical thinking progresses to pure thought in a series of binary splits, each of which is synthesized into new theses. Hegel maintained that knowledge of God, or the Absolute, can be achieved by rational thought. When the human consciousness has moved through this process and attained pure thought it has become identical with God, the Absolute Spirit.

Hegel was the first philosopher to recognize the historical dimension in the progression of philosophies. Great philosophical systems are valid within their own historical frameworks; as humanity learns more, it moves to more inclusive positions. Thinking is therefore never complete; it is constantly in need of revision, and each system is inevitably superseded. Reality is an all-inclusive rational unity in which everything has its necessary and logical place. The philosopher's job is to understand and explain the underlying rationale. Progress, according to Hegel, is achieved by the slow unfolding of historical forces rather than through the deliberate efforts of men and women.

Hegel was born on 27 August 1770 and was prepared for the Lutheran ministry from early childhood. His father, Georg Ludwig Hegel, a minor government official whose family had fled to Swabia in the sixteenth century from Carinthia (Austria) to escape religious persecution, was a disciplinarian with strong aristocratic convictions which shaped his son's attitude toward authority. His mother, Maria Magdelena Fromm Hegel, died when Georg Wilhelm Friedrich, the oldest of two sons and a daughter, was thirteen. From 1773 to 1775 he attended the German and Latin elementary schools, and in 1780 he was enrolled at the Gymnasium illustre, today the Eberhard-Ludwigs Secondary School in Stuttgart. At the gymnasium Hegel amassed considerable knowledge by translating or excerpting at length from a broad array of reading material, stretching from the Bible, Homer, Thucydides, and Sophocles to such contemporary writers as Johann Christoph Gottsched, Gotthold Ephraim Lessing, Christoph Wieland, and Christian Garve.

In 1785 he began a diary, partially in German and partially in Latin, which contains a personal assessment of his education at each step. The diary also reveals a growing antipathy toward organized religion, which he describes as an instrument of political oppression and a handmaiden of the state. Hegel yearned for a simpler religion, one that was closer to the people and free from the language of orthodoxy. In his later writings he sought to replace this language with a whole new vocabulary. The diary also records his growing disillusionment with contemporary social institutions.

In 1788 he graduated and was given a modest scholarship to study theology at the prestigious theological school at the University of Tübingen. A bastion of orthodoxy, the University

Hegel in his study (lithograph by L. Sebbers, 1828)

of Tübingen trained its theology students–seventy-five percent of a student body of two hundred–for minor government posts and careers in education and church service. Observing the desperate attempts of his teachers to defend orthodox positions against the challenges generated by the new discoveries in the natural sciences, Hegel recognized that a broader philosophical perspective, one that would integrate the growing body of new knowledge with the old, was needed. He saw dogma as the cause of the emerging animosity between religion and science. Scientists, he believed, were merely seeing the other face of God in nature as God gradually revealed Himself. His teacher Christian Storr opposed this attitude: espousing a "Supranaturalism" based on an orthodox interpretation of Christ's divinity as revealed through His miracles, Storr disputed the validity of scientific findings. Hegel felt that Storr should be replaced by a more up-to-date instructor.

As a student Hegel liked to drink, play cards, and discuss Jean-Jacques Rousseau's philos-

ophy. He was disinclined to talk about his own views, preferring to brood for days over the speculations of others. Such reticence, a tendency toward physical clumsiness, and occasional moodiness earned him the epithet "der Alte" (the old man). The French Revolution inspired him, and he was soon hoping for a similar upheaval in philosophical and religious thinking; it is said that Hegel's favorite expression in the years from 1789 to 1793 was "Kopf ab!" (Off with his head!). (On the other hand, the anecdote reported by a fellow student, Christian Leutwein, that Hegel and some other radical students planted freedom trees as an act of political provocation, has been dismissed as a fabrication.) Hegel shared a room with Friedrich Schelling and Friedrich Hölderlin, the latter of whom deepened Hegel's understanding of ancient Greek culture and mythology; neither roommate was impressed with Hegel's proficiency in classical Greek.

After he finished his studies Hegel took a position in October 1793 as a private tutor to the children of Carl Friedrich Steiger von Tschugg in Bern, Switzerland. Soon he felt isolated, far from the political mainstream. With Hölderlin's help he obtained a position as a private tutor in the home of the merchant Johann Gogol in Frankfurt. When his father died on 14 January 1799, Hegel decided to use his inheritance to pursue an academic career. His plan was to go to Bamberg to prepare for his academic debut. In the meantime, Schelling had been called to a professorial chair at the university in Jena, and he convinced the hesitant Hegel that more preparation was not necessary: he should come to Jena, the center of Germany's philosophical community, and establish himself as a private lecturer. Hegel had yet to publish, however, and therefore could not qualify for the needed certificate.

With the treatise *Differenz des Fichte'schen und Schelling'schen Systems der Philosophie* (1801; translated as *The Difference between Fichte's and Schelling's System of Philosophy*, 1977), the thirty-one-year-old Hegel entered the philosophical arena for the first time. His starting point was a survey of contemporary philosophy by Karl L. Reinhold, who, Hegel claimed, had completely overlooked major differences in the philosophies of Schelling and Johann Gottlieb Fichte. Furthermore, he asserted, Reinhold's procedure threatened to reduce all philosophy to mere logic. According to Hegel, Fichte, although claiming to be an interpreter of Immanuel Kant, had actually created a different philosophical system, not a critical but a subjective idealism. Fichte had produced a masterpiece of speculation but hardly a system, because he had not dealt with nature, morality, or aesthetics. There were also contradictions in Fichte's discussion of the Absolute Being: he had failed to show how this Being became conscious of itself. Schelling, on the other hand, had produced an objective idealism which avoided Fichte's one-sidedness by not identifying mind with the private subject. Hegel praised the unity of principle and method in Schelling's system. While he also pointed out some weaknesses in Schelling's objective idealism, Hegel's views at this point closely resemble Schelling's.

In this essay, Hegel also developed a clearer concept of the dialectical process. In contrast to Fichte, who had seen the antithesis as something outside the thesis, Hegel argued that contradictions within the thesis itself create the tension which gives rise to the antithesis. This internal pressure is inevitable and marks the way to higher levels of consciousness; therefore, all philosophical systems are caught up in the continuous unfolding of truth which manifests itself as a steady accumulation of knowledge. Thus all major philosophical systems are valid within their own historical contexts. Despite the conciliatory attitude inherent in such historicizing of philosophical viewpoints, Hegel's notion of continuous, never-really-completed thinking, which must be revised constantly, is at odds with any systematic presentation, since, by implication, each new finding subjects the entire system to revision. Perhaps Hegel published so little during his lifetime because he was searching for the latest viewpoint, the most current revelation, in hopes of creating a system which would not immediately be superseded.

If this first treatise bears the initial imprint of his dialectical method and his historical thinking, Hegel's dissertation shows his early and intense interest in the natural sciences. In *Dissertationi philosophicae de orbitis planetarum* (1801) he scrutinizes the natural laws regulating the distances between planets. Criticizing Sir Isaac Newton's failure to account for the differences in orbital spacing, he defends Johannes Kepler's contention that higher reason had produced the pattern of orbiting bodies. The failure to search for reason, Hegel insisted, was the fundamental weakness in contemporary science. All of Hegel's subsequent efforts to comprehend the unfolding of the Logos in the universe are marked by this devotion to understanding the higher purpose.

On his birthday in 1801 the examining board awarded him the *venia legendi,* and in the Winter semester 1801-1802 he gave his lectures on logic and metaphysics, on natural law, and on mathematics. Today, his lectures on the history of philosophy are generally regarded as his most significant achievement during his Jena years. These lectures confirm that the determining factor in the evolution of Hegel's system was what he regarded as the historical development of philosophical consciousness. With Schelling, Hegel edited the *Kritisches Journal der Philosophie* (Critical Journal of Philosophy), for which he wrote most of the articles, from August 1802 until May 1803. In the introduction to the journal he explained that its aims were to defend the unity of systematic philosophy against modern attempts at being original at all costs, at popularizing all systems, and at simply describing in logical, formalistic terms. In the essay "Glauben und Wissen" (Faith and Reason, 1802) he attacked Kant, Johann Georg Jacobi, and Fichte for regarding truth, the Absolute, or God as beyond human knowledge. Following the precepts of the Enlightenment, they had filled the cognitive void created by the limitations they had imposed on the human mind with some vague yearning or an all-encompassing sense of duty. In the essay "Über die wissenschaftlichen Behandlungsarten des Naturrechts" (Ways of Dealing Scientifically with Natural Law, 1802) he developed the idea that a "Volk" (national group) embodies an absolute ethical totality in which subjectively perceived morality and objectively imposed ethics are synthesized. His insistence that human consciousness was capable of attaining absolute knowledge and his supposition that the national group is the transmitter of a higher ethical force became key ingredients in his philosophy. These essays are, therefore, among the best sources for studying Hegel's emerging system.

By 1805 Hegel had achieved the status of associate professor of philosophy at Jena with a meager salary of only one hundred Taler a year. While many of his colleagues were leaving for more attractive positions elsewhere–Schelling had been called to Würzburg in 1803–Hegel's financial situation was deteriorating rapidly. Fewer and fewer students came to Jena. By the fall of 1806, with war between Prussia and France looming, Hegel was searching frantically both for another position and for a publisher. His first major work, *Die Phänomenologie des Geistes* (1807; translated as *The Phenomenology of Mind*, 1910) was almost completed. He found a publisher, the schizophrenic Joseph Anton Goebhardt, who was willing to print the work piecemeal. Hegel sent him the chapters one by one after he read them to his students. The book was finished amid the thunder of cannons as the Battle of Jena-Auerstedt raged on 13 and 14 October, virtually at Hegel's doorstep. With the concluding pages in his pocket he left for Bamberg, while French soldiers ransacked his quarters.

Three months later Hegel wrote a preface to *Die Phänomenologie des Geistes* in which he broke with Schelling and with many of his own recently expressed viewpoints. He had come to see all philosophical systems that advocate a direct insight into the Absolute as dangerous. Intuitive insight or mystical experience, Hegel maintains, is opposed to reflections of the mind and must be rejected. The philosopher's job is to reflect, understand, and work out the reason for and in the universe. The preface caused an uproar as students of the popular Schelling rushed to his defense. In a dogged attempt to avoid the language of orthodox religion and to replace it with a new world of thought, Hegel describes in the main body of *Die Phänomenologie des Geistes* how the human mind evolves from mere consciousness through self-awareness, reason, spirit, and religion to absolute knowledge. Asserting that the limitations Kant had placed on reason were unjustified, he demonstrates that the various forms of consciousness deceive each other and that such internal contradictions prompt one form to make room for a higher form. Cognition is a dialectical process in which each subject senses that its own experience with an object has been preceded by experiences shared by mankind throughout evolution. The development of living spirit is the course of history. Hegel also tries to reconcile the deep contradictions in the emerging structure of bourgeois society and to present a philosophy of religion. Whereas Fichte had argued, and Schelling had agreed, that human consciousness is incapable of attaining absolute knowledge because of its moral depravity, Hegel insists that consciousness can rise to an absolute perspective. The highest form of consciousness can rise to an absolute perspective. The highest form of consciousness is neither the moral spirit, as Fichte had maintained, nor art, as Schelling had concluded. Over both rise the higher forms of religion that eventually produce knowledge of the spirit which

knows and is certain of itself. At this stage, consciousness has achieved pure thought, the only reality. As pure, logical thought, the mind has arrived at the absolute perspective. Hegel spent the rest of his life trying to prove and expand upon the systematic speculations presented in *Die Phänomenologie des Geistes.*

In 1807 Hegel served as editor of the *Bamberger Zeitung* at a modest salary. He was glad to get away from Jena not only because of the war but also because he had fathered a son, Ludwig, by Christiana Charlotte Burkhardt-Fischer, the wife of his landlord. His respite was short-lived: he was soon groaning under the newspaper's yoke. He asked Friedrich Immanuel Niethammer, who had been instrumental in getting *Die Phänomenologie des Geistes* published, for help. Niethammer had become an influential member of the Bavarian education board, and he suggested that Hegel apply for the rector's position at the Ägidiengymnasium in Nuremberg. From 15 November 1808 until he received the summons to the University of Heidelberg in August 1816, Hegel served as professor of philosophical preparatory sciences and rector of the secondary school.

These eight years in Nuremberg were kind to Hegel. There, in 1811, the forty-one-year-old philosopher met and married the twenty-year-old Marie von Tucher, who bore him two sons: Karl, who became a professor of history at Erlangen, and Immanuel, who became the head of the Lutheran Synod in Brandenburg. Because the Tuchers, one of Nuremberg's foremost patrician families, expressed concern over their son-in-law's meager earnings, Hegel applied for professorial chairs wherever they became available: at Jena, Erlangen, Heidelberg, and Berlin. As he awaited the decision of the various boards he wrote primers and handbooks to supplement his classroom instruction. These developed into such challenging books as the *Wissenschaft der Logik* (1812-1816; translated as *Hegel's Science of Logic*, 1929) and the *Encyklopädie der philosophischen Wissenschaften im Grundrisse* (Encyclopedia of the Philosophical Sciences in Outline Form, 1817; translated as *The Logic of Hegel*, 1874).

Lenin maintained that no one can understand Marx's *Das Kapital* (Capital, 1867) without first comprehending Hegel's entire *Wissenschaft der Logik*. Marx considered Hegel's work as a metaphysical subterfuge that cloaks and yet describes the process inherent in the self-propulsion of capital. Hegel's title, at any rate, was meant as a provocation: logic was regarded by his contemporaries as the foundation for thinking, not as a science in itself. Hegel pitted this view of logic as a tool, as a way of reflecting on the form used to reach conclusions, against transcendental logic, the relationship of thought to reality. The first part, *Die objektive Logik* (Objective Logic), comprises two volumes, *Die Lehre vom Sein* (The Theory of Being, 1812) and *Die Lehre vom Wesen* (The Theory of Essence, 1813); part two consists of one volume, titled *Die Subjektive Logik oder die Lehre vom Begriff* (Subjective Logic; or, The Theory of Concepts, 1816). Hegel says that his goal is to become acquainted with that which in its alienated form is nature and in its self-understanding is spirit. Traditional logic, he maintains, is similar to the lifeless bones of a skeleton, thrown together in total disarray. Transcendental logic, he argues, is forever begging the question of how truth is attained. Hegel then confronts these two concepts with subjective logic, which, he claims, eliminates all separation between form and content, between thinking and the ultimate reality and truth–God, Being, eternity. Logic and metaphysics, Hegel says, are one and the same. Logic is the system of pure reason, the realm of pure thought. Here truth is as it really is, without a mask, of and for itself. A description of the structure of human consciousness, once consciousness has reached this stage of pure logical thought, is at the same time a description of God as He is in His eternal essence, before the creation of nature and the finite mind. At the level of pure thought, there is no opposition from subjectivity; thus this level corresponds to higher Being. Hegel's ponderous language and the way in which he incorporates the whole tradition of Western philosophy into his work presents even the most informed reader with major obstacles; for example, Hegel simply assumes that his audience is totally familiar with his two reference points, formal logic and Kant's transcendental logic.

In 1816 Hegel received answers to his letters of application. He was invited to join the faculty at Erlangen, but the invitation was worded in a cold, bureaucratic, almost insulting manner. The University of Berlin made the strange request that he respond to criticism that his eight-year absence from the university had caused a deterioration of his ability to lecture. This demeaning request was the work of the dean, Wilhelm Martin De Wette, who had already complained to the former Berlin police chief and now minister of education, Kaspar Friedrich von Schuckmann,

that Hegel was no more than a disciple of Schelling. Schuckmann, a Kantian, was alarmed by De Wette's characterization of Hegel's *Wissenschaft der Logik* as an obscure secret science and of Hegel's style of lecturing as confused, timid, embarrassed, completely void of clarity or fluency. By contrast, the Prorektor (vice president) at Heidelberg, Karl Daub, sent a warm and complimentary letter, saying that a refreshing ray of light would enter his life if he could welcome Hegel to the university he so dearly loved. Hegel accepted his invitation and arrived in Heidelberg on 19 October 1816.

At Heidelberg Hegel added a new lecture, on aesthetics, to his repertoire of logic, metaphysics, natural law, and the history of philosophy. He also edited the philosophical and philological sections of the *Heidelbergische Jahrbücher der Literatur,* for which he wrote the controversial "Verhandlungen in der Versammlung der Landstände des Königsreichs Württemberg im Jahre 1815 und 1816" (Deliberations in the Estates Assembly of the Kingdom of Württemberg in the Years 1815 and 1816, 1817). As Hegel observed, King Frederick had tried for two years to grant his subjects a more progressive constitution; but his efforts were blocked by the Estates, which regarded the new constitution as a threat to rank and privilege. Hegel accuses the Estates of having slept through the last twenty-five years and argues forcefully in favor of the king's more liberal position. Ironically, by championing the validity of abstract civil rights over the historical rights of the Estates, Hegel uses a progressive position to justify restoring power to the monarch.

In 1817 Hegel published his *Encyklopädie der philosophischen Wissenschaften im Grundrisse,* which was intended as no more than a guideline to help listeners follow his lectures. In 1827 and again in 1830 Hegel completely revised and expanded the book; each version is subject to a completely different interpretation. (The editors of his collected works [1832-1877] changed the character of the book once more by including uncorroborated statements Hegel allegedly made during his lectures.) In the encyclopedia he works out a detailed and systematic description of subjective and objective spirit. He subdivides the former into anthropology, phenomenology, and psychology; unfortunately, this phenomenology is different from that of *Die Phänomenologie des Geistes* and from phenomenology as it appears in the *Wissenschaft der Logik.* Such inconsistency complicates attempts at interpreting Hegel's thought. Ob-

Hegel around 1825 (painting by Jack Schesinger; Ullstein Bilderdienst)

jective spirit (nature philosophy) is subdivided into mechanics, physics, and organic physics (life). In the section on objective spirit he integrates the latest findings in chemistry, physics, and medicine into a coherent theory. His philosophy appealed to contemporary scientists because it emphasized the role of speculative thinking in the formulation of hypotheses subject to confirmation or refutation by empirical means. Hegel was seen as bridging the gap between the natural scientists and the hostile philosophers and theologians.

In the meantime, the Prussian minister of the interior and head of the educational committee, Karl von Stein zum Altenstein, worked diligently to procure for Hegel the chair of philosophy at the University of Berlin, which had been vacant since Fichte's death in 1814. He was opposed by Friedrich Schleiermacher, who feared

that philosophy would displace theology at the university, and by Friedrich Karl von Savigny, the professor of Roman law. Altenstein's ally was the theologian Philipp Konrad Marheinecke, who regarded Hegel as his counterpart in philosophy: whereas Marheinecke advocated a speculative theology which tried to mediate between the modern scientific spirit and the Christian tradition, Hegel was mediating between the natural scientists and the philosophers. On 26 December 1817 Altenstein wrote to Hegel, inviting him to take Fichte's chair and to help him develop various plans. A month later Hegel asked for details and whether an advance might be made to defray the cost of the move. It is clear from this exchange of letters that Hegel was being asked to play an important role in the reform of the Prussian educational system. After he arrived in the capital in the fall of 1818 he was consulted frequently by Altenstein and his assistant Johannes Schulze, with whom Hegel formed a lasting friendship.

The politicians were to carry out reforms worked out with Hegel's assistance. Moreover, the philosopher was to exert a calming influence on impatient students until the reforms could be implemented. Whenever Hegel refers to Prussia in his later philosophical works he is talking not about the Prussian state as it was but about a nation which was yet to be; his "Prussia" includes several institutions that were on the drawing boards at Berlin but had not yet been established. Thus, when critics deride Hegel as the "Prussian state philosopher," they fail to see that the Prussia Hegel discusses existed only in the minds of the reformers. It is to this emerging Prussia based on rational principles that he pays homage. He criticizes Plato's ideal state in the *Republic* because it was to be imposed on the people. He objects to the historical school of law because its proponents claimed, rather naively, that existing law must be rational because it existed, that there had to be some need for a particular law at the time of enactment. But for Hegel feudal law had evolved into an irrational and unjust system. His "Prussia" is the higher form of society. This social organization is to be founded on ethical principles to which the citizens will freely adhere. Hegel was certain not only that this Prussia was coming into being but also that its citizens would recognize the rationality of that state, in which the legal system would pursue not the letter of the law but its spirit.

Nevertheless, the publication in 1820 of his *Grundlinien der Philosophie des Rechts, oder Natur-*

recht und Staatswissenschaft (Outline of the Philosophy of Right; or, Natural Law and the Science of the State; translated as *Philosophy of Right*, 1896) provoked many contemporaries to derision and ridicule. It was the preface which caused the biggest commotion: his attack on Jakob Friedrich Fries, who had been suspended from the university for participating in the Wartburg Festival on 10 October 1817, cost Hegel several supporters. It has scarcely been noticed, however, that Hegel's castigation was not an argumentum ad hominem but the admonishment of a philosopher. According to Hegel, it is the duty of a philosopher to demonstrate his tenets and draw his conclusions in a systematic, logical way. Fries, however, was appealing to raw emotions, stirring up patriotic sentiment which was never rationally analyzed. Hegel objects to this "Brei des Herzens" (jelly of the heart) kept from the scrutiny of the brain. His position vis-à-vis Fries is therefore consistent with his criticism of Schelling's claims for intuitive insight or Friedrich Schlegel's and Ludwig Tieck's attempts to vindicate direct experience of the divine through art. Moreover, as a transplanted Swabian he resented Prussia's superpatriots and their heated appeals to mindless national sentiment.

Nineteenth-century interpretations of Hegel's philosophy of law tend to regard the work as a scientific justification of the Prussian police state. Modern analysts emphasize Hegel's ambiguous rhetoric, which tries to avoid any clear statement about existing political institutions. The most famous statement in the work, "was vernünftig ist, das ist wirklich; und was wirklich ist, das ist vernünftig" (what is reasonable is real; and what is real is reasonable), has been interpreted as an apology for the Prussian state, as an affirmation of the state *after* reforms are carried out, as a summons to seek out what is reasonable in the life of the nation, and as a demand that all that is unreasonable be destroyed in order to erect a state based on reason. According to a tongue-in-cheek account by the poet Heinrich Heine, who heard Hegel lecture at Berlin, the philosopher, whenever asked about these various interpretations, merely smiled benevolently, especially at the more radical conclusions drawn, and left final judgment up to the individual listener.

Hegel's starting point was the chapter in the *Encyklopädie der philosophischen Wissenschaften im Grundrisse* titled "Der objektive Geist" (The Objective Spirit). His purpose was to reconstruct theoretically the essential elements of contemporary life

and to reconcile these with life in the state as the most concrete form of ethics and morality. Hegel blends modern "proofs" of the autonomy of the individual with antiquity's concept of the integrated community. Distinguishing between the state and the simpler community of citizens, he rejects the notion of a social contract in favor of a more abstract idea of rights. In so doing, he shows the intense contradictions within the social framework. Social assimilation is poignantly depicted as the multifaceted dependency of all on all. Work in the bourgeois social order is both an emancipation from natural necessities and the continuation or extension of these necessities on a higher plane. Society produces both luxury and the endless increase of dependency and want. He tries to reconcile these contradictions within the state, which is alleged to be the reality of the ethical idea. He provoked considerable criticism by championing constitutional monarchy as the best form of government, and despite his connections with Altenstein and Schulze he was placed under surveillance by the police. His student and disciple Leopold von Henning was arrested. There is evidence that the lectures of 1817 were modified in 1820 so that they could be published; the early version, which is lost, apparently advocated individual freedom until the time when political reality became reasonable. Thus the Prussian authorities regarded Hegel as too liberal.

On the other hand, the way he treated two colleagues prompted his opponents to label Hegel a reactionary: his reaction to the suspension from the university of De Wette and his silencing of Friedrich Beneke. When the demented theology student Karl Sand murdered the playwright and Russian spy August von Kotzebue in 1819, De Wette sought to console the bereaved mother of the assassin in a letter which fell into the wrong hands. De Wette was suspended for expressions of sympathy which appeared to vindicate Sand. In the ensuing controversy at the university, Hegel maintained that the state had the right to suspend, without pay, academicians who utter inflammatory statements. Schleiermacher disagreed vehemently and branded Hegel a supporter of the ancien régime. It is not well known, however, that Hegel contributed generously to a fund established for De Wette after the suspension–despite De Wette's personal attacks on Hegel during the search for Fichte's successor.

Beneke was unrelenting in his attacks on Hegel. He insisted that the dialectical method was worthless and that all philosophy should be restructured on the basis of experience. In a series of lectures in 1822 Beneke claimed there was no Absolute, that all disciplines should be reorganized on the basis of human psychology. This denial of all higher Being, purpose, and meaning ran counter to everything Hegel stood for. Therefore, he denounced Beneke to Altenstein, who promptly revoked Beneke's *licentia docenti.* The ensuing debate over whether the Educational Committee, that is the state, had the right to revoke an academic license focused more on Hegel's abuse of power than on the atheistic tendency in Beneke's lectures. Hegel's only response came in the form of a defense against complaints that he was unnecessarily severe in his castigation of the Catholic church. Hegel emphasized that he was first and foremost a Lutheran philosopher whose bias for Protestantism was well known. He saw it as his job not only to defend Protestantism against attacks from atheists and Catholic dogmatists but also to provide a metaphysical system in support of religion. Overlooked by Hegel's detractors is his tacit consent to the reinstatement of Beneke at Berlin five years later.

The last work to appear during Hegel's lifetime, "Über die englische Reformbill" (On the English Reform Bill), appeared in the *Allgemeine preußische Staatszeitung* in 1831. Critics point to it as a prime example of Hegel's reactionary attitude without noting that more than one-third of the article was deleted by Prussian censors. Hegel argues that the bill weakened the monarchial principle, caused long-winded debates in Parliament, unjustifiably strengthened the peculiar right of Englishmen to private property, and defended the cruel treatment of Irishmen. He was most disturbed by what he regarded as a radical departure from the principles which had made England great. Older laws may have come about by chance and may contain some irrational features; nevertheless, they have many useful, rational functions. The reforms would weaken them and secure privileges for special-interest groups which could not be rationally defended. The suppressed last installment of this article was copied and circulated privately: it confirms that Hegel's criticism did not emanate from a reactionary viewpoint but rather sought to weigh the pros and cons of departing so markedly from a system that worked so well. With the passage of this bill, he maintained, there need be no more blind admiration for England nor blind disrespect for the political process in Germany.

In 1831 plague descended on Berlin from the east. The announcement that the epidemic was ending had hardly circulated when Hegel allegedly contracted cholera and died on 14 November. The diagnosis of cholera was questioned by Hegel's wife, and Hermann Glockner, who edited a collected edition of Hegel's works (1927-1940), concluded after a lengthy study that the philosopher actually died of a long-standing stomach ailment; he had complained of chronic pains in his digestive tract since a trip to Paris in 1827. He was buried next to Fichte. His friends and students began at once to publish his posthumous papers and to prepare his collected works.

The publication of the first work to emerge from these collaborative efforts split Hegel's students into two camps: a conservative and a radically progressive school. Less than a year after Hegel's death Marheinecke published the lectures on the philosophy of religion (translated, 1962), which he believed showed the development of Hegel's thought into a speculative reconciliation with Christianity. Even earlier Karl F. Göschel, in a work entitled *Aphorismen über Nichtwissen und Absolutes Wissen im Verhältnis zum christlichen Glaubensbekenntnis* (Aphorisms on Not-Knowing and Absolute Knowledge in Relation to the Christian Faith, 1829), had tried to reconcile faith with Hegel's arguments; others now attempted to interpret Hegel's philosophy in an orthodox Christian context. But Hegel's philosophy of religion offers a justification of religion in philosophical terms: it criticizes religious concepts and forms and says that religion is to terminate in philosophy. Scrutiny focused almost immediately on the Bible, as more radical exponents of Hegel's methods asked whether the four Gospels were historically valid and accurate. By 1835-1836, when the Tübingen theologian David Friedrich Strauss published *Das Leben Jesu, kritisch bearbeitet* (The Life of Jesus, Critically Treated), the two camps were irreconcilably divided. Strauss was skeptical about the historical foundation for the Gospel narratives, yet he believed that he could still preserve the inner core of Christian faith by applying Hegel's speculative methods. Ludwig Feuerbach and Karl Marx turned Hegel's ideas on religion to atheistic ends.

The deep division between the "Right Hegelians" and the "Young" or "Left Hegelians" also marks interpretations of Hegel's lectures on aesthetics and philosophy of history. The former, edited by Heinrich Hotho, were published from 1835 to 1838 as *Vorlesungen über die Aesthetik* (Lectures on Aesthetics; translated as *The Philosophy of Fine Art,* 1920). Aesthetics occupies a low level in Hegel's hierarchy. Poetry, painting, and sculpture enjoyed prominence in antiquity because they provided the only glimpses of the divine, the Absolute. As the bearer of insight into a higher world, art was supplanted by religion, which, in turn, was superseded by philosophy. Art serves more as an adornment than as a way of understanding; it provides, at best, a brief and incomplete view of the supreme realm. Beauty is the veil which covers truth, not truth itself. Art seeks to lift the veil, and when it succeeds, it rises to unity with the Absolute Spirit. During those fleeting moments when art attains truth, it approximates religion. The aesthetic experience is shortlived and must be expanded by logical thought. Thus, for Hegel, art is a limited form of knowledge, subordinate to religion and even more to philosophy.

These reflections are based on personal observations of a staggering number of works of art. Hegel challenges the academic disciplines concerned with literature, painting, and music to scrutinize their concepts and to analyze in detail those masterpieces which capture the essence of an era. Perhaps the greatest provocation the *Vorlesungen über die Aesthetik* contained for contemporaries was the directive to get out of self-absorbed flights of fantasy, out of uncontrolled subjectivity, and into the real world. He insisted that poets interact with nature instead of retreating into their own egos, which only leads to seclusion and self-glorification. Deriding the Romantics for their mystical approach to the Absolute, he prodded writers, artists, sculptors, and architects to get involved in the world outside, where they were sure to find the "Vernünftigkeit des Wirklichen" (rationality of reality). When those who heard Hegel's words stepped into the world surrounding them, however, they found not rationality but the misery and want that had accompanied industrialization. They saw their personal growth stymied by a rigid, illogically conceived class society which recognized birthright over talent. For this reason, they interpreted Hegel's notion of the Absolute in a revolutionary way: whatever was not rational was not real and, therefore, must be changed or eliminated. Hegel's aesthetics thus became the basis for a social theory of art.

In 1837 Eduard Gans published the last of Hegel's great lecture series, *Vorlesungen über die Philosophie der Geschichte* (translated as *The Philosophy of History,* 1899). Hegel begins with a reference to the last chapter in the *Grundlinien der Philosophie des Rechts,* where he states that the philosopher must assume that there is a rational purpose behind all phenomena; if there is none, then the philosopher can cease his work. World history is a record of the progress of freedom in human consciousness. The Orient recognized that only one man, the ruler, was genuinely free. The ancient Greeks knew that a few men, the citizens of the city-state, lived freely. The Reformation made it clear that all men are free. Freedom, as defined by the "Volksgeister" (spirits of various peoples) is the motivating force in human history, while the national spirits are the material used by the Weltgeist (World Spirit) on its way to self-realization. Each national group is given for a time the leadership of the world's development; after a while this leadership role is rescinded and given to another national group. Within these groups are "welthistorische Individuen" (world-historical individuals), such as Socrates, Alexander the Great, Julius Caesar, Jesus, and Napoleon, who sense the Absolute Spirit in its direct relationship to the times. The Weltgeist uses their subjective passions to realize not their goals but its own through the "List der Vernunft" (cunning of reason). The end of this process is the creation of freedom in reality. At the end of each period, philosophers reflect on the spirit of the age; such reflections serve as the basis for the next stage. Reflecting on his own age, Hegel saw the rise of liberalism with its desire for the participation of all as a danger because it appeared to have no concrete organization and to be guided by a subjective will. The lectures end with Hegel pointing to the Christian-Germanic culture as the latest and, therefore, highest stage in the evolution of human civilization. This conclusion does not mean that the Indo-European culture has achieved an identity with the Absolute Spirit, but rather that it now has the chance to move mankind to a higher plane.

With these statements, German Idealism comes to an end. Hegel completes the tradition which began with Kant and the Enlightenment; his successors produced no further all-embracing systems which attempted to understand and interpret the Absolute. On the contrary, philosophical scrutiny turned almost at once toward material reality. Hegel's successor in Berlin, Georg Andreas Gabler, was unable to reverse the trend toward materialism. Feuerbach argued that the Absolute Spirit did not create men but that men projected their aspirations, dreams, and ideals out into the universe and called the composite picture God.

Marx and Friedrich Engels insisted that Hegel was standing on his head and allegedly set him on his feet again by using his own dialectical method to prove that the Absolute did not manifest itself in social institutions, but rather that social institutions use God to justify their own illogical existence. Hegel's influence persisted in the method, vocabulary, and logic of materialism, but his search for the higher Being in and outside the human mind was abandoned.

Bibliographies:

Christoph Helferich, *G. W. Fr. Hegel* (Stuttgart: Metzler, 1979);

Kurt Steinhauer, ed., *Hegel Bibliography: Background Material on the International Reception of Hegel within the Context of the History of Philosophy* (Munich: Sauer, 1980).

Biographies:

Rudolf Haym, *Hegel und seine Zeit: Vorlesungen über Entstehung und Entwicklung, Wesen und Werth der Hegelschen Philosophie* (Berlin: Gaertner, 1857; reprinted, Hildesheim: Olms, 1962);

H. S. Harris, *Hegel's Development: Toward the Sunlight, 1770-1801* (Oxford: Clarendon Press, 1972);

Harris, *Hegel's Development: Night Thoughts (Jena 1801-1806)* (Oxford: Clarendon Press, 1983).

References:

Theodor Bodhammer, *Hegels Deutung der Sprache* (Hamburg: Meiner, 1969);

J. N. Findlay, *Hegel: A Re-examination* (New York: Macmillan, 1958);

Hans Georg Gadamer, *Hegels Dialektik* (Tübingen: Mohr-Siebeck, 1971);

François Grégoire, *Études Hégéliennes* (Louvain: Publications Universitaires de Louvain, 1958);

M. J. Inwood, *Hegel* (London & Boston: Routledge & Kegan Paul, 1983);

Walter Kaufmann, *Hegel: A Reinterpretation* (Garden City, N.Y.: Doubleday, 1965);

Alexandre Kojève, *Introduction to the Reading of Hegel*, edited by Allan Bloom, translated by

James H. Nichols, Jr. (New York: Basic Books, 1969; reprinted, Ithaca, N.Y.: Cornell University Press, 1980);

Quentin Lauer, *A Reading of Hegel's Phenomenology of Spirit* (New York: Fordham University Press, 1976);

Alasdair MacIntyre, ed., *Hegel: A Collection of Critical Essays* (Garden City, N.Y.: Doubleday, 1972);

Herbert Marcuse, *Reason and Revolution: Hegel and the Rise of Social Theory* (London & New York: Oxford University Press, 1941);

Michael John Petry, ed., *Hegel und die Naturwissenschaften* (Stuttgart & Bad Cannstatt: Holzboog, 1987);

Raymond Plant, *Hegel* (Bloomington: Indiana University Press, 1973);

Otto Pöggler, ed., *Hegel* (Freiburg & Munich: Alber, 1977);

Stanly Rosen, *G. W. F. Hegel: An Introduction to the Science of Wisdom* (New Haven & London: Yale University Press, 1974);

Andries Sarlemijn, *Hegelsche Dialektik* (New York & Berlin: De Gruyter, 1971);

Ivan Soll, *An Introduction to Hegel's Metaphysics* (Chicago: University of Chicago Press, 1969);

Robert Solomon, *In the Spirit of Hegel: A Study of G. W. F. Hegel's Phenomenology of Spirit* (New York: Oxford University Press, 1983);

William T. Stace, *The Philosophy of Hegel* (London & New York: Oxford University Press, 1924);

Charles Taylor, *Hegel* (Cambridge: Cambridge University Press, 1975);

Franz Wiedmann, *Hegel* (Hamburg: Rowohlt, 1965).

Papers:

The Hegel-Archiv is at the Rheinisch-Westfälische Akademie der Wissenschaft der Ruhr-Universität Bochum, Bochum, West Germany. Other collections of manuscripts and letters include the Houghton Library, Harvard University; the Deutsches Literaturarchiv, Marbach, West Germany; and the Nationale Forschungs- und Gedenkstätte der klassische Literatur: Goethe-Schiller-Archiv, Weimar, East Germany.

Heinrich Heine

(13 December 1797-17 February 1856)

Robert C. Holub

University of California, Berkeley

BOOKS: *Gedichte* (Berlin: Maurer, 1822);

Tragödien, nebst einem lyrischen Intermezzo (Berlin: Dümmler, 1823);

Reisebilder, 4 volumes (Hamburg: Hoffmann & Campe, 1826-1831)–comprises volume 1, "Die Heimkehr," "Die Harzreise," "Die Nordsee I"; volume 2, "Die Nordsee II," "Die Nordsee III," "Ideen: Das Buch Le Grand," "Briefe aus Berlin"; volume 3, "Reise von München nach Genua," "Die Bäder von Lucca"; volume 4, *Nachträge* "Die Stadt Lucca," "Englische Fragmente"; translated by Charles Godfrey Leland as *Pictures of Travel*, 1 volume (Philadelphia: Weik, 1855; London: Trübner, 1856);

Buch der Lieder (Hamburg: Hoffmann & Campe, 1827); translated by Leland as *Heine's Book of Songs* (Philadelphia: Leypoldt/New York: Christern, 1864); translated by Henry Sullivan Jarrett (under the pseudonym Stratheir) as *The Book of Songs* (London: Constable, 1913); German version republished (New York: Ungar, 1944);

Französische Zustände (Hamburg: Hoffmann & Campe, 1833);

Vorrede zu Heinrich Heines französischen Zuständen: nach der französischen Ausgabe ergänzt (Leipzig: Heideloff & Campe, 1833);

Zur Geschichte der neueren schönen Literatur in Deutschland, 2 volumes (Paris & Leipzig: Heideloff & Campe, 1833); republished as *Die romantische Schule*, 1 volume (Hamburg: Hoffmann & Campe, 1836); translated by S. L. Fleishman as *The Romantic School* (New York: Holt, 1882);

Der Salon, 4 volumes (Hamburg: Hoffmann & Campe, 1834-1840)–comprises volume 1, "Französische Maler: Gemäldeausstellung in Paris 1831," "Gedichte," "Aus den Memoiren des Herrn von Schnabelewopski"; volume 2, "Zur Geschichte der Religion und Philosophie in Deutschland," "Frühlingslieder"; volume 3, "Florentinische Nächte," "Elementargeister"; volume 4, "Der Rabbi von Bacha-

Heinrich Heine (Heinrich-Heine-Institut, Düsseldorf)

rach," "Gedichte," "Über die französische Bühne"; "Zur Geschichte der Religion und Philosophie in Deutschland" translated by John Snodgrass as *Religion and Philosophy in Germany: A Fragment* (New York: Houghton, Mifflin, 1882; London: Trübner, 1882);

De l'Allemagne, 2 volumes (Paris: Renduel, 1835); enlarged edition, 2 volumes (Paris: Lévy, 1855);

Über den Denunzianten: Eine Vorrede zum dritten Theile des Salons (Hamburg: Hoffmann & Campe, 1837);

Shakespeares Mädchen und Frauen: Mit Erläuterungen (Paris & Leipzig: Brockhaus & Avenarius, 1838 [dated 1839]);

Heinrich Heine über Ludwig Börne (Hamburg: Hoffmann & Campe, 1840);

Neue Gedichte (Hamburg: Hoffmann & Campe/ Paris: Dubochet, 1844);

Deutschland: Ein Wintermärchen (Hamburg: Hoffmann & Campe, 1844);

Atta Troll: Ein Sommernachtstraum (Hamburg: Hoffmann & Campe, 1847); translated by Thomas Selby Egan as "Atta Troll" in *Atta Troll and Other Poems* (London: Chapman & Hall, 1876); translated by Herman Scheffauer as *Atta Troll* (London: Sidgwick & Jackson, 1913; New York: Huebsch, 1914);

Der Doktor Faust: Ein Tanzpoem. Nebst kuriosen Berichten über Teufel, Hexen und Dichtkunst (Hamburg: Hoffmann & Campe, 1851); translated by Basil Ashmore as *Doktor Faust: A Dance Poem; Together with Some Rare Accounts of Witches, Devils, and the Ancient Art of Sorcery* (London: Nevill, 1952);

Romanzero (Hamburg: Hoffmann & Campe, 1851);

Les Dieux en exil (Brussels & Leipzig: Kiessling, 1853);

Vermischte Schriften, 3 volumes (Hamburg: Hoffmann & Campe, 1854)–comprises volume 1, "Geständnisse," "Gedichte 1853 und 1854," "Die Götter im Exil," *Die Göttin Diana*; volumes 2-3, *Lutezia*;

Heinrich Heine's Sämmtliche Werke, 7 volumes (Philadelphia: Weik, 1855-1861);

Heinrich Heine's Sämmtliche Werke: Rechtmäßige Original-Ausgabe, edited by Adolf Strodtmann, 24 volumes (Hamburg: Hoffmann & Campe, 1861-1895);

Memoiren und neugesammelte Gedichte, Prosa und Briefe: Mit Einleitung, edited by Eduard Engel (Hamburg: Hoffmann & Campe, 1884);

Sämtliche Werke, edited by Ernst Elster, 7 volumes (Leipzig: Bibliographisches Institut, 1887-1890);

Sämtliche Schriften, edited by Klaus Briegleb, 6 volumes (Munich: Hanser, 1968-1976);

Werke, Briefwechsel, Lebenszeugnisse: Säkularausgabe, edited by the Nationale Forschungs- und Gedenkstätten der klassischen deutschen Literatur in Weimar and the Centre National de la Recherche Scientifique in Paris, 5 volumes published (Berlin & Paris: Aufbau, 1970-);

Sämtliche Werke, edited by Manfred Windfuhr, 13 volumes published (Hamburg: Hoffmann & Campe, 1973-).

Editions in English: *The Poems of Heine, Complete: Translated in the Original Metres*, translated by Edgar Alfred Bowring (London: Bohn, 1861)–comprises "Memoir," "Book of Songs," "Pictures of Travel," "Atta Troll," "Germany, a Winter Tale," "Romancero," and "Latest Poems";

The Works of Heinrich Heine, translated by Leland and others, 12 volumes (London: Heinemann, 1891-1905; New York: Dutton, 1906)– comprises volume 1, "Florentine Nights," "The Memoirs of Herr von Schnabelewopski," "The Rabbi of Bacharach," "Shakespeare's Maidens and Women"; volumes 2-3, *Pictures of Travel;* volume 4, *The Salon; or, Letters on Art, Music, Popular Life and Politics;* volumes 5-6, *Germany;* volumes 7-8, *French Affairs;* volume 9, *The Book of Songs*, translated by Thomas Brooksbank; volume 10, *New Poems*, translated by Margaret Armour; volume 11, "Germany," "Romancero, Books I-II," translated by Armour; volume 12, "Romancero, Book III," "Last Poems," translated by Armour;

Heinrich Heine: Paradox and Poet, volume 2: *The Poems*, translated by Louis Untermeyer (New York: Harcourt, Brace, 1937);

The Poetry and Prose of Heinrich Heine, translated by Untermeyer, Aaron Kramer, Frederic Ewen, and others, edited by Ewen (New York: Citadel Press, 1948);

Selected Works, translated and edited by Helen M. Mustard and Max Knight (New York: Random House, 1973);

The Complete Poems of Heinrich Heine: A Modern English Version, translated by Hal Draper (Cambridge, Mass.: Suhrkamp/Insel, 1982; Oxford: Oxford University Press, 1982);

Poetry and Prose, edited by Jost Hermand and Robert C. Holub (New York: Continuum, 1982);

The Romantic School and Other Essays, edited by Hermand and Holub (New York: Continuum, 1985).

OTHER: *Kahldorf über den Adel in Briefen an den Grafen M. von Moltke*, edited by Heine (Nuremberg: Hoffmann & Campe, 1831);

Miguel de Cervantes, *Der sinnreiche Junker Don Quichote von La Mancha*, translated by Heine, 2 volumes (Stuttgart: Verlag der Klassiker, 1837-1838).

From the generation following Johann Wolfgang von Goethe there is perhaps no writer more controversial than Heinrich Heine. Although best known now for his early lyrics–which have been set to music more often than those of any other poet–during most of his life he was renowned for his witty prose, his political journalism, and his caustic satires. These were the writings which earned him a controversial reputation among his contemporaries and after his death. Frequently censored for his liberal views and his attacks on religion, he was despised by narrow-minded German nationalists for his cosmopolitan feelings and discriminated against by a bigoted German society for his Jewish origins. While his writings became extremely popular among enlightened sectors of the European intelligentsia, in his native land he was often subjected to scorn or ridicule. This prejudice against Heine culminated in the period of National Socialism, when he was retroactively stripped of his German background; during the Third Reich the author of the "Loreley," Heine's most celebrated poem, was listed as "an unknown poet."

This blatant discrimination on the part of fanatical racists is somewhat balanced, however, by Heine's tremendous impact on the most innovative minds of the nineteenth century. He was a close friend of Karl Marx during his Parisian exile in 1843-1844, and it is quite likely that the radical socialist was influenced by both Heine's wit and his political views. Richard Wagner used motifs from two of Heine's works for his operas *Der fliegende Hollander* (The Flying Dutchman, 1841) and *Tannhäuser* (1843-1844). Friedrich Nietzsche admired him as one of the greatest poets of the century and considered him to be one of the superior German stylists of all times. And Sigmund Freud was obviously thoroughly acquainted with his writings; many of the illustrations he uses in *Wit and Its Relation to the Unconscious* (1905) are taken from Heine's works. With regard to his reputation, then, Heine has been a subject of considerable dispute. Hailed as a genial poet and innovative prose writer by some, he has been vilified as a flighty poetaster and traitor to the fatherland by others.

In fact, controversy entered into Heine's life from–and around–the very moment of his birth. Although it is now presumed that he was born on 13 December 1797, this elementary biographical fact is by no means certain. No official record exists, and Heine himself, for unknown reasons, never confirmed this date. Indeed, he most often asserted that he was born two years later. Previous defamatory speculation that he lied in order to cover up his illegitimacy or to avoid service in the Prussian army has proven to be false. But no one has been able to ascertain why Heine consistently felt compelled to hide his actual age.

Heine's birth is not the only fact about his early life which is shrouded in mystery. Little information is available about his early years, and what there is is often of somewhat dubious validity. This much seems certain, however. Heine was one of four children–three sons and a daughter–born to Samson and Betty (van Geldern) Heine. He was named Harry by his parents, apparently to honor one of his father's associates. His childhood appears to have been rather uneventful. He attended a nursery school and a Hebrew school before entering the public school system in 1807. He was accepted into the lyceum in 1810 but never graduated, partially because of the turbulence surrounding the Napoleonic Wars, and partially because his family had planned for him to become a businessman. Accordingly he was enrolled in a business school in 1814. In 1816 he was apprenticed to a bank in Hamburg under the auspices of his uncle, Salomon Heine, one of the wealthiest financiers in Germany. Two years later his uncle set him up in his own business, but it was liquidated by early 1819, apparently because Salomon discovered that Samson was drawing money against his son's accounts.

After this brief and unsuccessful business career it was decided, probably by Uncle Salomon, that Heine should study law. In the autumn of 1819 he enrolled at the recently founded university in Bonn. Although he was several years older than the usual student, his behavior appears to have been quite typical for a young man of his times. He participated in a demonstration to commemorate the Battle of Leipzig shortly after his arrival in town, joined a nationalist student club in his first semester, and attended lectures on topics relating to German history and literature. After a year at Bonn, he transferred to the university in Göttingen, which had a fine reputation, particularly in the field of law. Here he was terribly unhappy, chiefly because both the faculty and the students lacked the nationalist enthusiasm he had experienced in Bonn. Heine joined a student club but was expelled, probably because of his Jewishness, which no doubt contributed to his dissatisfaction with the university. The misery of his first stay in Göttingen, however, lasted less than four months. Because he engaged in a duel with a fellow student, he was expelled from the university for a minimum of half a year.

After a short visit with his family in Hamburg, Heine was sent to Berlin to continue his studies. Berlin, like Bonn, was a relatively new university (founded in 1810), but it had already acquired a fine reputation. Heine seems to have enjoyed seminars there more than in Göttingen, and he attended lectures by some of the most eminent intellectuals of his times. Chief among these was Georg Friedrich Wilhelm Hegel, perhaps the most influential philosopher on the Continent. But more important than his studies were the social connections he made in the Prussian capital. He gained entrance to the salon of Rahel Varnhagen von Ense, a Jewish woman married to a liberal Prussian former diplomat, and mingled there with the important literati of Berlin society. He was also successful in finding a publisher for his first book, *Gedichte* (Poems, 1822). But perhaps most significant for him was his association with the Verein für Cultur und Wissenschaft der Juden (Society for Culture and Scholarship of the Jews). In association with other young Jewish intellectuals, Heine explored the role Jews had played in European culture and came to appreciate his own heritage. From his own researches Heine began a novel, "Der Rabbi von Bacherach" (The Rabbi from Bacherach, 1840), of which he completed less than three chapters.

Fortified by his sojourn in Berlin, Heine returned to Göttingen in 1824 to complete his degree in law. Aside from a two-month journey on foot through the Harz mountains in the fall of that year, he appears to have applied himself diligently to his studies. In May 1825 he passed his oral defense, and in July the title of doctor of law was conferred on him. Between these two dates another momentous change occurred in his life. In June he converted to Protestantism and was baptized Heinrich. For Jews who had any aspirations to hold governmental (including academic) positions, such a conversion was hardly unusual. Eduard Gans, who later became Hegel's successor in Berlin, and Heinrich Marx, Karl Marx's father, converted at about the same time. Heine himself insisted that it was his "Entreebillet zur europäischen Kultur" (entrance ticket to European culture). Still, considering his recent encounters with the Jewish tradition in Berlin and his reactions against others who converted, it is safe to assume that the decision was not made lightly.

By this time in his life Heine had already gained some notoriety as a writer. He had composed two dramas in the early 1820s, *Almansor* and *William Ratcliff*, first published in *Tragödien, nebst einem lyrischen Intermezzo* (Tragedies, with a Lyrical Intermezzo, 1823), but these were epigonic works which are largely forgotten today. His real talent lay in lyric poetry. Starting in 1817 he had begun to publish his verse in literary journals, and two small books appeared in 1822 and 1823. His literary reputation, however, rests largely on the collection of verse published in 1827 under the title *Buch der Lieder* (Book of Songs). It contained chiefly poems Heine had written during the late 1810s and early 1820s, revised and arranged in five sections or cycles: "Junge Leiden" (Young Sorrows), "Lyrisches Intermezzo" (Lyrical Intermezzo), "Die Heimkehr" (Homecoming), "Aus der Harzreise" (From the Harz Journey), and "Die Nordsee" (The North Sea). Although the second edition did not appear until a decade later, by the end of the nineteenth century it had become one of the best-selling books of poetry in the German language. Heine's most familiar poems, including those that so enchanted the composers of Romantic Lieder, are found in this volume.

Most of these early poems deal with the theme of unrequited love. Although they appear to be simply constructed from familiar romantic motifs, closer inspection reveals meticulous poetic craft and insight. Their outstanding feature is the turn or ironic twist which frequently concludes a poem. The reader is lulled into a false sense of security when he or she encounters the familiar imagery of lyrics from the Age of Goethe. But in the final lines Heine calls this imagery—and the ideology behind it—into question with a note of discord or ironic distancing. In this way the poem becomes a vehicle for self-reflection upon the role of the poet, the use of poetic motifs, and romantic poetry in general. To achieve their effect these poems therefore depend on subtle techniques of playing with and often disappointing the expectations of the reader. They are carefully designed to destroy the harmony they initially seem to posit, and thus they reaffirm in the form the thematic emphasis on unhappy love. Unfortunately, many of the most famous musical compositions for the poetry in *Buch der Lieder* fail to appreciate Heine's essentially ironic stance. These poems implicitly challenge the ideal of harmony and the idyllic world found in the literature of the preceding period. In accord with an era of turbulence and change in the social, political, and intellectual realm, they explore, on the level of emotions, dissonance and strife.

Although this poetry would later become an enormous success, Heine was unable to live by writing verse. In fact, the *Buch der Lieder* brought him no money at all for at least a decade after its publication. Since poetry was not a promising way to earn a living, Heine was forced to pursue other avenues. During the period between the attainment of his law degree in 1825 and his immigration to Paris in 1831 he traveled about Europe–journeying to England in 1827 and to Italy in 1828–while contemplating various career options. At the beginning of 1828 he assumed the only regularly paying position he ever held, editor of the *Neue allgemeine politische Annalen*, but he resigned after six months. He then ingratiated himself with a Bavarian minister of the interior in hopes of securing a professorship in Munich. He apparently wanted to lecture on German history, but a competitor was chosen above him. Heine even thought about entering the political arena. Toward the end of 1830 he waged an unsuccessful and half-hearted campaign to be appointed to a high post in the Hamburg city government. Since he had no experience and scant qualifications, it is not surprising that nothing ever came of this attempt.

Much more important for Heine during these years was his writing; it was during this period that he established himself as a major author on the German literary scene. In 1826 he met Julius Campe, a progressive publisher in Hamburg who recognized his genius and did much to promote his works. Heine sold him the rights to "Die Harzreise" (The Harz Journey), a prose work that had appeared in a literary journal, and Campe saw the opportunity to publish more than just an isolated travel description. He conceived the idea of using it and other similar works in a series; each volume would thus serve as advertisement for subsequent volumes. Accordingly, he brought out *Reisebilder I* (Travel Pictures I) in 1826, followed by second, third, and fourth volumes in 1827, 1829, and 1831. Although the sales were unimpressive at first, by the time Heine left Germany in 1831 the *Reisebilder* had made him a relatively famous writer, especially in the circles of young, liberal intellectuals.

The success of this series can be attributed largely to its controversial content and innovative form. Heine takes up matters of current concern and comments upon them in a witty and critical fashion. Because of censorship he had to be extremely cautious. Rarely does one find a sustained or direct treatment of an issue or personality. Most often · Heine operates with an apparently free-floating technique of associating ideas. Something he witnesses or experiences will remind him of a politically more sensitive topic which he then discusses with humor, allusions, and innuendos. Heine had developed this technique earlier in the 1820s in a set of correspondence articles, "Briefe aus Berlin" (Letters from Berlin, 1822), and in a short travel description, "Über Polen" (On Poland, 1823), but by the end of the decade he had obviously perfected his art.

"Die Harzreise" is the first and probably the best-known work in the *Reisebilder*. The framework is the journey through the Harz mountains which Heine undertook as a break from his studies in late 1824. In this work his attitudes are more clearly tied to the German Romantic tradition. Some of the main targets for his ironic barbs are those individuals and institutions which maintain senseless cultural conventions. Heine's narrative persona is presented as a friend of nature, love, and authentic feeling, someone who disdains poetic prescriptions and aesthetic pretentiousness. In this work the philistine, a frequent object of ridicule for Romanticism, is the epitome of all that Heine detests. But Heine's criticism, unlike that of most Romantics, extends beyond the realm of art into societal relations. He is concerned with restrictions not only to artistic creativity, but to human potential as well. Thus he takes society to task wherever it confines individual liberty. For this reason Heine frequently mocks rigid class distinctions and orthodox religious attitudes. Both serve to maintain a conservative order inimical to his progressive, emancipatory desires.

Perhaps the most imaginative work in the *Reisebilder* is "Ideen: Das Buch Le Grand." Consisting of twenty chapters of varying length, this work may be conveniently divided into four sections. In the first and last quarter of the work Heine assumes various personae: an Italian knight, an Indian count, a brokenhearted lover. In these parts the dominant themes are familiar from the Romantic canon: love, death, and suicide. At the close of the fifth chapter and throughout the next quarter of the book, the loosely structured narration shifts focus; the narrative persona, who is a somewhat distorted mirror of the author, begins to talk of his youth. The major event he discusses is the invasion of the French army into the German Rhineland at the beginning of the nineteenth century. Napoleon and the drum major Le Grand become symbols of emancipation for a backward, biased, and anesthetized Germany. In the third quarter of the work, after the demise of Napoleon and the death of Le Grand, the narrator reflects on a variety of themes including academic scholarship, the writing profession, and the political absurdities following the Congress of Vienna in 1815. The result is an amusing but critical collage of culture and society in an age of reactionary politics.

With the exception of "Die Nordsee I" and "Die Nordsee II" (The North Sea), the first cycles of German poetry written about the sea, the rest of the works in the *Reisebilder* exhibited similar tendencies. In their form an apparently loose association of ideas, they deliver nonetheless a powerful and decisive liberal message. Because of the conservative political and cultural establishment these works were bound to be seen as a challenge to the status quo. But the most controversial of the works in the *Reisebilder* is known less for its political critique than for its personal character assault. In "Die Bäder von Lucca" (The Baths of Lucca) Heine's penchant for literary polemics led him to lash out fiercely at a fellow writer, August Graf von Platen-Hallermünde. The feud between them apparently began when Heine published some epigrams ridiculing Platen at the end of "Nordsee III." Although they were composed by Heine's friend Karl Immermann, a noted playwright and novelist of the period, it appears that Platen was offended that Heine would dare to print them. He therefore countered with *Der romantische Oedipus* (The Romantic Oedipus, 1829), a satire of German literary life which included a few anti-Semitic swipes at Heine's Jewish background. Heine, who was especially sensitive about this matter anyway, suspected–wrongly, it turns out–that Platen was part of a Catholic-reactionary conspiracy which had prevented him from obtaining the professorship he had wanted in Munich. His assault was therefore especially harsh and all encompassing. Platen was taken to task for his metrical fastidiousness, his lack of originality, his aristocratic origins, and his bragging. But Heine also attacked him rather shamelessly for his homosexuality. In the prudish moral climate of the times such openness was unusual and attracted a great deal of attention. Heine was severely censured for this impropriety, even by some of his friends.

Although by 1830 Heine had acquired quite a reputation as a writer of both verse and prose, his future was nonetheless uncertain. Unable to live from his writings and unsuccessful at finding a secure position, hounded by the censors for his moral and political views and constantly fearing detention or incarceration, he decided to leave his native land for Paris. In May 1831 he arrived in the French capital, and outside of two visits to Germany in the 1840s and an occasional vacation, it remained his home until his death a quarter of a century later. Heine was exceedingly pleased with what he found there. Shortly after his arrival he remarked that if a fish in water were asked how it felt, it would reply, "Like Heine in Paris." It is not difficult to understand his enthusiasm. In Paris he found the stimulating political environment which was totally lacking in Germany. The French Revolution of 1830 had brought Louis Philippe, the bourgeois king, to the throne, but a spectrum of political parties from royalists to socialists thrived in a relatively open climate. Heine was also able to pursue his interests in Saint-Simonism, a philosophically based utopian doctrine which he had begun to study in Germany. But another reason he felt at home in Paris was because he fit well into the cultural life of the city. Several good translations of his work facilitated his acceptance into the best salons and literary circles. By the mid 1830s he had become acquainted with some of the most celebrated musicians and writers of the era, and in time he himself became a cultural figure to whom visitors flocked.

One of Heine's principal activities in the Parisian capital was to mediate French cultural and political events to the German public. During the first decade and a half of what began as a self-imposed exile, he was an on-the-scene correspondent for some of the more popular German newspapers and journals. One of the first projects he undertook after arriving in Paris was a series of reports on an art exhibit in 1831. Although many of the paintings on display were conceived before the July Revolution, Heine seeks to uncover the spirit of the new era in these works. The articles, originally published in the *Morgenblatt* in 1831, were collected under the title "Französische Maler" (French Painters) in the first volume of *Der Salon* (1834-1840). In the second half of the 1830s Heine performed a similar task for French theater. In the form of letters to August Lewald, the editor of the *Allgemeine Theater-Revue*, Heine dealt with recent trends on the French stage.

"Über die französische Bühne" (Concerning the French Stage; in volume 4 of *Der Salon*), like "Französische Maler," praises progressive trends in France, while questioning German backwardness. Heine's most successful writings about France were collections of correspondence articles he wrote during the 1830s and 1840s. *Französische Zustände* (Conditions in France, 1833) consists of reports published originally in early 1832 in the Augsburg *Allgemeine Zeitung*, while *Lutezia*, which appeared in book form in 1854 and is the longest work published by Heine, is an edition of articles composed in the early 1840s. In both works Heine shows himself to be an acute observer of the political and cultural scene. Using more intuition than investigative procedures, and writing in the witty, sometimes associative style that was his trademark, Heine analyzes various aspects of cultural and political progress in the most revolutionary European city of the early nineteenth century.

But Heine also endeavored to mediate German culture to the French. His two most important essays of the early 1830s, *Die romantische Schule* (The Romantic School) and "Zur Geschichte der Religion und Philosophie in Deutschland" (Concerning the History of Religion and Philosophy in Germany; published in volume 2 of *Der Salon*) attempt to correct the view of German intellectual life found in Mme de Staël's influential book *De l'Allemagne* (1813). It was especially important for Heine to combat de Staël's favorable portrayal of German Romanticism, and Heine's first essay contains a sustained discussion of and attack upon this current in German letters. *Die romantische Schule*, however, is more encompassing than its title suggests. For it includes observations on most of the major figures in German literature during the Age of Goethe. Indeed, the title under which this work was first published, *Zur Geschichte der neueren schönen Literatur in Deutschland* (Concerning the History of Recent Belles Lettres in Germany), is much more appropriate. What emerges from this literary history–which was one of the first of its kind to be written in German–is a view of two antagonistic tendencies in German culture. The first is identified with the Enlightenment, sensualism, Protestantism, and progressive politics; Gotthold Ephraim Lessing, Johann Gottfried von Herder, Friedrich von Schiller, Johann Heinrich Voß, and the Young Germans are placed in this tradition. Opposing it is a mystical, spiritualist, Catholic, and politically regressive turn to the Middle Ages

that Heine associates with the Romantic movement. Towering above both of these, although definitely allied with the Enlightenment heritage, is Goethe. By introducing this typology to deal with German literary history, Heine is attempting to discourage French intellectuals from their admiration of the German Romantics, while simultaneously showing them that Germany, too, possesses a critical and forward-looking literature.

The identical set of dichotomies structures Heine's essay on German religious and philosophical thought. Heine sets up an historical narrative according to which the spiritualism of the Catholic Middle Ages is gradually eroded by advances in the domain of German intellectual life. The major stages in this erosion process, which is also the path of political emancipation, are the focal points of the three sections. In the first Heine treats Martin Luther's clash with the Roman Catholic church as a pivotal point in breaking the hegemony of spiritualism. By opposing this foreign, intellectual oppression, Luther managed to assist in the creation of a positive and liberating national identity. Benedict de Spinoza appears as the hero of the second section because of his doctrine of pantheism, "the clandestine religion of Germany." Here Heine traces the materialist roots of pantheistic teachings and points to their potentially revolutionary implications. Although the final book deals with German idealist philosophy in general, there is little doubt that Immanuel Kant is the central figure. His *Kritik der reinen Vernunft* (Critique of Pure Reason, 1781) is likened to the French Revolution; it destroyed the last remnants of deism in German philosophy and made theology in any traditional sense a dead issue. Heine's reading of intellectual life in this work thus posits a basically emancipatory trajectory, and his exegetical practice elucidates the hidden stations on the enlightened road as well as the intellectual detours.

Heine's views were inherently oppositional, especially when one considers the repressive atmosphere in Germany at that time. But he appears to have limited his opposition to acts of the pen. He seems never to have been a member of any organized political group. It must have come as a surprise to him, therefore, when in 1835 the German Diet marked him as one of the leaders of the Young Germans and banned the sales of all his past and future works. The others mentioned in this official decree (Karl Gutzkow, Heinrich Laube, Theodor Mundt, and Ludolf Wienbarg) were also liberal writers; the conspiracy against

Heine with his wife, the former Crescence Eugénie Mirat, whom he called Mathilde (painting by Ernst Benedikt Kietz, 1851; courtesy of the Landschaftsverband Rheinland, Düsseldorf)

the state which the Diet perceived was clearly non-existent, the result of either mistaken identity or extreme paranoia. Heine–and most of the others–protested vehemently against this prohibition, and although total censorship was soon lifted, the ban definitely had a deleterious effect on the intellectual climate for the rest of the decade. Certainly this is part of the reason that the following five years were the least productive in Heine's literary career. Aside from a polemic against Wolfgang Menzel, a rabid nationalist who was one of the most vituperative critics of the Young Germans, and an attack on a group of Swabian poets, Heine published only a novel fragment, "Florentinische Nächte" (Florentine Nights), an essay on folklore entitled "Elementargeister" (Elementary Spirits)–both in volume 3 of *Der Salon*–and a preface to an edition of illustrations from Shakespeare, *Shakespeares Mädchen und Frauen* (Shakespeare's Maidens and Ladies, 1838). When he collected a few miscellaneous works for a volume which appeared in 1837, he suggested "das stille Buch" (the quiet book) or "Mährchen"

(fairy tales) as the title; either would have been appropriate.

Toward the end of the decade, however, Heine once again turned to bolder themes. Perhaps the most controversial of these dealt with the writer Ludwig Börne. On the surface Börne and Heine had much in common. Both were liberal Jews residing in France, and both wielded particularly sharp pens. During the early part of the decade they seem to have recognized these affinities and admired one another's work, but a process of estrangement obviously occurred. By the time Börne died in 1837 he and Heine were no longer on friendly terms. Some unfavorable remarks which Börne made in reviews of Heine's work and in private had increased the acrimony between the two men, and Heine soon seized the opportunity to distinguish his views from Börne's. The result was a book which was supposed to be titled "Ludwig Börne: Eine Denkschrift" (Ludwig Börne: A Memorial). To fuel the fires of controversy, however, Heine's publisher Campe gave it the unauthorized title *Heinrich Heine über Ludwig Börne* (1840)–a pun, since the German word *über* means both "about" and "over." In the Denkschrift Heine sets up two different types of radical positions. The Nazarene, associated with Börne, is narrowly political, antiartistic, petty, and Catholic. The Hellene, on the other hand, appreciates aesthetic excellence and understands that a true revolution must encompass more than political upheaval. Although it is never explicitly stated, Heine identifies himself with this preferred position.

Because of Börne's sterling reputation, even among adversaries, Heine's strategy backfired. He was almost universally condemned for what was perceived as an unjustified assault on a man of unimpeachable integrity. What made matters worse was that Heine had also cast aspersions on Jeanette Wohl; for a time Börne had lived with her and her husband, Salomon Strauss. Heine's innuendos concerning this ménage à trois occasioned a public scandal which led to a duel between Heine and Strauss; Heine escaped with a mere wounded hip. The more lasting outcome of this escapade was Heine's marriage to Crescence Eugénie Mirat. Mathilde, as Heine renamed her, was a poor salesgirl whom he had met in 1834 and with whom he had been living since 1836. Recognizing that he could be killed in his confrontation with Strauss, he decided to provide some measure of security for her, and they were wed a week before the duel in August 1841.

Despite the reception of the Börne book and its disastrous consequences, its appearance marks a positive turning point in Heine's literary career. Although in this book he consciously separated himself from the Republican oppositional party with which Börne was associated, his writing once again became more radical and more political during the early 1840s. This turn is partially due to the altered political atmosphere in Germany during the period known as the Vormärz (pre-March), which refers to the eight years directly preceding the March Revolution in 1848. With the death of Friedrich Wilhelm III of Prussia in 1840 and the ascension to the throne of his successor, Friedrich Wilhelm IV, progressive forces hoped for a fundamental change in German political life. These hopes were kindled during the initial years of his reign by reforms in censorship and an apparent willingness to tolerate oppositional views. But perhaps more important for the intellectual climate was the appearance of a strong contingent of left or young Hegelians, who attacked conservative bastions with journalistic enterprises and philosophically informed arguments. Heine was acquainted with the writings of many members of this diverse group, and he befriended for a time the most celebrated young Hegelian, Karl Marx, while he was in his Parisian exile during 1843-1844. Some of Heine's most rousing political verse was written for the radical newspaper *Vorwärts*, to which Marx was also a frequent contributor.

The culmination of Heine's political poetry occurred in 1844 with the mock epic *Deutschland: Ein Wintermärchen* (Germany: A Winter's Tale). In twenty-seven brief chapters containing clever rhymes and witty barbs the poem describes a fictitious coach trip from the French border to Hamburg. Heine had traveled to Hamburg in late 1843 to visit his mother, and the stations on his return home correspond, in reverse order, to the central episodes in the poem. Heine's biting satire has three major objects. First, he attacks the German government, especially Prussian bureaucracy and the limitations placed on individual freedom. Second, he criticizes a rabid nationalism which advocated political revolution without a liberation from religious and ethical bondage. And finally Heine takes to task the German people themselves for their Romantic quietism and political acquiescence to authority. To some extent all three are assailed in the central chapters (14-17), where in a dream the poet confronts the former kaiser of the Holy Roman Empire, Friedrich Barbarrosa. According to legend Barbarrosa and his army are asleep in the Kyffhäuser Mountain waiting for the proper moment to rise up and save Germany. Heine mocks this nationalist myth and the people who would place false hopes on revolutionary leadership coming from royalty. After arousing Barbarrosa's anger by mentioning the French Revolution, he concludes that the German people do not need a kaiser at all.

Atta Troll (1847), the other mock epic Heine wrote during the 1840s, has a somewhat different target. The title figure is a dancing bear who escapes from captivity only to be tracked down and killed by a team of odd hunters whose symbolic significance remains obscure. Atta Troll represents everything Heine objected to most in the German opposition. Prone to long-winded, empty speeches about freedom and equality, this "Tendenzbär" (tendentious bear) personifies the politically limited, religiously tainted, and ethically backward personality Heine had ridiculed in his caricature of Börne. And indeed, this work performs a function similar to that of the book on Börne. While in the earlier work he sought to distinguish his views from those of an apparent po-

Death mask of Heine by Joseph Fontana (Heinrich-Heine-Institut, Düsseldorf)

litical ally, in *Atta Troll* he endeavors to separate his notions of political poetry from the crudities of the poetasters during the Vormärz. In defending fantasy and the imagination as imperative for successful verse, Heine criticizes the trend during the 1840s to create poems consisting of revolutionary platitudes in rhyme.

Heine's radical phase came to an end toward the close of the decade, and three factors were generally responsible for this change. First was his growing preoccupation with what has been called the Erbschaftstreit (inheritance controversy). Salomon Heine had helped to support his nephew with a modest annual allowance, but when he died in 1844, his son Carl balked at continuing these payments. A huge struggle ensued, and the battle of the cousins was carried out on Heine's part with all the public pressure and private leverage he could muster. Heine eventually secured the money he wanted on the condition that he not print anything injurious to the reputation of his family. Far more important was Heine's rapidly deteriorating health, a condition which may have been exacerbated by the stress

of the inheritance controversy. Although the precise identity of Heine's ailment is uncertain—most commentators feel that it was some variety of syphilis—its effects were all too evident. He had suffered from severe headaches even as a young man, but during the mid 1840s he began to experience more serious symptoms. Among these were paralysis in various parts of his body, including his eyelids, severe spinal cramps, and tormenting pain. During the last eight years of his life he was completely bedridden, and this period has therefore come to be known as the Matratzengruft (mattress grave). Finally, the failure of the 1848 revolutions to achieve any of the political goals he so cherished probably dampened his spirits even further.

In this state of physical decay and spiritual depression, Heine underwent a conversion of sorts. Although he had been one of the harshest critics of religion all his life, during his final years he expresses a strong belief in a supreme being. Perhaps more significant for his writing was the abandonment of the sensualist position which had characterized his thought from the early 1820s. While his two ballet scenarios, *Der Doktor Faust* (1851) and *Die Göttin Diana* (published in volume 1 of *Vermischte Schriften*, 1854), the first of which was commissioned in 1846 for Her Majesty's Theatre in London, still advocate a pagan materialism, his later works tend to reject both sensualism and spiritualism as philosophical doctrines. Thus the tenor and content of his poetry from the Matratzengruft, the two collections *Romanzero* (1851) and "Gedichte 1853 und 1854" (in volume 1 of *Vermischte Schriften*), stand in marked contrast to both his early love poetry and his activist verse from the 1840s. While there is no decline in poetic craft or composition, thematically his verse now most often deals with the futility of existence and the ultimate victory of evil over good. That each collection contains a Lazarus cycle says much about the mood and content. Despite this pessimism in his later years, Heine did not completely relinquish his progressive political stance; his later lyrics still evidence a sense of moral outrage at social injustice, and quite a few treat contemporary topics with the satirical wit for which he had become so famous. But a sense of melancholy pervades even these poems, and like the soldier in the war for liberation in "Enfant Perdu," Heine knows that he must count on others who are younger and stronger to fight future battles.

The sufferings of Heine's final years were mitigated somewhat by a woman acquaintance, Elise Krinitz, who is better known by her pen name, Camille Selden, and whom Heine called La Mouche. He met her in 1855, and although Heine's physical state made a passionate affair impossible, the six poems he wrote to her demonstrate his genuine feelings. By the time she had appeared in his life, however, his condition had much deteriorated. Severe cramps and hemorrhaging became frequent occurrences; his pain was regularly relieved by rubbing morphine in an open wound. An end to his torment finally came on 17 February 1856. Three days later he was buried in Montmartre Cemetery on the outskirts of Paris.

Bibliographies:

Arnmin Arnold, *Heine in England and America: A Bibliographical Check-List* (London: Linden Press, 1959);

Gottfried Wilhelm and Eberhard Galley, *Heine Bibliographie*, 2 volumes (Weimar: Arion, 1960);

Franz Finke, "Heine-Bibliography 1954–1959," *Heine-Jahrbuch*, 3 (1964): 80-94;

Eva D. Becker, "Heinrich Heine: Ein Forschungsbericht 1945-1965," *Deutschunterricht*, 18, no. 4 (1966): 1-18;

Siegfried Seifert, *Heine-Bibliographie 1954-1964* (Berlin: Aufbau, 1968);

Jost Hermand, *Streitobjekt Heine: Ein Forschungsbericht 1945-1975* (Frankfurt am Main: Athenaüm, 1975);

Jeffrey L. Sammons, *Heinrich Heine: A Selected Critical Bibliography of Secondary Literature, 1956-1980* (New York: Garland, 1982);

Seifert and Albina A. Volgina, *Heine-Bibliographie 1965-1982* (Berlin: Aufbau, 1986).

Biographies:

Adolf Strodtman, *H. Heines Leben und Werke*, 2 volumes (Berlin: Duncker, 1867-1869);

Louis Untermeyer, *Heinrich Heine: Paradox and Poet*, volume 1: *The Life* (New York: Harcourt, Brace, 1937);

E. M. Butler, *Heinrich Heine: A Biography* (London: Hogarth Press, 1956);

Hans Kaufmann, *Heinrich Heine: Geistige Entwicklung und künstlerisches Werk* (Berlin: Aufbau, 1967);

Manfred Windfuhr, *Heinrich Heine: Revolution und Reflexion* (Stuttgart: Metzler, 1969);

Fritz Mende, *Heinrich Heine-Chronik seines Lebens und Werkes* (Berlin: Akademie-Verlag, 1970);

Joseph A. Kruse, *Heines Hamburger Zeit* (Hamburg: Hoffmann & Campe, 1972);

Michael Werner, ed., *Begegnungen mit Heine: Berichte der Zeitgenossen*, 2 volumes (Hamburg: Hoffmann & Campe, 1973);

Eberhard Galley, *Heinrich Heine*, 4th revised edition (Stuttgart: Metzler, 1976);

Jeffrey L. Sammons, *Heinrich Heine: A Modern Biography* (Princeton: Princeton University Press, 1979);

Mende, *Heinrich Heine: Studien zu seinem Leben und Werk* (Berlin: Akademie-Verlag, 1983);

Wolfgang Mädecke, *Heinrich Heine: Eine Biographie* (Munich: Hanser, 1985);

Ritchie Robertson, *Heine* (London: Holban, 1988).

References:

Akademie der Wissenschaften der DDR, eds., *Heinrich Heine und die Zeitgenossen: Geschichtliche und literarische Befunde* (Berlin: Aufbau, 1979);

Karl Wolfgang Becker, and others, eds., *Heinrich Heine: Streitbarer Humanist und volksverbundener Dichter* (Weimar: Nationale Forschungs- und Gedenkstätten der klassischen deutschen Literatur in Weimar, 1973);

Albrecht Betz, *Ästhetik und Politik: Heinrich Heines Prosa* (Munich: Hanser, 1971);

Klaus Briegleb, *Opfer Heine?: Versuche über Schriftzüge der Revolution* (Frankfurt am Main: Suhrkamp, 1986);

Jürgen Brummack, ed., *Heinrich Heine: Epoche–Werk–Wirkung* (Munich: Beck, 1980);

Barker Fairley, *Heinrich Heine: An Interpretation* (Oxford: Clarendon Press, 1954);

Wilhelm Grössmann, ed., *Geständnisse: Heine im Bewußtsein heutiger Autoren* (Düsseldorf: Droste, 1972);

Grössmann, ed., *Der späte Heine 1848-1856: Literatur–Politik–Religion* (Hamburg: Hoffmann & Campe, 1982);

Heinz Hengst, *Idee und Ideologieverdacht: Revolutionäre Implikation des deutschen Idealismus im Kontext der zeitkritischen Prosa Heinrich Heines* (Munich: Fink, 1973);

Jost Hermand, *Der frühe Heine: Ein Kommentar zu den "Reisebildern"* (Munich: Winkler, 1976);

Laura Hofrichter, *Heinrich Heine* (Oxford: Clarendon Press, 1963);

Gerhard Höhn, *Heine-Handbuch: Zeit, Person, Werk* (Stuttgart: Metzler, 1987);

Robert C. Holub, *Heinrich Heine's Reception of German Grecophilia: The Function and Application of the Hellenic Tradition in the First Half of the Nineteenth Century* (Heidelberg: Winter, 1981);

Rolf Hosfeld, ed., *Signaturen: Heinrich Heine und das 19. Jahrhundert* (Berlin: Argument, 1986);

Raymond Immerwahr and Hanna Spencer, eds., *Heinrich Heine: Dimensionen seines Wirkens* (Bonn: Bouvier, 1979);

Wolfgang Kuttenkeuler, *Heinrich Heine: Theorie und Kritik der Literatur* (Stuttgart: Kohlhammer, 1972);

Sol Liptzin, *The English Legend of Heinrich Heine* (New York: Bloch, 1954);

Willfried Maier, *Leben, Tat, Reflexion: Untersuchungen zu Heinrich Heines Ästhetik* (Bonn: Bouvier, 1969);

Günter Oesterle, *Integration und Konflikt: Die Prosa Heinrich Heines im Kontext oppositioneller Literatur der Restaurationsepoche* (Stuttgart: Metzler, 1972);

Klaus Pabel, *Heines "Reisebilder": Ästhetisches Bedürfnis und politisches Interesse* (Munich: Fink, 1977);

S. S. Prawer, *Franken-Stein's Island: England and the English in the Writings of Heinrich Heine* (Cambridge: Cambridge University Press, 1986);

Prawer, *Heine's Jewish Comedy: A Study of His Portraits of Jews and Judaism* (Oxford: Clarendon Press, 1983);

Prawer, *Heine the Tragic Satirist: A Study of the Later Poetry 1827-1856* (Cambridge: Cambridge University Press, 1961);

Wolfgang Preisendanz, *Heinrich Heine: Werkstrukturen und Epochenbezüge* (Munich: Fink, 1973);

Nigel Reeves, *Heinrich Heine: Poetry and Politics* (Oxford: Oxford University Press, 1974);

William Rose, *The Early Love Poetry of Heinrich Heine: An Inquiry into Poetic Inspiration* (Oxford: Clarendon Press, 1962);

Jeffrey L. Sammons, *Heinrich Heine: The Elusive Poet* (New Haven: Yale University Press, 1969);

A. I. Sandor, *The Exile of Gods: Interpretation of a Theme, a Theory and a Technique in the Work of Heinrich Heine* (The Hague: Mouton, 1967);

Hanna Spencer, *Heinrich Heine* (Boston: Twayne, 1982);

Dolf Sternberger, *Heinrich Heine und die Abschaffung der Sünde* (Düsseldorf: Claassen, 1972);

Benno von Wiese, *Signaturen: Zu Heinrich Heine und seinem Werk* (Berlin: Schmidt, 1976);

Stefan Bodo Wurffel, *Der produktiver Widerspruch: Heinrich Heines negative Dialektik* (Bern: Francke, 1986);

Susanne Zantop, ed., *Paintings on the Move: Heinrich Heine and the Visual Arts* (Lincoln: University of Nebraska Press, 1989).

Papers:
The Heine Archive is at the Landes- und Stadtbibliothek, Düsseldorf.

E. T. A. Hoffmann

(24 January 1776-25 June 1822)

Steven Paul Scher
Dartmouth College

BOOKS: *Fantasiestücke in Callot's Manier: Blätter aus dem Tagebuche eines reisenden Enthusiasten,* anonymous, 4 volumes (Bamberg: Kunz, 1814-1815)–comprises volume 1, "Jacques Callot," "Ritter Gluck," "Kreisleriana Nro. 1-6," "Don Juan"; volume 2, "Nachricht von den neuesten Schicksalen des Hundes Berganza," "Der Magnetiseur"; volume 3, "Der goldene Topf: Ein Märchen aus der neuen Zeit," translated by Thomas Carlyle as "The Golden Pot," in his *German Romance: Specimens of Its Chief Authors* (Edinburgh: Tait, 1827; Boston: Munroe, 1841); volume 4, "Die Abenteuer der Silvester-Nacht," "Kreisleriana"; revised (1819);

Die Vision auf dem Schlachtfelde bei Dresden: Vom Verfasser der Fantasiestücke in Callots Manier, anonymous (Bamberg: Kunz, 1814);

Die Elixiere des Teufels: Nachgelassene Papiere des Bruders Medardus, eines Capuziners. Herausgegeben von dem Verfasser der Fantasiestücke in Callots Manier, anonymous (Berlin: Duncker & Humblot, 1815-1816); translated anonymously as *The Devil's Elixir,* 2 volumes (Edinburgh & London: Blackwood, 1824); translated by Ronald Taylor as *The Devil's Elixirs* (London: Calder, 1963);

Kinder-Mährchen, by Hoffmann, Karl Wilhelm Contessa, and Friedrich de la Motte Fouqué, 2 volumes (Berlin: Realschulbuchhandlung, 1816-1817);

Nachtstücke, herausgegeben von dem Verfasser der Fantasiestücke in Callots Manier, anonymous, 2 volumes (Berlin: Realschulbuchhandlung, 1817)–comprises volume 1, "Der Sandmann," translated by J. Oxenford as "The Sandman," in Oxenford and C. A. Feiling's *Tales from the German* (New York: Harper, 1844; London: Chapman & Hall, 1844); "Ignaz Denner"; "Die Jesuiterkirche in G.," translated by Oxenford as "The Jesuits Church in G-," in *Tales from the German;* "Sanctus"; volume 2, "Das öde Haus"; "Das

E. T. A. Hoffmann in 1821 (drawing by Wilhelm Hensel; by permission of the Nationalgalerie, Berlin)

Majorat," translated by Robert Pierce Gillies as "Rolaudsitten; or, The Deed of Entail," in his *German Stories* (Edinburgh: Blackwood, 1826); "Das Gelübde"; "Das steinerne Herz";

Seltsame Leiden eines Theater-Direktors: Aus mündlicher Tradition mitgeteilt vom Verfasser der Fantasiestücke in Callots Manier, anonymous (Berlin: Maurer, 1819);

Klein Zaches genannt Zinnober: Ein Mährchen herausgegeben von E. T. A. Hoffmann (Berlin: Dümmler, 1819);

Die Serapions-Brüder: Gesammelte Erzählungen und Mährchen. Herausgegeben von E. T. A. Hoffmann, 4 volumes (Berlin: Reimer, 1819-1821)–comprises volume 1, "Der Einsiedler

157

Serapion"; "Rat Krespel," translated anonymously as "The Cremona Violin," in *Stories by Foreign Authors*, 2 volumes (New York: Scribners, 1898); "Die Fermate"; "Der Dichter und der Komponist"; "Ein Fragment aus dem Leben dreier Freunde"; "Der Artushof"; "Die Bergwerke zu Falun"; "Nußknacker und Mausekönig," translated by Mrs. Saint Simon as *Nutcracker and Mouse-king* (New York: Appleton, 1853); volume 2, "Der Kampf der Sänger"; "Eine Spukgeschichte"; "Die Automate"; "Doge und Dogaresse"; "Alte und neue Kirchenmusik"; "Meister Martin der Küfner und seine Gesellen," translated anonymously as "Master Martin and His Workmen," in *Beauties of German Literature: Selected from Various Authors* (London: Burns, 1847); "Das fremde Kind," translated anonymously as *The Strange Child: A Fairy Tale* (London: Rivington, 1852); volume 3, "Nachricht aus dem Leben eines bekannten Mannes"; "Die Brautwahl"; "Der unheimliche Gast"; "Das Fräulein von Scuderi," translated by Gillies as "Mademoiselle de Scuderi," in *German Stories*; "Spielerglück"; "Baron von B."; volume 4, "Signor Formica," translated anonymously as *Signor Formica: A Tale, in Which Are Related Some of the Mad Pranks of Salvator Rosa and Don Pasquale Capuzzi* (New York: Taylor, 1845); "Erscheinungen"; "Der Zusammenhang der Dinge"; "Die Königsbraut"; translated by Alexander Ewing as *The Serapion Brethren*, 2 volumes (London: Bell, 1886-1892);

Lebens-Ansichten des Katers Murr nebst fragmentarischer Biographie des Kapellmeisters Johannes Kreisler in zufälligen Makulaturblättern, 2 volumes (Berlin: Dümmler, 1820-1822); translated by A. R. Hope as "The Educated Cat," in *Nutcracker and Mouse King, and, The Educated Cat* (London: Unwin, 1892);

Prinzessin Brambilla: Ein Capriccio nach Jacob Callot (Breslau: Max, 1821);

Meister Floh: Ein Mährchen in sieben Abenteuern zweier Freunde (Frankfurt am Main: Wilmans, 1822); translated by G. Sloane as "Master Flea," in *Specimens of German Romance, Selected and Translated from Various Authors*, volume 2 (London: Printed for Whittaker, 1826); unexpurgated edition (Berlin: Bard, 1908);

Geschichten, Mährchen und Sagen, by Hoffmann, H. von den Hagen, and Heinrich Steffens (Breslau: Max, 1823);

Aus Hoffmann's Leben und Nachlass, edited by Julius Eduard Hitzig, 2 volumes (Berlin: Dümmler, 1823);

Die letzten Erzählungen von E. T. A. Hoffmann, edited by Hitzig, 2 volumes (Berlin: Dümmler, 1825)–comprises volume 1, "Haimatochare"; "Die Marquise de la Pivardiere"; "Die Irrungen: Fragment aus dem Leben eines Fantasten"; "Die Geheimnisse: Fortsetzung des Fragments aus dem Leben eines Fantasten"; "Der Elementargeist," translated by Oxenford as "The Elementary Spirit," in *Tales from the German;* "Die Räuber: Abenteuer zweier Freunde auf einem Schlosse in Böhmen"; volume 2, "Die Doppeltgänger"; "Datura fastuosa," translated anonymously as "The Datura Fastuosa: A Botanical Tale," *Dublin University Magazine*, 13 (1839): 707; "Meister Johannes Wacht"; "Des Vetters Eckfenster"; "Die Genesung: Fragment aus einem noch ungedruckten Werke";

Ausgewählte Schriften, 10 volumes (Berlin: Reimer, 1827-1828);

E. T. A. Hoffmann's Erzählungen aus seinen letzten Lebensjahren, sein Leben und Nachlaß, edited by Micheline Hoffmann, 5 volumes (Stuttgart: Brodhag, 1839);

Lied von E. T. A. Hoffmann (Altona: Hammerich, 1839);

E. T. A. Hoffmann's gesammelte Schriften, 12 volumes (Berlin: Reimer, 1844-1845);

E. T. A. Hoffmanns musikalische Schriften: Mit Einschluß der nicht in die gesammelten Werke aufgenommen Aufsätze über Beethoven, Kirchenmusik, etc. nebst Biographie, edited by H. vom Ende (Leipzig: Vom Ende, 1889);

E. T. A. Hoffmann, Sämtliche Werke in 15 Bänden, edited by Eduard Greisbach, 15 volumes (Leipzig: Hesse, 1900);

Das Fräulein von Scuderi: Erzählung aus dem Zeitalter Ludwig des Vierzehnten, edited by Gustav Gruener (New York: Holt, 1907);

Meister Martin der Küfner und seine Gesellen: Erzählung, edited by Robert Herndon Fife, Jr. (New York: Holt, 1907);

E. T. A. Hoffmanns Sämtliche Werke: Historisch-kritische Ausgabe, edited by Carl Georg von Maassen, 9 volumes (volumes 1-4, 6-7, Munich: Müller; volume 8, Berlin: Propyläen; volumes 9-10, Munich: Müller, 1908-1928);

E. T. A. Hoffmanns Werke in fünfzehn Teilen, edited by Georg Ellinger, 5 volumes (Berlin: Bong, 1912; revised, 1927);

E. T. A. Hoffmanns Tagebücher und literarische Entwürfe: Mit Erläuterungen und ausführlichen Verzeichnissen, edited by Hans Müller (Berlin: Paetel, 1915);

Sämmtliche Werke: Serapions-Ausgabe, edited by Leopold Hirschberg, 14 volumes (Berlin: De Gruyter, 1922);

E. T. A. Hoffmann: Musikalische Werke, edited by Gustav Becking, 3 volumes (Leipzig: Linnemann, 1922-1927);

Die Maske: Ein Singspiel in 3 Akten (1799), edited by Friedrich Schnapp (Berlin: Verlag für Kunstwissenschaft, 1923);

Dichtungen und Schriften sowie Briefe und Tagebücher: Gesamtausgabe, edited by Walther Harich, 15 volumes (Weimar: Lichtenstein, 1924);

Handzeichnungen E. T. A. Hoffmanns in Faksimileleichtdruck nach den Originalen, mit einer Einleitung: E. T. A. Hoffmann als bildender Künstler, edited by Walter Steffen and Hans von Müller (Berlin: Propyläen, 1925); revised edition, edited by Friedrich Schnapp (Hildesheim: Gerstenberg, 1973);

Der goldene Topf: Ein Märchen aus der neuen Zeit, edited by William Faulkner Mainland (Oxford: Blackwell, 1942);

E. T. A. Hoffmann: Poetische Werke, edited by Klaus Kanzog, 12 volumes (Berlin: De Gruyter, 1957-1962);

Gesammelte Werke: Neuausgabe, edited by Walter Müller-Seidel and others, 5 volumes (Munich: Winkler, 1960-1965); volume 5, part 1, revised by Friedrich Schnapp as *Schriften zur Musik: Aufsätze und Rezensionen* (Munich: Winkler, 1977); volume 5, part 2, revised by Schnapp as *Nachlese: Dichtungen, Schriften, Aufzeichnungen und Fragmente* (Munich: Winkler, 1981);

Liebe und Eifersucht (Die Schärpe und die Blume): Ein Singspiel-Libretto in drei Aufzügen, nach dem Spanischen des Calderón und der Schlegelschen Übersetzung, edited by Schnapp (Munich: Winkler, 1970);

E. T. A. Hoffmann: Ausgewählte musikalische Werke, edited by Georg von Dadelsen and others, 8 volumes published (Mainz: Schott, 1970-)—comprises volumes 1-3, *Undine;* volumes 4-5, *Die lustigen Musikanten;* volume 10b, *Miserere;* volume 11, *Sinfonia Es-dur; Recitativo ed Aria "Prendi, l'acciar ti rendo";* volume 12b, *Quintett c-moll für Harfe, zwei Violinen, Viola und Violoncello; Grand Trio E-dur für Klavier, Violine und Violoncello;*

Tagebücher: Nach der Ausgabe Hans von Müllers mit Erlauterungen, edited by Schnapp (Munich: Winkler, 1971);

Juristische Arbeiten, edited by Schnapp (Munich: Winkler, 1973);

E. T. A. Hoffmann, edited by Schnapp (Munich: Heimeran, 1974);

Gesammelte Werke in Einzelausgaben, edited by Rudolf Mingau and Hans-Joachim Kruse, 8 volumes published (Berlin & Weimar: Aufbau, 1976-);

Der Musiker E. T. A. Hoffmann: Ein Dokumentenband, edited by Schnapp (Hildesheim: Gerstenberg, 1981);

Sämtliche Werke, edited by Wulf Segebrecht, Hartmut Steinecke, and others, 2 volumes published (Frankfurt am Main: Deutscher Klassiker Verlag, 1985-).

Editions in English: *Hoffmann's Strange Stories: From the German,* translated by Lafayette Burnham (Boston: Burnham, 1855)—comprises "Life of Hoffmann," "The Cooper of Nuremberg" ("Meister Martin, der Küfner, und seine Gesellen"), "The Lost Reflection" ("Die Abenteuer der Sylvester-Nacht"), "Antonia's Song" ("Rat Krespel"), "The Walled-up Door" ("Das Majorat"), "Berthold, the Madman" ("Die Jesuiterkirche in G–"), "Coppelius, the Sandman" ("Der Sandmann"), "Salvator Rosa" ("Signor Formica"), "Cardillac, the Jeweler" ("Das Fräulein von Scuderi"), "The Pharo-bank" ("Spielerglück"), "Fascination" ("Der Magnetiseur"), "The Agate Heart" ("Das steinerne Herz"), "The Mystery of the Deserted House" ("Das öde Haus");

Hoffmann's Fairy Tales, translated by Burnham (Boston: Burnham, 1857)—comprises "The Adventures of Traugott" (Der Artushof "), "Annunziata" ("Doge und Dogaressa"), "The Chain of Destiny" ("Der Zusammenhang der Dinge"), "Ignaz Denner" ("Nachtstücke," part 1), "Little Zack" ("Klein Zaches");

Weird Tales by E. T. A. Hoffmann: A New Translation from the German, translated by John Thomas Bealby, 2 volumes (London: Nimmo, 1885; New York: Scribners, 1885)—comprises volume 1, "The Cremona Violin," "The Fermata," "Signor Formica," "The Sand-man," "The Entail," "Arthur's Hall"; volume 2, "The Doge and Dogess," "Master Martin the Cooper," "Mademoiselle de Scudéri," "Gambler's Luck," "Master Johannes Wacht";

Tales of Hoffmann, translated by Frederick Mac-Curdy Atkinson (London: Harrap, 1932; New York: Dodd, Mead, 1933)–comprises "The Interdependence of Things," "The Sandman," "The Mystery of the Deserted House," "The Lost Reflection," "The Walled-in Door";

The Tales of Hoffmann: Stories by E. T. A Hoffmann, translated out of the German by Various Hands (New York: Heritage Press, 1943)–comprises "The Sandman," translated by Bealby; "The Mines of Falun," translated by E. N. Bennett; "Councillor Krespel," translated by Barrows Munsey; "Don Juan," translated by Jacques Le Clercq; "The Mystery of the Deserted House," translated by Maria Labocceta; "The Vow," translated by F. E. Pierce; "Mademoiselle De Scudéry," translated by Bealby; "The Entail," translated by Bealby; "The Uncanny Guest," translated by Alexander Ewing; "Gambler's Luck," translated by Bealby;

Tales of Hoffmann, edited by Christopher Lazare (New York: Wyn, 1946; republished, New York: Grove Press, 1959)–comprises "Mademoiselle de Scudéry," "Don Juan," "Antonia's Song," "The Golden Pot," "The Doubles," "The Vow," "The Fermata," "Berthold the Madman," "Salvator Rosa," "The Legacy";

Tales from Hoffmann: Translated by Various Hands, edited by J. M. Cohen (London: Bodley Head, 1950; New York: Coward-McCann, 1951)–comprises "The Golden Pot," "The Sandman," "The Deed of Entail," "The Story of Krespel," "Mlle de Scudéri";

Eight Tales of Hoffmann, Newly Translated, translated by Cohen (London: Pan, 1952)–comprises "The Lost Reflection," "The Sandman," "The Jesuit Church in Glogau," "The Deserted House," "Councillor Krespel," "The Mines of Falun," "A Ghost Story," "Gamblers' Luck";

The King's Bride, translated by Paul Turner (London: Calder, 1959);

The Tales of Hoffmann: Newly Selected and Translated from the German, translated by Michael Bullock (New York: Ungar, 1963)–comprises "The Sandman," "Mademoiselle de Scudery," "Datura Fastuosa," "The King's Bride," "Gambler's Luck";

The Best Tales of Hoffmann, edited by E. F. Bleiler (New York: Dover, 1967)–comprises "The Golden Flower Pot," "Automata," "A New Year's Eve Adventure," "Nutcracker and the King of Mice," "The Sand-man," "Rath Krespel," "Tobias Martin, Master Cooper, and His Men," "The Mines of Falun," "Signor Formica," "The King's Betrothed";

Selected Writings of E. T. A. Hoffmann, edited and translated by Leonard J. Kent and Elizabeth C. Knight, 2 volumes (Chicago: University of Chicago Press, 1969)–comprises volume 1, "Ritter Gluck," "The Golden Pot," "The Sandman," "Councillor Krespel," "The Mines of Falun," "Mademoiselle de Scuderi," "The Doubles"; volume 2, "The Life and Opinions of Kater Murr," books 1 & 2;

Three Märchen of E. T. A. Hoffmann, translated by Charles E. Passage (Columbia: University of South Carolina Press, 1971)–comprises "Little Zaches, Surnamed Zinnober," "Princess Brambilla," "Master Flea";

Tales, edited by Victor Lange (New York: Continuum, 1982)–comprises "The Golden Pot," "Councillor Krespel," "Mademoiselle de Scudéri," "The Mines of Falun," "The Fermata," "The Deed of Entail," "The Sandman";

Tales of Hoffmann, edited and translated by R. J. Hollingdale (Harmondsworth, U.K. & New York: Penguin, 1982);

Nutcracker, translated by Ralph Manheim (New York: Crown, 1984; London: Bodley Head, 1984).

An ironist and humorist par excellence, the prolific storyteller E. T. A. Hoffmann occupies a prominent place in the canon of nineteenth-century European literature. He is regarded today as the influential, eccentric genius of German Romanticism, whose distinctive fictional universe foreshadows late-twentieth-century sensibility. Sophisticated as well as entertaining, Hoffmann's fiction is quintessentially Romantic in thematic orientation, milieu, aesthetic and philosophical outlook, and narrative stance–and yet it also strikes contemporary readers as astonishingly modern. At the height of his writing career, Hoffmann was a best-selling author in Germany, and soon after his premature death at age forty-six he became known on the Continent through translations as the author of "weird" and fantastic tales–particularly in France and Russia, but also in England. The prominent poets and writers demonstrably inspired by Hoffmann's oeuvre include Gerard de Nerval, Honoré de Balzac, Victor Hugo, Alfred de Musset, George Sand, Alexandre Dumas père, Prosper Mérimée, and Charles Baudelaire in France; Sir Walter Scott, Thomas Carlyle, Charles Dickens, Robert Louis Stevenson, the Brontës, Oscar Wilde, and G. K. Chesterton in England; Samuel Beckett in Ireland; Edgar Allan Poe, Nathaniel Hawthorne, and Washington Irving in America; Alexander Pushkin, Nikolai Gogol, Ivan Turgenev, Fyodor Dostoyevski, and Leo Tolstoy in Russia; Søren Kierkegaard, Hans Christian Andersen, Henrik Ibsen, and filmmaker Ingmar Bergman in Scandinavia; and Heinrich Heine, Hugo von Hofmannsthal, Thomas Mann, and Franz Kafka in German-speaking countries.

E. T. W. Hoffmann
born Königsberg in Prussia
on 24 January 1776
died Berlin on 25 June 1822
Court of Appeal Councillor
excellent
in office
as writer
as composer
as painter
Dedicated by his friends.

Perhaps this concise inscription on his tombstone captures best the existential dilemma that plagued the uncommonly talented Hoffmann throughout his life and shaped the all-pervasive dualistic worldview that he so consistently espoused: can one and the same individual live and work as an integral part of bourgeois society and be a free-spirited creative artist as well? Still today it is little known that Hoffmann was a multiply gifted man and artist: he was not only the successful author of fantastic and grotesque tales but also an eminent jurist, a Romantic composer of considerable merit, a talented painter, draftsman, and caricaturist, as well as an experienced man of the theater. Ironically, it is the inauthentic, trivializing nineteenth-century image of the "Hoffmann of the Tales" that lives on in public consciousness, perpetuated by Jacques Offenbach's popular opera *Les Contes d'Hoffmann* (*The Tales of Hoffmann*, 1881) which portrays the title hero as a self-dramatizing Romantic fabulist, notorious drinker, and womanizer. And while Tchaikovsky's *Nutcracker* continues to be a perennial favorite of audiences the world over, few of its admirers realize that the scenario for the ballet is based on Hoffmann's tale "Nußknacker und

Mausekönig" (1816; translated as *Nutcracker and Mouseking*, 1853). Typically, even Hoffmann's tombstone stands to remind posterity of his accomplishment as a legal official first and not as the writer and composer E. T. A. Hoffmann who, in honor of Mozart, his idol, substituted Amadeus for his third given name, Wilhelm. "Es ist in meinem Leben etwas recht Charakteristisches," he wrote to a friend in 1814, contemplating his new appointment as a judge in Berlin, "daß immer das geschieht was ich gar nicht erwartete, sey es nun Böses oder Gutes, und daß ich stets das zu thun gezwungen werde, was meinem eigentlichen tieferen Prinzip widerstrebt." (It is something genuinely characteristic of my life that what happens is invariably what I least expect, whether for the worst or for the best, and that I am always compelled to do what runs counter to my deepest convictions.)

Ernst Theodor Wilhelm Hoffmann spent the first twenty years of his life in Königsberg, a university town on the Baltic Sea known chiefly for its most famous son, the philosopher Immanuel Kant. Hoffmann was born into troubled family circumstances: his parents, Christoff Ludwig and Luise Albertine Doerffer Hoffmann, divorced when he was barely two years old. Hoffmann endured a lonely childhood in the depressing household of his maternal grandmother, a religious fanatic, where he lived with his neurotic and perennially ill mother, two spinster aunts, and his uncle Otto Wilhelm Doerffer, a pedantic philistine who was dismissed from legal practice for incompetence. Hoffmann's psychologically unstable father, a descendant of lawyers and a civil servant himself, moved away and was not heard from again. The desolate family atmosphere did not, however, altogether stifle the boy's budding intellectual and artistic curiosity. Oddly enough, it was Uncle Otto, an avid amateur chamber musician, who gave the precocious child his first music lessons and thus planted the seeds of Hoffmann's lifelong passion for music. More systematic musical study followed, and soon he became quite proficient in music theory; learned to play the piano, violin, harp, and guitar; and—at age thirteen—began to compose. During these formative years he received instruction in the visual arts as well and developed his talent for drawing and painting. His reading habits were also formed in his early teens. Hoffmann and his playmate Theodor Gottlieb von Hippel, later a leading Prussian legal administrator and lifelong loyal friend, devoured contemporary adventure stories and popular novels along with the classics of European literature, among them the works of Johann Wolfgang Goethe, Friedrich von Schiller, Jean Paul, William Shakespeare, Jonathan Swift, Laurence Sterne, Miguel de Cervantes, Jean-Jacques Rousseau, and Denis Diderot. Their particular favorites were Goethe's *Die Leiden des jungen Werthers* (The Sorrows of Young Werther, 1787), Sterne's *Sentimental Journey* (1768) and *Tristram Shandy* (1759-1767), and Rousseau's *Confessions* (1770).

In spite of his inclination toward the arts, Hoffmann yielded to family pressures and at age sixteen enrolled as a law student at Königsberg University. He pursued his legal studies conscientiously, passed his first law examination in 1795, and started working as a judicial aide at a local court. But, characteristically, when not on the job, he devoted himself totally to artistic pursuits–a double life-style he juggled throughout his career: "Sontag blühn bey mir Künste und Wissenschaften.... Die Wochentage bin ich Jurist und höchstens etwas Musiker, Sontags am Tage wird gezeichnet und Abends bin ich ein sehr witziger Autor bis in die späte Nacht." (On Sundays the arts and sciences are in flower for me.... Weekdays I am a jurist and at most a bit of a musician. In the daytime on Sundays I draw; in the evening and far into the night I am a very witty author.) Indeed, already in his late teens, in addition to musical composition, caricature drawing, and portrait and historical painting, the budding jurist experimented with writing fiction, though neither of the two novels he wrote at the time–the three-volume "Cornaro" and "Der Geheimnisvolle" (The Mystery Man)–survives.

While a law student, Hoffmann supported himself by giving music lessons. He fell in love with one of his pupils, Dora ("Cora") Hatt, an unhappily married woman ten years his senior. Though in 1796 he left Königsberg for a two-year stint as judiciary aide in the provincial Silesian town of Glogau, the passionate but hopeless affair was not terminated until 1798; it reappeared later in fictionalized form as the core of one of Hoffmann's best-known stories, "Das Majorat" (1817; translated as Rolaudsitten; or, The Deed of Entail, 1826). In this narrative, which demonstrably inspired Edgar Allan Poe's famous 1839 ghost story "The Fall of the House of Usher," the young lawyer-narrator Theodor visits a haunted castle and falls unhappily in love with the baroness Seraphine, who shares his passion for music.

In Glogau, Hoffmann stayed with the family of another lawyer uncle and continued to compose and paint in his spare time. After the break with Cora he became engaged, however half-heartedly, to his first cousin Minna Doerffer. Upon passing his second judicial examination in 1798, with the help of his uncle he received a transfer to a new legal post in Berlin. For the first time in his life, Hoffmann was in his element: the Prussian capital offered him the intellectual and cultural excitement provincial Glogau so sorely lacked. He threw himself with a vengeance into Berlin's rich opera, concert, and theater life, frequented literary salons, and even found time to study composition with Johann Friedrich Reichardt, a central figure of contemporary German music who was also Goethe's friend and consultant in musical matters.

In 1799 Hoffmann completed his first substantial creative effort, a singspiel titled *Die Maske* (The Mask), which was discovered and published in 1923. That he wrote both the text and the music is an early confirmation of the musico-literary aspirations that he sustained throughout his life. Clearly indebted to the Italian opera buffa tradition and particularly to Mozart's *Don Giovanni* (1787), Hoffmann's favorite opera, the music is competently crafted. The libretto anticipates many of his later thematic preoccupations such as the split personality, the occult, insanity, inherited sin, and the demonic.

Hoffmann's first Berlin stay was cut short in 1800 by his promotion, after his final law examination, to a new legal post in the Prussian administration, this time in the Polish provinces at a higher court in Posen. Once again, life in the hinterlands had an adverse effect on the urbane young man, who sought solace in drinking and socializing. The bitterly satirical caricatures he drew of fellow legal officials and members of the local military elite earned him a disciplinary transfer to Plock, a tiny and even more provincial Polish town totally devoid of culture. Shortly before leaving Posen for Plock, Hoffmann broke off his engagement to Minna Doerffer, and on 26 July 1802 he married Michaelina ("Mischa") Rorer, a good-natured, stable, and loyal twenty-three-year-old Polish woman with whom he enjoyed lasting domestic bliss. Mischa's unfaltering devotion and support could, however, only partially mitigate the interminable two years in Plock; his diary entries record continued drinking, illnesses, a persecution complex, death visions, and doppelgänger fantasies. Yet, at night Hoffmann continued to

Ausgearteter Fantasie
Graufenerregende Bilder
Des gährenden Hirns — des
Wahnfins schrekhafte Kinder —

nach W. Hoffmanns Handzeichn
von E. Neureuther?

Drawing by Hoffmann (etched by E. Neureuther)

compose and write. In 1803 he made it into print for the first time with a piece of musico-literary criticism, a short essay entitled "Schreiben eines Klostergeistlichen an seinen Freund in der Hauptstadt" (Letters from a Friar to His Friend in the Capital), which discusses the function of declamation and singing in drama. He also won honorable mention in a play-writing competition with a comedy called *Der Preis* (The Prize).

In 1804 the intervention of his friend Hippel rescued Hoffmann at last from his provincial "exile": he was appointed as government councillor in Warsaw. The Polish capital was a cultural haven at the time, and Hoffmann took full advantage of its offerings. His lasting friendship with Julius Eduard Hitzig, a fellow lawyer from Berlin and later his first biographer, also dates from the happy Warsaw years. Hitzig introduced him to the best of contemporary German literature, the

writings of Friedrich and August Wilhelm von Schlegel, Novalis, Ludwig Tieck, and Clemens Brentano. Hoffmann resumed composition in earnest and even got a chance to conduct regularly in public orchestral concerts a sampling of his own music, along with works by Christoph Willibald von Gluck, Franz Joseph Haydn, Wolfgang Amadeus Mozart, Luigi Cherubini, and Ludwig van Beethoven. For a while Hoffmann's musical career seemed well under way. He composed some of his best works during the Warsaw period, among them a singspiel based on Brentano's comedy *Die lustigen Musikanten* (The Merry Minstrels, 1805); a mass in D minor (1805); his only symphony, in E-flat major (1806); a quintet for harp and string quartet in C minor (1807); and an opera entitled *Liebe und Eifersucht* (Love and Jealousy, 1807), for which he also wrote a libretto inspired by Spanish dramatist Pedro Calderón de la Barca.

In October 1806 Napoleon's armies occupied the Polish capital and dissolved the Prussian administration. Hoffmann, along with other legal officials, suddenly found himself without a livelihood and had to leave Warsaw. He sent his wife and infant daughter Cäcilia (who died shortly after at the age of two) to stay with relatives in Posen and decided to try his luck in Berlin, where he returned in the summer of 1807. His brief second Berlin stay turned out to be disappointing. The Napoleonic invasion had left the Prussian capital in shambles, and Hoffmann, who was penniless, was unable to make ends meet either as a jurist or a free-lance artist. Finally, after a period of despair and even starvation, during which he nevertheless continued composing, painting, and drawing, he responded to a newspaper advertisement and accepted a position as music director of the theater in Bamberg in southern Germany. It seemed at last that Hoffmann might have a fair chance to fulfill his lifelong ambition to pursue the career of a professional musician.

Upon arrival in Bamberg in 1808, however, he found the theater nearly bankrupt, the artistic conditions debilitating, and the management fraught with internal strife. A few weeks after he assumed his duties as conductor and music director, he was unemployed once again. Though he retained his title, at the theater he merely functioned as artistic consultant and occasional composer of incidental music. To eke out a living, he gave piano and singing lessons. In 1810 he became hopelessly infatuated with fourteen-year-old Julia Mark, one of his voice pupils. The affair remained strictly one-sided, internalized, and sublimated in passionate diary entries. Julia was soon married off to a boorish Hamburg merchant, and Hoffmann never saw her again. But this all-consuming emotional experience, transfigured and poeticized, came to permeate many of Hoffmann's major narratives as a recurrent theme of the artist's idealized, unattainable beloved, forever the object of his infinite yearning and unfulfilled desire. For example, the Julia Mark affair forms the core of the 1814 story "Nachricht von den neuesten Schicksalen des Hundes Berganza" (An Account of the Latest Fortunes of the Dog Berganza), a fictionalized reminiscence about Hoffmann's time in Bamberg from the ironic perspective of a Cervantes-inspired talking dog. The motif also figures prominently as the Julia-Giulietta constellation in the tale "Die Abenteuer der Silvester-Nacht" (1815; translated as "A New Year's Eve Adventure," 1967) and in the Julia-Kreisler relationship of the novel *Lebens-Ansichten des Katers Murr nebst fragmentarischer Biographie des Kapellmeisters Johannes Kreisler in zufälligen Makulaturblättern* (1820-1822; translated as "The Life and Opinions of Kater Murr," in *Selected Writings of E. T. A. Hoffmann,* 1969).

Despite the emotional turmoil and pecuniary difficulties, the Bamberg years (1808-1813) were crucial for Hoffmann's evolving artistic career as musician, music critic, and writer of fiction. To be sure, throughout his Bamberg stay Hoffmann still regarded himself primarily as a musician. He composed here some of his finest music, such as the piano trio in E major (1809), a *Miserere* in B-flat minor (1809), the operas *Trank der Unsterblichkeit* (Potion of Immortality, 1808) and *Aurora* (1812), and began working on his musical magnum opus, the opera *Undine* (composed in 1813-1814). But while still composing, he turned increasingly to writing critical essays on the contemporary musical scene for the Leipzig *Allgemeine musikalische Zeitung*, the leading musical journal at the time. It was an ingenious blend of satirical music criticism and fantastic fiction that in February 1809 launched Hoffmann's career as both music critic and man of letters: the narrative "Ritter Gluck" (literally Sir Gluck, translated as "Ritter Gluck," 1969).

Hoffmann scholars unanimously agree that "Ritter Gluck," though a literary first, is an unusually accomplished piece which provides the key to understanding this multiply gifted writer: it embodies most of the traits and narrative strategies of his fictional universe that the term "Hoffmannesque" has come to signify. An extended anecdote rather than a short story, "Ritter Gluck"–subtitled "Eine Erinnerung aus dem Jahre 1809" (A Recollection from the Year 1809)–offers no real plot. In a Berlin outdoor café, the first-person narrator meets a curious old man, who claims to be a musician and raves mysteriously about having just been banished from the "kingdom of dreams," hospitable to true artistic talent, and condemned to reconcile his higher vision of truth with living in the philistine confines of the Prussian capital. The two become acquainted through a conversation praising the music of Mozart and Gluck and disparaging contemporary musical life in Berlin. Back at his lodgings, the stranger amazes the narrator by playing Gluck's 1777 opera *Armide* on the piano from a score of blank pages. Then, in the italicized concluding line of the story, the stranger at last reveals his identity: "*Ich bin der Ritter Gluck!*" (I am Chevalier Gluck!). The German title "Ritter" corresponds to the English "Sir" and implies knighthood, an honor that was indeed conferred on the composer Christoph Willibald Gluck, who died in 1787 in Vienna. But who, then, is Ritter Gluck, roving the streets of Berlin in 1809? A revenant, a mad musician who believes he is the great composer, or simply a creation of the daydreaming narrator? Who is the inquisitive narrator? And what about the parallel between the fictitious author of this musical reminiscence and the real author of the story, the struggling composer and budding writer E. T. A. Hoffmann? Typically, these and countless other questions remain unresolved, signifying that there are simply no clear-cut solutions to Hoffmann's puzzling narratives; ambiguity and multiple meanings reign supreme.

"Ritter Gluck" established Hoffmann's reputation as the author of a refreshingly original kind of music criticism. The numerous reviews of contemporary as well as earlier music that he regularly contributed to the *Allgemeine musikalische Zeitung* until 1815 combined broad aesthetic assessment and informed value judgments with competent yet not overly technical analysis. His insights into the creative process of the musical giants Giovanni Pierluigi da Palestrina, Johann Sebastian Bach, Gluck, Haydn, Mozart, and Beethoven are valid today and earned him recognition as the founder of modern music criticism. His Beethoven reviews, particularly that of the Fifth Symphony (1810), stand out as pioneering critical achievements. That Hoffmann considered reviewing music as a genuinely literary activity is borne out by the fact that his famous interpretive essay entitled "Beethovens Instrumental-Musik" (1814)–a recasting, without the analytical sections, of his reviews of the Fifth Symphony and two piano trios into a flowing narrative–became part of the first volume of his first literary publication in book form, the *Fantasiestücke in Callot's Manier: Blätter aus dem Tagebuche eines reisenden Enthusiasten* (Fantasy Pieces in the Manner of Callot: Sheets from the Diary of a Traveling Enthusiast, 1814-1815). It was in this epoch-making essay that Hoffmann, for the first time in the history of musical aesthetics, conjoined Haydn, Mozart, and Beethoven as the musical trinity that still perdures, pronounced Beethoven as a quintessentially Romantic artist, and formulated his influential definition of music as "die romantischste aller Künste, [. . .] denn nur das Unendliche ist ihr Vorwurf " (the most romantic of all the arts, [. . .] for its sole subject is the infinite). For Hoffmann, the term "Romantic" was a value judgment rather than a period designation. He interpreted Haydn, Mozart, and Beethoven as Romantic composers because he regarded them as the greatest, because in their works he could discern an unmediated aura of the demonic, the supernatural, and the inexpressible. A characteristic, musically inspired literary manifestation of Hoffmann's elusive romantic aura is the well-known fantasy piece "Don Juan" (1813; translated 1943), which has profoundly influenced critical appraisals of Mozart's opera, *Don Giovanni* (1787). This enigmatic narrative oscillates between an autobiographically charged fictional frame and a partial analysis of the opera based on a curiously biased interpretation of the ambivalent Don Giovanni-Donna Anna relationship.

In the spring of 1813 Hoffmann accepted an offer to become music director of an opera company that performed alternately in Dresden and Leipzig. Just before he left Bamberg, he signed a contract for the publication of his *Fantasiestücke,* the first two volumes of which were to collect most of his writings to date. Since he was still determined to make a name for himself as a musician, he requested that his publisher print the work anonymously: "Ich mag mich nicht nennen, indem mein Name nicht anders als durch eine gelungene musikalische Composition der Welt bekannt werden soll." (I do not wish to be named, for my name should become known to the world by means of a successful musical com-

position and not otherwise.) Even after he had become a best-selling author, Hoffmann adhered to this resolution: not one of his literary works appeared under his own name until 1816, when his opera *Undine* was successfully staged and enthusiastically received in Berlin.

Hoffmann's brief stint as opera conductor in Dresden and Leipzig (1813-1814) was also his last employment as a professional musician. As his notoriously bad luck would have it, once again he found himself in the midst of the Napoleonic wars: he had to shuttle between the two besieged cities and conduct performances between battles. Yet, during his hectic, nine-month tenure as commuting conductor, Hoffmann managed to complete his operatic masterpiece *Undine* and the first part of the two-volume novel *Die Elixiere des Teufels: Nachgelassene Papiere des Bruders Medardus, eines Capuziners. Herausgegeben von dem Verfasser der Fantasiestücke in Callots Manier* (1815-1816; translated as *The Devil's Elixir,* 1824). In Dresden he also wrote his best-known tale, "Der goldene Topf: Ein Märchen aus der neuen Zeit" (1814)–which was translated by Thomas Carlyle in 1827 as "The Golden Pot"–and contributed two major pieces of music criticism to the *Allgemeine musikalische Zeitung:* "Der Dichter und der Komponist" (The Poet and the Composer, 1813) and "Alte und neue Kirchenmusik" (Ancient and Modern Church Music, 1814).

Hoffmann himself considered "Der goldene Topf " as his best piece of writing. It is also perhaps his most representative work, for it illustrates best his poetics of story-telling: a characteristic fusion of fabulistic inventiveness, reader manipulation, and biting social satire imbued with humor and irony. Already the narrative's startling subtitle "A Modern Fairy Tale" signals the Hoffmannesque confrontation between the poetic fairy-tale world and the prosaic confines of every day. Like "Ritter Gluck," "Der goldene Topf " opens in a commonplace setting and concludes with an intimation of the supernatural as the realm of "true reality." Hoffmann formulates the principle for this paradigmatic story-telling strategy in a famous passage from the conversational frame of his *Die Serapions-Brüder: Gesammelte Erzählungen und Mährchen. Herausgegeben von E. T. A. Hoffmann* (1819-1821; translated as *The Serapion Brethren,* 1886-1892):

Ich meine, daß die Basis der Himmelsleiter, auf der man hinaufsteigen will in höhere Regionen, befestigt sein müsse im Leben, so daß jeder

a. die Nase.
b. die Stirn.
c. die Augen.
d. Dallasische Beafsteck.
   u. Portwein.
e. der Ironische Zug, oder
   die Mahrohen Muskel
f. das lange Kinn mifrathe.
   ne Schauspiele(Blandina etc)
g. Neuaptirte Haare oder
   Geistererscheinungen
h. Ein Halstuch.
i. Ein Kragen.

k. Ein Rokaermel mit
   willkührlichen Falten
l. Der Backenbart oder
   übernächtige Gedanken
   eines Mondsüchtigen
m. die Mephistophelesmusik.
   oder Rachgier u. Mordlust_
   Elixiere des Teufels.
n. fehlt
o. Das Ohr oder Kreislers
   Lehrbrief der weder ge.
   hört noch verstanden word.
p. Und so weiter

Self-portrait of Hoffmann (Archiv für Kunst und Geschichte, Berlin)

nachzusteigen vermag. Befindet er sich dann immer höher und höher hinaufgeklettert, in einem fantastischen Zauberreich, so wird er glauben, dies Reich gehöre auch noch in sein Leben hinein, und sei eigentlich der wunderbar herrlichste Teil desselben.

(I believe that the foot of the heavenly ladder, upon which we want to climb into higher regions, has to be anchored in life, so that everyone may be able to follow. If then, having climbed higher and higher, people find themselves in a fantastic, magical world, they will think that this realm, too, still belongs in their life and is actually its most wonderfully glorious part.)

"Der goldene Topf" is novelistic in form, dimension, and narrative technique. Hoffmann divides his tale into twelve vigils and gives each vigil elaborate and humorously elliptical headings that anticipate plot details intelligible only later in the appropriate narrative context. The basic story line is both disarmingly transparent and won-

drously blurred; it revolves around the typically romantic protagonist Anselmus, a young, handsome, and talented social misfit. Amiably shy and clumsy, the student Anselmus shuttles between ordinary life in contemporary Dresden and the supernatural realm of snakes, salamanders, fire lilies, witches, enchanted gardens, and exotic birds. He spends his leisure time in the company of pedantic bureaucrats like Registrar Heerbrand and Dean Paulmann, courting Paulmann's lovely, blue-eyed daughter Veronica, who is not disinclined. But Anselmus, given to poetic reverie, also leads an entirely different sort of existence in the world of myth and magic. Here his adventures are remote-controlled by Lindhorst, a salamander and prince of the spirits who, as the eccentric Privy Archivarius, is also a respected citizen of Dresden. In the mythical fairy-tale realm Anselmus's beloved and muse is Serpentina, the little blue-eyed golden-green snake, who also happens to be one of Lindhorst's marriageable daughters. By the end of the tale Anselmus has become a poet: his quest for knowledge and self-realization is fulfilled as he symbolically graduates from Veronica's philistine world into Serpentina's redemptive realm of the imagination and attains "life in poetry" in mythical Atlantis. His reward is a golden flowerpot that signifies endurance and growth. Hoffmann's poetic allegory of the fundamental "dualism of being" has come full circle.

Hoffmann had to wait for public recognition as composer and storyteller until he was offered a chance–through the intervention of his influential friend Hippel–to return to Berlin, where he spent the remaining eight years of his life as a literary celebrity and respected civil servant. In February 1814 the destitute and disillusioned thirty-eight-year-old composer-conductor was ready to opt for a more settled life-style: however reluctantly, he decided to abandon his dream of a musical career and accepted a position in the Prussian judicial system. Within a mere two years he acquired a reputation as a brilliant jurist and rose in the legal hierarchy from unpaid court councillor to judge on the supreme court of appeals.

By 1816 Hoffmann was well known as the author of *Fantasiestücke*, the four-volume collection of his narratives including "Ritter Gluck," "Don Juan," "Der goldene Topf," the famous Beethoven essay, and other "Kreisleriana" pieces (featuring his musician alter ego, the eccentric and opinionated Kapellmeister Johannes Kreisler); and his first novel, *Die Elixiere des Teufels*, became a bestseller overnight. This intriguingly complex, ingeniously constructed forerunner of the sophisticated crime thriller *and* the modern psychological novel–replete with violence, lust, inherited guilt, rape, murder, incest, insanity, persecution complex, mistaken identities, split personalities, and doppelgänger–conjures up the demonic powers that emanate from the darkest recesses of the subconscious. The story of the runaway monk Medardus is a suspenseful spine-chiller from start to finish: cursed by the sins of his degenerate ancestors and led by Satan, Medardus becomes inextricably entangled in a series of lurid criminal adventures, for which he atones by recording his experiences before he dies.

With fourteen performances the hit of the 1816-1817 Berlin theater season, the opera *Undine*–one of the long line of German Romantic operas which includes Karl Maria von Weber's *Der Freischütz* (1821) and Richard Wagner's *Lohengrin* (1850)–established at last Hoffmann's reputation as a composer, and he began to publish his writings under his own name. The *Undine* libretto, however, was provided by Friedrich de la Motte Fouqué, the author of the well-known fairy tale of the same title (1811): the erotic story of the water nymph Undine, frustrated in her attempt to become a loved and loving woman. But Hoffmann's long-awaited operatic success was soon eclipsed by his literary fame as the best-selling author of the *Fantasiestücke*, the *Elixiere des Teufels*, and the dozens of diverse narratives he published during his remaining six years. By 1818 he commanded such a devoted reading public that despite his phenomenal productivity he could not keep up with the ever-increasing requests and commissions from publishers for new works. Encouraged by the success of his *Fantasiestücke* model, Hoffmann gathered the enormous literary harvest of his last years in two multivolume collections: *Nachtstücke, herausgegeben von dem Verfasser der Fantasiestücke in Callots Manier* (Night Pieces, edited by the Author of the Fantasy Pieces in the Manner of Callot, 1817) and *Die Serapions-Brüder*. Only his second and last novel, *Kater Murr*, and three longer narratives were published separately in book form: *Klein Zaches genannt Zinnober: Ein Mährchen herausgegeben von E. T. A. Hoffmann* (1819; translated as "Little Zaches, Surnamed Zinnober," 1971), *Prinzessin Brambilla: Ein Capriccio nach Jacob Callot* (1821; translated as "Princess Brambilla," 1971), and *Meister Floh: Ein Mährchen in sieben Abenteuern*

zweier Freunde (1822; translated as "Master Flea," 1826).

The two volumes of *Nachtstücke* contain eight suspenseful stories, among them "Der Sandmann" (translated as "The Sandman," 1844), which inspired Freud's celebrated essay on the "uncanny" that led to his formulation of the Oedipal castration complex, and "Das Majorat." The title for his collection Hoffmann borrowed from painting terminology: "night piece" fittingly conveys the uncanny, nocturnal aura of mystery and impending doom that permeates these tales of horror, replete with telepathy, hallucinations, and optical illusions and populated with ghosts, villains, murderers, and madmen. That throughout the nineteenth century the supreme mastery of narration evident in these stories went unnoticed seems inexplicable today. It was chiefly on account of the *Nachtstücke* (and the novel *Die Elixiere des Teufels*) that for years the author was labeled "Gespenster-Hoffmann" (Hoffmann of the ghosts) and his entire oeuvre degraded by insensitive critics as inferior, trivial literature.

With twenty-eight narratives in four volumes, *Die Serapions-Brüder* constitutes Hoffmann's largest collection. Like the *Nachtstücke*, this last collection includes some of his best-known tales such as "Nußknacker," "Rat Krespel" (translated as "Councillor Krespel," 1943), "Die Automate" (translated as "Automata," 1967), and "Das Fräulein von Scuderi" (translated as "Mademoiselle de Scuderi," 1826). But unlike the *Nachtstücke*, which is unified by a prevailing spooky atmosphere, *Die Serapions-Brüder* brings together many different kinds of fiction. In seemingly random succession, stories based on mesmerism, animal magnetism, somnambulism, and clairvoyance alternate with genuine fairy tales; chronicle-inspired narratives follow critical essays on musical aesthetics and the poetics of opera; and the first example of modern crime fiction ("Scuderi") coexists with stories exploring the creative process in music, painting, and literature. The underlying fictional frame that interrelates the diverse narratives is Hoffmann's unobtrusive device for integrating his poetics of story-telling into his own fiction: a series of sophisticated conversations in which six friends, members of the literary Serapion Brotherhood, first narrate and then discuss their works. Ingeniously enough, all of this is fictional: the narratives as well as the frame which presents criticism of fiction that is itself fiction.

The extraordinary narrative virtuosity that Hoffmann attained in *Kater Murr* secures this truly Romantic yet astonishingly modern novel a prominent place among the handful of outstanding epic monuments in nineteenth-century European literature. That Hoffmann's favorite double-optics principle propels this unique novelistic experiment is hinted at in his elaborate, ironic title echoing Sterne's title *The Life and Opinions of Tristram Shandy, Gentleman*. Clearly, in *Kater Murr* there are two seemingly unrelated protagonists and two distinct narratives that are also generically different: the memoirs of Tomcat Murr and an anonymous biography of the musician Kreisler promise to converge under the same cover. Moreover, Hoffmann signs himself as the editor of the work. Meister Abraham, Murr's owner and Kreisler's close friend, the only figure who appears in both narratives, may also be Kreisler's unidentified biographer. The complex fictionalizing process comes full circle when the reader begins to suspect that Abraham and Kreisler are antithetical alter egos of the book's real author, E. T. A. Hoffmann.

Tomcat Murr's hilarious autobiographical disquisitions allow for plenty of vintage Hoffmannesque humor, parody, and satire. A delightfully unaware pseudointellectual with an overblown ego, Murr "unintentionally" unmasks contemporary society's pretensions, hypocrisy, and ignorance concerning the function and value of education, culture, and the arts. The feline author's "informed" account of cat and dog society evokes bourgeois societal conditions in Hoffmann's Germany so vividly that the two worlds virtually merge and animals become paradigmatic of humans. As Hoffmann's fictional musician alter ego, Johannes Kreisler figures prominently in the earlier *Kreisleriana* pieces. In *Kater Murr* he is an unappreciated composer-conductor in residence at the tiny court of an insignificant, intrigue-laden German principality. Like his creator, an ironist out of self-preservation, Kreisler embodies Hoffmann's conception of the exalted, disillusioned, and unfulfilled yet forever striving Romantic artist at odds with his social milieu.

By contrasting specific plot details in the Murr and Kreisler sections, Hoffmann skillfully integrates the heterogeneous narrative strains and character constellations of the novel. The complacent tomcat's reminiscences unfold in a coherent chronological sequence, while Kreisler's biography is presented in desultory, episodic fragments that reflect his eccentric, disjointed personal and artistic traits in tone, syntax, diction, and narrative structure. Kreisler's name (cir-

cler) subtly points to the circular compositional design underlying the Kreisler sections: though positioned first in the cycle of episodes, the opening Kreisler fragment is actually meant to conclude it as well. In a postscript to *Kater Murr*, "editor" Hoffmann reports Murr's death (his own real-life cat was also called Murr) and promises more of both stories to follow in a third volume, which he never wrote. Ironically, this purported open-endedness, too, is part of the novel's overall fictional design.

During his last years, the constitutionally fragile Hoffmann continued to lead his precarious double existence and somehow managed to sustain simultaneously his literary and legal careers while also frequenting Berlin's salons and cafés. But once more politics interfered with his life. After the Napoleonic wars a period of reaction set in and Prussia became a police state. In 1819 Hoffmann was appointed to a newly formed legal commission to investigate subversive and demagogic activities, an added burden that must have hastened the onset of final illness. As a member of the commission, he courageously defended liberal intellectuals and students charged with fabricated crimes. When it leaked out that in the humorous tale *Meister Floh* Hoffmann himself satirized police methods, the powerful and humorless chief of police started proceedings against him. The satirical passages had to be deleted before publication in the spring of 1822, and Hoffmann was interrogated and had to compose his own legal defense while on his deathbed. He escaped persecution only through his death from total paralysis of the nervous system on 25 June 1822.

E. T. A Hoffmann is recognized today as a major nineteenth-century writer. But beyond his well-established literary fame as the "author of the tales," he will also be remembered as a distinguished jurist and an important figure in music history, a pioneer of modern music criticism.

Letters:

E. T. A. Hoffmann im persönlichen und brieflichen Verkehr: Sein Briefwechsel und die Erinnerungen seiner Bekannten, edited by Hans von Müller, 4 volumes (Berlin: Paetel, 1912);

Briefe: Eine Auswahl, edited by Richard Wiener (Vienna: Rikola, 1922);

E. T. A. Hoffmann Briefwechsel, edited by Müller and Friedrich Schnapp, 3 volumes (Munich: Winkler, 1967-1969);

Selected Letters of E. T. A. Hoffmann, edited and translated by Johanna C. Sahlin (Chicago: University of Chicago Press, 1977).

Bibliographies:

Klaus Kanzog, "Grundzüge der E. T. A. Hoffmann-Forschung seit 1945: Mit einer Bibliographie," *Mitteilungen der E. T. A. Hoffmann-Gesellschaft*, 9 (1962): 1-30;

Kanzog, "E. T. A. Hoffmann-Literatur 1962-1965: Eine Bibliographie," *Mitteilungen der E. T. A. Hoffmann-Gesellschaft*, 12 (1966): 33-39;

Jürgen Voerster, *160 Jahre E. T. A. Hoffmann-Forschung: Eine Bibliographie 1805-1965* (Stuttgart: Eggert, 1967);

Hartmut Steinecke, "Zur E. T. A. Hoffmann-Forschung," *Zeitschrift für deutsche Philologie*, 89 (1970): 222-234;

Kanzog, "E. T. A. Hoffmann-Literatur 1966-1969: Eine Bibliographie," *Mitteilungen der E. T. A Hoffmann-Gesellschaft*, 16 (1970): 28-40;

Steinecke, "E. T. A. Hoffmann: Dokumente und Literatur 1973-1975," *Zeitschrift für deutsche Philologie*, 95 (1976): 160-163;

Kanzog, "Zehn Jahre E. T. A. Hoffmann-Forschung: E. T. A. Hoffmann-Literatur 1970-1980. Eine Bibliographie," *Mitteilungen der E. T. A. Hoffmann-Gesellschaft*, 27 (1981): 55-103;

Gerhard Salomon, *E. T. A. Hoffmann Bibliographie* (Hildesheim: Olms, 1983).

Biographies:

Georg Ellinger, *E. T. A. Hoffmann: Sein Leben und seine Werke* (Hamburg: Voss, 1894);

Walter Harich, *E. T. A. Hoffmann: Das Leben eines Künstlers*, 2 volumes (Berlin: Reiss, 1921);

Theo Piana, *E. T. A. Hoffmann als bildender Künstler* (Berlin: Das neue Berlin, 1954);

Gabrielle Wittkop-Ménardeau, *E. T. A. Hoffmann in Selbstzeugnissen und Bilddokumenten* (Reinbek: Rowohlt, 1966);

Friedrich Schnapp, ed., *E. T. A. Hoffmann in Aufzeichnungen seiner Freunde und Bekannten* (Munich: Winkler, 1974);

Ulrich Helmke, *E. T. A. Hoffmann: Lebensbericht mit Bildern und Dokumenten* (Cassel: Wenderoth, 1975);

Klaus Günzel, *E. T. A. Hoffmann: Leben und Werk in Briefen, Selbstzeugnissen und Zeitdokumenten* (Berlin: Verlag der Nation, 1976);

Arwed Blomeyer, *E. T. A. Hoffmann als Jurist. Eine Würdigung zu seinem 200. Geburtstag* (Berlin: De Gruyter, 1978);

Marcel Schneider, *Ernest Théodore Amadeus Hoffmann: Biographie* (Paris: Julliard, 1979);

Rüdiger Safranski, *E. T. A. Hoffmann: Das Leben eines skeptischen Phantasten* (Munich: Hanser, 1984);

Eckart Klessmann, *E. T. A. Hoffmann oder Die Tiefe zwischen Stern und Erde: Eine Biographie* (Stuttgart: DVA, 1988).

References:

Gerhard Allroggen, *E. T. A. Hoffmanns Kompositionen: Ein chronologisch-thematisches Verzeichnis seiner musikalischen Werke mit einer Einführung* (Regensburg: Bosse, 1970);

Horst S. Daemmrich, *The Shattered Self: E. T. A. Hoffmann's Tragic Vision* (Detroit: Wayne State University Press, 1973);

Hermann Dechant, *E. T. A. Hoffmanns Oper "Aurora"* (Regensburg: Bosse, 1975);

Klaus-Dieter Dobat, *Musik als romantische Illusion: Eine Untersuchung zur Bedeutung der Musikvorstellung E. T. A. Hoffmanns für sein literarisches Werk* (Tübingen: Niemeyer, 1984);

Hans Ehinger, *E. T. A. Hoffmann als Musiker und Musikschriftsteller* (Olten: Walter, 1954);

Heide Eilert, *Theater in der Erzählkunst: Eine Studie zum Werk E. T. A. Hoffmanns* (Tübingen: Niemeyer, 1977);

Brigitte Feldges and Ulrich Stadler, eds., *E. T. A. Hoffmann: Epoche–Werk–Wirkung* (Munich: Beck, 1986);

Paul Greeff, *E. T. A. Hoffmann als Musiker und Musikschriftsteller* (Cologne: Staufen, 1958);

Ernst Heilborn, *E. T. A. Hoffmann: Der Künstler und die Kunst* (Berlin: Ullstein, 1926);

Harvey Hewett-Thayer, *Hoffmann: Author of the Tales* (Princeton: Princeton University Press, 1948);

Werner Keil, *E. T. A. Hoffmann als Komponist: Studien zur Kompositionstechnik an ausgewählten Werken* (Wiesbaden: Breitkopf & Härtel, 1986);

Lothar Köhn, *Vieldeutige Welt: Studien zur Struktur der Erzählungen E. T. A. Hoffmanns und zur Entwicklung seines Werkes* (Tübingen: Niemeyer, 1966);

Peter von Matt, *Die Augen der Automaten: E. T. A. Hoffmanns Imaginationslehre als Prinzip seiner Erzählkunst* (Tübingen: Niemeyer, 1971);

Hans Mayer, "Die Wirklichkeit E. T. A. Hoffmanns," in his *Von Lessing bis Thomas Mann* (Pfullingen: Neske, 1959), pp. 198-246;

James M. McGlathery, *Mysticism and Sexuality: E. T. A. Hoffmann*, 2 volumes (Bern: Lang, 1981-1985);

McGlathery, ed., *Journal of English and German Philology*, special Hoffmann issue, 75 (1976);

Mitteilungen der E. T. A. Hoffmann-Gesellschaft (1938-);

Alain Montandon, ed., *E. T. A. Hoffmann et la musique* (Bern: Lang, 1987);

Kenneth Negus, *E. T. A. Hoffmann's Other World: The Romantic Author and His "New Mythology"* (Philadelphia: University of Pennsylvania Press, 1965);

Lothar Pikulik, *E. T. A. Hoffmann als Erzähler: Ein Kommentar zu den "Serapions-Brüdern"* (Göttingen: Vandenhoeck & Ruprecht, 1987);

Helmut Prang, ed., *E. T. A. Hoffmann* (Darmstadt: Wissenschaftliche Buchgesellschaft, 1976);

Jean F. A. Ricci, *E. T. A. Hoffmann, l'homme et l'oeuvre* (Paris: Corti, 1947);

Elke Riemer, *E. T. A. Hoffmann und seine illustratoren* (Hildesheim: Gerstenberg, 1978);

R. Murray Schafer, *E. T. A. Hoffmann and Music* (Toronto & Buffalo, N.Y.: University of Toronto Press, 1975);

Steven Paul Scher, ed., *Zu E. T. A. Hoffmann* (Stuttgart: Klett, 1981);

Wolf Segebrecht, *Autobiographie und Dichtung: Eine Studie zum Werk E. T. A. Hoffmanns* (Stuttgart: Metzler, 1967);

Hartmut Steinecke, ed., *Zeitschrift für deutsche Philologie*, special Hoffmann issue, 95 (1976);

Ronald Taylor, *Hoffmann* (London: Bowes & Bowes, 1963);

Hans-Georg Werner, *E. T. A. Hoffmann: Därstellung und Deutung der Wirklichkeit im dichterischen Werk* (Berlin & Weimar: Aufbau, 1971);

Ilse Winter, *Untersuchungen zum serapiontischen Prinzip E. T. A. Hoffmanns* (The Hague: Mouton, 1976).

Papers:
Only a few of E. T. A. Hoffmann's original papers and manuscripts, including letters, musical scores, and drawings, survived World War II. Most are in the Märkisches Museum der Stadt Berlin, East Germany; the E. T. A Hoffmann-Sammlung der Staatsbibliothek Bamberg; and the Handschriftenabteilung, Staatsbibliothek Preußischer Kulturbesitz, Berlin, West Germany.

Friedrich Hölderlin
(20 March 1770-7 June 1843)

Lawrence Ryan
University of Massachusetts—Amherst

BOOKS: *Hyperion oder Der Eremit in Griechenland,* 2 volumes (Tübingen: Cotta, 1797-1799); translated by Willard R. Trask as *Hyperion; or, The Hermit in Greece* (New York: Ungar, 1965); facsimile edition of German version (Frankfurt am Main: Stroemfeld/Roter Stern, 1979);

Gedichte, edited by Gustav Schwab and Ludwig Uhland (Stuttgart & Tübingen: Cotta, 1826)—includes *Der Tod des Empedokles,* translated by Michael Hamburger as *The Death of Empedocles, Quarterly Review of Literature,* 13 (1964): 93-121;

Sämtliche Werke, edited by Christoph Theodor Schwab, 2 volumes (Stuttgart & Tübingen: Cotta, 1846);

Sämtliche Werke: Historisch-kritische Ausgabe, edited by Norbert von Hellingrath, Friedrich Seebaß, and Ludwig von Pigenot, 6 volumes (volumes 1, 4, 5, Munich & Leipzig: Müller; volumes 2, 3, 6, Berlin: Propyläen, 1913-1923);

Sämtliche Werke, edited by Friedrich Beißner and Adolf Beck, 8 volumes (Stuttgart: Cotta/Kohlhammer, 1943-1985);

Sämtliche Werke und Briefe, edited by Günter Mieth, 2 volumes (Munich: Hanser, 1970);

Sämtliche Werke: Frankfurter Ausgabe, edited by Dietrich Sattler, 13 volumes to date (Frankfurt am Main: Roter Stern, 1975-   );

Homburger Folioheft, facsimile edition, edited by Sattler and Emery E. George (Basel: Stroemfeld/Roter Stern, 1986);

Stuttgarter Foliobuch, facsimile edition, edited by Sattler (Frankfurt am Main: Stroemfeld/Roter Stern, 1989);

Bevestigter Gesang: Die neu zu entdeckende hymnische Spätdichtung bis 1806, facsimile edition, edited by Dietrich Uffhausen (Stuttgart: Metzler, 1989).

Editions in English: Poems and Fragments, translated and edited by Michael Hamburger (London: Routledge & Kegan Paul, 1967; Ann Arbor: University of Michigan, 1967;

Friedrich Hölderlin in 1792 (pastel by Franz K. Hiemer; by permission of the Schiller-Nationalmuseum, Marbach)

2nd enlarged edition, Cambridge: Cambridge University Press, 1980);

Hyperion; Thalia Fragment, 1794, translated and edited by Karl W. Maurer (Winnipeg: Hölderlin Society, 1968);

Friedrich Hölderlin, Eduard Mörike: Selected Poems, translated by Christopher Middleton (Chicago: University of Chicago Press, 1972);

"On Tragedy: Notes on the *Oedipus*; Notes on the *Antigone*," translated by Jeremy Adler, *Comparative Criticism,* 5 (1983): 205-244;

"Philosophical Archaeology: Hölderlin's *Pindar Fragments*," translated, with an interpretation, by Adler, *Comparative Criticism,* 6 (1984): 23-46;

Hymns and Fragments, translated by Richard Sieburth (Princeton: Princeton University Press, 1984);

"On Tragedy, Part 2: 'The Ground of Empedocles'; On the Process of Becoming in Passing Away,'" translated by Adler, *Comparative Criticism,* 7 (1985): 147-173;

Selected Verse, edited and translated by Hamburger (London & Dover, N.H.: Anvil Press, 1986);

Essays and Letters on Theory, translated and edited by Thomas Pfau (Albany: State University of New York Press, 1988).

OTHER: *Die Trauerspiele des Sophokles,* translated by Hölderlin, 2 volumes (Frankfurt am Main: Wilmans, 1804)–comprises volume 1, *Ödipus der Tyrann*; volume 2, *Antigonä*; facsimile edition (Frankfurt am Main: Stroemfeld/ Roter Stern, 1986);

"On the Process of the Poetic Mind," translated by Ralph R. Read, in *German Romantic Criticism,* edited by A. Leslie Willson (New York: Continuum, 1982), pp. 219-237.

Denied recognition during his lifetime, Friedrich Hölderlin has come to be regarded as a central figure of the German Classical-Romantic period. Despite his achievements in the fields of the novel, drama, and poetic theory, and despite the important influence he exerted on the development of the philosophy of German Idealism, he is best known for his lyric poetry. Hölderlin's verse represents both the culmination of the German classical tradition, with its thematic and formal indebtedness to the literature of antiquity, and the highest expression of the German Romantic glorification of the poet, combining veneration of nature with the development of a national poetic ideal.

Johann Christian Friedrich Hölderlin was born in Lauffen, near Nürtingen, in Swabia, to Heinrich Friedrich Hölderlin and Johanna Christiana Heyn Hölderlin on 20 March 1770. His father died in 1772, and his mother remarried in 1774; her second husband, Johann Christoph Gock, mayor of Nürtingen, died in 1779. Hölderlin's mother was a constant admonishing presence throughout most of his life, forcing him continually to defend his preoccupation with poetry. After attending the local school in Nürtingen, Hölderlin enrolled in 1788 in the

Tübinger Stift, the theological seminary which has counted among its pupils such thinkers and poets as Johannes Kepler, Johann Albrecht Bengel, Friedrich Christoph Oetinger, Eduard Mörike, Wilhelm Hauff, and Friedrich Theodor Vischer. Georg Wilhelm Friedrich Hegel and Friedrich Wilhelm Joseph von Schelling, two of the leading figures of German Idealism, were fellow students of Hölderlin, and their exchange of ideas continued for some years after they left the seminary. At Tübingen Hölderlin was instructed in theology, Greek literature, and contemporary philosophy, all of which laid the groundwork for his later writings. He graduated from the seminary in 1793 on the basis of two theses, "Parallele zwischen Salomons Sprüchwörtern und Hesiods *Werken und Tagen*" (Parallel Between the Proverbs of Solomon and Hesiod's *Works and Days*) and "Geschichte der schönen Künste unter den Griechen" (History of the Fine Arts among the Greeks). An important influence was the French Revolution, which aroused in the seminarians high hopes for the realization of revolutionary political ideals in Germany. While still in Tübingen, Hölderlin wrote hymnic poems with such titles as "Hymne an die Freiheit" (Hymn to Freedom) and "Hymne an die Göttin der Harmonie" (Hymn to the Goddess of Harmony). They are lengthy, somewhat prolix rhymed poems that owe much to the example of Hölderlin's Swabian compatriot Friedrich Schiller, whom the younger poet revered and with whom he occasionally corresponded. Although several of these poems were published in various almanacs, they attracted little attention and are by no means characteristic of Hölderlin's most important work.

After graduating from the seminary, Hölderlin was unwilling to pursue the career of clergyman for which his training had befitted him, and instead, on Schiller's recommendation, took a position as private tutor with Schiller's friend Charlotte von Kalb at Waltershausen, in Thuringia. Although this position afforded him an opportunity to devote himself to the poetic and philosophical studies that were already his main concern, he soon encountered difficulties with his pedagogical duties, which led to termination of his employment. In early 1795 he moved to Jena, where he attended lectures at the university with the intention either of preparing himself for an academic career or of supporting himself by his writing. There he was in contact with Schiller, and also met Johann Wolfgang von Goethe and Johann Gottfried von Herder, but he was influenced most particularly by the philosopher Johann Gottlieb Fichte, whom he called "die Seele von Jena" (the soul of Jena). Fichte's epoch-making lectures on his "Wissenschaftslehre" (Theory of Knowledge), which laid the foundation of German Idealist philosophy, affected Hölderlin deeply. But Fichte's theory of the self-positing ego, inimical to nature as it was, plunged Hölderlin into a turmoil of self-doubt from which he had to struggle to emancipate himself. It is generally considered that his precipitous return from Jena to his native Nürtingen in mid 1795 was largely an attempt to escape from what he called the "Luftgeister mit den metaphysischen Flügeln" (airborne spirits with metaphysical wings).

Hölderlin's philosophical differences with Fichte first found expression in two jottings (unpublished until the 1960s) titled "Sein" (Being) and "Urteil" (Judgment), in which he questions Fichte's concept of the manifest self-consciousness of the "absolute ego" as the starting point of philosophy. For Hölderlin, self-consciousness is the establishment of an identity that presupposes a foregoing difference and is therefore by definition distinct from the ultimate oneness of Being, so that self-consciousness and the Absolute are mutually exclusive. (He expressed a similar idea in a letter to Hegel of 26 January 1795.) "Sein" and "Urteil" probably represent the first articulation of a criticism of Fichte that gave a new turn to the whole philosophy of Idealism; they also suggest the important influence that Hölderlin exerted on Hegel and Schelling, as does the document generally known as "Das älteste Systemprogramm des deutschen Idealismus" (The Oldest System-Program of German Idealism; unpublished until 1917), a two-page outline of a philosophic program which culminates in the call for "eine neue Mythologie" (a new mythology). It is in Hegel's handwriting but its authorship has been much disputed, and it has been variously attributed to Hegel, Schelling, and Hölderlin; the input of Hölderlin seems in any case to have been paramount.

Late in 1795 Hölderlin accepted a position as tutor with the family of Jakob Friedrich Gontard, a banker in Frankfurt am Main. Although disaffected by the stiffness of the city's social life, he soon developed a deep attachment to Susette Borkenstein Gontard, the wife of his employer. Under the name of Diotima, taken from that of the priestess of love in Plato's *Symposium*,

she began to figure in Hölderlin's writings as the object of his love and as the incarnation of eternal beauty. He describes himself as being in a "neue Welt" (new world), where his "Schönheitssinn" (sense of beauty) is assured beyond all uncertainty. In 1796, owing to the unrest caused by the Napoleonic wars, he accompanied Susette Gontard on a trip to Cassel and Bad Driburg in Westfalia, where he also made the acquaintance of the author Wilhelm Heinse. By September 1798, however, his relationship with Susette Gontard had created such tensions in the household that he was forced to give up his position and leave Frankfurt am Main for the nearby town of Homburg. He seems seldom to have seen Susette after his departure, but her letters to him, published in 1921 as *Die Briefe von Diotima* (Letters from Diotima) and often reprinted, constitute a moving testimony to their love.

The main work of this period is the novel *Hyperion oder Der Eremit in Griechenland* (2 volumes, 1797-1799; translated as *Hyperion; or, The Hermit in Greece,* 1965). Hölderlin had begun the novel during his student days in Tübingen and had revised it continually during his stays in Waltershausen and Jena. In 1794 a preliminary version was published under the title "Fragment von *Hyperion*" (Fragment of *Hyperion*) in Friedrich Schiller's literary journal *Neue Thalia.* This version of the novel is cast in the form of letters from Hyperion, a young late-eighteenth-century Greek, to his German friend Bellarmin. The letters depict his constant struggle to attain the moment of transcendent experience in which all conflict is resolved and temporality is suspended: "Was mir nicht Alles, und ewig Alles ist, ist mir Nichts" (What for me is not All, and eternally All, is nothing). In nature, in love, in a visit to Homeric sites, Hyperion experiences momentary intimations of his ideal, which constantly eludes him, so that his aspirations remain unfulfilled. The image of the "exzentrische Bahn" (eccentric path), which constantly diverges from the center of Being that it always seeks but can never permanently attain, becomes a symbol of the course of human existence.

In Jena Hölderlin had revised this version, partly in order to take account of his attempt to come to terms with the philosophy of Fichte. In a metrical version and a fragment entitled "Hyperions Jugend" (Hyperion's Youth), he abandoned the epistolary format in favor of a retrospective technique in which the older Hyperion looks back on his youth. The narrator, relating his story to a young visitor, acknowledges that the process of reflection has made him "tyrannisch gegen die Natur" (tyrannical toward nature), in that he has reduced nature to the material of self-consciousness. This theme echoes Hölderlin's criticism of Fichte's philosophy and its preoccupation with the autonomy of the "absolute ego." Hölderlin's new orientation finds expression in the Platonic view of love as the longing of the imperfect for the ideal, and in a new conception of beauty, which emerges as the only form in which the unity of Being, unattainable precisely because it is the object of striving, is incarnated: "jenes Sein, im einzigen Sinne des Worts . . . ist vorhanden–als Schönheit" (Being, in the unique sense of the word . . . is present–as Beauty). With this subordination of self-consciousness to the realization of beauty, Hölderlin establishes the conceptual framework that he follows in completing the novel.

The final version of the novel, the greater part of which was completed during the period he was in Frankfurt am Main, shows Hölderlin's increasing stylistic and formal mastery. He returns to the epistolary form of the first version, but now endows it with a particularly sophisticated structure. Hyperion presents a retrospective view of his life, beginning at the stage at which, after having lost his beloved and his friends, he returns bitterly disappointed to his native land, intending to take up the life of a hermit. The main focus is not the sequence of events but the act of narration itself. The seemingly disconnected fragments of his experience are integrated through the process of reflective recapitulation and gradually assume a dialectical structure in which union and separation, joy and suffering come to be seen as inseparable parts of a complex unity.

The first book of volume 1 presents fleeting moments of a joyous hope that is inevitably dashed: "Auf dieser Höh steh ich oft, mein Bellarmin! Aber ein Moment des Besinnens wirft mich herab. . . . O ein Gott ist der Mensch, wenn er träumt, ein Bettler, wenn er nachdenkt" (On these heights I stand often, Bellarmin! But a moment of reflection casts me down. O man is a god when he dreams, and a beggar when he thinks). This pattern is repeated in Hyperion's relationship with his mentor Adamas, who introduces him to the world of the ancient Greeks, and especially with his friend Alabanda, who is a political revolutionary. Together, Hyperion and Alabanda aspire to change the world, but their ways soon part, as Hyperion becomes disillusioned with the violence that is inseparable from revolutionary action. He accuses Alabanda of placing too much emphasis on the state, which has but a restrictive and regulatory function, and too little on the "unsichtbare Kirche" (invisible church) of all-enveloping enthusiasm, which is the only means of comprehensive regeneration. The conclusion of the first book laments the illusory nature of human fulfillment with a consistent hopelessness that is reminiscent of that of Goethe's Werther. It is at this point that the theme of beauty transforms Hyperion's strivings. The encounter with Diotima (narrated in the second book of the first volume) transports him to a realm of experience in which the ideal that is otherwise sought beyond the stars or at the end of time has become reality in the here and now. As such, it is not lost when no longer immediately present, but merely hidden, and can be recovered through the process of memory. Not only the person of Diotima, but also the culture of ancient Athens is an embodiment of the divine in this sense. In this view Athenian culture was a self-realization of divine beauty by virtue of the fact that God and man were ultimately one, and the forms of human self-expression–art, religion, political freedom, and even philosophy–were manifestations of their unity. The principle of "das Eine in sich unterschiedne" (the one that is differentiated within itself), which Hölderlin adapted from a formulation of Heraclitus, defines at once the essence of the Athenian and the nature of beauty–as opposed to the one-sidedness and fragmentation characteristic of the Egyptians and the Spartans, and, in Hölderlin's view, also of modern times.

Thus at the beginning of the second volume Hyperion thinks he has found in the Athenian realization of beauty a model that can be re-created in his own epoch. The belief enables him to take up again the political cause that he had previously rejected. He allies himself once more with Alabanda and participates in the Greek war of liberation against the Turks, hoping to forge a free state as a pantheon of beauty. Such a project is, however, doomed to failure, as the discrepancy between the high ideal and the reality of warfare and violence becomes apparent, and he is forced to recognize that it is folly to entrust a "Räuberbande" (band of robbers) with the founding of his Elysium. In despair, Hyperion plunges recklessly into battle, where death seems certain.

In fact, he is merely wounded, and spends several days in a coma. At this stage, Hyperion's relationships with both Alabanda and Diotima, who had represented opposite poles of his being, have undergone radical transformation. Whereas they had previously been dominant influences on him, their essential impulses are now subsumed in Hyperion himself, who combines the activism of the one with the harmony of the other. As a result, both characters recognize that Hyperion has absorbed into himself and thus superseded the essence of their being. Alabanda submits himself to the harsh judgment of the revolutionary confederates that he has betrayed by his association with Hyperion, and Diotima, caught up in Hyperion's passion for change, is fatally estranged from the innocent harmony that she had once embodied. A visit to Germany brings further disappointment, as Hyperion discovers the Germans' total lack of aesthetic sensibility. His "Letter on the Germans" has become a famous example of German cultural self-criticism.

When he returns to his native land from Germany, Hyperion has returned to the point at which the novel begins. Now, however, his past has become for him the consequence of a necessary interplay of forces, rather than of a series of isolated setbacks. He is "ruhig" (calm) as he realizes that suffering and death are inseparable from life, and is able through recollection to resolve dissonances into the harmony of song. Diotima's parting words, that he is neither crowned with the laurel wreath of fame nor decorated with the myrtle leaves of love, but that his "dichterische Tage" (poetic days) as priest of nature are now assured, provide a justification for his future poetic vocation that concludes the novel and lays the groundwork for the overriding theme of Hölderlin's later work.

From 1798 until 1800 Hölderlin was in Homburg. There he was befriended by Isaak von Sinclair, who had studied law in Tübingen and Jena, had been expelled from the University of Jena in 1795 because of his involvement with Jacobin political circles, and was now in the service of the Landgraf (count) of Hessen-Homburg. Hölderlin called Sinclair his "Herzensfreund (bosom friend) *instar omnium*" and accompanied him to the Congress of Rastatt in 1798-1799. The theme of the affinity of poet and hero (man of action), which occurs in several of Hölderlin's poems of this period, reflects his relationship to Sinclair. The ode "An Eduard" (To Edward) is actually addressed to Sinclair, to whom Hölderlin later dedi-

cated "Der Rhein" (The Rhine), one of his major poems. While in Homburg, Hölderlin made every effort to establish himself by his writing. Hoping for recognition from the court, he addressed an ode to the princess ("Der Prinzessin Auguste von Homburg") and some years later dedicated his translation of Sophocles' tragedies to her; his poem "Patmos," furthermore, was presented to the Landgraf. Hölderlin attempted to establish himself in the literary world by founding a journal called "Iduna," which would contain both original literary works and critical and historical essays; although he solicited the support of several literary figures, including Schiller, Schelling, and Goethe, the response was negligible. Indeed, his isolation and lack of recognition were such that he has become almost a prototype of the poet who fails to regain renown in his own time.

Hölderlin's major literary project in Homburg was his verse drama *Der Tod des Empedokles* (1826; translated as *The Death of Empedocles*, 1964), on which he had begun work while he was still in Frankfurt am Main. Its theme was taken from a legend of the pre-Socratic natural philosopher Empedocles, who was said to have thrown himself to his death in the volcano Etna. Empedocles is for Hölderlin the figure of a seer who, endowed with the ability to be the mouthpiece of nature, is, in his attempt to exploit his prophetic gifts, guilty of a hubris that can only be expiated by his return to nature through the act of his freely chosen death. His guilt is the "guilt of language," which desecrates the divine by articulating it in human words. The play is also the vehicle for Hölderlin's criticism both of established religion and of political rule, in that the priest Hermokrates and the archon Kritias are cast as opponents who endeavor to have Empedocles expelled and condemned. But in anticipation of his death, which is a spiritual reconciliation with nature, Empedocles regains the support of his people by articulating the prophetic vision of a coming festival of the gods at which his "einsam Lied" (lonely song) is to become a "Freudenchor" (chorus of joy) uniting the whole people.

The play is on the one hand an attempt to recreate the tragic drama of the Greeks, on the other a statement of Hölderlin's position in relation to questions of his own time. The declaration "Dies ist die Zeit der Könige nicht mehr" (This is no longer the time of kings), with which Empedocles rejects the crown proffered to him, is an affirmation of the republican principle derived ultimately from the French Revolution. But the problem of establishing an overriding "objective" necessity of Empedocles' death, according to the Greek conception of tragedy, caused Hölderlin considerable difficulty and led him to recast the play several times. After leaving the (comparatively extensive) first version and a shorter second version incomplete, he set down his reflections in an essay, "Grund zum Empedokles" (translated as "The Ground of Empedocles," 1985), which attempts to establish that, as Empedocles is a son of his time and of his country and conditioned by a particularly virulent conflict between nature and culture, his death is the means of reconciliation of this conflict: he is "ein Opfer seiner Zeit" (a victim of his time), who must be sacrificed so that the reconciliation achieved in him as an individual can be carried over into the life of his people. He is in a way a Christ figure, the prophet of a new age of peace that he cannot himself live to see. This conception finds expression in a third version of the play, which, however, also remains unfinished. One of the reasons Hölderlin abandoned his play, without publishing any of it, may be that he came to see that the prophetic vision of a new age was not really a theme suitable for tragic drama, the quintessentially Greek form, but was more appropriate to the lyric, whose origin is rather the isolation of the individual in a still-godless age.

It is in the lyric that Hölderlin was able to express himself most freely at all stages of his literary career. Whereas in Tübingen he had, until 1792, largely imitated the loose, rhymed forms of Schiller's poetry, he soon turned predominantly to the Classical ode. The ode, as it is understood in German literary history, is not the so-called Pindaric ode cultivated by English Romantic writers, but the Horatian ode, whose basic form is a four-line stanza, unrhymed, with an intricate metrical pattern. It had been adapted to the German language by Friedrich Gottlieb Klopstock and others, and gained in Hölderlin's work a new level of flexibility and expressiveness. In contrast to Klopstock, who experimented with many traditional ode forms and even invented new ones, Hölderlin confined himself almost entirely to the alcaic and the (third) asclepiadeic stanzas. In Frankfurt am Main he had written several short, almost epigrammatic odes, some of which were published in various journals and almanacs, but in the more mature odes written in Homburg he expanded the form to accommodate the full range of his themes. The odes are mostly apostrophes to divine, natural, or heroic beings, elevated in tone, and borne by a conviction to the poet's vocation: "Beruf ist mirs, zu rühmen Höhers" (It is my profession to extol higher things). The programmatic ode "Natur und Kunst, oder Saturn und Jupiter" (Nature and Art, or Saturn and Jupiter), for example, calls upon the Olympian god Jupiter, who embodies the rule of law and has banished his own father, the god of the Golden Age, to reinstate the latter and acknowledge his supremacy. In terms of the poem's metaphorical dimension, art must recognize its origin in and indebtedness to nature as the ground of its being. The poem "Der Abschied" (Leave-taking) laments the poet's parting from Diotima, which, anguishing though it is at first, ultimately yields to a poetic recollection of past happiness that transcends the sense of loss. "Der gefesselte Strom" (The Icebound Stream) depicts the river that in the spring bursts out of its frozen state to become the harbinger of regeneration, although it must lose itself as it flows into the sea. In this poem (as elsewhere) the river, the demigod of divine birth whose life-bringing sojourn on earth is but a prelude to his return to his origins, is a central image. Several odes–"Dichterberuf " (The Poet's Vocation), "Dichtermut" (The Courage of the Poet), "Der blinde Sänger" (The Blind Singer)– outline the theme of the poetic vocation with its immediacy to the divine and its consequent perils and blessings. An experimental poem written in Pindaric meters, "Wie wenn am Feiertage . . . " (As when on a Feast Day . . .), presents the situation of the poet in the figure of Semele, who, according to the myth, wished to see Jupiter with her own eyes but was fatally consumed by his radiance, giving birth to Dionysus. Just so should the poet stand bareheaded in the storms of the divine, in order to transmit the sacred fire to other human beings in the form of song. It is characteristic of Hölderlin's odes of the Homburg period to conclude with an affirmation of poetry.

During this time he also drafted several essays, which for the most part remained unfinished and were probably not intended for publication in their present form, but which contain the outline of a comprehensive theory of poetry. He was concerned on the one hand to define poetry as the articulation of the "infinite moment" of transcendent experience, and on the other hand to construct a system of poetic genres and forms. The essay "Über die Verfahrungsweise des poetischen Geistes" (On the Procedure of the Poetic Spirit) defines the "free choice" of poetic subject matter and the creation of a "Welt in der

Welt" a (World in the World) as the only means
of attaining self-consciousness. Thus poetry provides the answer to the philosophical question
raised by Fichte and becomes for Hölderlin–as
for other Romantic writers of his time–the highest expression of the human spirit. By shaping
the relationship of the human to the divine, it
also in a sense supersedes "positive" religion: "So
wäre alle Religion ihrem Wesen nach poetisch"
(Thus all religion is essentially poetic), as
Hölderlin asserts in the essay "Über Religion"
(On Religion).

The "Romantic" glorification of poetry was
balanced by a "Classical" adherence to formal clarity and exactitude. Not only did Hölderlin write
mainly in classical meters, but in addition his
whole conception of genres was based on ancient
Greek literature, with its three great models:
Homer for epic poetry, Sophocles for tragedy,
and Pindar–"das Summum der Dichtkunst" (the
ultimate perfection of poetry), as Hölderlin had
put it while still in Tübingen–for the lyric. In
Hölderlin's essay "Über den Unterschied der
Dichtarten" (On the Difference of Poetic Genres),
each kind of poetry is defined in terms of a basic
opposition: the underlying "heroic" impulse of
epic poetry is expressed all the more powerfully
because of its contrast with the "naive" concreteness of Homeric language; lyric poetry is "naive"
in its origin, in that it speaks with the voice of an
individual, but it soars to the expression of a
suprasensual, "idealistic" harmony; tragic poetry
is grounded in an "idealistic" intellectual perception of the whole, which can only be expressed in
the depiction of "heroic" conflict. It is apparent
from the use of the terms *naive, heroic,* and *idealistic* that Hölderlin's theory, while based on traditional divisions into genre, is also a self-contained
system in the spirit of Idealist thinking. He further proceeds to define poetic structure in terms
of these same three tones, which he even sets out
as a "Wechsel der Töne" (modulation of tones) in
tabular form. The tables also establish an overall
structure: by returning to its starting point at a
higher level of reflection, the poem effects a dialectical resolution of dissonances.

In mid 1800 Hölderlin moved to Stuttgart,
where he spent an unusually happy half year
with a friend he had first met in Jena, Christian
Landauer. He earned some money by giving lessons in philosophy, but soon sought another position as a children's tutor. In January 1801 he accepted a post with the family Gonzenbach in
Hauptwil, Switzerland, which he gave up after

*The young Hölderlin in Maulbronn (drawing by "Troy"; by
permission of the Schiller-Nationalmuseum, Marbach)*

only three months in order to return to
Nürtingen. The exact reason for the termination
of his employment is not known, but there are indications that his growing restlessness may have
been a first sign of the mental illness that later be-
fell him. His experience of the Swiss landscape
left traces in the elegy "Heimkunft" (Homecoming) and other poems.

At about this time, Hölderlin composed several lengthy poems in the elegiac form. In the German tradition, the elegy is not just a poem of
lamentation, but is written in elegiac couplets (consisting of an alternation of hexameter and pentam-
eter) adapted from Greek and Roman literature.
Building upon the work of such predecessors as
Goethe and Schiller, who had already adapted
this form to the needs of the German language,
Hölderlin was able to render it with consummate
mastery. His first elegy, "Menons Klagen um
Diotima" (Menon's Lament for Diotima), takes its
starting point in the separation of the lovers, but
opens into an enthusiastic invocation of a new
age of bliss. "Brod und Wein," perhaps his best-

known elegy, explores the historical progression from Greek antiquity to the present: the disappearance of the gods from Greece leads to a premonition of their reappearance in present-day Germany, which—in a conflation of the Classical and the Christian traditions centered in Dionysus and Christ respectively—is embodied in the symbols of bread and wine, common to both traditions. The elegies "Stuttgart" and "Heimkunft" take this process further and celebrate German heroes. More and more the elegies, which had begun by turning to the past, shift in emphasis toward the national future. The same applies to the long hexameter poem "Der Archipelagus" (The Archipelago), which celebrates the Greek victory over the Persians but ultimately evokes a development that encompasses Greek antiquity and the present day in a single grandiose sequence of the seasons, so that the "köstliche Frühlingszeit im Griechenlande" (precious springtime of Greece) is due to return the coming autumn in the perfection of maturity.

The elegies can thus be regarded as an intermediate stage leading to the later hymns, which are perhaps Hölderlin's most lasting achievement. In 1801 he began a series of poems in free rhythms in the tradition of the "hymn" (in the German sense), for which the obvious model was Pindar—though less in respect to meter (which in Pindar, as Hölderlin already knew, is closely regulated) than in the overall structure, specifically in the tripartite form that is characteristic of Pindar's poems. Most of Hölderlin's hymns contain six, nine, twelve, or fifteen stanzas, which are arranged in groups of three in a complex dialectical pattern. From various statements in his letters, it is clear that he regarded this new style—"das hohe und reine Frohlocken vaterländischer Gesänge" (the pure noble jubilation of patriotic songs)—as the attainment of his poetic goal, indeed as a fusion of nature and history that was previously achieved only in ancient Greece: "die Sangart überhaupt wird einen andern Charakter nehmen" (poetry altogether will take on a new character). It should be noted that the "patriotic" element does not so much involve the narrowly German as the modern, "sofern es von dem Griechischen verschieden ist" (insofar as it is distinct from the Greek). Hölderlin's view of the *querelle des anciens et des modernes* is one of the more significant variations of this theme, which was so prevalent in the literature of his time.

The later hymns conform to this conception. The poem "Der Rhein" combines the depiction of the river as a demigod that bursts its banks in order to transform the divine impulse into fruitful human activity with a reflection on the nature of genius and with a consideration of Rousseau, a problematical figure who in his closeness to the harmony of nature seems no longer to typify the heroic existence, and of Socrates, who retained sobriety when all around him were succumbing. The poem combines the immediate presence of the divine in nature with the timeless transcendence of the spirit in a vast panorama that embraces the whole range of interaction of the human and the divine in a concerted set of images. In "Patmos" the poet is transported to the isle of Patmos, site of the composition of the Gospel of John, which inaugurates a tradition that points from the Orient to the West, from the original revelation of the divine to its transmission in the form of the "fester Buchstabe" (the fixed letter) of biblical tradition. The poem "Friedensfeier" (Festival of Peace), whose final version was not discovered and published until 1953, celebrates a truce in the Napoleonic Wars, but at the same time envisages the coming of a somewhat mysterious "Fürst des Fests" (Prince of the Feast), who seems to combine elements of Napoleon, Christ, and other figures. But however controversial the question of the identity of Hölderlin's unnamed figure has remained, it is clear that his coming signals a reconciliation of nature and humanity, a new millenium. In the poem "Der Einzige" (The Unique One) the sweeping overview of the whole philosophical and religious tradition is called into question by what seems to be an irreconcilable conflict between the claims of Christ to a uniqueness that excludes the worship of all other gods (hence the title of the poem), and the mutual mediability of the polytheistic gods—and demigods—of antiquity. If Heracles as the conquering inaugurator and Dionysus as the purveyor of the communal spirit can be regarded as successive stages in the development of human culture, then the Christian claim to uniqueness threatens to disrupt continuity: thus the poem circles incessantly about the theme of the comparability of Heracles, Dionysus, and Christ, who ideally should be conceivable as forming a kind of three-leafed clover but whose respective claims tend to cause dissension rather than unity. That the poem remains unfinished, despite having been recast several times, is testimony to the vastness of Hölderlin's ambition: to reconcile the Greek and the Christian traditions in one comprehensive vision, to rewrite mythology, to dissolve the fixity of traditional names in order to re-create them out of their common matrix. More and more, the ambitiousness of Hölderlin's attempt to present the coming fulfillment as the culmination of European history strained his poetic capacities and led to a continual process of revision which affected several of his poems of this period.

After his return to Nürtingen from Switzerland in April 1801, Hölderlin had gained provisional consent from the publisher Johann Friedrich Cotta to bring out a collection of his poems. But the project was interrupted (and in effect aborted) by Hölderlin's decision to take yet another position as private tutor, this time with the family of D. C. Meyer, German consul in Bordeaux. He set out on foot for Strasbourg in December 1801, arriving in Bordeaux on 28 January 1802. Again, the circumstances of his stay and the reasons for its premature termination remain unclear. He left Bordeaux on 10 May and arrived in Strasbourg in early June, evidently after extensive wanderings that took him by way of Paris. On his arrival in Germany he received the shattering news of the death of Susette Gontard, who had succumbed to an infection she had caught from her children. He arrived home in Nürtingen in a distraught state, and from this time reports of his mental instability increased.

The poems that Hölderlin completed after his return show a certain shift, which has often been attributed to a growing doubt in the validity of his prophetic vision. The poem "Andenken" (Remembrance) is clearly influenced by the scenery of Bordeaux; although it culminates in the apparent definitiveness of the oft-quoted final verse "Was bleibet aber, stiften die Dichter" (But what lasts is founded by the poets), it is characterized by an uneasy alliance of private remembrance and gnomic utterance that gives it a hauntingly mysterious, not clearly definable tone. The same applies to "Mnemosyne," in which the theme of the death of Mnemosyne, the muse of memory, suggests that Hölderlin had reached a breaking point, at which the constituent elements of his unifying vision were threatened by disintegration. His later poems, which remain largely unfinished, attempt to incorporate ever more modern figures.

While his poetic production yielded few tangible results in the form of complete poems at this stage, Hölderlin turned his attention increasingly to translations from the Greek, and had his versions of Sophocles' *Oedipus Rex* and *Antigone*

published in 1804. His concern, however, was allied to that of his own poetry, in that he wished to make of his translations a kind of reinterpretation that would reestablish continuity between antiquity and the present. Indeed, he expressed the intention of "correcting" the artistic failing of Sophocles, who had underplayed the "Feuer vom Himmel" (fire from heaven) in which the "Oriental" origins of Greek culture are reflected. Hölderlin's translations are notable in that, despite certain inaccuracies, they convey more of the elemental power of the original than other German translations; they have often been performed on the stage. (The translation of *Antigone* forms the basis of a play by Bertolt Brecht and an opera by Carl Orff.) Hölderlin elaborated his views in several letters written in 1803 and 1804 to his publisher Friedrich Wilmans, and also in the commentaries that accompany his versions of Sophocles' plays. Here he suggests that Oedipus, who is driven out of his mind by the inability to comprehend his own origins, is the prototype of Greek tragedy, whereas Antigone, who asserts her own independence in defiance of the established order, anticipates the transition from the ancient Greek to the modern. At much the same time, Hölderlin translated some fragments from Pindar, which he supplied with comments that are less an explanation of Pindar's poems than a rather enigmatic exposition of some of Hölderlin's own concepts.

A request from the publisher Wilmans to contribute to his almanac for the year 1805 provided Hölderlin with the opportunity to publish several of his poems. He submitted a group of nine poems that had been written after his return from Bordeaux in 1802 and that he now collected under the title "Nachtgesänge" (Night Songs). The six odes among them are in the main reworkings of earlier poems which introduce a harsher and more discordant note. The well-known poem "Hälfte des Lebens" (Middle of Life), which contrasts a summer scene of peace and bliss with the windswept emptiness of portending wintry desolation, has often been read as a portrayal of Hölderlin's recognition of a turning point in his own life.

Following the publication of the Sophocles translations in 1804 and the "Night Songs" in 1805, several other poems by Hölderlin appeared in print, if not always with his permission: an old friend, Leo von Seckendorf, brought out the poems "Stuttgart" and "Die Wanderung" (The Journey) in his *Musenalmanach für das Jahr*

1807 (Almanac for the Muses for 1807) and other poems–"Der Rhein," "Patmos," and "Andenken" (Remembrance)–in the corresponding volume for 1808. But Hölderlin was able to work only sporadically by this time, and in June 1804 his friend Sinclair took him to Homburg once more and obtained for him a position (more of a sinecure, as Hölderlin's salary was paid out of Sinclair's pocket) as court librarian. Hölderlin was further unsettled by events of early 1805, when one Alexander Blankenstein denounced Sinclair for having allegedly conspired against the life of the Elector Friedrich II of Württemberg; Sinclair was accused of high treason and imprisoned for a time before being brought to trial (he was later acquitted), and Hölderlin was tangentially involved through his association with Sinclair. Although medical testimony to his insanity saved him from having to stand trial, he was deeply disturbed by the whole affair, which also unfavorably affected his friendship with Sinclair. Because the state of Hesse-Homburg was dissolved in 1806, Sinclair could no longer provide for Hölderlin in Homburg and asked Hölderlin's mother to take him back. By this time considered quite insane by most people who knew him, Hölderlin was forcibly removed from Homburg in September 1806 and delivered to the tender mercies of Ferdinand Autenrieth, who ran a clinic in Tübingen for the mentally ill. (It lies on the bank of the Neckar just above the Hölderlin Tower, and now houses various university departments.) Autenrieth is best known as the inventor of a face mask named after him, whose function was to prevent patients from screaming, and his treatment of Hölderlin did little to alleviate the latter's condition. In May 1807 Hölderlin was released as incurable, with the prognosis of having no more than about three years to live, and given over to the care of the carpenter Ernst Zimmer and his family, who lived just below the clinic. Hölderlin's room was in a tower by the riverbank, which (after having been burned down and rebuilt) is now known as the Hölderlin Tower and houses the Hölderlin-Gesellschaft (Hölderlin Society).

The three years allotted to Hölderlin became thirty-six. During that time he was lovingly cared for by the Zimmer family and treated in niggardly fashion by his mother, who, although living close by, did not once visit him and contrived to limit his access to the patrimony due to him. Hölderlin became an object of some notoriety to students and younger writers. Writers such as Justinus Kerner, Mörike, and Wilhelm Waiblinger have left accounts, with Waiblinger making him the subject of an essay titled *Friedrich Hölderlins Leben, Dichtung und Wahnsinn* (Friedrich Hölderlin's Life, Poetry and Madness, 1947). Although he may have continued to write for a short time in his previous style, most of the poetry that Hölderlin wrote during this period represents a distinct break: he reverted to simple rhyming four-line stanzas, devoted largely to stereotypical evocations of the seasons and reflections on the human condition, devoid of the intensity and breadth of vision of his earlier work. Many of the poems he distributed to visitors were signed with imaginary names–most often: Scardanelli–and provided with impossible dates. Hölderlin died peacefully in his sleep on 7 June 1843, at the age of seventy-three.

Although Hölderlin achieved comparatively little recognition during his lifetime, and during his final stay in Tübingen was unable to supervise the publication of his own work, there was some slight local interest in his writings. His novel *Hyperion* was republished in 1822, and in 1826 Gustav Schwab and Ludwig Uhland brought out an edition of some of the poems. The first edition with any claim to comprehensiveness was prepared by Christoph Theodor Schwab; comprising a larger selection of poetry, some letters, and the "Fragment von *Hyperion*," it appeared in 1846. Other editions appeared around the turn of the century, without exciting great resonance. The first real breakthrough occurred in the years preceding World War I, when Norbert von Hellingrath, who as a student in Munich had written a doctoral dissertation on Hölderlin's translations of Pindar, inaugurated a historical-critical edition. The fourth volume, which appeared in 1916 and for the first time designated the later poems as "Herz, Kern und Gipfel" (heart, core and pinnacle) of Hölderlin's work, had a sensational impact that established his reputation as a major poet. Several German Expressionist poets–Georg Trakl, Georg Heym, Johannes R. Becher, Ernst Stadler–as well as Stefan George and Rainer Maria Rilke felt a close affinity to him. Hölderlin's prophetic poetry came to be regarded by many as a proclamation for modern times, or as a timeless manifestation of the poetic essence. An influential case is that of the philosopher Martin Heidegger, who in the 1930s, after he had disassociated himself from the National Socialist order that he had at first embraced, turned to the glorification of Hölderlin.

After Hellingrath's death in World War I, the edition he had begun was completed by others. The fact that so many poems exist only in heavily reworked but not finally revised manuscripts has made the editing of Hölderlin's works a test of the editor's craft. The standard critical edition is the Große Stuttgarter Ausgabe (Large Stuttgart Edition), edited by Friedrich Beißner (eight volumes, published from 1943 to 1985), which breaks new ground in its presentation of variant readings; the letters and extensive biographical documents are edited by Adolf Beck. The more recent Frankfurt Edition (to date thirteen volumes, the first of which appeared in 1975) includes photocopies of manuscripts; and facsimile collections of manuscripts–the *Homburger Folioheft* (1986) and the *Stuttgarter Foliobuch* (1989)–have also been published in recent years, attesting to Hölderlin's now-established renown as a poet and thinker of international importance.

In 1943 the Hölderlin-Gesellschaft was established in Tübingen. It is responsible for the *Hölderlin-Jahrbuch* (Hölderlin Yearbook), the twenty-fifth volume of which appeared in 1987, and also conducts biennial meetings. The Hölderlin Archive, which has originals or copies of all extant manuscripts and a comprehensive collection of literature on Hölderlin, was founded in Tübingen in 1941; moved to Bebenhausen, near Tübingen, in 1943; and in 1970 was incorporated into the Württembergische Landesbibliothek (Württemberg State Library) in Stuttgart.

Letters:
Ausgewählte Briefe, edited by Wilhelm Böhm (Jena: Diederichs, 1910);
Briefe, edited by Erich Lichtenstein (Weimar: Lichtenstein, 1922);
Friedrich Hölderlins gesammelte Briefe, edited by Ernst Bertram (Leipzig: Insel, 1935);
Briefe, edited by Friedrich Seeba (Vienna: Kirschner, 1944);
Briefe zur Erziehung, edited by K. Lothar Wolf (Hamburg: Simons, 1950);
Einundzwanzig Briefe, edited by Bertold Hack (Frankfurt am Main: Beyer, 1966);
Dokumente seines Lebens: Briefe, Tagebücher, Aufzeichnungen/Hölderlin, edited by Hermann Hesse and Karl Isenberg (Frankfurt am Main: Insel, 1976).

Bibliography:
Maria Kohler, ed., *Internationale Hölderlin-Bibliographie* (Stuttgart: Frommann-Holzboog, 1985).

References:
Adolf Beck and Paul Raabe, *Hölderlin: Eine Chronik in Text und Bild* (Frankfurt am Main: Insel, 1970);
Friedrich Beißner, *Hölderlins Übersetzungen aus dem Griechischen* (Stuttgart: Metzler, 1933);
Beißner, *Reden und Aufsätze* (Weimar: Böhlau, 1961);
Maurice Benn, *Hölderlin and Pindar* (The Hague: Mouton, 1962);
Paul Bertaux, *Friedrich Hölderlin* (Frankfurt am Main: Suhrkamp, 1978);
Wolfgang Binder, *Friedrich Hölderlin: Studien* (Frankfurt am Main: Suhrkamp, 1987);
Binder, *Hölderlin-Aufsätze* (Frankfurt am Main: Insel, 1970);
Bernhard Böschenstein, *Hölderlins Rheinhymne* (Zurich: Atlantis, 1959);
Böschenstein, *Konkordanz zu Hölderlins Gedichten nach 1800* (Göttingen: Vandenhoeck & Ruprecht 1964);
David Constantine, *Hölderlin* (Oxford: Clarendon Press, 1988);
Martin Dannhauer, Hans Otto Horch, and Klaus Schuffels, eds., *Wörterbuch zu Friedrich Hölderlin*, volume 1: *Die Gedichte* (Tübingen: Niemeyer, 1983);
Howard Gaskill, *Hölderlin's "Hyperion"* (Durham, U.K.: University of Durham, 1984);
Robin Harrison, *Hölderlin and Greek Literature* (Oxford: Clarendon Press, 1975);
Martin Heidegger, *Erläuterungen zu Hölderlins Dichtung* (Frankfurt am Main: Klostermann, 1951);
Dieter Henrich, *Der Gang des Andenkens: Beobachtungen zu Hölderlins Gedicht* (Stuttgart: Klett-Cotta, 1986);
Henrich, "Hegel und Hölderlin," in his *Hegel im Kontext* (Frankfurt am Main: Suhrkamp, 1971), pp. 9-40;
Alfred Kelletat, *Hölderlin: Beiträge zu seinem Verständnis in unsrem Jahrhundert* (Tübingen: Mohr, 1961);
Werner Kirchner, *Der Hochverratsprozeß gegen Sinclair* (Marburg: Simons, 1949);
Günter Mieth, *Friedrich Hölderlin: Dichter der bürgerlich-demokratischen Revolution* (Berlin: Rütten & Loening, 1978);
Ernst Müller, *Hölderlin: Studien zur Geschichte seines Geistes* (Stuttgart: Kohlhammer, 1944);

Ronald Peacock, *Hölderlin* (London: Methuen/ New York: Barnes & Noble, 1973);

Allesandro Pellegrini, *Friedrich Hölderlin: Sein Bild in der Forschung* (Berlin: De Gruyter, 1965);

Lawrence Ryan, *Friedrich Hölderlin* (Stuttgart: Metzler, 1961; revised, 1967);

Ryan, *Hölderlins "Hyperion": Exzentrische Bahn und Dichterberuf* (Stuttgart: Metzler, 1965);

Ryan, *Hölderlins Lehre vom Wechsel der Töne* (Stuttgart: Kohlhammer, 1960);

Eric L. Santner, *Friedrich Hölderlin: Narrative Vigilance and the Poetic Imagination* (New Brunswick, N.J.: Rutgers University Press, 1986);

Jochen Schmidt, *Hölderlins Elegie "Brot und Wein"* (Berlin: Schmidt, 1968);

Schmidt, *Über Hölderlin* (Frankfurt am Main: Insel, 1970);

Richard Ungar, *Friedrich Hölderlin* (Boston: Twayne, 1984);

Wilhelm Waiblinger, *Friedrich Hölderlins Leben, Dichtung und Wahnsinn* (Hamburg: Ellermann, 1947).

Papers:
The Hölderlin Archive is at the Württembergische Landesbibliothek, Stuttgart.

Ernst von Houwald

(29 November 1778-28 January 1845)

Clinton Shaffer
University of North Carolina at Chapel Hill

BOOKS: *Romantische Akkorde,* edited by Wilhelm Contessa (Berlin: Dümmler, 1817);
Buch für Kinder gebildeter Stände (3 volumes, Leipzig: Göschen, 1819-1824; revised, 2 volumes, 1833)–includes "Der Christ und der Muhamedaner," translated by "S. T." as "The Christian and the Mahometan," in *"The Christmas Roses" and Other Tales* (London: Cundall, 1845);
Erzählungen (Dresden: Arnold, 1819);
Das Bild; Der Leuchtthurm; Die Heimkehr: Drei Trauerspiele (Stuttgart: Macklot, 1821);
Das Bild: Trauerspiel in fünf Akten (Leipzig: Göschen, 1821);
Fluch und Segen: Drama in zwei Acten (Leipzig: Göschen, 1821);
Der Leuchtthurm; Die Heimkehr: Zwei Trauerspiele (Leipzig: Göschen, 1821);
Fluch und Segen: Drama; Seinem Schicksal kann Niemand entgehen: Dramatisirtes Sprichwort (Stuttgart: Macklot, 1822);
Der Fürst und der Bürger: Ein Drama in drei Aufzügen (Leipzig: Göschen, 1823);
Die alten Spielkameraden: Lustspiel in zwei Aufzügen (Weimar: Hoffmann, 1823);
Die Feinde: Ein Trauerspiel in drei Aufzügen (Leipzig: Göschen, 1825);
Vermischte Schriften, 2 volumes (Leipzig; Göschen, 1825)–comprises volume 1, *Die Freistatt; Seinem Schicksal kann Niemand entgehen;* "Jacob Thau, der Hofnarr"; "Das Seetreffen bei Nacht"; volume 2, "Materialien zu einem Volkskalender"; "Scenen aus einem Bade"; "Das Begräbniß"; *Der Epilog zu Maria Stuart;* "Gedichte";
Gesammelte Schriften, 10 volumes (Vienna: Ludwig, 1826-1827);
Bilder für die Jugend, 3 volumes (Leipzig: Göschen, 1829-1832)–includes "Der Juwelier" and "Der Neujahrswunsch," translated anonymously as "The Goldsmith" and "The New Year's Wish," respectively, in *Cousin Natalia's Tales* (London: Cundall, 1841);

Ernst von Houwald in 1824 (lithograph by Eduard Meyer after drawing by Franz Krüger; courtesy of Dr. Götz Dieter Freiherr von Houwald)

Die Seeräuber: Ein Trauerspiel in fünf Acten (Leipzig: Göschen, 1831);
Abend-Unterhaltungen für Kinder: Erstes Bändchen (Leipzig: Göschen, 1833);
Ernst von Houwalds Sämmtliche Werke, edited by Friedrich Adami, 5 volumes (Leipzig: Göschen, 1851);
Klassische Märchen (Leipzig: Berndt's Verlag, 1877).

OTHER: *Die Freistatt: Tragisches Gemälde in einem Akt,* in *Almanach für Privatbühnen,* edited by Adolph Müllner (Leipzig: Göschen, 1819), pp. 193-230;

"Die Ahnung: Eine Epistel," in *Penelope: Taschenbuch für das Jahr 1820,* edited by Theodor Hell (K. G. T. Winkler) (Leipzig: Hinrichs, 1820), pp. 381-384;

"Wach auf! Ein Kranz von sieben Sonetten," and "Drei zusammenhängende romantische Episteln," in *Urania, Taschenbuch auf das Jahr 1820* (Leipzig: Brockhaus, 1820), pp. 323-331, 423-446;

"Das Begräbnis: Ein zweites Bruchstück aus meinen musikalischen Wanderungen," in *Penelope: Taschenbuch für 1821,* edited by Hell (Leipzig: Hinrichs, 1821), pp. 34-75;

"Wohin? Ein Sonettenkranz," in *Urania: Taschenbuch auf das Jahr 1821* (Leipzig: Brockhaus, 1821);

"An Fiona," in *Taschenbuch zum geselligen Vergnügen* (Leipzig: Gleiditsch, 1822), p. 271;

Seinem Schicksal kann Niemand entgehen: Dramatisiertes Sprichwort. Ein Schwank, in *Taschenbuch zum geselligen Vergnügen* (Leipzig: Göschen, 1822), pp. 153-203;

Der Brandenburgische Hausfreund: Ein Volkskalender, edited by Houwald, 3 volumes (Berlin: Dümmler, 1823-1825);

Die alten Spielkameraden: Lustspiel in zwei Aufzügen, in *Weimarisches dramatisches Taschenbuch* (Weimar: Hoffmann, 1823), n. pag.;

C. W. Contessa's Schriften, edited by Houwald, 9 volumes (Leipzig: Göschen, 1826);

"Einige Bruchstücke aus C. W. Contessa's Leben," edited by Houwald, in *Taschenbuch zum geselligen Vergnügen,* edited by Friedrich Kind (Leipzig: Göschen, 1828), pp. 211-246;

"Die Genesung: Cantate in 2 Abtheilungen," in *Penelope für 1830,* edited by Hell (Leipzig: Hinrichs, 1830), pp. 389-400;

"Das erste Lied," in *Deutscher Musenalmanach* (Leipzig: Weidmann, 1833), pp. 56-60;

Ein Buch für kleinere Kinder: Aus dem Französischen frei übersetzt von Cora von Mosch, foreword by Houwald (Leipzig: Göschen, 1838);

"Lenz und Winter," in *Deutscher Musenalmanach* (Leipzig: Weidmann, 1838), pp. 103-106.

Ernst von Houwald is best known as an author of Schicksalstragödien (fate tragedies) in the Romantic stage tradition of Zacharias Werner and Adolph Müllner. In contrast to his older con-temporaries and consistent with the bourgeois spirit of the early nineteenth century, Houwald placed less emphasis on inexorable fate as a grue-some and horrible force. Instead, aspects of the moving and sentimental combine to lend his drama enormous stage appeal–and to win him the scorn of such critics as Ludwig Tieck and Lud-wig Börne. Houwald's lifelong interest in peda-gogy and his devotion to humane principles helped him to achieve distinction in a second cre-ative field: as one of the period's most prolific and respected writers of literature for children and adolescents.

Christoph Ernst von Houwald was born on 29 November 1778 to Gottlob Karl Willibald von Houwald and Auguste von Houwald (née von Knoch) on his family's estate, Schloß Straupitz in Lower Lusatia; the family had been granted a pat-ent of nobility by King Gustav Adolf of Sweden in 1631. Although he was later named a Knight of the Red Order of the Eagle and received the Johannite Cross in acknowledgement of his lit-erary achievements, and although he was frequently–even on title pages–referred to as *Freiherr* (Baron), Houwald did not officially bear the title. Together with his brother Heinrich, Houwald was educated by a tutor until age fif-teen. At thirteen he composed his first poems and a five-act tragedy based on Schiller's history of the Thirty Years' War. In 1793 the brothers were enrolled in the Pädagogium, a secondary school in Halle; August Hermann Niemeyer, chancellor of the school served as Houwald's men-tor for many years. The strong pietistic sen-timent with which Niemeyer infused the Pädagogium would characterize most of Hou-wald's literary efforts. In addition, Houwald devel-oped a close friendship with the future dramatist Karl Wilhelm Contessa; even in the impromptu dramatic competitions between the two aspiring schoolboy writers, Houwald's affinity for the tragic emerged–frequently to be derided in Contessa's comedies.

In 1799 Houwald entered the University of Halle, where he lived with Contessa; for four years he studied law and public administration. With the inheritance he received upon his fa-ther's death in 1799 he purchased the estate Craupe. In 1805 he was named a provincial dep-uty for Lower Lusatia; the following year he mar-ried Auguste von Haberkorn, whose dowry in-cluded the estate Sellendorf. In addition to raising two foster children, the couple was to have nine children of their own.

Worsening economic conditions during the Napoleonic period made Houwald's land holdings more liabilities than assets: he was forced to sell Craupe and to lease Sellendorf. His administrative obligations also increased: following Napoleon's defeat at Leipzig in October 1813, Houwald directed the rearmament of a district of Saxony under the auspices of the provisional Russian government; in addition, he headed a commission channeling aid to war victims and arranging for the adoption of children orphaned by the war. In 1816 he took the widowed Contessa into his home together with the latter's son; the two remained a part of the household until 1824.

Though Houwald had published isolated poems in literary almanacs as early as 1805, initially under the pseudonyms "Ernst" and "Waluhdo," Contessa's presence spurred him on to more large-scale attempts. The first of these, *Romantische Akkorde* (Romantic Accords, 1817) is a collection of tales ranging from murder mystery to love story; *Erzählungen* (Tales, 1819) represents Houwald's only other substantial narrative offering to an adult audience.

In the six years following *Die Freistatt* (The Sanctuary, 1819) Houwald directed most of his creative attention toward the genre of the fate tragedy. *Die Freistatt* is a one-act drama depicting the reunion in death of a husband and wife separated by political circumstance. In this play and in *Die Heimkehr* (The Homecoming, 1821), a one-act work about a man who returns after a long absence only to discover that his wife has remarried, concealed identity and sudden revelation are central to the achievement of the effect desired by the fate dramatist. The former work received almost no critical attention and was performed only after Houwald's reputation was firmly established; *Die Heimkehr* was hailed by critics and paved the way for the successes of his better-known fate dramas.

In 1821 Houwald assumed the office of provincial syndic and became increasingly involved in political and administrative affairs; he moved his family to the estate Neuhaus bei Lübben in order to be closer to the provincial seat. He managed, however, to continue producing fate dramas in rapid succession. *Das Bild* (The Picture, 1821) was perhaps his greatest popular success; in typical fate drama fashion, it employs a talismanlike object—the picture of the title—to set in motion a plot of thwarted love, concealed and mistaken identity, and unwarranted vengeance. The rather inadequate development of its five

acts suggests that the author's preference for one- and two-act works was well advised.

Der Leuchtthurm (The Lighthouse, 1821) and *Fluch und Segen* (Curse and Blessing, 1822) are two-act dramas. The former, composed in frequently rhyming trochaic tetrameter as opposed to Houwald's customary iambic verse, again centers around coincidental encounters between long-lost family members and revelation of past misdeeds. *Fluch und Segen*, whose setting and action bear some resemblance to those of Werner's *Der vierundzwanzigste Februar* (The Twenty-fourth of February, 1815), the definitive Schicksalstragödie, uses similar devices. Originally conceived as a contribution to a philanthropic anthology on behalf of orphans, the work presents the self-sacrificing attempts of a child to ease his parents' financial difficulties. Houwald's divergence from the fate tragedy per se is his emphasis upon fate as the consequence of human action coupled with a pietistic assurance of the possibility of reconciliation and forgiveness. Characterization and dramatic development are subordinated to these convictions.

Nowhere is Houwald's ambivalence toward the conventional understanding of "fate" more obvious than in the one-act travesty *Seinem Schicksal kann Niemand entgehen* (No One Can Escape His Fate, 1822). In its depiction of the efforts of a pompous mayor to avoid a cuff on the cheek, prophesied to him a year ago to the day by a Gypsy woman, the work derides the fate tragedy conventions of ominous prediction and the *dies fatalis* (fateful day); the mayor does, of course, receive his slap when his mother accidentally strikes him with a flyswatter—a further jest at the convention of the fateful talisman or Schicksalswaffe (fateful weapon). Houwald displays a certain aptitude for comedy yet makes no further use of his skill beyond the insignificant *Die alten Spielkameraden* (The Old Playmates, 1823).

At the invitation of the director of the royal theater of Bavaria, Houwald composed *Der Fürst und der Bürger* (The Prince and the Burgher, 1823) to celebrate the wedding of Princess Amalie of Bavaria to the Prince of Saxony. Before it could be performed, however, the work was labeled inappropriate by influential circles in Munich; the embarrassed theater director avoided informing the author of this rejection for four months, ultimately blaming the delay on a fire in the theater. This work, together with the dramas *Die Feinde* (The Enemies, 1825) and *Die Seeräuber* (The Pirates, 1831), resulted in a decline in critical and popular enthusiasm for Houwald's dramas.

In 1824 Houwald joined in the founding of a savings bank in Lower Lusatia; based on a British model and serving diverse clientele, the institution was one of the first of its kind in Germany and had a long life.

The earliest volumes of Houwald's works for children had begun appearing in 1819. The three-volume *Buch für Kinder gebildeter Stände* (Book for Children of the Cultured Classes, 1819-1824) included a variety of literary forms. Like its successors, *Bilder für die Jugend* (Pictures for Youth, 1829-1832) and *Abend-Unterhaltungen für Kinder* (Evening Entertainments for Children, 1833), *Buch für Kinder gebildeter Stände* unabashedly pursues pedagogical ends. Occasionally the values to be inculcated transcend the Biedermeier admonition to be content with one's station in life: for example, in the short play *Der Schuldbrief* (The Promissory Note) a Jewish character exemplifies concern for his neighbor; the conclusion is reminiscent of the ideal of tolerance presented in Gotthold Ephraim Lessing's *Nathan der Weise* (Nathan the Wise, 1779).

Abend-Unterhaltungen für Kinder proved to be Houwald's last substantial publication; increasing administrative responsibilities allowed him little time for writing. He died on 28 January 1845 following a stroke suffered on the road between Neuhaus and Lübben.

Letters:

Dreihundert Briefe aus zwei Jahrhunderten, edited by Karl von Holtei, 2 volumes (Hannover: Rümpler, 1872; reprinted, Bern: Lang, 1971), II: 33-35;

Briefwechsel und Tagebücher des Fürsten Hermann von Pückler-Muskau, edited by Ludmilla Assing-Grimessi, 9 volumes (volumes 1-2, Hamburg: Hoffmann & Campe; volumes 3-9, Berlin: Wedekind & Schweiger, 1873-1876; reprinted, Bern: Lang, 1971), VII: 375-376; 435-437; VIII: 377-378;

Erinnerungen an Friedrich von Uechtritz und seine Zeit in Briefen von ihm und an ihn, edited by Heinrich von Sybel (Leipzig: Hirzel, 1886), pp. 380-381;

W. Pfeiffer, "Drei Briefe an Fouqué," *Euphorion,* 9 (1902): 674-677;

"Aus dem literarischen Briefwechsel Ernst von Houwalds," in *Die Niederlausitz in den Tagen des Klassizismus, der Romantik und des Bieder-*

meier, edited by Rudolf Lehmann (Cologne & Graz; Böhlau, 1958), pp. 160-253.

References:

Theodor Brüggemann, "Das Bild des Juden in der Kinder- und Jugendliteratur von 1750-1850," in *Das Bild des Juden in der Volks- und Jugendliteratur vom 18. Jahrhundert bis 1945,* edited by Heinrich Pleticha (Würzburg: Königshausen & Neumann, 1985), pp. 61-83;

Siegmund Hirsch, "Die Schicksalstragödie im Spottbild der Satire," *Zeitschrift für Deutschkunde,* 40 (1926): 276-284;

Herbert Kraft, *Das Schicksalsdrama: Interpretation und Kritik einer literarischen Reihe* (Tübingen: Niemeyer, 1974);

Albin Lenhard, "Didaktische Mimikry: Zur Kinder- und Jugendliteratur Ernst von Houwalds," in *Literatur für Kinder: Studien über ihr Verhältnis zur Gesamtliteratur,* edited by Maria Lypp (Göttingen: Vandenhoeck & Ruprecht, 1977);

Lenhard, "Die Rübezahlmärchen Ernst von Houwalds (1778-1845) im Rahmen seiner Kinder- und Jugendliteratur," *Schlesien,* 23 (1978): 221-234;

Jacob Minor, *Das Schicksalsdrama* (Berlin & Stuttgart: Spemann, 1884);

Minor, *Die Schicksals-Tragödie in ihren Hauptvertretern* (Frankfurt am Main: Rütten & Loening, 1883);

Minor, "Zur Geschichte der deutschen Schicksalstragödie und zu Grillparzers 'Ahnfrau,'" *Jahrbuch der Grillparzer-Gesellschaft,* 9 (1899): 1-85;

Otto Schmidtborn, *Christoph Ernst Frhr. v. Houwald als Dramatiker* (London: Johnson, 1968);

Friedrich Sengle, *Biedermeierzeit: Deutsche Literatur im Spannungsfeld zwischen Restauration und Revolution 1815-1848,* 3 volumes (Stuttgart: Metzler, 1972).

Papers:
Houwald's papers and letters are distributed among more than twenty libraries and archives in East and West Germany, Poland, Austria, and Switzerland; most possess only isolated manuscripts or letters. The most substantial collections are in the Archivdepot Lübben der Staatlichen Archivverwaltung Potsdam, Lübben, East Germany; the Deutsche Staatsbibliothek, East Berlin; the Deutsches Literaturarchiv/Schiller-Nationalmuseum, Marbach, West Germany; the Sächsische Landesbi-

bliothek, Dresden, East Germany; the Staatsarchiv, Sanssouci-Orangerie, Potsdam, East Germany; the Wissenschaftliche Allgemeinbibliothek des Bezirkes Potsdam, Potsdam; and the Zentrales Staatsarchiv/Dienststelle Merseburg, Merseburg, East Germany.

Therese Huber
(7 May 1764-15 June 1829)

Jeannine Blackwell
University of Kentucky

BOOKS: *Die Familie Seldorf: Eine Erzählung aus der französischen Revolution,* 2 volumes (Tübingen: Cotta, 1795-1796); modern edition, edited by Magdalene Heuser, 1 volume (Hildesheim: Olms, 1989);

Louise, ein Beitrag zur Geschichte der Convenienz: Roman (Leipzig: Brockhaus, 1796);

Erzählungen, as L. F. Huber, 3 volumes (Brunswick: Vieweg, 1801-1802)–includes "Ueber die Weiblichkeit in der Kunst, in der Natur und in der Gesellschaft," translated by Miss Eliza C. as "Female Experience," in *The German Novellist: A Choice Collection of Novels* (Görlitz: Anton, 1800);

Ludwig Ferdinand Hubers sämtliche Werke seit dem Jahr 1802, 2 volumes (Tübingen: Cotta, 1806-1810);

Bermerkungen über Holland aus dem Reisejournal einer deutschen Frau, as Therese H (Leipzig: Fleischer, 1811); translated by Rodney Livingstone as *Adventures on a Journey to New Holland, and The Lonely Deathbed,* edited by Leslie Bodi (Melbourne: Lansdowne Press, 1966);

L. F. Hubers gesammelte Erzählungen, fortgesetzt von Therese Huber geb. Heyne, 2 volumes (Stuttgart & Tübingen: Cotta, 1819);

Hannah, der Herrnhuterin Deborah Findling (Leipzig: Brockhaus, 1821);

Ellen Percy oder Erziehung durch Schicksale, 2 volumes (Leipzig: Brockhaus, 1822);

Jugendmuth: Eine Erzählung (Leipzig: Brockhaus, 1824);

Die Ehelosen, 2 volumes (Leipzig: Brockhaus, 1829);

Therese Huber (Ludwig Geiger, Therese Huber*)*

Erzählungen, edited by Victor Aimé Huber, 6 volumes (Leipzig: Brockhaus, 1830-1833);

Die Geschichte des Cevennenkriegs: Ein Lesebuch für Ungelehrte. Nach Memoiren und geschichtlichen Nachrichten erzählt von der verstorbenen Therese Huber (Stuttgart & Tübingen: Cotta, 1834);

Anthologie aus den Schriften von L. F. Huber (Hildburghausen & New York: Meyer, n.d.).

OTHER: Jean-Baptiste Louvet, *Emilie von Varmont: Eine Geschichte in Briefen. Aus dem Französischen übersetzt vom Verfasser des heimlichen Gerichts,* translated by Huber (Tübingen: Neue Allgemeine Deutsche Bibliothek, 1794);

Der Trostlose: Aus dem Französischen übersetzt vom Herausgeber der Friedenspreliminarien, translated by Huber (Berlin, 1794);

Madame de Charrière, as Abbé de la Tour, *Drei Weiber: Eine Novelle aus dem französischen Manuscript,* translated by Huber and Ludwig Ferdinand Huber (Leipzig: Brockhaus, 1795);

Adele von Senange oder Briefe des Lords Syndenham: Aus dem Französischen, translated by Huber and Ludwig Ferdinand Huber (Leipzig: Brockhaus, 1795);

Neueres französisches Theater, edited and translated by Huber and Ludwig Ferdinand Huber, 3 volumes (Leipzig: Brockhaus, 1795-1796);

Anna Charlotte Thiesen, as Caroline Stille, *Erzählungen für weibliche Jugend,* foreword by Huber (Leipzig: Reim, 1825);

Johann Georg Forsters Briefwechsel: Nebst einigen Nachrichten von seinem Leben, edited by Huber, 2 volumes (Leipzig: Brockhaus, 1829).

Therese Heyne Forster Huber reflected in her life and works many of the animosities of her time: German hatred of things French, particularly the Revolution; the politicization of German literature in the wake of Romanticism; reaction against "scribbling women"; and public conflict about marriage and civil divorce. As the unnamed editor of one of Germany's most influential cultural newspapers of the early nineteenth century, Johann Friedrich Cotta's *Morgenblatt für gebildete Stände* (Morning Daily for the Cultured Classes), she indirectly imposed new critical directions in German literature as Romanticism waned. She was long held in ill repute for attempting to divorce Georg Forster, supporter of the French Revolution, even though at the time of the couple's separation he was on a diplomatic mission to Paris representing the Rhenish German National Convention and advocating the incorporation of the Rhineland into France. Huber and Caroline Michaelis Böhmer Schlegel Schelling, those two infamous Göttingen professors' daughters, stood at the center of controversies about emancipation of the flesh, divorce for women, and the rift between Romanticism and proto-realism. In more modern times the two women have become the paradigms with which several literary historians have fought out the battle be-

tween Romanticism and its enemies. Such an ideologically charged life should, it would seem, make Therese Huber one of the most famous and infamous women of her time. Yet her association with the "losing side" in many of these controversies has relegated her to relative historical obscurity.

Therese Heyne was born on 7 May 1764 in the university town of Göttingen to Therese Weiß Heyne, whose reported adultery and neglect of her family left her daughter angry and traumatized after her death in 1775, and Christian Gottlob Heyne, a professor of ancient languages who had little involvement in domestic life. Professor Heyne's public persona was much brighter: as the teacher of August Wilhelm and Friedrich von Schlegel and as leader of an intellectual circle in Göttingen, he provided his students and daughter with fertile ground for later literary growth. Göttingen supplied Huber not only contact with her father's students but also friendships with other professors' daughters, Philippine Gatterer (later Engelhard) and Caroline Michaelis, and eventual marriage to the world traveler and natural scientist Georg Forster, arranged primarily by her father. Trips with relatives to a few German towns and to Switzerland had preceded her engagement at nineteen to the thirty-year-old who had sailed around the world with Captain Cook. They were married on 4 September 1785.

Their marriage was problematic from the start. It was not a love match; her passionate friendship for Friedrich Wilhelm Meyer, the university librarian, apparently complicated the Forsters' relationship. Therese found her husband physically repugnant and his sensuality oppressive. They spent the first two years at the university in Vilna, Poland, and then returned to Göttingen, where Therese's passion for Meyer was revived; she insisted on a move to Mainz when the opportunity arose in 1788. Yet there, as well, a family friend became closer to the wife than the husband: the career Prussian diplomat (and later translator, dramatist, and critic) Ludwig Ferdinand Huber and Therese fell in love. Again Forster tolerated and even encouraged their affair. The Forsters reestablished close ties with her old friend Caroline Michaelis Böhmer, by then a widow, who lived in their home in 1792 and 1793. Controversy still continues about the nature of Caroline's and Ludwig's friendship with Georg and Therese.

Between 1789 and 1793 Georg Forster became a leader of the pro-French Revolution faction in Mainz and accumulated heavy debts about which Therese knew nothing. The French Army of the Republic approached and besieged Mainz; it fell, and the German sympathizers helped organize the occupation. When German forces threatened to liberate the city from French hands, both Ludwig Huber, who was collaborating with the Forsters and supported the French cause yet was employed by the anti-French Prussians, and Forster, who was a leader of the losing side and deeply in debt, were in danger. Forster went to Paris, leaving behind his debts and the children (four were born, of whom two, Claire and Therese, survived infancy) with Therese and Ludwig; the family fled for Strasbourg and then Bôle, Canton Neuchâtel, Switzerland. Caroline Michaelis Böhmer, who was unmarried and pregnant by a French officer, was imprisoned.

Forster, mortally ill in Paris, died in January 1794 before divorce proceedings were completed. He had last seen the family at a Swiss border town in November of 1793. Therese married Ludwig Huber on 10 April 1794, amid sharp accusations and almost universal condemnation from the German intellectual community. With Huber she had six children, four of whom died in childhood (Sophie Albertine, Emanuel Honoré Michel, Emanuele Honorine Adele, and Clemence) and two who survived, Luise Emilie and Victor Aimé.

Even before their Swiss exile Therese had begun to write under the name of Ludwig Huber, and many of her writings from 1793 until his death in 1804 appeared under the name of the erstwhile dramatist or anonymously. Together they translated eighteen plays from the French, as well as several novels, letters, and stories, among them those of their friend Madame de Charrière. The Hubers left exile in 1798 to live in Tübingen, Stuttgart, and Ulm, where Ludwig had a series of governmental and editorial posts. Gradually Therese's initial translation work expanded into fiction; she also supplemented her husband's income by expanding on his writing and editing. She was not only trying to pay Forster's debts but also helping to support the family. Perhaps the best known and most significant of Therese Huber's first independent literary efforts is *Die Familie Seldorf: Eine Erzählung aus der französischen Revolution* (The Seldorf Family: A Story from the French Revolution, 1795-1796),

possibly the only contemporary novel of the French Revolution to appear in German.

Ludwig Huber's death in 1804 brought about a real isolation from intellectual life: what her controversial private life and her association with Georg Forster's politics had not accomplished, Ludwig Huber's quarrels with August Wilhelm and Friedrich von Schlegel over Romanticism had. She spent the next twelve years traveling or living with her grown children, writing, and working as a governess. As a widow without pension she struggled to support her three unmarried younger children and to find positions for them; yet she was unhappy in the role of elderly relative or governess and gladly accepted a position with the Cotta publishing firm.

In 1807 she became a regular contributor to the Cotta publishing undertakings and in 1816 became the editor of Cotta's *Morgenblatt für gebildete Stände* (Morning Daily for the Cultured Classes), albeit anonymously and without a contract. There she was responsible for the development of the *Literaturblatt* (Literary Magazine) as a feuilleton supplement to the paper. Among the many figures about whom she wrote critically in those years were Edward Gibbon, Jean Paul, E. T. A. Hoffmann, and Friedrich de la Motte-Fouqué.

In 1823 she was dismissed as editor. One explanation for her discharge is that she moved to Augsburg, acting on the rumor that Cotta was about to relocate the press in the city. Cotta did not move the press and gave her absence as the grounds for dismissal. But there are other speculations as well: possibly Cotta was trying to create a sinecure for his unsuccessful son, or as biographer Ludwig Geiger states, perhaps Cotta was angry that Huber had begun in 1821 to publish her novels with his archrival Brockhaus. But it is plausible to assume that the practical businessman realized the left-liberal agnostic Therese Huber was no longer representative of her times, in the growing reactionary climate of post-1815 Europe. Her pro-Napoleon stance and her conflicts with August von Kotzebue and implicit sympathy for his assassin, Karl Ludwig Sand, in 1819 are indicative of the directions she gave the newspaper. Although Cotta and his son replaced her as editors she continued to contribute to the paper until 1827.

Although Therese Huber's literary production cannot be definitively separated from Ludwig Huber's, research by Ludwig Geiger and Sabine Jordan differentiates them as nearly as

Silhouette of Therese Huber (by permission of the Schiller-Nationalmuseum, Marbach)

possible: essentially all prose works appearing under L. F. Huber's name are actually Therese's. Other works by her also most probably appeared in journals such as *Isis, Minerva, Flora, Selene, Urania,* and *Cornelia.*

Her six novels and more than sixty stories center on women and problematic relations between the sexes. Her radical women such as Sara in *Die Familie Seldorf* appear sporadically; much more frequent are her plain or ugly, uncomfortable or unhappy women characters, who are at odds with their society. She depicts women at crucial life stages–before marriage choices, at menopause, at the birth of first child or grandchild. She provides models for working women who reject marriage, although they suffer for it. While her work displays the Entsagung (resignation to one's fate) that typifies women's literature from 1800 to 1830, it is a forced and unwilling resignation to which her heroines succumb. She reveals as well an ardent feminine sensuality that is startling for a woman author in this period. A continuing concern for this mother of two unpropertied daughters was the plight of the poor unmarried woman; her last work, and the one of which she was herself most proud was *Die Ehelosen* (The Un-

married Women, 1829), a collection of vignettes on how women could lead productive, meaningful lives without matrimony.

A second theme prevalent in Huber's works is criticism of religious bigotry and religion itself: the tale "Urteil der Welt" (Judgment by the World, 1805) and the novel *Hannah, der Herrnhuterin Deborah Findling* (Hannah, the Moravian Deborah Findling, 1821) depict women who find deep contradictions in belief and action. Close in importance to Huber's critique of religion was her concern for girls' education, presented most forcefully in *Ellen Percy oder Erziehung durch Schicksale* (Ellen Percy or Education Through Fate, 1822).

Although her plot resolutions are often sentimental and her style is sometimes repetitive, the bitter social criticism and rejection of religious hypocrisy which are structured into her texts prefigure Young German texts and later feminist concerns. The religious critique foreshadows the works of Karl Gutzkow and Fanny Lewald; her writing on women's topics and political engagement are echoed in the works of authors such as Fanny Tarnow, Caroline Auguste Fischer, Luise Mühlbach, and Luise Otto-Peters. Yet there has been little scholarship devoted to her work and its influence on later women authors, and only recently has there been any attempt to separate her writings from those of her husband. An edition of her prolific correspondence is being prepared and should contribute to a clearer picture of her actual literary production.

Her death on 15 June 1829 was marked by a eulogy published in the *Morgenblatt* (14 August 1829), possibly written by Cotta himself, that describes the profound personal and political changes Therese Huber had witnessed and helped create: "Sie brachte aus den unter politischen Stürmen verlebten Jahren ihrer Jugend und ihres besten Alters zu diesem Geschäfte der Matrone eine reiche Lebenserfahrung, einen bei einem weiblichen Geiste höchst seltenen Ueberblick von Welt und Zeit und jenen allgemeinen Freiheitssinn, jenes Unabhängigkeitsgefühl, die Begeisterung für Wahrheit und Recht mit, die jeder Schriftsteller haben soll" (From those days of her youth and prime of life which were spent in political storms, she brought to this task of her matronly days [her work as editor] rich life experience; an understanding of the world and the age that is rare in a female mind; and that general belief in freedom, that feeling for independence, and that enthusiasm for truth and justice which every author should possess).

Letters:

"Briefe der Therese Huber an Caroline Pichler," *Jahrbuch der Grillparzer-Gesellschaft*, 17 (1907): 190-291;

A. Götze, "Unveröffentlichtes aus dem Briefwechsel der Frau von Staël (including a letter to Therese Huber)," *Zeitschrift für französische Sprache und Literatur*, 78 (1968): 193-228.

Biography:

Ludwig Geiger, *Therese Huber (1764-1829): Leben und Briefe einer deutschen Frau* (Stuttgart: Cotta, 1901).

References:

Barbara Becker-Cantarino, "Therese Forster-Huber und Polen," *Chloe: Beiheft zum Daphnis*, 7 (1988): 53-66;

Irma Brandes and Ursula Mauch, *Der Freiheit entgegen: Frauen der Romantik* (Esslingen & Munich: Bechtle, 1986), pp. 19-49;

Alfred Wilhelm Dove, *Die Forsters und die Humboldts: Zwei Paar bunter Lebensläufe zur*

allgemeinen deutschen Biographie beigetragen (Leipzig: Duncker & Humblot, 1881);

Ludwig Geiger, "Aus Therese Hubers Herzenleben," in his *Dichter und Frauen: Vorträge und Abhandlungen* (Berlin: Paetel, 1896);

Frieda Höfle, *Cottas Morgenblatt für gebildete Stände und seine Stellung zu Literatur und literarischer Kritik* (Berlin: Buchdruckerei Gutenberg, 1937), pp. 116-128;

Sabine Dorothea Jordan, *Ludwig Ferdinand Huber (1764-1804): His Life and Works* (Stuttgart: Akademisches Verlag Hans-Dieter Heinz, 1978);

Paul Kluckhohn, *Die Auffassung der Liebe in der Literatur des 18. Jahrhunderts und in der Romantik*, third edition (Tübingen: Niemeyer, 1966), pp. 287-293;

G. von König-Warthausen, "Therese Huber: Schriftstellerin, Redakteurin von Cottas *Morgenblatt*. 1764-1829," *Lebensbilder aus Schwaben und Franken*, 10 (1966): 215-232;

Wulf Köpke, "Immer noch im Schatten der Männer? Therese Huber als Schriftstellerin," in *Der Weltumsegler und seine Freunde*, edited by Detlev Rasmussen (Tübingen: Narr, 1988), pp. 116-132;

A. Leitzmann, *Georg und Therese Forster und die Brüder Humboldt: Urkunden und Umrisse* (Bonn: Röhrscheid, 1936);

"Ludwig and Therese Huber," *Die Grenzboten* (1859): 201-222, 254-267;

Marta Marthy, "Widersprüchlich–widerständig: Therese Huber," *Alternative*, 25 (1982): 106-116;

Helga Meise, "Der Frauenroman: Erprobungen der 'Weiblichkeit,' " in *Deutsche Literatur von Frauen*, edited by Gisela Brinker-Gabler, volume 1 (Munich: Beck, 1988), pp. 434-452;

Renate Möhrmann, *Die andere Frau: Emanzipationsvorsätze deutscher Schriftstellerinnen im Vorfeld der 48er Revolution* (Stuttgart: Metzler, 1977);

Helmut Peitsch, "Die Revolution im Familienroman: Aktuelles politisches Thema und konventionelle Romanstruktur in Therese Hubers *Die Familie Seldorf*," *Jahrbuch der deutschen Schillergesellschaft*, 28 (1984): 248-269;

Lydia Schieth, *Die Entwicklung des deutschen Frauenromans im ausgehenden 18. Jahrhundert* (Frankfurt am Main: Lang, 1987);

Christine Touaillon, *Der deutsche Frauenroman des 18. Jahrhunderts* (Vienna & Leipzig: Braumüller, 1919);

Eva Walter, *Schrieb oft, von Mägde Arbeit müde: Lebenszusammenhänge deutscher Schriftstellerinnen um 1800–Schritte zur bürgerlichen Weiblichkeit* (Düsseldorf: Schwan, 1985).

Papers:

Therese Huber's papers are widely scattered. Letters and personal items are at the Niedersächische Staats- und Universitätsbibliothek in Göttingen and letters are at the Schiller Nationalmuseum in Marbach; the Goethe and Schiller Archives in Weimar have documents pertaining to her marriages, the Huber family papers, and several letters. Other collections are at the Staats- und Universitätsbibliothek Hamburg, Sächsische Landesbibliothek Dresden, Staatsbibliothek Dessau, Bayerische Staatsbibliothek München, and the Württembergische Landesbibliothek. A clearinghouse for copies of works and letters by Therese Huber, as well as for research publications on her, is the Arbeitsstelle Therese Huber at the University of Osnabrück, Fachbereich Sprach- und Literaturwissenschaft, Dr. Magdalene Heuser, director.

Alexander von Humboldt
(14 September 1769-6 May 1859)

James Hardin
University of South Carolina

SELECTED BOOKS: *Mineralogische Beobachtungen über einige Basalte am Rhein: Mit vorangeschickten, zerstreuten Bemerkungen über den Basalt der ältern und neuern Schriftsteller* (Brunswick: Schulbuchhandlung, 1790);

Florae Fribergensis specimen plantas cryptogamicas praesertim subterraneas exhibens (Berlin: Rottmann, 1793);

Versuche über die gereizte Muskel- und Nervenfaser nebst Vermuthungen über den chemischen Process des Lebens in der Thier- und Pflanzenwelt, 2 volumes (Berlin: Decker, 1797);

Versuche über die chemische Zerlegung des Luftkreises und über einige andere Gegenstände der Naturlehre (Brunswick: Vieweg, 1799);

Über die unterirdischen Gasarten und die Mittel ihren Nachtheil zu vermindern: Ein Beytrag zur Physik der praktischen Bergbaukunde (Brunswick: Vieweg, 1799);

Voyage de Humboldt et Bonpland, by Humboldt, Aimé Bonpland, and others, 23 volumes (Paris: Schoell, 1805-1834)—comprises part 1, *Voyage aux régions équinoxiales du nouveau continent, fait en 1799, 1800, 1801, 1802, et 1804,* 3 volumes (1814-1834), translated by Helen Maria Williams as *Personal Narrative of Travels to the Equinoctial Regions of the New Continent, During the Years 1799-1804,* 7 volumes (London: Longman, Hurst, Rees, Orme & Brown, 1814-1829; volumes 1-2 republished, Philadelphia: Carey, 1815); section 2 of part 1, "Vues des Cordillères et monuments des peuples indigènes de l'Amérique," translated by Williams as *Researches, Concerning the Institutions & Monuments of the Ancient Inhabitants of America, with Descriptions & Views of Some of the Most Striking Scenes in the Cordilleras!* (London: Longman, Hurst, Rees, Orme & Brown, Murray & Colburn, 1814); part 2, *Recueil d'observations de zoologie et d'anatomie comparée, faites dans l'océan Atlantique, dans l'intérieur du nouveau continent et dans la mer du Sud pendant les années 1799, 1800, 1801, 1802, et 1803,* 2 volumes

Alexander von Humboldt (etching by P. Habelmann after a painting by Emma Gaggiotti-Richards)

(1811-1833); part 3, *Essai politique sur le royaume de la Nouvelle-Espagne,* 2 volumes (1811-1812), translated by John Black as *Political Essay on the Kingdom of New Spain: With Physical Sections and Maps Founded on Astronomical Observations and Trigonometrical and Barometrical Measurements* (3 volumes, London: Printed for Longman, Hurst, Rees, Orme & Brown, 1811; 2 volumes, New York: Riley, 1811); part 4, *Recueil d'observations astronomiques, d'opérations trigonométriques et de mesures barométriques, faites pendant le cours d'un voyage aux régions équinoxiales du nouveau conti-*

nent, depuis 1799 jusqu'en 1803, par A. de Humboldt; rédigées et calculées, d'après les tables les plus exactes, par Jabbo Oltmanns, 2 volumes (1810); part 5, *Essai sur la géographie des plantes: Accompagné d'un tableau physique des régions équinoxiales, fondé sur des mésures exécutées, depuis le dixième degré de latitude boréale jusqu'au dixième degré de latitude australe, pendant les années 1799, 1800, 1801, 1802 et 1803* (1805); part 6, *Botanique,* 15 volumes (1808-1834);

Ideen zu einer Physiognomik der Gewächse (Tübingen: Cotta, 1806);

Ansichten der Natur, mit wissenschaftlichen Erläuterungen (Tübingen: Cotta, 1808; revised and enlarged, 1826, 1849); translated by Elizabeth Juliana Sabine as *Aspects of Nature, in Different Lands and Different Climates: With Scientific Elucidations* (2 volumes, London: Longman, Brown, Green & Longmans, 1849; 1 volume, Philadelphia: Lea & Blanchard, 1849); German version republished as *Alexander von Humboldt's Ansichten der Natur* (New York: Gerhard, 1859);

Des lignes isothermes et de la distribution de la châleur sur le globe (Paris: Perronneau, 1817); translated anonymously as *Isothermal Lines and the Distribution of Heat over the Globe,* 2 volumes (Edinburgh, 1820-1821);

Essai géognostique sur le gisement des roches dans les deux continents (Paris: Levrault, 1823); translated anonymously as *A Geognostical Essay on the Superposition of Rocks in Both Hemispheres* (London: Longman, Hurst, Rees, Orme, Brown & Green, 1823);

Fragments de géologie et de climatologie asiatiques, 2 volumes (Paris: Gide, 1831);

Asie Centrale: Recherches sur les chaînes des montagnes et la climatologie comparée, 3 volumes (Paris: Gide, 1843);

Kosmos: Entwurf einer physischen Weltbeschreibung, 5 volumes (Stuttgart & Tübingen: Cotta, 1845-1862); translated by Elise C. Ollé, Benjamin H. Paul, and William S. Dallas as *Cosmos: A Sketch of a Physical Description of the Universe* (London: Bohn, 1848-1865);

Kleinere Schriften (Stuttgart & Tübingen: Cotta, 1853);

Gesammelte Werke, 12 volumes (Stuttgart: Cotta, 1889);

Alexander von Humboldt: Aus meinem Leben. Autobiographische Bekenntnisse, edited by Kurt-R. Biermann (Munich: Beck, 1987);

Alexander von Humboldt: Studienausgabe in sieben Bänden, edited by Hanno Beck, 1 volume published (Darmstadt: Wissenschaftliche Buchgesellschaft, 1987-).

PERIODICAL PUBLICATION: "Die Lebenskraft, oder Der rhodische Genius," *Die Horen* (July 1795).

Friedrich Wilhelm Karl Heinrich Alexander von Humboldt, one of the most famous men of his time, a polymath and Renaissance man in an age of genius, perhaps the greatest naturalist and explorer of the nineteenth century, was born in Berlin on 14 September 1769. He was the second son of the royal chamberlain Alexander Georg von Humboldt and Maria Elisabeth Colomb von Humboldt. His older brother, Karl Wilhelm, was to achieve European fame in his own right as politician, philologist, and philosopher.

After their father's death in 1779 the brothers were educated by energetic and demanding private tutors, under the supervision of their mother, at the family estate in Tegel, near Berlin. They studied the classics–concentrating, as was still the custom, on Virgil and Horace; French, the obligatory language of instruction and discourse and the scientific lingua franca; mathematics; drawing; and later, philosophy, law, and political science.

The tutors had given the boys some instruction in botany, and Alexander was able to apply Linnaeus's system of classification to the flora in the forests and parks near Castle Tegel. Even as a child he displayed a conspicuous interest in collecting and classifying plants, shells, and insects and as a result received the nickname "the little apothecary." At the age of sixteen the precocious Alexander attended lectures in physics and philosophy at the home of the physician Marcus Herz. There he learned of the electrical experiments of Benjamin Franklin and Alessandro Volta, one result of which was the installation–thought blasphemous by the orthodox clergy–of lightning rods at Castle Tegel.

Complying with his mother's wishes that he eventually enter the Prussian civil service, Humboldt studied finance at the small university in drab Frankfurt an der Oder (there was as yet no university in Berlin) in 1787-1788. It was there that he made the first of a series of close male friendships. There is something in these relationships of the fervent eighteenth-century cult of friendship, and also an unmistakable element of the homoerotic. His disinclination to marry and found a family in accordance with the expectations of society was part and parcel of his independent, austere attitude toward life; and many of his most significant scientific findings, often gained under incredibly demanding conditions and in the most exotic and hostile locales, might never have been made had he married. Wilhelm married Caroline von Dacheröden in 1791, and Alexander's occasional lengthy stays with the couple and their five children were the closest approximation to a family life ever enjoyed by the scientist.

In April 1789 he enrolled at the University of Göttingen, then the foremost German university, where he studied under such celebrated professors as the anatomist and anthropologist Johann Friedrich Blumenbach and the classicist and archaeologist Christian Gottlob Heyne, one of the first scholars to make a scientific analysis of Greek mythology. Displaying "Prussian" perseverance and industry, he read Plautus and Petronius with his Greek and Latin professor from nine until eleven on many nights.

In 1789 Humboldt was traveling along the Rhine with a geologist friend, collecting plant and mineral specimens. In comparing his observations of geologic formations along the Rhine with geological terms used by Pliny and Strabo, he found that Strabo's "basalt" seemed to correspond to the material that in contemporary parlance was called "Granit" (granite). This insight was only one of many that resulted from comparison of the authorities of antiquity with his own observations. The older literature provided in many instances the matrix, the classification system, and the theoretical underpinnings for entire branches of science; it also provided priceless data of a historical kind, such as Pliny the Younger's detailed description of the eruption of Mt. Vesuvius. It was thus of key significance that Humboldt was well read not only in belletristic but also in the great "scientific" literature of classical antiquity. In this accomplishment he was, in his youth, not atypical; but by the time he died, such learning had become a rare achievement.

Humboldt's research led him to the question of how basalt, and minerals generally, had come into being. Thus he became involved in the controversy over the "Neptunist" theory, which held that rocks had formed by water, and the "Plutonic" theory, which postulated a volcanic origin of minerals. Early in his life Humboldt was a Neptunist, but his observations in the Andes

were to convert him to Plutonism and were to call forth the criticism of Johann Wolfgang von Goethe, who was not friendly to the idea of revolutionary geological change. (Goethe's disagreement with Humboldt and the English geologist James Hutton is alluded to in the dialogue between Seismos and the Sphinxes in *Faust II* [1832], Act II).

The studies made along the Rhine resulted in his first major work, *Mineralogische Beobachtungen über einige Basalte am Rhein* (Mineralogic Observations on Basalts along the Rhine, 1790). In the same year as his Rhine trip he met a kindred soul in Georg Forster, author, renowned traveler, and companion of Captain James Cook. The two men traveled together to the Netherlands, Belgium, Great Britain, and France. In July 1790 they experienced at first hand the enthusiasm and tumult of the French Revolution, to which Humboldt was, like most German intellectuals, sympathetically inclined. In Mainz the two parted great friends, but they never saw one another again.

Between August 1790 and February 1792 Humboldt studied commerce and foreign languages in Hamburg and geology and mining in Freiberg, Saxony. The science of geology was new, and Humboldt plunged into it with typical energy. In February 1792 he completed his studies and received, at the age of only twenty-two, a responsible position as inspector of mines in the Bayreuth district. Humboldt became concerned about the welfare of the workers under his supervision and attempted to alleviate the hazards of their working conditions. In 1793 he established, at Steben in the Fichtel Mountains, the first training school for miners. In the same year he published *Florae Fribergensis specimen plantas cryptogamicas praesertim subterraneas exhibens*, dealing with the vegetation of the mines of Freiberg. He also experimented with the phenomena of animal magnetism after reading of the work of Luigi Galvani. In 1797 he published the extensive *Versuche über die gereizte Muskel- und Nervenfaser nebst Vermuthungen über den chemischen Process des Lebens in der Thier- und Pflanzenwelt* (Essays on Muscular Irritability with Conjectures on the Chemical Process of Life in the Animal and Plant Kingdoms).

In 1794 Humboldt's brother introduced him to Goethe, the leading European man of letters and a scientist in his own right. They were immediately drawn to one another, and there are striking similarities in the obsession of both men

Humboldt in 1847 (daguerreotype by Herman Blow; by permission of the Museum für Kunst und Gewerbe, Hamburg)

with the interrelatedness of all knowledge. The two met many times at Goethe's house in Weimar, where they discussed geological problems, Goethe's theories of anatomy, and the metamorphosis of insects. Goethe, who at this juncture was uncertain about how best to pursue his own multifaceted career and found the company of most persons distasteful or boring, seems to have been much stimulated by the intellect of his younger colleague. He reported to Duke Karl August that he could learn more in an hour of conversation with Humboldt, a veritable cornucopia of knowledge, than in a week of reading books. Others of the exclusive Weimar circle had a less favorable opinion. In a letter of 1797 Friedrich Schiller concluded that for all Humboldt's energy he would contribute little to science, since he lacked the ability to view nature imaginatively. Nonetheless, Schiller was sufficiently impressed by Humboldt to publish his philosophical allegory "Die Lebenskraft, oder Der rhodische Genius" (Life Power; or, The Genius of Rhodes) in the July 1795 number of his literary journal *Die Horen*.

Although his talent as a director of mines seemed to augur a promising career in the Prussian civil service, the ever-restless Humboldt came to the conclusion that he must undertake the scientific expeditions he had dreamed of since his youth. Accordingly, on becoming financially independent after his mother's death in 1796 he resigned his position and prepared for a

major expedition to the Americas to study anatomy, geodesy, astronomy, botany, geology, and meteorology. In May 1798 he traveled to Paris, where he made many friends and conducted experiments. Impatient and disappointed by the postponement of Captain Nicolas Baudin's proposed voyage of circumnavigation, he left Paris for Egypt but wound up in Spain instead. He developed revolutionary theories on the geological structure of Spain, and, more important, was granted permission to explore the Spanish possessions in America.

This immensely fruitful expedition, which lasted from 5 June 1799 until 3 August 1804, took Humboldt and the French naturalist Aimé Bonpland through some of the most spectacular, isolated, and perilous areas in the world; but Humboldt seemed to thrive on danger and physical exertion and was, as usual, tireless in his observations. He explored Venezuela; discovered the link between the Orinoco River and the Amazon; visited Cuba, where he was horrified at the practice of slavery; journeyed through Peru, where he was fascinated by what he saw of the remnants of the great Inca civilization; traveled through Colombia; spent a year in Mexico studying its volcanoes, minerals, and previously neglected pre-Columbian culture; and briefly visited the United States, where he conferred with President Thomas Jefferson. With this expedition, possibly the most significant of the era, Humboldt established the foundations of geography and meteorology. He studied the relationship between elevation, temperature, and organic life; invented the concept of isothermal lines; examined the earth's magnetic field; and investigated the origin of tropical storms, rocks, and volcanoes.

Except for the period from November 1805 until November 1807, when Humboldt resided in Berlin, he lived from 1804 until 1827 in Paris, then the scientific capital of the world. His primary goal in this period was to make public the results of his great expedition. It was to take nearly thirty years for him to write, sort, and classify his data and collections and to have illustrated, fund, and print *Voyage de Humboldt et Bonpland* (1805-1834), which was sold unbound for the princely sum of £383. The publication established Humboldt's fame, though he continued to live in relatively modest circumstances.

Humboldt had chosen Paris as a residence because it had the facilities he needed to write and publish his work. The Prussian king supported him with a generous yearly pension. But in 1827 Humboldt reluctantly accepted the king's invitation to move to Berlin, with an annual pension of five thousand talers and permission to live in Paris several months of each year. The king hoped that Berlin, then a provincial town compared with cities such as London and Paris, would, with the influence and reputation of scholars such as Humboldt, become the scientific and cultural center of Europe.

In Berlin Humboldt gave public lectures and initiated, presided over, and supported scientific enterprises and associations. A series of lectures in 1827-1828 on physical geography at the University of Berlin attracted an audience of over a thousand, consisting of students, professors, and (a sensation at the time) women. The course was to form the basis for Humboldt's great work *Kosmos: Entwurf einer physischen Weltbeschreibung* (1845-1862; translated as *Cosmos: A Sketch of a Physical Description of the Universe*, 1848-1865). He was also involved in politics and social affairs. He regarded the revolutions of 1848 favorably, and after their failure he did not cease to advocate universal political rights, to promote the emancipation of the Jews, or to help poor artists and scientists and victims of persecution.

Not until he was fifty-eight did Humboldt undertake–at the invitation of the czar–another major expedition. From May to November 1828 he made a journey of some nine thousand miles through Russia and Siberia. The journey yielded only moderate discoveries in the fields of mining, geology, geophysics, and climatology. Humboldt's *Fragments de géologie et de climatologie asiatiques* appeared in Paris in 1831.

In 1845, in his seventy-sixth year, Humboldt began to write one of the most extraordinary works of the period, *Kosmos*, an attempt to describe the underlying unity of the universe in a manner comprehensible to the general reader. In the preface Humboldt wrote that the most important aim of science is "in der Mannigfaltigkeit die Einheit zu erkennen, von dem Individuellen alles zu umfassen, was die Entdeckungen der letzteren Zeitalter uns darbieten, die Einzelheiten prüfend zu sondern und doch nicht ihrer Masse zu unterliegen ... " (to recognize unity in diversity, to comprehend all the single aspects as revealed by the discoveries of the last epochs, to judge single phenomena separately without capitulating to their sheer bulk . . .). *Kosmos* was to have four primary aims: to describe the earth physically; to provide an objective depiction of nature; to show "den Reflex der Natur auf die Einbildungskraft

und das Gefühl, als Anregungsmittel zum Naturstudium durch begeisterte Schilderungen ferner Himmelsstriche und naturbeschreibende Poesie (ein Zweig der modernen Literatur), durch veredelte Landschaft-Malerei, durch Anbau und contrastrirende Gruppirung exotischer Pflanzenformen (the action of nature on the imagination and emotion as an incentive to nature studies through enthusiastic descriptions of distant regions and a literature of travel [a branch of modern literature], by means of an ennobled landscape painting, and the growth and display of contrasting groups of exotic plants); and to provide an intellectual history of the development of the concept of the cosmos, the view of nature as a whole.

It is typical of Humboldt that this ambitious scientific work should deal explicitly with literature, that it should attempt to analyze the effect of nature on the imagination. And thus, while *Kosmos* is an invaluable compendium of what was known about the physical sciences in the mid-nineteenth century, its vision of a linkage between nature and spirit also reflects a survival of the humanism of late eighteenth-century Weimar. The encyclopedic character of the work ran contrary to the specializing currents of the age.

The book was never finished. Humboldt died on 6 May 1859, at the age of eighty-nine, while writing the fifth and final volume. A state funeral was ordered, house fronts in central Berlin were draped in black, and on 10 May 1859 a cortege consisting of royal chamberlains carrying Humboldt's decorations, Knights of the Order of the Black Eagle, members of the diplomatic corps, professors, municipal delegations, and six hundred students proceeded to the Berlin Cathedral to pay their last respects to the greatest explorer of the age. Humboldt was buried at Tegel next to his brother.

In anthropology Humboldt was among the first to call attention to the neglected Inca, Aztec, and Maya civilizations; in astronomy he is the first to observe a meteor shower with instruments and helped to establish the periodicity of such phenomena; in botany, with the collaboration of Bonpland, he collected sixty thousand plant specimens and described thirty-five hundred new species; in geography his observations were the basis for all future maps of Central and South America; in geology he was perhaps the first to link geological faults with volcanic activity and to show the effect of volcanism on the earth's structure. The list of achievements could be expanded at

*Humboldt in his library, 1856 (lithograph after a watercolor by Hildebrandt, by permission of the
Royal Geographical Society, London)*

will in the fields of meteorology, geophysics, oceanography, physiology, and zoology. It seems likely, although no specialized study has yet been done on the question, that his influence on the artists and literary figures of the epoch has been underrated and that it was all-pervasive.

Letters:

Briefe von Alexander von Humboldt and Varnhagen von Ense aus den Jahren 1827 bis 1858: Nebst Auszügen aus Varnhagen's Tagebüchern, und Briefen von Varnhagen und andern an Humboldt (Leipzig: Brockhaus, 1860; New York: Hauser, 1860); translated by Friedrich Kapp as *Letters of Alexander von Humboldt, Written between the Years 1827 and 1858 to Varnhagen von Ense: Together with Extracts from Varnhagen's diaries, and letters from Varnhagen and Others to Humboldt* (New York: Rudd & Carlson, 1860; London: Trübner, 1860);

Briefwechsel und Gespräche Alexander von Humboldt's mit einem jungen Freunde: Aus den Jahren 1848

bis 1856 (Berlin: Duncker, 1861);

Briefwechsel Alexander von Humboldt's mit Heinrich Berghaus aus den Jahren 1825 bis 1858, 3 volumes (Leipzig: Costenoble, 1863);

Correspondance, scientifique et littéraire, recueillie, publié et prédédé d'une notice et d'une introduction, par M. de La Roquette.... Suivie de la biographie des principaux correspondants de Humboldt, de notes et d'une table et ornée de deux portraits de A. de Humboldt, du facsimilé d'une de ses lettres et de figures intercalées dans le texte (Paris: Ducrocq, 1865);

Correspondance inédite scientifique et littéraire recueillie et publié par M. de La Roquette ... Suivie de la biographie des principaux correspondants de Humboldt et de notes, 2 volumes (Paris: Guérin, 1869);

Briefe an Christian Carl Josias Freiherr von Bunsen (Leipzig: Brockhaus, 1869);

Im Ural und Altai: Briefwechsel zwischen Alexander von Humboldt und Graf George von Cancrin, aus den Jahren 1827-1832 (Leipzig: Brockhaus, 1869);

Goethe's Briefwechsel mit den Gebrüdern von Humboldt (1795-1832), edited by F. Th. Bratranek (Leipzig: Brockhaus, 1876);

Briefwechsel zwischen A. v. Humboldt und Gauss: Zum hundertjährigen Geburtstage von Gauss am 30. April 1877, edited by Karl Bruhns (Leipzig: Engelmann, 1877);

Briefe Alexander's von Humboldt an seinen Bruder Wilhelm: Herausgegeben von der Familie von Humboldt in Ottmachau (Stuttgart: Cotta, 1880);

Jugendbriefe an Wilhelm Gabriel Wegener, edited by Albert Leitzmann (Leipzig: Göschen, 1896);

Lettres américaines d'Alexandre de Humboldt, 1798-1807: Précédées d'une notice de J.-C. Delamétherie et suivies d'un choix de documents en partie inédits, edited by E.-T. Hamy (Paris: Guilmoto, 1904);

Correspondence d'Alexandre de Humboldt avec François Arago (1809-1853), edited by Hamy (Paris: Guilmoto, 1907);

Briefe Alexander von Humboldt's an Ignaz von Olfers, edited by E. W. M. von Olfers (Nuremberg: Sebald, 1913).

References:

Alexander von Humboldt: Katalog einer Sammlung seiner Werke, Portraits und Schriften (Frankfurt am Main: Baer, 1912);

Ewald Banse, *Alexander von Humboldt: Erschließer einer neuen Welt* (Stuttgart: Wissenschaftliche Verlagsgesellschaft, 1953);

Aaron Bernstein, *Alexander von Humboldt und der Geist zweier Jahrhunderte: Sammlung gemeinverständlicher wissenschaftlicher Vorträge*, (Berlin: Virchow, 1869);

Rudolf Borch, *Alexander von Humboldt: Sein Leben in Selbstzeugnissen, Briefen und Berichten* (Berlin: Verlag des Druckhauses Tempelhof, 1948);

Douglas Botting, *Humboldt and the Cosmos* (London: Rainbird, 1973); translated into German by Annelie Hohenemser as *Alexander von Humboldt: Biographie eines großen Forschungsreisenden* (Munich: Prestel, 1974);

Karl Christian Bruhns, *Alexander von Humboldt: Eine wissenschaftliche Biographie*, 3 volumes (Leipzig: Brockhaus, 1872); translated by Jane and Caroline Lassell as *Life of Alexander von Humboldt*, 2 volumes (London: Longmans, Green/Boston: Lee & Shepard, 1873);

Alfred Gebauer, *Alexander von Humboldt, Forschungsreisender-Geograph-Naturforscher: Ein großer Sohn Berlins* (Berlin: Stapp, 1987);

Georg Heller, *Die Weltanschauung Alexander von Humboldt's in ihren Beziehungen zu den Ideen des Klassizismus* (Leipzig: Voigtländer, 1910);

Hermann Klencke, *Lives of the Brothers Humboldt, Alexander and Wilhelm* (New York: Harper, 1853);

Hermann Kletke, *Alexander von Humboldt's Reisen in Amerika und Asien*, 4 volumes (Berlin: Hasselberg, 1859-1861);

Mario Ferdinand Krammer, *Alexander von Humboldt: Mensch, Zeit, Werk* (Berlin: Wegweiser, 1951);

Walther Linden, *Alexander von Humboldt: Weltbild der Naturwissenschaft* (Hamburg: Hoffmann & Campe, 1940);

William Macgillivray, *The Travels and Researches of Alexander von Humboldt* (New York: Harper, 1832);

Willy Möbus, *Alexander von Humboldt, der Monarch der Wissenschaften* (Berlin: Pontes, 1948);

Friedrich Muthmann, *Alexander von Humboldt und sein Naturbild im Spiegel der Goethezeit* (Zurich: Artemis, 1955);

Halina Nelken, *Alexander von Humboldt: His Portraits and Their Artists. A Documentary Iconography* (Berlin: Reimer, 1980);

Heinrich Pfeiffer, ed., *Alexander von Humboldt: Werk und Weltgeltung* (Munich: Piper, 1969);

J. H. Schultze, ed., *Alexander von Humboldt: Studien zu seiner universalen Geisteshaltung* (Berlin: De Gruyter, 1959);

Richard Henry Stoddard, *The Life, Travels, and Books of Alexander von Humboldt* (London: Low, 1859; New York: Rudd & Carlton, 1859);

Helmut de Terra, *Humboldt: The Life and Times of Alexander von Humboldt* (New York: Knopf, 1955);

Rudolf Zaunick, ed., *Alexander von Humboldt: Kosmische Naturbetrachtung. Sein Werk im Grundriß* (Stuttgart: Kröner, 1958).

Papers:

Most of Alexander von Humboldt's remaining papers are in the Staatsbibliothek Preußischer Kulturbesitz, West Berlin; in the Cotta-Archiv housed in the Schiller-Nationalmuseum, Marbach, and in the Germanisches Nationalmuseum, Nuremberg.

Wilhelm von Humboldt
(22 June 1767-8 April 1835)

Charlotte B. Evans
Central Michigan University

BOOKS: *Prozeß des Buchdrucker Unger gegen den Oberkonsistorialrath Zöllner in Censurangelegenheiten wegen eines verbotenen Buchs* (Berlin: Unger, 1791);

Ästhetische Versuche. Theil I: Über Göthe's Hermann und Dorothea (Brunswick: Vieweg, 1799);

Rom (Berlin: Haude & Spener, 1806);

Berichtigungen und Zusätze zum ersten Abschnitte des zweyten Bandes des Mithridates über die cantabrische oder baskische Sprache (Berlin: Voß, 1817);

An die Sonne (Paris: Didot, 1820);

Prüfung der Untersuchungen über die Urbewohner Hispaniens vermittelst der Vaskischen Sprache (Berlin: Dümmler, 1821);

Über die Aufgabe des Geschichtschreibers (Leipzig: Meiner, 1822);

Über das Entstehen der grammatischen Formen, und ihren Einfluß auf die Ideenentwicklung (Berlin: Dümmler, 1823);

Über die Buchstabenschrift und ihren Zusammenhang mit dem Sprachbau (Berlin: Dümmler, 1826);

Über die unter dem Namen Bhagavad-gitá bekannte Episode des Mahá-bhárata (Berlin: Königliche Akademie der Wissenschaften, 1826);

Über vier Aegyptische, löwenköpfige Bildsäulen in den hiesigen Königlichen Antikensammlungen (Berlin: Dümmler, 1827);

Lettre à M. Abel-Rémusat, sur la nature des formes grammaticales en général, et sur le génie de la langue chinoise en particulier (Paris: Dondey-Dupré, 1827);

Ueber den Dualis: Gelesen in der Akademie der Wissenschaften am 26. April 1827 (Berlin: Königliche Akademie der Wissenschaften, 1828);

An Essay on the Best Means of Ascertaining the Affinities of Oriental Languages: Contained in a Letter to Sir Alexander Johnston (London, 1828);

Über die Verwandtschaft der Ortsadverbien mit dem Pronomen in einigen Sprachen (Berlin: Dümmler, 1830);

Über die Kawi-Sprache auf der Insel Java, nebst einer Einleitung über die Verschiedenheit des menschlichen Sprachbaues und ihren Einfluß auf die gei-

Wilhelm von Humboldt (etching by Eduard Eichens after a drawing by F. Krüger)

stige Entwicklung des Menschengeschlechts, 3 volumes (Berlin: Königliche Akademie der Wissenschaften, 1836-1839); introduction translated by George C. Buck and Frithjof A. Raven as *Linguistic Variability and Intellectual Development* (Coral Gables, Fla.: University of Miami Press, 1971);

Gesammelte Werke, edited by Carl Brandes, 7 volumes (Berlin: Reimer, 1841-1852);

Ideen zu einem Versuch, die Gränzen der Wirksamkeit des Staats zu bestimmen, edited by Eduard Cauer (Breslau: Trewendt, 1851); translated by Joseph Coulthard, Jr., as *The Sphere and*

Duties of Government (London: Chapman, 1854); translated by J. W. Burrow as *The Limits of State Action* (London: Cambridge University Press, 1969);

Sonette (Berlin: Reimer, 1853);

Abhandlungen über Geschichte und Politik (Berlin: Heimann, 1869);

Die sprachphilosophischen Werke Wilhelm von Humboldts, edited by Heymann Steinthal (Berlin: Dümmler, 1884);

Tagebuch von seiner Reise nach Norddeutschland im Jahre 1790, edited by Albert Leitzmann (Weimar: Felber, 1894; reprinted, Bern: Lang, 1970);

Sechs ungedruckte Aufsätze über das klassische Altertum, edited by Leitzmann (Leipzig: Göschen, 1896)—comprises "Über das Studium des Altertums und des Griechischen insbesondere," "Pindar," "Betrachtungen über die Weltgeschichte," "Über das antike Theater in Sagunt: An Goethe," "Latium und Hellas oder Betrachtungen über das klassische Altertum," "Geschichte des Verfalls und Unterganges der griechischen Freistaaten," "Anhang: Bruchstücke einer späteren Fassung der 'Skizze über die Griechen' ";

Gesammelte Schriften, edited by Leitzmann and others, 20 volumes (Berlin: Behr, 1903-1936);

Wilhelm von Humboldts ausgewählte philosophische Schriften, edited by Johannes Schubert (Leipzig: Dürr, 1910);

Über den Geschlechtsunterschied; Über die männliche und weibliche Form, edited by Fritz Giese (Langensalza: Wendt & Klauwell, 1917);

Über die deutsche Verfassung: Denkschriften an Freiherrn vom Stein und Friedrich von Gentz (1813/14) (Leipzig: Meiner, 1919);

Wilhelm von Humboldt: Eine Auswahl aus seinen politischen Schriften, edited by Siegfried A. Kähler (Berlin: Hobbing, 1922);

Kleine Schriften: Eine Auswahl aus den geistesgeschichtlichen Aufsätzen, edited by Otto Heuschele (Leipzig: Reclam, 1928)—comprises "Über Schiller und den Gang seiner Geistesentwicklung," "Über Goethes zweiten römischen Aufenthalt," "Über den Geschlechtsunterschied und dessen Einfluß auf die organische Natur," "Über die männliche und weibliche Form," "Über die Aufgabe des Geschichtschreibers," "Über das vergleichende Sprachstudium in Beziehung auf die verschiedenen Epochen der Sprachentwicklung";

Wilhelm von Humboldts philosophische Anthropologie und Theorie der Menschenkenntnis, edited by Fritz Heinemann (Halle: Niemeyer, 1929);

Schulpläne des Jahres 1809: "Über die innere und äussere Organisation der höheren wissenschaftlichen Anstalten in Berlin," 1810 (Hamburg: Selbstverlag der Universität Hamburg, 1946);

Wilhelm von Humboldt und Karl Freiherr vom Stein: Über Einrichtung landständischer Verfassungen in den Preußischen Staaten, edited by Arndt Schreiber (Heidelberg: Winter, 1949);

Wilhelm von Humboldt: Sein Leben und Wirken, dargestellt in Briefen, Tagebüchern und Dokumenten seiner Zeit, edited by Rudolf Freese (Berlin: Verlag der Nation, 1953);

Wilhelm von Humboldt: Schriften zur Anthropologie und Bildungslehre, edited by Andreas Flitner (Düsseldorf: Küpper, 1956);

Wilhelm von Humboldt: Bildung und Sprache, edited by Clemens Menze (Paderborn: Schöningh, 1959);

Wilhelm von Humboldt: Werke in fünf Bänden, edited by Flitner and Klaus Giel, 5 volumes (Darmstadt: Wissenschaftliche Buchgesellschaft / Stuttgart: Cotta, 1960-1981);

Schriften, edited by Walter Flemmer (Munich: Goldmann, 1964);

Studienausgabe in 3 Bänden, edited by Kurt Müller-Vollmer, 1 volume published (Frankfurt am Main & Hamburg: Fischer, 1970);

Schriften zur Sprache, edited by Michael Böhler (Stuttgart: Reclam, 1973).

Edition in English: *Humanist without Portfolio: An Anthology of the Writings of Wilhelm von Humboldt*, translated and edited by Marianne Cowan (Detroit: Wayne State University Press, 1963).

OTHER: Pindar, *Zweite olympische Ode: Metrisch übersetzt*, translated by Humboldt (Berlin: Unger, 1792);

Alexander von Humboldt, *Über die unterirdischen Gasarten und die Mittel, ihren Nachtheil zu vermindern*, foreword by Humboldt (Brunswick: Vieweg, 1799);

Aeschylus, *Agamemnon: Metrisch übersetzt*, translated by Humboldt (Leipzig: Fleischer, 1816);

"Denkschrift über Preußens ständische Verfassung," in *Denkschriften des Ministers Freiherrn vom Stein über deutsche Verfassungen*, edited by Georg H. Pertz (Berlin: Reimer, 1848);

"Nine Unpublished Sonnets by Wilhelm von Humboldt," translated and edited by Felix M. Was-sermann, *Germanic Review*, 26 (December 1951): 268-278;

"On the Historian's Task," translated by G. G. Iggers and K. von Moltke, *History and Theory*, 6, no. 1 (1967): 57-71; reprinted in *The Theory and Practice of History* (Indianapolis: Bobbs-Merrill, 1973), pp. 5-23;

"On the Spirit and the Organizational Framework of Intellectual Institutions in Berlin," translated by Edward Shils, *Minerva*, 8 (April 1979): 242-250.

PERIODICAL PUBLICATIONS: "Ideen über Staatsverfassung, durch die neue französische Konstitution veranlaßt," anonymous, *Berlinische Monatsschrift*, 19 (January 1792): 84-98);

"Über den Geschlechtsunterschied und dessen Einfluß auf die organische Natur," *Die Horen*, 1, no. 2 (1795): 99-132;

"Über die männliche und weibliche Form," *Die Horen*, 1, no. 3 (1795): 80-103;

"Über die gegenwärtige französische tragische Bühne: Aus Briefen," *Propyläen*, 3, no. 1 (1800): 66-109;

"Der Montserrat, bei Barcelona," *Allgemeine Geographische Ephemeriden*, 11, no. 3 (1803): 265-313;

"Rezension von Goethes zweitem römischen Aufenthalt," *Jahrbücher für wissenschaftliche Kritik*, 2 (1830): columns 353-374;

"Über die Behandlung der Angelegenheiten des Deutschen Bundes durch Preußen," edited by Christian Rössler, *Zeitschrift für preußische Geschichte und Landeskunde*, 9 (1872): 84-137.

Much acclaimed, often misjudged and misinterpreted, Wilhelm von Humboldt was one of the most original and influential thinkers in eighteenth-century German intellectual history. His contemporaries knew him as a sophisticated Prussian diplomat serving in several ambassadorial posts, as a reform-minded Prussian undersecretary of the interior, and as a tough negotiator and right hand of Karl August Hardenberg, chancellor of Prussia during the reorganization of Europe in the post-Napoleonic days. At his death only a few knew that he had also been intensely involved in linguistic studies, the field in which his most important mark in history would be made. His mind was so far-ranging, his intellect so penetrating, his interests so varied and esoteric that it is beyond any one person's competence to interpret his life's work. As a consequence it became

his fate to be interpreted by many, each of whom viewed him from a different area of expertise. This diversity of commentators, coupled with Humboldt's cumbersome style and exhaustive argumentation, led to interpretation and reinterpretation of his thought from various narrow viewpoints and to the neglect of his own writings.

Today Humboldt is perhaps most widely known as the founder of the university in East Berlin that bears his name. He was instrumental in creating a comprehensive system of public education that set the course for German schools and universities for more than a century and influenced Horace Mann in his reforms of American education. As one of the few who urged King Frederick William III to accept a constitutional monarchy for Prussia after the fall of Napoleon, he was unappreciated in that reactionary era; but today he is credited by historians with the most insightful and practicable proposal for a post-Napoleonic Prussia. He is also known as one of the founders of modern historiography. Of most revolutionary importance were his contributions to linguistics and philosophy of language. Here he found the common denominator for all his studies of the human intellect and paved the way for the modern theory of generative grammar. His close friendship with Friedrich Schiller and Johann Wolfgang von Goethe during their classical period led him at first to aesthetics, in which his theories reflect the general wave of Greek revivalism and his own fascination with the ancient Greek culture and ideals. From there he found his own way through anthropology to comparative language studies and ultimately to linguistic theory, where he ranks with Jacob Grimm and August Wilhelm Schlegel as one of the most illustrious stars of the time.

Born on 22 June 1767 into a wealthy Pomeranian aristocratic family, the son of Alexander Georg and Elisabeth Colomb von Humboldt, Friedrich Wilhelm Christian Karl Ferdinand von Humboldt lacked none of the educational opportunities that the enlightened society of Berlin had to offer. He and his younger brother Alexander, the future explorer and natural scientist, were tutored privately at home but also participated in the discussions of the circle around the philosopher Moses Mendelssohn, the physician Marcus Herz, and Herz's wife Henriette, the center of one of the most illustrious salons of the Enlightenment in Berlin. While studying at the universities of Frankfurt an der Oder and Göttingen, Humboldt preferred lectures on philosophy, history, and philology to the law curriculum which he was supposed to absorb, showing particular interest in ancient Greece and the Greek language. In 1790 he took a position in the Prussian judicial system, only to decide after barely a year that he was totally unsuited for a legal career. Relieved from his duties at his request, he carefully laid plans to pursue his private studies. He was enthusiastically supported in this decision by Caroline von Dacheröden, whom he married on 29 June 1791. This extraordinarily happy union proved a great source of inspiration and support to him, as his voluminous correspondence with his wife during their many forced separations bears out. Of the couple's eight children only five survived to adulthood.

Living at first on the Dacheröden estates, Humboldt was engrossed in Greek and Latin studies and corresponding with Schiller. A paper written during his student days on the relationship of religion and poetry to moral education, "Über das Verhältnis der Religion und der Poesie zu der sittlichen Bildung," had already contained ideas which became dominant themes in many of his later official documents: the state should stay out of religious matters and must grant its subjects freedom for personal development and education to the limit of their capabilities. In the years following his abrupt resignation he broadened these concerns about the conflicting rights of the state and the individual. In *Ideen zu einem Versuch, die Gränzen der Wirksamkeit des Staats zu bestimmen* (Ideas toward an Attempt to Define the Limits of the Efficacy of the State, 1851; translated as *The Sphere and Duties of Government*, 1854), written in 1792, he propounded the need for individual development instead of centrally planned action. In another paper of 1792, "Ideen über Staatsverfassung, durch die neue französische Konstitution veranlaßt" (Thoughts on Constitutions, apropos of the New French Constitution), Humboldt expressed his lack of confidence in the power of reason as the basis for a state, arguing that no nation is mature enough to be guided by reason alone.

Humboldt further pursued his ideas about education in "Über das Studium des Altertums und des Griechischen insbesondere" (About Classical Studies, Particularly Concerning the Greeks, written in 1793, published in 1896), focusing on the theme of Bildung (education, in the sense of developing one's talents to the maximum). In Humboldt's opinion, the Greek example should guide and inspire contemporary mankind to de-

velop into a more harmonious society. He returned to this subject in two unfinished essays written between 1806 and 1808, "Latium und Hellas" (1896) and "Geschichte des Verfalls und Unterganges der griechischen Freistaaten" (History of the Decline and Fall of the Greek City-States, 1896). All his life he made translations of ancient Greek writers, beginning with several odes of Pindar during the 1790s. He worked on translating Aeschylus's *Agamemnon* off and on for twenty years, finally finishing it in 1816. A perfect translation, he felt, is neither desirable nor possible; a translation must always retain the "otherness" of the original language.

When the Humboldts moved to Jena in 1794, a close and lasting friendship with Schiller and Goethe developed. Schiller appreciated Humboldt's coolly objective analysis and criticism and encouraged him to contribute to his journal *Die Horen*. Humboldt complied with two essays on the difference between the sexes: "Über den Geschlechtsunterschied und dessen Einfluß auf die organische Natur" (On Sexual Differences and Their Influence on Organic Nature) and "Über die männliche und weibliche Form" (On Male and Female Form), which were published in the journal in 1795. Intended to supplement Schiller's "Über die ästhetische Erziehung des Menschen in einer Reihe von Briefen" (Letters on Aesthetic Education, 1795) from an anthropological point of view, the essays were not well received.

The Jena years were frustrating and unproductive for Humboldt: while he envisioned a literary career in the classical mold, he was overshadowed in this field by the two literary giants of the age. Recognizing that this path would not lead him to success, he decided to leave Jena. His mother's death and the resulting inheritance enabled Humboldt to move his family in 1797 to Paris, where he made astute and detached observations on the members of the Directory and on the French national character. He remained in close touch with his Jena friends and their work and exchanged manuscripts with them. *Ästhetische Versuche* (Aesthetic Experiments), his planned comprehensive work on literary theory, the first part of which was published in 1799 as a review of Goethe's *Hermann und Dorothea* (1797), turned out to be one more disappointment for him. In spite of Schiller's warning that few readers would be able to understand the work, Humboldt expounded extensively upon his ideas of art, beauty, nature, and the epic as literary genre.

Schiller and friends in Jena. Back row: Goethe (left) and Wilhelm von Humboldt (third from left); Alexander von Humboldt on porch (Douglas Botting, Humboldt and the Cosmos, *Michael Joseph, 1973).*

Schiller proved to be right: the essay was largely unappreciated by Humboldt's contemporaries.

Humboldt's lifelong interest in languages received new impetus and direction through an extended trip to Spain, an experience which confirmed his inclination to make linguistic studies the center of his interest. He added Portuguese, Basque, Provençal, and Galician to the already impressive list of modern languages at his command. Basque in particular fascinated him because it provided insight into what he considered to be one of the more primitive peoples and cultures. His increasing fascination with languages was rooted in his interest in the characters of the people who spoke them: through language he wanted to discover the essence of a nation. But feeling that he was not ready to undertake a life devoted exclusively to linguistics, he accepted a diplomatic career in the service of Prussia.

This second public phase was to last for seventeen years, beginning in 1802 with Humboldt's appointment as minister plenipotentiary to the Vatican. The relatively undemanding post permitted him considerable time for his studies of the Basque, Icelandic, Gaelic, and American Indian languages. He enjoyed the leisurely life and the mild climate, but the Italian years were marred by the loss of three children and by the additional shock of Schiller's death. Only one publication dates from these years: his poem *Rom* (1806), in which history is depicted as cyclical and Italy takes on characteristics of ancient Greece. After Napoleon's defeat of Prussia in 1807 Humboldt asked for a leave of absence to administer his and Caroline's estates, which had fallen under foreign rule. He intended to return within a few months, but he was not to see Rome again.

In 1809, with permission to return to his Roman post denied and with government reform in Prussia in progress under the leadership of the Reichsfreiherr Karl von Stein, Humboldt accepted an assignment in the Ministry of the Interior. Coordinating school reform efforts, he formulated a theory of public education for all levels of society: primary schools based on the ideas of the Swiss educator Johann Heinrich Pestalozzi, Gymnasien (secondary schools) imbued with his own humanistic ideals, and a new university in Berlin to replace the many separate academies. Mainstays of the Gymnasium were to be mathematics, history, and languages, with no great concern for the natural sciences. The university was to be a community of scholars free to inquire and teach without restraints. While Frederick William III preferred an educational system that produced loyal, peaceful, religious, and obedient subjects rather than inquiring minds, Humboldt prevailed in many of his ideas: that humanistic studies constitute the core curriculum of the Gymnasium, that basic education be made available to all people, that the Gymnasium be the only avenue to the university, and that graduation requirements and teacher qualifications be standardized. But his proposal that every child have access to education according to his potential fell victim to elitist trends of the nineteenth century; and his successors, in establishing the new university, rejected his conception of a truly free institution of higher learning. The reactionary Prussian state was not ready for such liberal innovations, and Humboldt ran into increasing opposition from his superiors. He requested a transfer, and by June 1810 he was at his new post as Prussian ambassador to Vienna.

At first the Slavic and Hungarian languages provided new study subjects during his leisure hours, but soon Napoleon's defeat at Waterloo and the ensuing negotiations in Vienna threw Humboldt into the midst of new activities. Increasingly indispensable to Hardenberg, who had replaced Stein as chancellor, he was considered a cool and calculating negotiator and was feared for his sharp wit. For his diligence in guarding Prussian interests at the conference table, the king awarded him the Iron Cross. The outcome of the Congress of Vienna and the resulting loose confederation of German states was in general agreement with Humboldt's conception of post-Napoleonic Germany. While he did not want to enhance Austria's influence, he did not believe that the German people were ready to govern themselves as one state. He saw Germany mainly as a cultural community which he loved for its very diversity. He did not, however, succeed in his plan to provide for a unifying federal court system, guaranteeing civil rights and religious freedom to everyone; the German princes would not suffer such curtailment of their royal prerogatives. Moreover, Metternich, the quintessence of conservatism, who had begun to dislike Humboldt intensely, made him the object of intrigues and thereby limited his usefulness to Hardenberg. Incredibly, even these busy years could not keep him from his studies. Approached by J. C. Adelung and J. S. Vater to contribute to their four-volume linguistic publication *Mithridates* (1806-1816), Humboldt furnished a volume of corrections and additions on the Basque language in 1817.

After mediating several territorial disputes between German princes, Humboldt returned to Berlin and became a member of the Privy Council; but an appointment to a leading post in the government eluded him. Hardenberg was intent on staying at the helm, and Humboldt had made many enemies with his reform ideas. After reluctantly spending the year 1817-1818 in London as Prussian ambassador he insisted on returning to Berlin, where he served once more in the Ministry of the Interior. There he clashed with Hardenberg on matters of reform. Rejecting both French and American constitutional models, Humboldt outlined a proposal for a constitution that gave more power to the estates but limited the power of the king, the police, and the chancellor. The harshly repressive Carlsbad Edicts of 1819 provided the occasion for Humboldt to force Hardenberg to a showdown, but the king sided with Hardenberg and accepted Humboldt's resignation at the end of the year. Humboldt's memorandum to Stein on constitutional reforms,

"Denkschrift über Preußens ständische Verfassung" (Memorandum on Prussia's Constitution of Estates), became famous when it was published in 1848 during a revival of political liberalism and German nationalism. He wrote that political order should be based on the participation of the estates; that the nobility should be taxed; and that personal liberty, equality under the law, and freedom of the press should be guaranteed. Had this proposal been accepted, Prussia would have made an easy transition to a constitutional monarchy, and the rigid class system would have been phased out. But that time had not yet come.

Humboldt's biographer Paul R. Sweet speculates that Humboldt would have succeeded in substantially modifying the character of the Prussian government had he been willing to bide his time. But he chafed under Hardenberg's conservative restraints and was probably more ambitious than he cared to admit. The king granted him a pension and an estate of his choice, enabling the Humboldts to continue to live in comfort. In 1820 Humboldt retired to Tegel. When Hardenberg died in 1822, Humboldt was proposed as his successor, but his liberal ideas had created too much opposition and his enemies were implacable. Instead, he read papers at the Prussian Academy of Sciences and concerned himself with the American Indian, Arab, Tartar, Phoenician, ancient Egyptian, Sanskrit, Japanese, and Chinese languages.

After his retirement Humboldt began to evolve his philosophy of language. In correspondence with John Pickering and Peter Du Ponceau he argued that the grammatical deficiencies in primitive languages, such as those of the American Indians, limited the development of intellectual activities of the speakers. In a paper prepared for the Prussian Academy of Sciences in 1820, "Über das vergleichende Sprachstudium in Beziehung auf die verschiedenen Epochen der Sprachentwicklung" (On Comparative Linguistics with Reference to the Various Periods of Language Development, 1928), he noted that each language originates as an organism that already possesses its essential grammatical forms yet permits growth. A language grows according to its innate law, energized by a "Kraft" (force) which modern linguists call the generative principle. This inner law permits an infinite variety of expressions. In an 1821 paper for the Prussian Academy, *Über die Aufgabe des Geschichtschreibers* (On the Task of the Historian, 1822), he stated that history is not just a recounting of supposed facts but a re-creation and reinterpretation which requires intuitive understanding. The historian must find the original connection of things, a transcendental order which does not always agree with the manifest facts. Writing history involves a creative power not unlike that used in producing language.

The range of Humboldt's investigations during his last years is overwhelming: analyses of the Mexican, Chinese, Sanskrit, Kawi, Malayan, and South Sea Islands languages; academy papers on the *Bhagavad Gita* and the dual; and analyses of grammatical forms. His last and greatest work was *Über die Kawi-Sprache auf der Insel Java, nebst einer Einleitung über die Verschiedenheit des menschlichen Sprachbaues und ihren Einfluß auf die geistige Entwicklung des Menschengeschlechts* (On the Kawi Language on the Island of Java, with an Introduction on the Difference of Human Linguistic Structures and Its Influence on the Intellectual Development of Mankind, 1836-1839). Humboldt prepared the first volume for publication; the other two volumes were completed by Eduard Buschmann, a respected confidant of Humboldt's last years. In the nearly 350-page introduction to the first volume (translated as *Linguistic Variability and Intellectual Development*, 1971) Humboldt postulates that the actual process of speaking is only an external appearance of an inner force which he names "energeia"–the very essence, for him, of humanity.

After his wife's death in 1829 Humboldt immersed himself more and more in his studies. Yet, at the request of the king and in spite of failing eyesight and hearing, he participated in the planning of the new Prussian state museum in Berlin. In 1830, at the request of Schiller's son Ernst, he wrote "Über Schiller und den Gang seiner Geistesentwicklung" (translated as "Schiller and the Process of His Intellectual Development," 1913) as an introduction to his and Schiller's correspondence, edited by himself. He pays tribute to his old friend as the perfect combination of the real and the ideal, a true poet who infused his work with his own personality. He also analyzes the influence on Schiller of the philosophy of Immanuel Kant. In the same year Goethe published his account of his journey to Italy in 1790. In his review of this work, "Rezension von Goethes Zweitem römischen Aufenthalt" (1830), Humboldt tries to capture the spirit of Goethe's universality. He relives the memories of his own Roman years while eloquently describing Goethe

as a painter and sculptor, an observer of life and nature, and a scientist.

When the July 1830 revolution shook the German states, Humboldt remained uninvolved. Although diagnosed as having Parkinson's disease, he continued his studies of the languages of Southeast Asia, Indonesia, and Polynesia. With his body ailing but his mind unimpaired, he carried on a voluminous correspondence with the leading linguists, including John Pickering, Franz Bopp, and August Wilhelm Schlegel, until his death on 8 April 1835. Along with Caroline and other members of the Humboldt family, he lies buried in the park at Tegel.

Humboldt's 1,183 sonnets, written daily during the last three years of his life, are noteworthy not for their poetic quality but for shedding light on the inner life of the writer. They have never been published in their entirety, but Albert Leitzmann provides a note on each in volume 9 of his edition of Humboldt's *Gesammelte Schriften* (Collected Writings, 1903-1936).

Humboldt's vast correspondence is not available in one edition. His correspondence with Caroline takes up seven volumes and provides revealing insights into this remarkable marriage as well as the events of his time. Curiously, Humboldt's first popular acclaim came from his letters to "a friend," Charlotte Diede, published as *Briefe von Wilhelm von Humboldt an eine Freundin* (1847; translated as *Letters of Wilhelm von Humboldt to a Female Friend*, 1849). Humboldt hardly knew Diede, having met her only once during his student days, but upon her appeal he tried to help her in later years through a correspondence which was a mixture of stern admonitions, moral encouragement, and practical advice. Diede published his letters after his death, taking great liberties with the text, and they enjoyed almost instant best-seller success in many translations as proper reading for young ladies.

Letters:

Briefwechsel zwischen Schiller und Wilhelm von Humboldt: Mit einer Vorerinnerung über Schiller und den Gang seiner Geistesentwicklung, edited by Humboldt (Stuttgart & Tübingen: Cotta, 1830); Humboldt's introduction translated by F. H. King as "Schiller and the Process of His Intellectual Development: The Early Romantic School," in *The German Classics of the Nineteenth and Twentieth Centuries*, edited by Kuno Fischer and W. G. Howard, volume 4 (New York: German Publications Society, 1913), pp. 37-70;

Briefe von Wilhelm von Humboldt an eine Freundin, edited by Charlotte Diede, 2 volumes (Leipzig: Brockhaus, 1847); translated by Catherine M. A. Couper as *Letters of William von Humboldt to a Female Friend: A Complete Edition* (London: Chapman, 1849); translated by Charles G. Leland as *Letters to a Lady* (Philadelphia: Leypoldt / New York: Christern, 1864);

Wilhelm von Humboldt's Briefe an F. G. Welcker, edited by Rudolf Haym (Berlin: Gaertner, 1859);

Goethe's Briefwechsel mit den Gebrüdern von Humboldt (1795-1832), edited by F. T. Bratranek (Leipzig: Brockhaus, 1876);

Ansichten über Aesthetik und Literatur, von Wilhelm von Humboldt: Seine Briefe an Christian Gottfried Körner (1793-1830), edited by F. Jonas (Berlin: Schleiermacher, 1880);

Aus Wilhelm von Humboldts letzten Lebensjahren (Eine Mittheilung bisher unbekannter Briefe), edited by Theodor Distel (Leipzig: Barth, 1883);

Briefe von Wilhelm von Humboldt an Friedrich Heinrich Jacobi, edited by Albert Leitzmann (Halle: Niemeyer, 1892);

Briefe an Johanna Motherby von Wilhelm von Humboldt und E. M. Arndt: Mit einer Biographie Johanna Motherby's und Erläuterungen, edited by Heinrich Meisner (Leipzig: Brockhaus, 1893);

Briefe an Georg Heinrich Ludwig Nicolovius, edited by Haym (Berlin: Felber, 1894);

Wilhelm und Caroline von Humboldt in ihren Briefen 1788-1835, edited by Anna von Sydow, 7 volumes (Berlin: Mittler, 1906-1918; reprinted, Osnabrück: Zeller, 1968);

Briefwechsel zwischen Wilhelm von Humboldt und August Wilhelm Schlegel, edited by Leitzmann (Halle: Niemeyer, 1908);

Wilhelm von Humboldt in seinen Briefen, edited by Karl Sell (Leipzig & Berlin: Teubner, 1909);

Neue Briefe Wilhelm von Humboldts an Schiller, 1796-1803, edited by Friedrich Clemens Ebrard (Berlin: Paetel, 1911);

Wilhelm von Humboldt im Verkehr mit seinen Freunden: Eine Auslese seiner Briefe, edited by Theodor Kappstein (Berlin: Borngräber, 1917);

Die Brautbriefe Wilhelms und Karoliniens von Humboldt, edited by Leitzmann (Leipzig: Insel, 1921);

Wilhelm von Humboldts Briefe an Gottfried Hermann, edited by Leitzmann (Weimar: Böhlau, 1929);

Wilhelm von Humboldts Briefe an Johann Gottfried Schweighäuser, zum ersten Mal nach den Originalen herausgegeben und erläutert, edited by Leitzmann (Jena: Frommann, 1934);

Wilhelm von Humboldts Briefe an Karl Gustav Brinkmann, edited by Leitzmann (Leipzig: Hiersemann, 1939);

Wilhelm von Humboldts Briefe an Christian Gottfried Körner, edited by Leitzmann (Berlin: Ebering, 1940);

Wilhelm von Humboldt und sein Erzieher, mit ungedruckten Briefen Humboldts, edited by Leitzmann (Berlin: Akademie der Wissenschaften, 1940);

Briefe, edited by Leitzmann (Berlin: Akademie-Verlag, 1949);

Briefe, edited by Wilhelm Rössle (Munich: Hanser, 1952);

Wilhelm und Caroline von Humboldt: Ein Leben in Briefen, edited by Herbert Nette (Düsseldorf & Cologne: Diederichs, 1956);

Briefe an Christine Reinhard-Reimarus, edited by Arndt Schreiber (Heidelberg: Schneider, 1956).

Bibliography:
Fritz G. Lange, "Wilhelm von Humboldt," in *Grundriß zur Geschichte der deutschen Dichtung,* edited by Karl Goedeke, volume 14 (Berlin: Akademie, 1959).

Biographies:
Gustav Schlesier, *Erinnerungen an Wilhelm von Humboldt,* 2 volumes (Mannheim: Köhler, 1843-1845); translated by Juliette Bauer as *Lives of the Brothers Humboldt, Alexander and William* (London: Ingram, 1852);

Rudolf Haym, *Wilhelm von Humboldt: Lebensbild und Charakteristik* (Berlin: Gaetner, 1856; reprinted, Osnabrück: Zeller, 1965);

Otto Harnack, *Wilhelm von Humboldt* (Berlin: Hofmann, 1913);

Albert Leitzmann, *Wilhelm von Humboldt: Charakteristik und Lebensbild* (Halle: Niemeyer, 1919);

Paul Binswanger, *Wilhelm von Humboldt* (Frauenfeld & Leipzig: Huber, 1937);

Johann Albrecht von Rantzau, *Wilhelm von Humboldt* (Munich: Beck, 1939);

Ernst Howald, *Wilhelm von Humboldt* (Erlenbach-Zurich: Rentsch, 1944);

Friedrich Schaffstein, *Wilhelm von Humboldt: Ein Lebensbild* (Frankfurt am Main: Klostermann, 1952);

Eberhard Kessel, *Wilhelm von Humboldt: Idee und Wirklichkeit* (Stuttgart: Koehler, 1967);

Paul R. Sweet, *Wilhelm von Humboldt: A Biography*, 2 volumes (Columbus: Ohio State University Press, 1978-1980);

Peter Berglar, *Wilhelm von Humboldt: In Selbstzeugnissen und Bilddokumenten* (Reinbek: Rowohlt, 1979).

References:

Hans-Heinrich Baumann, "Die generative Grammatik und Wilhelm von Humboldt," *Poetica*, 4 (January 1971): 1-12;

Brigit Benes, *Wilhelm von Humboldt, Jacob Grimm, August Schleicher: Ein Vergleich ihrer Sprachauffassungen* (Winterthur: Keller, 1958);

Walter Horace Bruford, *The German Tradition of Self-Cultivation: "Bildung" from Humboldt to Thomas Mann* (London & New York: Cambridge University Press, 1975);

Ernst Cassirer, "Die Kantischen Elemente in Wilhelm von Humboldts Sprachphilosophie," in *Festschrift für Paul Hensel*, edited by J. Binder (Greiz: Chag, 1923);

Gordon A. Craig, "Wilhelm von Humboldt as Diplomat," in *Studies in International History*, edited by K. Bourne and D. C. Watt (London, 1967);

Charlotte B. Evans, "Wilhelm von Humboldts Sprachtheorie: Zum Gedächtnis seines 200. Geburtstages," *German Quarterly*, 40 (September 1967): 509-517;

Bruno Gebhardt, *Wilhelm von Humboldt als Staatsmann*, 2 volumes (Stuttgart: Cotta, 1896-1899; reprinted, Aalen: Scientia, 1965);

Wilhelm Grau, *Wilhelm von Humboldt und das Problem des Juden* (Hamburg: Hanseatische Verlagsanstalt, 1935);

Ole Hansen-Love, *La révolution copernicienne du langue dans l'oeuvre de Wilhelm von Humboldt* (Paris: Vrin, 1972);

Siegfried Kaehler, *Wilhelm von Humboldt und der Staat: Ein Beitrag zur Geschichte deutscher Lebensgestaltung um 1800*, second edition (Göttingen: Vandenhoeck & Ruprecht, 1963);

Irmgard Kawohl, *Wilhelm von Humboldt in der Kritik des 20. Jahrhunderts* (Ratingen: Henn, 1969);

Joachim H. Knoll and Horst Siebert, *Wilhelm von Humboldt: Politik und Bildung* (Heidelberg: Quelle & Meyer, 1969);

Ursula Krautkrämer, *Staat und Erziehung: Begründung öffentlicher Erziehung bei Humboldt, Kant, Fichte, Hegel und Schleiermacher* (Munich: Berchmans, 1979);

Ingrid Lecoq-Gellersen, *Die politische Persönlichkeit Wilhelm von Humboldts in der Geschichtsschreibung des deutschen Bildungsbürgertums: Historiographiegeschichtliche Studie zur Problematik des Intellektuellen in der Politik* (Bern, Frankfurt am Main & New York: Lang, 1985);

Jutta Leppin, "Some Observations on the Chomskian Interpretation of Wilhelm von Humboldt," *Archivum Linguisticum*, new series 8 (1977) ;

Robert Leroux, *L'Anthropologie comparée de Guillaume de Humboldt* (Paris: Societé d'Édition, 1958);

Leroux, *Guillaume de Humboldt: La formation de sa pensée jusqu'en 1794* (Paris: Societé d'Édition, 1932);

Leroux, "La philosophie de l'histoire chez Herder et Guillaume de Humboldt," in his *Mélanges Henri Lichtenberger* (Paris: Stock, 1934), pp. 144-166;

Bruno Liebrucks, *Sprache und Bewußtsein*, volume 2: *Wilhelm von Humboldt* (Frankfurt am Main: Akademische Verlagsgesellschaft, 1965);

Friedrich Meinecke, *The Age of German Liberation 1795-1815*, translated by P. Paret and H. Fischer (Berkeley, Los Angeles & London: University of California Press, 1977);

Clemens Menze, *Die Bildungsreform Wilhelm von Humboldts* (Hanover, Dortmund, Darmstadt & Berlin: Schroedel, 1975);

Menze, "Sprechen, Denken, Bilden. Eine Erörterung zu Grundaspekten der Sprachtheorie Wilhelm von Humboldts," *Pädagogische Rundschau*, 32 (1978): 475-489;

Menze, "Wilhelm von Humboldts Grundlegung der Theorie der Bildung des Menschen," *Vierteljahresschrift für wissenschaftliche Pädagogik*, 54 (1978): 485-505;

Robert L. Miller, *The Linguistic Relativity Principle and Humboldtian Ethnolinguistics* (The Hague & Paris: Mouton, 1968);

Kurt Müller-Vollmer, *Poesie und Einbildungskraft: Zur Dichtungstheorie Wilhelm von Humboldts* (Stuttgart: Metzler, 1967);

Richey Novak, *Wilhelm von Humboldt as a Literary Critic* (Bern: Lang, 1972);

Kenneth Russell Olson, *Wilhelm von Humboldt's Philosophy of Language* (Ann Arbor: University Microfilms, 1979);

Eduard Spranger, *Wilhelm von Humboldt und die Humanitätsidee* (Berlin: Reuther & Reichard, 1909); (Berlin: Reuther & Reichard, 1910; revised edition, Tübingen: Niemeyer, 1965);

Spranger, "Wilhelm von Humboldt und Kant," *Kant Studien,* 13 (1908): 57-129;

Heymann Steinthal, *Über Wilhelm von Humboldt* (Berlin: Dümmler, 1883);

Steinthal, *Der Ursprung der Sprache, im Zusammenhang mit den letzten Fragen alles Wissens. Eine Darstellung der Ansicht Wilhelm von Humboldts verglichen mit denen Herders und Hamanns* (Berlin: Dümmler, 1851).

Papers:

Photocopies of more than twelve thousand letters to and from Humboldt are in the Brief-Archiv of the University of Heidelberg. The manuscript department of the university has a complete record of materials of the family archives at Tegel and of the Leitzmann papers at Jena. Other manuscripts, mainly linguistic papers, are at the Staatsbibliothek in East Berlin and the Staatsbibliothek in West Berlin. The East German government denies access to the official documents from Humboldt's public service years in the archives at Merseburg. Other official documents are in the Geheimes Staatsarchiv in Dahlem, West Germany.

Justinus Kerner

(18 September 1786-21 February 1862)

Lee B. Jennings
University of Illinois at Chicago

BOOKS: *Die Reiseschatten,* as the Schattenspieler Luchs (Heidelberg: Braun, 1811); critical edition, by P. H. Scheffler (Stuttgart: Steinkopf, 1964);

Deutscher Dichterwald, by Kerner, Friedrich de la Motte Fouqué, Ludwig Uhland, and others (Tübingen: Heerbrandt, 1813);

Das Wildbad im Königreich Würtemberg (Tübingen: Heerbrandt, 1813);

Über die Besetzung der Physikate durch die Wahlen der Amtsversammlungen (Hall: Schwend, 1817);

Der rasende Sandler: Ein politisches dramatisches Impromptu, mit Marionetten aufzuführen (Stuttgart: Cotta, 1817);

Neue Beobachtungen über die in Würtemberg so häufig vorfallenden tödtlichen Vergiftungen durch den Genuß geräucherter Würste (Tübingen: Osiander, 1820);

Die Bestürmung der würtembergischen Stadt Weinsberg durch die hellen christlichen Haufen im Jahre 1525 und deren Folgen für die Stadt: Aus handschriftlichen Überlieferungen der damaligen Zeit dargestellt (Öhringen: Erbe, 1822);

Das Fettgift oder die Fettsäure und ihre Wirkung auf den thierischen Organismus: Ein Beitrag des in verdorbenen Würsten giftig wirkenden Stoffes (Stuttgart: Cotta, 1822);

Geschichte zweyer Somnambülen nebst einigen anderen Denkwürdigkeiten aus dem Gebiete der magischen Heilkunde und der Psychologie (Karlsruhe: Braun, 1824);

Gedichte (Stuttgart & Tübingen: Cotta, 1826);

Die Seherin von Prevorst: Eröffnungen über das innere Leben der Menschen und über das Hereinragen einer Geisterwelt in die unsere, 2 volumes (Stuttgart & Tübingen: Cotta, 1829; revised, 1832); translated by Catherine Crowe as *The Seeress of Prevorst: Being Revelations Concerning the Inner-Life of Man and the Inter-Diffusion of a World of Spirits in the One We Inhabit* (London & Edinburgh: Moore, 1845; New York: Harper, 1845);

Justinus Kerner (etching by A. Duttenhofer)

Sendschreiben an die Bürger des Oberamts Weinsberg, in Betreff der uns drohenden Cholera (Heilbronn: Schell, 1831);

Einige Worte in betreff der uns drohenden Cholera, vorgetragen in der Amtsversammlung zu Weinsberg am 28. September 1831 (Heilbronn: Schell, 1831);

Die Dichtungen von Justinus Kerner: Neue vollständige Sammlung in einem Band (Stuttgart & Tübingen: Cotta, 1834); enlarged as *Die Dichtungen von Justinus Kerner,* 2 volumes (Stuttgart & Tübingen: Cotta, 1841); volume 1 enlarged as *Die lyrischen Gedichte* (Stuttgart & Tübingen: Cotta, 1847; enlarged, 1854);

Geschichten Besessener neuerer Zeit: Beobachtungen aus dem Gebiete kakodämonisch-magnetischer Erscheinungen (Karlsruhe: Braun, 1834);

Eine Erscheinung aus dem Nachtgebiete der Natur durch eine Reihe von Zeugen gerichtlich bestätigt und den Naturforschern zu Bedenken mitgetheilt (Stuttgart & Tübingen: Cotta, 1836);

Das entstellte Ebenbild Gottes in dem Menschen durch die Sünde: Dargestellt in einer Folge von Predigten zur heiligen Fastenzeit, by Kerner and Alexander Fürst von Hohenlohe-Waldenburg-Schillingsfürst (Regensburg & Landshut: Manz, 1836);

Nachricht von dem Vorkommen des Besessenseyns, eines dämonisch-magnetischen Leidens und seiner schon im Alterthum bekannten Heilung durch magisch-magnetisches Einwirken, in einem Sendschreiben an den Herrn Obermedizinalrath Dr. Schelling in Stuttgart (Stuttgart & Augsburg: Cotta, 1836);

Der Bärenhäuter im Salzbade: Ein Schattenspiel (Stuttgart: Brodhag, 1837);

Das Bilderbuch aus meiner Knabenzeit: Erinnerungen aus den Jahren 1786 bis 1804 (Brunswick: Vieweg, 1849);

Der letzte Blüthenstrauß (Stuttgart & Tübingen: Cotta, 1852);

Die somnambülen Tische: Zur Geschichte und Erklärung dieser Erscheinung (Stuttgart: Ebner & Seubert, 1853);

Winterblüthen (Stuttgart: Cotta, 1859);

Ausgewählte poetische Werke (Stuttgart: Cotta, 1878);

Kleksographien (Stuttgart, Leipzig, Berlin & Vienna: Deutsche Verlags-Anstalt, 1890);

Sämtliche poetische Werke, edited by Josef Gaismaier, 4 volumes (Leipzig: Hesse, 1905);

Werke, edited by Raimund Pissin, 6 volumes (Berlin, Leipzig, Vienna & Stuttgart: Bong, 1914);

Ausgewählte Werke, edited by Gunter Grimm (Stuttgart: Reclam, 1981).

OTHER: *Poetischer Almanach für das Jahr 1812,* edited, with contributions, by Kerner (Heidelberg: Braun, 1812); republished as *Romantische Dichtungen* (Karlsruhe: Braun, 1818);

Herzog Christophs Leben, geschrieben von seinem Beichtvater: Nach dem Drucke von 1660, edited by Kerner (Hall: Schwend, 1817);

Gedichte des Leinewebers Johann Lämmerer, vom Lämmershof bei Gschwend, edited by Kerner (Gmünd: Ritter, 1819);

Des ungarischen Arztes Harst, eines Württembergers, erprobte Behandlung der Cholera, seinen Landleuten zugesandt, edited by Kerner (Heilbronn: Drechsler, 1831);

Blätter aus Prevorst: Originalien und Lesefrüchte des inneren Lebens, mitgetheilt von dem Herausgeber der Seherin von Prevorst, edited, with contributions, by Kerner, 12 volumes (Karlsruhe: Braun, 1831-1839);

Die Gesichte des Thomas Ignaz Martin, Landmanns zu Gallardon, über Frankreich und dessen Zukunft, im Jahre 1816 geschaut: Nach dem Französischen. Eine Zugabe zu den Blättern aus Prevorst, edited by Kerner (Heilbronn: Drechsler, 1835);

Magikon: Archiv für Beobachtungen aus dem Gebiete der Geisterkunde und des magnetischen und magischen Lebens, nebst anderen Zugaben für Freunde des Inneren, als Fortsetzung der Blätter aus Prevorst, edited by Kerner, 5 volumes (Stuttgart: Ebner & Seubert, 1840-1853);

W. Joukowsky (Vasilii Andreevich Zhukovski), *Das Mährchen von Iwan Zarewitsch und dem grauen Wolf,* introduction by Kerner (Stuttgart: Hallberger, 1852);

Franz Anton Mesmer aus Schwaben, Entdecker des thierischen Magnetismus: Erinnerungen an denselben nebst Nachrichten von den letzten Jahren seines Lebens zu Meersburg am Bodensee, edited by Kerner (Frankfurt am Main: Literarische Anstalt, 1856).

PERIODICAL PUBLICATION: "Mitteilungen aus dem Schiller-National-Museum III: Justinus Kerners Jugendgedichte," *Rechenschaftsberichte des schwäbischen Schillervereins,* 32 (1927-1928): 75-98.

The prevailing image of Justinus Kerner has been gleaned chiefly from autobiographical sources and from family memoirs. Kerner's letters and childhood autobiography, the biography written by his daughter Marie Niethammer, and his son Theobald's reliable but anecdotal account of goings-on in the Kerner house in Weinsberg present an innocuous picture of jovial eccentricity while suppressing Kerner's nearly pathological depressive tendency. At the same time, they trivialize his psychic research, which, he continually insisted, he undertook strictly as a natural scientist (he was a physician). It has been only recently that the dark side of Kerner, as well as his importance in the history of medicine, has received due scholarly attention. Outside of his native Swabian region in southwestern Germany, where he is still honored as a kind of genius loci and patriotic bard, Kerner is less remembered as a romantic poet than as an "occultist," that is, an early parapsychologist (perhaps the first one). He evolved no systematic theory of the paranormal but sought to proceed on a purely empirical basis. In an age of still unrestrained theorizing, this procedure was widely misunderstood, and, as he himself complained, his poetic bent was construed by some to discredit his occultistic work, a quite separate undertaking.

Justinus Kerner was born on 18 September 1786 to Christoph Ludwig and Friederika Luise Stockmayer Kerner and spent most of his childhood and youth in his birthplace, Ludwigsburg. His father was an Oberamtmann (regional administrator) who died in 1799, leaving his family in rather poor circumstances. In *Das Bilderbuch aus meiner Knabenzeit* (A Boyhood Picture-Book, 1849) Kerner describes himself as a somewhat ailing, highly imaginative, but energetic and contented child. Plans to commit him to the trade of pastry cook fortunately came to naught, and, after a period of apprenticeship in a textile mill, his way to the university at Tübingen was paved by an academic family friend.

Kerner's account of his childhood ends with his decision to study medicine, arrived at in typically intuitive fashion (he claims) when a gust of wind wafted a doctor's prescription into his path. At Tübingen, Kerner made the acquaintance of Ludwig Uhland and other aspiring poets caught up in the enthusiasm of the new romantic movement and contributed to a handwritten journal that they passed about. In the meantime he finished his dissertation on the auditory processes of various animals, living specimens of which he kept in his room.

On completing his studies, Kerner undertook a major journey. He went first to Hamburg to visit his brother Georg, a practicing physician who had once been a Jacobin in Paris. There Kerner's devotion to his fiancée, Friederike ("Rickele") Ehmann, was severely threatened by a sudden passion that he developed for his sister-in-law. By a roundabout route he traveled next to Vienna, ostensibly to observe hospitals, though puppet shows seemed to interest him more. Kerner was at least as much invigorated by life in the great cities as he was nostalgic for his Swabian homeland, which, as he came to recognize, was

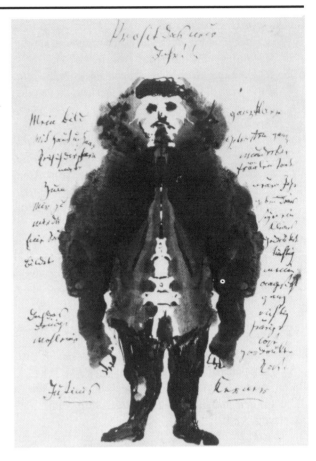

Inkblot self-portrait of Kerner with New Year's greeting (by permission of the Württembergische Landesbibliothek)

an economically and culturally deprived hinterland.

The trip was altogether so broadening as nearly to undermine the young doctor's sanity, given that he looked forward with little enthusiasm to a confining backwoods medical practice; but from it arose one of his major poetic works, *Die Reiseschatten* (Travel Shadows, 1811). The work takes its title from the popular Chinese shadow plays. It is hardly a true travel account, but rather a series of excursions into ethereal love-poetry, ghostly ballad, and broad, fantastic satire aimed at neoclassicists and philistines. The spontaneity of the work stamps it as a true Romantic product, worthy of more attention than it has hitherto received.

Kerner, upon his return, took up medical practice successively in Dürrmenz, Wildbad, and Gaildorf, treating mostly illiterate peasants and suffering the hardships of a rigorous apprenticeship, living in makeshift quarters and wading through mud for lack of a horse. Meanwhile, however, he contributed actively to poetic almanacs and sought to better his medical career through publication, beginning with *Das Wildbad im Königreich Würtemberg* (1813), a book praising the Wildbad spa. He had married Rickele in 1813, and the union developed a remarkable harmony, the more so as Rickele's resoluteness grew.

Kerner claimed in later years that he had always abhorred politics, but in fact he was heavily involved in the Württemberg constitutional struggles that arose in the wake of Napoleon's defeat and continued until 1819. No doubt under the tutelage of his brother Karl (recently a general in Napoleon's Russian campaign, then, for a time, Minister of the Interior), Kerner espoused the reform plan of the enlightened King Wilhelm I, which was decidedly more liberal and progressive than the one adhered to by the provincial diet. The latter chauvinistically insisted on restoration of the "Old Law," the obsolete former Württemberg constitution. Uhland was a vociferous exponent of the Old Law, and this, combined with his basic distrust of otherworldliness, led to an eventual rift between the two poets.

Kerner for a time contributed to political journals and pamphlets advocating a "free citizenry"; but as repressive forces gained control, he came to eschew politics, emerging only occasionally in later years with a poetic squib against revolutionary agitation or for monarchy. A curious product of his early political involvement is *Der rasende Sandler* (The Raging Sand-Blotter, 1817), a puppet play in which a local magistrate hysterically defends the manure heap of tradition.

Kerner, in the meantime, had moved to Weinsberg, the near-legendary site of his later activities, and had developed new enthusiasms. In a medical treatise on local cases of sausage poisoning, he described the symptoms of botulism (as it is now known) with a clinical accuracy that is still admired. At the same time, he began to employ Mesmer's "magnetic" therapy and to record his experiences with "somnambules" (patients who fell into trance states and appeared to show visionary and clairvoyant propensities) in the form of medical case histories.

It was a publication of this sort that established Kerner's fame, or, as some would say, his notoriety. *Die Seherin von Prevorst* (1829; translated as *The Seeress of Prevorst*, 1845) is the history of Friederike Hauffe, a merchant's wife from the nearby village of Prevorst, referred to Kerner for treatment in a state of advanced enervation. Initially reluctant to aggravate his patient's condi-

tion, he finally applied "magnetic" methods and became convinced that she not only possessed self-diagnostic and clairvoyant powers but was indeed in contact with spirits of the dead. He even recorded physical manifestations such as spirit rapping and objects moved "as if by an unseen hand." It was not so much the existence of a spirit world as such, but the idea of an "intrusion of a spirit world into our own" that vexed his critics. While Kerner's procedures often lack controls, and while alternative explanations for the described phenomena have been suggested, the work stands as a serious and open-minded attempt to explore the limits of contemporary scientific knowledge.

Kerner continued his occultistic writings in studies of local hauntings and poltergeist phenomena, notably in the Weinsberg prison, and of demonic possession. The latter researches caused him some official embarrassment, since he had employed the alcoholic tailor Dürr, a folk exorcist or shaman of dubious morals, as his assistant and had advocated using amulets and invoking Jesus' name, albeit for purely pragmatic reasons.

Kerner lived to hear of the American spiritualist movement and the table-tapping vogue. He was skeptical of these "American ghosts" and suggested the alternative explanation of *Nervengeist* (neural essence, a subtle medium not unlike ectoplasm, emanating from living persons). Already in his studies on possession Kerner had become more cautious about claiming spirit intervention. However, he clung to the belief that the souls of the dead dwell for centuries in a kind of purgatory, often in animal form, and he claimed to foresee the worst for himself in this "Middle Realm." Despite his penchant for macabre jokes, there can be no doubt as to the seriousness of Kerner's interest in the occult, which bordered on obsession. He had the misfortune, though, to present the world with a painstaking account of paranormal phenomena precisely at the dawn of a positivistic age.

Kerner was instrumental in collecting Friedrich Hölderlin's works for publication; as a medical student he had attended the aging schizophrenic poet. The Kerner house in Weinsberg became a gathering place for established and budding authors, notables, the curious, and various eccentrics. He befriended the arrogant, tormented poet Nikolaus Lenau and served as mentor to him. He was perhaps tempted to follow Lenau to America, where, he imagined, his children would one day swing on elephants' trunks.

Kerner in 1834 (drawing by C. Müller, by permission of the Schiller-Nationalmuseum, Marbach)

When Lenau returned, disenchanted, from his brief sojourn as a gentleman farmer in Ohio and later succumbed to syphilitic dementia, Kerner visited him and sadly concluded that his friend was hopelessly trapped in the "dream ring" (as the Seeress of Prevorst had once put it).

Kerner continued to write lyric poems throughout his lifetime. A few are still included in anthologies, but his early spontaneity seems to have deserted him in the area of poetry, only to emerge in other areas. His best poems invoke nature as a nurturing and devouring mother and suggest the downward pull of nature, its dominance over intellect, and the pain lying at its core. In this, Kerner illustrates the general transformation of romantic longing into a resignedly antimaterialistic Weltschmerz. (The railroad, he feared, would take the poetry out of traveling.) Though Kerner's gloom increased with age, he still often succeeded in reanimating his vivid poetic imagination to produce major works.

Das Bilderbuch aus meiner Knabenzeit is perhaps Kerner's most successful combination of vivid imagery with precise factual detail, valuable for its portrayal of a provincial, preindustrial Ludwigsburg and its flourishing eccentrics. Most bizarre, though somehow quintessential, is his *Kleksographien* (Blottograms), which was not published until 1890, though it was circulated privately during Kerner's lifetime. This series of Rorschachian inkblots was heavily doctored to resemble demons, butterflies, human figures, etc., with poetic commentaries. The figures are mostly those of lost souls, doomed to purgatory because of their egoism and rationalistic outlook while alive. Kerner can hardly be said to have "invented" the creative inkblot, but it became his trademark.

In later years Kerner was partially blind due to cataracts and could never bring himself to undergo surgery. It would be frivolous to claim that he was content to dwell upon the "inner eye," but it was as a visionary that he had his greatest impact. Kerner had held the office of *Oberamtsarzt* (regional medical administrator) since 1815. He retired from medical practice in 1851 and received pensions from the kings of Württemberg and Bavaria, who no doubt esteemed his efforts on behalf of the ancien régime and its vanishing graces.

Letters:

Justinus Kerners Briefwechsel mit seinen Freunden, edited by Theobald Kerner and Ernst Müller, 2 volumes (Stuttgart: Deutsche Verlags-Anstalt, 1897);

Ludwig Geiger, "Justinus Kerners Briefwechsel mit Varnhagen von Ense," *Zeitschrift für deutsche Philologie*, 31 (1899): 371-384;

Geiger, "Briefe von Justinus Kerner an Varnhagen von Ense," *Nord und Süd*, 92 (1900): 51-80;

Geiger, "Politische Briefe Justinus Kerners an Varnhagen von Ense," *Studien zur vergleichenden Literaturgeschichte*, 9 (1909): 1-21;

Briefe an Cotta, volume 2, edited by Herbert Schiller (Stuttgart: Cotta, 1927);

Briefwechsel zwischen Justinus Kerner und Ottilie Wildermuth 1853-1862, edited by Adelheid Wildermuth (Heilbronn: Salzer, 1927);

Justinus Kerner und sein Münchener Freundeskreis: Eine Sammlung von Briefen, edited by Franz Pocci (Leipzig: Insel, 1928);

Heinz Otto Burger, "Aus dem Kreise der schwäbischen Romantik: Unveröffentlichte Briefe von Justinus Kerner," *Euphorion*, 30 (1929): 332-365;

Otto Güntter, "Zur schwäbischen Romantik: Zwei Briefe von Kerner an Uhland," *Dichtung und Volkstum*, 38 (1937): 225-242;

Letters of Justinus Kerner to Graf Alexander von Württemberg, edited by L. A. Willoughby and Derek Hudson (Cambridge: Cambridge University Press, 1938);

Hartmut Fröschle, "Ein Dokument der Spätromantik. Der Briefwechsel zwischen Justinus Kerner und Johann Friedrich von Meyer," *Jahrbuch des Wiener Goethe-Vereins*, 80 (1976): 75-88.

Biographies:

Aimé Reinhard, *Justinus Kerner und das Kernerhaus zu Weinsberg: Gedenkblätter aus des Dichters Leben* (Tübingen: Osiander, 1862);

Marie Niethammer, *Justinus Kerners Jugendliebe und mein Vaterhaus* (Stuttgart: Cotta, 1877);

Walter Hagen, "Justinus Kerner: Arzt und Dichter, 1786-1862," in *Lebensbilder aus Schwaben und Franken*, volume 9, edited by Max Miller and Robert Uhland (Stuttgart: Kohlhammer, 1963), pp. 127-134;

Hartmut Fröschle, *Justinus Kerner und Ludwig Uhland. Geschichte einer Dichterfreundschaft*, Göppinger Arbeiten zur Germanistik 66 (Göppingen: Kümmerle, 1972);

Theobald Kerner, *Das Kernerhaus und seine Gäste*, second edition (Stuttgart: Deutsche Verlags-Anstalt, 1897; reprinted with index, Weinsberg: Justinus-Kerner-Verein, 1978);

Lee B. Jennings, *Justinus Kerners Weg nach Weinsberg (1809-1819): Die Entpolitisierung eines Romantikers* (Columbia, S.C.: Camden House, 1982);

Otto-Joachim Grüsser, *Justinus Kerner 1786-1862: Arzt–Poet–Geisterseher nebst Anmerkungen zum Uhland-Kreis und zur Medizin- und Geistesgeschichte im Zeitalter der Romantik* (Berlin: Springer, 1987).

References:

Andrea Berger-Fix, ed., *Justinus Kerner: Nur wenn man von Geistern spricht. Briefe und Klecksographien* (Stuttgart: Thienemann, 1986);

Heinz Büttiker, "Justinus Kerner: Ein Beitrag zur Geschichte der Spätromantik," Ph.D. dissertation, University of Zurich, 1952;

Alan P. Cottrell, "Justinus Kerner: Der Grundton der Natur," *German Quarterly*, 39 (1966): 173-186;

Heino Gehrts, "Justinus Kerners Forschungsgegenstand," *Neue Wissenschaft*, 10 (1961-1962): 130-143;

Gehrts, *Das Mädchen von Orlach: Erlebnisse einer Besessenen* (Stuttgart: Klett, 1966);

Walter Hagen, "Justinus Kerner als Ludwigsburger im politischen Geschehen der Jahre 1817 und 1848," *Ludwigsburger Geschichtsblätter*, 16 (1964): 127-134;

Lee B. Jennings, "Der aufgespießte Schmetterling: Justinus Kerner und die Frage der psychischen Entwicklung," *Antaios*, 10 (1968): 109-131;

Jennings, "Geister und Germanisten: Literarisch-parapsychologische Betrachtungen zum Fall Kerner-Mörike," in *Psi und Psyche: Neue Forschungen zur Parapsychologie*, edited by Eberhard Bauer (Stuttgart: Deutsche Verlagsanstalt, 1974), pp. 95-109;

Jennings, "Justinus Kerner und die Geisterwelt," *Neue Wissenschaft*, 14 (1966): 75-95;

Jennings, "Kerner, Lenau und der amerikanische Dämon," *Beiträge zur schwäbischen Literatur- und Geistesgeschichte*, 1 (1981): 96-106;

Jennings, "Zur Symbolik in Justinus Kerners 'Die Heimatlosen,'" *Beiträge zur schwäbischen Literatur- und Geistesgeschichte*, 3 (1985): 35-53;

Rudolf Lang, *Neues zur Seherin von Prevorst* (Innsbruck: Resch, 1983);

Karl Mayer, *Ludwig Uhland: Seine Freunde und Zeitgenossen*, 2 volumes (Stuttgart: Krabbe, 1867);

Emil Staiger, "Zwei schwäbische Lieder," in his *Die Kunst der Interpretation* (Zurich: Atlantis, 1955), pp. 205-221;

Heinrich Straumann, *Justinus Kerner und der Okkultismus in der deutschen Romantik* (Horgen-Zürich & Leipzig: Münster, 1928);

David Friedrich Strauss, *Justinus Kerner: Zwei Lebensbilder aus den Jahren 1839 und 1862* (Marbach: Schiller-Nationalmuseum, n.d.);

Bernhard Zeller, ed., *Das Sonntagsblatt für gebildete Stände* (Marbach: Schiller-Nationalmuseum, 1961).

Papers:

The main collection of Justinus Kerner's manuscripts is at the Schiller-Nationalmuseum/Deutsches Literaturarchiv, Marbach am Neckar; it is described by Werner Volke in *Jahrbuch der deutschen Schillergesellschaft*, 6 (1962): 556-581. Important holdings are also at the Württembergische Landesbibliothek, Stuttgart; the University library

Heinrich von Kleist

(18 October 1777-21 November 1811)

James M. McGlathery
University of Illinois at Urbana-Champaign

BOOKS: *Die Familie Schroffenstein: Ein Trauerspiel in fünf Aufzügen,* anonymous (Bern & Zurich: Gessner, 1803); translated by Mary J. and Lawrence M. Price as *The Feud of the Schroffensteins* (London: Badger, 1916);

Amphitryon: Ein Lustspiel nach Molière, edited by Adam H. Müller (Dresden: Arnold, 1807); translated by Marion Sonnenfeld as *Amphitryon: A Comedy* (New York: Ungar, 1962);

Penthesilea: Ein Trauerspiel (Tübingen: Cotta, 1808); translated by Humphry Trevelyan as *Penthesilea,* in *Five German Plays,* volume 2 of *The Classic Theatre,* edited by Eric Bentley (London: Mayflower, 1959; New York: Doubleday, 1959);

Erzählungen, 2 volumes (Berlin: Realschulbuchhandlung, 1810-1811)–comprises volume 1, "Michael Kohlhaas: Aus einer alten Chronik," translated by J. Oxenford as "Michael Kohlhaas," in *Tales from the German* (London: Chapman & Hall, 1844; New York: Harper, 1844); "Die Marquise von O . . . ," translated by Heinrich Roche as "The Marquise of O . . . ," in *Great German Stories* (London: Benn, 1929); "Das Erdbeben in Chili," translated by Norman Brown as "Earthquake in Chile," in *The Blue Flower* (New York: Roy, 1946); volume 2, "Die Verlobung in St. Domingo," translated by Martin Greenberg as "The Engagement in Santo Domingo," in *The Marquise of O-, and Other Stories* (New York: Criterion, 1960); "Das Bettelweib von Locarno," translated by Ernest N. Bennett as "The Beggar Woman of Locarno," in *German Short Stories* (London: Oxford, 1934); "Der Findling," translated by Greenberg as "The Foundling," in *The Marquise of O-, and Other Stories* (New York: Criterion, 1960); "Die heilige Cäcilie oder Die Gewalt der Musik, Eine Legende," translated by J. Oxenford as "St. Cecilia; or, The Power of Music: A Catholic Legend," in *Tales from the German* (London: Chapman & Hall, 1844; New York: Harper, 1844); "Der Zweikampf,"

Heinrich von Kleist in 1801 (miniature by Peter Friedel; the only likeness of Kleist known to have been executed from life, it is now in a private collection)

translated by Greenberg as "The Duel," in *The Marquise of O-, and Other Stories* (New York: Criterion, 1960);

Das Käthchen von Heilbronn oder Die Feuerprobe: Ein großes historisches Ritterschauspiel (Berlin: Realschulbuchhandlung, 1810); translated by Elijah B. Impey as *Kate of Heilbronn,* in *Illustrations of German Poetry* (London: Simkin, Marshall, 1841); translated by Frederick E. Pierce as *Kaethchen of Heilbronn or The Test of Fire: Great Historical Chivalric Drama in 5 Acts,* in *Romantic Drama,* volume 2 of *Fiction and Fantasy of German Romance: Selections from the German Romantic Authors, 1790-1830 in English Translation* (New York: Oxford, 1927);

Der zerbrochne Krug: Ein Lustspiel (Berlin: Real-schulbuchhandlung, 1811); translated by J. Krumpelmann as *The Broken Jug: A Comedy, Poet Lore*, 45 (1939): 146-209;

Germania an ihre Kinder (N.p., 1813);

Das erwachte Europa (Berlin: Achenwall, 1814);

Hinterlassene Schriften, edited by Ludwig Tieck (Berlin: Reimer, 1821)–includes *Die Hermannsschlacht: Ein Drama; Prinz Friedrich von Homburg: Ein Schauspiel*, translated by Francis Lloyd and William Newton as *Prince Frederick of Homburg*, in *Prussia's Representative Man* (London: Trübner, 1875); translated by Hermann Hagedorn as *The Prince of Homburg*, in *The German Classics of the Nineteenth and Twentieth Centuries*, edited by Kuno Francke and W. G. Howard, volume 4 (New York: German Publications Society, 1913); and "Fragment aus dem Trauerspiel Robert Guiskard, Herzog der Normänner";

Gesammelte Schriften, edited by Tieck, 3 volumes (Berlin: Reimer, 1826);

Gesammelte Schriften, edited by Tieck, revised by J. Schmidt (Berlin: Reimer, 1859);

Politische Schriften und andere Nachträge zu seinen Werken, edited by Rudolf Koepke (Berlin: Charisius, 1862);

Werke: Kritisch durchgesehene und erl. Gesamtausgabe, edited by E. Schmidt, G. Minde-Pouet, and R. Steig, 5 volumes (Leipzig: Bibliographisches Institut, 1904-1905);

Sämtliche Werke und Briefe, edited by Helmut Sembdner, 2 volumes (Munich: Hanser, 1985).

OTHER: *Phöbus: Ein Journal für die Kunst*, edited by Kleist and Adam H. Müller (volume 1, nos. 1-10, Dresden: Gärtner, 1808; nos. 11-12, Dresden: Walther, 1808);

Berliner Abendblätter, edited by Kleist (first quarter, nos. 1-77, Berlin: Hitzig, 1810; second quarter, nos. 1-76, Berlin: Kunst- und Industrie-Comptoir, 1811).

PERIODICAL PUBLICATION: "Über das Marionettentheater," *Berliner Abendblätter*, 12-15 December 1810; translated by Christian Albrecht-Gollub as "On the Marionette Theater," in *German Romantic Criticism: Novalis, Schlegel, Schleiermacher, and Others*, edited by A. Leslie Willson (New York: Continuum, 1982).

One of the most enigmatic of German writers, Heinrich von Kleist has been the object of critical debate and controversy from his appearance on the literary scene, in the first decade of the nineteenth century, to the present day. That his creative genius was of an exceptionally high order has never been disputed. It was rather the extremity and immoderation of his depictions that shocked his contemporaries, denying him the public and critical acclaim he coveted and believed he deserved. In his plays and stories, raging passions result in shattered skulls with brains oozing from them and suitors slain and devoured in the name of love. This very propensity has contributed to maintaining interest in his works, as have the shocking circumstances of his suicide.

Kleist's short life is almost as much a puzzle as his works. (His death came just a month after his thirty-fourth birthday; he never married.) In his plays and stories, the facts at least are clear; only their meaning is in doubt. Regarding his life, however, there is a dearth of information.

He was born in Frankfurt an der Oder on 18 October 1777. On his father's side the men in the family mostly served as officers in the Prussian army, some having risen to the rank of general; the Kleists thus were known throughout German-speaking countries as a military family. The expectation was, therefore, that Heinrich would follow that career, or at least one in the Prussian civil service. His father, Joachim Friedrich von Kleist, a captain in the Leopold von Braunschweig Regiment, died in June 1788, when Kleist was ten; the youth was sent to the Prussian capital Berlin to be educated. His mother, Juliane Ulrike von Kleist (née von Pannwitz) died in February 1793, by which time Kleist was a corporal in the King's Guard Regiment based at Potsdam. When he had his first experience of military service in an area of combat, with allied armies opposing French revolutionary forces at the Rhine, he was thus largely out in the world on his own; his mother's sister, an officer's widow, presided over the orphaned family back home in Frankfurt an der Oder.

In the spring of 1799 he turned his back on the secure military career that was expected of him to return home and take up studies at the small university there, with the intention possibly of becoming a professor. He attended the university only one year, 1799-1800, and never completed his studies. At the time of his resignation from the military there was no indication that he was thinking of pursuing a literary career. He threw himself instead into study of science and philosophy, and tried out his pedagogical skills by organizing and teaching a private course for a dozen aristocratic young women.

This attempt at pedagogy led at the end of the year to his proposal of marriage to one of the students, Wilhelmine von Zenge, two years his junior and the elder of two daughters of Kleist's neighbor, the local regimental commander. His engagement to Wilhelmine made the choice of a career more pressing. Her family would not consent to the marriage until his ability to support her properly was assured. It was for this reason that he broke off his studies at the university the year after having begun them, and went to Berlin in the summer of 1800 to seek a civil position in the Prussian bureaucracy. Late that August he interrupted this stay to embark on a mysterious journey.

The purpose of this trip, about which Kleist engaged in deliberate mystification, has remained one of the great secrets in his life. The journey led to a protracted visit in the Catholic, Franconian university city of Würzburg, on the Main river. The chances are that the goal was medical treatment, and probably for a sexual deficiency; but Kleist created the impression in letters to his fiancée and to his half sister Ulrike, the only member of his immediate family in whom he confided, that he was on a secret diplomatic or commercial mission related to the aim of his securing a civil position.

Not long after Kleist's return to Berlin he was writing to Ulrike that a career in the civil service would be impossibly uncongenial for him and to Wilhelmine that their marriage might need to be postponed–perhaps for as long as six years, until he could support them by writing about Kantian philosophy (much discussed at the time) or by teaching. He would need, he wrote, to go to Paris; Ulrike, whom he asked to help pay for the journey, accepted his perhaps only half-hearted invitation to join him. In justifying his need to get away, he reported that Kant's assertion that the existence of God and thus of any absolute could never be shown had destroyed his belief in man's ability to know the truth; he needed time to rethink his aims and purposes.

While there was in the winter of 1800 and early spring of 1801 still no hint that he was thinking of a literary career, the ensuing trip to Paris that spring and early summer carried him first to the Saxon capital Dresden, known as Florence on the Elbe, with its impressive architecture and cultivation of the arts. The famous Dresden gallery attracted him so strongly that he could hardly be persuaded to continue the journey. Then, as he and Ulrike traveled on toward Paris, they stopped to visit the elderly author Johann Wilhelm Gleim, who had been a friend of their distant relative Ewald Christian von Kleist, a poet who died from wounds received in the battle of Kunersdorf during the Seven Years' War. Paris itself was, of course, a center for artists and poets. By the end of his stay there, it was clear that Kleist, now just turned twenty-four, had determined to support himself and achieve fame as an author.

Kleist wrote to his fiancée that he would never return to his Prussian fatherland until he could do so honorably crowned with poetic laurels. He therefore begged her to join him in Switzerland, where he planned to take up farming while he strove for literary fame; but she declined, and their engagement was broken off. In Bern he was encouraged in his writing by a circle of three literary friends: Heinrich Zschokke, a young author and pedagogue prominent in Swiss politics; Heinrich Gessner, publisher and son of Salomon Gessner, the celebrated Swiss writer of idylls; and Ludwig Wieland, son of the well-known German author Christoph Martin Wieland. That winter of 1802 and spring of 1803, Kleist read to them from a play he was completing, the lovers' tragedy *Die Familie Schroffenstein* (1803; translated as *The Feud of the Schroffensteins*, 1916), which takes from Shakespeare's *Romeo and Juliet* its theme of family enmity standing in the way of young love.

This first of Kleist's works already bears the stamp of his peculiar genius. The dramatic tension is located so deeply and completely in the characters' emotions that there is essentially no reflection, only action. Thus, even the soliloquies are almost wholly expressions of passion, not contemplations of ideas; and in the dialogues, the characters' responses are often fragmentary or enigmatic, suggesting mental confusion or emotional conflict. Intensity of feeling produces frequent lapses of comprehension on the part of the characters, and occasional faintings. The spectator or reader is left with uncertainty, too, about the characters' intentions, motivations, and emotions, which often are indicated not by words, but by gestures. One of the marks of Kleist's greatness is thus that he does not tell his audience what to think about the action or how to understand it. The emotions of each character form a drama within the drama, because the characters typically know no more what to make of their own feelings and actions than they do of those around them.

The enmity between the families of the two lovers Ottokar and Agnes von Schroffenstein–they are first cousins, their mothers being sisters, while their fathers are more distantly related–has resulted from mistrust owing to the provision that if one of the lines of the family is left without an heir its estate falls to the other line. The situation enables Kleist to exploit the possibilities of confused perceptions about the motives of others, and inner doubt and uncertainty about the purity of one's own feelings and motivations. Also, since the tension between the families renders the young lovers' passion a forbidden one, the intensity of their romantic desire is that much greater, as in *Romeo and Juliet*. Kleist emphasizes this point by comingling, to a far greater extent than Shakespeare did, erotic passion and thoughts of suicide. In addition, Kleist makes his heroine the object of passion on the part of the hero's illegitimate brother, Johann, and of less intense attraction for two older men as well, her middle-aged suitor and relative Jeronimus and her blind old grandfather, Sylvius. The veiled role of erotic desire in motivating the characters' actions contributes significantly to the mysteriousness of their behavior and their mystification of themselves, one another, and Kleist's audience.

Kleist may have brought this play with him to Switzerland in almost completed form. It was, in any case, published there anonymously by Gessner's firm in 1803, not long after Kleist had returned to Germany. Still in Switzerland in the spring of 1802, he repaired to an island on the lake at Thun to devote himself to writing, perhaps the play that became the comedy *Der zerbrochne Krug* (1811; translated as *The Broken Jug*, 1939), but especially historical drama, probably including "Robert Guiskard, Herzog der Normänner" (Robert Guiskard, Duke of the Normans), which became for him, at this early stage, the test of his calling to poetic greatness.

The effort at proving his talent for historical drama perhaps contributed to his falling ill that summer, so that he had to leave the island to put himself under a physician's care in Bern. There he was joined in September by Ulrike, who rushed to his aid when she learned he was sick and needing money. By the time she reached Bern he had recovered; and they soon departed for Germany with Wieland, who had incurred the displeasure of the revolutionary government in Bern and been ordered to leave. The intention was to accompany Wieland home to visit his famous father; and although Wieland changed his plans and Ulrike journeyed homeward to Prussia, Kleist went on by himself to meet the elderly poet and stayed with him as his guest on his estate near Weimar. During this visit Kleist again struggled to progress with writing the play about the medieval Norman ruler, and remained with Wieland through the winter of 1802 to the following spring, when the romantic passion that the old author's youngest daughter conceived for the young poet occasioned his departure. He moved to Leipzig, and then on to Dresden, still unhappy with the results of his labors on "Robert Guiskard."

In Dresden a friend from his youth in the military, Ernst von Pfuel, who in later years was to become a high Prussian official, encouraged Kleist to turn his talents to comedy to distract himself from his torment with the serious play. When that remedy failed, Pfuel arranged to travel with him to Switzerland. From there they went to Paris, where, in October 1803, Kleist suffered a complete collapse of his hopes and, after arguing with Pfuel, set out for Normandy intending to seek death in the invasion of England Napoleon was planning. Instead, this crisis of suicidal despair ended with his being persuaded to return to Paris, once his identity was discovered, and then to accede to the Prussian ambassador's stipulation that, in view of his attempt to join the French forces, he accept a passport constraining him to return by direct route to his homeland. For unknown reasons, perhaps having to do with secret missions or activities of a political nature, but more likely because of despair over the prospect of having to explain himself to government authorities on his return to Prussia and over his failed ambitions for the Guiskard play, when he reached Germany, Kleist, who was ailing, remained in the Rhineland through the following spring, spending most of the time in Mainz as houseguest of a physician named Georg Christian Gottlob Freiherr von Wedekind, a friend of Wieland's, who took him in so that he could keep him under observation.

When Kleist finally presented himself to officials in Berlin in the summer of 1804, he was sharply reprimanded for his behavior; but, aided by intercession from friends and relatives, he was offered an appointment in the finance ministry.

The following spring, he accepted an offer to be allowed to study in Königsberg, at government expense, under the leading economist Christian Jakob Kraus, and arrived there the first week of May 1805. At this juncture he enjoyed the encouragement and support of highly placed officials. Karl Freiherr vom Stein zum Altenstein, particularly, who was soon to become finance minister, took a special interest in him as a promising prospective public servant. Yet Kleist continued to be devoted to his writing, which he likely had never ceased except for the period of despair in France. In Berlin, while waiting to receive civil appointment, he had attended the literary salons and worked on his manuscripts. Now in Königsberg, he increasingly withdrew to his writing and neglected the study of finance. During his second summer in Königsberg, he sought and received a leave of absence for health reasons, as a way of easing out of his commitment to pursue a career in civil service. He wrote at the time to Otto August Rühle von Lilienstern, a friend from his military youth who shared Kleist's interest in literature, that he intended for the rest of his life, "as long as that lasts," to do tragedies and comedies: "Du weißt, daß ich meine Karriere wieder verlassen habe.... Ich will mich jetzt durch meine dramatischen Arbeiten ernähren; und nur, wenn Du meinst, daß sie auch dazu nicht taugen, würde mich Dein Urteil schmerzen, und auch das nur, weil ich verhungern müßte. Sonst magst Du über ihren Wert urteilen, wie Du willst" (You know that I have left my career [in government service] again.... I want to support myself now through my dramatic works; and only if you think that they are not even good enough for that would your verdict pain me, and then only because I would have to starve to death. Otherwise, you may judge them as you wish).

Prussia's crushing defeat by Napoleon at Jena and Auerstedt on 14 October 1806 found Kleist still in Königsberg, to which the Prussian court fled in the face of Berlin's capture by the French. Civilian and military refugees followed the king and queen to East Prussia, so that Königsberg soon became overcrowded. Already having planned to move to a center of publishing to help further his aim of supporting himself from his writings, Kleist the following January set out for Dresden by way of Berlin. In the occupied Prussian capital, however, he was arrested and sent as a war prisoner to Châlons-sur-Marne, in France, evidently under the suspicion that as former military officers he and his traveling companions were on a mission for the Prussian government. During this captivity, which lasted until early July 1807, when the peace treaty was signed at Tilsit in East Prussia, Kleist was able for the most part to continue his writing, and enjoyed the satisfaction of learning that a second book of his had been published, the first since *Die Familie Schroffenstein* four years before.

This new work of Kleist's was the play *Amphitryon* (1807; translated as *Amphitryon: A Comedy*, 1962), an adaptation of Molière's comedy of the same title, in turn derived from Plautus's *Amphitruo*. As contemporary critics were quick to observe, Kleist transformed the French farce into something quite sublime, and introduced an element of idealization, transcendence, and mystery into the play's previously matter-of-fact sensuality. In particular, he deepened the relationship between the heroine Alkmene and the god Jupiter, who took the form of her husband Amphitryon in order to spend a night of love with her. Goethe, who read the play at the baths in Carlsbad that summer and was both fascinated and bothered by it, remarked in his diary (13 July 1807) that Kleist aimed at depicting a "Verwirrung des Gefühls" (confusion of emotions) in the main figures.

Following his release from prison at Châlons-sur-Marne, Kleist finally was able to reach his journey's original goal, Dresden, where Rühle von Lilienstern, to whom he had entrusted several of his completed manuscripts, was living and where *Amphitryon* had been published. Rühle had just had a much-discussed book published on a military subject; and the two friends, reckoning that they could make far more from their writings by publishing the books themselves, joined in a venture with Adam Heinrich Müller, a lecturer and publicist, who had been instrumental in the publication of *Amphitryon* and had written the preface for it. The positive critical reception of that play, together with the news that Goethe had accepted Kleist's other finished comedy, *Der zerbrochene Krug*, for production at the court theater in Weimar, contributed to Kleist's being lionized by literary circles in Dresden. Thus, with his thirtieth birthday in the fall of 1807, his dream of literary fame and of supporting himself from his writings appeared about to be fulfilled, after six years of ardent striving and of doubt and despair.

Almost immediately, these high hopes were dashed. An ambitious literary periodical, *Phöbus*, edited by Kleist and Müller, was announced and promoted with a pretentious exuberance that won it only enemies and no friends, so that long before 1808 was out the enterprise was doomed, and the issues of that first and only year were brought to completion late and with great difficulty. Goethe's production of *Der zerbrochene Krug* failed in Weimar; and Kleist's resulting attacks on Goethe, blaming him for the failure, further cast a shadow over him with the public. The underlying reason for the defeat of Kleist's hopes, however, surely was the peculiar nature of his poetic gift. He was simply a problematic genius.

The failure of Kleist's comedy on the stage was attributed to what Goethe and others viewed as a lack of a truly dramatic plot. The scene is set entirely in the courtroom of a Dutch village magistrate; and the drama revolves around the gradual revelation that the judge himself is the culprit in the case at hand, which involves a broken jug and an attempt on a maiden's honor. Like all of Kleist's plays and stories, the comedy is a masterpiece of finely drawn psychological depiction, which was undoubtedly a reason for Goethe's having wanted to produce it. The audience in Weimar rejected the play chiefly because they found it boring; but there were also complaints about offenses against good taste and propriety, perhaps because of the eroticism expressed in some of the characters' emotional outbursts.

The tragedy *Penthesilea* (1808; translated, 1959), excerpted in the first issue of *Phöbus* and published as a book that same year, most strikingly reveals Kleist's unsettling peculiarities as an author. Kleist wrote at the time, to his relative by marriage Marie von Kleist, his intimate, older friend and benefactress at the Prussian court, that the play contained "der ganze Schmutz zugleich und Glanz meiner Seele" (the whole filth as well as splendor of my soul; it has been debated whether Kleist wrote *Schmutz*, filth, or *Schmerz*, pain). The drama is a depiction of intense romantic passion, rendered extreme because the heroine, the title character, is queen of the Amazons, and is therefore prohibited from choosing a lover instead of merely accepting the one that falls to her by the luck of battle. While her society dictates that Penthesilea shall capture a warrior solely to mate with him to produce daughters who will guarantee the survival of the all-female state, feminine vanity coupled with erotic desire makes her yearn to captivate Achilles with her charms, as much or more than to vanquish him on the battlefield. Faced with her inability to defeat him, she complains to her sister Amazons that they should allow her to become

his captive and concubine; but ashamed at having thus impulsively divulged her secret wish, she reacts to Achilles' renewed invitation to combat by calling forth the whole machinery of destruction at her command to run him down like a hunted animal and then to eat the flesh of his corpse. When she learns that he called her out to battle only to surrender to her, she dies of a broken heart, but happy that her charms had moved him after all. The play's bizarre eroticism, especially in association with murder, lust, and suicidal urges, turned public favor away from Kleist. The enigmatic behavior of his characters in *Die Familie Schroffenstein* and *Amphitryon* had fascinated his readers; but Penthesilea's desperate passion struck them as offending against decency and propriety.

In 1807 the first of Kleist's stories to be published, "Das Erdbeben in Chile" (collected in *Erzählungen* [Stories], volume 1, 1810; translated as "Earthquake in Chile," 1946), appeared–under the title "Jeronimo und Josephe," the names of the hero and heroine–in a leading periodical, the publisher Johann Friedrich Cotta's *Morgenblatt für gebildete Stände* (Morning Paper for the Cultivated Classes), shortly after Kleist's arrival in Dresden. It tells of the tragic fate of a young couple who, on the verge of death and suicide, are spared by a terrible earthquake only to be slain by an angry crowd of churchgoers eager to find scapegoats for the sinfulness that they believe has brought God's judgment on the city in the form of the natural disaster. The tale appears to have been favorably received and certainly did not detract from Kleist's positive, enthusiastic reception in his first months in Dresden. The same cannot be said of his next published story when it appeared in his journal *Phöbus* in 1808. Opinions on "Die Marquise von O . . . " (collected in *Erzählungen*, volume 1; translated as "The Marquise of O . . . ," 1929) were divided, with women readers in particular finding embarrassing or revolting this tale about a rape that occurs while the heroine is in a faint, and about which she and the reader learn only after she has become pregnant. Here Kleist aimed once again at depicting the "confusion of emotions" of which Goethe spoke in regard to *Amphitryon;* but as with *Penthesilea,* his focus on uncontrolled erotic passion alienated many in his audience.

Following the failure of his publishing venture centered around the journal *Phöbus*, and the disappointing reception given *Penthesilea* and "Die Marquise von O . . . " by readers and *Der zerbrochene Krug* in Goethe's production, Kleist set his hopes on a play better suited for success in the theater. This was the "Grand Historical Chivalric Play" *Das Käthchen von Heilbronn oder Die Feuerprobe* (Katie of Heilbronn; or, The Trial by Fire, 1810; translated as "Kate of Heilbronn," 1841), which he tailored especially for the Vienna stage, hoping to make use of the good contacts with the Austrian court he had established in Dresden through the embassy secretary Joseph von Buol-Mühlingen and the connections he had made, via Adam Müller, with the author and government official Friedrich von Gentz. Though *Das Käthchen von Heilbronn* is thoroughly Kleistian, particularly in the emotional violence attendant upon the aristocratic hero's struggle to suppress his passion for the beautiful burgher heroine, it is still quite recognizable as a romantic and extremely tender love story and remains a popular favorite with theater audiences. This success did not become assured until after Kleist's death, however, and then at first only with texts substantially adapted for the stage.

Das Käthchen von Heilbronn was performed during Kleist's lifetime, and in Vienna, but not until early spring of 1810. One reason for the delay was the outbreak of hostilities between Austria and France. Anticipating that turn of events, on the first day of 1809 Kleist sent the manuscript of another play, the patriotic drama *Die Hermannsschlacht* (The Battle of Teutoburg Forest, published in *Hinterlassene Schriften* [Posthumous Writings], 1821), to his contact with the Viennese theaters, Heinrich Joseph von Collin, secretary to the court and a writer himself, suggesting that the play might be performed first, before *Das Käthchen von Heilbronn*, because its topicality would make its success more certain. On 9 April Austria declared war on France; and at the end of the month Kleist left Dresden with an Austrian passport and headed via Prague for Vienna, but failed to reach there because Napoleon captured the Austrian capital on 13 May. In Prague, Kleist and his traveling companion, the young scholar Friedrich Christoph Dahlmann (later, with Jacob and Wilhelm Grimm one of the seven Göttingen professors who protested the revocation of Hannover's constitution in 1837), sought, with others, to establish a journal, *Germania*, to agitate for Napoleon's defeat. Austria was decisively beaten on 5 July at Wagram, however; and Kleist was prevented from making a name for himself as a patriotic publicist, and thus from joining the ranks of others in his Romantic genera-

tion, including Friedrich Schlegel in Vienna and Ernst Moritz Arndt in Berlin, who found employment through their enthusiasm for the cause of liberation from French domination.

Information is scant about Kleist's life from July 1809 to the following February. Clearly, though, his travels in this period home to Frankfurt an der Oder, to Berlin, and westward to the other Frankfurt, on the Main, concerned his financial plight and his desperate need to secure a future for himself as a writer.

In the end, Kleist returned to the capital of his native Prussia. Arriving in Berlin at the beginning of February 1810, he renewed contacts with literary friends and made new ones, drawing especially close to Achim von Arnim and Clemens Brentano. Again he frequented the literary salons, particularly that of Rahel Levin (better known as Rahel Varnhagen von Ense because of her marriage a few years later), and met such important publishers as Georg Andreas Reimer, Johann Daniel Sander, and Julius Eduard Hitzig. *Penthesilea* had been published by Cotta in the fall of 1808; and at the beginning of 1810, Kleist had sent the manuscript of *Das Käthchen von Heilbronn* to him. When Cotta indicated, though, that he would not be able to publish the volume by the end of the year, Kleist offered it to Reimer, whose Realschulbuchhandlung produced it that autumn, followed by *Der zerbrochene Krug* in February 1811. Reimer likewise published a volume of Kleist's tales in fall 1810, and the next summer brought out a second one.

Kleist's hopes for financial survival, though, came in the fall of 1810, pinned on a publishing project of a new sort, a daily newspaper edited by him and called *Berliner Abendblätter* (Berlin Evening Newspages). The venture was initially greeted with enthusiasm, partly because the paper was the only one in the city to appear each weekday, and was thus able to provide brief reports of events such as crimes and fires almost immediately after they happened. Entertaining anecdotes and other short pieces of excellent quality were offered, too, as well as essays on contemporary economic, political, and cultural matters of interest, most of them authored by Kleist and his collaborators, who included Arnim, Brentano, Friedrich de la Motte Fouqué, Wilhelm Grimm, and Adam Müller, among others. The first issue of the *Abendblätter* appeared on 1 October 1810. Before the end of the year, Hitzig withdrew as its publisher; and with the new firm, August Kuhn, publisher of the established journal *Der Frei-*

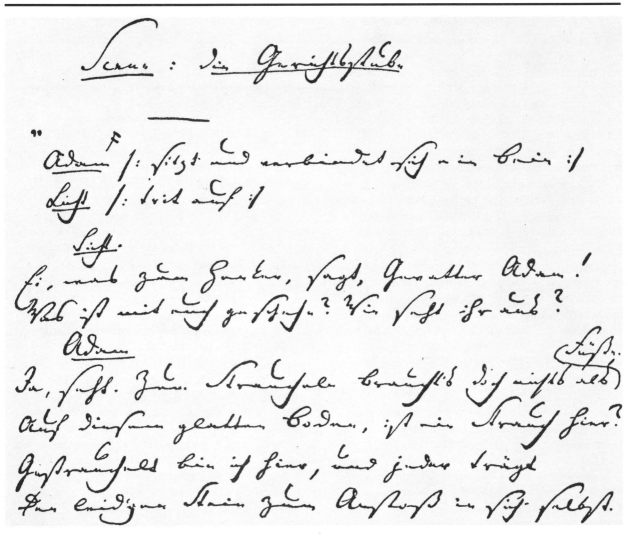

First page of the manuscript for Kleist's comedy, Der zerbrochne Krug *(Bilderatlas zur Geschichte der Deutschen Nationalliteratur, 1895)*

müthige (The Frank Talker), the *Abendblätter* limped along through the second quarter of its first year before ceasing publication at the end of March 1811. Though the venture failed, it occasioned some of Kleist's finest prose, from his masterful recastings of material from other journals to brilliantly ironic satirical pieces and the enigmatic fictional dialogue "Über das Marionettentheater" (1810; translated as "On the Marionette Theater," 1982), of which dozens of critical and scholarly interpretations have appeared.

A major reason for Kleist's turn to the newspaper venture was that the Berlin stage seemed to be closed to his plays; and except for the three-evening, heavily attended run of *Das Käthchen von Heilbronn* in Vienna, he was not making headway in other major theater cities either. About

the time of the performance of *Das Käthchen von Heilbronn* in Vienna in the spring of 1810, it was planned that Kleist's new play, *Prinz Friedrich von Homburg* (published in *Hinterlassene Schriften;* translated as *Prince Frederick of Homburg,* 1875), would be performed at the private theater of Anton Heinrich, Prince of Radziwill, husband of Princess Luise of Prussia, and then at Berlin's Nationaltheater; but when it was learned that the hero and title character, a young Prussian officer, becomes terrified at the sight of the grave being dug for him, prominent persons in the army and at court became indignant, and the plan to perform the play was abandoned. Then, that summer, the much-celebrated actor and playwright August Wilhelm Iffland, director of the Nationaltheater, rejected *Das Käthchen von Heilbronn* for performance there.

Prinz Friedrich von Homburg was Kleist's third play on a historical subject, after the unfinished "Robert Guiskard" and *Die Hermannsschlacht*. Only the first ten scenes of "Robert Guiskard," a play about the Norman leader's plan to conquer Constantinople in 1085, have survived, and only in the version published in Kleist's journal *Phöbus* in the double issue for April and May 1808 (and later included in *Hinterlassene Schriften*). This fragment, though, suffices to demonstrate how powerful a drama it might have become had he been able to finish it. These scenes again reveal Kleist's use of dramatic gesture and unfinished utterance paired with Homeric similes, hyperbolic metaphor, convoluted rhetoric, and disrupted word order—all to indicate the emotional conflicts and secret thoughts and feelings of the characters. Yet "Robert Guiskard" is anomalous in having no romantic interest, only a moral and political one. Moreover, the central figure is dying of the plague and is much debilitated at the opening of the play. These differences may explain why, of all of Kleist's major works that have survived, "Robert Guiskard" is the only one he never finished. He did complete *Die Hermannsschlacht,* for example, a consummately political drama (indeed, very much a propaganda piece, using the German defeat of Roman legions in the Teutoburg forest in 9 A.D. to urge revolt against Napoleonic influence and rule in Germany). But in this play the central figure, far from being sickly, is entirely robust and in condition thoroughly to savor his triumph in the end. Romantic drama, too, is not lacking in the play. The work's poetic interest is owing largely to the susceptibility of the German leader's wife to the flattering attentions of a young Roman diplomat and the—typically Kleistian—emotional conflict this produces in her.

Prinz Friedrich von Homburg is as much a love story as a piece about political and moral issues. With this drama, which may have supplanted or superseded "Robert Guiskard" in Kleist's poetic imagination, he largely returned to depiction of erotic desire and its sublimations evident in the earlier plays, from *Die Familie Schroffenstein* to the comedies *Amphitryon* and *Der zerbrochene Krug* and on to the romantic dramas *Penthesilea* and *Das Käthchen von Heilbronn*. To be sure, the issue in *Prinz Friedrich von Homburg* is whether the young prince is guilty of insubordination and treason for disobeying orders to delay his cavalry charge and whether he should be executed for it. Yet the prize of which he dreams

and which makes him yearn to win laurels on the battlefield is quite specifically marriage to the elector's pretty niece; and that is the very reward Brandenburg's ruler apparently accords him, once Homburg has shown his greater heroism by proving he is ready to accept death as punishment for his questionable deed.

Among Kleist's stories, "Michael Kohlhaas," of which the beginning was published in *Phöbus,* is the most political, especially with the completion he gave it for the first volume of *Erzählungen,* where it appeared with "Das Erdbeben in Chile" and "Die Marquise von O . . . ," both of which had appeared in finished form earlier. Kohlhaas, a subject of the elector of Brandenburg, is a horse trader who doggedly, singlemindedly, and violently seeks restitution for a cruel wrong done him by a member of the neighboring Saxon nobility. The tale, based on a chronicle from Luther's time, has been a favorite with readers for its historical realism and narrative objectivity, but has been criticized for the seemingly pointless, drawn-out story toward the end about a gypsy woman and a mysterious capsule containing a secret prophecy concerning the future of Saxony's ruling family. Often overlooked is that the tale is also a love story. The immediate occasion for Kohlhaas's murderous rampage is his wife's death as a consequence of his efforts to win justice (this is where the fragment in *Phöbus* broke off); grief over her loss is uppermost in his mind in the climactic scene when he visits Luther to justify his behavior; and the dead wife herself proves to have sought to protect him from beyond the grave as his guardian angel, in the form of the gypsy woman.

Political history and romance are mixed, too, in the first story of the second volume of Kleist's *Erzählungen,* "Die Verlobung in St. Domingo" (translated as "The Engagement in Santo Domingo," 1960), set during the black Haitians' revolt against the whites in the wake of the refusal to accept freedom and equality for the blacks as ordered by the revolutionary government in France in 1794. (Kleist's interest in these events was aroused evidently by his having been imprisoned in 1807 temporarily in the same Fort Joux in France where the black Haitian leader Toussaint l'Ouverture had been held captive and died in 1804.) The second tale of the volume, "Das Bettelweib von Locarno" (translated as "The Beggar Woman of Locarno," 1934), while not political, does contain an element of class resentment, in that the woman has been treated gruffly by an

Italian aristocrat and returns from the grave to haunt his castle; but the short piece is chiefly a masterful ghost story, memorable in its lack of explanation of the apparition and for the suicidal horror and despair it produces in the central figure. "Der Findling" (translated as "The Foundling," 1960), the third of these five stories, likewise involves class tension. A rich Roman merchant, widowed and still more recently grieving over the death of his child by his first wife, rescues a youth from the plague and adopts him to replace the dead son. When the youth reaches maturity he attempts to rape the benefactor's young wife, taking advantage of her romantic love for an aristocratic Genovese youth who had died as a result of his heroic rescue of her when she was a girl and whom the adopted foundling resembles, especially when dressed in appropriate costume. The succeeding tale, "Die heilige Cäcilie oder Die Gewalt der Musik, Eine Legende" (translated as "St. Cecilia; or, The Power of Music: A Catholic Legend," 1844), has a religious rather than a political or social subject. Four young Dutch brothers involved in a planned attack on a convent in Aix-la-Chapelle during the period of iconoclasm in the wake of the Reformation fall strangely insane after a young nun, pale from having just arisen from her sickbed, has appeared in the convent church to direct the playing of an old Italian Mass. As in Kleist's ghost story, there is no single, satisfactory explanation of this mystery. The concluding story, "Der Zweikampf" (translated as "The Duel," 1960), which is the last work from Kleist's pen that has been preserved, has a religious subject, too. A duel is fought to seek God's judgment of a woman's virtue; and as a consequence, a tender love story unfolds and competes for the reader's attention with the question of whether God's hand is evident in the duel's result.

Volume 2 of Kleist's *Erzählungen* appeared at the beginning of August 1811; but this gratification was not enough to sustain him. He was unable to earn enough from publication of his plays and stories to survive financially. A last, desperate hope for supporting himself was reinstatement as a military officer (that request was languishing in the files at the time of his death). Ulrike had lent or given him money time and again over the years, much to his shame; but when he visited her in September to ask for enough to outfit himself for the prospective officer's commission, he met with a rebuke from her

and several relatives who were with her in the family home in Frankfurt an der Oder.

Kleist's financial plight and other disappointments deepened his sense of loneliness. After the breaking off of his engagement to Wilhelmine von Zenge he had resolved never to marry and to devote himself entirely to his writing. In Dresden, on the way to Paris with Ulrike in the spring of 1801, he had drawn close to the two von Schlieben sisters, Caroline and Henriette, impoverished aristocrats; and during his later residence in Dresden, from late summer 1807 to spring 1809, he and Adam Müller reportedly quarreled over Sophie von Haza, the wife of Müller's former employer (Müller married her soon after she divorced her husband). Other women also played roles in Kleist's life; most were concerned for his welfare and survival and drawn to him because of his poetic genius. Of all of them, he was closest to his relative by marriage, Marie von Kleist, and felt that she best understood his poetic aspirations. When he died, however, it was in the company of a friend's wife who suffered from an incurable uterine cancer, and who accepted his offer to end her life and then his own. In the late afternoon of 21 November 1811, beside Lake Wannsee near Potsdam, Kleist shot Henriette Vogel through the chest and then discharged a second pistol in his mouth. Both died instantly; and after the investigation of the deaths, they were buried side by side at the spot the following evening.

The double suicide was reported throughout Europe and attracted much attention and debate, thereby helping to keep Kleist's memory alive and ultimately to stimulate critical interest in his works. Later in the century Prussia's political ascendance caused him to be praised for patriotic reasons. It was not until the vogue of literary naturalism in Germany in the 1880s and 1890s, though, that analysis of his works began in earnest, in this case emphasizing his depiction of the characters as creatures of biology and society. In the early decades of the twentieth century, during the period of expressionism and with the rise of intellectual history, interest became focused first on death mysticism in his works, and then on the crisis he suffered over Kant's philosophy and reported in his letters to his fiancée in the spring of 1801. The arrival of existentialism in the late 1920s and early 1930s caused this crisis to assume new importance in criticism of Kleist's work, showing him to be a poet of man's struggle with an incomprehensible universe. Under Hitler, both the Prussian patriotic and existentialist views of Kleist were appropriated by National Socialists to portray him as a poet of Germany's tragic mission and destiny for greatness. Kleist criticism after World War II has largely reflected the existentialist approach; but since the 1960s there has been increasing emphasis on social, political, and historical aspects of his works. This orientation has moved Western criticism closer to the Marxist approach of Eastern European scholars, whose views in turn arose in reaction and response to earlier nationalist and existentialist perspectives. In the huge literature on Kleist that numbers books in the hundreds and articles in the thousands (a complete bibliography has not yet been prepared), many other critical viewpoints are also represented, including psychoanalytically oriented studies.

Letters:

Heinrich von Kleists Leben und Briefe: Mit einem Anhange, edited by Eduard von Bülow (Berlin: Besser, 1848);

Briefe an seine Schwester Ulrike, edited by August Koberstein (Berlin: Schroeder & Hermann Kaiser, 1860);

Briefe an seine Braut: Zum ersten Male nach den Originalhandschriften, edited by Karl Biedermann (Breslau: Schottlaender, 1884);

Letters of Heinrich von Kleist: With a Selection of Essays and Anecdotes, edited by Philip B. Miller (New York: Dutton, 1982).

Bibliographies:

Richard Kade, "Heinrich von Kleist," in Karl Goedeke, *Grundriß zur Geschichte der deutschen Dichtung aus den Quellen,* revised by Edmund Goetze, volume 6 (Leipzig, Berlin & Dresden: Ehlermann, 1898), pp. 96-104;

Alexander von Weilen, "Zur Kleist-Literatur des Jahres 1911," *Zeitschrift für die österreichischen Gymnasien,* 63 (1912): 198-218;

Georg Minde-Pouet, "Neue Kleistliteratur," *Das literarische Echo,* 15 (1912-1913): columns 968-978;

Minde-Pouet, "Kleist-Bibliographie 1914-1921," *Jahrbuch der Kleist-Gesellschaft,* 1 (1921): 89-169;

Minde-Pouet, "Kleist-Bibliographie 1922," *Jahrbuch der Kleist-Gesellschaft,* 2 (1922): 112-163;

Minde-Pouet, "Kleist-Bibliographie 1923 und 1924 mit Nachträgen," *Jahrbuch der Kleist-Gesellschaft,* 3-4 (1923-1924): 181-230;

Paul Kluckhohn, "Das Kleistbild der Gegenwart: Bericht über die Kleistliteratur der Jahre 1922-25," *Deutsche Vierteljahrsschrift für Literaturwissenschaft und Geistesgeschichte,* 4 (1926): 798-830;

Minde-Pouet, "Kleist-Bibliographie 1925-1930 mit Nachträgen," *Jahrbuch der Kleist-Gesellschaft,* 11-12 (1929-1930): 60-193;

Minde-Pouet, "Kleist Bibliographie 1931 bis 1937 mit Nachträgen," *Jahrbuch der Kleist-Gesellschaft,* 17 (1933-1937): 186-263;

Roger Ayrault, *La Légende de Heinrich von Kleist: Un poète devant la critique* (Paris: Nizet et Bastard, 1934);

Kluckhohn, "Kleist-Forschung 1926-1943," *Deutsche Vierteljahrsschrift für Literaturwissenschaft und Geistesgeschichte,* 21 (1943): 45-87;

Helmut Kreuzer, "Kleist-Literatur 1955-1960," *Der Deutschunterricht,* 13, no. 2 (1961): 116-135;

Eva Rothe, "Kleist-Bibliographie 1945-60," *Jahrbuch der Deutschen Schiller-Gesellschaft,* 5 (1961): 414-547;

Horst Schiller, ed., *Heinrich von Kleist 1777-1811: Auswahlbibliographie über Leben, Werk und Zeit* (Frankfurt an der Oder & Berlin: Zentralinstitut für Bibliothekswesen, 1962);

Werner Preuss, "Hundertfünfzig Jahre Kleist-Forschung," *Wissenschaftliche Zeitschrift der Pädagogischen Hochschule Potsdam: Gesellschafts- und Sprachwissenschaftliche Reihe,* 10 (1966): 243-262;

Helmut Sembdner, *Kleist-Bibliographie 1803-62: Heinrich von Kleists Schriften in frühen Drucken und Erstveröffentlichungen* (Stuttgart: Eggert, 1966);

Manfred Lefèvre, "Kleist-Forschung 1961-1967," *Colloquia Germanica,* 3 (1969): 1-86;

Helmut G. Hermann, "Der Dramatiker Heinrich von Kleist: Eine Bibliographie," in *Kleists Dramen: Neue Interpretationen,* edited by Walter Hinderer (Stuttgart: Reclam, 1981), pp. 238-289.

Biographies:

Max Morris, *Heinrich von Kleists Reise nach Würzburg* (Berlin: Skopnik, 1899);

Reinhold Steig, *Heinrich von Kleists Berliner Kämpfe* (Berlin & Stuttgart: Spemann, 1901);

Steig, *Neue Kunde zu Heinrich von Kleist* (Berlin: Reimer, 1902);

Otto Brahm, *Das Leben Heinrichs von Kleist*, fourth revised edition (Berlin: Egon Fleischl, 1911);

Heinrich Meyer-Benfey, *Kleists Leben und Werke: Dem deutschen Volke dargestellt* (Göttingen: Hapke, 1911);

Heinz Ide, *Der junge Kleist* (Würzburg: Holzner, 1961);

Heinz Politzer, "Auf der Suche nach Identität: Zu Heinrich von Kleists Würzburger Reise," *Euphorion*, 61 (1967): 383-399; reprinted in his *Hatte Ödipus einen Ödipus-Komplex?: Versuche zum Thema Psychoanalyse und Literatur* (Munich: Piper, 1974), pp. 182-202;

Helmut Sembdner, *Heinrich von Kleists Nachruhm: Eine Wirkungsgeschichte in Dokumenten* (Berlin: Schünemann, 1967);

Sembdner, *Dichter über ihre Dichtungen: Heinrich von Kleist* (Munich: Heimeran, 1969);

Katharina Mommsen, *Kleists Kampf mit Goethe* (Heidelberg: Stiehm, 1974);

Sembdner, *In Sachen Kleist: Beiträge zur Forschung* (Munich: Carl Hanser, 1974);

Joachim Maass, *Kleist: Die Geschichte seines Lebens* (Bern & Munich: Scherz, 1977); abridged as *Kleist: A Biography*, translated by Ralph Manheim (New York: Farrar, Straus & Giroux, 1983);

Sembdner, *Heinrich von Kleists Lebensspuren: Dokumente und Berichte der Zeitgenossen*, revised and enlarged edition (Frankfurt: Insel, 1977);

Hermann F. Weiss, *Funde und Studien zu Heinrich von Kleist* (Tübingen: Niemeyer, 1984).

References:

Ruth K. Angress, "Kleist's Treatment of Imperialism: 'Die Hermannsschlacht' and 'Die Verlobung in St. Domingo,' " *Monatshefte für deutschen Unterricht, deutsche Sprache und Literatur,* 69 (1977): 17-33;

Hermann Behme, *Heinrich von Kleist and C. M. Wieland* (Heidelberg: Winter, 1914);

John C. Blankenagel, *The Dramas of Heinrich von Kleist: A Biographical and Critical Study* (Chapel Hill: University of North Carolina Press, 1931);

Günter Blöcker, *Heinrich von Kleist oder das absolute Ich*, second edition (Berlin: Argon, 1962);

Friedrich Bruns, "Die Motivierung aus dem Unbewußten bei Heinrich von Kleist," in *Studies in Honor of Alexander Rudolph Hohlfeld* (Madi-

son: University of Wisconsin Press, 1925), pp. 47-77;

Sigurd Burckhardt, *The Drama of Language: Essays on Goethe and Kleist*, edited by Bernhard Blume and Roy Harvey Pearce (Baltimore: Johns Hopkins University Press, 1970);

Ernst Cassirer, *Heinrich von Kleist und die kantische Philosophie* (Berlin: Reuther & Reichard, 1919); republished in his *Idee und Gestalt: Goethe, Schiller, Hölderlin, Kleist: Fünf Aufsätze* (Berlin: Bruno Cassirer, 1921), pp. 153-200;

Dorrit Cohn, "Kleist's 'Marquise von O . . .': The Problem of Knowledge," *Monatshefte für deutschen Unterricht, deutsche Sprache und Literatur*, 67 (1975): 129-144;

Josef Collin, "Heinrich von Kleist, der Dichter des Todes: Ein Beitrag zur Geschichte seiner Seele," *Euphorion*, 27 (1926): 69-112;

Donald H. Crosby, "Psychological Realism in the Works of Kleist: 'Penthesilea' and 'Die Marquise von O . . . ,' " *Literature and Psychology*, 19, no. 1 (1969): 3-16;

Peter Dettmering, *Heinrich von Kleist: Zur Psychodynamik seiner Dichtung* (Munich: Nymphenburger Verlagshandlung, 1975);

Denys Dyer, *The Stories of Kleist: A Critical Study* (New York: Holmes & Meier, 1977);

John Martin Ellis, *Heinrich von Kleist: Studies in the Character and Meaning of His Writings* (Chapel Hill: University of North Carolina Press, 1979);

Ellis, *Kleist's "Prinz Friedrich von Homburg": A Critical Study* (Berkeley: University of California Press, 1970);

Gerhard Fricke, *Gefühl und Schicksal bei Heinrich von Kleist: Studien über den inneren Vorgang im Leben und Schaffen des Dichters* (Berlin: Junker & Dünnhaupt, 1929);

Franziska Füller, *Das psychologische Problem der Frau in Kleists Dramen und Novellen* (Leipzig: Haessel, 1924);

John Gearey, *Heinrich von Kleist: A Study in Tragedy and Anxiety* (Philadelphia: University of Pennsylvania Press, 1968);

Ilse Graham, *Heinrich von Kleist: Word into Flesh: A Poet's Quest for the Symbol* (Berlin: De Gruyter, 1977);

Friedrich Gundolf, *Heinrich von Kleist* (Berlin: Bondi, 1922);

Dieter Harlos, *Die Gestaltung psychischer Konflikte einiger Frauengestaltungen im Werk Heinrich von Kleists: Alkmene, Die Marquise von O, Penthesilea, Käthchen von Heilbronn* (Frankfurt am Main: Lang, 1984);

Ingeborg Harms, " 'Wie feilgender Sommer': Eine Untersuchung der Höhlenszene' in Heinrich von Kleists *Familie Schroffenstein*," *Jahrbuch der Deutschen Schiller-Gesellschaft*, 28 (1984): 270-314;

Robert E. Helbling, *The Major Works of Heinrich von Kleist* (New York: New Directions, 1975);

Hanna Hellmann, *Heinrich von Kleist: Darstellung des Problems* (Heidelberg: Winter, 1911);

Walter Hinderer, ed., *Kleists Dramen: Neue Interpretationen* (Stuttgart: Reclam, 1981);

Johannes Hoffmeister, "Beitrag zur sogenannten Kantkrise Heinrich von Kleists," *Deutsche Vierteljahresschrift für Literaturwissenschaft und Geistesgeschichte*, 33 (1959): 574-587;

Werner Hoffmeister, "Die Doppeldeutigkeit der Erzählweise in Heinrich von Kleists 'Die heilige Cäcilie oder die Gewalt der Musik,' " in *Festschrift für Werner Neuse*, edited by Herbert Lederer and Joachim Seyppel (Berlin: Die Diagonale, 1967), pp. 44-56;

Hans Heinz Holz, *Macht und Ohnmacht der Sprache: Untersuchungen zum Sprachverständnis und Stil Heinrich von Kleists* (Frankfurt am Main: Athenäum, 1962);

Peter Horn, "Hatte Kleist Rassenvorurteile?: Eine kritische Auseinandersetzung mit der Literatur zur 'Verlobung in St. Domingo,' " *Monatshefte für deutschen Unterricht, deutsche Sprache und Literatur*, 67 (1975): 117-128;

Jahresgabe der Heinrich von Kleist-Gesellschaft, 1962, 1964, 1965-1966, 1968, edited by Walter Müller-Seidel (Berlin: Schmidt, 1962-1969);

Klaus Kanzog, *Edition und Engagement: 150 Jahre Editionsgeschichte der Werke Heinrich von Kleists*, 2 volumes (Berlin: De Gruyter, 1979);

Kleist-Jahrbuch (1980-1986);

Friedrich Koch, *Heinrich von Kleist: Bewusstsein und Wirklichkeit* (Stuttgart: Metzler, 1958);

Max Kommerell, "Die Sprache und das Unaussprechliche: Eine Betrachtung über Heinrich von Kleist," in his *Geist und Buchstabe der Dichtung: Goethe, Schiller, Kleist, Hölderlin*, fourth edition (Frankfurt am Main: Klostermann, 1956), pp. 243-317;

Helmut Koopmann, "Das 'rätselhafte Faktum' und seine Vorgeschichte: Zum analytischen Charakter der Novellen Heinrich von Kleists," *Zeitschrift für deutsche Philologie*, 84 (1965): 508-550;

Hans Joachim Kreutzer, *Die dichterische Entwicklung Heinrich von Kleists: Untersuchungen zu sei-

nen Briefen und zu Chronologie und Aufbau seiner Werke* (Berlin: Schmidt, 1968);

Clara Kuoni, *Wirklichkeit und Idee in Heinrich von Kleists Frauenerleben* (Leipzig: Huber, 1937);

Robert Labhardt, *Metapher und Geschichte: Kleists dramatische Metaphorik bis zur 'Penthesilea' als Widerspiegelung seiner geschichtlichen Position* (Kronberg im Taunus: Scriptor, 1976);

Örjan Lindberger, *The Transformations of Amphitryon* (Stockholm: Almqvist & Wiksell, 1956);

Georg Lukács, "Die Tragödie Heinrich von Kleists," in his *Deutsche Realisten des 19. Jahrhunderts* (Bern: Francke, 1951), pp. 19-48;

Thomas Mann, "Kleists 'Amphitryon': Eine Wiedereroberung," in his *Gesammelte Werke in zwölf Bänden*, volume 9: *Reden und Aufsätze*, part 1 (Frankfurt am Main: Fischer, 1960), pp. 187-228;

Hans Mayer, *Heinrich von Kleist: Der geschichtliche Augenblick* (Pfullingen: Neske, 1962);

James M. McGlathery, *Desire's Sway: The Plays and Stories of Heinrich von Kleist* (Detroit: Wayne State University Press, 1983);

Heinrich Meyer-Benfey, *Das Drama Heinrich von Kleists*, 2 volumes (Göttingen: Hapke, 1911-1913);

Walter Müller-Seidel, *Versehen und Erkennen: Eine Studie über Heinrich von Kleist* (Cologne & Graz: Böhlau, 1961);

Müller-Seidel, ed., *Heinrich von Kleist: Aufsätze und Essays* (Darmstadt: Wissenschaftliche Buchgesellschaft, 1967);

Heinz Politzer, "Kleists Trauerspiel vom Traum: 'Prinz Friedrich von Homburg,' " *Euphorion*, 64 (1970): 200-220; republished in Politzer's *Hatte Ödipus einen Ödipus-Komplex?: Versuche zum Thema Psychoanalyse und Literatur* (Munich: Piper, 1974), pp. 156-181;

William C. Reeve, *In Pursuit of Power: Heinrich von Kleist's Machiavellian Protagonists* (Toronto: University of Toronto Press, 1987);

Ewald Rösch, "Bett und Richterstuhl: Gattungsgeschichtliche Überlegungen zu Kleists Lustspiel *Der zerbrochene Krug*," in *Kritische Bewahrung: Beiträge zur deutschen Philologie: Festschrift für Werner Schröder zum 60. Geburtstag*, edited by Ernst-Joachim Schmidt (Berlin: Schmidt, 1974), pp. 434-475;

Alfred Schlagdenhauffen, *L'Univers Existentiel de Kleist dans le Prince de Hombourg* (Paris: Société d'Édition les Belles Lettres, 1953);

Jochen Schmidt, *Heinrich von Kleist: Studien zu seiner poetischen Verfahrensweise* (Tübingen: Niemeyer, 1974);

Schriften der Kleist-Gesellschaft, 1 (1921)-19 (1939);

Gerhard Schulz, "Kleists 'Bettelweib von Locarno': Eine Ehegeschichte?," *Jahrbuch der Deutschen Schiller-Gesellschaft*, 18 (1974): 431-440;

Walter Silz, *Heinrich von Kleist: Studies in His Works and Literary Character* (Philadelphia: University of Pennsylvania Press, 1961);

Ernst Ludwig Stahl, *Heinrich von Kleist's Dramas* (Oxford: Blackwell, 1948);

Anthony Stephens, " 'Eine Träne auf den Brief': Zum Status der Ausdrucksformen in Kleists Erzählungen," *Jahrbuch der Deutschen Schiller-Gesellschaft*, 28 (1984): 315-348;

Siegfried Streller, *Das dramatische Werk Heinrich von Kleists* (Berlin: Rütten & Loening, 1966);

Rudolf Unger, *Herder, Novalis und Kleist: Studien über die Entwicklung des Todesproblems in Denken und Dichten vom Sturm und Drang zur Romantik* (Frankfurt am Main: Diesterweg, 1922), pp. 88-143;

Ulrich Vohland, *Bürgerliche Emanzipation in Heinrich von Kleists Dramen und theoretischen Schriften* (Bern: Herbert Lang/Frankfurt am Main: Peter Lang, 1976);

Hermann J. Weigand, "Das Motiv des Vertrauens im Drama Heinrichs von Kleist," *Monatshefte für deutschen Unterricht, deutsche Sprache und Literatur*, 30 (1938): 233-245;

Weigand, "Das Vertrauen in Kleists Erzählungen," *Monatshefte für deutschen Unterricht und deutsche Sprache und Literatur*, 34 (1942): 49-63, 126-144;

Hans Wolff, *Heinrich von Kleist als politischer Dichter* (Berkeley: University of California Press, 1947).

Papers:
Heinrich von Kleist's papers are in the Westdeutsche Bibliothek, Marburg; the Staatsbibliothek Berlin; the Universitätsbibliothek Tübingen; and the Universitätsbibliothek Heidelberg.

Theodor Körner

(23 September 1791-26 August 1813)

Mark R. McCulloh

Davidson College

BOOKS: *Den Manen Carl Friedrich Schneiders von Seinen hier studierenden Freunden* (Freiberg, 1809);

Unserm Freunde . . . Biedermann, anonymous (Leipzig, 1810);

Knospen (Leipzig: Göschen, 1810); translated by Charles W. Hubner as *Wild Flowers: Poems* (New York: Author's Publishing Company, 1877);

Kurze Darstellung der kirchlichen Feierlichkeit bei der Vereidung und Einseegnung des preußischen Freijägerkorps . . . nebst der . . . Rede von Herrn Prediger Peters (Breslau: Max, 1813);

Drei deutsche Gedichte (Berlin: Nicolai, 1813);

Zwölf freie deutsche Gedichte: Nebst einem Anhang, edited by Wilhelm Kunz (Leipzig: Weygand, 1813); enlarged by Christian Gottfried Körner as *Leyer und Schwerdt: Einzige rechtmäßige, von dem Vater des Dichters veranstaltete Ausgabe* (Berlin: Nicolai, 1814); translated by W. B. Chorley as *The Lyre and the Sword, with a Life of the Author and His Letters* (London: Hamilton, Adams, 1834);

Jägerlied fürs Königl. Preußische Freikorps (N.p., 1813);

Lied zu der feyerlichen Einseegnung des k. preußischen Freykorps am 27. März 1813 (Breslau: Kreuzers-Scholz, 1813);

Dramatische Beyträge, 3 volumes (Vienna: Wallishauser, 1813-1815)—comprises volume 1, *Toni: Ein Drama in drei Aufzügen,* translated by William Stursberg as *Toni: A Drama in Three Acts* (New York, 1864); *Die Braut: Lustspiel in einem Aufzuge; Der grüne Domino: Ein Lustspiel in Alexandrinern, in einem Aufzuge; Der Nachtwächter: Eine Posse in Versen in einem Aufzuge;* volume 2, *Der vierjährige Posten: Singspiel in einem Aufzug,* translated by Samuel Gordon as *The Faithful Sentry: Opera in One Act* (London: St. Cecilia, 1899); *Der Vetter aus Bremen: Ein Spiel in Versen und einem Aufzug; Joseph Heyderich oder Deutsche Treue,* translated by J. Pym Johnston as *Joseph Heyderich; or, Military Fidelity: An Authentic Incident, Dra-*

Theodor Körner (chalk drawing by his sister Emma; courtesy of the Körnermuseum, Dresden)

matised in One Act (London: Senior, 1838); *Hedwig, die Banditenbraut: Drama in drei Aufzügen,* translated by Mrs. Burton Daveny as *Hedwig; or, Love and Gratitude: A Drama in Three Acts* (Norwich, U.K.: Miller, 1878); *Die Gouvernante: Eine Posse in einem Aufzuge;* volume 3, *Zriny: Ein Trauerspiel in fünf Aufzügen,* translated by R. E. de Beer as *Sigeth and Zriny* (London: Wildy, 1936); *Rosamunde: Ein Trauerspiel in fünf Aufzügen,* translated anonymously as *Rosamond: A Tragedy* (London: Kidd, 1830);

An das Volk der Sachsen: Im April 1813, anonymous (N.p., 1813);

Für Theodor Körner's Freunde (Dresden: Gärtner, 1814);

Gedichte vor und im heiligen Kriege gesungen (N.p., 1814);

Lob teutscher Helden gesungen, by Körner and Ernst Moritz Arndt (N.p., 1814);

Theodor Körners poetischer Nachlaß: Vermischte Gedichte und Erzählungen, edited by Christian Gottfried Körner and C. A. Tiedge, 2 volumes (Leipzig: Hartknoch, 1814-1815);

Sämmtliche Werke: In Auftrage der Mutter des Dichters herausgegeben (Berlin: Nicolai, 1834);

Körners Werke in zwei Teilen: Auf Grund der Hempelschen Ausgabe neu herausgegeben, edited by Augusta Weldler-Steinberg, 2 volumes (Berlin: Bong, 1908);

Theodor Körners sämtliche Werke: Hundertjahr-Jubelausgabe, edited by Eugen Wildenow (Leipzig: Hesse & Becker, 1913);

Körners Werke, edited by Hans Zimmer, 2 volumes (Leipzig & Vienna: Bibliographisches Institut, 1916).

Edition in English: *A Selection from the Poems and Dramatic Works of Theodor Körner,* translated by Mme Lucien Davésiès de Pontès (London: Williams & Norgate, 1850)–includes *The Expiation (Die Sühne), Antonia (Toni), Hedwig, Rosamond (Rosamunde), The Fisherman's Daughter (Das Fischermädchen), On Hate and Love (Haß und Liebe), The Spirits of the Mountain (Die Bergknappen), The Fight with the Dragon (Der Kampf mit dem Drachen), Alfred the Great (Alfred der Große), The Doves (Die Tauben), The Harp (Die Harfe),* and *The Roses (Die Rosen).*

Were it not for a small group of patriotic poems immortalized by his reputed Heldentod (hero's death) in battle against the forces of Napoleon, Theodor Körner would probably deserve mention as nothing more than a minor poet and dramatist whose influential father, Dr. Christian Gottfried Körner, cultivated the acquaintance of many central literary figures of Goethe's day. In fact, Goethe counted the elder Körner among his friends and consequently promoted the brief career of Körner's only son, Theodor, with several acts of patronage. Yet it was not Goethe's patronage, nor any critical consensus on the quality of the younger Körner's works, that established him as a figure of literary and cultural importance in the German-speaking world, but the patriotic expression of his characteristic impulsiveness and single-mindedness at a time of great tumult in Europe. On 15 March 1813 in a dramatic gesture that came only two weeks after Prussia joined

with Russia to oppose Napoleon, Körner bid his fiancée farewell and abandoned his career in Vienna in order to join the Prussian cavalry forces. He was killed near Schwerin on 26 August 1813 and quickly was endowed with a kind of martyrdom. Indeed, through his act of self-sacrifice he personified the unification of the poet and the man of action; he represented the sensitive and exuberant young artist whose creative vigor as a writer is also matched by worldly deeds of great historical import. For many at the time who read his poems of liberation and love for the fatherland (or heard these performed as songs), he came to embody the spirit of the age. Later, after liberal-democratic hopes for a unified Germany were betrayed by the restoration of the old order in the wake of Napoleon's defeat, Körner's martyrdom became a revolutionary symbol. Significantly, the student Carl Ludwig Sand is said to have carried with him a copy of Körner's *Leyer und Schwerdt* (1814; translated as *The Lyre and the Sword,* 1834) when, on 23 March 1819, he assassinated August von Kotzebue, who was then serving as a representative of the Russian government in Mannheim.

Körner was born in Dresden on 23 September 1791, the son of a distinguished jurist in the service of Saxony. Both Körner's mother, Maria Jacobine Stock, and his father pursued literary interests, and their home in Dresden often was the scene of high-toned gatherings of artists and literati, for their circle of friends included Goethe, Heinrich von Kleist, Alexander and Wilhelm Freiherr von Humboldt, Karl Friedrich Zelter, Christian Garve, Friedrich Nicolai, Ludwig Tieck, Friedrich and August Wilhelm von Schlegel, and Novalis, to name but a few. Dr. Körner was an especially close friend of Friedrich Schiller, whose ballads were undoubtedly among the first poems encountered by young Körner.

Körner's father held unconventional attitudes toward the education of children and attempted to raise his son as "naturally" as possible according to the tenets of Jean Jacques Rousseau and the pedagogue Johann Friedrich Herbart. Strict discipline was avoided, replaced by moral encouragement. Körner, who was a sickly child in his earliest years, remained in his father's house until his seventeenth year. He received instruction at home from private tutors, including one student of Johann Heinrich Pestalozzi. Körner showed a talent for mathematics and the natural sciences but did not advance in the study of languages, which did not appeal to him.

At seventeen Körner entered the Freiberg Bergakademie (School of Mines), probably on the advice of Novalis, who himself had studied at Freiberg and was a frequent visitor in the Körner home. Indeed, Körner pursued his theoretical interests under Novalis's teacher, Abraham Gottlob Werner, and remained in Freiberg almost two years. Yet the practical side of mineralogy did not ultimately suit the restless youth, and his romantic enthusiasm for the simple life and the "eternal night" of the mines, as expressed in some early poems such as "Berglied" (Song of the Mountain) and "Bergmannsleben" (Life of the Miner), did not translate into a career in mineralogy. His sojourn in the Oberlausitz and the Silesian mountains under the tutelage of Count von Gessler in the summer of 1809 gave him practical experience in the mines but doubtlessly awakened a stronger passion for the artistic over the scientific description of nature. The lyrical poems "Buchwald" and "Sonnenaufgang auf der Riesenkoppe" (Sunrise on the Riesenkoppe) are the product of his experience of the Silesian landscape.

In 1810 Körner abandoned his studies at Freiberg and moved to Leipzig to read philosophy. There he published his first collection of poems in a small volume titled *Knospen* (1810; translated as *Wild Flowers*, 1877). Student life in Leipzig at that time was polarized by enmity between the aristocratic and liberal bourgeois contingents, and Körner joined in the conflict on the side of the liberals with characteristic ardor. After a duel and subsequent arrest, he was forced to flee in the spring of 1811, making his way via Berlin (where he enrolled briefly at the new University) to Karlsbad, where he spent the summer convalescing from an attack of fever. He began writing poems on the local landscape and the folk legends of the region, as well as some of his first love poems. In the meantime, Körner's father, who believed that the atmosphere at German universities had proved too provocative for his son's "fiery" temperament, arranged for him to go to Vienna, where he might regain his academic stability under the influence of Wilhelm von Humboldt and the Schlegels. He changed subjects once again and began reading history at the University of Vienna as recommended by Humboldt, but by that time he had determined to become a dramatist and pursued his studies exclusively for the purpose of collecting material for historical drama.

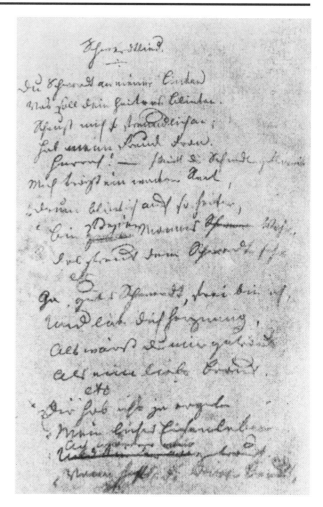

Manuscript for Körner's last poem, from his notebook, 23 August 1813 (Bilderatlas zur Geschichte der Deutschen Nationalliteratur, 1895)

In Vienna in the autumn of 1811 Körner completed his first truly ambitious works, the verse comedies *Die Braut* (The Fiancée), *Der grüne Domino* (The Green Domino), and *Der Nachtwächter* (The Nightwatchman), all clearly showing the influence of Kotzebue. Körner seems to have had no difficulty getting his plays performed. More comedies followed, but Körner was also at work on serious historical dramas. His writing was, as always, prolific. In 1812 alone he was working on several historical or quasi-historical plays: *Toni*, *Rosamunde*, and *Zriny*, which is generally considered his best play. These followed the success in Vienna of several light theater pieces and farces that, though tightly constructed and amusing, rely too obviously on unoriginal motifs (trifling obstacles to marriage, mistaken identity, and so forth) for their comic effect. Two of the last comedies, *Der Vetter aus Bremen* (The Cousin from Bremen) and *Die Gouvernante* (The Governess), met with considerable popular acclaim. *Die Gouvernante,* a harmless satire of the stuffy and overprotective older generation, entered the repertory in Berlin and had over sixty performances. All of these plays were published in his three-volume collection, *Dramatische Beyträge* (Dramatic Contributions), which appeared from 1813 to 1815.

Yet it was Körner's wish to be taken seriously as a dramatist. *Die Sühne,* his first real effort in that regard, is a Schicksalstragödie, a tragedy of fate in the tradition of Zacharias Werner's *Vierundzwanzigster Februar* (The Twenty-fourth of February, 1810). It is a one-act tale of royal obsession, intrigue, and murder, and while Goethe favored it with a premier in Weimar, the censors in Vienna would not allow it to be performed. *Toni,* on the other hand, was performed before enthusiastic audiences in the Austrian capital in the summer of 1812 but owed much of its success to the talent of Körner's fiancée, Antonie ("Toni") Adamberger, who performed the title role. The play is essentially a dramatization of Kleist's 1811 novella "Die Verlobung in St. Domingo" (translated as "The Engagement in Santo Domingo," 1960), which Körner had read in the July 1811 issue of a Viennese journal. As such the play is disappointing, being too hurried in its development and too blatant in its pathos. Like most of Körner's work, it was composed in haste. Nonetheless, Goethe presented the play in Weimar and wrote Körner's father of his son's youthful talent and great promise.

Körner's next play, *Zriny,* was his first noncomedy to be performed not only in Vienna but also in Berlin, then Dresden. The story centers around the sixteenth-century Hungarian general Nicholas Zrinyi and his heroic but doomed defense of the city of Svigetvar against the Turkish armies of Suleiman the Magnificent. The theme of patriotic resistance to tyrannical invaders clearly suggests a subversive allegory of Napoleonic domination of the Germans, although the primary controversy surrounding the play was caused by the obvious issue of Hungarian nationalism within the Austrian empire. Yet despite the compelling mood of impending disaster created by Körner, the play has an oddly static effect due in large part to the absence of any profound character development, as Hans Zimmer has pointed out in his 1916 edition of Körner's works. There is much in this tragedy, as in the others by Körner, that bears the mark of Schiller's influence in style as well as content; Körner was especially passionate about Schiller's Freiheitsideal (ideal of liberty as a universal goal of human history). In fact, Körner was soon given the epithet "Vienna's second Schiller."

Rosamunde is a quieter, subtler tragedy, based on the story of Henry II's illicit love for "Fair Rosamond" in Thomas Percy's *Reliques of Ancient English Poetry* (1765). It is a play that, like the other tragedies, shows women in major roles, although the women here also suffer Körner's pallid characterization. Evidently Körner drained the English Rosamond of her passion and impulsivity at least partly on purpose, making her pure and spiritual so as to fit the role to Antonie Adamberger's dramatic requirements and proclivities. The character of Henry's beloved thus acquires a crippling ambiguity, functioning more as a second, better wife than as an extramarital rival for Queen Eleanor; the erotic attraction of Henry and his mistress is attributed to Rosamunde's self-proclaimed "weakness." Because of the virtually chaste characterization of the leading role, *Rosamunde* met with considerable interest in Victorian England, where Körner became the best known of the minor German poets.

Körner would never see *Rosamunde* performed. The tumultuous events of 1813 would soon interrupt his literary career. Meanwhile, Goethe (who in the winter of 1816 presented *Rosamunde* in Weimar) invited the young poet-dramatist to be his guest for a time in Weimar, but Körner declined when he received word he had been appointed Theaterdichter (theater poet) to the Viennese Court, a position he took up in January of 1813. Körner's last dramatic composition, *Joseph Heyderich; oder Deutsche Treue* (1813-1815; translated as *Joseph Heyderich; or Military Fidelity,* 1838), like his short story "Woldemar," was based on accounts of Austrian campaigns against Napoleon in Italy. This one-act sketch of a modest corporal's brave sacrifice is made cumbersome by its unrelenting patriotic fervor and the obsequiousness of the main character.

Before his death Körner finished several opera libretti and was beginning to make a name for himself among composers. Beethoven had discussed a collaborative effort with him, as had Louis Spohr. Körner's youthful musical interests (many of his poems were written to hymns and folk songs, and he himself was an accomplished singer) might have led him on to great achievements under the guidance of such luminaries. At least one opera, *Der vierjährige Posten* (1813; translated as *The Faithful Sentry*, 1899) stood the test of time to be revived in England in 1899.

Körner's most famous works are the poems associated with his death. Like so many young men and women of his day, Körner was impassioned by the liberal-democratic vision of a unified German nation freed from French domination, and he wrote a number of ebulliently patriotic poems before and after joining, in March 1813, the Prussian forces marshaling against Napoleon. The most famous poem of this final period is the rousing "Lützows wilde Jagd" ("Lützow's Wild Chase"), a tribute to the commander of the volunteer unit in which Körner served. In the following decades many composers, including Zelter, Carl Loewe, and Carl Maria von Weber, set the poem to music, but Franz Schubert's 1815 rendition is probably best known. "Was uns bleibt" is a notable song of undaunted determination to struggle and maintain, in the face of almost certain defeat, a kind of Graeco-Christian ideal of the new Germany. Other renowned poems are "Abschied vom Leben," written as he lay suffering from his first set of wounds on 17 and 18 June 1813, and "Frisch auf, mein Volk, die Flammenzeichen rauchen" (Arise, my people, the signal fires are burning!). These and others became well known through Wilhelm Kunze's publication of Körner's *Zwölf freie deutsche Gedichte* (Twelve Free German Poems) in November 1813, although the author was already dead at the time, and through the larger posthumous collection *Leyer und Schwerdt*, which was published by Körner's father in 1814. From the latter collection, the famous "Schwerdtlied" (Sword Song) or "Du Schwerdt an meiner Linken" (Thou sword at my left) is supposed to have been written after Körner was mortally wounded in a skirmish at Gadebusch in Mecklenburg on 26 August 1813, although some scholars dismiss as fiction this romantic vision of the poet composing a rallying, sixteen-stanza song as he lies dying.

Intent on honoring their son's memory and preserving his work, Körner's parents acted to collect and make available all of his writings. His father edited and published *Theodor Körners poetischer Nachlaß* within a year after the appearance of *Leyer und Schwerdt*. In 1834 Maria Körner released a new edition of his collected works. Not all voices praised the youthful poet, however, in life or in death. Some contemporaries were quite frank in their distaste for his prolific work; Heinrich Heine and Friedrich Hebbel both consid-

ered him a writer of little talent. Ludwig Tieck was critical. Yet in the years after Körner's death by sword his fame grew, fueled by harsh repression in the German-speaking states. Liberal journals such as *Die Gartenlaube* cultivated his memory, and an admiring "cult" took shape. Right-wing patriots accepted him as a national poetic figure of legendary proportions during the Prussian wars of conquest in the latter half of the nineteenth century, and statues in his honor were erected in Dresden and elsewhere.

The centennials of Körner's birth in 1891 and his death in 1913 were accompanied by substantial scholarly attention, whereas by the second half of the twentieth century he was virtually forgotten due to the general rejection in Germany of most forms of patriotic rhetoric in the wake of two disastrous World Wars, and to the growing conviction that Körner never should have received recognition as anything but a "third-rate" writer. On the occasion of the sesquicentennial of his death in 1963, only two critical articles appeared. Körner has been celebrated more enthusiastically in the German Democratic Republic, where he has been recognized since 1954 as a Russophile and a soldier of liberation.

By all accounts, Goethe's quiet support of Körner's ambitions was given more out of respect for the young man's father than out of unequivocal admiration for the young man's work. Körner's very nature was opposed to that of the established Goethe. Körner was impetuous, unrestrained, and wrote much and corrected little–a truly romantic figure, perhaps, but hardly of the same predilections as the older Goethe, who had long since returned to the disciplined aesthetics of the classics. As Körner himself put it to his father in a letter of 20 May 1812, "du kennst mich, mein warmes Blut, meine ungeschwächte Kraft, meine wilde Phantasie . . . mein kindliches Herz" (you know me, my hotbloodedness, my undiminishing power, my wild phantasy . . . my childish heart). In addition to these qualities, his patriotic fervor was hardly shared by Goethe, who was cosmopolitan in sympathy and whose respect for Napoleon is well known. Thus, the fame Körner would achieve as a patriot-poet was of little value in Goethe's mind. In any case, Körner appeared briefly on the literary horizon in the Age of Goethe largely because of the circumstances of his birth and death.

Letters:
Theodor Körners Briefwechsel mit den Seinen, edited

234

by A. Weldler-Steinberg (Leipzig: Quelle & Meyer, 1910).

Biographies:
E. Peschel and E. Wildenow, *Theodor Körner und die Seinen*, 2 volumes (Leipzig: Seemann, 1898);
Karl Berger, *Theodor Körner* (Bielefeld & Leipzig: Velhagen & Klasing, 1912).

References:
W. Barton, "Theodor Körners Schwanengesang," *Jahrbuch der Wittheit zu Bremen*, 8, no. 4 (1964): 23-39;
Erhard Jöst, "Der Heldentod des Dichters Theodor Körner," *Orbis Litterarum*, 32 (Summer 1977): 310-340;
R. Musiol, *Theodor Körner und seine Beziehungen zur Musik* (Ratibor: Simmich, 1893);

Edith Rothe, "Nochmals: Theodor Körner–Sänger und Held?," *Neue Deutsche Literatur*, 3 (March 1955): 115-118;
V. Stockley, *German Literature as Known in England 1750-1830* (London: Routledge, 1929), pp. 201-206;
Helena Szepe, "Opfertod und Poesie: Zur Geschichte der Theodor-Körner-Legende," *Colloquium Germanica*, 9 (Spring 1975): 291-304.

Papers:
Theodor Körner's papers are at the Institut und Museum für Geschichte der Stadt Dresden and the Museum für Geschichte der Stadt Leipzig. All but a handful of personal effects and documents were lost in the bombardment that destroyed the Körner Museum in Dresden during World War II.

Wilhelm Müller
(7 October 1794-1 October 1827)

H. M. Waidson
University of Wales, Swansea

BOOKS: *Bundesblüthen,* by Müller, Graf Friedrich von Kalckreuth, Graf Georg von Blankensee, Wilhelm Hensel, and Wilhelm von Studnitz (Berlin: Maurer, 1816);

Rom, Römer und Römerinnen: Eine Sammlung vertrauter Briefe aus Rom und Albano mit einigen späteren Zusätzen und Belegen, 2 volumes (Berlin: Duncker & Humblot, 1820);

Sieben und siebenzig Gedichte aus den hinterlassenen Papieren eines reisenden Waldhornisten (Dessau: Ackermann, 1821);

Lieder der Griechen, 2 volumes (Dessau: Ackermann, 1821-1822; volume 1 republished, enlarged by the poem "Byron," 1825);

Neue Lieder der Griechen, 2 volumes (Leipzig: Brockhaus, 1823);

Gedichte aus den hinterlassenen Papieren eines reisenden Waldhornisten (Dessau: Ackermann, 1824); republished as *Lieder des Lebens und der Liebe* (Dessau: Ackermann, 1824);

Homerische Vorschule: Eine Einleitung in des Studium der Ilias und Odyssee (Leipzig: Brockhaus, 1824);

Neueste Lieder der Griechen (Leipzig: Voß, 1824);

Missolunghi (Dessau: Published by the author, 1826);

Lyrische Reisen und epigrammatische Spaziergänge (Leipzig: Voß, 1827);

Vermischte Schriften, edited by Gustav Schwab, 5 volumes (Leipzig: Brockhaus, 1830);

Gedichte, edited by Schwab, 2 volumes (Leipzig: Brockhaus, 1837);

Gedichte: Vollständige kritische Ausgabe, edited by J. T. Hatfield (Berlin: Behr, 1906);

Rheinreise von 1827 sowie Gedichte und Briefe, edited by Paul Wahl (Dessau: Schwalbe, 1931).

OTHER: *Blumenlese aus den Minnesingern: Erste Sammlung,* edited by Müller (Berlin: Maurer, 1816);

Christopher Marlowe, *Doktor Faustus,* translated by Müller (Berlin: Maurer, 1818);

Askania: Zeitschrift für Leben, Literatur und Kunst,

Wilhelm Müller (after an oil painting by Hensel)

edited by Müller, 6 issues (Dessau: Ackermann, 1820);

Bibliothek deutscher Dichter des siebzehnten Jahrhunderts, edited by Müller, 10 volumes (Leipzig: Brockhaus, 1822-1827);

Egeria: Sammlung italienischer Volkslieder, aus mündlicher Überliefarung und fliegenden Blättern, edited by Müller, completed by O. L. B. Wolff (Leipzig: Fleischer, 1829).

PERIODICAL PUBLICATIONS: "The Earliest Poems of Wilhelm Müller," edited by James Taft Hatfield, *Publications of the Modern Language Association,* 13 (1898);

"Unpublished Letters of Wilhelm Müller," edited by Hatfield, *American Journal of Philology,* 24 (1903).

Wilhelm Müller was caught up and influenced by the urge to find simplicity and homeliness in the folk-song tradition, while at the same time his verse reflected his widely ranging knowledge of German and European literature. His work as editor, reviewer, and translator demonstrates his critical ability, his alert understanding, and his energy. He was liberal in politics, happy that Napoleon's defeat in 1815 might mean freedom for German people from foreign domination. He became impatient with the censorship imposed in the years following and sponsored enthusiastically the cause of the Greeks in their struggle against Turkish oppression. In his political interests he had something in common with the Young German movement. Some of his lyrical poems are widely known through having been set to music by Franz Schubert in some of his finest songwriting. Although the music of the two song cycles is particularly outstanding, the poet's words have their positive contribution to make too, with their evocation both of an idyllic and of a tragic landscape.

Johann Ludwig Wilhelm Müller was the son of Christian Leopold Müller, a tailor in Dessau, and Maire Leopoldine Cellarius Müller. His mother gave birth to seven children, of whom only Wilhelm attained adulthood, and she herself died when he was fourteen. At the age of eighteen Müller enrolled in the newly founded Berlin University to study language, literature, and history. He joined the Prussian army in February 1813, the time of the national uprising against Napoleon. He returned to Berlin to study in November 1814 and began to have contact with literary figures there. Literature soon became his major interest. In addition to writing his own verse, he also engaged in editorial enterprises. His translation of Christopher Marlowe's *Doctor Faustus* (1818) gained him acclaim and was reprinted several times. Between November 1817 and Easter 1818 he toured Italy as traveling companion to a courtier, Baron von Sack, and after a disagreement with the baron, he remained in Rome for the summer of 1818. Müller had popular success with his fluently written, cheerful, and informative account of varied aspects of life in Italy, mainly in and near Rome, in a series of letters titled *Rom, Römer und Römerinnen* (Rome, Roman Men and Roman Women, 1820). In 1819 he obtained a post as teacher, mainly of classics, at the Bürgerschule at Dessau; he was appointed as director of the ducal library in 1820 and found this post more congenial. On 21 May 1821 he mar-

ried Adelheid von Basedow, the granddaughter of the educationist Johann Bernhard von Basedow. Theirs was a happy marriage which produced a daughter, Auguste, and a son, Friedrich Max. This was an important time for Müller as a writer as well, for his substantial collection of original poems *Sieben und siebenzig Gedichte aus den hinterlassenen Papieren eines reisenden Waldhornisten* (Seventy-seven Poems from the Posthumous Papers of a Traveling Horn-player, 1821) had been published, as well as the collection *Lieder der Griechen* (Songs of the Greeks, 1821-1822).

The sequence of poems "Die schöne Müllerin" (The Beautiful Miller's Daughter), which opens *Sieben und siebenzig Gedichte aus den hinterlassen Papieren eines reisenden Waldhornisten* was set to music by Schubert and by other composers. "Die schöne Müllerin" originated as a group undertaking by Müller and some friends gathered in Berlin toward the end of 1816. The poet distances himself from the action by means of an ironic prologue and epilogue but otherwise uses the point of view of the protagonist, a miller's apprentice. The apprentice follows the brook which has enchanted him; it leads him to the mill and to the miller's daughter, with whom he falls in love. In "Ungeduld" (Impatience), the protagonist wants to write everywhere the phrase "Dein ist mein Herz, und soll es ewig bleiben" (Yours is my heart and shall remain so eternally). The apprentice's happiness in love is darkened by the realization that his beloved prefers his rival, the huntsman. He seeks and finds death in the stream.

Most of the poems in the book use regular rhythms and rhyme schemes in the folk-song manner. The ten poems of "Johannes und Esther" are serious in their description of two lovers against a contemporary Christmastime background. "Reiselieder" (Travel Songs) center upon lovers who are separated by their work from their beloved ones. "Ländliche Lieder" (Rural Songs) is again concerned with the separation of lovers, while "Die Monate" (The Months) is a sonnet sequence. "Musterkarte" (Model Card) which concludes this collection, contains the somber ballad "Der Glockenguss zu Breslau" (The Casting of the Bell in Breslau) in its twelve poems.

The collection *Gedichte aus den hinterlassenen Papieren eines reisenden Waldhornisten* (Poems from the Posthumous Papers of a Traveling Horn-player, 1824) contains the sequence "Die Winterreise," which Schubert composed as a song cycle shortly before his death. If, in "Die schöne

Wilhelm Müller's birthplace circa 1880. The house was destroyed in 1945 in an air raid (Cecilia C. Baumann, Wilhelm Müller: The Poet of the Schubert Song Cycles*).*

Müllerin," the miller's apprentice moves from isolation to a community in springtime, the protagonist in "Die Winterreise," a single man rejected by a woman who prefers a wealthier suitor, prepares to go off alone in winter. The emotional response to the cold is graphically presented in "Gefrorene Tränen" (Frozen Tears) and "Erstarrung" (Congealment). "Der Lindenbaum" (The Linden Tree) has become, with Schubert's music, probably the best known of these poems; this is the song, a wanderer's vision of home, with which Hans Castorp, at the end of Thomas Mann's *Der Zauberberg* (1924; translated as *The Magic Mountain*, 1927), confronts his experience of the war in 1914. Frost has given the young man's black hair a gray, elderly impression ("Der greise Kopf," The Aged Head). His loss of hope is evoked by the image of the last leaf being blown off a tree ("Letzte Hoffnung," Last Hope). As he passes unseen at night in "Im Dorfe" (In the Village) the young man declares that he has now finished with dreaming, but in "Täuschung" (Disillusionment) he admits the charm of self-deception. The final poem of the cycle, "Der Leiermann" (The Hurdy-gurdy Man) describes the pathos of an old man who offers his art to a world that ignores him; shall the poet go with him and combine his verse with the old man's

music? Perhaps, for all the bitter irony of the hurdy-gurdy man as a symbol for society's evaluation of the imaginative artist there is a note of hope; the protagonist finally considers turning to a fellow human being in the real world for companionship and collaboration.

The remaining sequences in the collection seem slight when compared with "Die Winterreise." "Tafellieder für Liedertafeln" (Festive Songs for Male Choirs) celebrate the pleasures of wine-drinking. The bucolic poems of "Ländliche Lieder" (Rural Songs) are lighthearted in their delineation of the aspirations of young lovers. The theme of the wanderer is again presented in a group of six poems ("Wanderlieder," Songs of Wandering). The light verse of "Devisen zu Bonbons" (Mottoes for Bonbons) is reminiscent of the rococo.

In the 1820s Müller's sponsorship of the Greek struggle against the Turks in *Lieder der Griechen, Neue Lieder der Griechen* (New Songs of the Greeks, 1823), *Neueste Lieder der Griechen* (Newest Songs of the Greeks, 1824), and *Missolunghi* (1826) led to his being called "Griechen-Müller." The introductory poem of *Lieder der Griechen* urges the reader to be actively concerned about present-day Greece: "Das Alt' ist neu geworden, die Fern' ist euch so nah, / Was ihr erträumt so lange, leibhaftig steht es da . . ." (The old has become new, the distant is so close to you, what you have dreamt of so long is there, in flesh and blood . . .). An Austrian newspaper is criticized for its failure to sponsor the Greek cause in "Die Griechen an den Österreichischen Beobachter," (The Greeks to the Austrian Observer). "Die Ruinen von Athen an England" (The Ruins of Athens to England) expresses sharp indignation toward the British for their removal of precious Greek statuary to England. "Greichenlands Hoffnung" (The Hope of Greece) asserts that freedom will come only from the determination of the Greeks, not from foreign intervention. In "Die Eule" (The Owl) the owl calls for help on behalf of the harassed and helpless Greek women, children, and priests. Even if other countries are inactive, God has made a covenant with the sons of Hellas in "Der Bund mit Gott" (The Covenant with God). The death of Lord Byron at Missolunghi in 1824 is celebrated in heroic language; the poem "Byron" (1825), like much of Müller's verse associated with the Greek cause, uses long-lined rhyming couplets. Its elegiac mood is introduced by an initial quotation from Byron: "My task is done, my song has ceased, my theme / Has died into an echo." The fall of Missolunghi into Turkish hands in 1826 is remembered with sadness in four poems.

The mid 1820s were a time of busy literary activity for Müller, both as critic and editor as well as lyricist; he showed much interest in seventeenth-century German poetry and in Homer, as well as modern Greek and Italian folk songs. *Lyrische Reisen und epigrammatische Spaziergänge* (Lyrical Travels and Epigrammatic Walks), the last published collection of his verse in his lifetime, appeared in 1827. As the title indicates, the poet often gives here impressions of visits to unfamiliar places, as in "Lieder aus dem Meerbusen von Salerno" (Songs from the Bay of Salerno). "Ständchen in Ritornellen" (Serenades in Ritornelli) reveals Müller's interest in Italian folk song. Another section, "Reime aus den Inseln des Archipelagus" (Rhymes from the Islands of the Archipelago), collects adaptations of popular modern Greek songs. A fortnight's stay near Dresden provides the impetus for the sequence "Frühlingskranz" (Spring Wreath) which includes an effective evocation of the advent of the divine spirit over the earth in "Pfingsten" (Whitsuntide). The poems of "Muscheln von der Insel Rügen" (Shells from the Island of Rügen) are the outcome of a summer visit in 1825. Here scenes

from fisherfolk's daily lives are presented in "Muscheln" (Shells) and "Die Mewe" (The Sea Gull), while "Vineta," with its theme of the submerged city, has become one of Müller's best known poems. On 7 June 1826 Heinrich Heine sent a copy of his recently published *Die Nordsee* (The North Sea) to Müller, writing appreciatively of the latter's work: "Ich habe sehr früh schon das deutsche Volkslied auf mich einwirken lassen, . . . aber ich glaube erst in Ihren Liedern den reinen Klang und die wahre Einfachheit, wonach ich immer strebte, gefunden zu haben. Wie rein, wie klar sind Ihre Lieder und sämmtlich sind es Volkslieder" (I let the German folk song have its effect on me at a very early stage, . . . but I believe that I first found in your songs the pure sound and the true simplicity which I always sought. How pure and clear are your poems, and all of them are folk songs). The poems in "Lieder aus Franzensbad bei Eger" (Songs from Franzensbad, near Eger) are an outcome of the author's summer visit of 1826, while "Die schöne Kellnerin von Bacharach und ihre Gäste" (The Beautiful Waitress of Bacharach and Her Guests) consists of drinking songs. Two collections, each of a hundred epigrams, round off the volume; a model for Müller here was the work of Friedrich Logau.

Throughout the autumn and winter of 1826-1827 Müller continued to be active as a writer, but in the spring of 1827 he took leave from his library work, traveled, and was reputed to be looking ill; he died on 1 October 1827. As Cecilia C. Baumann has written: "Wilhelm Müller is not just the poet of the Schubert song cycles. A versatile and prolific poet, translator, literary critic, editor, scholar, and prose writer, his creative work brought him recognition far away from provincial Dessau . . . Müller's achievements during his short life are remarkable." He will no doubt be most widely remembered for having provided Schubert's musical imagination with a congenial and felicitous basis for two inspired song cycles, but his other poetry also forms a varied and characteristic contribution to German writing of the early nineteenth century.

References:

Cecilia C. Baumann, *Wilhelm Müller: The Poet of the Schubert Song Cycles. His Life and Works* (University Park & London: Pennsylvania State University Press, 1981);

Alan P. Cottrell, *Wilhelm Müller's Lyrical Song-Cycles: Interpretations and Texts* (Chapel Hill: University of North Carolina Press, 1970);

Arnold Feil, *Franz Schubert, "Die schöne Müllerin" und "Die Winterreise": Mit einem Essay "Wilhelm Müller und die Romantik" von Rolf Vollmann* (Stuttgart: Reclam, 1975);

Dietrich Fischer-Dieskau, *Schubert: A Biographical Study of His Songs*, translated by Kenneth S. Whitton (London: Cassell, 1976);

Günter Hartung, "Wilhelm Müller und das deutsche Volkslied," *Weimarer Beiträge*, 23 (1977);

Klaus Günther Just, "Wilhelm Müllers Liederzyklen 'Die schöne Müllerin' und 'Die Winterreise,'" *Zeitschrift für Deutsche Philologie*, 83 (1964);

Heinrich Lore, *Wilhelm Müller als Kritiker und Erzähler: Ein Lebensbild mit Briefen an F. A. Brockhaus und anderen Schriftstücken* (Leipzig: Brockhaus, 1927);

Helen Meredith Mustard, *The Lyrical Cycle in German Literature* (New York: King's Crown Press, 1946);

John Nollen, "Heine und Wilhelm Müller," *Modern Language Notes*, 17 (May 1902): 261-276;

Nigel Reeves, "The Art of Simplicity: Heinrich Heine and Wilhelm Müller," *Oxford German Studies*, 5 (1970);

Reinhold Steig, "Wilhelm Müllers Übersetzung von Marlowes Faust," *Euphorion*, 13 (1906).

Novalis
(Friedrich von Hardenberg)
(2 May 1772-25 March 1801)

William Arctander O'Brien
University of California, San Diego

EDITIONS: *Schriften,* edited by Friedrich Schlegel and Ludwig Tieck, 2 volumes (Berlin: Realschulbuchhandlung, 1802)–includes *Heinrich von Ofterdingen: Ein nachgelassener Roman,* translated by Palmer Hilty as *Henry von Ofterdingen* (New York: Ungar, 1964); "Geistliche Lieder"; and *Die Lehrlinge zu Sais,* translated by Ralph Manheim as *The Novices of Sais* (New York: Valentin, 1949);

Schriften, edited by Tieck and Schlegel, 2 volumes (Berlin: Realschulbuchhandlung, 1826)–includes "Die Christenheit oder Europa";

Schriften, edited by Paul Kluckhohn, Richard Samuel, Hans-Joachim Mähl, and Gerhard Schulz, 6 volumes (Stuttgart: Kohlhammer, 1975-1983);

Werke, Tagebücher und Briefe Friedrich von Hardenbergs, edited by Mähl and Samuel, 3 volumes (Munich: Hanser, 1978-1987).

Editions in English: "The Story of Hyacinth and Roseblossom," translated by Lillie Winter, in *German Classics of the Nineteenth and Twentieth Centuries,* edited by Kuno Francke and W. G. Howard, volume 4 (New York: German Publications Society, 1913;

Hyacinth and Rosebud, Eros and Fabel, translated by Florence Bryan and Kathe Roth (Aberdeen: Selma, 1955);

Sacred Songs of Novalis, translated by Eileen Hutchins (Aberdeen: Selma, 1956);

Hymns to the Night and Other Selected Writings, translated by Charles E. Passage (New York: Liberal Arts Press, 1960)–includes "Hymns to the Night," "Christianity or Europe," "Klingsohr's Fairy Tale," and selected aphorisms;

"Selected Aphorisms and Fragments," translated by Alexander Gelley, in *German Romantic Criticism,* edited by A. Leslie Willson (New York: Continuum, 1982), pp. 62-83–includes selections from "Pollen," "Miscellaneous Observations," "Logological Frag-

Novalis as a young man (oil portrait by Franz Gareis; photo by Foto-Kind, Weißenfels, used by permission of the Museum Weißenfels)

ments," "Dialogues 1 & 2" and "Monologue";

Selections from "Miscellaneous Writings," 6 "Dialogues," "Monologue," and the fragment "On Goethe," in *The Romantic Ironists and Goethe,* edited by Kathleen Wheeler (Cambridge: Cambridge University Press, 1984), pp. 83-111;

Hymns to the Night, translated by Dick Higgins, revised edition (New Paltz, N.Y.: McPherson, 1984).

PERIODICAL PUBLICATIONS: "Klagen eines Jünglings," *Der Neue Teutsche Merkur*, 37 (April 1791): 410-413;

"Blüthenstaub," *Athenaeum: Eine Zeitschrift*, 1 (April 1798): 70-106;

"Blumen," *Jahrbücher der Preußischen Monarchie unter der Regierung von Friedrich Wilhelm III.*, 2 (June 1798): 184ff;

"Glauben und Liebe, oder der König und die Königin," *Jahrbücher der Preußischen Monarchie unter der Regierung von Friedrich Wilhelm III.*, 2 (July 1798): 269-286;

"Hymnen an die Nacht," *Athenaeum: Eine Zeitschrift*, 3 (August 1800): 188-204; translated by Charles E. Passage as "Hymns to the Night" in *Hymns to the Night and Other Selected Writings* (New York: Liberal Arts Press, 1960).

Poet, aphorist, novelist, mystic, literary and political theoretician, student of philosophy and the natural sciences, Friedrich von Hardenberg–best known by his pen name, Novalis–was one of the most striking figures of German Romanticism. Hardenberg's theoretical writings helped establish the program of Early or Jena Romanticism, and his literary compositions rank among the most radical examples of Romantic experimentation in form. His best-known works remain the fragment collection "Blüthenstaub" (1798; selections translated as "Pollen," 1982), the rhapsodic essay "Die Christenheit oder Europa" (1799; translated as "Christianity or Europe," 1960), the poetic cycle "Hymnen an die Nacht" (1800; translated as "Hymns to the Night," 1960), and the unfinished novel *Heinrich von Ofterdingen* (1802; translated as *Henry von Ofterdingen*, 1964). The last two writings especially have secured Hardenberg's place in the history of letters, although his voluminous notebooks, which comprise the greatest part of his literary remains, have attracted much recent critical attention for their imaginative and often strikingly advanced treatment of literary, scientific, and philosophical issues. Both practical and enthusiastic, Hardenberg regarded his work in letters as a mere avocation beside his career in the Saxon civil service, and he published scarcely eighty pages of writings before his death at the age of twenty-eight. Celebrated or condemned in the nineteenth and early twentieth centuries primarily as the sweet poet of "the blue flower" (a striking image from *Heinrich von Ofterdingen* that came to symbolize the Romantic movement), Hardenberg has come to be recognized not only as an expressive and innovative poet of the German language, but as a daring, resourceful, and rigorous thinker at the threshold of modernity.

A direct descendant of twelfth-century Saxon nobility, the Freiherr (Baron) Georg Friedrich Philipp von Hardenberg was the second oldest of eleven children born into the quiet Pietistic household of Auguste Bernhardine (née von Bölzig) and Heinrich Ulrich Erasmus Freiherr von Hardenberg. Raised on the family estate of Oberwiederstedt, about eighty kilometers north of the cultural and academic centers of Leipzig and Jena, Hardenberg was a weak and slow child, who suddenly emerged as a sensitive and imaginative boy upon recovery from a prolonged case of dysentery in his ninth year. A brief visit for instruction with the religious Herrnhuter community in Neudietendorf appears to have ended unsuccessfully, and he was sent to live for a year with his uncle, a prestigious aristocrat of the ancien régime and Commander of the Teutonic Order at the opulent Lucklum castle. After having acquainted himself with the good library and more worldly society of his uncle, in 1785 Hardenberg rejoined his family at their new home in Weißenfels. At about this time he began to write poetry in the style of Friedrich Klopstock, Christoph Martin Wieland, and Gottfried August Bürger. In May 1789 a meeting with Bürger followed a correspondence in which the young admirer had exulted that a letter was written to him by the same hand that once wrote "Lenore" and wrestled with Homer.

In 1790, after studying at the Eisleben gymnasium under the distinguished classicist C. D. Jani, Hardenberg moved to Jena to begin university studies in jurisprudence. He quickly attached himself to the professor of Kantian philosophy, Karl Leonhard Reinhold, and to his history professor, the thirty-one-year-old Friedrich Schiller. Schiller, a lifelong acquaintance and influence, encouraged Hardenberg's interest in history, philosophy, poetry, and–at the request of the boy's father–his foundering study of jurisprudence. Hardenberg idolized his teacher, helped nurse him through severe illness in the winter of 1792, and followed his advice to transfer to the university at Leipzig in the fall. His feelings of inferiority before Schiller led directly to Hardenberg's first publication, the poem "Klagen eines Jünglings" (A Youth's Lament). A sentimental prayer for more manly "Sorgen, Elend und Beschwerden" (cares, misery and hardships), the poem was printed under the signature v. H***g. in Wieland's *Der Neue Teutsche Merkur* of April 1791.

At Leipzig Hardenberg met Friedrich Schlegel, who, though only two months older, assumed the role of mentor for his provincial friend. The two neglected their formal studies and abandoned themselves to a raucous student life, while Schlegel led Hardenberg deeper into the study of Kant, introduced him to more contemporary literature and criticism, and awakened his delight in the wit and paradox that would henceforth enliven his writing. In 1792 Hardenberg transferred to the University of Wittenberg. There he finally applied himself to his studies, and in the summer of 1794 he passed the state examinations in jurisprudence with the highest grade.

Having made little headway in securing a government post through a distant relative, the Prussian minister Karl August von Hardenberg, in October Hardenberg accepted a position as administrative assistant for the district director Coelestin August Just in Tennstedt. By November Hardenberg had embarked upon the experience that would prove decisive in his life: on a business trip to nearby Grüningen, he met and fell deeply in love with the twelve-year-old Sophie von Kühn. Everyone who met her, including Goethe, Schlegel, and Ludwig Tieck, would later agree that Sophie was a remarkable girl, and in his most detailed description of her, a sketch entitled "Klarisse," Hardenberg notes that she was devoted to her family, rather formal, fond of tobacco, not overly fond of poetry, and, perhaps most important: "Sie *will nichts seyn*–Sie *ist* etwas" (She *wants to become nothing*–She *is* something). The two became secretly engaged in March, but in November Sophie fell ill with a tuberculosis-related liver tumor. A series of painful operations ensued, and after much suffering she died on 19 March 1797, followed a month later by Hardenberg's favorite brother, Erasmus. The deaths plunged Hardenberg into a prolonged period of mourning and a meditation on death that would decisively alter the nature of his work.

The two years with Sophie had been intellectually fruitful. Hardenberg had immersed himself in the philosophy of Johann Gottlieb Fichte and produced the long "Fichte-Studien" (Fichte Studies) notebooks of 1795 and 1796. Here Hardenberg grapples with problems of the self, perception, religion, ontology, and semiotics, and makes the statement central to all his work:

"Spinotza stieg bis zur Natur–Fichte bis zum Ich, oder der Person. Ich bis zur These Gott" (Spinoza ascended to Nature, Fichte to the Ego or Person; I to the thesis, God). In the summer of 1795 he met Fichte along with the poet Friedrich Hölderlin at a gathering where, his host noted, much was spoken about how many questions still remained open for philosophy in regard to religion. After Sophie von Kühn's death, by which time he had returned to Weißenfels to assist his father's directorate of the Saxon salt mines, he studied Spinoza, Kant, Schelling, Goethe, the pietistic writer Nikolaus Ludwig Zinzendorf, the mystical philosophers Johann Kasper Lavater and Tiberius Hemsterhuis, the Scottish physician John Brown, and other philosophical, mystical, and alchemical writers.

In December 1797, after stopping on the way to meet Schelling, Hardenberg arrived at the Mining Academy in Freiberg for a year and a half of studies. Under the direction of Abraham Gottlob Werner and W. H. Lampadius, two of the foremost scientists of the day, he studied geology, mineralogy, chemistry, surveying, mining, and mining law, and worked in the mines three or four times a week. Hardenberg, who during his stay at the academy often slept only five hours a night and planned his time to the quarter hour, managed to continue his other readings and his notebooks, as well as to socialize with Fichte, Schiller, Goethe, Friedrich Schlegel and his brother August Wilhelm, and his friends in the Saxon Diet, Hans Georg von Carlowitz and Dietrich von Miltitz. In the summer of 1798 he produced his first major publications, the fragment collections "Blüthenstaub" and "Glauben und Liebe, oder der König und die Königin" (Faith and Love, or the King and Queen). In both, Hardenberg took up the pseudonym Novalis, a name derived from the phrase *de novali* and used by his early forebears from the estate Von der Rode.

"Blüthenstaub" filled thirty-seven pages of the first issue of the Schlegel brothers' epoch-making journal, the *Athenaeum*, with 114 prose fragments–a genre raised to new heights by the Romantics. Ranging in length from two lines to two pages, the fragments address issues in philosophy, literature, religion, and politics. This diversity is explained by the collection's motto: "Freunde, der Boden ist arm, wir müßen reichlichen Samen / Ausstreuen, daß uns doch nur mäßige Erndten gedeihn" (Friends, the soil is poor, we must richly scatter seeds to produce even a modest harvest). Enthusiastic over the French Revolution and the rapid literary development of Germany, the contributors to the *Athenaeum* had great ambitions, as Hardenberg programmatically states in "Blüthenstaub": "Wir sind auf einer Mißion: zur Bildung der Erde sind wir berufen" (We are on a mission: we are called to the education of the world). Such a project, which would now inform all of Hardenberg's work, clearly shows a debt to the enlightened pedagogy of Schiller and Gotthold Ephraim Lessing, but also the change it has undergone in its "Romanticization." No longer elaborated in a discursive treatise but in a fragmentary and disparate text, the Romantic project of "universal education" rejects an enlightened, totalizing concept of history, and instead envisions a pervasive reevaluation of values and institutions for which the goal–playfully called by Hardenberg "the Golden Age"–remains infinitely deferred. The "end of history" is no longer a historical goal for Hardenberg but a question of personal salvation. As he states in one of the most famous and "Fichtecizing" fragments of "Blüthenstaub": "Nach Innen geht der geheimnißvolle Weg. In uns, oder nirgends ist die Ewigkeit mit ihren Welten, die Vergangenheit und Zukunft" (Inward goes the mysterious path. In us or nowhere is eternity with its worlds, the past and future).

The political and personal, practical and mystical, revolutionary and reactionary task set forth by the Early Romantics at first provoked general incomprehension, a response that greeted Hardenberg's "Glauben und Liebe" even from the Prussian throne. Forty-three political aphorisms preceded by two pages of poetic "Blumen" (Flowers), "Glauben und Liebe" was printed in the 1798 *Jahrbücher der Preußischen Monarchie unter der Regierung von Friedrich Wilhelm III.* (Journal of the Prussian Monarchy under Friedrich Wilhelm III), a monthly magazine devoted to the young Prussian monarch and Queen Louise, both of whom had been greeted as paragons of political and domestic virtue upon succession to the throne in 1797. "Glauben und Liebe" puts forth a complex and highly metaphorical theory of political institutions. Praising the Prussian king and queen in their own right, it also presents them as educating their subjects for the eventual replacement of monarchy with new, republican institutions–which Hardenberg still describes with metaphors of monarchial rule. Thus, while Hardenberg heaps exorbitant praise on the actual king and queen, he simultaneously uses

Sketch of Novalis as a boy (photo by Foto-Kind, Weißenfels, used by permission of the Museum Weißenfels)

them as figures for political conceptualization, as in the claim: "Der König ist das gediegene Lebensprinzip des Staats; ganz dasselbe, was die Sonne im Planetensystem ist" (The king is truly the principle of life in the state; quite the same as the sun in the planetary system). Paradoxes abound in formulations such as: "kein König ohne Republik, und keine Republik ohne König" (No king without a republic, and no republic without a king) and: "Alle Menschen sollen thronfähig werden" (All men should become fit for the throne). Notwithstanding Hardenberg's disclaimer that he was writing in a "Tropen und Räthselsprache" (a language of tropes and riddles), the court made its disapproval known, the censor stopped publication of the final installment entitled "Politische Aphorismen" (Political Aphorisms), and even Friedrich Schlegel voiced his disapproval, advising his friend either to find a new pseudonym or to abandon hopes for publishing ever again.

While in Freiberg, Hardenberg greatly expanded his reflections on the underlying linguistic and cognitive structures that permitted something like "a language of tropes and riddles" or even scientific language. In groups of fragments with titles such as "Logologische Fragmente" (translated as "Logological Fragments," 1982) and "Poëticismen" (Poeticisms), he develops a theory of "Magic Idealism." Extending the thought of Kant and Fichte, Hardenberg claims, "Die Welt . . . ist überhaupt a priori von mir belebt" (The world . . . is animated by me a priori), and he seeks to control this animation through the magic of language: "Magie ist = Kunst, die Sinnenwelt willkührlich zu gebrauchen" (Magic is = the art of using the world of the senses arbitrarily). To systematize these observations further, he embarked on a large encyclopedic project, the "Allgemeine Brouillon" (General Notebooks) of 1798-1799. Differing from the encyclopedias of the eighteenth century, which present individual fields of knowledge under separate headings, the "Allgemeine Brouillon" tries to show the underlying unity of all knowledge through analogical discussions of "chemische Musik" (chemical music), "poetische Physiologie" (poetic physiology), "mathematische Philosophie" (mathematical philosophy), and "physicalische Geschichte" (physical history), among many other similarly combinative topics.

While Hardenberg's theoretical studies reached their most abstract point in Freiberg, he soon established relationships with two people who would rivet his attention more closely than ever to his professional career and to literature. In January 1798 Hardenberg met Julie von Charpentier, the daughter of the Freiberg official and former mineralogy instructor Johann Friedrich Wilhelm von Charpentier. A year later they were engaged, a step Hardenberg seems to have undertaken not entirely without calculation and with a pronounced ambivalence (he wrote to Friedrich Schlegel that a very interesting life appeared to await him–still, he would rather be dead). In any case, he energetically returned to work in Weißenfels in May 1799, filled with hopes for financial independence and marriage. The following month on a visit to Jena he met the young Ludwig Tieck, already a popular writer. The two instantly struck up a close friendship, read the mystical writings of Jakob Böhme together, and even planned joint literary projects. Hardenberg entered upon his most intense period of professional and literary activity, producing by the following fall the essay "Die Christenheit oder Europa," the novelistic fragment *Die Lehrlinge zu*

Sais (translated as *The Novices of Sais*, 1949), and the first of the poems known as "Geistliche Lieder" (Spiritual Songs, translated as *Sacred Songs of Novalis*, 1956).

Die Lehrlinge zu Sais is an essay-length prose text composed of first- and third-person meditations on nature that are loosely bound together by the general narrative setting of novices arriving in the ancient Egyptian city of Sais in search of the *Ursprache*, or primeval language. In the brief first part, "Der Lehrling" (The Novice), a first-person narrator muses on nature as a "große Chiffernschrift" (a great script of ciphers) written in a language no one understands, "weil sich die Sprache selber nicht verstehe, nicht verstehen wolle" (because the language does not understand itself, nor want to understand). He compares it to "die ächte Sanscrit" (genuine Sanskrit), which only speaks "um zu sprechen, weil Sprechen ihre Lust und ihr Wesen sey" (in order to speak, because speaking is its pleasure and its essence). This simultaneously skeptical and mystical conception of language–which Hardenberg also expounds in his brief poetical manifesto "Monolog" (translated as "Monologue," 1982)–receives amplification in the longer second part of *Die Lehrlinge zu Sais*, "Die Natur" (Nature). Here a marginal narrator introduces numerous soliloquies on nature and language that echo the views of Hardenberg's own teachers. One of the voices makes the extreme claim–especially remarkable given the Romantics' supposed cult of nature: "Man kann nicht sagen, daß es eine Natur gebe, ohne etwas überschwengliches zu sagen, und alles Bestreben nach Wahrheit in den Reden und Gesprächen von der Natur entfernt nur immer mehr von der Natürlichkeit" (One cannot say that nature exists, without saying something excessive; and all striving after truth in speeches and conversations about nature only progressively distances one from naturalness). Yet if in *Die Lehrlinge zu Sais* one voice denies the ability of language truthfully to represent nature, the teacher's voice claims at its conclusion that nature still serves as an instrument of higher understanding if it provokes an overwhelming feeling of *Sehnsucht*, of longing for a transcendent unity that never appears as such, but only in diversity, difference, and change. This desire for a lost unity is succinctly dramatized within the second part of *Die Lehrlinge zu Sais* by the story "Hyacinth und Rosenblüthe" (translated as "The Story of Hyacinth and Roseblossom," 1913), an allegorical fairy tale in which Hyacinth abandons his childhood home and his beloved to search for knowledge, only to recover Roseblossom far from home, in a dream within the temple of Isis.

Hardenberg's skepticism regarding language as a medium of truthful representation and his by no means contradictory belief in its practical power coalesced in his attempts to generate new cultural mythologies in "Die Christenheit oder Europa" and the "Geistliche Lieder." Opening with the words, "Es waren schöne, glänzende Zeiten" (They were beautiful, sparkling brilliant times), "Die Christenheit oder Europa" is cleverly posed between historical account and fairy tale. In presenting a mythical history of Europe from the Middle Ages to the present, Hardenberg strives to incite readers both to a reevaluation of modern European history and to personal transformation. Employing the triadic structure of unity, fall, and redemption, the essay rhapsodically recalls the Catholic Middle Ages as a time of cultural and spiritual integration, laments Europe's spiritual disintegration through the Reformation and Enlightenment, and announces the imminent return of "die Regierung Gottes auf Erden" (God's reign upon earth), which it sees foreshadowed in the political turmoil of the French Revolution and in the cultural growth of Germany. "Die Christenheit oder Europa" ends with the insistence that this political and cultural renewal can take place only through religion: "Nur die Religion kann Europa wieder aufwecken" (Only religion can reawaken Europe). The text produced great embarrassment among Hardenberg's friends. In presenting the Middle Ages not as the Dark Ages but as a period of high culture to inspire Germany, Hardenberg was building upon the groundwork of a new, Romantic appreciation of the past that Tieck and Heinrich Wackenroder had already laid in place; but in his effusive celebration of Catholicism and the Counter-Reformation, his hyperbolic criticism of the Reformation, Protestantism, and the Enlightenment, and his explicit fusion of republican politics with mystical religion, Hardenberg went beyond the pale of even the most liberal Romantic propriety. Acting on the advice of Goethe and the Berlin theologian Friedrich Schleiermacher, the Schlegels refused to publish the manuscript in the *Athenaeum*–and it was first printed twenty-five years later, probably through an error.

The twelve poetical songs now grouped together as the "Geistliche Lieder" were undertaken as a more modest project and met with more immediate success. Having found the church songs of the eighteenth century to be overly intellectual, dogmatic, and obscure, Hardenberg set about the composition of more accessible and evocative ones. He succeeded in producing poems that express tender religious sentiments in an imaginative, mystical, and at times erotic language, poems that preserve their popular appeal with a deceptively simple style and vocabulary. Although their orthodoxy remains a matter of debate, several of the songs quickly found their way into church songbooks, where they can still be found today.

The fall of 1799 marked the high point of Early Romanticism, as Hardenberg, Tieck, Schleiermacher, the scientist J. W. Ritter, and Friedrich and Dorothea Schlegel met regularly at the home of August and Caroline Schlegel in Jena. Hardenberg, a brilliant speaker and, according to Tieck, a virtuoso in the social arts, read his new works aloud to this group, who spurred him on to his most productive year. Although professional duties in Tennstedt occupied most of his attention, and his health continued to deteriorate from the tuberculosis that had begun to afflict him the previous year, Hardenberg began work on his two most ambitious literary projects: the poetic cycle "Hymnen an die Nacht" and the quintessentially Romantic novel *Heinrich von Ofterdingen.*

"Hymnen an die Nacht," published in the final issue of the *Athenaeum* in August 1800, immediately became Hardenberg's most successful work in his lifetime, and continues to be his most-read work to the present day. The first four hymns, written almost entirely in rhythmic prose, elaborate the basic argument of the text. In the first hymn, after initially praising the light as a "König der irdischen Natur" (king of earthly nature), the poet announces a turn "Abwärts . . . zu der heiligen, unaussprechlichen, geheimnißvollen Nacht" (downward . . . to the holy, ineffable, mysterious night). The poet's nostalgia for the daylight is overcome by the appearance of a mediatrix, his "zarte Geliebte" (tender beloved) with whom he experiences a sexual-mystical union, which proves at first to be only transitory. In the second hymn, the poet returns to day and laments the transitoriness of the night. The brief third hymn, perhaps Hardenberg's most famous piece of writing, recounts the central experience of the "Hymnen an die Nacht," a vision with striking–and artfully reworked–similarities to his 1796 diary account of an experience at Sophie von Kühn's grave. The poet tells how he once

Novalis's engagement ring, with inscription: "Sophia sey mein Schuz Geist" (Sophia be my guardian spirit) (Photo by Foto-Kind, Weißenfels, used by permission of the Museum Weißenfels)

stood, overcome with grief, at the burial mound of the "Gestalt meines Lebens" (shape of my life). Suddenly he feels a "Dämmerungsschauer" (twilight shudder). A heavenly sleep overcomes him, the mound seems to rise up, time to blow away, and the beloved almost to resurrect before him. The poet claims that this vision was "der erste, einzige Traum" (the first and only dream), after which he feels only an "ewigen, unwandelbaren Glauben an den Himmel der Nacht und sein Licht, die Geliebte" (an eternal, immutable faith in the heavenly Night and in its light, the beloved). The fourth hymn, after affirming the poet's now cheerful return to the day and his inner fidelity to the night, concludes by breaking forth with jubilant song in praise of the night and "des Todes / Verjüngende Flut" (death's rejuvenating flood). The fifth hymn sharply changes the direction of the "Hymnen an die Nacht" by translating this history of personal salvation into a mythical history of Western religion from an-

cient Greece to Christianity. After alternating between prose and verse, it ends with a song in praise of the Resurrection as mankind's victory over death, and of the Virgin Mary as the eternal mother who awakens the human longing for immortality. The sixth and final hymn, the ten-stanza poem "Sehnsucht nach dem Tode" (Longing for Death) recapitulates the major themes of the "Hymnen an die Nacht" and ends with the poet's yearning for his celestial home, where "Ein Traum bricht unsre Banden los / Und senkt uns in des Vaters Schoß" (A dream at last our bonds does snap / And lays us in our Father's lap).

Heinrich von Ofterdingen, a Bildungsroman based freely on accounts of the medieval poet Heinrich von Ofterdingen, was Hardenberg's final and most extensive literary production. It traces the growth of its protagonist through adolescence on his way to becoming a poet—a goal never attained in the incomplete novel. Formally daring, *Heinrich von Ofterdingen* mixes a realistic and morally elevated narration with dreams, fairy tales, operatic songs, mystical dialogues, discourses on poetry, and fantastic adventures. The first part, "Die Erwartung" (Anticipation), begins with Heinrich's dream within a dream of the blue flower—a vision that fills him with a longing he cannot understand. The second through fifth chapters trace Heinrich's journey to Augsburg with his mother and their encounters with businessmen, former crusaders, an Arabian woman, and a wise miner, all of whom share their stories with the boy. In the sixth chapter the pair arrives at his grandfather's house in Augsburg, where Heinrich falls in love with Mathilde, the daughter of his grandfather's friend and adviser, the poet Klingsohr. Heinrich and Klingsohr discuss poetry, history, and politics into the eighth chapter, in which Heinrich and Mathilde promise eternal love in a series of avowals that would later become the clichés of Romantic love, but are here spoken with a fairy-tale simplicity. The first part of the novel ends with "Klingsohrs Märchen" (Klingsohr's Fairy Tale), an obscure allegory of universal renewal filled with scientific, alchemical, mystical, philosophical, and literary allusions. When the novel's second, unfinished part, "Die Erfüllung" (Fulfillment), begins, Mathilde has died, and Heinrich is roaming the world as a pilgrim. The novel abruptly breaks off as Heinrich speaks with Sylvester, his father's former teacher, about nature, education, and religion.

Although Hardenberg had detailed plans for the continuation of the novel and wrote some of his finest poetry to include within it, his rapidly deteriorating health prevented him from finishing it. While writing the first part, Hardenberg had continued to make literary and professional plans, and even obtained a promotion as district director for the area around Weißenfels. Yet while he remained free from pain, he grew progressively weaker. In October 1800, when he received word that a younger brother had drowned, Hardenberg suffered a severe hemorrhage and was forced to cease virtually all professional and literary activity. Over the winter of 1800-1801, even speaking became tiring for him, and in the spring he sent for his friends. On 25 March 1801, as Friedrich Schlegel sat beside him in Weißenfels, Hardenberg fell asleep listening to his brother Karl play piano and died peacefully at noon. Less than a year and a half later Tieck and Schlegel issued the first two-volume collection of his works, including *Heinrich von Ofterdingen, Die Lehrlinge zu Sais,* "Geistliche Lieder," and some unpublished fragments. By 1837 the collection had gone through five editions and had assured Novalis's place in the world of letters.

Letters:

Friedrich Schlegel und Novalis: Biographie einer Romantikerfreundschaft in ihren Briefen, edited by Max Preitz (Darmstadt: Gentner, 1957).

Bibliography:

Richard Samuel, "Zur Geschichte des Nachlasses Friedrich von Hardenberg (Novalis)" *Jahrbücher der deutschen Schillergesellschaft,* 2 (1958): 301-347;

Samuel, *Novalis (Friedrich von Hardenberg): Der handschriftliche Nachlaß des Dichters. Zur Geschichte des Nachlasses* (Gerstenberg: Hildesheim, 1973).

Biographies:

Sophie von Hardenberg, *Friedrich von Hardenberg (genannt Novalis): Eine Nachlese aus den Quellen des Familienarchivs* (Gotha: Perthes, 1873);

Heinz Ritter-Schaumburg, *Novalis und seine erste Braut* (Stuttgart: Urachhaus, 1986);

Hermann Kurzke, *Novalis* (Munich: Beck, 1988).

References:

Heinz Bollinger, *Novalis: Die Lehrlinge zu Sais. Versuch einer Erläuterung* (Winterthur: Keller, 1954);

Kenneth S. Calhoon, "Language and Romantic Irony in Novalis' *Die Lehrlinge zu Sais,*" *Germanic Review,* 56 (Spring 1981): 51-61;

Manfred Dick, *Die Entwicklung des Gedankens der Poesie in den Fragmenten des Novalis* (Bonn: Bouvier, 1967);

Martin Dyck, *Novalis and Mathematics* (Chapel Hill: University of North Carolina Press, 1960);

Manfred Frank, *Das Problem "Zeit" in der deutschen Romantik* (Munich: Winkler, 1972);

Richard W. Hannah, *The Fichtean Dynamic of Novalis' Poetics* (Bern: Lang, 1981);

Klaus Hartmann, *Die freiheitliche Sprachauffassung des Novalis* (Bonn: Bouvier, 1987);

Josef Haslinger, *Die Ästhetik des Novalis* (Königstein: Hain, 1981);

J. F. Haussmann, "Die deutsche Kritik über Novalis von 1850-1900," *Journal of English and Germanic Philology,* 12 (1913): 211-244;

Haussmann, "German Estimates of Novalis from 1800 to 1850," *Modern Philology,* 9 (January 1911): 399-415;

Bruce Haywood, *Novalis: The Veil of Imagery. A Study of the Poetic Works of Friedrich von Hardenberg* (Cambridge: Harvard University Press, 1959);

Friedrich Hiebel, *Novalis: German Poet, European Thinker, Christian Mystic* (Chapel Hill: University of North Carolina Press, 1954);

Frank and Gerhard Kurz, "Ordo inverus: Zu einer Reflexionsfigur bei Novalis, Hölderlin, Kleist und Kafka," in *Geist und Zeichen,* edited by H. Anton and others (Heidelberg: Winter, 1977), pp. 75-97;

Alice Kuzniar, *Delayed Endings: Nonclosure in Novalis and Hölderlin* (Athens: University of Georgia Press, 1987);

Nikolaus Lohse, *Dichtung und Theorie: Der Entwurf einer dichterischen Transzendentalpoetik in den Fragmenten des Novalis* (Heidelberg: Winter, 1988);

György Lukács, "On the Romantic Philosophy of Life: Novalis," in his *Soul and Form,* translated by Anna Bostock (Cambridge: Massachusetts Institute of Technology Press, 1974);

Hans-Joachim Mähl, *Die Idee des goldenen Zeitalters im Werk des Novalis* (Heidelberg: Winter, 1965);

Mähl, "Novalis," in *Deutsche Dichter der Romantik,* edited by Benno von Wiese (Berlin: Schmidt, 1971), pp. 190-224;

Wilfried Malsch, *"Europa": Poetische Rede des Novalis. Deutung der französischen Revolution und Reflexion auf die Poesie in der Geschichte* (Stuttgart: Metzler, 1965);

Géza von Molnár, "Another Glance at Novalis' 'Blue Flower,'" *Euphorion,* 67 (1973): 273-286;

Von Molnár, *Novalis' "Fichte Studies"* (The Hague: Mouton, 1970);

Von Molnár, *Romantic Vision, Ethical Context. Novalis and Artistic Autonomy* (Minneapolis: University of Minnesota Press, 1987);

John Neubauer, *Bifocal Vision: Novalis' Philosophy of Nature and Disease* (Chapel Hill: University of North Carolina Press, 1971);

Neubauer, *Novalis* (Boston: Twayne, 1980);

William Arctander O'Brien, "Twilight in Atlantis: Novalis' *Heinrich von Ofterdingen* and Plato's *Republic,*" *Modern Language Notes,* 95, no. 5 (1980): 1292-1332;

Heinz Ritter, *Novalis' Hymnen an die Nacht* (Heidelberg: Winter, 1974);

Gerhard Schulz, *Novalis in Selbstzeugnissen und Bilddokumenten* (Reinbek: Rowohlt, 1969);

Schulz, "Die Poetik des Romans bei Novalis," *Jahrbuch des Freien Deutschen Hochstifts* (1964): 120-157;

Schulz, ed., *Novalis: Beiträge zu Werk und Persönlichkeit Friedrich von Hardenbergs,* second edition (Darmstadt: Wissenschaftliche Buchgesellschaft, 1986);

Elisabeth Stopp, " 'Übergang vom Roman zur Mythologie': Formal Aspects of the Opening Chapters of *Heinrich von Ofterdingen,* Part II," *Deutsche Vierteljahrsschrift für Literaturwissenschaft und Geistesgeschichte,* 48 (1974): 318-341;

Friedrich Strack, *Im Schatten der Neugier: Christliche Tradition und kritische Philosophie im Werk Friedrich von Hardenbergs* (Tübingen: Niemeyer, 1982).

Papers:

The Freies Deutsches Hochstift, Frankfurt am Main, holds the largest collection of Novalis's extant manuscripts. The Biblioteka Jagiellońska of Kraków University has collections of his poetic juvenalia and professional writing. The Museum Weißenfels has a collection of Hardenberg family correspondence, several of Novalis's personal possessions, and the oil portrait of Novalis by Franz Gareis.

August von Platen

(24 October 1796-5 December 1835)

Jeffrey L. Sammons
Yale University

BOOKS: *Lyrische Blätter* (Leipzig: Brockhaus, 1821);

Ghaselen (Erlangen: Heyder, 1821);

Vermischte Schriften (Erlangen: Heyder, 1822);

Neue Ghaselen (Erlangen: Junge, 1823);

Schauspiele: Erstes Bändchen (Erlangen: Heyder, 1824);

An König Ludwig: Ode (Erlangen: Palm, 1825);

Sonette aus Venedig (Erlangen: Heyder, 1825); translated by R. B. Cooke as *Sonnets from Venice* (Boston: Badger, 1923);

Die verhängnisvolle Gabel: Ein Lustspiel in fünf Akten (Stuttgart & Tübingen: Cotta, 1826);

Ihren hochverehrtesten Gönnern am ersten Tage des Jahres 1826 in tiefster Ehrfurcht dargebracht von der dekretirten Zetteltragerin Pitz in Erlangen, anonymous (N.p., 1826);

Gedichte (Stuttgart & Tübingen: Cotta, 1828; enlarged edition, 1834);

Schauspiele, 2 volumes (Stuttgart & Tübingen: Cotta, 1828);

Der romantische Oedipus: Ein Lustspiel in fünf Akten (Stuttgart & Tübingen: Cotta, 1829);

Geschichten des Königreichs Neapel von 1414 bis 1443 (Frankfurt am Main: Sauerländer, 1833);

Die Liga von Cambrai: Geschichtliches Drama in drei Akten (Frankfurt am Main: Sauerländer, 1833);

Die Abbassiden: Ein Gedicht in neun Gesängen (Stuttgart & Tübingen: Cotta, 1835);

Gedichte aus dem ungedruckten Nachlasse (Strasbourg: Literarisches Comptoir, 1839; enlarged edition, Strasbourg: Schuler, 1841);

Gesammelte Werke in einem Bande (Stuttgart & Tübingen: Cotta, 1839);

Gesammelte Werke, 7 volumes (volumes 1-5, Stuttgart & Tübingen: Cotta / volumes 6 & 7, Leipzig: Dyk, 1843-1852);

Polenlieder (Frankfurt am Main: Literarische Anstalt, 1849);

Poetischer und litterarischer Nachlaß, edited by J. Minckwitz, 2 volumes (Leipzig: Dyk, 1852);

August von Platen (Staatsbibliothek Berlin)

Der Sieg der Gläubigen: Ein geistliches Nachspiel, edited by C. Vogt (Geneva: Lauffer, 1857);

Platens Tagebuch 1796-1825, edited by V. Engel-
    hardt and K. Pfeufer (Stuttgart & Augs-
    burg: Cotta, 1860);
Die Tagebücher: Aus der Handschrift des Dichters, edit-
    ed by G. von Laubmann and L. von Scheff-
    ler (Stuttgart: Cotta, 1896-1900);
*Dramatischer Nachlaß: Aus den Handschriften der
    Münchener Hof- und Staatsbibliothek,* edited by
    Erich Petzet (Berlin: Behr, 1902);
*August Graf von Platens sämtliche Werke in zwölf Bän-
    den: Historisch-kritische Ausgabe,* edited by
    Max Koch and Erich Petzet (Leipzig: Hesse,
    [1910]).

August von Platen was one of several German post-Romantic poets who strove to overcome Romantic lyricism by restoring poetry's spoken, verbal quality and by pursuing a more
precisely defined imagery. Platen's particular strategy was to reach out to the forms of the international cultural patrimony, in which he was extremely erudite. He mastered a dozen languages,
including Latin and Greek, the French of his social class, English, Italian, Spanish, Portuguese,
Dutch, Danish, and Persian. Among German
poets he was the most complex metrician since
Friedrich Gottlob Klopstock in the eighteenth century and the most ingenious rhymer before Christian Morgenstern in the twentieth century. His
personal life, even by the standards of poets, was
exceptionally unhappy.

Platen was descended from a prominent
and sometimes influential noble family scattered
in Germany from north to south, but, though he
bore the title of count, his branch was obscure
and relatively poor; his father was a Prussian forestry official in Ansbach. When Ansbach passed
to Bavaria in 1806, Platen became a page at the
Munich court and subsequently an officer in the
Bavarian infantry. His regiment was in the field
at the time of Waterloo but saw no action. Platen
hated military life: he chafed under the mindless
drill and authoritarian spirit and was disheart-
ened by the absence of culture and poetic sensibility among his fellows. His commander disliked
him, and three times he was put under arrest,
once for several weeks, for being away without
leave. But he won the goodwill of the Bavarian
king, Maximilian Joseph, and crown prince, the future Ludwig I, with the result that he was able to
study on extended leave at the University of
Erlangen, allegedly preparing for a diplomatic career but in fact deepening his cultural learning
and developing his literary abilities. He never

took a degree, but in 1828 he was granted a
small annual stipend as a member of the Bavarian Academy of Sciences and spent much of his
time traveling, primarily in Italy, which became
his true spiritual home.

The central feature of his personality, upon
which all else turns, was his homosexuality,
which caused him profound misery. He grieved
at his incurable difference from others and was
never able to find a partner with whom he could
share his hunger for affection for any length of
time; he was the loneliest and most isolated of unrequited lovers. At the same time he was extremely chaste; he would break with friends if he
suspected them of licentiousness. He sublimated
his inclination into an aesthetic contempla-
tiveness, elevated above all worldly and sensual aspects. One of his recurrent homoerotic images is
the tulip, borrowed from Persian poetry; as a
flower without a fragrance, it appeals only to the
higher, immaterial sense of sight. These proclivities, along with his maladroitness in human relations and his chronic poor judgment in managing his life and career, led him into a horrible
blunder in the late 1820s. In 1827 the satirist
Karl Immermann contributed to the second volume of Heinrich Heine's *Reisebilder* (1826-1831;
translated as *Pictures of Travel,* 1855) a series of epigrams spoofing the fashion of Orientalizing poetry, clearly directed against Platen among others.
Platen struck back with an "Aristophanic" comedy, *Der romantische Oedipus* (1829), portraying
Immermann as an obsolescent Romantic, which
he was not, and sniping at Heine with witless anti-
Semitic jibes. Platen knew virtually nothing of
Heine and therefore had no notion of how dangerous an adversary he could be, while Heine had
been following Platen's career with close attention. In *Die Bäder von Lucca* (The Baths of
Lucca), in the third volume of the *Reisebilder*
(1829), Heine replied with one of his most fero-
cious polemics, scoffing at Platen's formalistic poetry as acrobatic and lifeless and at his sublimation
of the erotic as prudishly repressive, quite unjustly accusing him of reactionary allegiances,
and above all drenching the polemic in derisive allusions to Platen's homosexuality. The sorry episode damaged the careers and reputations of
both men. For most of his few remaining years
Platen wandered forlornly around Italy, admiring great works of art. In 1835 he fled the cholera to Sicily; in Syracuse he died as pathetically
as he had lived, from an overdose of anticholera
medicine.

Platen's poetic corpus can be clearly organized by genre: ballads, romances, and songs; occasional poems; political poems; ghazels; sonnets; odes and hymns; epigrams; and the epic. It is perhaps the ghazels with which his name is most readily associated. The ghazel is a Persian form beginning with a rhymed couplet and then repeating the same rhyme in alternate lines for the remainder of the poem; the rhyme can be a phrase of several syllables, sometimes as many as eight. The model for the form was the Persian poet Hafiz (1326?-1390), whose verse Platen studied and translated. Hafiz was also the model for Goethe's *West-östlicher Divan,* but Platen's poems are much closer in form to the originals and explicitly exploit their homoerotic imagery in a way that would have been quite foreign to Goethe. Reading a number of Platen's ghazels in succession can have quite a hypnotic effect, and this effect is undoubtedly intended, for Platen believed that poetry should be ceremonious and transporting and should be chanted in singsong as ancient poetry was. At least the equal of his ghazels in their formal achievement, however, are his sonnets, all of which are Petrarchan in form. Platen was the most accomplished sonneteer in the German language between the seventeenth century and the great experiments of Rainer Maria Rilke. Outstanding among them is a series about Venice, written during a sojourn in that city in 1824. His odes, Pindaric hymns, eclogues, and idylls employ not only Greek and Latin meters and strophic forms, but often even more complex patterns of Platen's own devising; sometimes, like Klopstock before him, he provided the pattern in metrical notation at the beginning of the poem. Many critics and literary historians are skeptical of verse of this type, believing it incongruent with the stress pattern of Germanic languages. But Platen's employment of these forms is not only homage to the ancients; it is a mode of countering Romantic lyricism with a harsher versification that juxtaposes and silhouettes heavily stressed individual words.

For Platen was not out of touch with his own age; his political poetry, as well as his private comments, show that it is an error to perceive him, as Heine did, as a reactionary aristocrat; he was a firm liberal, hostile to repression, tyranny, and obscurantism, even intimating traces of republican ideas. His *Polenlieder* (Polish Songs), expressing outrage at the Russian and Prussian suppression of the Polish revolution in 1831, could not be safely published until after

Platen as a Bavarian cadet (oil painting by unknown artist, in private collection)

the 1848 revolution. His pugnacious and irritable, admittedly sometimes priggish view of the contemporary literary and cultural scene is articulated in his epigrams; some of them betray the influence of the English poet he most enthusiastically admired: Alexander Pope. The epic, however, the dream of many a nineteenth-century German poet, was finally to elude him. Some fragments of an epic poem on the Hohenstaufen dynasty make one grateful that it was not continued. Instead he completed an amusing mock-epic, *Die Abbassiden* (The Abbassids, 1835), with motifs drawn from *The Arabian Nights* and a theme of mutual religious tolerance. It turned out to be one of the lightest and most cheerful of all his works.

Platen also experimented constantly with dramas. Apart from his "Aristophanic" comedies, *Die verhängnisvolle Gabel* (The Fateful Fork, 1826), a spoof of the fashionable fate tragedy, and the ill-fated *Der romantische Oedipus,* they include *Der Turm mit sieben Pforten* (The Tower with Seven Gates, 1825), a one-act comedy concerning the rescue of an imprisoned damsel from the despotic

Bey of Tunis; *Der gläserne Pantoffel* (The Glass Slipper, 1824), a conflation of Cinderella and Sleeping Beauty; and *Der Schatz des Rhampsenit* (The Treasury of Rhampsinitus, 1823), drawn from an anecdote of Herodotus that relates how a crime wave was stanched by making the thief king (years later Heine was to take up the story again in a poem). An attempt at a Shakespearean drama with a medieval setting, *Treue um Treue* (Loyalty for Loyalty, 1825), was Platen's only stage success in his lifetime but is not likely to impress modern readers. The same is true of his talky, static historical drama, *Die Liga von Cambrai* (The League of Cambrai, 1833), an attempt to heroize the republican spirit of Venice. He had more success with a prose work of popularized history, *Geschichten des Königreichs Neapel* (Stories of the Kingdom of Naples, 1833). From the age of seventeen until shortly before his death Platen also kept a detailed diary, parts of which are written in English, French, and Portuguese; he titled it "Memorandum meines Lebens" (Memorandum of My Life) and shaped it into an ongoing autobiography. Because of its frankness it could not be published in full until the end of the nineteenth century, when it appeared under the title *Die Tagebücher: Aus der Handschrift des Dichters* (1896-1900).

Few have ever doubted Platen's high-mindedness, his unremitting efforts to improve and perfect himself, or his sincere and cosmopolitan love of great literature and art. But he has always been difficult to evaluate as a poet. Many observers have found his habit of adapting the classical forms of past literature imitative and epigonic. His pronounced aestheticism has sometimes been dismissed as escapist. Heine was not the only observer to see in Platen's dexterity with meter and rhyme a kind of parlor trick, an exhibit of overcoming difficulties, rather than an utterance proceeding from the inner self. Enlightened people of contemporary times will find it easier to commiserate with his sad isolation as a homosexual in an unsympathetic environment, but his narcissistic introversion cramped his vision and hobbled his spirit. Because he lacked an inventive freedom of the imagination, his perpetual, unvarying lament for unachievable love and friendship in much of his verse can be monotonous. A certain monotony, too, is generated by his metrical obsessions; he held to his metrical patterns with strict regularity, so that much of his poetry beats along pedantically, lacking the counterpoint of meter and rhythm of which his despised con-temporary Heine was a master. Curiously, his most complex meters in his odes and hymns, just because they violate the normal stress patterns of German, are among his more subtle and satisfying rhythmical effects.

Platen was constantly, especially in his younger years, beset by fears that he lacked talent and imagination; his occasionally vainglorious public pronouncements, in which he proclaimed himself the successor of Goethe and even of Homer, were, as Heine shrewdly perceived, nothing but neurotic symptoms of crippled self-esteem. His love of great poetry not only inspired him but also oppressed him with the anxiety of influence. Yet among much in his work that is merely brave and well-intentioned there are also some moments of exceptional refinement and depth. A criticism on more modern principles of his metrics and the leitmotivic variations in his recurring images can elevate his stature considerably. With his intertwined themes of love, beauty, sorrow, and death he can be interpreted as a harbinger of later nineteenth-century poets. Creative writers who have turned their attention to him have sometimes come to regard him with admiration. Among them is Thomas Mann, who delivered a perceptive lecture on Platen in 1930 and had already borrowed for a novella the title of one of Platen's best-known poems, "Tristan" (1825), which begins: "Wer die Schönheit angeschaut mit Augen, / Ist dem Tode schon anheimgegeben" ("He who has gazed upon beauty with his own eyes / Is already yielded up to death"). More recently, in 1985, the homosexual, avant-garde writer Hubert Fichte published as one of the last works of his life an impassioned defense of Platen. Further attention to Platen on modern interpretive principles, while unlikely to make of him a poet of the first rank, should illuminate his genuine achievements and his significant place in the history of European poetry.

Letters:

Der Briefwechsel des Grafen August von Platen, edited by Ludwig von Scheffler and Paul Bornstein, 4 volumes (Munich & Leipzig: G. Müller, 1911-1931; Hildesheim & New York: Georg Olms, 1973).

Bibliography:

Fritz Redenbacher, *Platen-Bibliographie. Zweite, bis 1970 fortgeführte Auflage* (Hildesheim & New York: Georg Olms, 1972).

Biographies:

Max Koch, *Platens Leben und Schaffen* (Leipzig: Hesse, 1910);

Rudolf Schlösser, *August Graf von Platen*, 2 volumes (Munich: Piper, 1910-1913).

References:

Stuart Atkins, "A Humanistic Approach to Literature: Critical Interpretations of Two Sonnets by Platen," *German Quarterly*, 25 (1952): 258-276;

Claude David, "Sur le lyrisme de Platen," *Formenwandel: Festschrift zum 65. Geburtstag von Paul Böckmann*, edited by Walter Müller-Seidel and Wolfgang Preisendanz (Hamburg: Hoffmann und Campe, 1964), pp. 383-392;

Richard Dove, *The "Individualität" of August von Platen* (Frankfurt am Main & Bern: Lang, 1983);

Hubert Fichte, *"Deiner Umarmungen süße Sehnsucht": Die Geschichte der Empfindungen am Beispiel der französischen Schriften des Grafen August von Platen-Hallermünde* (Tübingen: Konkursverlag, 1985);

Gerald Gillespie, "Romantic Oedipus," in *Goethezeit: Studien zur Erkenntnis und Rezeption Goethes und seiner Zeitgenossen. Festschrift für Stuart Atkins*, edited by Gerhart Hoffmeister (Bern & Munich: Francke, 1981), pp. 331-346;

Vincent J. Günther, "August Graf von Platen," in *Deutsche Dichter des 19. Jahrhunderts: Ihr Leben und Werk*, edited by Benno von Wiese (Berlin: Erich Schmidt Verlag, 1969), pp. 77-96;

Günter Häntzschel, "August von Platen," in *Zur Literatur der Restaurationsepoche 1815-1848*, edited by Jost Hermand and Manfred Windfuhr (Stuttgart: Metzler, 1970), pp. 108-150;

Heinrich Henel, "Epigonenlyrik: Rückert und Platen," *Euphorion*, 55 (1961): 260-278;

Hans Kuhn, "Sind Klassiker unsterblich? Platens Fortleben in den Anthologien," *Orbis litterarum*, 22 (1967): 101-128;

Hans H. Lewald, *Platens geistiges Bild* (Essen: Zeitungsverlag Ruhrgebiet, 1958);

Jürgen Link, *Artistische Form und ästhetischer Sinn in Platens Lyrik* (Munich: Fink, 1971);

Thomas Mann, "August von Platen," in his *Leiden und Größe der Meister: Neue Aufsätze* (Berlin: Fischer, 1933), pp. 163-180; republished in his *Adel des Geistes* (Stockholm: Bermann-Fischer, 1945), pp. 503-517;

Hans Mayer, "Der Streit zwischen Heine und Platen," in his *Außenseiter* (Frankfurt am Main: Suhrkamp, 1975), pp. 207-223;

Kurt Partl, "Die Spiegelung romantischer Poetik in der biedermeierlichen Dichtungsstruktur Mörikes und Platens," in *Zur Literaturkritik der Restaurationsepoche 1815-1848*, edited by Jost Hermand and Manfred Windfuhr (Stuttgart: Metzler, 1970);

Jeffrey L. Sammons, "Platen's Tulip Image," *Monatshefte*, 52 (1960): 293-301;

Friedrich Sengle, "August Graf von Platen (1796-1835)," in his *Biedermeierzeit: Deutsche Literatur im Spannungsfeld zwischen Restauration und Revolution 1815-1848*, volume 3: *Die Dichter* (Stuttgart: Metzler, 1980), pp. 415-467;

Hans-Joachim Teuchert, *August Graf von Platen in Deutschland: Zur Rezeption eines umstrittenen Autors* (Bonn: Bouvier, 1980);

Walter Weiss, "August von Platen," in his *Enttäuschter Pantheismus: Zur Weltgestaltung der Dichtung in der Restaurationszeit* (Dornbirg: Vorarlberger Verlagsanstalt, 1962), pp. 123-155.

Papers:

August von Platen's papers are held in the Staatsbibliothek, Munich; the Universitätsbibliothek, Tübingen; the Cotta Archive, Schiller-Nationalmuseum, Marbach am Neckar; the Platen Archive, Stadtarchiv, Erlangen; and the Staatsbibliothek Preußischer Kulturbesitz, West Berlin.

Ferdinand Jakob Raimund

(1 June 1790-5 September 1836)

Erich P. Hofacker, Jr.
University of Michigan

BOOKS: *Sämmtliche Werke*, edited by Johann N. Vogl, 4 volumes (Vienna: Rohrmann & Schweigert, 1837)–comprises *Der Alpenkönig und der Menschenfeind*, translated by J. Baldwin Buckstone as *The King of the Alps: A Romantic Drama in 3 Acts*, in *Lacy's Acting Edition of Plays*, No. 6 (London, 1852); *Der Bauer als Millionär; oder, Das Mädchen aus der Feenwelt; Der Verschwender*, translated by Erwin Tramer as *The Spendthrift* (New York: Ungar, 1949); *Der Diamant des Geisterkönigs: Zauberspiel; Der Barometermacher auf der Zauberinsel: Zauberposse; Die gefesselte Fantasie: Original-Zauberspiel; Moisasur's Zauberfluch: Zauberspiel; Die unheilbringende Krone oder König ohne Reich, Held ohne Muth, Schönheit ohne Jugend;*

Dramatische Meisterwerke, edited by A. Zeising (Stuttgart: Hoffmann, 1869);

Sämmtliche Werke: Nach den Original- und Theater-Manuscripten nebst Nachlaß und Biographie, edited by C. Glossy and A. Sauer, 3 volumes (Vienna: Konegen, 1881);

Sämtliche Werke, 2 volumes (Stuttgart & Berlin: Cotta, 1895);

Raimund-Liederbuch: Lieder und Gesänge aus Friedrich Raimunds Werken, edited by W. A. Bauer (Vienna: Schroll, 1924);

Sämtliche Werke: Historisch-kritische Säkularausgabe, edited by Fritz Brukner and Eduard Castle, 6 volumes (Vienna: Schroll, 1924-1934).

Ferdinand Jakob Raimund in 1829 (lithograph by Joseph Kreihuber)

The works of Ferdinand Jakob Raimund, written for the "Wiener Volkstheater" (Viennese popular theater), were an important contribution to nineteenth-century European drama. Like Shakespeare and Molière, with whom he has been compared, Raimund was both an actor and a playwright. His unpretentious yet inspired plays raised the old Viennese "Possen"–uncultured and often crude comedies in the tradition of the Italian commedia dell'arte–to poetic heights. Raimund's sense of morality and his mild pedagogic inclination imbued the then-popular fairy and magic plays with a new ethical quality. With the poet's belated literary recognition, his ever-popular comedies moved out of the sphere of the Volkstheater and took their proper place in the repertoire of Vienna's venerable Burgtheater.

Raimund was born in Vienna on 1 June 1790. His father and grandfather, both lathe operators, had come from Prague in 1769. Jakob Raimann, his father, soon married Anna Katharina Merz, the daughter of the craftsman to whom he was apprenticed. After the death of his father-in-law, Jakob assisted in the operation

255

of a family flour-milling business, eventually becoming a master turner and a citizen of Vienna.

All of Raimund's brothers and sisters were placed in foster homes soon after birth, and nine of them died before he was born. Ferdinand was the only child to remain with his parents, who were determined to give this last child a proper bourgeois upbringing. In 1797 the family moved from the outskirts of town to the center so that he would be close to St. Anna's, the best school in Vienna. It was, by chance, located in the vicinity of the "Nationaltheater nächst der k.k. Burg" (the National Theater next to the royal imperial castle), later called the Burgtheater. The association of the boy's godfather with this most important playhouse of Vienna certainly contributed to Raimund's early enthusiasm for the stage. When his parents died in 1804, only an older married sister remained to care for the fourteen-year-old.

Apprenticed in 1804 to a baker with a concession at the Burgtheater, Raimund's daily exposure to the theater turned his long-held desire to become an actor to firm resolve. Inspired by the eloquent performances of the famous tragedian Ferdinand Ochsenheimer, he suddenly forsook the baker's ovens, penciling on the paper onto which he had just placed some sugared nuts: "Diese vierzig Nuss' sind meine letzte Buss" (these forty nuts are my last penance). The reference was to his disregard for the instructions of his now-deceased father to avoid the stage. In later years Raimund said, "Man wollte mich zwingen, einen anderen Stand zu wählen, als den eines Künstlers, aber ich konnte von meinen romantischen Träumen nicht lassen und wollte lieber hungern, als meinem Entschlusse entsagen." (People wanted to force me to choose a different craft than that of an artist, but I couldn't forsake my romantic dreams and was ready to go hungry rather than to renounce my decision.) He made the rounds of the theater directors in Vienna in 1808 but was rejected by each of them because he could not properly pronounce the letter "R." Therefore he had to begin his acting career with an unknown troop of roving players who performed in country towns in Austria and Hungary. After a two-year struggle with hunger and despair he joined the troop of Christoph Kuntz, which did not travel but instead had regular summer and winter engagements. Raimund now received good theatrical training, in compensation for low wages, and he was able to choose his roles. His preference was for comic characters and "Intriganten" (intriguers). In 1814, at the age of twenty-four and with six years of acting experience behind him, Raimund finally returned to Vienna to join the ensemble of the smallest and least important of the three Volkstheater, the Josefstädter Theater, located in the suburb of Josefstadt. There, too, he played second-ranked comic roles and "Intriganten." He had a successful debut as the peasant Feldkümmel in August von Kotzebue's comedy *Die Belagerung von Saragossa* (The Siege of Saragossa). As Franz Moor in Friedrich Schiller's *Die Räuber* (The Robbers, 1781), Raimund astounded the audience by mimicking perfectly, down to the smallest detail, the performance in that role of Ferdinand Ochsenheimer. Even the final words to the audience at the end of the play, followed his model exactly. He gave a perfect imitation of Ochsenheimer in the role of Gessler in Schiller's *Wilhelm Tell* (1804) and in dramas with a medieval setting. Raimund found his role model for the popular plays set in Vienna in Ignaz Schuster who, a few years later, was to become his main competitor for the favor of the audience. Since Schuster was humpbacked and successfully used this deformity to comic effect, especially in playing Viennese "Spiessbürger" (narrow-minded and often slightly ridiculous citizens), Raimund imitated the trademark with a pillow under his costume. Theater critics were divided in their response to his mimicry.

Raimund's original performances displayed a natural stage presence. He worked hard to build up a solid reputation so that he might join the ensemble of the Leopoldstädter Theater, the best of the Wiener Volkstheater. In 1815 he made a guest appearance there with Luise Gleich, a colleague from the Josefstädter Theater, performing in the comedy *Die Musikanten am Hohenmarkt* (The Musicians of Highmarket). He began to ad lib, first adding couplets and later creating new scenes. In 1816 he was selected as one of the six best players at the Josefstädter Theater and was made director of the ensemble. Raimund abandoned his mimicry and the critics acknowledged his acting potential: "Dieser echt lustige, humoristische Schauspieler gewinnt mit jedem Tag" (this really humorous comedian is improving day by day). He was called a born comedian, and it was asserted "selbst seine Ernsthaftigkeit gehört dem Komischen an" (even his seriousness was in the realm of the comic). Raimund's wit and gift for extemporization could save even a poor play from disaster.

In 1817 he joined the ensemble of the Theater in der Leopoldstadt and, in 1818, created a public scandal there with the actress Therese Grünthal, with whom he was living. Insults were hurled; Raimund slapped Therese and struck her with his cane in the theater lobby. Despite his apology from the stage, he spent three days in prison in irons. The scandal did not hurt his reputation in the least, and he was declared the public's favorite actor of the popular stage. Soon after, he performed the role of Fritz in *Der lustige Fritz* (Carefree Fritz), one of the many contemporary parodies of serious and moralistic dramas. Fritz, the spoiled son of the operator of a secondhand store, contracts many debts and sees in a dream the error of his ways. Raimund's performance of the play's ditty, "Wer a Geld hat, kann . . ." (Whoever has money can . . .), turned it into a popular song by adding successive verses cataloguing all imaginable human pleasures. Raimund established rapport with his audience not only with his prepared text changes but also by inserting extemporaneous comments on every topic but politics. His role in *Die travestierte Zauberflöte* (The Travestied Magic Flute), whose witticisms played on Mozart's *Die Zauberflöte* (1791), raised his popularity to new heights only a year after he had come to the Leopoldstädter Theater. On theater programs his name now appeared in larger type than others and popular playwrights began to write special roles for him, particularly those in which a character undergoes a transformation and those employing the quodlibets or light-hearted repartees, in which Raimund excelled.

At about this time Raimund met Antonie (Toni) Wagner, his one true love. For business reasons, this nineteen-year-old daughter of a café owner engaged in conversation with admiring male patrons. Raimund was soon taking walks through town with Toni, who saw evidence of his popularity in the many pictures, painted by Moritz von Schwird, of the comedian with the curly blond hair. He was the only actor of his day to be accorded this honor. A year later, Raimund called on Toni's parents to ask for her hand, only to be refused in no uncertain terms. The Wagner family had gained substantial wealth and reputation in business, primarily through the energy and enterprise of Frau Wagner, whose word was law. She objected to Raimund's profession, which was not highly esteemed among the bourgeoisie; she was also familiar with the scandal over Therese Grünthal. Soon after Frau Wagner's refu-

sal Raimund became seriously ill. He considered his family background no less bourgeois than that of the Wagners; only through an unfortunate turn of fate, the early death of his parents, had he become impoverished.

During this period of depression he was consoled by Luise Gleich, whom he had known since his first acting days in Vienna. The nature of the solace of the young, attractive, and not at all prudish actress made Raimund feel obliged to marry her. (Luise complained that her honor had been compromised and demanded satisfaction through the blessing of the Church.) On the morning of the scheduled ceremony, however, the couple had a spat in which the bridegroom was bitten on the finger and consequently left the bride waiting at the altar. "Aber beissen–am Hochzeitstage! I bitt' Ihne–das kann jo a Viech umbringen!" (But biting me, on our wedding day! If you please– that would do even an animal in!). The public soon learned of the incident and booed its favorite the next time he appeared on stage. When Raimund was not persuaded by the public mood, trickery was used to bring the recalcitrant bridegroom to heel. A respected citizen invited him to his home to discuss the matter and soon bested him with his persuasive arguments. At that point, Luise and her father, Joseph Alois Gleich, entered from a side door, the former begging his forgiveness for injury, the latter imploring him to marry Luise. Unable to withstand the pressure, Raimund consented. Through a second door, a priest and altar boy entered and immediately performed the ceremony. The wedding took place in April 1820 and, in October, "Amalia Reimann, vulgo Raimund" was born; Raimund naturally assumed he was the father. After the wedding, Toni received an emotional letter of farewell to which she replied with birthday greetings on June 1. Their correspondence continued in secret, without the knowledge of Luise or the elder Wagners.

Raimund's marriage was short-lived. Claiming physical abuse, the young wife returned to her parents' home in July 1821, and a divorce was granted the following January. In the summer, the so-called Kinderballettskandal, or Children's Ballet Scandal, became public and Raimund learned that he had been duped by Luise and her father. Gleich, the author of two hundred popular plays, was one of the most important Viennese playwrights of the period. Because of his extravagant life-style, however, he was never out of debt. For ten years, since she was thirteen, Luise had regularly been given to Prince Alois Kaunitz von Reitberg by her father in return for five hundred florins and valuable presents. Over the years, the wealthy Kaunitz had sexually used 113 girls, mostly minors, including many from the famous Viennese Children's Ballet. Police reports indicated that the most recent rendezvous between Kaunitz and Luise had been in the month of her marriage to Raimund.

The performances of the actor-playwright were now being more closely watched by the censors because of his frequent improvisations; occasionally, a play was withdrawn from the stage. His success continued unabated, although during his marriage he often suffered from depression. In May 1821 the theater was reorganized and the players' contracts were renegotiated. Raimund now received a generous salary commensurate with his acting skills and reputation, but even though his future seemed secure, inner peace eluded him. The continuance of his rendezvous with Toni depended upon the surreptitious aid of her sisters and the widow of a theater make-up artist, in whose apartment they met. Whenever Raimund spotted Toni in her parents' café in the midst of her admirers, with whom she conversed jovially, he fell into despair; Toni was similarly jealous of the actresses with whom Raimund performed. Their letters were full of recriminations in which they spoke of separation, but neither could bear to take that step. Since Austrian law forbade the marriage of a divorced person, they swore eternal fidelity before the figure of the Virgin Mary in a country chapel at Mariazell on 10 September 1822. Raimund was soon forced to secure the dismissal from the theater ensemble of Luise Gleich; for her part, Luise publicly and falsely cited Raimund as the father of three of her children, born in 1823, 1828, and 1830.

By this time the actor no longer found the plays of other dramatists sufficient for his continued success. His acting seemed to be routine and less compelling. The time for a new writer of popular comedies was at hand. Through his additions of dialogue and a closing aria, Raimund's name had first appeared as an author on a play-bill in 1822. He was then thirty-two years old and had been performing on the stages of Vienna for eight years. When the play written for his annual actor's benefit performance prescribed for him in his new contract did not suit him, he replaced it with his own comedy, *Der Barometermacher auf der Zauberinsel* (The Barome-

ter Maker on the Magic Island, published in 1837). The play was in the tradition of the Viennese theater, but the plot was borrowed from a fairy tale, "The Princess with the Long Nose." The work demonstrated Raimund's talent as a dramatist, aided by his extensive acting experience, and also his skill at adapting epic material to drama. This comedy came at the beginning of a wave of "Zauberspiele" (magic plays), which populated South Sea island settings with the Viennese petit-bourgeoisie. The main character, the fairy-tale prince Tutu, undergoes a burlesque transformation and reappears as Bartholomäus Quecksilber (Bartholomew Quicksilver), a failed Viennese maker of barometers. As was customary in the local "Volksstück" (popular play), he enters with an aria and a monologue. Raimund made generous use of music throughout the play, including duets and choral pieces, in addition to arias and melodies which introduced the various roles, in the manner of a leitmotif. Since Quecksilber had been a failure in Vienna, he was sailing the world, looking for a better location to ply his trade, only to be shipwrecked and washed up onto a distant island. A fairy gives him the instruments and materials of his trade as well as a talisman, which practically insures his success in all his undertakings. He immediately tries to marry the fairy and becomes involved in an assortment of adventures; in the end, he chooses the chambermaid. Quecksilber rules the island as Prince Tutu and acts just as the average petit-bourgeois of Vienna would. Raimund was quite successful with this first comedy.

Ever since his audience had shown him so little sympathy in his plight with Luise Gleich, Raimund's feelings toward the public had cooled, and he had become increasingly distrustful of people in general. He bought a horse and carriage and employed a driver-manservant, so that he could escape Vienna and unnecessary human contact whenever his acting schedule permitted. He was fond of romantic landscapes and particularly enjoyed exploring old castle ruins. Although his hypochondria and depression were now worsening, he had, by December 1824, written and begun to perform a new play for his annual actor's benefit. *Der Diamant des Geisterkönigs* (The Diamond of the Spirit King, published in 1837) was borrowed in part from the story of Alasnam and the King of the Genies in *The Arabian Nights*. He used only the episode of the pink statue; however, motifs from several other sources were also included: the trials of his hero Eduard, for example, have their origin in the tests by fire and water of Mozart's *Die Zauberflöte.* The traditional folk-play plot involves the acquisition of inherited wealth through the discovery of an enchanted diamond statue. Although Raimund's comic figures Florian and Mariandl still possess stereotyped aspects of the folk clown, the beginnings of individual characterization are perceptible. In the original fairy tale the spirit king demands something concrete in exchange for the pink statue, specifically, a fifteen-year-old girl who has never felt the desire for a man. Raimund elevates the ethical horizon, however, and introduces, instead of material compensation for the statue, a test of truthfulness. The least truthful women are to be found just in the realm of King Veritatius, who wishes to hear only the "truth" that is pleasant to his own ears.

This comedy was even more enthusiastically received than *Der Barometermacher.* It was performed beyond Austrian borders in Munich and Berlin. Translations into Czech, Italian, and Polish appeared, as well as a Danish version by Hans Christian Andersen. *Der Diamant des Geisterkönigs* played many months in Vienna, and the fiftieth performance was still a sell-out. Finally, at the end of May 1825, Raimund's nerves suddenly could no longer stand the strain. When he returned to the stage four months later, Toni and her mother were in the audience to greet him and to witness the seemingly endless applause. He was presented with a commemorative medal. In the course of the year, Toni began to visit Raimund at his apartment and her mother appeared to accept him, since he was a well-paid and famous actor-playwright. Despite these encouraging signs, he continued to suffer bouts of depression accompanied by severe headaches and stomach cramps. He continued to flee the city and to seek solace in nature; occasionally, however, he appeared extroverted, enjoyed company, and told stories and jokes in great good humor. In September 1826 Raimund experienced one of his last great triumphs with a play other than his own, *Glück in Wien* (Happiness in Vienna), and his critical and popular acclaim were almost universal.

Raimund's third comedy was *Der Bauer als Millionär; oder, Das Mädchen aus der Feenwelt* (The Peasant as a Millionaire; or, The Girl from the Fairy World, published in 1837). Here he did not borrow motifs from literary sources but invented a simple plot of his own on the theme of the transitoriness of all material things. It portrays the trans-

Raimund as Aschenmann, 1827 (lithograph by Joseph Kriehuber, after a drawing by Moritz von Schwind)

formation of the peasant Fortunatus Wurzel, who becomes a millionaire–a turn of events which, in the popular plays of the day, could be attributed only to magic–and shows how he lost his wealth through a life of self-indulgence and injustice toward others. The conflict of good and evil is built into a lively and typically Viennese parody of the world of the fairies. Raimund includes the usual love story of folk comedy, fraught with obstacles. Lottchen is the child of a fairy and was raised as a foster child by Fortunatus Wurzel. She is not spoiled by wealth as he is, and her marriage to Karl, the young fisherman, brings happiness to the couple and also breaks the spell cast upon her fairy mother as a punishment for arrogance. While the companions of the lovers are simple folk figures, the Viennese "Schnackerl-Noblesse"–or gossipy, would-be aristocrats–keep company with the fairies and put on airs. Eventually, the magic spell through which Wurzel received his wealth is broken, and he suddenly becomes old and poor. The scene in which the allegorical figure of youth takes leave of the arrogant peasant is one of the most beautiful in German theater and this role brought fame to the actress Therese Krones. Fortunatus Wurzel becomes an ash collector, a familiar figure of the Viennese street scene and a symbol of transitoriness. The suffering which this reversal of circumstances entails has a healing effect; he becomes satisfied with his lot in life and is not embittered. In the tradition of Viennese local drama since the seventeenth-century baroque, Raimund made liberal use of allegorical figures in this comedy. In conjunction with the fairy realm, youth and age, hate, envy, and satisfaction appear, as do various figures of ancient mythology. As in other comedies by Raimund, many characters in *Der Bauer als Millionär* were based on persons the playwright knew: Lottchen was thought to represent a sister of his beloved Toni who had helped the lovers find a meeting place. Because of its "human content," the play was one of Raimund's most successful, and it has never lost its popularity. At the hundredth performance, Moritz von Schwind made six handsome lithographs of the players in the principal roles, including Raimund as "Aschenmann." The song "Brüderlein fein" (Nice Little Brother), bidding farewell to youth, became an enchanting folk song which may be heard still today in collections of Viennese melodies.

Raimund's next dramatic effort was not very successful. The plot of *Die gefesselte Fantasie* (Fettered Imagination, published in 1837), was again the playwright's invention, and its theme was once more the conflict between good and evil, the struggle between the powers of light and darkness. An oracular utterance by Apollo gives impetus to the plot. A poetry contest, a distant echo of the great events of the Athenians, is held in order to usher in the marriage of Queen Hermine and her beloved, the shepherd Amphio. The fairy sisters Vipria and Arrogantia make use of the Viennese harpist "Nachtigall" (Nightingale) to frustrate the wedding plans. Apollo later serves as the deus ex machina to assist in the victory of good over evil. Critics spoke of the Shakespearian power of Raimund's text, but the audience of the popular theater was not accustomed or inclined to enjoy esoteric comedies on themes from Greek antiquity, and the play closed after relatively few performances.

With *Moisasur's Zauberfluch* (Moisasur's Magic Spell, published in 1837) Raimund continued along the path of elevated drama. Allegories and symbols as well as allusions to Shakespeare increased in frequency. Once again, good struggles with evil. In genuinely folksy scenes, a poor but compassionate quarryman and his wife confront hard-hearted, rich peasants. In the allegorical frame story, Moisasur, the demon of evil, puts a curse on Queen Alzinde of India. In her "Tugendheiligtum" (sanctuary of virtue) her high moral standards dictate a readiness to sacrifice her own life for Hoanghu, her spouse. As the plot progresses, the curse takes effect: everything is taken from Alzinde–her youth, beauty, and royal position–but she retains her youthful spirit, "damit sie zehnfach jeden Schmerz empfinde und die Erinnerung ihres Glücks sie quäle" (so that she will experience her pain tenfold and the remembrance of her happiness will torment her). That her anguish may be increased, the curse of Moisasur specifies that Alzinde is to cry tears of diamonds and thus expose herself to crass human greed. In the role played by Raimund himself, the deadly sin of avarice is exemplified in Gluthahn, a wealthy Viennese farmer who is hypocritical, envious, and cynical. The sadism and general meanness with which he torments his wife to her death are antithetical to the sacrificial love of Alzinde for her husband. Legal proceedings, in which Alzinde is sentenced to death as a witch, signal the end of the local Viennese element introduced with Gluthahn, and thereafter the drama ascends to grandiose heights. The demon Moisasur had set a condition for Alzinde's deliverance: "Nur dann, wenn Alzinde im Arm des Todes Freudentränen weint, kehrt ihr zurück, was ihr mein Zauberfluch entriss" (only when Alzinde weeps tears of joy in the arms of death will she be given once again what my magic spell took from her). Thus, the joy of the Queen of India at the prospect of death restores life.

This comedy was not considered humorous enough to play well in das Theater in der Leopoldstadt and therefore premiered at the Theater an der Wien (Theater on the Vienna River), owned by one Carl Carl, an aggressive businessman whose design to control all three Volkstheater in Vienna had been frustrated only by Raimund's influence. Carl himself played the role of Gluthahn to perfection by giving expression to his own personality. Although *Moisasur's Zauberfluch* was performed for several years and did better than *Die gefesselte Fantasie*, its success nevertheless was limited. The Viennese theater world reacted in typical fashion to the play, making it the subject of a parody, *Moisasur's*

Hexenspruch (The Witch's Spell of Moisasur), which trivialized its serious undertone.

Early in 1828 the Leopoldstädter Theater changed hands, and Raimund was named artistic director. His initial optimism quickly cooled, however, when he learned of the plans of the new owner, Rudolf Steinkeller, who knew little about theater operation and was primarily interested in increased profits through reduced expenditures. Within two years the best Viennese popular theater had gone bankrupt. Raimund took every opportunity to escape Vienna and the depressing conditions at the theater. During his first absence, Steinkeller dismissed twenty actors, entirely against his director's wishes.

On 17 October 1828 Raimund's new comedy, *Der Alpenkönig und der Menschenfeind* (The King of the Alps and the Misanthrope, published in 1837) had its premiere in the Leopoldstädter Theater. It was a very different play from the preceding two in that allegories and symbols had been replaced by masterfully sketched individuals; its success surpassed even that of *Der Bauer als Millionär*. A comparison of Fortunatus Wurzel in the earlier play with Herr von Rappelkopf in *Der Alpenkönig und der Menschenfeind* illustrates the playwright's progress in character development. Raimund had introduced a certain lightness and human warmth into the serious plot, which had been inherently lacking in the earlier abstract allegorical figures. Rappelkopf is not a misanthrope purely by nature but because his relationship to the world has become unbalanced; it is a subjective reaction of his choleric temperament and his tendency to hypochondria, a problem also in Raimund's personality. One day, when he is walking in the forest, he meets Astragalus, the King of the Alps, who convinces him that he himself is to blame for his misanthropy. Astragalus possesses a fatherly kindness as well as an element of magic which helps in the "Bekehrung" (change in the mind-set), of Rappelkopf. In his self-examination, the misanthrope can see himself reflected in a revealing mirror image. The plot direction is indicated in the promise of the King of the Alps to the daughter of Rappelkopf: "Erkennen wird mit seinem Wahnsinn rechten," meaning that her father's self-recognition of his nature will contend with his unnatural antagonism toward his fellow man. As a result, "Die Sterne werden bald zur Brautnacht winken" (the stars will soon signal a bridal night), for her father will sanction her marriage to her beloved.

The simple idea that a person might change through a personal examination of his nature is skillfully carried out. *Der Alpenkönig und der Menschenfeind* is a confessional play in which Raimund recognizes and tries to come to terms with his own feelings of disdain for others. In his letters to Toni are complaints about envious individuals, schemers, and enemies of all sorts whose numbers Raimund overestimated, just as he failed to recognize his many friends and admirers. Rappelkopf soothes his anger in the solitude of nature; Raimund found solace in the Viennese Forest, the areas around Brühl and the village of Gutenstein, or in the foothills of the Alps. Though society was imperfect, Raimund viewed nature as a well-ordered, divine creation where man can find peace and healing, symbolized by the King of the Alps. Herr von Rappelkopf was able to find a permanent cure for his malady; however, Raimund's healing was only temporary: with each return to civilization he reverted to his former tormented state of mind. Rappelkopf's long-suffering wife is called Antonie or Toni in the first draft of the play. Her abiding love despite mistreatment suggests Raimund's apology for Toni Wagner's difficult times when he himself was at odds with the world.

Franz Grillparzer praised Raimund's approach in this play: "Ein psychologisch wahreres, an Entwicklungen reicheres Thema hat noch kein Lustspieldichter gewählt" (no writer of comedy has chosen a theme that incorporates more psychological truth and greater development). Although he did not see the play, the aged Goethe responded positively when given a resumé of the first act: "Der Gedanke ist nicht übel und verrät Theaterkenntnis" (the idea is not bad and reveals a knowledge of the theater). *Der Alpenkönig und der Menschenfeind* played on many stages: in Pressburg in 1829 with Johannes Nepomuk Nestroy, Raimund's later rival, as Rappelkopf; in Linz, Prague, and Hamburg; in 1830 in Berlin and Dresden; in English translation and subsequently adapted to the British stage by the actor John Baldwin Buckstone. The comedy was so popular that it ran continuously for three months in the Adelphi Theater in London in 1831. *Der Alpenkönig und der Menschenfeind*, more than any other play by Raimund, belongs to world theater literature.

Except for the continuing success of this play, 1829 was not a good year for Raimund. Irritated by the economy measures of Steinkeller, he continued to use every opportunity to absent himself from Vienna and to work on a new play. *Die unheilbringende Krone* (The Unpropitious Crown, published in 1837), which premiered in December, was his only complete failure. Thematically, the play relates to *Moisasur's Zauberfluch*, whose characters in the final scenes utter profundities in grandiose diction. *Die unheilbringende Krone* begins with similar scenes and opaquely presents a struggle between good and evil. In comparison to the simple concepts of the previous work, the plot was too complicated for the audience of the "Volkstheater," the triadic subtitle suggests: *König ohne Reich, Held ohne Mut, Schönheit ohne Jugend* (King without a Kingdom, Hero without Courage, Beauty without Youth). To solve the dilemma posed by the comedy, not one or two but three conditions must be fulfilled. After twelve performances, the play was dropped from the repertoire. Its failure worsened the relationship between Raimund and Rudolf Steinkeller, who had allegedly invested eight thousand florins in its production. In April 1830 Raimund legally terminated his contract as artistic director, which was to have run another eight months. In June he appeared opposite the famous comedian Ignaz Schuster in a favorite local comedy, *Evakathel und Schnudi*. There was long and thunderous applause as the old rivals bowed hand in hand at the end of the performance.

Now free of contract obligations, Raimund appeared only in guest roles in the three "Wiener Volkstheater" as well as in Prague, Munich, Hamburg, and Berlin. His long-standing wish was fulfilled: he and Toni were able to share an apartment in the house of her parents. She accompanied him on excursions and, in the summer, lived with him in the beautifully situated town of Gutenstein. The poet nevertheless continued to be plagued by bouts of depression and his old nervous ailments. Homeopathic treatments produced temporary improvements but no permanent cure. When friends complained of his persistent melancholy and hypochondria, Raimund answered: "Sie sein vüll glücklicher als i; Sie hab a rosenfarbnes Bluet, das allweil lusti in Ihne uma laauft; habe z'Haus a guets Weiba und schöni Kinder. Was hab' i? Ruhm? No ja. 's is halt wahr. Aba was hab i z'Haus? Nix. Wann i mi'm Spülln ferti bin, so find' i a eifersüchtige, dummi Person [Toni], di mi z'Tod sekkiert." (You are much happier than I am; you have good red blood coursing through your veins that keeps you in good humor; at home you have a wife and beautiful children. What do I have? Fame?

Well, yes. It's true. But what do I have at home? Nothing. When I finish a performance I find at home a jealous, stupid person [Toni] who just nags me to death).

Late in October 1830, shortly after leaving the Leopoldstädter Theater, Raimund began a forty-one-evening guest appearance in the Theater an der Wien, playing mostly in his own comedies. The following February, he began in Munich, but after only three performances he was overtaken by a spell of deep melancholy and nervousness, accompanied by severe headaches and stomach distress. He had no appetite and could not sleep. On the advice of physicians who urged him to take a trip to the mountains, he went to Garmisch and Partenkirchen. At an inn where he had stopped for an hour's rest, a trained bird was whistling the first measure of a popular song from *Der Bauer als Millionär*. Raimund was so moved and strengthened that he immediately returned to Munich and finished his scheduled guest appearance. In June 1831, under the spell of the mountainous area he loved and acting on a suggestion of Franz Grillparzer to write another comedy similar to *Der Alpenkönig und der Menschenfeind*, the playwright began to work on "Die Gewitternacht im Himalaja" (Stormy Night in the Himalayas). He made little progress, however, and the manuscript has been lost. In 1831 and 1832 Raimund continued his busy schedule of guest appearances in Germany. Between these he frequently sought rest and relaxation with Toni and his friends, away from the large cities. January through April 1833 found him back for a thirty-three-performance guest appearance at the Josefstädter Theater, where he had first performed in Vienna.

In his last comedy, *Der Verschwender* (published in 1837; translated as *The Spendthrift*, 1949), he abandoned the unnatural bombast of *Die unheilbringende Krone* and returned to the familiar Viennese tone and nuance of his most successful works. *Der Verschwender* was one of the last plays to be written in the now fading tradition of the Zauberspiel. The critical realism of the rising actor-playwright Johannes Nepomuk Nestroy was displacing the old romantic idealism. Raimund was well aware of the new direction of the sharp-tongued "Wiener Aristophanes" (Viennese Aristophanes). He attended a performance of Nestroy's *Lumpazivagabundus* (1833) and abhorred both the play and its title. Raimund forbade Nestroy to take roles in his plays because Nestroy, with his sarcastic wit, interpreted them in a vulgar and cynical manner. Raimund knew that the old era was coming to an end. In *Der Verschwender*, through magic, the fairy Cheristane is ready to do everything possible for Julius Flottwell, the spendthrift whom she loves platonically. But when she has sacrificed her last magic pearl for him, her power on earth is at an end. She can no longer influence his fate, and he himself must create his fortune, good or bad. Flottwell is as wasteful with the time allotted to him on earth as he is with the money he has received for Cheristane's pearls. Accordingly, he gives away to her a year of his life, which is personified as a beggar who becomes his constant companion and practically extorts as many presents from him as possible. Cheristane saves these presents for Flottwell and through their later return is able to save him from complete ruin. For in his late years and through his own foolishness, Flottwell becomes impoverished. Opposite Flottwell is his servant Valentin, the role performed by the playwright himself. The modest rise of this simple cabinetmaker, who embodies benevolence and charity, is contrasted with the steep descent of the once-enormously rich Flottwell. Indeed, the latter spends his last years with his former servant, the lives of both made more tolerable by the return of the presents Flottwell had once given to the beggar-emissary of Cheristane. In the first two acts, Valentin is the traditional Viennese comic character, but in the third, set twenty years later, he has become the exponent of the philosophy voiced in the popular song, "Da streiten sich die Leut herum wohl um den Wert des Glückes" (to think people will argue about the value to be placed on happiness). After *Der Bauer als Millionär* and *Der Alpenkönig und der Menschenfeind*, *Der Verschwender* was Raimund's third great success and one of the comedies which remain popular today. Raimund performed in it forty-one times during his fifty-two-performance second guest appearance in the Josefstädter Theater, January through April 1834. It was also a great financial success which enabled him to buy a country house and land in his beloved Gutenstein.

Raimund continued to accept many invitations for guest performances in and outside Vienna. In August 1836, while playing with a dog, he noticed two small bites, which quickly healed. Shortly after that, he and Toni made a pilgrimage to the chapel at Mariazell where, fourteen years earlier, they had sworn eternal fidelity. Upon their return to Gutenstein, they learned that the dog had been shot by a farmer who thought it rabid. Raimund left immediately for Vienna to see a physician but stopped in the village of Pottenstein at an inn, The Golden Stag, to wait out a storm. Ever more fearful that he would feel an aversion to water, which was taken to be a sure sign of rabies infection, he could not sleep. Around 4:00 A.M. he opened the window, complaining of feeling hot and of an anxiety greater than he had ever before experienced. To comfort him, Toni went to get a glass of water, but during her brief absence, Raimund put a pistol barrel into his mouth and shot himself. He died seven days later, on 5 September 1836. An autopsy revealed no sign of rabies infection. Ferdinand Jakob Raimund was buried at Gutenstein, at the site he had chosen nine years before. It was not until the year after his death that his plays were first published, in the four-volume *Sämmtliche Werke* (Collected Works).

Letters:
Ferdinand Raimunds Liebesbriefe, edited by Fritz Brukner (Vienna: Moritz Perles, 1914).

References:
Wolfgang Bender, "Verkennung und Erkennung in Ferdinand Raimunds Zauberspiel *Der Alpenkönig und der Menschenfeind*," *Germanisch-Romanische Monatsschrift*, 18 (1968): 58-71;

Hans Buczkowski, "Der Tod im Goldenen Hirschen. Ferdinand Raimund und Pottenstein. Zum 150. Todestag des Dichters am 5. September 1986," *Morgen*, 10 (1986): 203-205;

Roger Crockett, "Raimund's *Der Verschwender*. The Illusion of Freedom," *The German Quarterly*, 58 (1985): 184-193;

Claude David, "Ferdinand Raimund: *Moisasurs Zauberfluch*," in *Das deutsche Lustspiel*, edited by Steffen Hans, volume 1 (Göttingen: Vandenhoeck & Ruprecht, 1968), pp. 120-143;

Günther Erken, "Ferdinand Raimund" in *Deutsche Dichter des 19. Jahrhunderts*, edited by Benno von Wiese (Berlin: E. Schmidt, 1979), pp. 362-384;

Grete Fink-Töbich, *Das Schicksal setzt den Hobel an. Der Lebensroman Ferdinand Raimunds* (Klagenfurt: Heyn, 1969);

Rolf Geissler, "Raimunds *Verschwender* oder Der gute Mensch im Biedermeier," *Jahrbuch der Grillparzer-Gesellschaft*, 16 (1984/1986): 105-112;

Laurence V. Harding, *The Dramatic Art of Ferdinand Raimund and Johannes Nestroy: A Critical Study* (The Hague: Mouton, 1974);

Jürgen Hein, "Gefesselte Komik. Der Spielraum des Komischen in Ferdinand Raimunds Volkstheater," *Austriaca*, 8, no. 14 (1982): 73-86;

Hugo von Hofmannsthal, "Ferdinand Raimund" in *Gesammelte Werke, Prosa III.* (Frankfurt am Main: Fischer, 1952), pp. 471-478;

Margaret Jacobs, "Legitimate and Illegitimate Drama: Ferdinand Raimund's *Der Alpenkönig und der Menschenfeind* and John Baldwin Buckstone's *The King of the Alps*," *German Life and Letters*, 31 (1977/1978): 41-52;

Kurt Kahl, *Raimund (Friedrichs Dramatiker des Welttheaters, 35)* (Velber: Friedrich, 1967);

Heinz Kindermann, *Ferdinand Raimund: Lebenswerk und Wirkungsraum eines deutschen Volksdramatikers* (Vienna & Leipzig: Luser, 1940);

John Michalski, *Ferdinand Raimund* (New York: Twayne, 1968);

Corliss Edwin Phillabaum, "The Theater of Ferdinand Raimund: The Maid from Fairyland or The Peasant as Millionaire, Mountain King and Misanthrope," Ph.D. dissertation, Ohio State University, 1962;

Heinz Politzer, "Alt-Wiener Theaterlieder," *Forum*, 7, 8 (1960, 1961): 26-29;

Hermann Pongs, "Ferdinand Raimund: *Der Alpenkönig und der Menschenfeind*" in Hermann Pongs, *Das Bild in der Dichtung* (Marburg: Elwert, 1973);

W. Pötscher, "Euripides *Herakliden* und Ferdinand Raimunds *Der Bauer als Millionär*," *Literaturwissenschaftliches Jahrbuch*, 17 (1976): 343-347;

Dorothy Prohaska, *Raimund and Vienna: A Critical Study of Raimund's Plays in their Viennese Setting* (Cambridge: Cambridge University Press, 1970);

Prohaska, "Raimund's Contribution to the Viennese Popular Comedies," *The German Quarterly*, 42 (1969): 352-367;

Raimund Almanach, edited by the Raimund-Gesellschaft (Vienna: Bergland, 1963-);

August Sauer, "Ferdinand Raimund. Eine Charakteristik," in *Gesammelte Reden und Aufsätze* (Vienna & Leipzig: Fromme, 1903), pp. 240-274;

W. G. Sebald, "Die Mädchen aus der Feenwelt. Bemerkungen zu Liebe und Prostitution mit Bezügen zu Raimund, Schnitzler und Horwáth," *Neophilologus*, 67 (1983), Heft 1: 109-117;

Reinhard Urbach, "Zufriedenheit bei Ferdinand Raimund," *Austriaca*, 9 (1975): 107-126;

Michael Wachsmann, "Spielebenen als Stilebenen in Ferdinand Raimund," Ph. D. dissertation, University of Munich, 1975;

Edith Wagesreiter-Castle, "Schillerische Züge in Raimunds Dichterantlitz," *Österreich in Geschichte und Literatur* 19 (1975): 257-288;

Hans Weigel, "Ferdinand Raimund oder die Flucht in die Zwiespalt," *Neue Deutsche Hefte*, 6 (1959/1960): 503-516.

Papers:

The first draft of each of Ferdinand Raimund's dramas is in the manuscript collection of the Stadtbibliothek Wien. Final versions prepared by copyists for promptbooks, literary censors, and sale to theater directors are in the manuscript collections of the Stadtbibliothek Wien and the Österreichische Nationalbibliothek, Vienna. Almost all of Raimund's private and business correspondence has been preserved in the Stadtbibliothek Wien.

Friedrich Wilhelm Joseph von Schelling

(27 January 1775-20 August 1854)

Martin Donougho
University of South Carolina

BOOKS: *Ueber die Möglichkeit einer Form der Philosophie überhaupt* (Tübingen: Heerbrandt, 1795);

Vom Ich als Princip der Philosophie oder über das Unbedingte im menschlichen Wissen (Tübingen: Heerbrandt, 1795); translated by Fritz Marti as "Of the I as Principle of Philosophy, or on the Unconditional in Human Knowledge," in *The Unconditional in Human Knowledge: Four Early Essays (1794-1796)* (Lewisburg, Pa.: Bucknell University Press, 1980), pp. 63-149;

Ideen zu einer Philosophie der Natur (Leipzig: Breitkopf & Härtel, 1797); revised as *Ideen zu einer Philosophie der Natur, als Einleitung in das Studium dieser Wissenschaft* (Landshut: Krüll, 1803); translated by Errol Harris and Peter Heath as *Ideas for a Philosophy of Nature as Introduction to the Study of that Science* (Cambridge & New York: Cambridge University Press, 1988);

Von der Weltseele: Eine Hypothese der höheren Physik zur Erklärung des allgemeinen Organismus (Hamburg: Perthes, 1798); revised as *Erklärung des allgemeinen Organismus: Nebst einer Abhandlung über das Verhältniß des Realen und Idealen in der Natur, oder Entwicklung der ersten Grundsätze der Naturphilosophie an den Principien der Schwere und des Lichts* (Hamburg: Perthes, 1806; revised again, 1809);

Erster Entwurf eines Systems der Naturphilosophie: Zum Behuf seiner Vorlesungen (Jena & Leipzig: Gabler, 1799);

Einleitung zu einem Entwurf eines Systems der Naturphilosophie. Oder: Ueber den Begriff der speculativen Physik und die innere Organisation eines Systems dieser Wissenschaft (Jena & Leipzig: Gabler, 1799);

System des transcendentalen Idealismus (Tübingen: Cotta, 1800); translated by Heath as *System of Transcendental Idealism* (Charlottesville: University of Virginia Press, 1978);

Bruno oder über das göttliche und natürliche Princip der Dinge: Ein Gespräch (Berlin: Unger,

Friedrich Wilhelm Joseph von Schelling (Bildarchiv der Österreichischen Nationalbibliothek, Vienna)

1802); translated by Michael G. Vater as *Bruno; or, On the Natural and the Divine Principle of Things* (Albany: State University of New York Press, 1984);

Vorlesungen über die Methode des academischen Studium (Tübingen: Cotta, 1803); translated by Ella S. Morgan as *On University Studies*, edited by Norbert Guterman (Athens: Ohio University Press, 1966);

Philosophie und Religion (Tübingen: Cotta, 1804);

Ueber das Verhältniß der bildenden Künste zu der Natur: Eine Rede zur Feier des 12ten Oktobers als des Allerhöchsten Namenfestes Seiner Königlichen Majestät von Baiern gehalten in der öffentli-

chen Sitzung der Akademie der Wissenschaften (Munich: Krüll, 1807); translated by A. Johnson as *The Philosophy of Art: An Oration on the Relation between the Plastic Arts and Nature* (London: Chapman, 1845);

F. W. J. Schelling's philosophische Schriften (Landshut: Krüll, 1809)–comprises "Vom Ich als Princip der Philosophie oder Über das Unbedingte in menschlichen Wissen"; "Philosophische Briefe über Dogmatismus und Kriticismus," translated by Marti as "Philosophical Letters on Dogmatism and Criticism," in *The Unconditional in Human Knowledge*, pp. 156-218; "Abhandlungen zur Erläuterung des Idealismus der Wissenschaftslehre"; "Über das Verhältniß der bildenden Künste zu der Natur . . . (Mit Zugabe einiger Anmerkungen)"; "Philosophische Untersuchungen über das Wesen der menschlichen Freyheit und die damit zusammenhängenden Gegenstände," translated by James Gutmann as *Of Human Freedom* (Chicago: Open Court, 1936);

F. W. J. Schelling's Denkmal der Schrift von den göttlichen Dingen etc. des Herrn Friedrich Heinrich Jacobi und der ihm in derselben gemachten Beschuldigung eines absichtlich täuschenden, Lüge redenden Atheismus (Tübingen: Cotta, 1812);

Ueber die Gottheiten von Samothrace vorgelesen in der öffentlichen Sitzung der Baier'schen Akademie der Wissenschaften am Namenstage des Königs, den 12. Oct. 1815: Beylage zu den Weltaltern (Stuttgart & Tübingen: Cotta, 1815); translated by Robert F. Brown as "The Deities of Samothrace," in his *Schelling's Treatise on "The Deities of Samothrace"* (Missoula, Mont.: Scholar's Press, 1976);

Philosophische Untersuchungen über das Wesen der menschlichen Freiheit und die damit zusammenhängenden Gegenstände (Reutlingen: Ennslin, 1834);

Schelling's Erste Vorlesung in Berlin: 15. November 1841 (Stuttgart & Tübingen: Cotta, 1841); translated by Frederic Henry Hedge as "Schelling's Introductory Lecture in Berlin, 15th November 1841," *The Dial* (Boston), 3 (January 1843): 398-404;

Friedrich Wilhelm Joseph von Schellings sämmtliche Werke, 14 volumes (Stuttgart & Augsburg: Cotta, 1856-1861)–includes in volume 5 (1859), "Philosophie der Kunst," pp. 353-736, translated by Douglas W. Stott as *The Philosophy of Art* (Minneapolis: University of Minnesota Press, 1988); in volume 8

(1857), "Die Weltalter: Bruchstück," pp. 195-344, translated by Frederick de Wolfe Bolman, Jr., as *The Ages of the World* (New York: Columbia University Press, 1942); in volume 10 (1861), "Zur Geschichte der neueren Philosophie: Münchener Vorlesungen," pp. 1-200; as volume 11 (1856), *Einleitung in die Philosophie der Mythologie;* as volume 12 (1857), *Philosophie der Mythologie;* as volume 13 (1858), *Philosophie der Offenbarung;*

Clara oder Zusammenhang der Natur mit der Geisterwelt: Ein Gespräch (Stuttgart: Cotta, 1862);

Schellings Werke: Nach der Originalausgabe in neuer Anordnung herausgegeben, edited by Manfred Schröter, 12 volumes (Munich: Beck & Oldenbourg, 1927-1959);

Die Weltalter: Fragmente. In den Urfassungen von 1811 und 1813, edited by Schröter (Munich: Beck & Oldenbourg, 1946);

Initia philosophiae universae: Erlanger Vorlesung WS 1820/21, edited by Horst Furhmans (Bonn: Bouvier, 1969);

Grundlegung der positiven Philosophie: Münchner Vorlesungen WS 1832/33 und SS 1833, edited by Fuhrmans (Turin: Bottega d'Erasmo, 1972);

Stuttgarter Privatvorlesungen, edited by Miklos Vetö (Turin: Bottega d'Erasmo, 1973);

Werke: Historisch-kritische Ausgabe, edited by Hans Michael Baumgartner, Wilhelm Jacobs, Hermann Krings & Hermann Zeltner, 4 volumes published (Stuttgart & Bad Cannstatt: Fromann-Holzboog, 1976-);

Das Tagebuch 1848: Philosophie der Mythologie und demokratische Revolution, edited by Hans Jörg Sandkühler (Hamburg: Meiner, 1988).

Editions: *Vom Ich als Princip der Philosophie*, edited by Otto Weiss (Leipzig: Meiner, 1911);

Ideen zu einer Philosophie der Natur, edited by Weiss (Leipzig: Meiner, 1911);

Von der Weltseele, edited by Weiss (Leipzig: Meiner, 1911);

Vorlesungen über die Methode des academischen Studium, edited by Weiss (Leipzig: Meiner, 1911);

Philosophische Briefe über Dogmatismus und Kriticismus, edited by Otto Braun (Leipzig: Meiner, 1914);

Philosophische Untersuchungen über das Wesen der menschlichen Freiheit, edited by Christian Herrmann (Leipzig: Meiner, 1925);

Bruno, oder Über das göttliche und natürliche Prinzip der Dinge, edited by Herrmann (Leipzig: Meiner, 1928);

System des transzendentalen Idealismus, edited by Walter Schulz (Hamburg: Meiner, 1957);

Über das Verhältniß der bildenden Künste zu der Natur, edited by Lucia Sziborsky (Hamburg: Meiner, 1983).

PERIODICAL PUBLICATIONS: "Über Mythen, historische Sagen und Philosopheme der ältesten Welt," *Memorabilien: Eine philosophisch-theologische Zeitschrift der Geschichte und Philosophie der Religionen,* 5 (1793): 1-68;

"Philosophische Briefe über Dogmatismus und Kriticismus," anonymous, *Philosophisches Journal einer Gesellschaft Teutscher Gelehrten,* 2, no. 3 (1795): 173-239;

"Die letzten Worte des Pfarrers zu Drottning auf Seeland," as Bonaventura, *Musen-Almanach für das Jahr 1802* (1802): 118-128, 241-243;

"Über Dante in philosophischer Beziehung," anonymous, *Kritisches Journal der Philosophie,* 2, no. 2 (1803): 35-50; translated by Henry Wadsworth Longfellow as "Dante's Divina Commedia," *Graham's Magazine,* 36 (June 1850): 351-354.

Friedrich Wilhelm Joseph von Schelling might well be dubbed "the philosopher of Romanticism." He was close to Friedrich Hölderlin, the Schlegels, Novalis, and Ludwig Tieck; he theorized about their central concerns, such as consciousness, mythology, religion, nature, and art; above all, in his early thinking he made the philosophy of art the "organon" of philosophy as a whole. But Schelling may be thought Romantic in yet another sense: he tended to promote one system after another, almost in fragments, as if (to quote Georg Wilhelm Friedrich Hegel's jibe) he were carrying on his philosophical education in public. Henry Crabb Robinson, a student at the University of Jena in the early 1800s, relates in his diary that one evening Schelling asked whether the serpent was not characteristic of English philosophy; Robinson replied that his countrymen thought it emblematically German, since it shed its coat each year. Schelling had the last laugh, explaining that the English saw only the coat, not what was beneath. Schelling's philosophy is indeed more of a piece than his critics have alleged. There is a consistency between what Schelling called his early "negative" philosophy, which is marked by a restless Fichtean search for certification and systematization, and his later "positive" philosophy, which is more religious and existential, almost a repudiation of philosophical system. It is this second phase that

influenced such thinkers as Samuel Taylor Coleridge, Søren Kierkegaard, Karl Jaspers, and Martin Heidegger.

Schelling was born on 27 January 1775 in Leonberg in the Duchy of Württemburg to Joseph Friedrich and Gottliebin Maria Cless Schelling. His father was a pastor who in 1777 became professor of oriental languages at the Bebenhausen seminary near Tübingen. Intellectually precocious, Schelling attended school at Bebenhausen and at Nürtingen prior to entering the Tübingen Stift (seminary) at the unusually early age of fifteen and a half. He received a master's degree in philosophy in 1792 and another master's in theology in 1795. Like his friends and fellow seminarians Hölderlin and Hegel, he came under the influence of the philosophy of Jean-Jacques Rousseau and embraced the ideals of the French Revolution. He responded to Johann Gottlieb Fichte's *Grundlagen der gesammten Wissenschaftslehre* (1794; translated as *Science of Knowledge,* 1970) with enthusiasm, determined at the same time to test the system's claims; his *Ueber die Möglichkeit einer Form der Philosophie überhaupt* (On the Possibility of a Form of any Philosophy) and *Vom Ich als Princip der Philosophie oder über das Unbedingte im menschlichen Wissen* (translated as "Of the I as Principle of Philosophy, or on the Unconditional in Human Knowledge," 1980), both written in 1795, began a ten-year dialogue with Fichtean idealism. His next work, "Philosophische Briefe über Dogmatismus und Kriticismus" (1795; translated as "Philosophical Letters on Dogmatism and Criticism," 1980) attempts to balance an absolute object, such as is found in the philosophy of Spinoza, against a Fichtean absolute subject. Schelling declares that the proper task of philosophy lies in explaining the existence of the world by linking the two poles. Schelling's main response to Fichte was to try to open up to speculative thought that dark continent of nature or the non-ego, inaugurating with *Ideen zu einer Philosophie der Natur* (Ideas toward a Philosophy of Nature, 1797) a series of efforts in what he called "Naturphilosophie" (philosophy of nature). Nature was not to be consigned, as in Fichte's system, to material for the ego's moral striving but was to be viewed as slumbering spirit. This conception of nature links Schelling with the Romantics.

After three years as a house tutor (a formative experience shared with other underemployed intellectuals such as Fichte, Hölderlin, and Hegel), two of them spent in Leipzig, Schelling was invited in 1798 to teach at the University of Jena. There he favorably impressed Johann Wolfgang von Goethe. He also befriended the Romantics Friedrich Schlegel, Novalis, and Tieck and the scientists Henrik Steffens and Gotthilf Heinrich von Schubert. In 1802-1803 he co-edited the *Kritisches Journal der Philosophie* with Hegel.

From this period comes his *System des transcendentalen Idealismus* (1800; translated as *System of Transcendental Idealism*, 1978, which inaugurates the phase in his development which is known as "Identitätsphilosophie" (Philosophy of Identity) because it supposes one ultimate ground for everything). The work comprises three parts: the first deduces consciousness from sensation through intuition and reflection to abstractive intelligence; the second, practical part moves from the Kantian will through social and political institutions to history, seen as the progressive discovery of freedom, a drama in which human beings are not just the actors but also the authors; the third part attempts to synthesize the poles of transcendental philosophy, which moves from spirit to nonspirit, and Naturphilosophie, which moves in the opposite direction. It is in the third part that art, aesthetic intuition, and productive genius find their proper place as the keystone of the arch of philosophy, uniting conscious and unconscious activities, spirit and nature, ideal and real. The priority of art recurs in slightly altered guise in Schelling's lectures on art, published as "Philosophie der Kunst" (1859; translated as *The Philosophy of Art*, 1988), where art exemplifies the "Indifferenzpunkt" (indifference-point) between the real and the ideal that is the hallmark of the Identitätsphilosophie. In these two works Schelling formulates in philosophical terms the Romantic apotheosis of art and philosophy. Schelling also tried his hand at literature: in 1802 he published some poems under the pseudonym "Bonaventura," which led some to suppose him the author of the *Nachtwachen von Bonaventura* (1804; translated as *The Night Watches of Bonaventura*, 1971); in the twentieth century the work has been attributed to Clemens Brentano, E. T. A. Hoffmann, Caroline Schlegel-Schelling, and Friedrich Gottlob Wetzel.

Bruno oder über das göttliche und natürliche Princip der Dinge (1802; translated as *Bruno; or, On the Natural and the Divine Principle of Things*, 1984) signals a turn away from Fichtean method toward a more mystical attitude influenced by Neoplatonism. This tendency is strengthened in

Schelling, circa 1801 (portrait by Friedrich Tieck; Roger Cardinal, German Romantics in Context [London: Studio Vista, 1975])

the 1804 essay *Philosophie und Religion* (Philosophy and Religion), in which the finite and fallen world is taken to be the self-expression of an eternally creative principle. The work is heavily influenced by the thought of the seventeenth-century mystic Jakob Böhme, to which Schelling had been introduced by Franz von Baader.

In 1803 Schelling married Caroline Schlegel, the former wife of August Wilhelm Schlegel, and moved to the University of Würzburg. In 1806 he moved to Munich, where he was appointed secretary to the Academy of Arts and was ennobled. Caroline died in 1809, and although Schelling married a friend of hers, Pauline Gotter, in 1810, the death was a blow from which he found it difficult to recover.

Perhaps this experience only served to confirm him in his turn to more religious topics, specifically the problem of evil. "Philosophische Untersuchungen über das Wesen der menschlichen Freyheit und die damit zusammenhängenden Gegenstände" (Philosophical Investigations into the Essence of Human Freedom and Related Matters, 1809; translated as *Of Human Freedom*, 1936) expressly poses the problem of how God could have brought evil into the world. Schelling argues that evil arises not in God but in the disunity inherent in finite human existence; evil makes freedom and choice possible. Friedrich Heinrich Jacobi, president of the Bavarian Academy, mistook the position for pantheism; embittered by the ensuing controversy, Schelling published little for the rest of his life.

He continued to lecture, however, moving to Erlangen in 1820 and to Munich in 1827. In the second phase of his development, the period of his positive philosophy, Schelling's thinking turned against Fichtean speculation, which, he argued, dealt only with ideas, not with existence; insight was obtainable only through religion. Starting with "Die Weltalter" (1857; translated as *The Ages of the World*, 1942), written in 1811, Schelling undertook an extended study of mythology and revelation, understanding both as the evolution and expression of the divine in history. He did not believe that myths could be decoded, like allegories; he borrowed Coleridge's neologism *tautegory* (that which speaks only to itself) to describe the myth's mode of signifying. The results of his investigations appeared as *Philosophie der Mythologie* (Philosophy of Mythology, 1857) and *Philosophie der Offenbarung* (Philosophy of Revelation, 1858).

In 1841 Schelling was called to the University of Berlin to eradicate Hegelian pantheism. The audience for his eagerly awaited inaugural lecture included Kierkegaard, Jacob Burckhardt, Friedrich Engels, and Mikhail Bakunin; by all accounts it proved a disappointment. In 1846 Schelling gave up lecturing. He retired to Munich and set about preparing his manuscripts for publication. He died in 1854 in Bad Ragaz, Switzerland.

Schelling's later theosophical mode of thinking influenced the pan-Slavist movement in Russia, and the often proto-existentialist expression of this phase has been taken up by Paul Tillich, Jaspers, and Heidegger. Of greater moment for literary history is Schelling's earlier privileging of art. He was the first to formulate a Romantic philosophy: a philosophy centered on art, one that puts aesthetic self-expression at the heart of things. This philosophy influenced many poets and thinkers; Coleridge's *Biographia Literaria* (1817) is indebted to Schelling.

Letters:
Fichtes und Schellings philosophischer Briefwechsel aus dem Nachlasse beider, edited by I. H. Fichte und K. Fr. A. Schelling (Stuttgart & Augsburg: Cotta, 1856);

Aus Schellings Leben: In Briefen, edited by Gustav Plitt, 3 volumes (Leipzig: Hirzel, 1869-1870);
Briefe und Dokumente, edited by Horst Fuhrmanns, 3 volumes (Bonn: Bouvier, 1962-1975);
Schelling und Cotta: Briefwechsel 1803-1849 (Stuttgart: Klett, 1965).

Bibliographies:
Guido Schneeberger, *Friedrich Wilhelm Joseph von Schelling: Eine Bibliographie* (Bern: Francke, 1954);
Hans Jörg Sandkühler, *Friedrich Wilhelm Joseph Schelling* (Stuttgart: Metzler, 1970);
Hermann Zeltner, *Schelling-Forschung seit 1954* (Darmstadt: Wissenschaftliche Buchgesellschaft, 1975);
Daniel Breazeale, "English Translations of Fichte, Schelling, and Hegel: An Annotated Bibliography," *Idealistic Studies,* 6, no. 3 (1976): 279-297.

Biographies:
Kuno Fischer, *Schellings Leben, Werke und Lehre,* third edition (Heidelberg: Winter, 1902);
Xavier Tilliette, ed., *Schelling im Spiegel seiner Zeitgenossen* (volumes 1 & 2, Turin: Bottega d'Erasmo, 1974, 1980; volume 3, Milan: Mursia, 1987);
Manfred Frank and Gerhard Kurz, eds., *Materialien zu Schellings philosophischen Anfängen* (Frankfurt am Main: Suhrkamp, 1975).

References:
Ernst Behler, "Schellings Ästhetik in der Überlieferung von Henry Crabb Robinson," *Philosophisches Jahrbuch,* 83 (1976): 133-183;
Frederick Copleston, "Schelling," in his *A History of Philosophy,* volume 7, part 1 (London: Burns & Oates, 1963), pp. 120-182;
Jacques Derrida, "Languages and Institutions of Philosophy," *Recherches Semiotiques/Semiotic Inquiry,* 4, no. 2 (1984): 91-154;
James Engell, *The Creative Imagination: Enlightenment to Romanticism* (Cambridge: Harvard University Press, 1981);
Joseph L. Esposito, *Schelling's Idealism and Philosophy of Nature* (Lewisburg, Pa.: Bucknell University Press, 1977);
Emil Fackenheim, "Schelling's Philosophy of the Literary Arts," *Philosophical Quarterly,* 4 (October 1954): 310-326;

Manfred Frank, *Eine Einführung in Schellings Philosophie* (Frankfurt am Main: Suhrkamp, 1985);

Eduard von Hartmann, *Schellings philosophisches System* (Leipzig: Haacke, 1897);

Nicolai Hartmann, *Die Philosophie des deutschen Idealismus. I: Fichte, Schelling und die Romantik* (Berlin: De Gruyter, 1923);

Rudolf Haym, *Die romantische Schule: Ein Beitrag zur Geschichte des deutschen Geistes* (Berlin: Gaertner, 1870; Darmstadt: Wissenschaftliche Buchgesellschaft, 1972);

G. W. F. Hegel, *Differenz des fichte'schen und schelling'schen System der Philosophie* (Jena, 1801), translated by H. S. Harris and Walter Cerf as *The Difference between Fichte's and Schelling's System of Philosophy* (Albany: State University of New York Press, 1977);

E. D. Hirsch, *Wordsworth and Schelling: A Typological Study of Romanticism* (New Haven: Yale University Press, 1960);

Dieter Jähnig, *Schelling: Die Kunst in der Philosophie*, 2 volumes (Pfullingen: Neske, 1966-1969);

Karl Jaspers, *Schelling: Größe und Verhängnis* (Munich: Piper, 1955);

Hinrich Knittermeyer, *Schelling und die romantische Schule* (Munich: Reinhardt, 1929);

Werner Marx, *The Philosophy of F. W. J. Schelling: History, System, and Freedom*, translated by Thomas Nenon (Bloomington: Indiana University Press, 1984);

Hans Jörg Sandkühler, *Friedrich Wilhelm Joseph Schelling* (Stuttgart: Metzler, 1970);

Manfred Schröter, "Bericht über den Münchener Schelling-Nachlaß," *Zeitschrift für philosophische Forschung*, 8 (1954): 437-445;

H. M. Schueller, "Schelling's Theory of the Metaphysics of Music," *Journal of Aesthetics and Art Criticism*, 15 (1956-1957): 461-476;

Walter Schulz, *Die Vollendung des deutschen Idealismus in der Spätphilosophie Schellings* (Stuttgart: Kohlhammer, 1955);

George J. Seidel, "Creativity in the Aesthetics of Schelling," *Idealistic Studies*, 4 (1974): 170-180;

Peter Szondi, "Schellings Gattungspoetik," in his *Poetik und Geschichtsphilosophie II* (Frankfurt am Main: Suhrkamp, 1974), pp. 185-307;

Xavier Tilliette, *L'Absolu et la Philosophie* (Paris: Presses Universitaires de France, 1987);

Tilliette, *Schelling: Une philosophie en devenir*, 2 volumes (Paris: Vrin, 1970);

Alan White, *Absolute Knowledge: Hegel and the Problem of Metaphysics* (Athens: Ohio University Press, 1983);

White, *Schelling: An Introduction to the System of Freedom* (New Haven: Yale University Press, 1983);

Hermann Zeltner, *Schelling* (Stuttgart: Fromann, 1982).

Papers:

Most of Schelling's papers, which had been stored at the Bavarian State Library, were destroyed in 1944 during the bombing of Munich. The Literaturarchiv der Deutschen Akademie der Wissenschaften, East Berlin, contains about one thousand letters to and from Schelling, lecture manuscripts, and diaries. There are also some letters in the Schiller National Museum at Marbach, West Germany.

Dorothea Schlegel

(24 October 1763-3 August 1839)

Joachim J. Scholz
Washington College

BOOK: *Florentin: Ein Roman*, edited by Friedrich Schlegel, volume 1 (Lübeck & Leipzig: Bohn, 1801).

OTHER: *Geschichte der Jungfrau von Orleans: Aus altfranzösischen Quellen, mit einem Anhang aus Hume's Geschichte von England*, translated by Dorothea Schlegel, edited by Friedrich Schlegel (Berlin: Sander, 1802);

Geschichte der Margaretha von Valois, Gemahlin Heinrichs IV. Von ihr selbst beschrieben: Nebst Zusätzen und Ergänzungen aus den französischen Quellen von Friedrich Schlegel, edited and translated by Schlegel (Leipzig: Junius, 1803);

Sammlung romantischer Dichtungen des Mittelalters: Aus gedruckten und handschriftlichen Quellen, edited by Dorothea and Friedrich Schlegel, includes translations by Dorothea Schlegel (Leipzig: Junius, 1804);

Lother und Maller: Eine Rittergeschichte aus einer ungedruckten Handschrift, translated by Dorothea Schlegel, edited by Dorothea and Friedrich Schlegel (Frankfurt am Main: Wilmans, 1805);

Germaine de Staël, Corinne oder Italien, translated by Friedrich and Dorothea Schlegel, 4 volumes (Berlin: Unger, 1807-1808).

Dorothea Schlegel (anonymous pastel portrait; by permission of the Historisches Bildarchiv, Bad Berneck)

German Romanticism has long enjoyed the distinction of having included many prominent women in its fold, from the tragically melancholic poetess Caroline von Günderode to the great conversationalists Rahel Levin and Bettina von Arnim. As the wife of Friedrich Schlegel, German Romanticism's founding father, Dorothea Schlegel naturally occupied an important position among her notable sisters. Yet in spite of her many personal contacts and her considerable literary productivity, Dorothea Schlegel has to this day remained a curiously neglected figure. Her devout subservience to the genius of Friedrich Schlegel—a subservience which accounts for her willingness to have all her books published under her husband's name or auspices—and the unhealthy influence which she is said to have exercised on his growing religious bigotry have not helped to endear her to contemporary critics and thus leave her one of the last preeminent women of that period to await reappraisal.

The eldest daughter of Moses Mendelssohn, Germany's first noted Jewish philosopher, Brendel (as Dorothea was called before her association with Friedrich Schlegel) was born in Berlin on 24 October 1763. Although she grew up in the enlightened and emancipated atmosphere which the reign of Frederick II had brought to the capital of Prussia, in 1783 (or, some literary historians suggest, as early as 1778) she was asked to conform to customary practices and marry the honorable but intellectually limited Jewish banker Simon Veit. The Veits had four sons, two of whom survived infancy and later became important painters in the Romantic school of the Nazarenes. Little is known about the married life of Brendel Veit. By the late 1790s much of her activity seemed to have evolved around the fashionable salons of her close friends Henriette Herz and Rahel Levin, and it was in these surroundings that in September 1797 she met twenty-five-year-old Friedrich Schlegel.

Already one of Germany's foremost literary critics, Friedrich Schlegel had come to Berlin from Jena, where his sharp attacks on Friedrich Schiller had made him a cultural persona non grata. Ebullient and arrogant, yet underneath it all vulnerable and still smarting from his unrequited love for his brother's recent bride, Caroline Schlegel, he soon found himself involved in a passionate affair with the thirty-four-year-old Brendel Veit, whose unquestioning admiration became increasingly indispensable and gratifying to him. In fall 1798 Dorothea achieved an amicable separation from Veit, and in early 1799 she was granted a divorce which left her with a modest allowance and a limited right to the education of her younger son.

Very much in accord with his faith in the sociable origins of Romantic creativity was Friedrich's immediate determination to see Dorothea become active in literary affairs. If his suggestion to translate fashionable memoirs and novels from the French was motivated by his own financial predicaments, he thought highly enough of his mistress to insist that she should contribute to his and his brother August Wilhelm's cherished *Athenäum*, their programmatic journal of Romantic tastes and judgments. Two book reviews in the second volume of the *Athenäum* give evidence of the agility with which Dorothea adapted herself to her new occupation and how quickly she learned to speak with the voice of her recently acquired Romantic convictions.

In September 1799 Friedrich Schlegel returned to Jena, and one month later Dorothea Veit, with considerable trepidation, joined the household in which for the next two years they lived in close quarters with the fastidiousness of August Wilhelm and the intimidating charm of his wife Caroline. Dorothea learned Italian in order to read Dante and unleashed with her stanzaic improvisations a veritable frenzy of poetic pro-

ductivity among the Schlegels. For Friedrich, nevertheless, the quintessentially Romantic art form was not poetry but the novel. What wonder that Dorothea, egged on by her new friends, found herself writing a novel barely two months after her arrival in Jena. The unfinished *Florentin*, whose first and only part was published in January 1801, contains the story of a Romantic hero par excellence: a birth shrouded in mystery, a cruel education at the hands of devious priests, escape, military career, easy vagabondage, amorous adventures, an artistic vocation, much of this taking place in Venice, Rome, Paris, and London. In search of the truth about his existence, the hero finally comes to Germany before intending to leave Europe to join the republican armies of the United States. Hints of an approaching revelation concerning the hero's origins abound but are left unresolved.

Florentin attempts to combine the typical fate of the Romantic hero with the idea of a personal development toward social responsibility, a Bildung (development) that was exemplarily described in Goethe's novel *Wilhelm Meister's Lehrjahre* (Wilhelm Meister's Apprenticeship, 1795-1796). It was, of course, apparent that Dorothea's effort represented a successful amalgamation of several literary trends rather than a truly original contribution to any one of them. Less digressive and stylistically more controlled than other romantic works in this genre, the influence of *Florentin* on the novels of Joseph von Eichendorff and Achim von Arnim has been recognized. Still, attempts to advance the literary reputation of *Florentin* beyond its present stature as a charming but otherwise derivative invention have failed.

In spite of the intellectual and social stimulation she received, Dorothea soon found her life in Jena to be a difficult one. Only six weeks after her arrival, she wrote to her friends in Berlin about the disturbing relationship between Caroline Schlegel and the young philosopher Friedrich Wilhelm Joseph von Schelling. While Dorothea and Friedrich Schlegel saw in the blossoming affair a perfidious betrayal of the admired August Wilhelm, the latter seemed curiously unaffected by what went on around him and in the end even turned against the two warning voices. By 1801 Friedrich and Dorothea felt isolated. They were also in great financial straits and quite desperate to move on. Into this period of outward uncertainty falls Dorothea Schlegel's first substantial achievement as a translator.

Dorothea Schlegel circa 1790 (oil painting by Anton Graff; by permission of the Nationalgalerie Stiftung Preussischer Kulturbesitz, Berlin)

Geschichte der Jungfrau von Orleans (History of the Maid of Orleans, 1802) is an expanded translation of the anonymous *Mémoires concernant la Pucelle d'Orleans* and was in part instigated by the widespread interest which Schiller's recent *Die Jungfrau von Orleans* (1801) had aroused in Germany. The translation–which modernizes, adds to, and shortens the text in ways no longer acceptable to modern practitioners of the craft–is, by the standards of the early nineteenth century, remarkably successful and enjoyed considerable respect and popularity.

After a brief stay in Dresden, Friedrich went to Paris, where Dorothea joined him in November 1802. Friedrich's new journalistic venture, *Europa*, to which Dorothea contributed several smaller pieces, quickly proved a failure and left them almost destitute. As before, Dorothea tried to help by taking on a second translation from the French, *Geschichte der Margaretha von Valois* (History of Margaretha of Valois, 1803), containing the memoirs of the first wife of the French king Henry IV.

Prospects of a professorship at a reopened university in Cologne and rewarding contacts with several patricians from that city enticed Friedrich Schlegel to leave Paris in April 1804. Shortly before, Dorothea had converted to Protes-

tantism, as did many Jewish women of her time. Her long liaison with Friedrich was legalized on 6 April 1804, just before the move to Cologne. In Cologne Dorothea Schlegel was buoyed by the friendly and respectful reception she and her husband received in their new surroundings. In his *Europa*, Friedrich had argued for a decisive turn to the Middle Ages in search for poetic and religious motives. Now in Cologne, this ancient center of German medieval Catholicism, the Schlegels immediately felt a sense of spiritual homecoming which would eventually culminate in their conversion to Catholicism in 1808. While Friedrich labored on his studies of Sanskrit, it was Dorothea who followed through on her husband's ideas by translating two medieval sources. The "Geschichte des Zauberers Merlin" (Story of the Magician Merlin, in *Sammlung romantischer Dichtungen des Mittelalters* [Collection of Romantic Writings of the Middle Ages], 1804) belongs to the rich cycle of tales of King Arthur's round table. Dorothea's intentions were, once again, literary rather than editorial as she created a work in which medieval motives are effectively heightened by the introduction of subtle romantic touches. Dorothea was much less successful as a translator of a fifteenth-century German dialect source that provided the basis for her edition of *Lother und Maller* (1805). Here she failed not so much by what she presented as by what she left out. The robust sensuality of the original grated on her increasingly narrow understanding of Christian morality and was promptly deleted, as was the most distinguishing mark of this otherwise rather common story of knightly friendship and loyalty, the castration of Lother at the court of France. Only once more did Dorothea submit herself to the strenuous task of a lengthy translation. Since spring 1804 August Wilhelm Schlegel had accompanied the famous Madame de Staël on her travels through Europe, and from November 1806 to April 1807 Friedrich Schlegel had been invited to join his brother at her estate in Normandy. As so often before, Dorothea, left behind, was called upon to express their gratitude by translating Madame de Staël's latest novel, her highly romantic *Corinne, ou d'Italie* (1807).

Though Dorothea's literary productivity came to an end with the four-volume *Corinne oder Italien* (1807-1808), she continued as a writer of distinction in her many letters. Several collections of her correspondence provide a surprisingly vigorous documentation of her life and times. Most of all, these letters should help to dispel the not uncommon notion that Dorothea played the role of an evil demon in her gifted husband's life. While it is true that Catholicism became the firm and unbending measuring rod of all her actions and opinions, after the Schlegels' conversion in 1808 her letters clearly outline a life that stood in dire need of rigorous determination and fortitude. Friedrich Schlegel's growing apathy, together with his chronic inability to find a secure position in life, demanded great strength and loyalty on her part. The physical and spiritual welfare of her two sons, the younger of whom she agreed to return to his father during her stay in Cologne, also required much patient foresight. Unwavering in her love for her second husband as well as the two sons of her first marriage, Dorothea Schlegel succeeded in the end in creating around herself a new family from which not even her first husband was totally excluded by a sense of respectful gratitude.

Friedrich Schlegel, his hopes for a professorship in Cologne finally dashed, in 1808 moved toward uncertain prospects in Vienna. Dorothea followed him several months later. In April 1816 she joined her husband in Frankfurt am Main, where he had been appointed councillor to the Austrian legation to the German diet. When he was dismissed in early 1818, she declared herself willing to live with her two sons in Rome, in order not to be a financial burden in Friedrich's efforts to reestablish himself in Vienna. Her correspondence from Rome constitutes a particularly valuable record not only of her personality in later years but also for the unique insights it provides into the cultural life of that city's important colony of German artists. Two years later, in 1820, Dorothea finally returned to the side of her husband in Vienna. On 12 January 1829 Friedrich died of a stroke while on a lecture tour in Dresden. Dorothea, left in very modest circumstances, was prevailed upon in 1830 to move to Frankfurt am Main, into the home of her younger son, Philipp Veit, who had just been appointed director of the city's most famous art col-

lection. The letters of her widowhood, which are a significant part of Josef Körner's *Briefe von und an Friedrich und Dorothea Schlegel* (1926), reveal a woman who remained an astute observer of the literary scene until her death on 3 August 1839 at the age of seventy-five.

Letters:

Dorothea v. Schlegel geb. Mendelssohn, und deren Söhne Johannes und Philipp Veit: Briefwechsel, 2 volumes, edited by J. M. Raich (Mainz: Kirchheim, 1881);

Briefe von Dorothea und Friedrich Schlegel an die Familie Paulus, edited by Rudolf Unger (Berlin: Behr, 1913);

Caroline und Dorothea Schlegel in Briefen, edited by Ernst Wieneke (Weimar: Kiepenheuer, 1914);

Der Briefwechsel Friedrich und Dorothea Schlegel 1818-1820 während Dorotheas Aufenthalt in Rom, edited by Heinrich Finke (Munich: Kösel & Pustet, 1923);

Briefe von und an Friedrich und Dorothea Schlegel, edited by Josef Körner (Berlin: Askanischer Verlag, 1926).

Biographies:

Margareta Hiemenz, *Dorothea v. Schlegel* (Freiburg im Breisgau: Herder, 1911);

Bertha Meyer, *Salon Sketches: Biographical Studies of Berlin Salons of the Emancipation* (New York: Bloch, 1938), pp. 21-47.

References:

Franz Deibel, *Dorothea Schlegel als Schriftstellerin im Zusammenhang mit der romantischen Schule* (Berlin: Palaestra 40, Mayer & Müller, 1905);

Heinrich Finke, *Über Friedrich und Dorothea Schlegel* (Cologne: Bachem, 1918), pp. 64-119;

J. Hibberd, "Dorothea Schlegel's *Florentin* and the Precarious Idyll," *German Life and Letters*, 30 (April 1977): 198-207.

Friedrich Schlegel

(10 March 1772-12 January 1829)

Klaus Peter
University of Massachusetts–Amherst

BOOKS: *Die Griechen und Römer: Historische und kritische Versuche über das Klassische Alterthum* (Neustrelitz: Michaelis, 1797);

Geschichte der Poesie der Griechen und Römer (Berlin: Unger, 1798);

Lucinde: Ein Roman, Erster Theil (Berlin: Fröhlich, 1799); abridged and translated by Paul Bernard Thomas as *Lucinda*, in *The German Classics of the Nineteenth and Twentieth Centuries*, volume 4 (New York: Lyon, 1913), pp. 124-174;

Charakteristiken und Kritiken, 2 volumes, by Friedrich and August Wilhelm Schlegel (Königsberg: Nicolovius, 1801);

Alarcos: Ein Trauerspiel in zwei Aufzügen (Berlin: Unger, 1802);

Über die Sprache und Weisheit der Indier: Ein Beitrag zur Begründung der Alterthumskunde: Nebst metrischen Übersetzungen indischer Gedichte (Heidelberg: Mohr & Zimmer, 1808); translated by E. J. Millington as "On the Language and Wisdom of the Indians," in *The Aesthetic and Miscellaneous Works of Friedrich von Schlegel* (London: Bohn, 1849);

Gedichte (Berlin: Hitzig, 1809);

Über die neuere Geschichte: Vorlesungen gehalten zu Wien im Jahre 1810 (Vienna: Schaumburg, 1811); translated by Lyndsey Purcell and R. H. Whitelock in *A Course of Lectures on Modern History, to Which Are Added Historical Essays on the Beginning of Our History, and on Caesar and Alexander* (London: Bohn, 1849);

Geschichte der alten und neuen Litteratur: Vorlesungen gehalten zu Wien im Jahre 1812, 2 volumes (Vienna: Schaumburg, 1815); translated by J. G. Lockhart as *Lectures on the History of Literature, Ancient and Modern* (Edinburgh: Blackwood, 1818; Philadelphia: Hobson, 1818);

Sämmtliche Werke, 10 volumes (Vienna: Mayer, 1822-1825);

Die Drey ersten Vorlesungen über die Philosophie des Lebens: Als Abdruck für die Zuhörer (Vienna: Schaumburg, 1827);

Friedrich Schlegel (after the portrait by E. Hader; by permission of the Bildarchiv der Österreichischen Nationalbibliothek, Vienna)

Philosophie des Lebens: In fünfzehn Vorlesungen gehalten zu Wien im Jahre 1827 (Vienna: Schaumburg, 1828); translated by A. J. W. Morrison in *The Philosophy of Life and Philosophy of Language in a Course of Lectures* (London: Bohn, 1847; New York: Harper, 1848);

Philosophie der Geschichte: In achtzehn Vorlesungen gehalten zu Wien 1828 (Vienna: Schaumburg, 1829); translated by James Burton Robertson as *The Philosophy of History, in a Course of Lectures, Delivered at Vienna, by Friedrich von Schlegel*, 2 volumes (London: Saunders & Otley, 1835);

Philosophische Vorlesungen insbesondere über Philosophie der Sprache und des Wortes (Vienna: Schaumburg, 1830); translated by Morrison in *The Philosophy of Life and Philosophy of Language in a Course of Lectures* (London: Bohn, 1847; New York: Harper, 1848);

Philosophische Vorlesungen aus den Jahren 1804 bis 1806: Nebst Fragmenten vorzüglich philosophisch-theologischen Inhalts, aus dem Nachlaß des Verewigten, edited by C. J. H. Windischmann, 2 volumes (Bonn: Weber, 1836-1837);

Sämmtliche Werke, 15 volumes and 4 supplements (volumes 1-15, Vienna: Mayer, 1846; supplements 1-4, Bonn: Hanstein, 1846);

Friedrich Schlegel 1794-1802: Seine prosaischen Jugendschriften, edited by J. Minor (Vienna: Konegen, 1882);

Kritische Friedrich Schlegel-Ausgabe, edited by E. Behler and others, 24 volumes to date (Paderborn: Schöningh / Zurich: Thomas, 1958-).

OTHER: *Athenäum: Eine Zeitschrift*, edited, with contributions, by Friedrich and August Wilhelm Schlegel (Berlin, 1798-1800);

Dorothea Schlegel, *Florentin: Ein Roman*, edited by Friedrich Schlegel (Lübeck & Leipzig: Bohn, 1801);

Geschichte der Jungfrau von Orleans: Aus altfranzösischen Quellen, mit einem Anhang aus Hume's Geschichte von England, edited by Friedrich Schlegel, translated by Dorothea Schlegel (Berlin: Sander, 1802);

Geschichte der Margaretha von Valois, Gemahlin Heinrichs IV. Von ihr selbst beschrieben: Nebst Zusätzen und Ergänzungen aus den französischen Quellen von Friedrich Schlegel, edited and translated by Schlegel (Leipzig: Junius, 1803);

Europa: Eine Zeitschrift, edited, with contributions, by Schlegel (Frankfurt am Main: Wilmans, 1803-1805);

Lessings Gedanken und Meinungen aus dessen Schriften, edited by Schlegel, 3 volumes (Leipzig: Junius, 1804);

Sammlung romantischer Dichtungen des Mittelalters: Aus gedruckten und handschriftlichen Quellen, edited by Friedrich and Dorothea Schlegel (Leipzig: Junius, 1804);

Lother und Maller: Eine Rittergeschichte aus einer ungedruckten Handschrift, edited by Friedrich and Dorothea Schlegel (Frankfurt am Main: Wilmans, 1805);

Poetisches Taschenbuch für das Jahr 1805 (1806), edited by Schlegel, 2 volumes (Berlin: Unger, 1805-1806);

Germaine de Staël, Corinne oder Italien, translated by Friedrich and Dorothea Schlegel, 4 volumes (Berlin: Unger, 1807-1808);

Österreichische Zeitung, edited by Schlegel (1809);

Deutsches Museum, edited, with contributions, by Schlegel (1812-1813);

Concordia: Eine Zeitschrift, edited by Schlegel (1820-1823).

Friedrich Schlegel is best known for the essays and aphorisms he published in the journal *Athenäum* (1798-1800), which he and his older brother August Wilhelm edited. The literary theory he developed in these texts is an important expression of early German Romanticism and is regarded today by many scholars as the first theory of modern European literature, that is, a literature no longer bound by set norms and traditional rules. Schlegel compared the new freedom which this theory proclaimed for literature with the new political freedom for which the French had just fought; he and his friends, particularly Friedrich von Hardenberg, who wrote under the pseudonym Novalis, saw the cultural revolution in Germany they heralded as one of the radical changes taking place throughout Europe–in philosophy and literature, in the sciences, and in the arts as well as in politics. But the same Friedrich Schlegel who was a champion of revolutionary change in his earlier years supported C. W. L. Metternich's restoration policies after 1815. The son of a Protestant pastor, Schlegel converted to Catholicism in 1808 and publicized his new convictions in a wide range of philosophical, historical, and religious books, articles, and lectures. He became known throughout Germany and Europe for his reactionary views. Consequently, he was attacked by such liberals as Heinrich Heine, whose judgment of Schlegel in *Die romantische Schule* (1836; translated as *The Romantic School*, 1882) had an effect well into the twentieth century.

Thus there were two Schlegels, the young one and the older one, and the debate about the "true" Schlegel has never quite ended. In the twentieth century Schlegel's ideas have influenced modern writers as diverse as György Lukács, Thomas Mann, and Robert Musil, and it is a tribute to his powers as a literary theorist and as a philosopher that his views can provoke strong arguments pro and con even today. The history of Schlegel scholarship is characterized by these arguments, which reflect the various points of view, literary and political, that Schlegel's ideas inspired. Perhaps because he was one of the most controversial authors of the Age of Goethe, he is also one of the most fascinating. And this may be the reason why he seems to be more modern, even today, than most writers of that time.

The Schlegels had a long family tradition. Since the seventeenth century members had been prominent clergymen, lawyers, civil servants, and writers. Johann Adolf Schlegel (1721-1793), Friedrich Schlegel's father, enjoyed a successful career as a Protestant minister. When Friedrich (whose full name was Karl Wilhelm Friedrich Schlegel) was born, his father held an important pastorate in Hannover, and later he held high-ranking positions in the hierarchy of the Protestant church. Among Johann Adolf Schlegel's thirteen brothers and sisters two brothers stand out: the playwright and critic Johann Elias Schlegel (1719-1749) and Johann Heinrich Schlegel (1724-1780), who became a royal librarian in Copenhagen and published a two-volume history of the Danish kings. Johann Adolf Schlegel himself had literary ambitions and served for a short time as editor of the *Bremische Beiträge*, an influential literary journal of the time. He and his wife had seven children; their two youngest sons, August Wilhelm and Friedrich, achieved fame as the "Brüder Schlegel," thereby carrying on the illustrious tradition of the family. Friedrich Schlegel was very aware of the obligation this tradition imposed upon him, and it troubled him deeply when his own work fell short of this standard.

He was not an easy child. Lonely, given to brooding, and in poor health, he was sent to live with relatives in the country; his family hoped, too, that an apprenticeship in a bank in Leipzig in 1788 might start him on a solid middle-class career. But this project proved to be a total failure: after a short time Schlegel returned to Hannover, deeply disappointed because he had not succeeded. At this critical juncture in his life he turned to studying ancient Greece, a study which determined his future. Rapidly he acquired an extraordinary knowledge of ancient culture and, eventually, of modern culture as well. In 1790 and 1791 he joined his older brother August Wilhelm at the University of Göttingen—to study law, but in effect to pursue his newfound interests. August Wilhelm became his hero, and, indeed, during this year in Göttingen the close friendship between the brothers began. August Wilhelm Schlegel, who had already translated Dante and Shakespeare, was studying philology and publishing his first literary articles and reviews. His example inspired Friedrich in his development as a scholar and writer, and the bond between the two did not end when August Wilhelm finished his studies in 1791 and moved to Amsterdam; Friedrich continued his studies in Leipzig. The correspondence of the brothers—only Friedrich's letters have survived—is important for its documentation of Friedrich's intellectual development in these early years. The letters also give insight into his character. He compares himself with Hamlet, deplores his own melancholy, and speaks of his dissatisfaction with everything, including friendship and love.

In January 1794 he moved to Dresden. During Friedrich Schlegel's stay in Leipzig August Wilhelm had supported him not only morally and intellectually but also financially. In Dresden Friedrich expected the additional help of his sister Charlotte, who lived there with her husband. And in Dresden he hoped to be able finally to realize some of his many literary plans. In the famous Dresden gallery of Greek sculptures he looked for further inspiration. Friedrich Schlegel's ambition was to become the Winckelmann of literature. What Johann Joachim Winckelmann, in his *Geschichte der Kunst des Altertums* (Art History of Ancient Greece, 1764), had attempted to do for the arts, he planned to do for literature, namely, to combine a study of Greek literary history with the development of an aesthetic norm. The main results of these efforts were two books. Both were designed as first volumes of much larger projects, but neither project was continued.

In 1797 Schlegel published *Die Griechen und Römer* (The Greeks and the Romans), and in 1798 *Geschichte der Poesie der Griechen und Römer* (History of the Poetry of the Greeks and Romans) appeared. The first of these books included the essay "Über das Studium der griechischen Poesie" (Concerning the Study of Greek Literature). Here, in this most important text of that period, Schlegel presents the concept of a philosophy of history which became prominent in German Idealism; today this concept is associated principally with Georg Wilhelm Friedrich Hegel. Schlegel tried to establish a logical relationship between Greek and modern culture. The terms he introduced to characterize the two cultures are *objectivity* and *interest*. At the time of ancient Greece, he maintains, literature was part of the totality of Greek culture. A "natural" unity of all expressions of culture and social life was the basis for their "objectivity" and made them beautiful. This unity has been destroyed in modern times by the emergence of "subjectivity," the development of individual interests. Modern culture, therefore, is characterized by competing interests, and this lack of unity has produced an ever-deepening cultural crisis. In the eighteenth century, Schlegel believed, this crisis had reached the point that the future of mankind was at stake. If this crisis could not be ended, catastrophe seemed unavoidable.

To fully understand Schlegel's thesis it is necessary to look at the political situation of that time. Schlegel had come to admire the French Revolution, largely through the influence of Caroline Böhmer. This young woman, with whom August Wilhelm Schlegel had fallen in love, had experienced the French occupation of Mainz and become an avid republican in the process. After her capture and release by the Prussians, she convinced Friedrich Schlegel of the importance of the French events. The philosophy of history which he set forth in "Über das Studium der griechischen Poesie" combines this political interest with a scholarly one: as the French Revolution in Schlegel's eyes had restored the Greek polis, a democratic republic, so, he felt, the study of ancient culture could lead to the restoration of a society characterized by "objectivity." The new objectivity should not, and could not, Schlegel maintained, be a mere imitation of the old. The point of his argument is rather that the new objectivity should be a product of subjectivity; that is, what the Greeks were given by nature now was to be created by man.

These ideas formed the basis for the well-known texts of 1798 and 1800 which Schlegel contributed to the *Athenäum*. Before 1798, however, significant changes occurred in his life. In December 1795 Friedrich Schiller invited August Wilhelm Schlegel to participate in his new journal, *Die Horen*. He accepted the invitation and, after having married Caroline Böhmer, moved in July 1796 to Jena, where Friedrich Schlegel joined the young couple. The brothers' relationship with Schiller was difficult. August Wilhelm Schlegel worked with him, but Schiller and Friedrich Schlegel disliked each other, and their relations became actively hostile. Friedrich Schlegel, excluded from *Die Horen*, associated himself in Berlin with Johann Friedrich Reichardt, who published a journal called *Deutschland*. Friedrich contributed important articles on Gotthold Ephraim

Lessing and Georg Forster and sharply critical reviews of Schiller's work which finally, in May 1797, prompted the break between Schiller and August Wilhelm Schlegel as well. When the Berlin censors found *Deutschland* too revolutionary, Reichardt retitled the journal *Lyceum der schönen Künste* and invited Friedrich Schlegel to be an editor. In July 1797 Schlegel moved to Berlin. But soon he had disagreements with Reichardt and left the *Lyceum* in November. At this point he suggested to his brother that they start their own journal, the *Athenäum*. The first issue appeared in May 1798.

The *Athenäum* became the main voice of Early German or Jena Romanticism. The Brothers Schlegel were the main contributors. One of those in the circle of friends associated with Jena Romanticism was Friedrich von Hardenberg (Novalis), whom Friedrich Schlegel had first met in Leipzig in 1792 and who had become a close friend and collaborator. The group also included two friends Schlegel had met in Berlin: Friedrich Schleiermacher, a theologian who in Berlin was minister at the Charité, a hospital for the poor, and with whom Schlegel shared an apartment; and novelist and playwright Ludwig Tieck. Caroline Schlegel, August Wilhelm Schlegel's wife, was probably the center of the entire group; another member was Dorothea Veit, a writer who was the daughter of the philosopher Moses Mendelssohn. Friedrich Schlegel had met her in Berlin and had fallen in love with her. At the time she was unhappily married to the banker Simon Veit. She and Schlegel began to live together in 1798; in 1799 she got a divorce, and they were married in April 1804.

The *Athenäum* appeared twice a year in 1798, 1799, and 1800. Although the journal was received with great interest in literary circles, the first issue had a printing of 1,250 copies, not all of which were sold, and after the second issue in 1800 the publication was discontinued by the publisher. The content of the *Athenäum*, consisting of rather esoteric philosophy and literature, was of interest only to a relatively small audience of insiders. Friedrich Schlegel's most important contributions were the Fragmente and the unfinished essay "Über Goethes Meister" (On Goethe's Meister), both in 1798, and in 1800 a series of fragments entitled "Ideen" (Ideas) and the "Gespräch über die Poesie" (Dialogue on Poetry).

While in Dresden Schlegel had discovered the philosophy of Johann Gottlieb Fichte, whom he met in Jena where Fichte was teaching at the university. Schlegel's texts in the *Athenäum* are deeply indebted to Fichte. How thoroughly he studied and worked with Fichte's philosophy is documented in the *Philosophische Lehrjahre* (Philosophical Years of Apprenticeship), an extensive collection of notes about philosophical topics which Schlegel started to write in 1796. The notes were not intended for publication, but they provided him with ample material for his works. Today the *Philosophische Lehrjahre* fills two volumes of the critical edition of Schlegel's works which began to appear in 1958. Like Hegel, Friedrich von Hölderlin, and Friedrich Wilhelm Joseph von Schelling, whose works are unthinkable without Fichte, Schlegel viewed the *Grundlage der gesamten Wissenschaftslehre* (The Basis of All Doctrines of Science, 1794), Fichte's most important philosophical text, with a critical mind. He agreed with Fichte when he criticized Immanuel Kant for limiting the powers of the "I," but the "absolute I" of the *Wissenschaftslehre*, Schlegel felt, is "abstract"; it isolates the "I" from nature and from history. In terms of his essay "Über das Studium der griechischen Poesie" Schlegel saw Fichte's absolute "I" as an extreme expression of modern subjectivity. He demanded therefore that the "I" reflect its own limitations in order to become more "objective." This process he described dialectically: the "I" lives up to its full potential only through self-abnegation. Because this process–Schlegel called it a process of "Selbstschöpfung und Selbstvernichtung" (self-creation and self-destruction)–is endless, all activities of the subject are by necessity incomplete. This belief explains, in philosophical terms, Schlegel's choice of literary forms: the Fragment and the essay.

The best known of the fragments published in the *Athenäum* is No. 116, in which he defines the idea of Romantic literature. It begins: "Die romantische Poesie ist eine progressive Universalpoesie" (romantic literature is a progressive universal literature). It is universal because it is supposed to include all genres and, in addition, establish links with philosophy and rhetoric, with the other arts, and theoretically with all expressions of human activity. This universality, of course, can never be fully realized. Hence, romantic literature is progressive; that is, it is characterized by constant movement, by constant growth, and it is never completed. With revolutionary vigor it breaks through all traditional barriers and aims for total freedom, for the "absolute" or the "infinite." In his essay about Goethe's novel

Wilhelm Meisters Lehrjahre (Wilhelm Meister's Apprenticeship, 1795-1796) Schlegel speaks of his admiration for Goethe. Although his notes of that period indicate that he did not consider the novel "Romantic," he praises features of the text that seem to show that it is. Goethe was flattered by Schlegel's commentary, and, indeed, the essay is one of Schlegel's finest texts. In 1799 Schleiermacher published *Über die Religion: Reden an die Gebildeten unter ihren Verächtern* (translated as *On Religion: Speeches to Its Cultured Despisers*, 1892), which had a sensational success among the friends in Jena. Schleiermacher pleaded for a concept of religion which defines religion as "Sinn für das Universum" (sense for the universe), a pantheistic view heavily indebted to Spinoza. Schlegel's "Ideen" as well as his "Gespräch über die Poesie" reflect this view. He describes the longing for the absolute, for the infinite in religious terms. In the "Gespräch über die Poesie" Schlegel asks for a new mythology for which he claims the Orient as a model, rather than Greece. Clearly, Schlegel's texts of 1800 show a shift in his thinking. He moved away from Greece, from Goethe, and from Fichte. Spinoza and the Orient point in a different direction.

During this time, in 1799, Schlegel wrote and had published his only novel, *Lucinde*. In the *Gespräch über die Poesie* he declared the novel to be identical with romantic literature per se and developed a theory which takes its chief examples from Jean Paul, Laurence Sterne, and Diderot. Schlegel saw his own *Lucinde* in this tradition as an "arabesque" or "grotesque" work. With its untraditional form which combines narrative with reflections, letters, dialogue, and essays, Schlegel anticipated features of the twentieth-century novel. But as untraditional as its form is the novel's content. The text celebrates the love between Julius and Lucinde, easily recognizable as fictional counterparts to Schlegel and Dorothea Veit. And a shocked audience, including most of Schlegel's friends, not only read about an extramarital love affair but, in addition, was exposed to explicit erotic details.

In September 1799 Schlegel had returned to Jena where he hoped to secure a professorship at the university. He was granted the right to lecture (*venia legendi*) in October 1800. In the winter semester 1800-1801 he lectured about "Transzendentalphilosophie." But when success eluded him he gave up teaching. His life in Jena was financially uncertain, and when the circle of friends in Jena disintegrated in 1801, Schlegel left. Novalis died in March. Schlegel and Schleiermacher quarreled about philosophical differences. Caroline Schlegel and Dorothea Veit did not get along, and Caroline fell in love with Schelling. August Wilhelm Schlegel went to Berlin. Friedrich Schlegel followed him there but did not find a source of income. He decided to go to Paris. There he planned to study Oriental philosophy and languages and make a living by introducing the French to the most recent German philosophy and literature. He and Dorothea Veit arrived in Paris in July 1802. But Paris, too, was a disappointment. Schlegel's far-reaching European ambitions of that time are reflected in his second journal, *Europa* (1803-1805), which he edited from Paris. His contributions to the journal were substantial. Here he articulated his view that the Orient was destined to save Europe from the crisis he had diagnosed.

Schlegel was not received in Paris as eagerly as he had hoped; the lectures he gave there were attended mainly by German emigrants and tourists. Two of these tourists made it possible for him to return to Germany. The brothers Sulpiz and Melchior Boisserée, wealthy young men from Cologne, appreciated his knowledge and in 1804, when they had to go home, asked him to join them. Before they left Paris Schlegel and Veit were married. In Cologne Schlegel continued his lecture series, publicly and privately as well. In Paris he had become interested in the German Catholic past; in Cologne his interest became more intense. He was fascinated by the Catholic milieu in Cologne, its Gothic architecture, and the art of the Middle Ages which the Boisserées collected. The study of the seventeenth-century mystic Jakob Böhme caused him to denounce the pantheistic religion and the aestheticism of the *Athenäum* years. These experiences led to his conversion to Catholicism, which took place in April 1808.

This conversion opened new possibilities. When Madame de Staël, the well-known French writer and socialite, came to Berlin in 1804, she was so impressed with August Wilhelm Schlegel that she invited him to accompany her to her castle at Coppet, on Lake Geneva. He was to help her with her book *De l'Allemagne* and be a tutor for her children. Friedrich Schlegel visited there from Cologne. In 1807 August Wilhelm Schlegel accompanied Madame de Staël to Vienna where he presented his successful lecture series on the history of dramatic art and literature; in the large audience were many members of the nobility. With these new connections he helped pave the way for his brother's move to Vienna. Friedrich Schlegel, who at one time viewed Paris as the center of Europe, was disappointed with the French capital, and not merely for personal reasons. He did not think Napoleon was the right person to unify Europe. In line with his new interests he had come to believe instead that only Austria with her long tradition and political experience was capable of saving the old continent. Only the Austrian emperor was a "true" emperor; Napoleon was a "false" one.

For some time Schlegel had been looking for an opportunity to move to Vienna. He arrived there in June 1808. In March of the following year he obtained a position with the Austrian government as "Hofsecretär." In April 1809 Austria declared war on Napoleon, and Schlegel was ordered to join the Austrian army where he edited the *Österreichische Zeitung*, an army newspaper. After the war had ended with Austria's defeat and the peace treaty of Schönbrunn, Schlegel returned to Vienna in the beginning of 1810 and followed the example of his brother in presenting a series of lectures, *Über die neuere Geschichte* (published in 1811; translated in 1849 as *A Course of Lectures on Modern History*), to an illustrious audience. He used the occasion to praise Austria's "true" emperorship and to denounce Napoleon as the incarnation of everything that was wrong with modern Europe. In the following years he edited his third journal, his *Deutsches Museum* (1812-1813); it also served to strengthen the German resistance against French domination. When Napoleon finally was defeated in 1814 Schlegel played a role in planning a new order for Europe and especially for Germany. At the Congress of Vienna (1814-1815) and in newspaper articles he fought for the restoration of what he called the "altdeutsche Kaisertum," the German imperial rule of the Middle Ages which had lasted until Napoleon abolished it in 1806. This view, however, did not agree with Metternich's ideas and the Deutsche Bund (German Federation), which the Congress decided to establish; indeed, the federation had nothing to do with the old order Schlegel had in mind. Nevertheless, in 1815 Metternich appointed him a member of the Austrian delegation to the Bundestag in Frankfurt, the central organ of the new federation. But here Schlegel involved himself mainly with church matters. With his orthodox religious views he was of little help for Metternich's political plans. In September 1818 Metternich finally

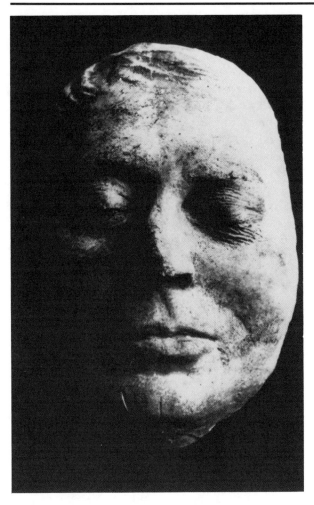

Friedrich Schlegel's death mask (by permission of the Staatliche Kunstakademie, Düsseldorf)

ordered him to return to Vienna.

His early retirement from politics allowed Schlegel again to concentrate on his cultural and in particular on his philosophical interests. His fourth journal, the *Concordia* (1820-1823), became the most important voice of Viennese, that is, Catholic, Romanticism. In addition to Schlegel himself, contributors were Adam Müller, Franz Baader, Carl Ludwig von Haller, and other representatives of the Catholic opposition to liberal politics and ideas. In his programmatic essay, "Signatur des Zeitalters" (Signature of the Age), Schlegel again condemns the moral decay of modern Europe and argues for the restoration of the social order of the Middle Ages. Another one of his essays, "Von der Seele" (About the Soul), is typical of his religious speculations regarding the loss of paradise. For an edition of his collected works–ten volumes published from 1822 to 1825–he reworked his earlier texts, some of which, among

them the Fragmente from the *Athenäum* and *Lucinde*, he deliberately left out because they agreed too little with his present views. In 1812 he undertook a lecture series in Vienna dealing with his latest ideas about literature: *Geschichte der alten und neuen Literatur* (Lectures on the History of Literature, Ancient and Modern). In the last two years of his life he developed his late philosophy in three new lecture series. He presented the first one, *Philosophie des Lebens* (The Philosophy of Life), in Vienna in 1827, the second one, *Philosophie der Geschichte* (The Philosophy of History), a year later in Vienna, and the third one, *Philosophie der Sprache und des Wortes* (Philosophy of Language and of the Word), in 1828 and 1829 in Dresden. In all three series, which were published in book form in 1828 and 1829 (and translated into English, 1835-1847), he combined earlier ideas about the crisis of the world in general and of Europe in particular with views taken from the Bible. On 12 January 1829 he died in Dresden of a stroke; he is buried in that city.

Bibliography:

Volker Deubel, "Die Friedrich-Schlegel-Forschung 1945-1972," *Deutsche Vierteljahrsschrift*, 47 (1973): 48-181.

References:

Jean-Jacques Anstett, *La Pensée religieuse de Friedrich Schlegel* (Paris: Société d'Édition Les Belles Lettres, 1941);

Ernst Behler, "Friedrich Schlegels Theorie der Universalpoesie," *Jahrbuch der Deutschen Schillergesellschaft*, 1 (1957): 211-252;

Behler, "Friedrich Schlegels Theorie des Verstehens: Hermeneutik oder Dekonstruktion?," in *Die Aktualität der Frühromantik*, edited by Behler and Jochen Hörisch (Paderborn: Schöningh, 1987), pp. 141-160;

Behler, *Die Zeitschriften der Brüder Schlegel: Ein Beitrag zur Geschichte der deutschen Romantik* (Darmstadt: Wissenschaftliche Buchgesellschaft, 1983);

Behler, ed., *Friedrich Schlegel in Selbstzeugnissen und Bilddokumenten* (Reinbek: Rowohlt, 1966);

Klaus Behrens, *Friedrich Schlegels Geschichtsphilosophie (1794-1808): Ein Beitrag zur politischen Romantik* (Tübingen: Niemeyer, 1984);

Raimund Belgardt, *Romantische Poesie: Begriff und Bedeutung bei Friedrich Schlegel* (The Hague: Mouton, 1969);

Klaus Briegleb, *Ästhetische Sittlichkeit: Versuch über Friedrich Schlegels Systementwurf zur Begründung der Dichtungskritik* (Tübingen: Niemeyer, 1962);

Hans Dierkes, *Literaturgeschichte als Kritik: Untersuchungen zu Theorie und Praxis von Friedrich Schlegels frühromantischer Literaturgeschichtsschreibung* (Tübingen: Niemeyer, 1980);

Hans Eichner, *Friedrich Schlegel* (New York: Twayne, 1970);

Eichner, "Friedrich Schlegel's Theory of Romantic Poetry," *Publications of the Modern Language Association*, 71 (December 1956): 1018-1041;

Hans-Joachim Heiner, *Das Ganzheitsdenken Friedrich Schlegels: Wissenssoziologische Deutung einer Denkform* (Stuttgart: Metzler, 1971);

Heinrich Henel, "Friedrich Schlegel und die Grundlagen der modernen literarischen Kritik," *Germanic Review*, 20 (1945): 81-93;

Raymond Immerwahr, "Friedrich Schlegel's Essay 'On Goethe's Meister,'" *Monatshefte*, 49 (January 1957): 1-21;

Immerwahr, "The Subjectivity or Objectivity of Friedrich Schlegel's Poetic Irony," *Germanic Review*, 26 (1951): 173-191;

Richard Littlejohns, "The 'Bekenntnisse eines Ungeschickten': A Re-Examination of Emancipatory Ideas in Friedrich Schlegel's 'Lucinde,'" *Modern Language Review*, 72 (July 1977): 605-614;

Franz-Norbert Mennemeier, *Friedrich Schlegels Poesiebegriff: Dargestellt anhand der literaturkritischen Schriften. Die romantische Konzeption einer objektiven Poesie* (Munich: Fink, 1971);

Willy Michel, *Ästhetische Hermeneutik und frühromantische Kritik: Friedrich Schlegels fragmentarische Entwürfe, Rezensionen, Charakteristiken und Kritiken (1795-1801)* (Göttingen: Vanderhoeck & Ruprecht, 1982);

Hugo Moser and Benno von Wiese, eds., *Friedrich Schlegel und die Romantik* (Berlin: Schmidt, 1970);

Armand Nivelle, *Frühromantische Dichtungstheorie* (Berlin: De Gruyter, 1970);

Klaus Peter, *Friedrich Schlegel* (Stuttgart: Metzlersche Verlagsbuchhandlung, 1978);

Peter, "Friedrich Schlegel und Adorno: Die Dialektik der Aufklärung in der Romantik und heute," in *Die Aktualität der Frühromantik*, edited by Behler and Jochen Hörisch (Paderborn: Schöningh, 1987), pp. 219-235;

Peter, "Friedrich Schlegels Lessing: Über die Aufklärung und ihre Folgen in der Romantik," in *Humanität und Dialog: Lessing und Mendelssohn in neuer Sicht*, edited by Erhard Bahr and others (Detroit: Wayne State University Press, 1982), pp. 341-352;

Peter, *Idealismus als Kritik. Friedrich Schlegels Philosophie der unvollendeten Welt* (Stuttgart: Kohlhammer, 1973);

Karl Konrad Polheim, *Die Arabeske: Ansichten und Ideen aus Friedrich Schlegels Poetik* (Munich, Paderborn & Vienna: Schöningh, 1966);

Helmut Schanze, *Friedrich Schlegel und die Kunsttheorie seiner Zeit* (Darmstadt: Wissenschaftliche Buchgesellschaft, 1985);

Ingrid Strohschneider-Kohrs, *Die romantische Ironie in Theorie und Gestaltung* (Tübingen: Niemeyer, 1960);

Heinz-Dieter Weber, *Friedrich Schlegels "Transzendentalpoesie": Untersuchungen zum Funktionswandel der Literaturkritik im 18. Jahrhundert* (Munich: Fink, 1973);

Werner Weiland, *Der junge Friedrich Schlegel oder Die Revolution in der Frühromantik* (Stuttgart: Kohlhammer, 1968).

Papers:

Schlegel's papers are at the Görres-Gesellschaft in Munich, the university library in Bonn, the Stadtarchiv in Cologne, the city library in Trier, and the Westdeutsche Bibliothek in Marburg.

Friedrich Schleiermacher

(21 November 1768-12 February 1834)

Edward T. Larkin
University of New Hampshire

BOOKS: *Über die Religion: Reden an die Gebildeten unter ihren Verächtern,* anonymous (Berlin: Unger, 1799; revised and enlarged edition, Berlin: Reimer, 1821); translated by John Oman as *On Religion: Speeches to Its Cultured Despisers* (London: Kegan Paul, Trench, Trübner, 1892; New York: Harper, 1958);

Monologen: Eine Neujahrsgabe (Berlin: Spener, 1800); translated by Horace Leland Friess as *Schleiermacher's Soliloquies* (Chicago: Open Court, 1926);

Vertraute Briefe über Friedrich Schlegels Lucinde, anonymous (Lübeck & Leipzig: Bohn, 1800);

Predigten (Berlin: Reimer, 1801);

Grundlinien einer Kritik der bisherigen Sittenlehre (Berlin: Realschulbuchhandlung, 1803);

Zwei unvorgreifliche Gutachten in Sachen des protestantischen Kirchenwesens zunächst in Beziehung auf den Preußischen Staat (Berlin: Realschulbuchhandlung, 1804)—comprises "Über die bisherige Trennung der beiden protestantischen Kirchen," "Über die Mittel, dem sogenannten Verfall der Religion vorzubeugen";

Die Weihnachtsfeier: Ein Gespräch (Halle: Schimmelpfennig, 1806); translated by W. Hastie as *Christmas Eve: A Dialogue on the Celebration of Christmas* (Edinburgh: Clark, 1890); translated by Terrence N. Tice as *Christmas Eve: Dialogue on the Incarnation* (Richmond, Va.: John Knox Press, 1967);

Über den sogenannten ersten Brief des Paulos an den Timotheos: Ein kritisches Sendschreiben an J. C. Cass (Berlin: Realschulbuchhandlung, 1807);

Predigten: Zweite Sammlung (Berlin: Reimer, 1808);

Gelegentliche Gedanken über Universitäten im deutschen Sinn: Nebst einem Anhang über eine neu zu errichtende (Berlin: Realschulbuchhandlung, 1808);

Kurze Darstellung des theologischen Studiums zum Behuf einleitender Vorlesungen (Berlin: Realschulbuchhandlung, 1811);

Predigten: Dritte Sammlung (Berlin: Reimer, 1816);

Friedrich Schleiermacher (lithograph by Gentili after a drawing by F. Krüger)

Über die für die protestantische Kirche des preußischen Staats einzurichtende Synodalverfassung: Einige Bemerkungen (Berlin: Reimer, 1817);

Über die Schriften des Lukas: Ein kritischer Versuch (Berlin: Reimer, 1817); translated by Connop Thirlwall as *A Critical Essay on the Gospel of St. Luke* (London: Taylor, 1825);

Predigten: Vierte Sammlung. Predigten über den christlichen Hausstand (Berlin: Reimer, 1820);

Der christliche Glaube nach den Grundsätzen der evangelischen Kirche im Zusammenhange dargestellt, 2 volumes (Berlin: Reimer, 1821-1822; revised, 1830-1831); translated as *The Christian Faith,* edited by H. R. Mackintosh and J. S.

Stewart (Edinburgh: Clark, 1928; Philadelphia: Fortress Press, 1976);

Ueber das liturgische Recht evangelischer Landesfürsten: Ein theologisches Bedenken, as Pacificus Sincerus (Göttingen: Vandenhoeck & Ruprecht, 1824);

Predigten: Fünfte Sammlung. Christliche Festpredigten (Berlin: Reimer, 1826);

Predigten: Sechste Sammlung. Predigten in Bezug auf die Feier der Uebergabe der augsburgischen Confession (Berlin: Reimer, 1831);

Predigten über das Evangelium Marci und den Brief Pauli an die Kolosser, edited by Friedrich Zabel, 2 volumes (Berlin: Herbig, 1835);

Friedrich Schleiermacher's sämmtliche Werke, edited by Ludwig Jonas, Alexander Schweitzer, Friedrich Lücke, and others, 30 volumes (Berlin: Reimer, 1835-1864); part 1, volume 6, *Das Leben Jesu,* edited by K. A. Rütenik (1864), translated by S. Maclean Gilmour as *The Life of Jesus* (Philadelphia: Fortress Press, 1975);

Christliche Sittenlehre in Vorlesungen (Winter-Semester 1822-1823): Aus Nachschriften, edited by Jonas, 2 volumes (Gotha: Perthes, 1891);

Kleinere theologische Schriften, 2 volumes (Gotha: Perthes, 1893);

Schleiermachers Sendschreiben über seine Glaubenslehre an Lücke, edited by Hermann Mulert (Giessen: Töpelmann, 1908); translated by James Duke and Francis Fiorenza as *On the Glaubenslehre: Two Letters to Dr. Lücke* (Chico, Calif.: Scholars Press, 1981);

Ungedruckte Predigten Schleiermachers aus den Jahren 1820-1828: Mit Einleitungen und mit einem Anhang ungedruckte Briefe von Schleiermacher und Henriette Herz, edited by Johannes Bauer (Leipzig: Nachfolger, 1909);

Abhandlungen gelesen in der Königlichen Akademie der Wissenschaften, edited by Otto Braun (Leipzig: Erkardt, 1911)–comprises "Über die wissenschaftliche Behandlung des Tugendbegriffes," "Versuch über die wissenschaftliche Behandlung des Pflichtbegriffs," "Über den Unterschied zwischen Naturgesetz und Sittengesetz," "Über den Begriff des Erlaubten," "Über den Begriff des höchsten Gutes: 1.-2. Abhandlung," "Über den Beruf des Staates zur Erziehung," "Über den Begriff des großen Mannes";

Friedrich Schleiermachers Ästhetik, im Auftrage der Preußischen Akademie der Wissenschaften und der Literatur-Archiv-Gesellschaft zu Berlin nach den bisher unveröffentlichten Urschriften zum er- *sten Mal herausgegeben,* edited by Rudolf Odebrecht (Berlin & Leipzig: De Gruyter, 1931);

Friedrich Schleiermachers Dialektik: Im Auftrage der Preußischen Akademie der Wissenschaften auf Grund bisher unveröffentlichten Materials herausgegeben, edited by Odebrecht (Leipzig: Hinrichs, 1942);

Hermeneutik, nach den Handschriften neu herausgegeben, edited by Heinz Kimmerle (Heidelberg: Winter, 1959); translated by James Duke and Jack Forstman as *Hermeneutics: The Handwritten Manuscripts* (Missoula, Mont.: Scholars Press, 1977).

Editions: *Der christliche Glaube nach den Grundsätzen der evangelischen Kirche im Zusammenhang dargestellt,* edited by Martin Redeker (Berlin: De Gruyter, 1960);

Vorlesungen über die Aesthetik: Aus Schleiermachers handschriftlichem Nachlasse und aus den nachgeschriebenen Heften von Carl Lommatzsch, edited by Carl Lommatzsch, originally published as Part 3, volume 7 of *Friedrich Schleiermacher's sämmtliche Werke,* 1842 (Berlin & New York: De Gruyter, 1974);

Monologen: Nebst der Vorarbeiten, edited by Friedrich Michael Schiele (Hamburg: Meiner, 1978);

Die praktische Theologie nach den Grundsätzen der evangelischen Kirche im Zusammenhang dargestellt, edited by Jacob Frerichs, originally published as Part 1, volume 13 of *Friedrich Schleiermacher's sämmtliche Werke,* 1850 (Berlin: De Gruyter, 1983);

Kritische Gesamtausgabe, edited by Hans-Joachim Birkner, Gerhard Ebeling, Hermann Fischer, Heinz Kimmerle, and Kurt-Victor Selge, 5 volumes to date (Berlin & New York: De Gruyter, 1984-   ).

Edition in English: *Selected Sermons,* translated by Mary F. Wilson (New York: Funk & Wagnalls, 1889; London: Hodder & Stoughton, 1890).

OTHER: T. Fawcett, *Predigten: Aus dem Englischen,* translated by Schleiermacher, 2 volumes (Berlin: Mylius, 1798);

Hugh Blair, *Hugo Blairs Predigten, aus dem Englischen aufs neue übersetzt,* volume 5, translated by Schleiermacher (Leipzig: Weidmann, 1802);

Plato, *Platons Werke,* translated by Schleiermacher, 6 volumes (Berlin: Realschulbuchhandlung, 1804-1809); introductions translated by William Dobson as *Schleiermacher's Introductions to the Dialogues of Plato* (Cambridge: Deighton, 1836).

Friedrich Schleiermacher was the preeminent clergyman of the Age of Goethe. The theological thought of this small, delicate, yet polemical man culminated in the revolutionary belief that religious faith, grounded in individual feeling that is itself the product of historical and cultural awareness, is the quintessential characteristic of human experience. Typical of the Romantic spirit, Schleiermacher, who has been called the father of modern scientific theology, was opposed to religion as dogmatic precept or as rationalistic speculation. While his primary sphere of influence was in theology and ecclesiastical policymaking, Schleiermacher was also passionately engaged in the political, philosophical, and, to a lesser extent, the literary discussions of his time. A charismatic and eloquent preacher, he was a spirited advocate of the unification of the German people and of the divided Protestant church. An exacting scholar, he lectured and wrote on all the major branches of philosophy and introduced hermeneutic analysis with his translations of the Platonic dialogues.

One of five children, Friedrich Daniel Ernst Schleiermacher was born in Breslau (today Wroclaw, Poland) on 21 November 1768. His father, Gottlieb Schleiermacher, was a Reformed chaplain in the Prussian army. His mother, Katharina Maria Stubenrauch Schleiermacher, was the youngest daughter of a Reformed Prussian court chaplain and sister of Samuel Stubenrauch, the professor of theology at the University of Halle.

Concerned about the corrupting influence of rationalistic theology on their children, the Schleiermachers enrolled Friedrich and his sister Charlotte—who was to remain Schleiermacher's lifelong confidante—in the Moravian school in Niesky, near Görlitz, in the spring of 1783. At this school Schleiermacher developed an appreciation for Greek and Latin and was permanently imbued with the Pietistic belief that religion entailed a personal, enrapturing experience of Christ.

At age sixteen Schleiermacher entered the more rigorous academic program at the relatively isolated Moravian seminary in Barby to prepare for a career in the ministry. He quickly became disenchanted with the lack of free inquiry which pervaded the institution, where he learned of the leading intellectual discussions of the day only

through the prejudices of his instructors. Together with his classmate and friend, Carl Gustav von Brinkmann, Schleiermacher surreptitiously read Goethe's *Die Leiden des jungen Werthers* (The Sorrows of Young Werther, 1774) and the *Jenaer Literaturzeitung*. Schleiermacher increasingly came to accept rationalistic theology, and he soon found it difficult to accept the necessity of Christ's sacrifice or the possibility of eternal damnation.

Uncertain of the authenticity of his calling to the ministry, Schleiermacher left Barby in April 1787 and matriculated as a student of theology at the University of Halle. There he lodged with his uncle, Professor Stubenrauch, who reinforced his nephew's embrace of rationalistic theology. Schleiermacher, who had rejected his father's wishes that he study something practical such as mathematics or French, diligently contemplated the transcendental idealism of Immanuel Kant, largely through J. A. Eberhard's criticisms of the Königsberg philosopher. At about this time he also attempted a translation of Aristotle's *Nicomachean Ethics*.

In May 1789 Schleiermacher accompanied his uncle to Drossen, near Frankfurt an der Oder, where the latter had accepted a position as pastor. In Drossen Schleiermacher was plagued by poor health and heightened skepticism, from which he sought relief in the satirical writings of Christoph Martin Wieland and Michel de Montaigne. His essays from this period reveal that he was troubled by Kant's apparently unbridgeable separation of morality from happiness.

In May 1790 Schleiermacher passed the theological examination in Berlin to qualify as a Reformed minister, having performed well in all areas except dogmatics. Through the influence of a family friend, the renowned clergyman Friedrich Samuel Gottfried Sack, he received a position as a private tutor to the children of Count Dohna in Schlobitten in East Prussia. In addition to his tutoring obligations Schleiermacher gave weekly sermons, which are characterized both by rationalistic morality and by warm, inward-looking piety. He flourished in the congenial atmosphere of Schlobitten for three years, and despite his political differences with the count—Schleiermacher lauded the French Revolution on the grounds that it evolved out of the French character and experience—he left the Dohna estate on amicable terms in May 1793.

Schleiermacher passed the second theological examination in April 1794 and was appointed assistant pastor in Landsberg in Brandenburg. In Landsberg he perfected his oratorical skills; he also translated the sermons of the Scotsman Hugh Blair and actually considered a career as a translator. Through the writings of Friedrich Heinrich Jacobi, Schleiermacher acquainted himself with the thought of Benedict Spinoza, whose philosophy was widely condemned as pantheistic. Schleiermacher was attracted to Spinoza's notion of the mutual interdependence between the finite individual and the infinite, as well as to the universal order which informs his philosophy; but he was critical of Spinoza's lack of interest in the individual human personality. In attempting to meld the philosophies of Kant and Spinoza, Schleiermacher hoped to account for both individuality and universality.

In September 1796 Schleiermacher was named Reformed pastor of the Charité Hospital in Berlin. In the Prussian capital he was a frequent and vocal participant in the salon of Henriette Herz, the beautiful, well-educated but unhappily married wife of the noted physician Dr. Marcus Herz, who had been a pupil of Kant's. Through his association with Frau Herz, for whom he developed a strong affection, Schleiermacher met Friedrich Schlegel, with whom he established a close friendship. The two men read Greek poetry and contemporary literature together and for a time shared an apartment. Schlegel introduced Schleiermacher to the intellectual world of Berlin and proposed that they translate the works of Plato. It soon became clear, however, that Schleiermacher was the more interested and dependable scholar in this project.

Schleiermacher shared much emotionally and intellectually with Schlegel and the other Romantics. His Romantic leanings–his accentuation of feeling and inwardness and his interest in the infinite–predate his relationship with Schlegel. On the other hand, Schleiermacher was more interested in the reality of the present than were the early Romantic writers. Schleiermacher had written some poetry and had considered writing a novel and a tragedy on the political revolution; he also edited and contributed to the Romantic journal *Das Athenäum*. But Schleiermacher made no pretense of being a writer; he was a preacher. He was less interested in literary production than in reconciling religious feeling with critical theory.

Nevertheless, at Schlegel's insistence he continued to write. The result was *Über die Religion: Reden an die Gebildeten unter ihren Verächtern* (trans-

Schleiermacher's family (drawing by F. W. Kantzenbach)

lated as *On Religion: Speeches to Its Cultured Despisers*, 1892), which appeared anonymously in 1799 and in a revised, less pantheistic version in 1821. By virtue of its forceful subjective argumentation and its powerful emotional appeal the work has been viewed as expressive of the Romantic aesthetic. Written in a dithyrambic manner, *Über die Religion* expounds a new basis for religion. Seeking to reclaim religion from the intellectual oblivion into which the Enlightenment had cast it, Schleiermacher directs his remarks not to atheists or agnostics but to those Romantics who were so infused with the idealistic culture of the time. He accepts, especially in the first edition, that art has a special affinity to religion and that both are sources of knowledge of the infinite. But he insists that the Romantic quest for greater self-fulfillment and variety can best be served through religion, for religion, according to Schleiermacher, is an intrinsic element in the self-consciousness of the fully developed man. In contrast to the theologians of the Enlightenment, according to whom religion is intellectually subordinate to morality, metaphysics, or dogmatics, Schleiermacher boldly asserts the primacy and independence of religion. He maintains that religion is not analyzable by speculative reason but is a mystical oneness with the universe. Religion is not dogma, not knowing, not acting; it is not subject to scientific or moral dissection. On the contrary, it entails an "Anschauung und Gefühl des Universums" (intuition and feeling of the universe). Religion is the consciousness of the immanence of the infinite in the world. The soul senses God, the seemingly impersonal reason of all being, knowledge, and volition, and then fuses its own individuality with infinity.

During four weeks in late 1799 Schleiermacher composed *Monologen* (1800; translated as *Schleiermacher's Soliloquies*, 1926), as a philosophical companion piece to *Über die Religion*. The five lyrical reflections, written in iambic and hexametric verse, elucidate the essential nature and significance of the individual in the cosmos and reflect Schleiermacher's increasing departure from Kant's concept of universal reason. Schleiermacher praises individuality as the highest inner life of man. The process of individuation occurs not only through societal interaction but also through inward differentiation or "Eigentümlichkeit" (particularity), that which endows the individual with a unity of life and an inalienable identity. The core of the individual is the particular manifestation of reason in him; consequently, the Kantian ethics of obligation to an absolute law can be replaced by one founded on inner development and organic growth and can take into consideration the vicissitudes of human experience. But Schleiermacher does not avow an ethics of subjectivism, insisting that self-cultivation and self-knowledge occur only in fellowship with others.

In May 1800 Schleiermacher published anonymously *Vertraute Briefe über Friedrich Schlegels Lucinde* (Confidential Letters about Lucinde), which some mistook for the second part of Schlegel's novel *Lucinde* (1799). But Schleiermacher's defense of the novel, in a series of letters by fictional characters praising the physical and spiritual union portrayed in the work, seems to be based more on friendship than on the literary or philosophical merits of the text, and Schleiermacher later withdrew many of the claims he set forth in the letters. In fact, a close reading of the letters and of Schlegel's response suggests that there was less agreement between the two men than is generally assumed. While Schlegel

seems to understand the conflation of spiritual and sensuous love portrayed in the novel as the result of the inevitable workings of an absolute entity, Schleiermacher emphasizes the necessity of human endeavor and is more cognizant of the legitimate demands society places on love; he praises the work but is grateful that it is not typical but unique. Similarly, Schlegel's notion of the unrestricted artist as a divine assistant in the creation of the world is incongruent with Schleiermacher's contention that art, like other domains of human activity, can mirror the ideal but is ultimately limited by the reality of a finite world.

In the spring of 1802 Schleiermacher accepted a position as court preacher in Stolpe, a provincial town in Pomerania, at least partially because he hoped that Eleonore Grunow, the unhappily married wife of a Berlin pastor, might follow him there. But when she resolved to stay in Berlin with her husband, Schleiermacher absorbed himself in his Plato translation. He wanted to demonstrate not only the correct chronology of the dialogues, which had been Schlegel's original intent, but also the validity of his hermeneutic approach. By analyzing each dialogue with utmost care he believed that he could reveal the author's inner development. Although the project was never completed, Schleiermacher's translations and commentaries are still considered valuable to Plato scholarship. He also continued to write poetry, mainly sonnets and madrigals, and worked on *Grundlinien einer Kritik der bisherigen Sittenlehre* (Foundation of a Critique of Earlier Ethical Theories, 1803). In this ponderous tome he seems primarily interested in demonstrating the inadequacies and contradictions of earlier ethical theories. He is highly critical of Kant for having universalized reason, thereby removing ethics from the idiosyncrasies of history. Schleiermacher contends that ethics is a descriptive science of the laws and principles to which human beings conform; it deals with the interpenetration of the reasonable and the natural. Ethics involves a moral agent acting in accord with his individuated rational nature and with the community and institutions in which he lives.

In 1804 Schleiermacher accepted a position as extraordinary professor of theology and university preacher at the University of Halle, the foremost Prussian university. Because of his theological views and close ties to the Romantics, he was given a cool reception by the predominantly rationalistic theology faculty at Halle. In addition

287

to lecturing on ethics, dogmatics, and New Testament exegesis, Schleiermacher continued his translation of Plato and used his hermeneutic method to argue on the basis of internal evidence that 1 Timothy was not written by St. Paul (1807).

In January 1806 Schleiermacher published his most literary work, *Die Weihnachtsfeier: Ein Gespräch* (translated as *Christmas Eve: A Dialogue on the Celebration of Christmas,* 1890). This cycle of three short stories and three speeches given at a middle-class Christmas celebration illuminates the significance of the Christmas feast from a variety of perspectives. Schleiermacher appears to reject his character Leonhart's rationalistic view that Christ as a historical figure has little to do with the evolution of Christianity; his sympathies lie rather with his namesake, Ernst, who emphasizes the inner feeling engendered by knowledge of the historical Jesus, and with Eduard, who argues that salvation is the realization that one's life is grounded in eternal being. Both historicity and emotional attachment are necessary to Christianity in Schleiermacher's view. The eternal being must enter history in order to bring about the perfection of humanity. Schleiermacher accentuates the primacy of the family, making the woman the representative of the soul of the Christmas festival, and underscores the importance of music as an approximation of religious feeling by having his characters sing some of Novalis's religious hymns.

In 1806 the French occupied Halle and closed the university. Schleiermacher delivered patriotic sermons at the university church and participated in secret missions to meet with members of the political reformist movement. In 1808 his former pupil, Alexander von Dohna, who had been named Minister of the Interior, appointed Schleiermacher to a position in the Department of Education. In May 1809 he settled in Berlin, became pastor of Trinity Church, and married the young widow Henriette von Willich, with whom he had five children and adopted two others.

In July 1809 Schleiermacher received an appointment to the theology faculty at the new University of Berlin, the basic philosophy and organization of which he had outlined in 1808 in *Gelegentliche Gedanken über Universitäten im deutschen Sinn: Nebst einem Anhang über eine neu zu errichtende* (Timely Thoughts on Universities from a German Viewpoint: With an Appendix on One To Be Newly Established). In this essay he argues that the new university must be indepen-

dent of the state and must encourage a broad view of learning rather than emulating the French technical school. Schleiermacher became dean of the theology faculty at the university in September 1810.

In his sermons Schleiermacher insisted that the war against France was an instrument of God, through which the inevitable unification of the German people would be realized. He blessed the soldiers before they went into battle and was himself a member of a local unit of the Landsturm, a military support unit composed of university professors.

By 1813, however, Schleiermacher was no longer convinced that victory over the French would guarantee German unity. Moreover, when the constitution promised by the king did not materialize and when the reforms proposed by the former chancellor, Karl vom Stein, failed to take effect, he recognized that his liberal views placed him in jeopardy. His open criticism in the *Preußische Zeitung* of the government's handling of the war brought a reprimand from King Friedrich Wilhelm III, and in July 1814 he was dismissed from the Department of Education. After a speech before the Royal Academy on 24 May 1818, in which he subtly suggested that the Prussian government did not reflect the will of the people, Schleiermacher's classes and sermons were carefully monitored.

Schleiermacher was again at odds with the government for his public support of the activities of liberal political societies and for his support of the theologian Wilhelm Martin De Wette, who had offered comfort to the mother of the seminary student Karl Sand; Sand had assassinated the playwright August von Kotzebue on 23 March 1819 and had been executed.

With the publication of the repressive Carlsbad Decrees in 1819 Schleiermacher realized that he could no longer openly defy the government. In a series of lectures titled *Die Lehre vom Staat* (The Doctrine of the State), published as volume 8 of part 3 of his collected works (1845), Schleiermacher made it clear that the German nation could arise only as a product of time and tradition; the prerequisite level of consciousness—on the part both of the leadership and of the people—was still lacking. Like Plato, Schleiermacher maintained that the ideal form of government was a monarchy in which the king acted in the interests of the people.

In 1822 the issue of the unification of the Reformed and Lutheran churches again brought

Schleiermacher into a combative relationship with the state. Schleiermacher had long sought to bring about the reconciliation of the two churches; but when the king's unification plan as implemented by Minister of the Interior Karl von Altenstein included a common, indiscriminate, and therefore unacceptable liturgy, the Berlin pastor vociferously protested. It was not until 1824 that Schleiermacher was able to say that he no longer feared arrest or punishment.

Schleiermacher's principal theological work, *Der christliche Glaube nach den Grundsätzen der evangelischen Kirche im Zusammenhange dargestellt* (The Christian Faith Presented in Relation to the Principles of the Evangelical Church; translated as *The Christian Faith*, 1928), was published in 1821-1822 and revised in 1830-1831. Schleiermacher delineates his positions on such theological issues as creation, salvation, and justification, and offers his conception of the organization of the theological disciplines. He asserts that "Das Woher des Abhängigkeitsgefühls" (the feeling of dependence) is the constitutive element of religion. This feeling of dependence is equivalent to a feeling of identity; that is, the individual becomes conscious of his own identity in his utter dependence on God. The individual's life unity is created by his relation to God. Consciousness of absolute dependence is equivalent to immediate self-consciousness or God-consciousness. Each individual must appropriate to his or her self-consciousness the relationship to Jesus Christ, who then becomes the center of the individual's inner religious consciousness.

During his final years Schleiermacher underwent a process of rehabilitation by the government. In 1831 he was awarded the Red Eagle Cross, Third Class, and on a trip to Denmark and Sweden in 1833 he received many gifts and awards. On 12 February 1834 he died of pneumonia. His coffin was carried by twelve students and followed by more than one hundred coaches, and thousands of Berliners lined the streets to mourn his passing.

Letters:

Aus Schleiermachers Leben in Briefen, edited by Wilhelm Dilthey and Ludwig Jonas, 4 volumes (Berlin: Reimer, 1858-1863); volumes 1 and 2 translated by Frederica Rowan as *The Life of Schleiermacher as Unfolded in his Autobiography and Letters*, 2 volumes (London: Smith, Elder, 1860);

Friedrich Schleiermachers Briefwechsel mit seiner Braut, edited by Heinrich Meisner (Gotha: Perthes, 1919);
Schleiermacher als Mensch: Sein Werden und Wirken. Familien- und Freundesbriefe, edited by Meisner, 2 volumes (Gotha: Perthes, 1922-1923);
Briefe Schleiermachers, edited by Hermann Mulert (Berlin: Propyläen, 1923).

Bibliographies:

Terrence Tice, *Schleiermacher Bibliography* (Princeton: Princeton Theological Seminary, 1966);
Tice, *Schleiermacher Bibliography 1784-1984* (Princeton: Princeton Theological Seminary, 1985).

Biographies:

Wilhelm Dilthey, *Leben Schleiermachers* (Berlin: Reimer, 1870);
Friedrich W. Kantzenbach, *Friedrich Daniel Ernst Schleiermacher in Selbstzeugnissen* (Hamburg: Rowohlt, 1967);
Martin Redeker, *Friedrich Schleiermacher: Leben und Werk* (Berlin: De Gruyter, 1968); translated by John Wallhausser as *Schleiermacher: Life and Thought* (Philadelphia: Fortress Press, 1973).

References:

Karl Barth, *Protestant Thought* (New York: Harper & Row, 1959);
Richard Brandt, *The Philosophy of Friedrich Schleiermacher* (New York: Harper & Row, 1941);
Keith Clements, *Friedrich Schleiermacher: Pioneer of Modern Theology* (London: Collins, 1987);
Richard Crouter, "Hegel and Schleiermacher in Berlin: A Many-Sided Debate," *Journal of the American Academy of Religion*, 60 (1980): 285-306;
Jerry F. Dawson, *Friedrich Schleiermacher: The Evolution of a Nationalist* (Austin & London: University of Texas Press, 1966);
Hans Dierkes, "Friedrich Schlegels *Lucinde*, Schleiermacher und Kierkegaard," *Deutsche Vierteljahrsschrift*, 57 (1983): 431-449;
Dierkes, "Die problematische Poesie: Schleiermachers Beitrag zur Frühromantik," in *Internationaler Schleiermacher-Kongreß Berlin 1984*, edited by Kurt-Victor Selge, volume 1 (Berlin & New York: De Gruyter, 1985), pp. 61-98;
Daniel Fallon, "Friedrich Schleiermacher and the Idea of the University: Berlin, 1810-1817," in his *The German University: A Heroic Ideal in Conflict with the Modern World* (Boulder,

Colo.: Colorado University Press, 1980), pp. 32-36;

Manfred Frank, "The Text and its Style: Schleiermacher's Hermeneutic Theory of Language," *Boundary*, 11 (1983): 11-28;

Robert W. Funk, ed., *Schleiermacher as Contemporary* (New York: Herder & Herder, 1970);

Brian Albert Gerrish, *A Prince of the Church: Schleiermacher and the Beginnings of Modern Theology* (Philadelphia: Fortress Press, 1984);

Thomas Lehnerer, *Die Kunsttheorie Friedrich Schleiermachers* (Stuttgart: Klett-Cotta, 1987);

Richard R. Niebuhr, *Schleiermacher on Christ and Religion: A New Introduction* (New York: Scribners, 1964);

Kurt Nowak, *Schleiermacher und die Frühromantik: Eine literaturgeschichtliche Studie zum romantischen Religionsverständnis und Menschenbild am Ende des 18. Jahrhundert in Deutschland* (Göttingen: Vandenhoeck & Ruprecht, 1986);

Hermann Patsch, *"Alle Menschen sind Künstler": Friedrich Schleiermachers poetische Versuche* (Berlin & New York: De Gruyter, 1986);

Peter Szondi, "Schleiermachers Hermeneutik heute," *Sprache im technischen Zeitalter*, 58 (1976): 95-111;

Dora Van Vranken, "Friedrich Schleiermacher as a Critic," Ph.D. dissertation, Stanford University, 1973.

Papers:
The Literaturarchiv of the Deutsche Akademie der Wissenschaften, Berlin, has Schleiermacher's diaries, daily calendars, manuscripts, correspondence, letters, copies of lectures, and family papers.

Arthur Schopenhauer

(22 February 1788-21 September 1860)

Martin Donougho
University of South Carolina

BOOKS: *Ueber die vierfache Wurzel des Satzes vom zureichenden Grunde: Eine philosophische Abhandlung* (Rudolstadt: Hof-Buch- und Kunst-
handlung, 1813; revised and enlarged
edition, Frankfurt am Main: Hermann,
1847; edited by Julius Frauenstädt, Leipzig:
Brockhaus, 1864; edited by Michael Land-
mann and Elfriede Tielsch, Hamburg: Meiner, 1970); translated by Mme. Karl Hille-
brand as "On the Fourfold Root of the
Principle of Sufficient Reason," in *Two Essays by Arthur Schopenhauer* (London: Bell,
1889); translated by F. E. J. Payne in *The Fourfold Root of the Principle of Sufficient Reason* (La-
salle, Ill.: Open Court, 1974);

Ueber das Sehn und die Farben: Eine Abhandlung
(Leipzig: Hartknoch, 1816; enlarged, 1854;
edited by Frauenstädt, Leipzig: Brockhaus,
1870); chapter 1 translated by Payne as "On
Vision," in *The Fourfold Root of the Principle
of Sufficient Reason*, pp. 237-255;

*Die Welt als Wille und Vorstellung: Vier Bücher, nebst
einem Anhange, der die Kritik der Kantischen Philosophie enthält* (Leipzig: Brockhaus, 1819; revised and enlarged, 2 volumes, 1844; revised and enlarged again, 2 volumes, 1854;
edited by Frauenstädt, 2 volumes, 1873);
translated by Richard B. Haldane and John
Kemp as *The World as Will and Idea*, 3 volumes (London: Trübner, 1883-1886; Boston:
Ticknor, 1887; reprinted, New York: AMS
Press, 1977); translated by Payne as *The
World as Will and Representation*, 2 volumes (Indian Hills, Col.: Falcon's Wing Press, 1958;
reprinted, New York: Dover, 1966);

*Ueber den Willen in der Natur: Eine Erörterung der Be-
stätigungen, welche die Philosophie des Verfassers,
seit ihrem Auftreten, durch die empirischen Wissenschaften erhalten hat* (Frankfurt am Main:
Schmerber, 1836; revised and enlarged edition, edited by Frauenstädt, Leipzig: Brockhaus, 1867); translated anonymously as *The
Will in Nature: An Account of the Corrobora-
tions Received by the Author's Philosophy from*

Arthur Schopenhauer (etching by M. Lämmel)

the Empirical Sciences (New York: Eckler,
1877; reprinted, Ann Arbor, Mich.: University Microfilms, 1982); translated by Hille-
brand as "On the Will in Nature," in *Two Essays by Arthur Schopenhauer*;

*Die beiden Grundprobleme der Ethik, behandelt in zwei
akademischen Preisschriften* (Frankfurt am
Main: Hermann, 1841; revised and enlarged edition, Leipzig: Brockhaus, 1860)–
comprises "Ueber die Freiheit des menschlichen Willens," translated by Konstantin
Kolenda as *Essay on the Freedom of the Will* (Indianapolis: Bobbs-Merrill, 1960; Oxford:
Blackwell, 1985); "Ueber das Fundament
der Moral," translated by Arthur Brodrick

Bullock as *The Basis of Morality* (London: Sonnenschein, 1903; New York: Macmillan,
1903); translated by Payne as *On the Basis of
Morality* (Indianapolis: Bobbs-Merrill, 1965);
*Parerga und Paralipomena: Kleine philosophische
Schriften*, 2 volumes (Berlin: Hayn, 1851; revised and enlarged edition, edited by Frauenstädt, Berlin: Hahn, 1862; edited by Arthur
Hübscher, Stuttgart: Reclam, 1953); selections translated by Thomas Bailey Saunders
as *Religion: A Dialogue; and Other Essays* (London: Sonnenschein, 1899; New York: Macmillan, 1899; reprinted, Freeport, N.Y.:
Books for Libraries Press, 1972)–comprises
"Religion: A Dialogue," "A Few Words on
Pantheism," "On Books and Reading," "On
Physiognomy," "Psychological Observations," "The Christian System," "The Failure
of Philosophy," "The Metaphysics of Fine
Art"; selections translated by Saunders as
*The Wisdom of Life: Being the First Part of Ar-
thur Schopenhauer's Aphorismen zur Lebensweis-
heit* (London: Sonnenschein, 1890)–
comprises "Introduction," "Division of the
Subject," "Personality, or What a Man Is,"
"Property, or What a Man Has," "Position,
or a Man's Place in the Estimation of Oth-
ers"; selections translated by Saunders as
*Counsels and Maxims: Being the Second Part of
Arthur Schopenhauer's Aphorismen zur Lebens-
weisheit* (London: Sonnenschein, 1890; New
York: Macmillan, 1899; reprinted, St. Clair
Shores, Mich.: Scholarly Press, 1970)–
comprises "General Rules," "Our Relation
to Ourselves," "Our Relation to Others,"
"Worldly Fortune," "The Ages of Life"; se-
lections translated by Saunders as *Studies in
Pessimism: A Series of Essays* (London:
Sonnenschein/New York: Macmillan, 1890;
reprinted, St. Clair Shores, Mich.: Scholarly
Press, 1970)–comprises "On the Sufferings
of the World," "On the Vanity of Existence,"
"On Suicide," "Immortality: A Dialogue,"
"Further Psychological Observations," "On
Education," "On Women," "On Noise," "A
Few Parables"; selections translated by Saun-
ders as *The Art of Literature: A Series of Essays*
(London: Sonnenschein, 1890; New York:
Macmillan, 1897)–comprises "On Author-
ship," "On Style," "On the Study of Latin,"
"On Men of Learning," "On Thinking for
Oneself," "On Some Forms of Literature,"
"On Criticism," "On Reputation," "On Ge-
nius"; selections from volume 2 translated

by R. J. Hollingdale as *Essays and Aphorisms*
(Harmondsworth, U.K.: Penguin, 1970); en-
tire work translated by Payne as *Parerga and
Paralipomena: Short Philosophical Essays*, 2 vol-
umes (Oxford: Clarendon Press, 1974);
*Aus Arthur Schopenhauer's handschriftlichem Nachlaß:
Abhandlungen, Anmerkungen, Aphorismen und
Fragmente*, edited by Frauenstädt (Leipzig:
Brockhaus, 1864);
Arthur Schopenhauer's sämmtliche Werke, edited by
Frauenstädt (6 volumes, Leipzig: Brockhaus,
1873-1874; revised and enlarged by Hüb-
scher, 7 volumes, 1937-1950);
Arthur Schopenhauer's sämmtliche Werke, edited by
Eduard Grisebach, 6 volumes (Leipzig: Rec-
lam, 1891);
*Handschriftlicher Nachlaß: aus den auf der Königli-
chen Bibliothek in Berlin verwahrten Manuskript-
büchern*, edited by Grisebach, 4 volumes
(Leipzig: Reclam, 1891-1893)–comprises volume 1, *Balthasar Gracian's Hand-Orakel und
Kunst der Weltklugheit*, translated by Schopenhauer; volume 2, *Einleitung in die Philosophie
nebst Abhandlungen*; volume 3, *Anmerkungen
zu Locke und Kant*; volume 4, *Neue Paralipomena*;
Arthur Schopenhauers sämtliche Werke, edited by
Paul Deussen, 13 volumes (Munich: Piper,
1911-1942);
Reisetagebücher aus den Jahren 1803-1804, edited
by Charlotte von Gwinner (Leipzig: Brockhaus, 1923);
*Der junge Schopenhauer: Aphorismen und Tagebuch-
blätter*, edited by Hübscher (Munich: Piper,
1938);
Der handschriftliche Nachlaß, edited by Hübscher, 5
volumes (Frankfurt am Main: Kramer, 1966-
1975)–comprises volume 1, *Frühe Manuskripte (1804-1818)*, translated by Valerie
Egret-Payne as *Manuscript Remains: Early
Manuscripts (1804-1818)* (Oxford: Berg,
1988); volume 2, *Kritische Auseinandersetzun-
gen (1809-1818)*, translated by Payne as *Critical Debates (1809-1818)* (Oxford: Berg,
1988); volume 3, *Berliner Manuskripte
(1818-1830)*; volume 4, part 1, *Die Manu-
skriptbücher der Jahre 1830 bis 1852*; volume
4, part 2, *Letzte Manuskripte; Gracians Hando-
rakel*; volume 5, *Randschriften zu Büchern; Eri-
stische Dialektik oder Die Kunst, Recht zu behal-
ten* (Zurich: Haffmans, 1983);
*Metaphysik des Schönen: Aus dem handschriftlichen
Nachlaß*, edited by Volker Spierling (Munich: Piper, 1985);

Theorie des gesammten Vorstellens, Denkens und Erkennens: Aus dem handschriftlichen Nachlaß, edited by Spierling (Munich: Piper, 1986);

Metaphysik dem Natur: Aus dem handschriftlichen Nachlaß, edited by Spierling (Munich: Piper, 1987);

Metaphysik der Sitten: Aus dem handschriftlichen Nachlaß, edited by Spierling (Munich: Piper, 1988);

Die Reisetagebücher, edited by Ludger Lutkehaus (Zurich: Haffmans, 1988).

Editions in English: *Select Essays of Arthur Schopenhauer*, translated by Garritt Droppers and C. A. P. Dachsel (Milwaukee: Sentinel, 1881) –comprises "Biographical Sketch," "The Misery of Life," "Metaphysics of Love," "Genius," "Aesthetics of Poetry," "Education";

Selected Essays of Arthur Schopenhauer: With Biographical Introduction and Sketch of His Philosophy, translated by Ernest Belfort Bax (London: Bell, 1891)–comprises "Life and Philosophy of Schopenhauer," "Sketch of a History of the Doctrine of the Ideal and Real," "Fragments of the History of Philosophy," "On Philosophy and Its Method," "Some Reflections on the Antithesis of Thing-In-Itself and Phenomenon," "Some Words on Pantheism," "On Ethics," "On the Doctrine of the Indestructibility of Our True Nature by Death," "On Suicide," "Contributions to the Doctrine of the Affirmation and Negation of the Will-to-live," "On the Metaphysics of the Beautiful and on Aesthetics," "On Thinking for Oneself," "On Reading and Books," "On Women";

The Art of Controversy, and Other Posthumous Papers, selected and translated by Saunders (London: Sonnenschein/New York: Macmillan, 1896)–comprises "The Art of Controversy," "On the Comparative Place of Interest and Beauty in Works of Art," "Psychological Observations," "On the Wisdom of Life: Aphorisms," "Genius and Virtue";

On Human Nature: Essays (Partly Posthumous) in Ethics and Politics, selected and translated by Saunders (London: Sonnenschein/New York: Macmillan, 1897)–comprises "Human Nature," "Government," "Free-will and Fatalism," "Character," "Moral Instinct," "Ethical Reflections";

Transcendent Speculations on Apparent Design in the Fate of the Individual, translated by David Irvine (London: Watts, 1913).

One of the leading German metaphysicians of the nineteenth century, Arthur Schopenhauer is exceptional in having had a widespread influence outside of philosophy; among his admirers may be counted such figures as Richard Wagner, Friedrich Nietzsche, Tolstoy, and Thomas Mann. Within philosophy itself, Schopenhauer is important for having broken with his Idealist contemporaries both in espousing a down-to-earth materialism and in forsaking philosophic jargon in favor of a limpid and vigorous literary style. He put forward a metaphysics of the will which approached life in concrete terms (his psychological insights often anticipate Freud) and resulted in a pessimistic attitude to the cosmos. Schopenhauer held that there are two ways to combat the tyranny of the will. The first is through art, at its most exalted in music; it is this aspect that entitles him to be thought of as the exemplarily Romantic philosopher, expounding (in Thomas Mann's phrase) a "Künstlerphilosophie [artist's philosophy] par excellence." The second path lies in an ethic of asceticism and self-overcoming; Schopenhauer was one of the first Western thinkers to take seriously Hindu and Buddhist philosophy.

Schopenhauer was born on 22 February 1788 in Danzig (today Gdansk, Poland). His father, Heinrich Schopenhauer, was a successful businessman of Dutch extraction who so despised absolutist government that when Danzig was annexed to Prussia in 1793 he moved his family and business to Hamburg. Schopenhauer's mother, Johanna Henriette Trosiener Schopenhauer, was of an artistic temperament and had some success as a writer. The family traveled a good deal, and the young Schopenhauer spent several years touring with them through France, England (including several months at a mediocre school in London), Switzerland, and Austria, as well as throughout Germany. In his travels Schopenhauer developed a love of natural beauty, along with a hatred of the human cruelty he witnessed everywhere. He also acquired a facility in several languages; as a thinker Schopenhauer was to be a cosmopolitan who admired English and French models more than German (his library had comparatively few books in that language).

After his father's death–probably by suicide–in 1805 Schopenhauer honored a promise he had made to enter business, although he found commerce distasteful. He remained in Hamburg only a year, after which he persuaded his mother to let him continue his education–first at a gymnasium in Gotha, where he was expelled for a prank, and then in 1808 at his mother's house in Weimar, where she had established a literary salon. He entered the University of Göttingen as a student of medicine in 1809. His interests were, however, captured by the lectures of the skeptic Gottlob Ernst Schulze, who encouraged him to read the works of Plato and Immanuel Kant; these authors, together with Schulze's stylistic clarity and emphasis on will, had a lasting effect on Schopenhauer's thinking. In 1811 Schopenhauer began philosophical studies at the University of Berlin. He attended lectures by Johann Gottlieb Fichte and Friedrich Schleiermacher but quickly tired of them, not for the last time exercising his biting sarcasm on other thinkers.

During the Wars of Liberation in 1813 he withdrew to Rudolstat to finish his dissertation, which was published the same year with the title *Ueber die vierfache Wurzel des Satzes vom zureichenden Grunde* (translated as "On the Fourfold Root of the Principle of Sufficient Reason," 1889). Schopenhauer always considered it the proper introduction to his thought, even though its abstractness and Kantian terminology make it rather forbidding. He argues that human knowledge presupposes the unprovable principle that everything must have a ground or reason. Knowledge takes four main forms: empirical representations of real objects; logical judgment and reasoning; mathematical knowledge; and knowledge of the self and its motives. Schopenhauer argues that human beings are not, as Kant thought, free agents but are ruled by a universal will.

On Schopenhauer's return to Weimar Goethe publicly acclaimed the work, and the two men cooperated on studies of the theory of color. The essay that Schopenhauer wrote on the subject did not meet with Goethe's approval, however. Schopenhauer had to ask Goethe for the return of the manuscript so that he could publish it, and it appeared under the title *Ueber das Sehn und die Farben* (On Vision and Colors, translated as "On Vision," 1974) in 1816. Schopenhauer's concerns had in the meanwhile taken a new turn thanks to his making the acquaintance of the well-known orientalist Friedrich Mayer, who introduced him to the *Upanishads* and various Buddhist texts. These works had a profound effect on his subsequent thinking.

Schopenhauer did not remain long at Weimar. After several quarrels with his mother—who, like her son, was headstrong, nervous, and self-centered—he left the house and never saw her again. From 1814 to 1818 he lived in Dresden, engaged in writing his greatest achievement, *Die Welt als Wille und Vorstellung* (translated as *The World as Will and Idea*, 1883-1886). The work appeared in 1819 (the printer said that Schopenhauer's behavior in correspondence was that of a cabman rather than a philosopher).

In the preface Schopenhauer writes that his book has a single idea—which nevertheless takes hundreds of pages (and indeed took the rest of his life) to develop: the world is but appearance, beneath whose illusory features lurks an implacable, irrational, impenetrable, merciless will; the workings of this will are unknown to human agents. The Vorstellungen (representations) that constitute the empirical world are subject to the principle of sufficient reason, which states that everything is causally determined. Language consists of representations of representations; its purpose is not to depict reality but is the purely instrumental one of communication (Nietzsche's theory of language was heavily influenced by Schopenhauer). The will behind the appearances is a monistic force or energy underlying and expressing itself in the phenomenal world. The will is thus extended beyond the human realm to nature in general: in human affairs it manifests itself in the ubiquity of desire—the sexual drive in particular—and in the unconscious determination of behavior.

The will can never be grasped as it is in itself; all one can know are its typical forms of expression, which Schopenhauer calls "Ideen" (Ideas) in the Platonic sense. Art—the topic of the third part of the book—offers both insight into and relief from the relentless action of the will. In revealing the forms the will takes in the world the work of art produces a disinterested and distanced attitude in both the creator and the spectator. Art is not caught up in the practical world of values and usefulness; it has nothing to do with individual objects connected by causal relationships. The highest art, music, escapes the realm of individuation altogether (at least so far as it is "pure" music, unsullied by words); music is not like the other arts, a copy of the Ideas but a copy of the will itself. The other arts speak only of shadows, while music speaks of the essence of the will. It is hardly surprising that the lyrical pages Schopenhauer devotes to this art of arts should have inspired musicians and musically inclined writers such as Wagner, Nietzsche, Hans Pfitzner, Marcel Proust, and Thomas Mann.

But art offers only a temporary exit from the phenomenal world—the world of suffering, of

Schopenhauer as a young man (painting by Ludwig Sigismund Ruhl; by permission of Historia-Photo, Bad Sachsa)

practical affairs, of causal determinism. The more lasting path is not aesthetic but ethical. The individual, Schopenhauer argues, ought to overcome the chains of desire that enslave him to the will; the ideal is disillusioned, ascetic turning away from the world. It would be better not to have been born; yet suicide is a mistake, since it rules out the possibility of self-overcoming.

Die Welt als Wille und Vorstellung excited little comment or interest on its publication (nor on its revision in 1844, at which time Schopenhauer added fifty chapters to the work). Undeterred by the book's failure, in 1820 Schopenhauer obtained permission to teach classes at the University of Berlin, deliberately choosing to lecture at the same time as Georg Wilhelm Friedrich Hegel, whom he termed a "charlatan" and "that intellectual Caliban." But Hegel was then entering upon the period of his greatest popularity, and Schopenhauer failed to attract an audience. In a state of nervous collapse he escaped to Italy. But he soon had to return to Berlin to answer a charge of battery brought by a seamstress: Schopenhauer, who hated noise (and wrote an amusing essay [1851; translated, 1890] on the topic), had been enraged by her loud chattering on the landing outside his room; in the ensuing altercation he pushed her, and she fell down a flight of stairs. He lost the case and was obliged to pay her a monthly allowance until her death. (When she finally died, twenty years later, he commented, "Obit anus, abit onus" [The old woman dies, the burden is lifted]). The experience served only to make him more misanthropic and misogynous–his diatribe "Über die Weiber" (1851; translated as "On Women," 1890) is notorious.

In 1831 Schopenhauer moved to Frankfurt to escape a cholera epidemic, and after 1833 he scarcely left the city. There he entered on the life for which he has become famous: almost in a parody of Kant, he dressed in an old-fashioned way, ate at strictly regular times, and took his daily walk in the company of his much-loved poodle Atma. Apart from occasional visits to the theater and reading the newspapers at the public library, he was the model of a scholarly recluse.

Besides a posthumously published translation of the seventeenth-century Spanish Jesuit Baltasar Gracián's *Hand-Orakel und Kunst der Weltklugheit* (Manual Oracle and Art of Worldly Wisdom, 1891), he wrote three more books. *Über den Willen in der Natur* (1836; translated as *The Will in Nature*, 1877) argues that his philosophy has received support from the empirical sciences. *Die beiden Grundprobleme der Ethik* (The Two Basic Problems of Ethics, 1841) comprises the two essays "Ueber die Freiheit des menschlichen Willens" (translated as *Essay on the Freedom of the Will*, 1960) and "Ueber das Fundament der Moral" (translated as *The Basis of Morality*, 1903). The former is an economical exposition of the problem of freedom and determinism that is still worth reading. In 1851 appeared a large collection of essays titled *Parerga und Paralipomena* (literally, Byproducts and Omissions; translated, 1974). Here Schopenhauer indulges to the full his literary and polemical skills, writing with verve on religion, ethics, aesthetics, literary style, philosophical method, university education, suicide, noise, women, and many other topics. He planned a five-volume edition of his collected works which was to carry the motto "*non multa*" (not a lot), but he was unable to complete the project (the first such collection was published by his literary executor, Julius Frauenstädt, in 1873-1874). The Schopenhauerian corpus remains a spare one.

Gradually Schopenhauer began to attract a following. The initial interest came from England–appropriately for someone who admired English political and cultural traditions. In 1853 John Oxenford, a translator of Goethe, wrote a short article on Schopenhauer for the *Westminster Review* titled "Iconoclasm in German Philosophy." It was at once translated into German and widely read. Favorable reactions quickly followed in France and Italy. Within a short time his ideas were being disseminated in German universities, and admirers began visiting him in his rooms at the Englischer Hof.

Schopenhauer had little time to enjoy this adulation. Heart trouble was diagnosed in 1857, and after a second heart attack in 1860 he developed an inflammation of the lungs. His doctor found him dead in his chair on the morning of 21 September of that year. In accordance with his wishes, his gravestone bore only the words "Arthur Schopenhauer."

His influence was largely posthumous. The moment for his ideas came later: they served as a bridge between earlier idealist systems and late nineteenth-century naturalism, irrationalism, and Lebensphilosophie (life philosophy). His appeal has been to artists and cultural critics as much as to philosophers and is literary or imaginative as much as intellectual, although twentieth-century analytic philosophy has shown some interest in Schopenhauer's metaphysics, largely thanks to the influence of Ludwig Wittgenstein.

Those influenced by his ideas include, above all, Wagner, who in 1857 sent the philosopher an inscribed copy of *Der Ring des Nibelungen* (1848); it was not acknowledged. Most of Wagner's mature operas–especially *Tristan und Isolde*–are unthinkable without their Schopenhauerian scaffolding; Wagner's privileging of music above words and his characteristic themes of renunciation and sympathy come straight from *Die Welt als Wille und Vorstellung*. It is true that Wagner sees redemption being won less through art than through love, and sexual love at that; but the importance of sexuality is stressed by Schopenhauer, too. Both Schopenhauer and Wagner worked powerfully upon the imagination of the young Nietzsche: the Dionysian/Apollonian polarity art as the justification of the world, the will to power, the eternal return are all transformations of Schopenhauerian leitmotifs. And Thomas Mann read Schopenhauer at a crucial moment during the writing of his novel *Buddenbrooks* (1901; translated, 1924) and fell into what he

called a "metaphysical intoxication." Other German-language writers influenced by Schopenhauer include Wilhelm Raabe, Wilhelm Busch, Gerhardt Hauptmann, Hugo von Hofmannsthal, Karl Kraus, Theodor Sturm, Richard Dehmel, Frank Wedekind, Ernst Jünger, Arno Schmidt, and Thomas Bernhard. To these may be added, in French literature, Émile Zola, Guy de Maupassant, Jules Laforgue, Joris Karl Huysmans, Marcel Proust, André Gide, and Samuel Beckett, and among English writers, Joseph Conrad (who conceived the artist's task as "above all to make you *see*" and modeled Axel Heyst's father in *Victory* [1915] on Schopenhauer), Thomas Hardy (the "immanent will"), and George Gissing. In other literatures there are Tolstoy, Ivan Turgenev, Andrei Bely, August Strindberg, Italo Svevo, and Jorge Luis Borges–the writer who, perhaps, could best of all have endorsed the opening line of Schopenhauer's masterwork: "Die Welt ist meine Vorstellung" (The world is my representation).

Letters:

Briefwechsel zwischen Arthur Schopenhauer und Johann August Becker, edited by Johann Karl Becker (Leipzig: Brockhaus, 1883);

Schopenhauer-Briefe: Sammlung meist ungedruckter oder schwer zugänglicher Briefe von, an und über Schopenhauer. Mit Anmerkungen und biographischen Analekten, edited by Ludwig Schemann (Leipzig: Brockhaus, 1893);

Schopenhauer's Briefe an Becker, Frauenstädt, v. Doss, Lindner und Asher: Sowie andere, bisher nicht gesammelte Briefe aus den Jahren 1813 bis 1860, edited by Eduard Grisebach (Leipzig: Reclam, 1894);

Arthur Schopenhauers Briefwechsel und andere Dokumente, edited by Max Brahn (Leipzig: Insel, 1911);

Der Briefwechsel zwischen Arthur Schopenhauer und Otto Lindner, edited by Robert Gruber (Vienna & Leipzig: Hartleben, 1913);

Briefe, Aufzeichnungen, Gespräche, edited by Paul Wiegler (Berlin: Ullstein, 1916);

Schopenhauer und Brockhaus: Zur Zeitgeschichte der "Welt als Wille und Vorstellung." Ein Briefwechsel, edited by Carl Gebhart (Leipzig: Brockhaus, 1926);

Arthur Schopenhauer: Mensch und Philosoph in seinen Briefen, edited by Arthur Hübscher (Wiesbaden: Brockhaus, 1960);

Gesammelte Briefe, edited by Hübscher (Bonn: Bouvier, 1978).

Bibliographies:

Arthur Hübscher, *Schopenhauer-Bibliographie* (Stuttgart & Bad Cannstatt: Fromann-Holzboog, 1981);

David Cartwright, "An English-Language Bibliography of Works on Schopenhauer," *Schopenhauer-Jahrbuch*, 68 (1987): 257-266.

Biographies:

Eduard Grisebach, *Schopenhauer: Geschichte seines Lebens* (Berlin: Hofmann, 1876);

Helen Zimmern, *Arthur Schopenhauer: His Life and His Philosophy* (London: Longmans, Green, 1876; revised edition, London: Allen & Unwin, 1932);

William Wallace, *Life of Arthur Schopenhauer* (London: Scott, 1890; reprinted, St. Clair Shores, Mich.: Scholarly Press, 1970);

Kuno Fischer, *Arthur Schopenhauer* (Heidelberg: Winter, 1893); revised as *Schopenhauers Leben, Werke und Lehre* (Heidelberg: Winter, 1898);

Walther Schneider, *Schopenhauer: Eine Biographie* (Vienna: Bermann-Fischer, 1937);

Arthur Hübscher, *Arthur Schopenhauer: Ein Lebensbild* (Leipzig: Brockhaus, 1938);

Volker Spierling, ed., *Schopenhauer im Denken der Gegenwart* (Munich: Piper, 1987);

Die Schopenhauer-Welt: Ausstellung der Staatsbibliotek Preußischer Kulturbesitz und der Stadt- und Universitätsbibliotek Frankfurt am Main zu Arthur Schopenhauers 200. Geburtstag (Frankfurt am Main: Kramer, 1988).

References:

Bernhard Adamy, "Künstlerphilosophie par excellence: Zur Schopenhauer-Rezeption der deutschen Literatur," *Schopenhauer-Jahrbuch* (1988): 483-496;

Philip Alperson, "Schopenhauer and Musical Revelation," *Journal of Aesthetics and Art Criticism*, 40 (Winter 1981): 155-166;

J. O. Bailey, *Thomas Hardy and the Cosmic Mind: A New Reading of "The Dynasts"* (Chapel Hill: University of North Carolina Press, 1956);

Bernard Bykhovskiĭ, *Schopenhauer and the Ground of Existence*, translated by Philip Moran (Amsterdam: Grüner, 1984);

William Caldwell, *Schopenhauer's System in Its Philosophical Significance* (Edinburgh & London: Blackwood, 1896);

David Cartwright, "Kant, Schopenhauer, and Nietzsche on the Morality of Pity," *Journal of the History of Ideas*, 45, no. 1 (1984): 83-98;

John Churchill, "Wittgenstein's Adaptation of Schopenhauer," *Southern Journal of Philosophy*, 21 (1983): 489-502;

Frederick Copleston, *Arthur Schopenhauer, Philosopher of Pessimism* (London: Burns, Oates & Washbourne, 1946; reprinted, London: Search Press, 1975);

Raymond Didier, *Schopenhauer* (Paris: Seuil, 1979);

S. Morris Engel, "Schopenhauer's Impact on Wittgenstein," *Journal of the History of Ideas*, 7 (1969): 285-302;

Michael Fox, ed., *Schopenhauer: His Philosophical Achievement* (Brighton, U.K.: Harvester, 1980);

Patrick Gardiner, *Schopenhauer* (Harmondsworth, U.K.: Penguin, 1963);

Helen Garwood, *Thomas Hardy: An Illustration of the Philosophy of Schopenhauer* (Philadelphia: Winston, 1911);

A. Phillips Griffiths, "Wittgenstein and the Fourfold Root of the Principle of Sufficient Reason," *Proceedings of the Aristotelian Society*, supplementary volume L (1976): 1-20;

D. W. Hamlyn, *Schopenhauer* (London: Routledge, 1980);

Gabriele von Heesen-Cremer, "Zum Problem des Kulturpessimismus: Schopenhauer-Rezeption bei Künstlern und Intellektuellen 1871-1918," in *Ideengeschichte und Kunstwissenschaft: Philosophie und bildende Kunst im Kaiserreich*, edited by Ekkehard Mai, Stephan Waetzoldt, and Gerd Wolandt (Berlin, 1983), pp. 45-70;

Hilde Hein, "Schopenhauer and Platonic Ideas," *Journal of the History of Philosophy*, 4 (1966): 133-144;

Erich Heller, *The Ironic German: A Study of Thomas Mann* (London: Secker & Warburg, 1958);

Max Horkheimer, "Die Aktualität Schopenhauers," *Schopenhauer-Jahrbuch*, 42 (1961): 12-25; translated as "Schopenhauer Today," in *The Critical Spirit: Essays in Honor of Herbert Marcuse*, edited by Robert K. Wolff and Barrington Moore (Boston: Beacon Press, 1967), pp. 124-141;

Arthur Hübscher, *Denker gegen den Strom: Schopenhauer gestern–heute–morgen* (Bonn: Bouvier, 1973);

Christopher Janaway, *Self and World in Schopenhauer's Philosophy* (Oxford: Oxford University Press, 1989);

Gerald Judzinski, *Leiden an der "Natur": Thomas Bernhards metaphysische Weltdeutung im Spiegel der Philosophie Schopenhauers* (Frankfurt am Main & New York: Lang, 1984);

Yasuo Kamata, *Der junge Schopenhauer: Genese des Grundgedankens der Welt als Wille und Vorstellung* (Frankfurt am Main & Munich: Alber, 1988);

Fritz Kaufmann, *Thomas Mann: The World as Will and Representation* (Boston: Beacon Press, 1957);

Israel Knox, *The Aesthetic Theories of Kant, Hegel, and Schopenhauer* (New York: Humanities Press, 1958);

Búrge Kristiansen, *Thomas Manns Zauberberg und Schopenhauers Metaphysik* (Bonn: Bouvier, 1986);

Bryan Magee, *The Philosophy of Schopenhauer* (Oxford: Clarendon Press, 1983);

Thomas Mann, *Schopenhauer* (Stockholm: Bermann-Fischer, 1938);

Sigrid McLaughlin, *Schopenhauer in Russland: Zur literarischen Rezeption bei Turgenev* (Wiesbaden: Harrassowitz, 1984);

McLaughlin, "Tolstoy and Schopenhauer," *California Slavic Studies*, 5 (1970): 187-245;

Franz Mockrauer, "Unknown Schopenhauer Documents," *Times Literary Supplement*, 27 June 1936;

Friedrich Nietzsche, *Schopenhauer als Erzieher*, volume 3 of his *Unzeitgemäße Betrachtungen* (Chemnitz: Schmeitzer, 1874); translated by R. J. Hollingdale as "Schopenhauer as Educator," in *Untimely Meditations* by Nietzsche (Cambridge: Cambridge University Press, 1983);

John Oxenford, "Iconoclasm in German Philosophy," *Westminster Review*, new series 3 (1853): 388-407;

Alexis Philonenko, *Schopenhauer: Une philosophie de la tragédie* (Paris: Vrin, 1980);

Otto Pöggeler, "Schopenhauer und das Wesen der Kunst," *Zeitschrift für philosophische Forschung*, 14 (1960): 353-389;

Ulrich Pothast, *Die eigentlich metaphysische Tätigkeit über Schopenhauers Ästhetik und ihre Anwendung durch Samuel Beckett* (Frankfurt am Main: Suhrkamp, 1982);

T. J. Reed, "Kafka und Schopenhauer: Philosophisches Denken und dichterisches Bild," *Euphorion*, 59 (1956): 160-172;

Clément Rosset, *L'Estétique de Schopenhauer* (Paris: Presses Universitaires de France, 1969);

Alfred Schmidt, *Idee und Weltwille: Schopenhauer als Kritiker Hegels* (Munich: Hanser, 1988);

Schmidt, *Die Wahrheit im Gewande der Lüge: Schopenhauers Religionsphilosophie* (Munich: Piper, 1986);

Jean W. Sedlar, *India in the Mind of Germany: Schelling, Schopenhauer and Their Times* (Washington, D.C.: University Press of America, 1982);

Georg Simmel, *Schopenhauer und Nietzsche: Ein Vortragszyklus* (Leipzig: Duncker & Humblot, 1907); translated by Helmut Loiskandle, Deena Weinstein, and Michael Weinstein as *Schopenhauer and Nietzsche* (Amherst: University of Massachusetts Press, 1986);

Bernhard Sorg, *Zur literarischen Schopenhauer-Rezeption im 19. Jahrhundert* (Heidelberg: Winter, 1975);

Volker Spierling, ed., *Materialien zu Schopenhauers "Die Welt als Wille und Vorstellung"* (Frankfurt am Main: Suhrkamp, 1984);

J. P. Stern, "The Aesthetic Re-Interpretation: Schopenhauer," in his *Re-Interpretations: Seven Studies in Nineteenth-Century German Literature* (London: Thames and Hudson, 1964), pp. 156-207;

Alan Walker, "Schopenhauer and Music," *Times Literary Supplement*, 3 January 1975, pp. 11-12;

Julian Young, "Schopenhauer's Critique of Kantian Ethics," *Kantstudien*, 75 (1984): 191-212;

Young, "The Standpoint of Eternity: Schopenhauer on Art," *Kantstudien*, 78, no. 4 (1987): 425-441;

Young, *Willing and Unwilling: A Study in the Philosophy of Arthur Schopenhauer* (The Hague: Nijhoff, 1987).

Papers:

Schopenhauer left many manuscripts and notes for revision to his executor, Julius Frauenstädt. The notes have been lost, but the manuscripts are part of the Preußischer Kulturbesitz of the Staatsbibliothek, Berlin. There is also a sizable collection of manuscripts and letters in the Schopenhauer-Archiv, Frankfurt am Main.

Johanna Schopenhauer

(9 July 1766-16 April 1838)

T. H. Pickett
University of Alabama

BOOKS: *Fernows Leben* (Tübingen & Stuttgart: Cotta, 1810);

Erinnerungen von einer Reise in den Jahren 1803, 1804 und 1805, 2 volumes (Rudolstadt: Hof-, Buch- und Kunstverlag, 1813-1814);

Novellen, fremd und eigen (Rudolstadt: Hof-, Buch- und Kunstverlag, 1816);

Reise durch das südliche Frankreich (Rudolstadt: Hof-, Buch- und Kunstverlag, 1817);

Reise durch England und Schottland, 2 volumes (Leipzig: Brockhaus, 1818);

Ausflucht an den Rhein und dessen nächste Umgebungen im Sommer des ersten friedlichen Jahres (Leipzig: Brockhaus, 1818);

Gabriele: Ein Roman, 3 volumes (Leipzig: Brockhaus, 1819-1820);

Johann van Eyck und seine Nachfolger, 2 volumes (Frankfurt am Main: Wilmans, 1822);

Die Tante: Ein Roman, 2 volumes (Frankfurt am Main: Wilmans, 1823);

Reise von Paris durch das südliche Frankreich bis Chamouny, 2 volumes (Leipzig: Brockhaus, 1824);

Erzählungen, 8 volumes (Frankfurt am Main: Sauerländer, 1825-1828);

Sidonia: Ein Roman, 3 volumes (Frankfurt am Main: Wilmans, 1827-1828);

Der Bettler von Sanct Colomba; Margaretha von Schottland: Zwei Novellen (Frankfurt am Main: Sauerländer, 1830);

Sämtliche Schriften, 24 volumes (Leipzig: Brockhaus / Frankfurt am Main: Sauerländer, 1830-1831);

Ausflug an den Niederrhein und nach Belgien im Jahre 1828, 2 volumes (Leipzig: Brockhaus, 1831);

Meine Großtante: Aus den Papieren eines alten Herrn (Stuttgart: Hoffmann, 1831);

Neue Novellen, 3 volumes (Frankfurt am Main: Sauerländer, 1832);

Die Reise nach Italien: Novelle (Frankfurt am Main: Sauerländer, 1835);

Richard Wood: Roman, 2 volumes (Leipzig: Brockhaus, 1837);

Johanna Schopenhauer, circa 1830 (by permission of the Schopenhauer-Archiv, Frankfurt am Main)

Jugendleben und Wanderbilder: Aus Johanna Schopenhauers Nachlaß, 2 volumes, edited by Adèle Schopenhauer (Brunswick: Westermann, 1839);

Nachlaß, 2 volumes, edited by Adèle Schopenhauer (Brunswick: Westermann, 1839);

Erinnerungen (Munich & Regensburg: Habbel & Naumann, 1924);

Johanna Schopenhauer: Ihr glücklichen Augen. Jugenderinnerungen; Tagebücher; Briefe, edited by Rolf Weber (Berlin: Verlag der Nation, 1979).

Johanna Schopenhauer is known to literary history as the author of travelogues that remain of interest as lively portrayals of early nineteenth-century life in Great Britain and France. She also played an important role as a *salonière* in Weimar and as a friend of Goethe. As the author of several romantic novels she explored the experience of young women who found themselves coerced into unwanted marriages. Finally, she was the mother of the important philosopher Arthur Schopenhauer, and her relationship with him is of some note.

Johanna Henrietta Trosiener, the daughter of Christian Heinrich Trosiener, a wealthy merchant, was born in Danzig (today Gdansk, Poland) on 9 July 1766. Her native language was German, though she learned Polish from the family servants. In 1785 she married another substantial merchant, Heinrich Floris Schopenhauer. The couple moved to Hamburg in 1793, just as Danzig was being annexed by Prussia.

The Schopenhauers had two children, Arthur and Adèle, both of whom accompanied them on extended journeys to Great Britain and France during the early years of the nineteenth century. In 1805 Heinrich Schopenhauer drowned; his death may have been suicide. Johanna moved to Weimar with the intention of educating herself and beginning a life there which corresponded more closely to her own intellectual ambitions. She arrived in Weimar on the eve of the Battle of Jena in late 1806.

In Weimar Schopenhauer established a biweekly evening tea, a kind of open house, to which members of the bourgeoisie as well as distinguished visitors in town could come. Her gatherings provided nonaristocratic society a meeting place in a provincial ducal seat that had otherwise little to offer those who could not appear at court.

Goethe was the most famous of those regularly attending Schopenhauer's gatherings in her rented house, and during the next decade every cultural pilgrim who made his or her way to Weimar came to her home in hope of meeting the great writer. Yet Goethe was not the sole attraction at Schopenhauer's, if one can believe the reports that often referred to the lively conversation and Johanna's talent for being a good hostess and purveyor of comfortable hospitality. Indeed, she was able to maintain these soirees long after Goethe stopped gracing them with any regularity.

Opinion about Johanna Schopenhauer seems to be sharply divided between those who found her too self-centered and assertive and those who appreciated her gifts as a hostess and an entertaining writer of travelogues and romantic novels. Though she lacked any systematic education, she began a course of study on her arrival in Weimar which she continued under the tutelage of her friend, the art historian Carl Ludwig Fernow.

It was the premature death of Fernow that led to Schopenhauer's first venture into writing for publication. After writing a biography of Fernow, Schopenhauer found a champion in the great publisher Johann Friedrich Cotta, who took over the business of getting the work into print. Cotta also settled a considerable debt Fernow had left and assisted in providing his destitute and orphaned children with some support.

It had been Fernow who advised Johanna's son to give up his commercial career in Hamburg in order to prepare himself for university study. Soon Arthur Schopenhauer was visiting his mother in Weimar, and the advent of his presence proved a very unhappy one. He was contentious, and Johanna was strong and assertive. The quarrels between mother and son became so acute that she finally closed the doors of her house to him.

There were many points on which mother and son did not agree, but the presence in her household of Mueller von Gerstenbergk was a constant source of irritation for Arthur. Since Arthur was not disposed to forgive, the relationship was terminated permanently in 1814.

The estrangement from her son did not deter Johanna Schopenhauer from developing further as a writer after the initial publication of Fernow's biography. The appearance in 1813 and 1814 of her two-volume travelogue of her sojourn in Great Britain, *Erinnerungen von einer Reise in den Jahren 1803, 1804 und 1805* (Recollections of a Journey in the Years 1803, 1804 and 1805), proved that she was not merely an amateur writer.

Her descriptions of what she saw during those years in Britain are lively and detailed. Though she still considered herself a dilettante, her prose proved interesting enough to attract a readership. For the modern traveler to Britain it remains interesting, especially since so many of the sites she describes have since become a standard part of every serious tourist agenda. Her descriptions are accompanied, moreover, by useful

Johanna and Adèle Schopenhauer in 1806 (painting by Karoline Bardua; by permission of the Goethe Nationalmuseum, Weimar)

maps by which a reader can trace her travels. The systematic organization of the text makes it easy to coordinate the reading with the maps as guide.

Schopenhauer also published an account of her 1817 visit to France, but she had already begun to try her hand at writing fiction by 1816 when she published *Novellen, fremd und eigen* (Novellas, Strange and Peculiar). The growth of her reputation as a writer can be gauged by the appearance of a biographical sketch of her in Brockhaus's *Zeitgenossen* (Contemporaries), which provided readers with the early nineteenth-century equivalent of personality sketches.

It was the collapse of the Danzig firm in which she and her daughter, Adèle, had invested all their fortune that changed Schopenhauer's attitude toward her writing and transformed her into an earnest professional. Her son managed, interestingly enough, to extract his own part of the fortune from the financial debacle, and he supported himself for most of his life on the interest. After 1819 Johanna and Adèle were dependent upon what could be earned with the pen.

The disaster occurred during a period in which Schopenhauer was working on her first full-

scale novel. Necessity brought out in her a shrewd talent she henceforth displayed for negotiating effectively with publishers. Brockhaus published her next work, the three-volume novel *Gabriele*, in 1819 and 1820.

There was talk of a break between Schopenhauer and Goethe in 1821, but the aging poet was, in any case, seriously ill that winter, and the frequency of his appearances at her soirees had diminished since 1810. Goethe's rejection of the Gothic in art may also have contributed to their disagreement, for Schopenhauer had cultivated a close friendship with Sulpiz Boisserée, one of the great advocates and sponsors of the Gothic and of the completion of the Cologne cathedral.

By the time of her financial loss, Schopenhauer's soirees had become a thing of the past. Goethe had withdrawn from society, and her own health had begun to suffer as well. In 1823 she suffered a stroke that left her feet partially paralyzed. There are also reports from contemporaries that she had become extremely overweight.

Schopenhauer might have left Weimar in 1819 had her friend Mueller von Gerstenbergk been successful in seeking employment elsewhere. There was nothing to hold her to the little ducal seat. As it was, she remained until 1829, publishing another successful novel, *Sidonia*, in 1827 and 1828, as well as a shorter work of fiction, *Meine Großtante: Aus den Papieren eines alten Herrn* (My Great Aunt: Taken from the Papers of an Old Man), in 1831.

The themes of Schopenhauer's first three novels are very similar. In each a young girl finds her intense adolescent romance interrupted by adults who do not approve and who separate her from her lover. These protagonists are then married to cold, older men whom they serve loyally but without passion. The narrative focuses upon a childlike consciousness that is surrounded by a hostile society. Minor characters are presented with a single neurosis or trait that distinguishes each. Her main figures are characterized by a rejection of conventional society, including marriage and family relationships.

In the two larger novels, *Sidonia* and *Gabriele*, the heroine is ultimately rescued by the kind and loving intervention of a person somehow related to her mother's youthful romance that serves as a background for her own story. In *Meine Großtante* the plot is more complex, and the title refers to the frame in which the story is set. An aging man discovers in his grandmother's papers the tale of her half sister, who was sent to the south of France on her mother's death. When she came of age, she was brought back to the harshness of a family that no longer really knew or valued her. The theme of a coerced and unhappy match is employed as the stepparents force their daughter into marriage with a hated suitor. The additional twist occurs when the reader discovers that the mysterious person who arrives and rescues the protagonist from her unhappy match is neither a cousin nor male. In fact the protagonist is shown to have actually married another female, and the element of lesbian love is blatant.

In 1830 Schopenhauer and her daughter settled in Bonn; the milder climate of Rhenish country, it was hoped, would have a salubrious effect upon her failing health. Her daughter spent a good deal of her own resources nursing her mother. Schopenhauer produced a final novel, *Richard Wood*, which was published in 1837. In that year she was also awarded a pension by the ruling duke of Sachsen-Weimar. She moved to Jena, where she died on 16 April 1838. Her last work further developed the Romantic theme that pitted individual consciousness against a hostile and sometimes corrupt society and a reality in which circumstances conspired to obstruct the achievement of the protagonist's desire.

Letters:

Johanna Schopenhauer: Briefe an Karl von Holtei, edited by Karl von Holtei (Leipzig: Brockhaus, 1870);

Damals in Weimar: Erinnerungen und Briefe von und an Johanna Schopenhauer, edited by H. H. Houben (Berlin: Rembrandt, 1929).

References:

Karl von Holtei, ed., "Arthur Schopenhauers Enterbung durch seine Mutter," in his *Kleine Blumen, Kleine Blätter aus Biedermeier und Vormärz* (Dessau: Rausch, 1925);

Detlev W. Schumann, "Goethe und die Familie Schopenhauer," in *Studien zur Goethezeit. Erich Trunz zum 75. Geburtstag*, edited by Hans-Joachim Mähl and Eberhard Mannack (Heidelberg: Carl Winter Universitätsverlag, 1981).

Gotthilf Heinrich Schubert

(26 April 1780-1 July 1860)

Roland Hoermann
University of California, Davis

BOOKS: *Dissertatio inauguralis medica continens Dubitata quaedam supra hominum a nativitate surdorum medelam galvanismo . . .* (Jena: Fromann & Wesselhoeft, 1803);

Die Kirche und die Götter: Ein Roman, 2 volumes (Penig: Dienemann, 1804);

Ahndungen einer allgemeinen Geschichte des Lebens, 2 volumes (Leipzig: Reclam, 1806-1821);

Ansichten von der Nachtseite der Naturwissenschaft (Dresden: Arnold, 1808; revised edition, 1840);

Neue Untersuchungen über die Verhältnisse der Größen und Eccentricitäten der Weltkörper (Dresden: Arnold, 1808);

Handbuch der Naturgeschichte, zweiter Theil: Handbuch der Geognosie und Bergbaukunde (Nuremberg: Schrag, 1813);

Die Symbolik des Traumes (Bamberg: Kunz, 1814; revised and enlarged, 1821; revised and enlarged again, Leipzig: Brockhaus, 1840);

Handbuch der Naturgeschichte, erster Theil: Handbuch der Mineralogie (Nuremberg: Schrag, 1816);

Altes und Neues aus dem Gebiet der innren Seelenkunde, 5 volumes (Leipzig: Reclam, 1817-1849);

Die Urwelt und die Fixsterne: Eine Zugabe zu den Ansichten von der Nachtseite der Naturwissenschaft (Dresden: Arnold, 1822; revised edition, 1839);

Handbuch der Naturgeschichte, fünfter Theil: Handbuch der Kosmologie (Nuremberg: Schrag, 1823);

Wanderbüchlein eines reisenden Gelehrten nach Salzburg, Tirol und der Lombardey (Erlangen: Palm & Enke, 1823; revised edition, 1834);

Lehrbuch der Naturgeschichte, für Schulen und zum Selbstunterricht (Erlangen: Heyder, 1823; revised editions in 1827, 1830, 1832, 1834, 1839; nineteenth and last edition in Frankfurt am Main, 1856); translated by W. F. Kirby as *Natural History of the Animal Kingdom for the Use of Young People* (London, 1889);

Gotthilf Heinrich Schubert (lithograph by Schreiner; courtesy of the Bildarchiv der Österreichischen Nationalbibliothek, Vienna)

Allgemeine Naturgeschichte, oder Andeutungen zur Geschichte und Physiognomik der Natur (Erlangen: Palm & Enke, 1826); revised as *Die Geschichte der Natur,* 3 volumes (Erlangen: Palm & Enke, 1835-1837); republished in two volumes as *Das Weltgebäude, die Erde und die Zeiten des Menschen auf der Erde* and *Abriß der Mineralogie* (Erlangen: Palm & Enke; 1852-1853);

Reise durch das südliche Frankreich und durch Italien, 2 volumes (Erlangen: Palm & Enke, 1827-1831);

Die Geschichte der Seele (Stuttgart & Tübingen: Cotta, 1830; revised, 1833; revised and enlarged, 2 volumes, 1850);

Von dem Vergehen und Bestehen der Gattungen und Arten . . . (Munich, 1830);

Kurze Geschichte der Reformation und des Reformators in Schottland Johannes Knox (Nuremberg: Raw, 1831);

Lehrbuch der Sternkunde für Schulen und zum Selbstunterrichte (Munich: Weber, 1831; revised and enlarged edition, Munich: Weber, 1832; revised and enlarged again, Erlangen: Heyder, 1847);

Von einem Feststehenden in der Geschichte der sichtbaren Natur und des in ihr wohnenden Menschen: Eine Anrede (Stuttgart: Cotta, 1837);

Lehrbuch der Menschen- und Seelenkunde, zum Gebrauch für Schulen und zum Selbststudium (Erlangen: Heyder, 1838);

Reise in das Morgenland in den Jahren 1836 und 1837, 2 volumes (Erlangen: Palm & Enke, 1838; revised edition, 1840);

Erzählungen, 4 volumes (Erlangen: Palm & Enke, 1840-1856);

Die Krankheiten und Störungen der menschlichen Seele (Stuttgart: Cotta, 1845);

Spiegel der Natur: Ein Lesebuch zur Belehrung und Unterhaltung (Erlangen: Palm, 1845; revised edition, 1854); translated by William Furness as *Mirror of Nature* (Philadelphia: Thomas-Cowperthwait, 1849; London: Tweedie, 1854);

Ueber Ahnen und Wissen: Ein Vortrag aus dem Kreise der Abendunterhaltungen im Museum zu München in December 1846 (Munich: Literarisch-artistische Anstalt, 1845);

Biographien und Erzählungen (Erlangen: Heyder, 1847-1848);

Der neue Robinson, oder Die Schicksale des Philipp Ashton, während seines erzwungenen Aufenthaltes unter den Seeräubern und auf der Insel Roatan: Eine wahre Geschichte für die deutsche Jugend (Stuttgart: Steinkopf, 1849);

Johann Tobias Kiessling und einige seiner Freunde nach ihrem Leben und Wirken (Leipzig: Brockhaus, 1850); translated anonymously as *The Life of John Tobias Kiesling, of Nuremberg* (London: Religious Tract Society, 1837);

Seebilder: Ein Buch zur Unterhaltung und Belehrung (Erlangen: Palm & Enke, 1850);

Der Meeresstrom: Eine Erzählung für die Jugend (New York: Amer.-Traktat Gesellschaft, 1850?); translated anonymously as *The Ocean Current* (London: Leeds, 1849); translated as *The Whirlpool* (Bath, 1852);

Die Zaubereisünden in ihrer alten und neuen Form betrachtet (Erlangen: Palm & Enke, 1854);

Der Erwerb aus einem vergangenen und die Erwartungen von einem zukünftigen Leben: Eine Selbstbiographie, 3 volumes (Erlangen: Palm & Enke, 1854-1856);

Vermischte Schriften, 2 volumes (Erlangen: Palm & Enke, 1857-1860);

Parabeln aus dem Buche der sichtbaren Werke (Munich: Cotta, 1858);

Die Ruhestunden eines alten Auswanderers (Düsseldorf, 1858);

Erzählende Schriften für christlich gebildete Leser jeden Standes und Alters (Erlangen: Palm & Enke, 1882).

OTHER: *Bibliotheca castellana, portugués y proenzal*, edited by Schubert (Altenburg: Rink, 1804);

L. C. de Saint-Martin, *Vom Geist und vom Wesen der Dinge, oder philosophische Blicke auf die Natur der Dinge und den Zweck ihres Daseyns, wobei der Mensch überall als die Lösung des Räthsels betrachtet wird*, translated by Schubert (Leipzig: Reclam, 1812);

Züge aus dem Leben des Johann Friedrich Oberlin, gewesenen Pfarrers im Steinthal bei Straßburg, edited by Schubert (Nuremberg: Raw, 1828; revised and enlarged, 1832); translated by Mrs. Sydney Williams as "Memoirs of John Frederic Oberlin," in her *Memoirs of Felix Neff, John Frederic Oberlin and B. Overberg* (Bristol: Wright & Albright/London: Hamilton & Adams, 1840);

Erinnerungen an Bernard Overberg und Michael Wittmann, edited by Schubert (Erlangen: Heyder, 1835); translated anonymously as *Memoir of Bernard Overberg* (London: Seeley, 1838);

Johann Friedrich Oberlin, *Berichte eines Visionärs über den Zustand der Seelen nach dem Tode: Aus dem Nachlaße Johann Friedrich Oberlins*, edited by Schubert (Leipzig: Brockhaus, 1837);

Johann M. Bernatz, *Bilder aus dem Heiligen Lande*, commentary by Schubert (Stuttgart: Steinkopf, 1839);

Helene Louise Elisabeth von Mecklenburg, *Erinnerungen aus dem Leben ihrer königlichen Hoheit Helene Louise, Herzogin von Orléans, gebornen Prinzessin von Mecklenburg-Schwerin: Nach ihren eignen Briefen zusammengestellt*, edited by Schubert (Munich: Cotta, 1859);

Adolf Kenngott, *Illustrierte Mineralogie,* explanatory texts by Schubert (Esslingen & Stuttgart: Schreiber, 1888).

No German writer is more representative of the Romantic polymath in the Age of Goethe than Gotthilf Heinrich Schubert. Yet Schubert was neither an original thinker nor a truly creative author. Rather, he belonged to a curiously Romantic breed of medical scientist who sought in nature a unifying moral principle underlying the development of all life forms. As a gifted lecturer and popularizer who explored the interfaces between philosophy, religion, and the biological sciences, he represented a bridge between Johann Gottfried Herder's humanistic-Spinozan pantheism and the new idealist organicism of Friedrich Wilhelm von Schelling's Naturphilosophie (philosophy of nature). Briefly a member of the same Dresden circle of Romantic practitioners as the famed dramatist Heinrich von Kleist, Schubert is credited with Kleist's interest in somnambulist and hypnotic trances, split consciousness, clairvoyant spells of fainting, and amnesiac ecstasy or rage. A prolific writer, Schubert had a knack for anticipating breaking waves of public interest; he thus stimulated the renowned writer E. T. A. Hoffmann to develop his motifs of reincarnative premonition, of the soul-life of the *Ich* (ego) and of the *Doppelgänger* (double), while furnishing the impetus for Hoffmann's adaptation of the Eddic myth of Creation to the birth of modern man's reflective faculty. Written with a warm, tutorial charm, Schubert's tracts are mixtures of anecdotal, sensationalist-effusive, and scientifically prophetic commentary on the inevitable rightness of God's evolutionary plan, in which the principle of evil or conflict plays only a minute role. The developmental line of his innovative psychic vision, receiving significant enhancement in the writings of Carl Gustav Carus, approaches the threshold of modern Freudian theory and Jungian parapsychological symbolism. Possessed of a Romantic soul, Schubert had a productive lifetime of pedagogic commitment because of the broad range of personal and epistolary exchange he cultivated with the leading figures of the Age of Goethe. The impact of his presence was in no small measure the result of his capacity for naive and sensitive enthusiasm, unpretentious kindliness, and his devout faith in mankind and in his Pietist roots.

Schubert was born to Christian Gottlob and Magdalena Werner Schubert, in Hohenstein, Saxony, on 26 April 1780. His formative years were spent in this small town, an economically depressed Lutheran pastoral milieu connected with the Moravian brotherhood. When Schubert was a small boy, his piety alternated in importance with his love of nature, which was attested by his collection of bird skeletons and his rock collection from the surrounding Erzgebirge mountains. Later, the youth tried his hand at writing a book about whaling, undertook potentially dangerous scientific experiments to his parents' distress, and brooded over riddles of physics and astronomy. After a somewhat profligate start at the college-preparatory gymnasium in the county seat of Greiz, the contrite Schubert convinced his father to send him in 1796 to the more rigorous humanistic academy in Weimar, where he soon became a protegé of the school's head examiner, Johann Gottfried Herder (whose son Emil became Schubert's lifelong friend).

In this period, the seventeen-year-old student engaged in a good deed of the kind that became characteristic of his life: he met a talented but destitute teenager whose father, a weaver, could not afford to send him to the boarding school in Weimar. Schubert "adopted" the boy, inviting him to be his roommate and to share his weekly allowance from home for the duration of their schooling.

The dean of Germany's Sturm und Drang (Storm and Stress) literary movement, Herder solidified in his young pupil a nascent belief in the spiritual unity and goodness of God's universal laws of Creation. Graduating in Weimar in 1799, young Schubert acceded to his father's wish by beginning the study of theology at the University of Leipzig. After two unfruitful semesters in this discipline, Schubert was able to transfer into medicine as a means of continuing his passionate boyhood interest in the natural sciences.

Together with his lifelong friend F. G. Wetzel, another maverick writer-scientist, Schubert moved in April of 1801 to the thriving mecca of Romanticism, the University of Jena, where they continued their medical studies. Here both were exhilarated by the lectures of the philosopher Schelling, in which Schelling explained his emerging Naturphilosophie with its doctrine of the creative opposition between nature and mind. A young physicist at Jena, Johann Wilhelm Ritter, whose unitary galvano-electrical principle linked the chemistry of material and psychic phenomena throughout the natural world, was another important influence on Schubert's thinking. At Jena Schubert also became interested in the work of the Scotsman John Brown and the Brownian movement, whose homeopathic therapy dealt with the stimulus-irritability polarity of all organic behavior.

With the conferral of Schubert's doctoral degree in 1803, one of his professors offered him an investigative post in South Africa. Seeking permission for such an important relocation, Schubert traveled to his parents in Hohenstein, where he fell in love "at first sight" with his sister's girlfriend Henriette Martin, of nearby Bärenwalde, and promptly abandoned plans for Africa. Schubert and Martin were married. He began practicing medicine in Altenburg, but his professional generosity resulted in the young couple's financial distress growing to such dimensions that a friend urged Schubert to turn the tide of his fortunes by writing a book and selling it to a publisher. Within three weeks the twenty-three-year-old physician had completed his first (and only) novel, *Die Kirche und die Götter* (The Church and the Gods). Encompassing 531 pages in two volumes in 1804, the imitative work has no coherent plot but involves noble sentiments and relationships interlaced with generally quite effective nature description–all in all, a feat attesting to Schubert's considerable potential.

Because Schubert aspired most of all in life to a teaching post in the natural sciences at an institution of higher learning, he felt it necessary also to study the physical sciences, especially applied geology. To this end, after selling his practice and retiring their debts, he and his wife moved (with a mere forty talers to their name) in 1805 to Freiberg, Saxony, where Schubert enrolled in the Academy of Mining Geology to hear the lectures of Abraham Gottlob Werner concerning the evolutionary laws of systematic geognosy. With the encouragement of both Schelling and Ritter (the latter of whom located a distinguished publisher in C. H. Reclam), Schubert was able to complete here the first volume of his "sensational" *Ahndungen einer allgemeinen Geschichte des Lebens* (Speculations Concerning a Universal History of Life, 1806). In this first major work, Schubert delineates how the total existence of Earth's organic and inorganic realms comprises a single mighty organism which aims at a higher consummation by means of its polarized interactivity and the revelatory design of a supreme intelligence. This dialectic of opposition and resolution (which the author traces from Schelling back to Heraclitus) is at the core of Schubert's thinking, for without

this contrastive tension he saw no possibility of either life or death.

Derived from the primary dialectic is the secondary, potentiating principle of *Streben* or *Steigerung* (self-surpassing fulfillment), which has the power to generate progressively higher levels of interrelatedness between Nature's forms as well as a more direct recognition (*Anschauung*) of the motive force behind all being. The organism possessed of the self-surpassing drive experiences its crucial premonitions of fulfillment during *cosmic impulses* when a kind of conflagration of forces consumes the natural form's individuality. Such threshold "breakthroughs" propel a natural structure onto an exponentially higher plane of interrelatedness and tension amid higher forms of opposition, gradually developing the form's heightened insight until it becomes part of an ultimate metaphysical unity. During heightened states of self-transformation, the individual entity radiates the force of its yearning and striving to lesser forms in its environment, thereby "infecting" them with a corresponding escalation of innovative fulfillment.

Among the premonitory cosmic impulses, Schubert includes gravitational pull (*Schwere*), death, consummation of love, spiritual visions in art and religion, and phenomena of the subconscious. Nature's forms thus constitute a hieroglyphic revelation of divine teleology to the deciphering natural scientist. The developmental continuum from the inorganic to the organic proceeds, according to Schubert, from water, through stone (granite to slate to sandstone to coal), metals, minerals, plant and animal life, corporeal (sun)light, and finally to the lightness of air.

Consonant with German nature mysticism, Schubert in *Ahndungen einer allgemeinen Geschichte des Lebens* views death as a liberating cosmic impulse freed of the Christian judgment of original sin. Celebrating the promise of final sacred reunion, the physical consummation of love anticipates and organically prefigures such transcendent release. Schubert sees the self-surpassing yearning for transformation manifesting itself as a drive for self-dissolution everywhere among nature's oppositions: thus acids and bases seek each other in order to achieve potentiating transformation in the form of neutralized salts, even as the organic body's languorous self-effacement in the love act achieves temporary equilibrium of the sexual polarity. The author rounds out volume 1 of his *Ahndungen einer allgemeinen Geschichte des*

Lebens by taking a cue from Herder's fifth book of the *Ideen zur Philosophie der Geschichte der Menschheit* (1784-1791; translated as *Outlines of the Philosophy of Man,* 1800) when he asserts that the transformational world of soul (*Seele*) begins with plants and ends with man, while the world of the spirit (*Geist*) begins with man and ends with God.

With the conclusion of Werner's lectures in Freiberg in 1806, Schubert decided to settle with his wife in Dresden, where an adequate library would allow him to continue his project and resolve fundamental questions he had raised. Here he made the acquaintance of Kleist, Adam Müller, and Karl August Böttiger (all three of whom were active in the publications of the journal *Phöbus*) and became friends with Caspar David Friedrich, the most important of the Romantic landscape painters. Upon the urging of the *Phöbus* triumvirate (and prompted by his need of funds), Schubert agreed to participate in a subscription series of evening lectures for upper-class Dresden society during the winter of 1807-1808. The unexpected success of Schubert's initial cluster of readings paved the way for him to publish later that year his series of talks under the title *Ansichten von der Nachtseite der Naturwissenschaft* (Views Concerning the Dark Side of the Natural Sciences, 1808). The volume elicited a stir among nonspecialists throughout the German and foreign lands and was promptly translated into many European languages, including Russian.

As a result of these lectures, Schubert came to be recognized as one of the leading Romantic scientists engaged in exposing Nature's unitary process of evolutionary design, so as to embrace even abnormal extremes of human behavior at the periphery (the "night side," or unnatural aspects, of natural science). In one of the lectures Schubert reported on the miraculous embalming effect of Nature's saltpeter in recounting the "Falun-miner" incident in his eighth lecture. The lecture inspired a series of literary works dealing with the young Swedish miner's death, state of perfect organic arrest, eventual reexcavation, and "timeless reunion" with his former fiancée a lifetime later, as she approached her death. In steady succession following Schubert's account there appeared a short story by Johann Peter Hebel, a ballad by Achim von Arnim, a tale by E. T. A. Hoffmann, and a five-act verse drama by the Austrian author Hugo von Hofmannsthal.

As in the *Ahndungen einer allgemeinen Geschichte des Lebens,* Schubert's method of formu-lating his inquiry in the *Ansichten von der Nachtseite der Naturwissenschaft* involves analogy and the principle of reciprocal interaction (*Wechselwirkung,* a concept related to those of polarity and potentiation). He focuses here, too, on that unifying principle of a *Weltseele* (world-soul) that has organized teleological-Christian evolution in terms of nature's ladder of self-surpassing metamorphosis. He illustrates in his *Ansichten von der Nachtseite der Naturwissenschaft* this potentiated transformational pattern for Nature's individual organic unit, as well as for epochal historical development and for the psychic development of the soul, by offering a commentary to a symbolic series of oil sketches entitled *Die vier Tageszeiten* (The Four Times of Day) by his friend the landscape painter Friedrich. Schubert's elaboration of Friedrich's portrayals, *Morning, Noon, Evening,* and *Night,* appears to have influenced the Dresden artist's final versions of 1820 that have become familiar to the art world.

Beginning with Geist (Spirit) within the world-soul, each of nature's forms exhibits a symbiotic habitation of "higher-within-lower" forces, explaining why all forms exist in precarious and ephemeral balance between being and becoming. Schubert interprets Goethe's "Das Märchen" (The Fairy Tale, 1795) as an illustration of his own principle of self-surpassing transformation–which Goethe embodies in his figure of the golden snake at the threshold of what Schubert would call a cosmic impulse–and to demonstrate the prophetic movement of the trancelike experience characteristic of the "night side" of human consciousness as well. The influence of Schubert's *Ansichten von der Nachtseite der Naturwissenschaft* is evident in works by his contemporaries. A clear correlation exists between Schubert's tenth lecture and the cosmic moments of reincarnative premonition found in E. T. A. Hoffmann's *Meister Floh* (Master Flea, 1822). Phenomena of split consciousness occur in Kleist's *Penthesilea* (1808), *Das Käthchen von Heilbronn* (1810), and *Prinz Friedrich von Homburg* (1821), while Arnim made use of this Schubertian "discovery" in his "Die Majoratsherren" (The Heirs in Primogeniture, published in *Taschenbuch zum geselligen Vergnügen* in 1819).

Those familiar with Hoffmann will recognize the influence of several of Schubert's lectures, treating a pantheistic era of harmony followed by mankind's act of power-hubris, his isolation from the Nature matrix, and his disoriented nadir of imprisonment within a world of self-reflective cogitation. One of the few avenues still open to this dislocated "modern man" for divining the natural world's harmonious raison d'être is the marginal sanity of altered states of consciousness (somnambulism, ecstatic visions and clairvoyance, dreams, trances and mental aberrations). In these states the subject's longing (*Sehnsucht*) for truth has driven him into a sublimated consciousness that exposes the subject-seer to a premature experience of oneness with the terrifying Absolute. With the limits of his personal individuation now obscured, the aberrant "prophet's" reentry into the cocoon of his outgrown personality poses a traumatic choice and hazardous passage. On the generic level, Schubert views such crises of "untimely development" or premature derailment as evolutionary maladaptations. Both Hoffmann's story "Der Magnetiseur" (The Hypnotist, 1814) and Justinus Kerner's *Die Seherin von Prevorst* (1829; translated as *The Seeress of Prevorst*, 1845), which is dedicated to Schubert, demonstrate a parapsychological access to metaphysical truth that is clearly indebted to *Ansichten von der Nachtseite der Naturwissenschaft,* as well as to his later *Die Symbolik des Traumes* (The Symbolism of Dreams, 1814).

Anticipating Jung's theories of depth psychology and the collective unconscious, Schubert was convinced that a premonitory knowledge of the holistic truth revealed in these extrasensory states resides in the primal myths of all peoples. It is the task of a new era of humankind to raise this knowledge to the level of conscious, spontaneously assimilated truth in everyday life. By affirming the continuing and simultaneous evolution of nature on God's hierarchical ladder, Schubert placed himself in opposition to the binary taxonomy of Linnaeus as well as to the mechanical atomism of Immanuel Kant.

Due to the intercession of Schelling and Schubert's former Jena mentor Ritter, he was able to escape his perennial state of financial distress by accepting in April 1809 the directorship of the newly founded Nuremberg Polytechnic Academy. In 1807 a daughter, Selma, had been born to Schubert and his wife; three years later the family grew with the adoption of Adeline, the orphaned two-year-old daughter of Ritter, who in 1810 died penniless in Munich. In 1812, with the death of his wife Henriette, Schubert seemed on the point of being overwhelmed by his sorrow and responsibilities; however, during a visit in 1813 with the parents of his dead wife, Schubert became better acquainted with Hen-

riette's niece, Julie, and a happy second marriage followed for him several months later. This new relationship provided him with emotional support when the academy was dissolved because of insufficient enrollments three years later. The chief impact of these seven years in Nuremberg was in the sphere of Schubert's personal religious development, as his contacts with the Pietist brotherhood of The Awakened Ones in various parts of Germany led him to study the mystical works of Jakob Böhme and Friedrich Christoph Oetinger. At this point he was persuaded by fellow physician, clairvoyant, and pupil of Werner, the philosopher-theologian Franz Xaver von Baader, to translate the tract *De l'esprit des choses* by the eighteenth-century visionary follower of Böhme, the Marquis de Saint-Martin, whose ideas surfaced clearly in Schubert's next major work, *Die Symbolik des Traumes.*

This work is the first modern attempt to understand the significance of the symbolic imagery contained in dreams. Dream visions are further intermittent evidence of a higher realm's premonitory awakening in human beings, maintains Schubert, for these visions–like other "night-side" states–represent that realm's temporary but incendiary consuming of the lower encasing structure of individuality in order to link one with humankind's unfathomed (past and future) spiritual life. Specifically, dream symbols have always spoken in God's revelatory language of natural creation which was universally intelligible to earlier man, Schubert declares. As abstract thought processes have alienated modern man from God's "natural" revelation, divine communication appears to have rigidified into an obscure system of mystic hieroglyphs. Man's chief remaining access to his withdrawn God is through the mediation of the "world-soul," whose sacred language is that of dreams and of God's hieroglyphic landscape. Like Novalis and Ludwig Tieck, Schubert believed that God's natural relationship to man lies half-buried in his unconscious primal memory as well as in the symbolical subtexts of poetic masterpieces and in inspired prophecy. Such prophetic vision emanates from man's soul and is "der versteckte Poet in uns" (the hidden poet in us) who speaks in dreams–an idea that appealed greatly to Romantics of the middle (or Heidelberg) and the later (or Berlin) phases of German Romanticism.

Although Schubert seldom, in any of his works, speaks of evil, he claims in *Die Symbolik des Traumes* to have detected in the dreams of certain subjects indications of intermittent dominance by a negative genius, which also (like a corresponding affirmative genius) derives from the world of Spirit. Moreover, in the case of a criminal-to-be, negative genius has a prophetic function. In this context, Schubert elaborates the influential concept of the Doppelgänger that hinges on the phenomenon of split or reversed personality, whose negative identity appears only in the somnambulistic, dream, or lunatic state. Schubert's interpretation of the ominous figure of the double shows congruence with Tieck's earlier literary formulations in the novella "Der getreue Eckhart und der Tannenhäuser" (The Trusty Eckhart and Tannenhäuser, 1799) or in the fairy tale "Der Runenberg" (1804), as well as direct influence on Hoffmann's *Die Elixiere des Teufels* (The Devil's Elixir, 1815-1816).

Following the closure of the Polytechnic Academy in Nuremberg that caused his brief unemployment, and after a desperate, three-year period as educator for the children of Grand Duke Friedrich Ludwig of Mecklenburg-Schwerin in the northern provincial town of Ludwigslust, Schubert acquired reappointment under the Bavarian ministry of education, this time as a professor of natural history at the University of Erlangen. Returned to the environs of Nuremberg in 1819 where he again found himself among congenial colleagues, lecturing in the areas of botany, forestry, geology, and the life sciences, Schubert demonstrated an enormous productivity. He held university administrative posts, engaged in voluntary tutorial and seminar instruction, and wrote numerous science manuals and travel memoirs. His prestige earned him an invitation to join the faculty of the new University of Munich in 1827 as a colleague of the first professor of natural history, Lorenz Oken. Oken was known as an empiricist; Schubert favored an integrative-generalist approach, and often there was tension between the two men. Schubert's appointment carried with it the adjunct conservatorship of the zoological museum of the Bavarian Academy of Science, another bone of contention between the two rivals. Schelling's presence and renown enabled the mild-mannered Schubert to retain his positions, and Oken moved to Zurich in 1833.

One of Schubert's long-held desires was fulfilled in this period when he was able to give lectures on anthropology and psychology while simultaneously preparing a book on the spiritual nature and destiny of man. This large volume, which Schubert perceived as the pinnacle of his scholarly achievement, appeared under the title of *Die Geschichte der Seele* (The Development of the Soul, 1830). The author announces an almost missionary involvement with his material in the foreword. His text traces the human soul from its initial stages as a psyche that symbolizes its received *physical* stimuli, ascends to a recognition of its essential humanity as an evolving human *soul,* and finally culminates as *Spirit* in an increasing identification with the absolute oneness of God. This tripartite scheme reveals man's soul caught between the stage of physical transformation and proliferation, on the one hand, and the stage of Spirit, on the other, where creative impulse and transformational design originate. In this mediate, self-contradictory state of physical individuation, the soul's overriding quality is its longing for release and higher fulfillment. For Schubert, the soul with its longing is the product of the basic opposition between life (a centripetal force) and death (a centrifugal force). The process that the soul undergoes begins with a soul developing the metaphysical drive of yearning, which is directed through a gradually evolving consciousness of self into a religious consciousness, toward confluence first in Nature's world-soul and then with the universe of Spirit.

Recognizing that his capacities no longer permitted full participation in professorial activities, Schubert agreed to accept retirement in 1853 in exchange for the title of Geheimrat (privy councilor), which enabled him to attain the lowest of the nonhereditary aristocratic ranks and alter his surname to von Schubert. After completing his three-volume autobiography, *Der Erwerb aus einem vergangenen und die Erwartungen von einem zukünftigen Leben* (The Rewards of a Past and the Expectations of a Future Life, 1854-1856), he devoted the last years of his life exclusively to publishing works that served the purpose of Christian edification, especially books for young people, and religious biographies.

Letters:

Gotthilf Heinrich Schubert in seinen Briefen: ein Lebensbild, edited by G. Nathanael Bonwetsch (Stuttgart: Belser, 1918).

References:

Ernst Busch, "Die Stellung Gotthilf Heinrich Schuberts in der deutschen Naturmystik und in der Romantik," *Deutsche Vierteljahrsschrift für*

Literaturwissenschaft und Geistesgeschichte, 20 (1942): 305-339;

Adalbert Elschenbroich, *Romantische Sehnsucht und Kosmogonie: Eine Studie zu Gotthilf Heinrich Schuberts "Geschichte der Seele" und deren Stellung in der deutschen Spätromantik* (Tübingen: Niemeyer, 1971);

H. J. Hahn, "G. H. Schubert's Principle of Untimely Development," *German Life and Letters,* 37 (1984): 336-353;

Peter Krebs, *Die Anthropologie des Gotthilf Heinrich von Schubert* (Cologne: Orthen, 1940);

John Neubauer, "The Mines of Falun: Temporal Fortunes of a Romantic Myth of Time," *Studies in Romanticism,* 19 (Winter 1980): 475-496;

Hans Querner, "Ordnungsprinzipien und Ordnungsmethoden in der Naturgeschichte der Romantik," in *Romantik in Deutschland: Ein interdisziplinäres Symposium,* edited by R. Brinkman (Stuttgart: Metzler, 1978), pp. 214-225;

A. Rössler, ed., *Gotthilf Heinrich Schubert: Gedenkschrift zum 200. Geburtstag des romantischen Naturforschers* (Erlangen: Universitätsbund, 1980).

Papers:

Schubert's papers are in the University Library at Erlangen and comprise 2,355 letters, manuscripts, lecture notebooks, and diaries. The Bavarian State Library in Munich has 153 letters from Schubert to C. G. Barth and 87 letters from Schubert to F. A. Koethe.

Ludwig Tieck

(31 May 1773-28 April 1853)

Donald H. Crosby
University of Connecticut

BOOKS: *Thaten und Feinheiten renommirter Kraft-
und Kniffgenies,* 2 volumes (Berlin: Himburg, 1790-1791);

Abdallah: Eine Erzählung (Berlin & Leipzig: Nicolai, 1793);

Eine Geschichte ohne Abentheuerlichkeiten, as Peter Leberecht, 2 volumes (Berlin & Leipzig: Nico-
lai, 1795-1796);

Geschichte des Herrn William Lovell, 3 volumes (Berlin & Leipzig: Nicolai, 1795-1796);

*Der betrügliche Schein, oder: Man muß nicht glauben,
was man sieht* (Berlin & Leipzig: Nicolai,
1796);

Ritter Blaubart: Ein Ammenmährchen, as Peter
Leberecht (Berlin & Leipzig: Nicolai, 1797);

*Herzensergießungen eines kunstliebenden Klosterbru-
ders,* by Tieck and Wilhelm Heinrich Wackenroder (Berlin: Unger, 1797); translated by
Mary Hurst Schubert as "Confessions from
the Heart of an Art-Loving Friar," in *Confessions and Fantasies* (University Park & London: Pennsylvania State University Press,
1971), pp. 79-160;

*Der gestiefelte Kater: Ein Kindermärchen in drey
Akten, mit Zwischenspielen, einem Prologe und
Epiloge,* as Peter Leberecht (Bergamo: Published by the author, 1797); translated by
Lillie Winter as "Puss in Boots," in *The German Classics of the Nineteenth and Twentieth Centuries,* edited by Kuno Francke and W. G.
Howard, volume 4 (New York: German Publications Society, 1913), pp. 194-293;

*Die sieben Weiber des Blaubart: Eine wahre Familienge-
schichte,* as Gottlieb Färber (Berlin: Nicolai,
1797);

Der Abschied: Ein Traumspiel in zwey Aufzügen (Berlin: Langhoff, 1798);

Alla-Moddin (Berlin: Langhoff, 1798);

*Ein Schurke über den andern oder die Fuchsprelle:
Ein Lustspiel in drei Aufzügen* (Berlin: Langhoff, 1798);

*Franz Sternbalds Wanderungen: Eine altdeutsche Ge-
schichte,* 2 volumes (Berlin: Unger, 1798);

Ludwig Tieck (Bibliothèque Nationale, Paris)

Phantasien über die Kunst, für Freunde der Kunst, by
Tieck and Wackenroder (Hamburg: Per-
thes, 1799); translated by Schubert as "Fantasies on Art for Friends of Art," in *Confessions and Fantasies,* pp. 161-197;

Sämmtliche Schriften, 12 volumes (Berlin & Leipzig: Nicolai, 1799);

Romantische Dichtungen, 2 volumes (Jena: Frommann, 1799-1800);

*Das Ungeheuer und der verzauberte Wald: Ein musikali-
sches Mährchen in vier Aufzügen* (Bremen: Wilmans, 1800);

Kaiser Octavianus: Ein Lustspiel in zwei Theilen
(Jena: Frommann, 1804);

311

Phantasus: Eine Sammlung von Mährchen, Erzählungen, Schauspielen und Novellen, 3 volumes (Berlin: Realschulbuchhandlung, 1812-1816); translated by Julius C. Hare, James Anthony Froude, and others as *Tales from the Phantasus* (London: Burns, 1845);

Sämmtliche Werke, 30 volumes (Vienna: Grund, 1817-1824);

Leben und Tod der heiligen Genoveva: Ein Trauerspiel (Berlin: Reimer, 1820);

Gedichte, 3 volumes (Dresden: Hilscher, 1821-1823);

Der Geheimnißvolle: Novelle (Dresden: Hilscher, 1823);

Die Gemälde: Novelle (Dresden: Arnold, 1823); translated by G. Cunningham as *The Pictures* in *Foreign Tales and Traditions,* 2 volumes (Glasgow: Blackie, Fullarton, 1829);

Novellen, 7 volumes (Berlin: Reimer/Breslau: Max, 1823-1828); enlarged as *Gesammelte Novellen,* 14 volumes (Breslau: Max, 1835-1842); "Der blonde Eckbert"; "Der getreue Eckart"; "Der Runenberg"; "Die Elfen"; "Der Pokal," translated by Thomas Carlyle as "The Fair-Haired Eckbert"; "The Trusty Eckart"; "The Runenberg"; "The Elves"; "The Goblet," in *German Romance: Specimens of Its Chief Authors,* 4 volumes (London: Tait/ New York: Scribner's, 1827);

Die Verlobung: Novelle (Dresden: Arnold, 1823);

Musikalische Leiden und Freuden: Novelle (Dresden: Arnold, 1824);

Die Reisenden: Novelle (Dresden: Arnold, 1824);

Dramaturgische Blätter, 3 volumes (Breslau: Max, volumes 1-2; Leipzig: Brockhaus, volume 3, 1825-1852);

Pietro von Abano oder Petrus Apone: Zaubergeschichte (Breslau: Max, 1825); translated anonymously as "Pietro of Abano," *Blackwood's Magazine,* 46 (1839): 288;

Der Aufruhr in den Cevennen: Eine Novelle in vier Abschnitten. Erster und zweiter Abschnitt (Berlin: Reimer, 1826); translated by Mme. Burette as *The Rebellion in the Cevennes: An Historical Novel,* 2 volumes (London, 1845);

Der Alte vom Berge, und: Die Gesellschaft auf dem Lande: Zwei Novellen (Breslau: Max, 1828); translated by J. C. Hare as *The Old Man of the Mountain* (London: Moxon, 1831);

Schriften, 28 volumes (Berlin: Reimer, 1828);

Novellenkranz, 5 volumes (Berlin: Reimer, 1831-1835);

Epilog zum Andenken Goethes: Nach Darstellung der Iphigenie in Dresden den 29. März 1832 (Dresden, 1832);

Der junge Tischlermeister: Novelle in sieben Abschnitten, 2 volumes (Berlin: Reimer, 1836);

Sämmtliche Werke, 2 volumes (Paris: Tétot, 1837);

Vittoria Accorombona: Ein Roman in fünf Büchern, 2 volumes (Breslau: Max, 1840); translated anonymously as *The Roman Matron; or, Vittoria Accorombona: A Novel* (London: Bury St. Edmunds, 1845);

Gedichte: Neue Ausgabe (Berlin: Reimer, 1841);

Kritische Schriften, 4 volumes (Leipzig: Brockhaus, 1848-1852);

Bibliotheca Tieckiana (Berlin, 1849);

Epilog zur hundertjährigen Geburtsfeier Goethes (Berlin: Hertz, 1849);

Die Sommernacht: Eine Jugenddichtung (Frankfurt am Main: Sauerländer, 1853); translated by Mary C. Rumsey as *The Midsummer Night; or, Shakespeare and the Fairies* (London, 1854);

Nachgelassene Schriften: Auswahl und Nachlese, edited by Rudolf Köpke, 2 volumes (Leipzig: Brockhaus, 1855);

Werke: Kritisch durchgesehene und erläuterte Ausgabe, edited by G. L. Klee, 3 volumes (Leipzig: Bibliographisches Institut, 1892);

Das Buch über Shakespeare: Handschriftliche Aufzeichnung. Aus seinem Nachlaß herausgegeben, edited by Henry Lüdecke (Halle: Niemeyer, 1920).

Editions in English: *Puss in Boots* (*Der gestiefelte Kater*), edited and translated by Gerald Gillespie (Austin: University of Texas Press, 1974);

The Land of Upside Down (*Die verkehrte Welt*), translated by Oscar Mandel and Maria K. Feder (Rutherford, N.J.: Fairleigh Dickenson University Press, 1978).

OTHER: *Straußfedern,* edited by Tieck, Johann Karl August Musaeus, and Johann Georg Miller, 8 volumes (Berlin & Stettin: Nicolai, 1795-1798);

William Shakespeare, *Der Sturm: Ein Schauspiel, für das Theater bearbeitet,* translated and adapted by Tieck (Berlin & Leipzig: Nicolai, 1796) –includes Tieck's essay "Ueber Shakespeares Behandlung des Wunderbaren";

Volksmährchen, edited by Tieck as Peter Leberecht, 3 volumes (Berlin: Nicolai, 1797);

Miguel de Cervantes Saavedra, *Leben und Thaten des scharfsinnigen Edlen Don Quixote von La*

Mancha, translated by Tieck, 4 volumes (Berlin: Unger, 1799-1801);

Poetisches Journal, edited by Tieck (Jena: Frommann, 1800);

Musen-Almanach für das Jahr 1802, edited by Tieck and August Wilhelm Schlegel (Tübingen: Cotta, 1802);

Friedrich von Hardenberg, *Novalis Schriften,* edited by Tieck and Friedrich Schlegel (Berlin: Realschulbuchhandlung, 1802-1805);

Minnelieder aus dem Schwäbischen Zeitalter, edited by Tieck (Berlin: Realschulbuchhandlung, 1803);

F. Müller, *Mahler Müller's Werke,* edited by Tieck, F. Batt, and Le Pique, 3 volumes (Heidelberg: Mohr & Zimmer, 1811);

Alt-Englisches Theater: Oder Supplement zum Shakespear, edited and translated by Tieck, 2 volumes (Berlin: Realschulbuchhandlung, 1811);

Frauendienst, oder: Geschichte und Liebe des Ritters und Sängers Ulrich von Lichtenstein, von ihm selbst beschrieben, revised and edited by Tieck (Stuttgart & Tübingen: Cotta, 1812);

Deutsches Theater, edited by Tieck, 2 volumes (Berlin: Realschulbuchhandlung, 1817);

Heinrich von Kleist, *Hinterlassene Schriften,* edited by Tieck (Berlin: Reimer, 1821);

Shakespeare's Vorschule, edited by Tieck, 2 volumes (Leipzig: Brockhaus, 1823-1829);

William Shakespeare: Dramatische Werke, translated by A. W. Schlegel and revised by Tieck and others (Berlin: Reimer, 1825-1833);

Kleist, *Gesammelte Schriften,* edited by Tieck, 3 volumes (Berlin: Reimer, 1826);

K. W. F. Solger: *Nachgelassene Schriften und Briefwechsel,* edited by Tieck and F. von Raumer, 2 volumes (Leipzig: Brockhaus, 1826);

Leben und Begebenheiten des Escudero Marcus Obregon: Oder Autobiographie des Spanischen Dichters Vicente Espinel, translated, with a foreword, by Tieck, 2 volumes (Breslau: Max, 1827);

F. von Uechtritz, *Alexander und Darius: Trauerspiel,* foreword by Tieck (Berlin: Vereinsbuchhandlung, 1827);

Braga: Vollständige Sammlung klassischer und volksthümlicher deutscher Gedichte aus dem achtzehnten und neunzehnten Jahrhundert, introduction by Tieck, 10 volumes (Dresden: Wagner, 1827-1828);

J. M. R. Lenz, *Gesammelte Schriften,* edited by Tieck, 3 volumes (Berlin: Reimer, 1828);

Johann Gottfried Schnabel, *Die Insel Felsenburg oder wunderliche Fata einiger Seefahrer: Eine Geschichte aus dem Anfange des achtzehnten Jahrhunderts,* edited by Tieck, 6 volumes (Breslau: Max, 1828);

F. L. Schröder, *Dramatische Werke,* introduction by Tieck, 4 volumes (Berlin: Reimer, 1831);

L. von Bülow, *Das Novellenbuch, oder hundert Novellen nach alten italiänischen, spanischen, französischen, lateinischen, englischen und deutschen bearbeitet,* foreword by Tieck, 4 volumes (Leipzig: Brockhaus, 1834-1836);

Sophie Bernhardi, née Tieck, *Evremont: Roman,* edited by Tieck, 3 volumes (Breslau: Max, 1836);

Shakespeare, *Vier Schauspiele,* translated by Tieck (Stuttgart & Tübingen: Cotta, 1836);

Cervantes Saavedra, *Die Leiden des Persiles und der Sigismunda,* introduction by Tieck, translated by Dorothea Tieck, 2 volumes (Leipzig: Brockhaus, 1838);

F. Berthold, *König Sebastian,* edited by Tieck, 2 volumes (Dresden & Leipzig: Arnold, 1839);

A. A. Afzelius, *Volkssagen und Volkslieder aus Schwedens älterer und neuerer Zeit,* foreword by Tieck, 3 volumes (Leipzig: Kollmann, 1842);

F. Berthold, *Gesammelte Novellen,* edited by Tieck, 2 volumes (Leipzig: Brockhaus, 1842);

K. Förster, *Gedichte,* edited by Tieck, 2 volumes (Leipzig: Brockhaus, 1843);

F. Laun, *Gesammelte Schriften,* revised, with a prologue, by Tieck, volume 1 (Stuttgart: Scheible, Rieger & Sattler, 1843);

Johann Wolfgang von Goethe, *Goethes ältestes Liederbuch,* edited by Tieck (Berlin: Schultze, 1844);

Sophocles, *Sämmtliche Tragödien,* foreword by Tieck (Berlin: Förstner, 1845);

Hardenberg, *Novalis Schriften: Dritter Theil,* edited by Tieck and E. von Bülow (Berlin: Reimer, 1846);

Norwegische Volksmährchen, foreword by Tieck (Berlin: Simion, 1847);

J. Ford, *Dramatische Werke,* volume 1, foreword by Tieck (Berlin: Simion, 1848);

D. Helena, *Lieder II,* foreword by Tieck (Berlin: Nicolai, 1848);

F. Lehmann, *Streit und Friede,* foreword by Tieck (Berlin: Paetel, 1851);

L. Wahl, *Mährchen,* foreword by Tieck (Berlin: Hollstein, 1852);

Mucedorus, ein englisches Drama aus Shakespeares Zeit, translated by Tieck (Berlin: Gronau, 1893).

Of the pioneers of the German Romantic movement around the turn of the nineteenth century, none was more daring–or more durable–than Ludwig Tieck. For more than five decades his name was virtually synonymous with German Romanticism; there was hardly a genre of this most multifarious of literary movements that he did not explore, if not actually inspire. Literary historians surveying the first half of the nineteenth century would be hard-pressed to name a German author who could not boast of a personal acquaintance with Tieck or who had not benefited from his conversation and counsel. Hailed by his youthful contemporaries as the founding poet of the Romantic movement, Tieck lived long enough to become its poet laureate as well. By the time he died in 1853 Romanticism had all but ceased to exist as a formal literary movement. Yet even to describe Tieck as the doyen of German Romanticism scarcely does justice to the esteem in which he was held for most of his long lifetime. Up to Goethe's death Tieck shared with the great poet recognition as Germany's preeminent man of letters; after Goethe's demise in 1832 the accolade was accorded to Tieck alone. Who else could have claimed to have conversed with Mozart, Beethoven, and Wagner; to have discussed philosophy with Fichte and Schelling, folklore with the Grimm Brothers, the art of translation with August Wilhelm Schlegel, poetry with Goethe, Novalis, and Kleist, and Shakespeare with Coleridge?

Johann Ludwig Tieck was born on 31 May 1773 into a middle-class family in Berlin, the capital of what was then the state of Prussia. His father, also named Johann Ludwig, was a ropemaker by trade. Well-read for his time and for his calling, he took an active interest in civic affairs and could lay claim to the honor of having been received by the King of Prussia, Frederick the Great. Tieck's mother, Anna Sophie Schale Tieck, was a sensitive, gentle, and pious woman who, while deferring to her ambitious and autocratic husband, nevertheless took an active part in the education of young Tieck. Evenings in the enlightened Tieck household were graced by readings and recitations either of biblical tales or contemporary German literature. One work which especially inflamed young Tieck's imagination was *Götz von Berlichingen* (1773), the popular "Storm

and Stress" play by Johann Wolfgang von Goethe. Like Goethe, to whom he was later compared, Tieck was privileged to have a puppet theater at his disposal, and, like the older poet, he was soon captured by the magic of theatrical illusion. Although circumstances were to deny him his ambition of becoming a professional actor, Tieck never ceased to be a man of the theater.

Young Tieck's love of learning, evidenced at an early age and encouraged by his parents, mandated his enrollment at a progressive gymnasium, where his obvious academic gifts–especially his talent for foreign languages–could be developed. Among the friends he made at the gymnasium was Wilhelm Heinrich Wackenroder, who was later to write, with Tieck's collaboration, one of the most important works of early German Romanticism: *Herzensergießungen eines kunstliebenden Klosterbruders* (1797; translated as "Confessions from the Heart of an Art-Loving Friar," 1971). Despite the demands posed by his studies, Tieck found time to sample the abundant offerings of the many theaters which thrived in Berlin, where even a schoolboy's allowance sufficed to purchase inexpensive tickets. By the time he completed his gymnasium studies in 1792 Tieck was a passionate theatergoer and admirer of the dramas of Goethe, Schiller, and Shakespeare.

Scholarship has recorded more than thirty works written during Tieck's gymnasium years, among them dramas, comedies, farces, epic fragments, translations, and lyric poetry. While this juvenilia is predictably uneven in quality, its sheer volume clearly presaged the arrival of an uncommon literary talent. The young author's free play of fantasy, his fascination with the gruesome and the horrific, and his ventures into the realm of irrationality gave hints of the Romantic poet to come.

In the spring of 1792 Tieck matriculated at the Prussian university of Halle as a student of theology, but the separation from home, his beloved sister Sophie, and his friend Wackenroder, together with boredom brought on by academic routine, left him dispirited and restless. Late in the fall of the same year he transferred to the university at Göttingen, where he found the Anglophilic atmosphere of the province of Hannover more congenial and the curriculum at the university more stimulating. Theology, for which he evidently had little heart, was quickly forgotten in favor of philosophy, English literature, and writing. Although happy with his new university, whose excellent library was equal even to Tieck's passion for reading, and appreciative of the flexibility of a student's life at Göttingen, Tieck frequently fell victim to bouts of depression. Manic mood swings, episodes of melancholia, and even hallucinations posed a threat to his further development as a writer.

In 1793 Wackenroder and Tieck undertook a journey through Franconia which culminated in an extended sojourn in Nuremberg. The city of Albrecht Dürer and Hans Sachs made a powerful impression on the young friends. From this visit sprang that veneration of the German Middle Ages which, especially in Tieck's works, became one of the characteristics of German Romanticism. It was the spirit of Dürer, too, which sparked the proselytizing fervor of those pages of *Herzensergießungen eines kunstliebenden Klosterbruders* and of Tieck's novel *Franz Sternbalds Wanderungen* (Franz Sternbald's Journeys, 1798), dedicated to the praise of German art. A different but related source of inspiration awaited the friends in Dresden, where their sober Protestantism was all but overwhelmed by the richness of Roman Catholic rituals in the Dresden cathedral. This experience was to bear fruit both in Tieck's "Catholic" works, such as his play *Leben und Tod der heiligen Genoveva* (Life and Death of St. Genoveve, 1799), and in his prolonged flirtation with conversion to Catholicism.

The plethora of stimuli to which Tieck had been exposed soon translated into creative activity. Although only twenty-one, Tieck thought of himself as a student only in a formal sense; the professional writer was about to be born. In his final semester at Göttingen—a brief transfer to Erlangen had proved unsatisfying—Tieck undertook his first major translation project, a prose version, with embellishments, of Shakespeare's *The Tempest*. The translation was published in 1796 together with a perceptive essay, "Ueber Shakespeares Behandlung des Wunderbaren (Shakespeare's Treatment of the Marvelous). This work marked the formal beginning of what was to become a lifetime preoccupation with Shakespeare.

In 1794 Tieck met the Berlin publisher Christoph Friedrich Nicolai, who offered the aspiring young writer employment as a sort of literary jack-of-all-trades. On the surface, the match would seem to have been an odd one: Nicolai was the Nestor of the waning Rationalist school of German literature, whereas Tieck's emerging literary persona was colored by the dawn of the new Romantic era. Yet the engagement turned

out to be a productive one for both parties: Nicolai was happy to have in his employ a writer of Tieck's speed and adaptability, and Tieck was grateful for the opportunity to earn a living exclusively by his pen. It was during these early years of employment that Tieck found time to complete his first major opus, *Geschichte des Herrn William Lovell* (Story of Mr. William Lovell, 1795-1796). A rambling, often disjointed work, the three-volume epistolary novel follows the travels and adventures of a protagonist torn between sensual and spiritual love, between self-indulgence and the ordered discipline of nature. In a reversal of the developmental pattern common to so many German novels, Lovell's diverse experiences lead him ever deeper into a moral labyrinth. Like Goethe's Faust, Lovell belatedly tries to turn away from evil and to return to nature, but he is denied redemption, and, after a final series of sordid adventures, he is killed in a duel. Though by no means autobiographical, *Geschichte des Herrn William Lovell* reflects the dualism, the mood swings, and the adolescent instability of young Tieck. To that extent the novel, for all its flaws, was a necessary summing-up for Tieck, a literary catharsis which cleansed his psyche and prepared him for the tasks yet to come.

In 1797, though still in the employ of Nicolai, Tieck began the publication, under the pseudonym Peter Leberecht, of an extended series titled *Volksmährchen* (Folktales). Some of these tales were epic, some dramatic; some were derivative, some original. All of them flew in the face of Rationalist dogma, which held that folktales, like folk poetry, were too primitive or even barbaric to be subsumed under the rubric of literature. These seminal volumes, whose appearance roughly coincided with the publication of the founding journal of Romanticism, *Das Athenäum* (edited by August Wilhelm and Friedrich Schlegel), generated concepts now recognized as perdurable components of German Romanticism: reverence for indigenous literature; the depiction of the shifting moods of the German forest; the integration of hallucinations and dreams into story plots; the free play of fancy; and the effacement of the boundary between the rational and the irrational. Without being aware of it—Tieck was always a natural, unreflective writer rather than a theoretician—he became the progenitor of an entirely new genre, the Kunstmärchen (literary fairy tale), which was to become one of the most successful experiments essayed by Tieck and fellow Romantics such as Novalis, Clemens Bren-

Tieck posing for a bust by David d'Angers in the studio of Karl Christian Vogel von Vogelstein (painting by Vogel von Vogelstein; by permission of the Nationalgalerie, Berlin)

tano, and E. T. A. Hoffmann.

Among the tales found in Tieck's *Volksmährchen* are "Ritter Blaubart" (Sir Bluebeard), a new version of the ancient Bluebeard legend, and "Die schöne Magelone" (The Fair Magelone), a re-creation of a twelfth-century story which originated in Provence. Tieck interspersed throughout his tale seventeen poems, fifteen of which were selected by Johannes Brahms for his song cycle *Die Magelone-Lieder*. It is in the pages of the *Volksmährchen,* too, that one finds two of Tieck's best-known works: "Der blonde Eckbert" (Blond Eckbert) and *Der gestiefelte Kater* (Puss in Boots, 1797). The former is an original tale which, although written hastily under the pressure of a publication deadline, has come to be regarded as a paradigm for the Romantic Kunstmärchen, especially in its blending of old and new elements. From the indigenous folktale Tieck borrowed the chronology of the indefinite past ("Once upon a time . . . "), the ambiance of the forest, a simple narrative style, and such commonplaces as a mysterious house deep in the woods, an old woman hobbling on a cane, and an enchanted bird which lays a jeweled egg. Build-

ing on this foundation Tieck made significant additions: a narrative frame distinguishing the real world from the world of enchantment, characters more complex than those found in the traditional folktale, syntactically complicated descriptive passages, a subplot, and a complex and somewhat ambiguous depiction of crime and punishment. Perhaps the most striking innovation in the tale is the mood Tieck creates, in part through detailed word pictures of the secluded forest refuge but chiefly through the songs sung by the enchanted bird, all of them variations on the theme of Waldeinsamkeit (meditative solitude in deep woods). The motif of Waldeinsamkeit, with its mysterious overtones, sometimes inviting, sometimes threatening, keynotes that mixture of awe and fear which was to become so characteristic of the Romantic perception of nature.

Like "Der blonde Eckbert," the play *Der gestiefelte Kater* was written with great speed; Tieck claimed to have finished it in one night. Yet, along with "Der blonde Eckbert," *Der gestiefelte Kater* has survived as his best-known literary creation. Based on a folktale retold by the seventeenth-century French writer Charles Perrault, the play centers around the story of the humanoid cat who gains a kingdom for his master. From this starting point Tieck embarks upon a far-ranging satire aimed in equal parts against the stuffy literalism of the Rationalists, the vapidity of popular playwrights of his day (especially August Wilhelm Iffland and August von Kotzebue), and the bad taste and intellectual shallowness of run-of-the-mill theater audiences. Withal, *Der gestiefelte Kater* is less a polemic than a spoof, and compared with the sharp attacks made by Goethe and Schiller against their contemporaries, the satire in *Der gestiefelte Kater* strikes today's reader as almost good-natured. Yet neither historical interest in the objects of Tieck's satire—most of the individuals targeted have passed into obscurity—nor the play's pervasive humor can account for its durability; what made the play unique for its time was Tieck's employment of a technique which can be broadly defined as Romantic irony. For as the fairy-tale plot of the *Der gestiefelte Kater*—intersecting with an apparently unrelated subplot—moves toward its conclusion, the illusion of a theatrical performance is constantly interrupted. The spectators become part of the performance by commenting aloud on the merits (or demerits) of the play; the actors fall out of their roles and rail at the spectators; the backstage technicians are integrated into the action; and even the fictive author of the play is called before the curtain to defend his creation. All the while the actual author—Tieck himself—toys both with the material and the reader, and by so doing asserts a new right claimed by the Romantic poet: the sovereign license to step outside (or inside) his creation and to regard it with detachment. Although playwrights before Tieck had ventured the experiment of inserting a "play within a play," none had ever attempted so ambitious a restructuring of the canonical relationship among actors, the audience, and the hitherto invisible author.

More serious in purpose than *Der gestiefelte Kater* were *Herzensergießungen eines kunstliebenden Klosterbruders*, *Phantasien über die Kunst, für Freunde der Kunst* (1799; translated as "Fantasies on Art for Friends of Art," 1971), and *Franz Sternbalds Wanderungen*, three works which also date from these highly productive years. Although Tieck's role in the composition of the *Herzensergießungen* was subordinate to that of his friend Wackenroder, he was in every sense a collaborator and fully deserves the recognition accorded him by posterity. The book consists of a series of short narratives connected by a common

theme: the veneration of medieval painters and their paintings. Devoted chiefly to a discussion of Italian masters—among them Raphael, Leonardo da Vinci, and Michelangelo—the book is balanced by a lofty panegyric to the German master Dürer. The volume concludes with two chapters written by Wackenroder depicting the life and career of a fictional musician, Joseph Berglinger. In these pages music is elevated to the exalted level of art and nature, because it, too, is deemed a divine language capable of mediating between God and man. Yet music, like nature, is Janus-faced: the intoxicating ecstasies described by Wackenroder barely conceal the destructive potential of music, a theme later taken up by such German authors as Kleist, Hoffmann, and Thomas Mann.

For *Phantasien über die Kunst*, published the year after Wackenroder's death, Tieck could claim a greater share of the joint effort, although the influence of his friend is apparent throughout. Here music, rather than painting, is given the highest rank among the arts because of its unique properties: intangible yet indisputably real, by turns emotional and cerebral, unlimited in its expressive qualities, music is seen as being universal in the wordless power of its divine language. Taken together with Wackenroder's depiction of the intoxicating effect of music in the Berglinger sections of the *Herzensergießungen eines kunstliebenden Klosterbruders*, the *Phantasien über die Kunst* forms the foundation of musical aesthetics for the Romantic movement. It is surely no coincidence that Tieck's other writings dating from this period, especially his lyric poetry, teem with musical effects: repeatedly Tieck combines assonance, rhyme, and rhythm to evoke the sounds and moods of music. This sort of verbal music would soon add a new dimension to the lyrics of Clemens Brentano, Heinrich Heine, and Joseph von Eichendorff.

Tieck's third important work of this period, *Franz Sternbalds Wanderungen*, was entirely of his own authorship. Several sources of inspiration can be descried for this novel, which—setting a pattern for the open-ended Romantic novel—was never completed: Tieck's conscious attempt to write a Romantic counterpart to Goethe's classical developmental novel *Wilhelm Meisters Lehrjahre* (Wilhelm Meister's Apprenticeship, 1795-1796); his need of a literary outlet after the sudden death of Wackenroder; and his determination to propagate the veneration of German art in the spirit of *Herzensergießungen eines kunstliebenden*

Klosterbruders. Set in the time of Dürer, the novel chronicles the adventures of a young painter who, after studying with the great master, leaves his native Nuremberg and journeys far and wide in the hope of rising to the level of his beloved mentor and model. Like Wilhelm Meister, Sternbald finds the path of human experience full of unforeseeable turns and twists; like Meister, too, he is educated through vicissitudes of life, through encounters with confidantes, mentors, and lovers. Unlike Goethe's hero, however, Sternbald is denied a journey's end; when Tieck's narrative breaks off, Sternbald is still a quester, still an unfinished artist. In form, too, Tieck's novel diverges from its model. In place of Goethe's taut design there is the rambling, ruminative narrative structure familiar from *Geschichte des Herrn William Lovell;* in place of the songs of Mignon and the harpist–which for all their atmospheric quality supply integral components to Goethe's plot–the reader finds long lyrical effusions which in fact retard the action. These diversions, made worse through Tieck's predilection for digressive polemics, weaken the novel's structure and give the work at times an almost improvisatory character. Tieck's strengths, on the other hand, emerge in stronger relief when his novel is not compared with its model; the reader can then savor the younger writer's ability to create musical verse, to conjure up marvelous varicolored landscapes, and to re-create the magic of the German forest. Above all, it is Tieck's limpid prose, imbued with music, color, and nature mysticism, which allows *Franz Sternbalds Wanderungen* to transcend its flaws and to assert its position as a landmark of early Romantic fiction.

Whatever its shortcomings, the novel established Tieck as an author to be reckoned with; his days of supplying hackwork to Nicolai were over. The appearance of *Franz Sternbalds Wanderungen* also led to a meeting with Goethe, who, despite understandable reservations about the novel, received its author with restrained cordiality. These two very different writers–often set against one another by malicious partisans–were to maintain a collegial, if somewhat distant relationship over the next thirty years. Most important for Tieck, however, was the fact that the immediate resonance that his novel found among like-minded literati of his own generation paved the way for his acceptance into that elite circle of poets, thinkers, theoreticians, and theologians who charged the final years of the eighteenth century with unparalleled intellectual dynamism: the

so-called Jena Romanticists. Among their ranks were Friedrich Schlegel, August Wilhelm Schlegel, Friedrich Wilhelm Schelling, Johann Gottlieb Fichte, Friedrich Schleiermacher, and Novalis. Complementing this formidable male circle were two women intellectuals who were, by the standards of the day, emancipated: Caroline Schlegel, the wife of August Wilhelm, and Friedrich's wife, Dorothea Veit Schlegel. Although the circle of the Jena Romanticists was frequently broken by comings and goings, by mutual antipathies and even by infidelities, the intellectual energy generated in the few years of its precarious existence was sufficient to fuel the Romantic movement for decades to come.

For Tieck, his entrée into the Jena circle signaled the end of his increasingly tenuous relationship with the house of Nicolai, which had published an unauthorized edition of his writings. In a sense the break was only a formality, since Tieck's artistic development had been drawing him, independently but ineluctably, toward the new school of Romantic theory established by the Schlegel brothers. Although a warm personal friendship with the brothers was slow to flower, Tieck immediately felt a rapport with each. With the mercurial Friedrich–the premier theoretician of the Romantic movement–he shared a love of Goethe's poetry and an interest in Spanish literature, Shakespeare, and Dante; in the more reserved August Wilhelm he recognized a congenial admirer of Elizabethan poetry, a keen student of the art of translation, and, above all, a passionate exponent of the dramas of Shakespeare. One of the first fruits of Tieck's collaboration with the Schlegel brothers was his translation of Cervantes's *Don Quixote*, undertaken at the urging of August Wilhelm. Despite Tieck's less-than-perfect grasp of Spanish, the translation, in four volumes published from 1799 to 1801, turned out to be true to the spirit of the original and quickly gained acceptance as the standard German version of Cervantes's masterpiece. Tieck's interaction with the philosophers of the Jena circle–Fichte, Schelling, and the Danish-born Henrik Steffens–was less immediately productive, in part because Tieck was never much of an abstract thinker but chiefly because his poetic intuition had already anticipated, or at least paralleled, the abstract concepts of the theoreticians. Thus the unprepossessing *Der gestiefelte Kater* may be viewed as a farcical representation of Fichte's doctrine of the supremacy of the ego, and "Der blonde Eckbert" contains at least the germ of the philosophy of nature mysticism expounded by Schelling and Steffens.

Of this circle of newly found friends, colleagues, and fellow Romantics only one came close to filling the void left in Tieck's life by the death of Wackenroder: the fine-nerved mining engineer Friedrich von Hardenberg, who called himself Novalis. At the time of their meeting Novalis stood at the threshold of his career as a poet, a career which was to be cut short by his early death from tuberculosis. Although a year older than Tieck, Novalis looked up to the author of the *Volksmährchen* and *Franz Sternbalds Wanderungen* with something akin to reverence; in a remarkable letter to Tieck he praised his new friend's uncommon insight and sensitivity, and described their meeting as having opened a new book in his life. Tieck, for his part, was happy to escape the superheated atmosphere of Jena for occasional sojourns at Novalis's residence in Weißenfels, where the two men could exchange ideas at leisure. Although echoes of Tieck's language and thought can be heard in Novalis's *Geistliche Lieder* (Spiritual Songs) and his *Hymnen an die Nacht* (Hymns to the Night), it is his allegorical novel *Heinrich von Ofterdingen* (1802; translated as *Henry von Ofterdingen*, 1964) which most clearly bears Tieck's imprint. It was during the hours spent together at Weißenfels that Novalis filled out the plan of his ambitious novel, which like Tieck's *Franz Sternbalds Wanderungen*, was to serve as a Romantic counterbalance to *Wilhelm Meisters Lehrjahre*. After Novalis's death in 1801 Tieck–once again mourning a beloved friend–gave some thought to completing the novel in line with Novalis's intentions, but wisely elected to give it to the world in its uncompleted form.

Inevitably, the daily contact with brilliant and original thinkers and artists supplied a powerful stimulus to Tieck's own creative energies. The years 1799 and 1800 brought the publication of Tieck's two-volume *Romantische Dichtungen* (Romantic Writings), much of which was conceived on his frequent visits to Jena during this time period. The collection includes two major dramas: *Prince Zerbino oder Die Reise nach dem guten Geschmack* (Prince Zerbino; or, The Trip in Search of Good Taste) and *Leben und Tod der heiligen Genoveva*. Described by Tieck as being something of a continuation of *Der gestiefelte Kater, Prinz Zerbino* does indeed share some of the characters, and much of the method, of the earlier play. Like most sequels, however, it falls short of the original, and today it is valued

chiefly as a document showing Tieck at a turning point of his career, in what one might call his Jena phase. *Prinz Zerbino* is a far more ambitious work than *Der gestiefelte Kater*, and, unlike the earlier play, could hardly have been written "in one night." As a tour de force of form it invites admiration with its plays-within-plays, its constant creation and destruction of illusion, and a new technique, the "playback" or reversal of the action, which anticipates the theater of the absurd of the twentieth century. Unfortunately, in his attempt to outdo himself, or perhaps to impress the Schlegels, Tieck burdened the play with too many satires (including one on his bête noir Nicolai), too many lyrical interludes, and too many obscure topical references. In place of the organized chaos of *Der gestiefelte Kater*–which derives at least a modicum of coherence from the fairy tale which forms its frame–Tieck substituted chaos for the sake of chaos. Brilliant and witty in its individual sections, *Prinz Zerbino* never coheres as a whole work of art.

Leben und Tod der heiligen Genoveva, conceived of as a serious play from the start, has little in common with the rollicking *Prinz Zerbino*. Based on an old legend, it tells the story of a noblewoman who is falsely accused of adultery. Sentenced to death, she is spared by a kindly retainer. Abandoned in the woods, she gives birth to a son whom she nourishes with doe's milk. Eventually she is found by her husband, who, convinced of her innocence, restores her to her rightful position. There was much in this time-honored legend to appeal to Tieck: the medieval ambience; the fairy-tale plot; the faint echoes of mythology; and the suggestion of the inexplicable or miraculous. Rather than expound the subject matter with the dramatic tautness of, say, Schiller, Tieck bent his talents to re-creating the essence of what he perceived as medieval, that "Mondbeglänzte Zaubernacht" (moonlit magic night) he was to apostrophize in other works. In Tieck's hands *Leben und Tod der heiligen Genoveva* became a lyrical drama, with mood replacing action, and with musical effects softening conflicts and confrontations. As in "Der blonde Eckbert," nature is no mere backdrop but an organic component of the plot, always weaving its wondrous spell. Even Goethe, who was normally cool to the "new school" of literature and kept his distance from the Jena circle, was charmed by the prismatic colors of Tieck's verse, his shimmering images and beguiling rhymes. After Tieck had read the play aloud to him, the great poet praised the colors, flowers, mirrors, and magic arts Tieck had conjured up. As a lyrical drama *Leben und Tod der heiligen Genoveva* does, in fact, point the way to Goethe's *Faust, Part II* (1832), a work which often eschews the concreteness and confrontations of traditional drama in favor of long, atmospheric lyrical interludes. Like *Prinz Zerbino*—indeed, like virtually all Romantic dramas—*Leben und Tod der heiligen Genoveva* is what Germans call a *Lesedrama*, a play more likely to be read than to be performed on stage. There is every evidence that Tieck, a consummate man of the theater, had a reading public rather than theater audiences in mind when he wrote *Prinz Zerbino* and *Leben und Tod der heiligen Genoveva*. He politely declined offers from the theater director Iffland and from Goethe himself to produce altered stage versions of *Leben und Tod der heiligen Genoveva* and *Prinz Zerbino*, respectively. Keenly aware of his talents, Tieck was conscious of his limitations as well.

In the summer of 1800 Tieck's Jena phase came to an end. The Jena Romanticists were beginning to go their separate ways, and Tieck, who had enriched his mind as a houseguest of August Wilhelm Schlegel, now had to cope with the practical problem of supporting himself and his family. In April 1798 he had married Amalie Alberti, and the next year brought the birth of their daughter Dorothea, who would one day herself become a translator of Shakespeare. In addition to caring for his family, Tieck had to come to terms with his deteriorating physical condition: physically robust in his youth, he began to be subject to bouts of rheumatoid arthritis, the effects of which eventually distorted his once-handsome figure. The years 1800 to 1802 were spent in restless commuting among Hamburg, Berlin, and Dresden as Tieck fruitlessly sought some steady employment which would relieve him from the financial and psychological burden of having to live from manuscript to manuscript. Somehow his energies were adequate to producing, in these hectic years, another major work: the two-part drama *Kaiser Octavianus* (Emperor Octavian, 1804). In many ways a valedictory to early German Romanticism, the play would be Tieck's last large-scale literary work for years to come. In style and content the work suggests a synthesis of the two dramas immediately preceding it. The "open form" and frequent excursions into humor recall *Prinz Zerbino*, while the main plot—there are several identifiable plots—dealing with the slandering of a virtuous woman, her banishment, her trials, and her even-

tual exoneration, clearly harks back to *Leben und Tod der heiligen Genoveva*. What *Kaiser Octavianus* is really about, however, is the play of fancy itself, the sovereign freedom of the poet to be guided only by his creative whim. Taking full advantage of his license as a Romantic poet, Tieck carries the reader to exotic lands and peoples, summons up the chivalric spirit of the Middle Ages, invokes the shades of Shakespeare and Calderón, and through the power of poetry pleads for the renewal of the era of miracles, mysticism, love, and faith. The play includes several now-familiar features: disjointed action, arbitrary transitions, and above all, long lyrical interludes marked by a stunningly virtuosic employment of verse forms and the evocation of shimmering, multihued images. Generations after the publication of *Kaiser Octavianus*, literary historians would be citing, as a motto for German Romanticism, the verses spoken by Romanze (Romance), the allegorical figure of the Prologue who symbolizes the spirit of poetry: "Mondbeglänzte Zaubernacht,/Die den Sinn gefangen hält,/Wundervolle Märchenwelt,/Steig' auf in der alten Pracht!" (Moonlit magic night,/Holding the mind in thrall,/Wondrous world of fairy tale,/Rise up in the splendor of old!). As a vehicle for stage performance, *Kaiser Octavianus*–like *Prinz Zerbino*, *Leben und Tod der heiligen Genoveva*, and indeed virtually every play by Tieck–was stillborn. Its value remains unquestioned, however, as a document which gives form, substance, and poetic realization to the theories and aspirations of an entire literary movement.

From 1802 until 1810 Tieck lived at Ziebingen, near Frankfurt an der Oder, where he and his family–another daughter, Agnes, was born in 1802–were in effect permanent houseguests of Wilhelm von Burgsdorff, an old friend from Tieck's university days. With the composition of *Kaiser Octavianus* Tieck brought to a close the extraordinary series of early Romantic works to which he owes his fame. Although he had another fifty years of life and literary productivity remaining, he would never again enjoy the accolades which had been accorded to the author of *Der gestiefelte Kater* and *Franz Sternbalds Wanderungen*. From his new base in Ziebingen, Tieck continued his many literary projects, including co-editorship with Friedrich Schlegel of the writings of his departed friend Novalis and research on his long-planned work *Das Buch über Shakespeare* (The Book About Shakespeare)–a work he never completed, although portions

Tieck in 1827 (from a drawing by Vogel von Vogelstein; by permission of the Bildarchiv der Nationalbibliothek, Vienna)

were posthumously published in 1920. Gregarious as always, he also cultivated new friends, among them the young painter Philipp Otto Runge. The two men had much to give one another: Tieck, the collaborator on *Herzensergießungen eines kunstliebenden Klosterbruders*, was delighted to have a conversational partner to whom he could pour out his undiminished enthusiasm for the great Italian and German masters; Runge was fascinated to have before him in the flesh the author of *Franz Sternbalds Wanderungen*. Like the progenitors of literary Romanticism, Runge was searching for a new form of art, a method of pictorial representation which reflected the new spirit of the times; he sought a means of expression more reflective of spontaneity than of classical formalism. Because Runge–along with Caspar David Friedrich–became the leading exponent of the Romantic school of painting, the claim can be made that Tieck's influence, so easily documented in the works of the writers who came after him, lived on in the pictorial medium as well. A more immediate by-product of the friendship with Runge, however, was *Minnelieder aus dem Schwäbischen Zeitalter* (Minnesongs from the

Swabian Era, 1803), edited by Tieck. Illustrated by Runge and introduced with a long essay by Tieck, the collection of 220 songs paid tribute to the outpouring of courtly-love poetry in the twelfth century, which, together with the epics *Parzival, Tristan und Isolde,* and *Das Nibelungenlied,* constitutes the literary glory of the German medieval era.

It was *Das Nibelungenlied,* sometimes called the national epic of the Germans, which next occupied Tieck during his residence in Ziebingen. Hampered by crippling bouts of rheumatism; often subjected to periods of depression, which had plagued him since his youth; always pressed for money; and feeling trapped in a deteriorating marriage, Tieck welcomed the opportunity to immerse himself in the distant world of medievalism he knew and loved so well. In the *Nibelungenlied* he found much to occupy him. The epic falls into two parts, with part one recounting the love story of the hero Siegfried–here portrayed as a mortal prince–and the Burgundian princess Kriemhild, the betrayal of Brünnhild, and the slaying of Siegfried by the scheming vassal Hagen; part two, "Kriemhilds Rache" (Kriemhild's Revenge), integrates the fiction of the Siegfried-Kriemhild-Brünnhild triangle with the historical slaughter of the Burgundian tribe at the hands of the Huns in 436 A.D. After centuries of neglect this amalgam of Germanic mythology, fiction, and history had surfaced around 1800 as part of the movement of revitalized nationalism which also placed emphasis on indigenous folk poetry and folktales. Eager to present his fellow Germans with a translation of the Middle High German epic, Tieck attacked the project with scholarly dedication, even journeying to Rome to study sources found in the Vatican Library. Like the complete *Buch über Shakespeare,* however, Tieck's edition never saw the light of day. A certain dilatory spirit which had crept into his writing habits, coupled with a perfectionist's mania for revision, consigned this work, too, to his unpublished papers. Highly praised by contemporaries (including the poet Clemens Brentano) who heard Tieck recite from his translation, the work lay discarded while inferior translations by Friedrich Heinrich von der Hagen and Karl Simrock gained recognition as the standard Modern High German renditions.

Despite his growing physical handicap, Tieck managed to undertake extensive travels during the years 1811 to 1817; often he was away from Ziebingen for months at a time visiting

Prague, Berlin, or Baden-Baden. In May 1817 Tieck fulfilled a lifetime's wish by visiting England, a trip instigated by his ever-useful friend and benefactor Burgsdorff. Tieck had scarcely set foot on English soil when he made straight for London and its theaters. For weeks he indulged his love for the stage, rarely missing an evening's performance. To his good fortune, the repertories of the various theaters were rich in Shakespeare productions: over the short period of his stay he saw performances of *Cymbeline, Julius Caesar, Henry IV*, part 1, *Hamlet, Macbeth, Coriolanus, The Merchant of Venice, Richard III* (with the celebrated actor Edmund Kean in the title role), and *Othello*. Yet his critical eye was not beguiled by the realization of his lifelong dream: he found the interpretations of Shakespeare ill-conceived and the acting style too pompous and rhetorical. All in all Tieck seems to have enjoyed himself more in the British Museum, where the first-hand information he gathered on Elizabethan literature was sufficient for *Shakespeare's Vorschule* (Pre-Shakespearean Drama), two volumes edited by Tieck and published in 1823 and 1829. Tieck's sojourn in London included a reunion with Samuel Taylor Coleridge, whom he had met some years before. Despite language difficulties on both sides, the two poets found enough collegial rapport to enjoy a meeting in which each expounded, at length, his views on poetry in general and English literature–of which Tieck by now had encyclopedic knowledge–in particular. Yet the real high point of the visit to England came with Tieck's trip to Shakespeare's birthplace, Stratford-upon-Avon, which Tieck felt was beckoning to him like a gleaming shrine. The pilgrimage made so deep an impression on Tieck that years later he was able to give a fictional account of it in the novella "Der Mondsüchtige" (The Moonstruck One, 1831).

It was to fiction, specifically the newly emergent form of the novella, that Tieck turned in the middle years of his long career. In so doing he found himself, if not quite rejuvenated, revitalized as a writer. Already in the years 1812 to 1816 Tieck had published an extended collection of mixed works–plays and tales–under the title of *Phantasus*. Some of the works, such as *Der gestiefelte Kater* and "Der Runenberg" (The Runic Mountain), stem from his earlier Romantic period; others–two plays and three tales–are new. Both in the arrangement of the collection and in the content of the most recent works, especially the tales, Tieck gave evidence of essaying a new

style of composition, if not indeed a new genre. Strictly speaking, the technique Tieck employed in organizing his collection was not new at all, since it is modeled after Boccaccio's *Decameron*, in which individual stories are framed by informal discussions held among cultured men and women. Nor was he the first German poet to borrow the Boccacian technique: Goethe had employed the same device in his *Unterhaltungen deutscher Ausgewanderten* (Conversations of German Émigrés, 1795). Typically, Tieck added a new dimension to the inherited technique: instead of using the conversations as mere transitional bridges between tales, he gave them a life of their own by extending them over many pages. As for the tales themselves, they do not entirely fit the accepted definitions of a novella as developed by later critics: the novella is shorter than the novel, with fewer characters and a more limited time frame; it has more dramatic tautness than the tale, often with what Tieck called a Wendepunkt (turning point) determining the direction of the plot; and it is basically realistic in content, with none of the fantastic excursions of the Kunstmärchen. Tieck claimed that he was moving toward a new, that is, un-Romantic, style in the tales of *Phantasus*, and there is some justification for his claim, provided that the reader overlooks "Die Elfen" (The Elves) a charming tale but one which might have been written in 1798: it is a throwback to Tieck's early Romantic period, full of fantasy and enchantment. The next tale, however, "Der Pokal" (The Goblet), meets in part Goethe's oft-quoted definition of a novella as an unheard-of event which might actually have taken place, since it is based on an experience Tieck had in Florence, where he came to the aid of a young woman who had stumbled on the steps of a church. This incident, though by no means "unheard-of," evidently left enough of an impression to serve as the factual germ of "Der Pokal." In the story Tieck expands the everyday incident into a love-at-first-sight romance and uses it as a starting point for an extended tale of thwarted love and wasted lives. By and large the story remains on the realistic plane associated with a novella, but Tieck tests the story's realism by adding supernatural properties to the goblet. The third tale in *Phantasus*, "Liebeszauber" (Love's Magic) is a horror story set in a realistic milieu; like E. T. A. Hoffmann's "Der Sandmann" (The Sandman), which appeared around the same time, it deals with the duplicity of the world of appearances. Despite unresolved contradictions and the intrusion of the uncanny–at one point a dragon materializes–the psychological realism of the story, especially in the blending of the themes of terror and guilt, is compelling.

It was from these tentative beginnings that Tieck evolved, in the course of the next two decades, into one of Germany's leading Novellendichter (novella writers). In 1819 Tieck moved to Dresden, where was appointed Dramaturg (literary historian and editor) of the Dresden theater, a position which at last assured him of a steady income. Relieved of the day-to-day pressure of finding means of support, Tieck was able to concentrate his energies on writing. The result was a steady stream of novellas, few of which one would label masterpieces, but most of them eminently readable. In their social orientation and restrained realism, novellas such as "Die Gemälde" (The Portraits, 1823) and "Die Verlobung" (The Betrothal, 1823) served as well-turned models of the new genre. One of the best-known–and most ambitious–of this series of novellas is *Der Aufruhr in den Cevennen* (The Uprising in the Cévennes Mountains, 1826). Based on the revolt of Calvinists in the south of France in the year 1703, the story in effect defines a subgenre of the novella, the historical novella, a form taken up later in the nineteenth century by Conrad Ferdinand Meyer. Of the later novellas–those written in the 1830s–only one has retained its popularity up to the present day: "Des Lebens Überfluss" (Life's Abundance). In a relaxed pace and with mellow humor Tieck unfolds the tale of a young couple, cut off from parental assistance, trying to live by their wits in the midst of a brutally cold winter. Making the most of their virtual imprisonment in a garret, they pass the time through enlightening conversations, always maintaining an exemplary civility toward one another. In a desperate attempt to keep warm, they begin sawing away at their staircase and using it for firewood, with predictably amusing complications. Having learned of their plight, the girl's parents end their estrangement and come to the couple's aid, thereby giving the story a happy ending. Reading this unprepossessing novella, the student of Tieck's life and works realizes that almost a full lifetime–more than forty years–separates the aging author of "Des Lebens Überfluss" from the youthful enthusiast who, before the turn of the nineteenth century, had penned the Volksmährchen and "Der blonde Eckbert." In place of the enchanted landscapes of the early Tieck one finds the homely confines of an urban garret; replacing the symbolic "blue flower" of early German Romanticism are the frosted flowers the penurious couple find on their unheated window panes; instead of the unlimited poetic amplitude of the Kunstmärchen, the reader finds the modest parameters of realism of the novella. The world had changed greatly since the heady days of the Jena Romanticists, and Tieck had changed with it.

One more late work is of interest: *Vittoria Accorombona* (1840; translated as *The Roman Matron*, 1845), which was planned as a historical novella along the lines of *Der Aufruhr in den Cevennen* but which grew into a novel. Composed over a four-year period, the novel had its roots in Tieck's student days, when he had read John Webster's play *The White Devil* (1612). Set in sixteenth-century Italy, *Vittoria Accorombona* might almost be read today as a feminist statement. To escape the clutches of a lecherous cardinal, Vittoria agrees to marry his dissolute nephew. A liaison with a charismatic duke leads to dual murders and the arrest of Vittoria, but the duke is able to use his position and his wiles to free and then marry Vittoria. A change of popes results in a puritanical witch-hunt against sinners, however, and Vittoria is assassinated by a spurned suitor. Free of the discursiveness and slack form of Tieck's earlier novels, *Vittoria Accorombona* illustrates again the protean character of Tieck's literary persona, his lifelong ability to adapt to new trends, styles, and forms. The strictness of form in *Vittoria Accorombona* indicates that Tieck understood fully that the time for lyrical excursions, formal experiments, and open-ended novels had passed. Significantly, Tieck refused to beautify late-Renaissance Italy, to gloss over ugly political and social realities, as he had once idealized the Middle Ages: the corruption, cruelty, and bigotry of sixteenth-century Italy are unsparingly set forth. Even the theme of love, so tenderly developed in *Kaiser Octavianus*, is used in *Vittoria Accorombona* as a cipher for the destructive power of passion.

Tieck's declining years were spent in Berlin; thus in a sense his long life came full circle. Yet these years were not happy ones. Despite his stature as the last towering figure of Romanticism, indeed of the Age of Goethe, the aging poet had been treated shabbily in his last years in Dresden, and it was almost as a supplicant that he appealed to Wilhelm IV of Prussia for an appointment at the Prussian theaters. The appointment came, albeit grudgingly, and Tieck was to spend his final decade struggling against pain and infirmity to carry out his duties as Dramaturg and stage director. Amid many failures and frustrations one success stood out: his staging of Shakespeare's *A Midsummer Night's Dream* in Potsdam in 1843. At last, the greatest Shakespeare authority of his day was able to bring his knowledge to bear on a practical realization of what he felt was the true Elizabethan spirit. Inevitably, Tieck had to make compromises, including the accommodation of Felix Mendelssohn's delightful but un-Elizabethan music, but the production met general acclaim and became a fixture of the repertory in Berlin and other cities for decades. It could be argued that only Max Reinhardt's dazzling production of the same play in Berlin early in the twentieth century eclipsed Tieck's authoritative interpretation.

Tieck died in Berlin on 28 April 1853, just a month before his eightieth birthday. To the end, despite illness and pain, he had kept up his reading, his correspondence, his editing, and even his writing. As always, his door remained open to aspiring artists and writers, some of whom came only to see the shell of a famous man, others who genuinely sought his counsel and support. Among the latter was that late-blooming Romantic Richard Wagner, whose opera *Tannhäuser* owed much to Tieck's tale "Der getreue Eckart und der Tannenhäuser" (1799), and who wished to discuss his planned opera *Lohengrin* with the aged man who had no peer as a re-creator of the spirit of the German Middle Ages. Visits such as Wagner's in 1847 were all the more welcome because Tieck's last years were spent in loneliness. His wife had died in 1837; his beloved daughter and literary protegée Dorothea in 1841; his brother Friedrich in 1851. Of his former friends, mentors, and colleagues, few were left: Wackenroder, Novalis, the Schlegels, and Goethe had long since passed into the realm of shadows and legends. Tieck had not only outlived these giants, he had in a sense outlived himself: he had become an anachronism in an era which, inexorably, was taking on a more "modern," more realistic coloration. Today Tieck occupies a position in German literature not unlike the one assigned to him in the declining years of his own time: he is regarded as an important author, but not a great one. He is remembered chiefly as the creator of "Der blonde Eckbert," *Leben und Tod heiligen Genoveva*, *Der gestiefelte Kater*, and *Franz Sternbalds Wanderungen*. Of his volumes of lyric poetry, few have yielded poems for anthologies; of his many plays, none can be found in theater repertories; of his many novellas, only a few enjoy currency.

But Tieck deserves to be remembered for more than this scant handful of works. Just at a time when early German Romanticism was in danger of being overwhelmed by a surfeit of pure theory, Tieck, acting on poetic intuition alone, demonstrated that Romanticism "worked," that it was a viable form of literary creativity. Alone among the Jena Romanticists, Tieck remained an inspiration to the succeeding waves of middle and late Romantic writers, and to painters and musicians as well. Together with the Schlegel brothers he helped turn the gaze of his fellow Germans, in a nationalistic era, to the literary treasures of other nations: of Spain, Italy, and especially England. Unselfish in his dedication to literature, he helped rescue from obscurity the works of J. M. R. Lenz, Novalis, and Heinrich von Kleist. For more than fifty years, in fame and in obscurity, in good health and bad, this tireless *praeceptor Germaniae* stood as a living link to the greatness of Germany's literary past. His influence upon generations of German writers, as well as English, French, Danish, Russian, and American authors, has been enormous. Hence while it is true that the bulk of his works lies dormant on dust-covered library shelves, Ludwig Tieck cannot be measured against conventional standards of popularity. Like Romanticism itself, his spirit knows no chronological boundaries.

Biographies:

Rudolf Köpke, *Ludwig Tieck. Erinnerungen aus dem Leben des Dichters nach dessen mündlichen und schriftlichen Mitteilungen*. 2 volumes (Leipzig: Brockhaus, 1855; reprinted, 1 volume, Darmstadt: Wissenschoftliche Buchgesellschaft, 1970);

Roger Paulin, *Ludwig Tieck: A Literary Biography* (New York: Oxford University Press, 1985).

References:

Paul Johann Arnold, "Tiecks Novellenbegriff," *Euphorion*, 23 (1921): 258-278;

Richard Benz, *Die deutsche Romantik: Geschichte einer geistigen Bewegung* (Leipzig: Reclam, 1937);

Gordon Birrell, *The Boundless Present: Space and Time in the Literary Fairy Tales of Novalis and Tieck* (Chapel Hill: University of North Carolina Press, 1979);

Anneliese Bodensohn, *Ludwig Tiecks "Kaiser Octavian" als romantische Dichtung* (Frankfurt am

Main: Diesterweg, 1937; reprinted, Hildesheim: Gerstenberg, 1973);

Richard Brinkmann, *Romantik in Deutschland: Ein interdisziplinäres Symposion* (Stuttgart: Metzler, 1978);

Walter Bruford, *Die gesellschaftlichen Grundlagen der Goethezeit* (Frankfurt am Main, Berlin & Vienna: Ullstein, 1975);

Pauline Bruny, "Ludwig Tiecks Künstlerdichtungen," Ph.D. dissertation, University of Vienna, 1934;

Willi Busch, *Das Element des Dämonischen in Ludwig Tiecks Dichtungen* (Delitzsch: Walter, 1911);

Alan Corkhill, *The Motif of "Fate" in the Works of Ludwig Tieck* (Stuttgart: Akademischer Verlag, 1978);

Corkhill, "Perspectives on the Language in Ludwig Tieck's Epistolary Novel *William Lovell*," *German Quarterly*, 58 (Spring 1985): 173-183;

Walter Donat, *Die Landschaft bei Ludwig Tieck und ihre historischen Voraussetzungen* (Hildesheim: Gerstenberg, 1973);

Kurt J. Fickert, "The Relevance of the Incest Motif in *Der blonde Eckbert*," *Germanic Notes*, 13, no. 3 (1982): 33-35;

Gail Finney, "Self-Reflexive Siblings: Incest as Narcissism in Tieck, Wagner, and Thomas Mann," *German Quarterly*, 56, no. 2 (1983): 243-256;

Christa Franke, *Philipp Otto Runge und die Kunstansichten Wackenroders und Tiecks* (Marburg: Elwert, 1974);

Sonia Fritz-Grandjean, *Das Frauenbild im Jugendwerk von Ludwig Tieck als Mosaikstein zu seiner Weltanschauung* (Bern: Lang, 1980);

Lisa Galanski, "Romantische Ironie in Tiecks 'Verkehrter Welt': zum Verständnis einer artistischen Theaterkomödie aus Berliner Frühromantik," *Recherches Germaniques*, 14 (1984): 23-57;

Janis Gellinek, "*Der blonde Eckbert:* A Tieckian Fall from Paradise," in *Lebendige Form: Interpretationen zur deutschen Literatur. Festschrift für Heinrich E. K. Henel*, edited by Jeffrey L. Sammons and Ernst Schürer (Munich: Fink, 1970), pp. 147-166;

Hans Geulen, "Zeit und Allegorie im Erzählvorgang von Ludwig Tiecks Roman *Franz Sternbalds Wanderungen*," *Germanisch-Romanische Monatsschrift*, 18 (July 1968): 281-298;

Frauke Gries, "Two Critical Essays by Ludwig Tieck: On Literature and its Sociological

Aspects," *Monatshefte für den deutschen Unterricht, deutsche Sprache und Literatur*, 66 (Summer 1974): 157-165;

Reinhold Grimm, "Zur Vorgeschichte des Begriffs 'Neuromantik,'" in *Das Nachleben der Romantik in der modernen deutschen Literatur*, edited by Wolfgang Paulsen (Heidelberg: Stiehm, 1969), pp. 32-50;

Klaus Günzel, *König der Romantik: Das Leben des Dichters Ludwig Tieck in Briefen, Selbstzeugnissen und Berichten* (Tübingen: Wunderlich, 1981);

Dieter H. Haenicke, "Ludwig Tieck und 'Der blonde Eckbert,'" in *Vergleichen und Verändern: Festschrift für H. Motekat*, edited by Albrecht Goetze and Günther Pflaum (Munich: Hueber, 1970), pp. 170-187;

Rudolf Haym, *Die romantische Schule: Ein Beitrag zur Geschichte des deutschen Geistes* (Berlin: Gaertner, 1870; reprinted, Hildesheim: Olms, 1961);

Christoph Hering, "Die Poetisierung des Alltäglichen in Tiecks 'Peter Leberecht,'" *Monatshefte*, 49 (December 1957): 361-370;

Harvey W. Hewett-Thayer, "Tieck's Novellen and Contemporary Journalistic Criticism," *Germanic Review*, 3 (October 1928): 328-360;

Valentine C. Hubbs, "Tieck, Eckbert, und das kollektive Unbewusste," *Publications of the Modern Language Association*, 71 (September 1956): 686-693;

Hubbs, "Tieck's Romantic Fairy Tales and Shakespeare," *Studies in Romanticism*, 8 (Summer 1969): 229-234;

Ricarda Huch, *Die Romantik*, 2 volumes, seventh edition (Leipzig: Haessel, 1918);

Raymond M. Immerwahr, "*Der blonde Eckbert* as a Poetic Confession," *German Quarterly*, 34 (March 1961): 103-117;

Immerwahr, *The Esthetic Intent of Tieck's Fantastic Comedy* (St. Louis: Washington University, 1953);

Paul Kluckhohn, *Die deutsche Romantik*, 2 volumes (Bielefeld: Klasing, 1924);

Paul Gerhard Klussmann, "Die Zweideutigkeit des Wirklichen in Ludwig Tiecks Märchennovelen," *Zeitschrift für deutsche Philologie*, 83 (1964): 426-452;

Victor Knight, "The Perceptive Non-Artist: a Study of Tieck's *Der Runenberg*," *New German Studies*, 10 (Spring 1982): 21-31;

Werner Kohlschmidt, "Der junge Tieck und Wackenroder," in *Die deutsche Romantik: Poetik, Formen und Motive*, edited by Hans Steffen (Göttingen: Vandenhoeck & Ruprecht, 1967), pp. 30-44;

Helmut Kreuzer, "Tiecks 'Gestiefelter Kater,' " *Deutschunterricht,* 15 (December 1963): 33-44;

Otto K. Liedke, "Tieck's 'Der blonde Eckbert.' Das Märchen von Verarmung und Untergang," *German Quarterly,* 44 (May 1971): 311-316;

W. J. Lillyman, " 'Des Lebens Überfluß': The Crisis of a Conservative," *German Quarterly,* 46 (May 1973): 393-409;

Lillyman, "Ludwig Tieck's 'Der Runenberg,' The Dimension of Reality," *Monatschefte,* 62 (Fall 1970): 231-244;

Lillyman, *Reality's Dark Dream: The Narrative Fiction of Ludwig Tieck* (Berlin & New York: De Gruyter, 1978);

Percy Matenko, *Tieck and America* (Chapel Hill: University of North Carolina Press, 1954);

Robert Minder, *Un Poète romantique allemand: Ludwig Tieck (1773-1853)* (Paris: Societé d'édition Les Belles lettres, 1936);

Roger Paulin, "Der alte Tieck: Forschungsbericht," in *Zur Literatur der Restaurationsepoche 1815-1848: Forschungsreferate und Aufsätze,* edited by Jost Hermand and Manfred Windfuhr (Stuttgart: Metzler, 1970), pp. 247-262;

Paulin, "Ohne Vaterland kein Dichter: Bermerkungen über historisches Bewußtsein und Dichtergestalt beim späten Tieck," *Literaturwissenschaftliches Jahrbuch,* 13 (1972): 125-150;

Julius Petersen, *Die Wesensbestimmung der deutschen Romantik* (Leipzig: Quelle & Meyer, 1926; reprinted, Darmstadt: Wissenschaftliche Buchgesellschaft, 1968);

Helmut Prang, ed., *Begriffsbestimmung der Romantik* (Darmstadt: Wissenschaftliche Buchgesellschaft, 1968);

Wolfdietrich Rasch, "Blume und Stein. Zur Deutung von Ludwig Tiecks Erzählung 'Der Runenberg,' " in *The Discontinuous Tradition,* edited by Petrus F. Ganz (Oxford: Clarendon Press, 1971), pp. 113-128;

Rasch, "Die Zeit der Klassik und der frühen Romantik," in *Annalen der deutschen Literatur,* second edition, edited by Hans Otto Burger (Stuttgart: Metzler, 1971), pp. 465-550;

Victoria L. Rippere, "Ludwig Tieck's 'Der blonde Eckbert': A Psychological Reading," *Publications of the Modern Language Association,* 85 (May 1970): 473-486;

Gerhard Schneider, *Studien zur deutschen Romantik* (Leipzig: Koehler & Amelang, 1962);

Rolf Schröder, *Novelle und Novellentheorie in der frühen Biedermeierzeit* (Tübingen: Niemeyer, 1970);

Uwe Schweikert, "Jean Paul und Ludwig Tieck," *Jahrbuch der Jean-Paul-Gesellschaft,* 8 (1973): 23-77;

Wulf Segebrecht, ed., *Ludwig Tieck: Wege der Forschung* (Darmstadt: Wissenschaftliche Buchgesellschaft, 1976);

Friedrich Sengle, *Biedermeierzeit: Deutsche Literatur im Spannungsfeld zwischen Restauration und Revolution, 1815-1848,* 2 volumes (Stuttgart: Metzler, 1971-1972);

Emil Staiger, "Ludwig Tieck und der Ursprung der deutschen Romantik," in his *Stilwandel* (Zurich & Freiburg: Atlantis, 1963), pp. 175-204;

Ralf Stamm, *Ludwig Tiecks späte Novellen: Grundlage und Technik des Wunderbaren* (Stuttgart, Berlin, Cologne & Mainz: Kohlhammer, 1973);

Hans Steffen, ed., *Die deutsche Romantik: Poetik, Formen und Motive* (Göttingen: Vandenhoeck & Ruprecht, 1967);

Gerhard Storz, *Klassik und Romantik: Eine stilgeschichtliche Darstellung* (Mannheim, Vienna & Zurich: Bibliographischer Institut, 1972);

Fritz Strich, *Deutsche Klassik und Romantik oder Vollendung und Unendlichkeit* (Munich: Meyer & Jessen, 1922);

Marianne Thalmann, "Hundert Jahre Tieckforschung," *Monatshefte,* 46 (March 1953): 113-123;

Thalmann, *Ludwig Tieck, "Der Heilige von Dresden"* (Berlin: De Gruyter, 1960);

Thalmann, *Ludwig Tieck, der romantische Weltmann aus Berlin* (Bern: Francke, 1955);

Thalmann, *Das Märchen und die Moderne* (Stuttgart: Kohlhammer, 1961);

Thalmann, *Zeichensprache der Romantik* (Heidelberg: Stiehm, 1967);

James Trainer, "The Incest-Theme in the Works of Tieck," *Modern Language Notes,* 76 (December 1961): 819-824;

Trainer, *Ludwig Tieck. From Gothic to Romantic* (London, The Hague & Paris: Mouton, 1964);

Harry Vredeveld, "Ludwig Tieck's 'Der Runenberg': An Archetypical Interpretation," *Germanic Review,* 49 (May 1974): 200-214;

Karlheinz Weigand, *Tiecks William Lovell: Studie zur frühromantischen Antithese* (Heidelberg: Winter 1975);

Benno von Wiese, "Ludwig Tieck: Des Lebens Überfluss," in *Die deutsche Novelle von Goethe bis Kafka* (Düsseldorf: Bagel, 1960), pp. 117-133;

Edwin H. Zeydel, "Die ersten Beziehungen Ludwig Tiecks zu den Brüdern Schlegel," *Journal of English and German Philology*, 27 (1928): 16-41;

Zeydel, "Ludwig Tieck und das Biedermeier," *Germanischromanische Monatsschrift*, 26 (1938): 352-358;

Zeydel, *Ludwig Tieck, The German Romanticist: A Critical Study* (Princeton: Princeton University Press, 1935; reprinted, Hildesheim & New York: Olms, 1971).

Papers:
Ludwig Tieck's papers are at the Staatsbibliothek Preußischer Kulturbesitz, West Berlin.

Ludwig Uhland

(26 April 1787-13 November 1862)

Edward M. Batley

University of London Goldsmiths' College

BOOKS: *Dissertatio inauguralis juridica de juris Romani servitutum natura dividua vel individua* (Tübingen: Schramm, 1810);

Deutscher Dichterwald, by Uhland, Justinus Kerner, Friedrich de la Motte Fouqué, and others (Tübingen: Heerbrandt, 1813);

Gedichte (Stuttgart & Tübingen: Cotta, 1815; enlarged editions, 1820, 1831); translated by Alexander Platt as *Poems of Uhland* (Leipzig: Volckmar, 1848);

Sechs vaterländische Gedichte (Stuttgart: Würtemberg, 1816);

Keine Adelkammer! Flugschrift vom Jahr 1817 (N.p., 1817);

Vaterländische Gedichte (Stuttgart & Tübingen: Fues, 1817);

Ernst, Herzog von Schwaben: Ein Trauerspiel in fünf Aufzügen (Heidelberg: Mohr & Winter, 1818);

Ludwig der Baier: Schauspiel in fünf Aufzügen (Berlin: Reimer, 1819);

Walther von der Vogelweide, ein altdeutscher Dichter (Stuttgart & Tübingen: Cotta, 1822);

Sagenforschungen, volume 1, *Der Mythus von Thôr nach nordischen Quellen* (Stuttgart & Tübingen: Cotta, 1836);

Alte hoch- und niederdeutsche Volkslieder, mit Abhandlung und Anmerkungen: Erster Band (Stuttgart & Tübingen: Cotta, 1844-1845);

Dramatische Dichtungen (Heidelberg: Winter, 1846);

Neun Reden für den Anschluß Oesterreichs an Deutschland, gehalten in der Paulskirche von den Abgeordneten Eisenmann, Reiter, . . . Uhland, . . . (Frankfurt am Main: Sauerländer, 1848);

Bodman: Beitrag zur schwäbischen Sagenkunde (Vienna: Manz, 1859);

Gedichte und Dramen, 3 volumes (Stuttgart: Cotta, 1863);

Die Todten von Lustnau (Vienna: Gerold, 1863);

Schriften zur Geschichte der Dichtung und Sage, 8 volumes (Stuttgart: Cotta, 1865-1873);

Gesammelte Werke, edited by Hermann Fischer, 6 volumes (Stuttgart: Cotta, 1892); repub-

Ludwig Uhland in 1818 (painting by Morff)

lished, 3 volumes (Darmstadt: Wissenschaftliche Buchgesellschaft, 1977);

Werke: Kritisch durchgesehene und erläuterte Ausgabe, edited by Ludwig Fränkel, 2 volumes (Leipzig & Vienna: Bibliographisches Institut, 1893);

Gedichte: Vollständige kritische Ausgabe, edited by E. Schmidt and J. Hartman, 2 volumes (Stuttgart: Cotta, 1898);

Sämtliche Werke, edited by Ludwig Holthof (Stuttgart: Deutsche Verlags-Anstalt, 1901);

Werke, edited by Hartmut Fröschle and Walter Scheffler (Munich: Winkler, 1980-1984);

Werke, edited by Hans-Rüdiger Schwab (Frankfurt am Main: Insel, 1983).

"Genial in verse, erudite in prose, noble in his political career, amiable in his private life, and unostentatiously reverent of things divine. . . ." Alexander Platt's characterization of Ludwig Uhland sprang directly from his personal acquaintance with this eminent Swabian Romantic. It was printed in the "Biographical Notice" to his English translations of Uhland's poetry published in 1848, a year to be remembered for the Austro-Hungarian and Prussian revolutions, the gathering momentum toward unifying the German nation, and Uhland's election to the new German Assembly in Frankfurt am Main. Neither dazzlingly brilliant nor renowned for invention, Uhland brought a charm, directness, and comprehensibility to poetry which superseded the grand and mystical design of Novalis and the critical and creative thinking of the Schlegel brothers. Commonly regarded as excelling in balladry and undramatic in his plays, Uhland's threefold contribution to German Romanticism as poet, politician, and scholar was significant and distinctive.

Johann Ludwig Uhland was born on 26 April 1787 to Johann Friedrich and Rosine Elizabeth Uhland. A native of Tübingen, the heart of Swabia and his family home for generations, Uhland was soon aware of the Germanic traditions which formed the cultural life of that part of southern Germany. His father was the university secretary, and his grandfather Ludwig Joseph Uhland, a poet in his own right, had been a professor of history and theology. Uhland began writing poems while at the Latin school which he first attended in 1793: hexameters in Latin, simple rhymes in German, and verses bespeaking a melancholy with which the poet was as yet insufficiently familiar to portray convincingly. The Scottish songs collected by James Macpherson between 1760 and 1763 and attributed to the Gaelic poet Ossian had inspired Johann Gottfried Herder during his student days at the University of Königsberg, and these and the poetry of Ludwig Hölty were among the earlier models which influenced the young poet's development.

In 1801 Uhland's father was awarded a grant so that his talented son might benefit from a university education. To prepare himself for the Tübingen Faculty of Law, where he registered four years later, Uhland took private lessons in classical languages and literature. Even greater inspiration came to him from the old heroic lays of German literature, whose fresh evocative imagery he found preferable to the lucidity of the classics and the rhetoric of contemporary writers. In 1805 he was inspired to learn Ro-

mance and Nordic languages in order to read in the original the folk songs which had been translated and collected by Herder in 1778 and 1779, and he became an avid reader of Arnim and Brentano's edition of German folk songs, *Des Knaben Wunderhorn* (The Boy's Cornucopia), published between 1805 and 1808. Among the better known of the Uhland ballads composed at this time are: "Die Kapelle" (The Chapel), which sings of the chapel on the hill of Wurmlingen and of the transience of life; "Schäfers Sonntagslied" (Shepherd's Sunday Song), evoking the sense of awe inspired in the poet by nature; and the mysteriously ambivalent "Das Schloß am Meer" (Castle by the Sea). "Entschluß" (Decision) shows the gentle irony and delicacy of the poet's touch and reveals the modesty of his personality.

Uhland's Romantic balladry tells movingly melancholy stories of a fulfilled or frustrated love which occasionally shifts into the demonic. Poems like "Abschied" (Farewell) contain lines memorable for the immediate appeal of their musical and rhythmic balance, doubtless a by-product of the poet's sensitivity to word and melody: "Was klinget und singet die Straß' herauf?" (What rings and sings from the street below?). Chivalric and patriotic echoes of the Germanic past replace the classical inheritance which had dominated the greater part of the earlier Age of Enlightenment.

At the university Uhland befriended other like-minded poets, among them Karl Meyer and Justinus Kerner. Bound together by their common interest in literature, German traditions, the idea of German nationhood, the folk songs of *Des Knaben Wunderhorn*, and the Middle Ages, their view of the past differed from the idealistic visions of the early Romantics as they sought to recapture its true historical character. Roused by Johann Friedrich Cotta's *Morgenblatt für gebildete Stände* (Morning Paper for the Educated Classes), which praised classical antiquity and the Enlightenment, they produced a rival *Sonntagsblatt für gebildete Stände* (Sunday Paper for the Educated Classes), in which, in 1807, Uhland published an essay on the concept of Romanticism. Here he wrote of man surrounded by the infinite, the eternal mystery of godhead and world; more than an imaginary vision of the Middle Ages, Romanticism was the high poetry of eternity, representing in images what words themselves could not express, a book of strange and magical images which preserve man's links with the dark world of the spirits. Romanticism was the shimmering rainbow, according to the Edda, a bridge across which the gods may move down to meet mortal man or the chosen few may move up to meet them. Uhland saw infinity in the beauty of nature which was both around him and within, yet his youthful zest and exuberance were balanced and contained by the careful design of his poems, resulting in their characteristic simplicity and clarity. Many of Uhland's poems were written during his student days.

With the faculty examinations of 1808 successfully behind him, Uhland sought and gained qualifications which would allow him to work as an advocate. A doctoral dissertation consumed most of his time for the next two years, although he continued to produce memorable poems such as "Klein Roland" (Little Roland), "Der gute Kamerad" (The Good Comrade), and "Der Wirtin Töchterlein" (The Innkeeper's Daughter). No sooner had he been awarded his Doctor of Law in 1810 than Uhland honored his father's wishes by traveling to Paris to study the Code Napoleon, the law which had governed Germany since the signing of the Rhine Alliance on 7 July 1806. Arriving in the French capital on 25 May, he was soon distracted from his original purpose by the medieval and Old French manuscripts to which the Bibliotheque Imperiale afforded him immediate access. There he read the old folktales of Heymon's children as well as those of Floire and Blanscheflur; collected material to be used later in historic ballads such as "Taillefer"; and wrote his essay on Old French epic poetry.

Returning home early in 1811, Uhland took up the practice of law. In his spare time he collaborated with Gustav Schwab and Justinus Kerner to publish an almanac of poetry. In 1812 a move to Stuttgart enabled him to work unsalaried for the Minister of Justice, a post from which he resigned in 1814. Unpretentious and unambitious, Uhland wished only for a relatively secure life which would afford him an opportunity to continue writing poetry. Now more frequently at home, he wrote a number of occasional poems as well as some of his most important ballads, among them "Des Sängers Fluch" (The Singer's Curse) and "Schwäbische Kunde" (Passed on from Swabia). Uhland's first major publication was an anthology of his poetry which was printed by Cotta in 1815. Not immediately successful, it was supplemented from time to time, running to nineteen editions by 1851 and forty by 1869. The postponement of Uhland's popularity has been attributed to the tranquillity which marks

the collection and which was at odds with the political turmoil of those earlier years. In the quieter period which followed, his songs, many of which were set to music by Conradin Kreuzer, were soon celebrated throughout Germany and beyond.

Uhland's interest in the Germanic past, its chivalry, history, language, and legends, found a natural complement in the tendencies of his own age, which were aimed at achieving the belated political unity of a great nation. The victory over Napoleon at the Battle of Leipzig in 1813 had liberated the country from French dominion and accelerated the process of nascent nationhood. It was hardly surprising that the call of patriotism should be widely heard in German poetry at the time, nor that it should figure in Uhland's poetry, too. Opposed to King Frederick of Württemberg's continued sympathy with the French cause and frustrated at the delay in framing former privileges in a new constitution, Uhland had his poems express his own political convictions in support of the struggle for independence and nationhood. Celebrating the third anniversary of the victory over the French on 18 October 1813, he exhorted the German princes to carry out the promises which had then been made. At a public meeting in 1848 where he spoke in favor of German unity, Uhland's audience was so moved by his words that they burst spontaneously into the first line of his patriotic song, "Wenn heut ein Geist herniederstiege" (If today a spirit should come down).

The subject matter of two of Uhland's dramas, *Ernst, Herzog von Schwaben* (Ernst, Duke of Swabia, 1818) and *Ludwig der Baier* (Ludwig the Bavarian, 1819), arose out of his work as a historian and collector of Germanic legends. Both take German unity as their central theme, using the message of the past to guide contemporary politicians toward Germany's future. On 28 and 29 October 1819, the year in which Uhland had been elected delegate for Tübingen in the Assembly of the Württemberg Estates, the ceremony to celebrate the acceptance of the constitution included a performance in Stuttgart of *Ernst, Herzog von Schwaben*. Set in the year 1030, the play depicts the conflict between the Holy Roman Emperor Konrad II and his stepson, Ernst, Duke of Swabia. Ending with the defeat of the latter by vastly superior forces, it pleads for unity by depicting the German tragedy of disunity and the final massacre of noble qualities such as bravery, chivalry, honor, truth, and loyalty unto death. Like

Death mask of Uhland (photograph by M. Clausen; by permission of the Bildarchiv der Österreichischen Nationalbibliothek)

Walther's songs, the play sings of the beauty of German noblewomen and of the kind of patriotism which rates the future of the country higher than personal ambition or individual life. The rich imagery of harvest is contrasted to the barrenness wrought by conflict, and in such fullness that it reflects Uhland's affectionate appreciation of his own Swabian countryside. The final words of Gisela at her son Ernst's heroic death link the play to the legend which was to live on as an inspiration to others. It also provided the subject matter for Uhland's inaugural lecture, which was delivered on 22 November 1832, three years after he assumed the Chair of German Literature in Tübingen.

Ludwig der Baier was inspired by a competition for the best play to celebrate the opening of the new court theater in Munich in October 1818. Set in 1314, Uhland's play dramatizes the noble conflict between the Bavarian Emperor Ludwig and Frederick of Austria, followed by their selfless reconciliation, which he regarded as symbolic of the unity to be achieved by the German people. However, the delicate nature of Bavaria's relations with the Pope and Austria at that time

prevented the play from taking a prize. Although Uhland's plays are generally dismissed as poetic rather than dramatic, they sustain a momentum which, together with the rousing rhetoric of his iambic blank-verse pentameters, sound a healthy note of patriotism reminiscent of Goethe's *Götz von Berlichingen* (1773) and the German military dramas of the late eighteenth century. The moral sublimity attained by Ludwig and Frederick in their final symbolic embrace as joint rulers of the Empire constitutes the tradition of self-effacing moral grandeur developed by Uhland's immediate predecessor and fellow Swabian, Friedrich Schiller. Other plays which Uhland began were never completed.

Uhland's engagement to Emilie Vischer was postponed for some time, partly as a result of his insecure future, partly because of his continued intellectual dependence upon his mother, who was doubtless one of the causes of the shyness and awkwardness for which she continually rebuked him. Applications for a lectureship at the University of Basel and a librarianship in Frankfurt were both unsuccessful. However, in 1819 he was elected to Württemberg's provincial government as the representative for Tübingen, an office which secured financial independence and paved the way for a short engagement followed by marriage on 29 May 1820.

With the parliamentary recess, the couple was able to honeymoon in Switzerland, where they visited St. Gallen, Schwyz, and the Emmenthal. Upon their return to Tübingen, Uhland's social and civic duties soon consumed most of his time. Politics and scholarship became his major interests, and although there was little time for poetry, earlier anthologies of his poems were now running to new editions. Taking up an earlier plan to write an account of medieval poetry, Uhland published in 1822 a substantial essay on the work of Walther von der Vogelweide, which was long to be regarded as one of the most important scholarly contributions on the work of this renowned medieval lyricist. Uhland opens the essay by identifying two complementary features of Germanic literature: its common inheritance, that is, the view of the Middle Ages presented in legend, image, and word; and the poetry created by the talents of particular individuals. Uhland's idea that there was a collective vision of the Middle Ages, with "Bild" (image) as its surest representation, echoed the thinking of his own Romantic age. Walther was for him its most talented exponent, a poet who, like Uhland, was keenly interested in the politics of his age, but who traveled more extensively, made a living from his poetry, and on the whole sang of his own contemporary world. Due to the almost total absence of other evidence, Uhland uses Walther's poetry to deduce some of the circumstances of his life. He knew Johann Jakob Bodmer's 1748 essay on Walther's poetry and Gleim's and Tieck's anthologies of 1779 and 1803 respectively, but his own essay set out on an original path to deduce biographical data and facets of personality from purely poetic evidence. Recent scholarship has more or less confirmed the conclusions presented in the essay.

As literary studies consumed more and more of his time, Uhland felt the growing burden of his political responsibilities. As a result he declined to stand for reelection in 1826. Since 1806 the insane Friedrich Hölderlin had been living in his tower on the banks of the Neckar, and now Uhland collaborated with Gustav Schwab to produce an anthology of their fellow Swabian's poetry. This and other work by Uhland made him known to other contemporary scholars of German language and literature, particularly Karl Lachmann, who had responded enthusiastically

to his essay on Walther. On 29 December 1829 he was awarded the Chair of German Literature at the University of Tübingen, and in May 1830 he opened the semester with lectures on the history of poetry from the thirteenth to the sixteenth centuries, the song of the Nibelungs, and the history of Romance and Germanic legends. In addition he offered a so-called "Stylistikum," where students submitted their own poems and essays for criticism.

Scarcely had Uhland settled into his new post than he found himself reelected in 1833 to Parliament, but five years later he abandoned his seat in the chamber to resume his studies. Back in Tübingen he concentrated on the literature and culture of the Middle Ages, work which was interrupted only by journeys to Vienna and North Germany. In the libraries of Dresden and Leipzig he searched for old texts; his interest focused upon folk songs, several of which he jotted down during his travels. He planned to publish an anthology of Low and High German folk songs which, unlike Arnim and Brentano's edition of *Des Knaben Wunderhorn*, would be faithful to the original texts and accompanied by sources and notes. Uhland's reputation as a scholar of German literature grew. The Berlin Academy made him a corresponding member, and the University of Tübingen awarded him a doctorate in philosophy.

In the meantime, the political situation within Germany had changed considerably. The Customs Union of 1844 had brought the federal states more closely together, and the call for political union made itself increasingly audible. A single army was to be created and German law unified. Uhland believed firmly in this vision of nationhood, and in 1848 it was decreed that seventeen representatives drawn from all the German States should be charged with the task of revising the constitution. Uhland was elected to represent Tübingen-Rottenburg, and he dedicated himself wholeheartedly to the process of unification. The town and university of Tübingen honored him with a torchlight procession prior to his departure for Frankfurt on 27 March. Yet the National Assembly did not live up to the hopes invested in it. Discussions were inconclusive, and even the rump Parliament, transferred to Stuttgart, proved unproductive. When Parliament was forcibly dissolved by the Württemberg militia, Uhland was in the front row of protesting delegates. He had no alternative but to return to his scholarly pursuits in Tübingen, although from time to time he still gave advice on political issues, remaining firmly opposed to the hegemony of Prussia which by then seemed a fait accompli.

The final years of Uhland's life included journeys to Berlin, Frankfurt, and Lake Constance. The last time he spoke publicly was at the Schiller festival in Stuttgart in 1859, where he expressed regret at the continued fragmentation of Germany. Disillusioned as he was, Uhland could not accept the high public honor of the Prussian Order "Pour le mérite," an award instigated on his behalf by Alexander von Humboldt, or the Bavarian Order of Maximilian. When he attended Justinus Kerner's funeral on 21 February 1862, Uhland caught a chill from which he never recovered, and he died later in the year on 13 November.

References:

Ricarda Huch, "Schwaben und Uhland," in *Alte und neue Götter: Die Revolution des neunzehnten Jahrhunderts in Deutschland* (Berlin & Zurich: Deutsch-Schweizerische Verlagsanstalt, 1930);

Karl Mayer, *Ludwig Uhland, seine Freunde und Zeitgenossen,* 2 volumes (Stuttgart: Krabbe, 1867);

Harry Maync, *Uhlands Jugenddichtung* (Berlin: Ebering, 1899);

Walther Reinöhl, *Uhland als Politiker* (Tübingen: Mohr, 1911);

Gerhard Schneider, "Uhland und die schwäbische Romantik," in *Studien zur deutschen Romantik* (Leipzig: Kocher & Amelang, 1962);

Hermann Schneider, *Uhland: Leben, Dichtung, Forschung* (Berlin: Hofmann, 1920);

Gerhard Storz, *Schwäbische Romantik: Dichter und Dichterkreise im alten Württemberg* (Stuttgart, Berlin, Cologne & Mainz: Kohlhammer, 1967);

Hellmut Thomke, *Zeitbewußtsein und Geschichtsauffassung im Werk Uhlands,* volume 9 of *Sprache und Dichtung* (Bern: Haupt, 1962).

Karl August Varnhagen von Ense

(21 February 1785-10 October 1858)

T. H. Pickett

University of Alabama

BOOKS: *Testimonia Auctorum de Merkelio, das ist: Paradiesgärtlein für Garlieb Merkel* (Cologne: Hammer, 1806);

Erzählungen und Spiele, by Varnhagen and W. Neumann (Hamburg: Schmidt, 1807);

Die Versuche und Hindernisse Karl's: Eine Deutsche Geschichte aus neuerer Zeit: Erster Theil (Berlin & Leipzig, 1809);

Geschichte der hamburgischen Begebenheiten während des Frühjahrs 1813 (London & Hamburg: Perthes, 1813);

Hanseatische Anregungen (Bremen, 1814);

Deutsche Ansicht der Vereinigung Sachsens mit Preußen (Tübingen: Cotta, 1814);

Gedichte während des Feldzugs 1813 (Friedrichstadt: Bade und Fischer, 1814);

Geschichte der Kriegszüge des Generals von Tettenborn während der Jahre 1813 und 1814 (Stuttgart & Tübingen: Cotta, 1814);

Deutsche Erzählungen (Stuttgart & Tübingen: Cotta, 1815);

Deutsche Frühlingskränze für 1815, by Varnhagen, Isidorus (pseudonym for F. A. O. H. Graf von Loeben), and others; edited by J. P. von Hornthal, 2 volumes (Bamberg: Kunz/Bamberg & Würzburg: Göbhardt, 1815-1816);

Vermischte Gedichte (Frankfurt am Main: Varrentrapp, 1816);

Biographische Denkmale, 5 volumes (Berlin: Reimer, 1824-1830; enlarged edition, 1845-1846);

Fürst Blücher von Wahlstadt (Berlin: Reimer, 1826);

Leben des Grafen von Zinzendorf (Berlin: Reimer, 1830);

Die Sterner und die Psitticher: Novelle (Berlin: Vereinsbuchhandlung, 1831);

Zur Geschichtschreibung und Litteratur: Berichte und Beurtheilungen: Aus den Jahrbüchern für wissenschaftliche Kritik und andern Zeitschriften gesammelt (Hamburg: Perthes, 1833);

Angelus Silesius und Saint-Martin (Berlin: Veit, 1834);

Karl August Varnhagen von Ense

Leben des Generals Freiherrn von Seydlitz (Berlin: Duncker & Humblot, 1834);

Leben des Generals Hans Karl von Winterfeldt (Berlin: Duncker & Humblot, 1836);

Denkwürdigkeiten und vermischte Schriften, 9 volumes (volumes 1-4, Mannheim: Hoff; volumes 5-9, Leipzig: Brockhaus, 1837-1859); *Denkwürdigkeiten des eignen Lebens* translated by Sir A. Duff Gordon as *Sketches of German Life and Scenes from the War of Liberation* (London: Murray, 1847); *Denkwürdigkeiten de eigen Lebens* republished and edited by Joachim Kühn, 2 volumes (Berlin: Volksverband der Bücherfreunde, 1922-1925);

Leben der Königin von Preußen Sophie Charlotte (Berlin: Duncker & Humblot, 1837);

Leben des Feldmarschalls Grafen von Schwerin (Berlin: Duncker & Humblot, 1841);

Leben des Feldmarschalls Jakob von Keith (Berlin: Duncker & Humblot, 1844);

Hans von Held: Ein preußisches Karakterbild (Leipzig: Weidmann, 1845);

Karl Müller's Leben und kleine Schriften (Berlin: Reimer, 1847);

Schlichter Vortrag an die Deutschen über die Aufgabe des Tages (Berlin: Reimer, 1848);

Leben des Generals Grafen Bülow von Dennewitz (Berlin: Reimer, 1853);

Aus dem Nachlasse: Blätter aus der preußischen Geschichte, edited by Ludmilla Assing, 5 volumes (Leipzig: Brockhaus, 1868);

Aus dem Nachlaß: Biographische Portraits von Varnhagen von Ense: Nebst Briefen von Koreff, Clemens Brentano, Frau von Fouqué, Henri Campan und Scholz, edited by Assing (Leipzig: Brockhaus, 1871; facsimile reprint, Bern: Lang, 1971);

Literaturkritiken; Mit einem Anhang: Aufsätze zum Saint-Simonismus, edited by Klaus F. Gille (Tübingen: Niemeyer, 1977);

Kommentare zum Zeitgeschehen: Publizistik, Briefe, Dokumente 1813-1858, edited by Werner Greiling (Leipzig: Reclam, 1984).

OTHER: *Musenalmanach auf das Jahr 1804 (1805, 1806)*, edited by Varnhagen and Adelbert von Chamisso, 3 volumes (Leipzig: Schmidt, 1804-1806);

I. P. V. Troxler, *Über die Schweiz; von einem schweizerischen Vaterlandsfreunde*, edited by Varnhagen (Stuttgart & Tübingen: Cotta, 1815);

Angelus Silesius (pseudonym for J. Scheffler), *Geistliche Sprüche*, introduction by Varnhagen (Berlin: Dümmler, 1820);

Silesius, *Geistreiche Sinn- und Schluß-Reime aus dem Cherubinischen Wandersmann*, edited by Varnhagen (Hamburg: Langhoff, 1822);

Goethe in den Zeugnissen der Mitlebenden: Beilage zu allen Ausgaben von Goethe's Werken. Erste Sammlung zum 28. August, 1823, edited by Varnhagen (Berlin: Dümmler, 1823);

J. B. Erhard, *Denkwürdigkeiten des Philosophen und Arztes Johann Benjamin Erhard*, edited by Varnhagen (Stuttgart & Tübingen: Cotta, 1830);

Achim von Arnim, *Sämmtliche Werke*, volumes 1-3 & 5-8, edited by Varnhagen (Berlin: Veit, 1830-1840);

Rahel: Ein Buch des Andenkens für ihre Freunde, edited by Varnhagen (Berlin: Duncker & Humblot, 1833; enlarged, 3 volumes, 1834);

K. L. von Knebel, *Literarischer Nachlaß und Briefwechsel*, edited by Varnhagen and Thomas Mund, 3 volumes (Leipzig: Reichenbach, 1835);

W. Neumann, *Schriften: Zwei Teile*, introduction by Varnhagen (Leipzig: Brockhaus, 1835);

Gallerie von Bildnissen aus Rahel's Umgang und Briefwechsel, edited by Varnhagen, 2 volumes (Leipzig: Reichenbach, 1836);

Ueber Rachel's Religiosität: Von einem ihrer älteren Freunde, edited by Varnhagen (Leipzig: Reichenbach, 1836);

A. F. Näke, *Wallfahrt nach Sesenheim*, edited by Varnhagen (Berlin: Duncker & Humblot, 1840);

A. F. Bernhardi and S. Bernhardi, *Reliquien: Erzählungen und Dichtungen*, introduction by Varnhagen, 3 volumes (Altenburg: Pierer, 1847);

J. G. von Reinhold, *Dichterischer Nachlaß*, edited by Varnhagen, 2 volumes (Leipzig: Brockhaus, 1853);

F. von Gentz, *Tagebücher*, introduction and afterword by Varnhagen (Leipzig: Brockhaus, 1861).

Karl August Varnhagen von Ense made a career as critic, journalist, memoirist, biographer, literary arbiter, and promoter of the cause of representative government and social reform. His position is, perhaps, unique in nineteenth-century German literature. His vision was focused upon society, and he saw himself as part of a social transformation that would bring political emancipation to Europe. He cultivated a network of correspondents that included the major figures of his age, and he worked within the limits of this vast epistolary labor to promote his liberal views wherever he could.

Varnhagen was born to middle-class parents on 21 February 1785 in Düsseldorf. His father, Johann Andreas Jakob Varnhagen, was a Rhenish physician, a Catholic, and an avid supporter of the French Revolution. His mother, whose maiden name was Kunz, was Protestant and was native to Alsace, on the French side of the Rhine. While Varnhagen was still very young the family moved to Strasbourg, where his father took up a lectureship at the university. From 1792 to 1794 Varnhagen accompanied his father on a series of journeys in which the elder Varnhagen was apparently attempting to reestablish himself professionally. In late 1794 the family finally settled in Hamburg, where on 5 June 1799 Varnhagen's father died, leaving them impoverished.

It was through the intervention of a family friend that the fifteen-year-old Varnhagen was sent to Berlin to the Pepiniere, a school for military physicians. By 1803 he had left the Pepiniere without completing his training and worked as a tutor in Berlin. When his first job with the Cohen family terminated with the family's bankruptcy, he found another tutoring position with the banking family Hertz in Hamburg. The generous support of the Hertz family enabled him to study at the Johanneum Gymnasium in Hamburg in 1805 where he learned Greek. In 1806 he matriculated at the University of Halle and studied under Friedrich August Wolf. In 1807 he and his friend Wilhelm Neumann published *Erzählungen und Spiele* (Tales and Games).

When Napoleon's victory at Jena and Auerstedt led to the closing of the university, Varnhagen joined many students who moved to Berlin, and it was there that he met his future wife, Rahel Levin. In Berlin he also established a friendship with Adelbert von Chamisso, a young French nobleman who would make his mark as a German poet. In 1809 Rahel persuaded him to resume studying medicine at Tübingen, where he became friends with several members of the Swabian school, including Justinus Kerner and Ludwig Uhland. Varnhagen had been at school only a short while when he abandoned his studies to join the Austrian army. Though he was wounded at the Battle of Deutsch-Wagram on 6 July 1809, he soon managed to win the confidence of his superior officer, Imperial Prince Wilhelm von Bentheim.

Varnhagen's close attachment to Bentheim enabled him to gain access to the highest levels of Austrian society and to observe the customs of the nobility. While visiting Bentheim's castle, he discovered the records of a noble family, the von Ense genannt Varnhagen, to which he claimed kinship. Thereafter he took on the noble predicate "von Ense" and used the title until 1826, when it was challenged in Berlin. As Prince Bentheim's personal adjutant, he accompanied his benefactor to Paris where he even participated in an audience with Napoleon. At this point in his life Varnhagen was characterized by his friends as precocious and irascible. He was known for his boundless energy and organizational skills, as well as for his status-seeking ambitions. By 1812 he left the Austrian service, however, realizing that there was no future there, and he returned to Berlin to be with Rahel.

Watercolor portrait of Varnhagen by Franz Krüger (by permission of the Staatliche Museen zu Berlin)

In 1813 Varnhagen joined the cavalry of Baron Tettenborn, whom he had met while in Paris with Bentheim. It was while riding with Tettenborn's cossacks against the French that he gained the experience he used to write his first successful works—*Hanseatische Anregungen* (Hanseatic Allusions), *Deutsche Ansicht der Vereinigung Sachsens mit Preußen* (German View of the Union of Saxony with Prussia), *Gedichte während des Feldzugs 1813* (Poems during the 1813 Campaign), and *Geschichte der Kriegszüge des Generals von Tettenborn während der Jahre 1813 und 1814* (Stories of the Military Expeditions of General von Tettenborn during the Years 1813 and 1814), presumably eyewitness accounts of the campaigns in which he had participated. These works appeared in 1814 and won Varnhagen a considerable reputation among German patriots, contributing to his appointment to the Prussian delegation under Chancellor Hardenberg to the Congress of Vienna. Within the delegation Varnhagen served as something of a press officer, placing articles and even writing a book that supported Prussian political objectives, such as the annexation of Saxony.

Varnhagen's work with the Prussian delegation gave him sufficient means to marry Rahel Levin. She was fifteen years older than Varnhagen and had enjoyed a period of cultural eminence during the first generation of the Romanticist movement in Berlin. During the last decade of the eighteenth century, Rahel had presided over a salon that numbered among its frequenters a royal prince and his in-law, a Prince de Radziwil.

Varnhagen's appointment after the Congress as Prussian attaché to the grand ducal court at Karlsruhe went beyond his wildest dreams of a career. He would have been satisfied with much less and had indeed spoken earlier of a modest civil service position that would permit him time enough to write. Though initially he had some difficulty at court because of his junior status and because he was married to a Jew, Varnhagen soon distinguished himself. His old commander Baron Tettenborn played an important role in saving the dynasty ruling in Baden, which prevented the grand duchy's annexation by Bavaria or some other power, and Varnhagen was his most important confederate.

At this time Varnhagen seemed to his rivals and contemporaries to be perched on the edge of a brilliant career. He had always impressed his acquaintances and friends as being brilliant, talented, and ambitious, if a bit irritable, imprudent, and acerbic. In fact, his career as a diplomat ended in circumstances that were never made clear publicly but which had an aura of disgrace. The first mistake Varnhagen made was becoming too closely involved with the parliamentary opposition in Karlsruhe. His activities offended the grand duke, who in 1819 requested his removal. The foreign ministry in Berlin was probably not adverse to recalling Varnhagen; his habit of ignoring the chain of command and directing his extensive, and frequently audacious, dispatches directly to Berlin rather than via Stuttgart had antagonized his immediate superior. Worst of all, Varnhagen devoted much energy to promoting the virtues of parliamentary government and praising the conduct of the parliamentarians in Karlsruhe, in direct contradiction to reports from other sources on the increasingly serious state of affairs within the polarized government of Baden.

Varnhagen's recall was not ultimately disastrous, though for the next three years his status remained questionable. After turning down a ministerial post in the United States, Varnhagen was placed in semiretirement and apparently worked only on a contract basis for the foreign minister. The enforced hiatus enabled him to become a man of letters.

In addition to continuing his journalistic work as a political and cultural commentator, Varnhagen began publication of the *Biographische Denkmale* (Biographical Monuments) in 1824. These "monuments" were issued in five volumes, some including more than one biography. The style was uniquely Varnhagen's. His success came from his ability to portray a milieu, and the oblique Biedermeier style displayed just enough of the elegiac to appeal to readers of the time. In these biographies Varnhagen presents indurate characters confronted with great obstacles, and he seems in these works to be most interested in how individuals behave when subjected to extraordinary stress.

The first volume deals with Germans who made their successes outside Germany and who confronted situations in which the odds were very much against them. Yet these characters are all shown in their rugged, even brutal, and occasionally sentimental acts. Varnhagen describes, for instance, Marshall Gebhard Leberecht von Blücher's coarse, blustering courage and undisciplined private life and, in another narrative, the sentimental and murderous behavior of Prince Dessau.

Biography was not the only genre in which Varnhagen excelled. In 1826 he founded, along with Eduard Gans, the Hegelian *Jahrbücher für wissenschaftliche Kritik* (Yearbooks for Scientific Criticism) and served for several years as a contributing editor. In 1833 Varnhagen collected his reviews from the journal in a volume entitled *Zur Geschichtschreibung und Litteratur* (On the Writing of History and Literature).

When his beloved wife, Rahel, died on 7 May 1833 after an extended illness, Varnhagen was convinced that an age had come to an end. Goethe had not been dead long, and conservative tendencies were apparent in both state and society. Varnhagen resolved to provide the dim new present with vivid reminders of the brightest hopes of the past two decades or more in which he himself had even played a peripheral role. The privately sponsored publication of *Rahel: Ein Buch des Andenkens für ihre Freunde* (Rahel: A Memorial for her Friends) appeared in 1833.

Varnhagen distributed the limited edition gratis among his correspondents.

In the book Varnhagen posed in the guise of pious editor, friend, and bereaved husband, but he was actually propagating a new consciousness. Recent research indicates that Rahel had worked with him prior to her death in preparing the volume, which was composed of excerpts from her journals and letters. The success of the book was remarkable, and Varnhagen published an enlarged edition in 1834. Varnhagen carried on his work of re-creating the liberal past with the publication of a similar miscellany entitled *Gallerie von Bildnissen aus Rahel's Umgang und Briefwechsel* (A Gallery of Portraits from Rahel's Circle and Correspondence) in 1836.

While Varnhagen continued his industrious production of biographies, contributing to an insatiable demand during that period for such work, he was also promoting young radicals and encouraging them in their pursuit of social change. Varnhagen's interest in proto-socialist configurations is well documented and can be traced to his and Rahel's embracing of Saint-Simonianism during the late 1820s. News of Parisian developments had been conveyed to the Varnhagens by Heinrich Heine and the American socialist Albert Brisbane.

In 1837 Varnhagen developed a new vehicle for his work in the nine-volume *Denkwürdigkeiten und vermischte Schriften* (Things Worthy of Note and Miscellaneous Writings), which might be regarded as the prototype of the modern digest. Installments appeared at irregular intervals until 1846, and in 1859 Varnhagen's niece, Ludmilla Assing, published a final posthumous number. In the course of the period, Varnhagen provided a full autobiographical account of his life up to his recall from his post in Baden.

Some of the ambivalence that has confounded Varnhagen's critics and admirers is evident during the insurrections in 1848. Though Varnhagen was ardently supportive of the democratic movement, he published a moderate tract arguing for the establishment of a constitutional monarchy. His vacillation between moderate public stances and private radical positions can be understood in the context of his conciliatory personality, his refusal to participate openly in causes that had little actual chance of realization, and his advanced age. Varnhagen was sixty-three in 1848.

Varnhagen's eminence as a cultured figure was due, in part, to the influence of his autobiographical narrative. During his lifetime he was known to many throughout Europe's elite as an observer of high society in action. But though Varnhagen's memoirs seem to be a dazzling record of life at the top, they also provide glimpses of the social conflict, deprivation, inequity, and insecurity lurking behind the glitter, pomp, and power. This ambiguity is reflected also in Varnhagen's self-portrait, which emerges as a mass of evasions, half-truths, and contradictions. He is always on the periphery and plays no authentic historical role in the events he records.

Varnhagen's other biographies hold no surprises but portray notables from the pantheon of Prussian heroes and heroines. At the same time, he injects into his narratives a constant argument for democratic ideas and representative political institutions, for the abandonment of caste and class, and for the establishment of an equitable social order.

Finally, the extraordinary extent of Varnhagen's prodigious correspondence gives an indication of his involvement with other luminaries of his age: Thomas Carlyle, George Henry Lewes, Richard Monckton Milnes, Harriet Grote, and Sarah Austin in England and Albert Brisbane in America. The enormous investment of time and energy that such correspondence entailed was not frivolously expended but, in virtually every case, was aimed at the promotion of social and political reform in Europe and in particular in Germany. Varnhagen died on 10 October 1858 in Berlin.

Letters:

Briefe an eine Freundin. Aus den Jahren 1844 bis 1853, edited by Amely Bölte (Hamburg: Hoffman und Campe, 1860);

Aus dem Nachlaß Varnhagens von Ense: Briefe von Stägemann, Metternich, Heine und Bettina von Arnim, edited by Ludmilla Assing (Leipzig: Brockhaus, 1865);

Aus dem Nachlaß: Blätter aus der preußischen Geschichte, 5 volumes, edited by Assing (Leipzig: Brockhaus, 1868);

Briefwechsel zwischen Varnhagen und Rahel, 6 volumes, edited by Assing (Leipzig: Brockhaus, 1874-1875);

The Letters of Varnhagen von Ense to Richard Monckton Milnes, Anglistische Forschungen 92, edited by Philip Glander (Heidelberg: Carl Winter, 1965);

"George Henry Lewes's Letters to K. A. Varnhagen von Ense," edited by T. H. Pickett, *Mod-*

ern Language Review, 80 (July 1985): 513-532;

The Letters of the American Socialist Albert Brisbane to K. A. Varnhagen von Ense, Anglistische Forschungen 193, edited by Pickett and Francoise de Rocher (Heidelberg: Carl Winter, 1986);

"Letters from J. M. Neverov and N. A. Mel'gunov to K. A. Varnhagen von Ense (1837-1845)," edited by Mark R. McCulloh and Pickett, *Germano-Slavica,* 5, no. 4 (1986): 131-174.

Biographies:

Carl Misch, *Varnhagen von Ense in Beruf und Politik*

(Gotha: Perthes, 1925);

Konrad Feilchenfeldt, *Varnhagen von Ense als Historiker* (Amsterdam: Erasmus, 1970);

Terry H. Pickett, *The Unseasonable Democrat: Karl August Varnhagen von Ense (1785-1858),* Modern German Studies 14 (Bonn: Bouvier Grundmann, 1985).

Papers:

Varnhagen's papers are held by the Varnhagen Collection, Manuscript Department, Jagiellonian University Library, Uniwersytet Jagiellonski, al. Mickiewicza 22, 30-059 Krakow, Poland.

Rahel Varnhagen von Ense

(26 May 1771-7 March 1833)

Doris Starr Guilloton
New York University

BOOKS: *Rahel: Ein Buch des Andenkens für ihre Freunde: Als Handschrift gedruckt,* edited by Karl August Varnhagen von Ense (Berlin: Duncker & Humblot, 1833; enlarged as *Rahel: Ein Buch des Andenkens für ihre Freunde,* edited by Varnhagen, 3 volumes (Berlin: Duncker & Humblot, 1834); translated by Mrs. Vaughan Jennings as *Rahel: Her Life and Letters* (London: King, 1876).

Gesammelte Werke, 10 volumes, edited by Konrad Feilchenfeldt, Uwe Schweikert, and Rahel E. Steiner (Munich: Matthes & Seitz, 1983).

Champion of individualism and humanism during the Romantic period in Germany, Rahel Varnhagen became famous for her literary salon in Berlin during the Napoleonic era. In her day she was considered the German Madame de Staël. She was perceived as a pioneer of women's intellectual emancipation by her contemporaries, including Goethe, Heinrich Heine, Johann Gottlieb Fichte, and Friedrich Daniel Ernst Schleiermacher. Her some ten thousand letters, according to Jean Paul "possibly the greatest treasure of our times," are the most lively documentation of the circles in which she moved. Imbued with social and intellectual concerns, the letters reveal a soaring undaunted spirit that could not be quelled by the dual dilemma of her restricted status as a woman and a Jew. As a woman, albeit financially comfortable, she could not acquire a formal education, a profession, or a public position. Nor could she aspire to the legal emancipation granted in Prussia to select Jewish men, such as her father and two brothers. As a result, like many other women in her position, she eventually converted to Christianity, assumed a Christian name, and married into the Gentile nobility.

Born in Berlin on 26 May 1771, Rahel Levin was the oldest of four children of a well-to-do jewel merchant and financier. She was able to educate herself and presciently choose as her literary models Goethe, Jean Paul, and Sebastian

Rahel Varhagen von Ense (from an engraving in the Upsala University Library)

Roch Nicolas Chamfort. The unique style of her correspondence reflects her peerless independence of thought. The richness of her vocabulary and syntax, which stems in part from the Yiddish culture of her childhood, lends a breath of fresh air to the literary German of her time. Her all-encompassing intellectual curiosity and her enormous energy, unfettered by convention, add a conversational note to the German epistolary prose of her day.

From early on, her writings, marked by political liberalism and extraordinary humanitarianism, reveal her deep involvement with the events of her times. Her adult life spanned the decade after the French Revolution through the Napoleonic Wars and the period of the Restoration. Historic events and the changing political climate had a profound effect on her life. Her first salon disintegrated and her friends were dispersed when the French entered Berlin in 1806. Opened in 1819, her second salon was a welcome forum for the open exchange of opinions in the face of restrictive laws devised to suppress free speech and the free press until 1832. In her last years she developed her own brand of broadened liberalism, blending the utopian socialism of Saint-Simon and the Swedenborgian mysticism of the French philosopher Saint Martin. She firmly believed in the perfectibility of the individual and of society. "So denk' ich mir das ganze Dasein progressiv...," she wrote to her brother Ludwig Robert on 5 February 1816, "darum denk' ich auch wahr und wirklich, daß das Erdenleben nicht eine steife, tote Wiederholung ist, sondern ein schreitendes Ändern und Entwickeln wie alles ... und bin auf Grosses, Neues gefaßt, mit einem Wort, auf Wunder der Erfindung, der Gemütskraft, der Entdeckung, Offenbarung, Entwicklung." (I think that our whole existence is progressive.... I therefore truly think that life on earth is not rigid, dead repetition, but a continuous change and development, as everything ... and I am prepared for great new things, in a word, for miracles of invention, emotional power, discovery, revelation and evolution.)

Rahel Levin's personal relationships documented in her vast correspondence reveal a passionately involved human being. Her earliest attachment was to David Veit, a student of medicine with whom she shared a warm intellectual friendship and an early enthusiasm for Goethe between 1790 and 1793. Of deep emotional consequence was her engagement to the handsome Karl Finckenstein, whom she met in 1795. His aristocratic background and her Jewishness were obstacles which he was neither willing to brave nor honest enough to admit. This inconstant relationship disintegrated in 1800; however, the next year in Paris she met the good-looking Wilhelm Bokelmann. Love at first sight on both sides resulted in a fervent correspondence which ultimately was of little consequence. Her most pas-

sionate and tragic entanglement ensued in Berlin with the Spanish diplomat Don Raphael d'Urquijo, to whom she was engaged from 1802 to 1804. Eventually d'Urquijo's jealousy and his lack of intellectual interests led to conflicts which could not be reconciled. In 1809 Rahel became enraptured by a platonic friendship with a much younger man, Alexander von der Marwitz. She spent two weeks with him in Dresden in 1811, only to find him among the wounded in Prague. He lost his life in battle in 1814. Friedrich von Gentz is the most famous among her suitors. Known as publicist and politician, he was first an advocate of the French Revolution and later an ultramontane conservative and close advisor to Prince von Metternich. Their eloquent love letters bear witness to a lifelong passion never consummated.

On 27 September 1814 Levin married Karl August Varnhagen von Ense, a writer and Prussian diplomat fourteen years her junior. Their relationship, based on common intellectual and social interests and unflinching moral support, was quite happy according to her written testimony. The couple participated in the Vienna Congress of 1815 and, after a brief sojourn in Frankfurt, they moved to Karlsruhe (Baden) in 1816, where his diplomatic post lasted only three years. His democratic-liberal views, shared by his wife, were probably incompatible with the constitutional conservatism of their environment. Happy to return to Berlin, Rahel Varnhagen prevailed upon her husband not to accept a diplomatic mission to the United States. In Berlin, where he retired in 1824, he acted as cohost of her second salon. As the most significant chronicler and biographer of the great figures of his times his contributions to German letters were invaluable.

During the four decades of her adult life spent in Berlin, Rahel Varnhagen lived in several different homes. Even though she had a following everywhere, both in good and bad times, three places were of particular importance: the mansard of her parents' house on Jägerstrasse which harbored her first salon at the turn of the century, and the homes she shared with her husband from 1814 until her death.

When Varnhagen was not in Berlin, she enjoyed traveling in Germany and abroad. Summers were spent at the renowned Bohemian spa Teplitz or in Baden-Baden, which provided stimulating places for meeting with old and new friends. At the turn of the century she stayed a year and a half in Paris in the company of illustrious Frenchmen, as well as Germans like Wilhelm and Karoline von Humboldt. Absorbing and observing French culture, she found it to be different from her own only in certain details. A dozen years later, in 1813, threatened by the events of the war, she felt compelled to leave Berlin again and to establish residency in Prague, where she stayed until the summer of 1814. There, despite her arthritis, she tended the wounded of both sides, organized hospital facilities, and appealed to donors for badly needed money. Prague at that time was also the center for anti-Napoleonic coalitionists and Prussian refugees. It was there that she renewed her acquaintance with old friends like Gentz, Alexander von der Marwitz, and her onetime lover d'Urquijo, as well as artists like Ludwig Tieck, Clemens Brentano, and Carl Maria von Weber. The next five years were spent in Austria and southwest Germany, as she followed her husband's diplomatic postings.

Varnhagen's idealism, evident in her attitude toward men and women of all nations, including the downtrodden and the impoverished, was a clear note in her salons, where she promoted the Humboldtean view that the purpose of man is to develop his greatness to the fullest according to his abilities. She also extended this vision to the issue of women. Comments surfaced in her salon and in her correspondence which called for greater freedom for women in private and public life. She extolled true partnership in a couple without its legalization through marriage, she urged social and economic rights for unwed mothers and their illegitimate children, and she demanded educational equality for women as well as vocational opportunity and access to the public domain. Her nurturing bent lead to philanthropic activities in times of war and during epidemics not only in Prague, but also in Berlin during the outbreak of cholera in 1831. Her concern for human welfare extended to an interest in international pacifism: she dreamed of European women of all classes, if not yet the men, organizing against war.

Varnhagen's most significant involvement in public life was the maintenance of her salons in Berlin, where intellectuals gathered to discuss literature, art, politics, and current events as well as personal matters. Despite financial difficulties in the early years, she managed to conduct her first salon from 1789 until the Napoleonic invasion of 1806. Later, under more favorable circumstances, a second salon flourished from 1819 until shortly before her death in 1833. Famous

scholars and scientists, philosophers and poets were her guests: among others, Alexander and Wilhelm von Humboldt, Fichte, Schleiermacher, August Wilhelm and Friedrich Schlegel, Tieck, Adelbert von Chamisso, Friedrich de la Motte Fouqué, and Heinrich Heine. Aristocrats such as Prince Louis Ferdinand of Prussia and Prince Hermann of Pückler-Muskau, foreign diplomats like Karl Gustav von Brinckmann, sympathizers of the ancien régime, and supporters of *Junges Deutschland* (Young Germany), a literary group of revolutionary liberals, frequented her salons.

Others she encountered outside the salon, like Goethe, Jean Paul, Madame de Staël, Marquis Astolphe de Custine, and Heinrich von Kleist, also felt her magnetism. Goethe, whom Varnhagen had met on several occasions–in Karlsbad in 1795, during mutual visits in Frankfurt in 1815, and in Weimar between 1825 and 1829–was fascinated by her mind. In turn, she held up Goethe as a literary model against the critical views of the young Romantics in her first salon and made him the subject of a cult in her second salon, promoting a progressive image of him.

During her stay in Berlin in 1804 Madame de Staël characterized Varnhagen as a genius, following an engaging conversation of one and a half hours, but no deeper rapprochement took place despite their commonly shared belief in man. Other women of significance–such as Henriette Hertz and Bettina von Arnim, who had their own salons in Berlin, aristocrats such as Countess Karoline of Schlabrendorf and Countess Josephine of Pachta, and commoners and actresses like Auguste Brede, Friederike Unzelmann, and "the German Ninon de l'Enclos" Pauline Wiesel–were among her close friends.

Varnhagen's ideas must be culled essentially from her correspondence and diaries, which are available in dispersed editions. Her primary interest was communication; writing for her was a social obligation. Even though the spontaneous style of her letters creates an impressionistic allure, they are primarily significant for their documentary value as a literary, autobiographical, and social record. During her lifetime selected letters were published in more than a dozen issues of a Berlin newspaper and in several journals in which the work of writers such as Fouqué and Ludwig Börne also appeared. In 1834, the year after her death, her husband edited and published three volumes of her letters and diaries–interspersed with biographical anecdotes and a selection of her aphorisms which he had gleaned

Varnhagen in 1822 (painting by Wilhelm Hensel; courtesy of the German Information Center, New York)

from her conversation—titled *Rahel: Ein Buch des Andenkens für ihre Freunde* (Rahel: A Memorial Book for her Friends). Thomas Carlyle, one of many who appreciated her writings, declared her in his *Critical and Miscellaneous Essays* (1838) "a singular biographic phenomenon of her century; a woman of genius, of true depth and worth . . . a woman equal to the highest thought of her century . . . the highest philosopher, a poet, or artist was not above her, but of a like element and rank with her." Heine, upon reading her letters, experienced a shock of recognition: "Als ich ihren Brief las, war's mir, als wär', ich traumhaft im Schlafe aufgestanden und hätte mich vor den Spiegel gestellt und mit mir selbst gesprochen. . . ." (When I read Rahel's letters, it was as if I had gotten up dreaming and had looked in the mirror and spoken to myself.)

In 1983, one hundred and fifty years after her death, all of her writings were published in a landmark edition comprising one critical volume and nine volumes of primary material, including her diaries and correspondence with over one hundred and twenty correspondents, foremost among them her husband, her brothers, her lovers, and her friends.

Letters:

Gallerie von Bildnissen aus Rahel's Umgang und Briefwechsel, 2 volumes, edited by Karl August Varnhagen von Ense (Leipzig: Reichenbach, 1836);

Aus dem Nachlaß Varnhagen's von Ense: Briefwechsel zwischen Rahel und David Veit, 2 volumes in 1, edited by Ludmilla Assing (Leipzig: Brockhaus, 1861);

Aus dem Nachlaß Varnhagen's von Ense: Briefwechsel zwischen Varnhagen und Rahel, 6 volumes (Leipzig: Brockhaus, 1874-1875);

Aus Rahel's Herzensleben: Briefe und Tagebuchblätter, edited by Assing (Leipzig: Brockhaus, 1877);

Briefwechsel zwischen Karoline von Humboldt, Rahel und Varnhagen, edited by Albert Leitzmann (Weimar: Böhlau, 1896);

Rahel Varnhagen: Ein Frauenleben in Briefen, selected, with an introduction, by Augusta Weldler-Steinberg (Weimar: Kiepenheuer, 1912; second edition, revised, 1917; third edition, revised, 1925);

Rahel und ihre Zeit: Briefe und Zeugnisse, edited by Bertha Badt (Munich: Rentsch, 1912);

Rahel und Alexander von der Marwitz in ihren Briefen: Ein Bild aus der Zeit der Romantiker, edited by Heinrich Meisner (Gotha: Perthes, 1925);

Briefwechsel, 4 volumes, edited by Friedhelm Kemp (Munich: Kösel, 1966-1968; revised edition, Munich: Winkler, 1979-);

Rahel Varnhagen: Jeder Wunsch wird Frivolität genannt, edited by Marlis Gerhardt (Darmstadt & Neuwied: Luchterhand, 1983).

Biographies:

Mrs. Vaughan Jennings, *Rahel: Her Life and Letters* (London: King, 1876);

Otto Berdrow, *Rahel Varnhagen: Ein Lebens- und Zeitbild* (Stuttgart: Greiner & Pfeiffer, 1900);

Ellen Key, *Rahel: Eine biographische Skizze,* translated from the Swedish by M. Franzos (Leipzig, 1907); translated by Arthur G. Chater as *Rahel Varnhagen: A Portrait* (New York & London: Putnams, 1913);

Hannah Arendt, *Rahel Varnhagen: The Life of a Jewess,* translated by Richard and Clara Winston (London: Leo Baeck Institute, 1957); published in German as *Rahel Varnhagen: Lebensgeschichte einer deutschen Jüdin aus der Romantik* (Munich: Piper, 1959); English version revised as *Rahel Varnhagen: The Life of a Jewish Woman* (New York: Harcourt Brace Jovanovich, 1974).

References:

Alan Bird, "Rahel Varnhagen von Ense and some English Assessments of her Character," *German Life and Letters,* 26 (April 1973): 183-192;

Christa Burger, "Arbeit und Ich: Zu Rahel Varnhagens Schreibprojekt," *Merkur,* 37 (January 1983): 116-120;

Ingeborg Drewitz, "Dialog als Schicksal: Zu den Briefen der Rahel Varnhagen," in her *Zeitverdichtung: Essays, Kritiken, Portraits* (Vienna, Munich & Zurich: Europa Verlag, 1980), pp. 79-86;

Drewitz, "Rahel," in her *Berliner Salons: Gesellschaft und Literatur zwischen Aufklärung und Industriezeitalter* (Berlin: Haude & Spener, 1965), pp. 48-72;

Konrad Feilchenfeldt, "Die Anfänge des Kults um Rahel Varnhagen und seine Kritiker" in *Juden im Vormärz und in der Revolution von 1848* (Stuttgart & Bonn: Burg, 1983), pp. 214-232;

Lore Feist, *Rahel Varnhagen: Zwischen Romantik und Jungem Deutschland* (Eberfeld: Hofbauer, 1927);

Emma Graf, *Rahel Varnhagen und die Romantik* (Berlin: Felber, 1903);

Doris Starr Guilloton, "Rahel Varnhagen und die Frauenfrage in der deutschen Romantik: Eine Untersuchung ihrer Briefe und Tagebuchnotizen," *Monatshefte,* 69 (Winter 1977): 391-403;

Guilloton, "Toward a New Freedom: Rahel Varnhagen and the German Woman Writers before 1848," in *Woman as Mediatrix: Essays on Nineteenth-Century European Woman Writers,* edited by Avriel H. Goldberger (New York, Westport, & London: Greenwood Press, 1987), pp. 133-143;

Kay Goodman, "The Impact of Rahel Varnhagen on Women in the Nineteenth Century," *Amsterdamer Beiträge zur Neueren Germanistik,* 10 (1980): 125-153;

Goodman, "Poesis and Praxis in Rahel Varnhagen's Letters," *New German Critique,* no. 27 (Fall 1982): 123-139;

Käte Hamburger, "Rahel und Goethe," in *Rahel Varnhagen: Gesammelte Werke,* edited by Konrad Feilchenfeldt, Uwe Schweikert, and Rahel E. Steiner (Munich: Matthes & Seitz, 1983), pp. 179-204;

Deborah Hertz, "Inside Assimilation: Rebecca Friedländer's Rahel Varnhagen," in *German Women in the Eighteenth and Nineteenth Centuries: A Social and Literary History,* edited by Ruth-Ellen B. Joeres and Mary Jo Maynes (Bloomington: Indiana University Press, 1986), pp. 271-288;

Hertz, "The Varnhagen Collection in Krakow," *American Archivist,* 44 (Summer 1981): 223-228;

Ursula Isselstein, "Una romantica donna tedesca (Rahel Levin)," *L'Orsaminore,* 9 (1982): 13-22;

Clara Malraux, *Rahel, ma grande soeur: Un Salon littéraire à Berlin au temps du romantisme* (Paris: Ramsay, 1980);

Percy Matenko, "Ludwig Tieck and Rahel Varnhagen: A Re-Examination," *Publications of the Leo Baeck Institute. Year Book 20* (New York: 1975), pp. 225-246;

C[laire] May, *Rahel Varnhagen: Ein Berliner Frauenleben im 19. Jahrhundert* (Berlin: Das Neue Berlin, 1951);

Margarita Pazi, "Rahel Varnhagen im Ganzen," *Neue Deutsche Hefte,* 32 (1985): 562-566;

Herbert Scurla, *Begegnungen mit Rahel: Der Salon der Rahel Levin* (Berlin: Verlag der Nation, 1962);

Scurla, *Rahel Varnhagen: Die große Frauengestalt der deutschen Romantik* (Düsseldorf: Claassen, 1978);

Jean-Edouard Spenlé, *Rahel: Mme Varnhagen von Ense. Histoire d'un Salon Romantique en Allemagne* (Paris: Hachette, 1910);

Hilde Spiel, "Rahel Varnhagen: Tragic Muse of the Romantics," in *Festschrift, Acta Neophilologica* (Ljubljana, 1980), pp. 13-21;

Liliane Weissberg, "Writing on the Wall: Letters of Rahel Varnhagen," *New German Critique,* 36 (Fall 1985): 157-173.

Papers:

Most of Varnhagen's manuscripts are in the Varnhagen Archive at the Jagiellonian Library of Krakow, where its accessibility is under some restriction.

Johann Heinrich Voß

(20 February 1751-29 March 1826)

Gerda Jordan
University of South Carolina

BOOKS: *Vermischte Gedichte und prosaische Aufsätze*
(Frankfurt am Main & Leipzig: auf Kosten
der Verlagscasse, 1784);

Gedichte, 2 volumes (volume 1, Hamburg: Hoffmann; volume 2, Königsberg: Nicolovius,
1785-1795);

*Über des Virgilischen Landgedichts Ton und Ausle-
gung* (Altona: Hammerich, 1791);

Mythologische Briefe, 2 volumes (Königsberg: Nicolovius, 1794); revised and enlarged as *Mythologische Briefe,* 5 volumes (volumes 1-3, Stuttgart: Metzler; volumes 4-5, Leipzig: Lehn-
hold, 1827-1834);

Luise: Ein laendliches Gedicht in drei Idyllen (Königsberg: Nicolovius, 1795); translated by James
Cochrane as *Louisa* (Edinburgh: Johnstone,
1852);

Idyllen (Königsberg: Nicolovius, 1801);

Sämmtliche Gedichte, 7 volumes (Königsberg: Nicolovius, 1802);

*Zeitmessung der deutschen Sprache: Beilage zu den
Oden und Elegien* (Königsberg: Nicolovius,
1802);

Ueber Gleims Briefsammlung und letzten Willen (Heidelberg: Mohr & Zimmer, 1807);

Ueber Götz und Ramler: Kritische Briefe (Mannheim:
Schwan & Götz, 1809);

Abriß meines Lebens (Rudolstadt: Fröber, 1818);

*Bestätigung der Stolbergischen Umtriebe, nebst einem
Anhang über persönliche Verhältnisse* (Stuttgart:
Metzler, 1820);

*Voß gegen Perthes: Abweisung einer mystischen Injurien-
klage & Zweite Abweisung einer mystischen Inju-
rienklage,* 2 volumes (Stuttgart: Metzler,
1822);

Antisymbolik, 2 volumes (Stuttgart: Metzler,
1824-1826);

Sämmtliche Gedichte: Auswahl der letzten Hand, 4 volumes (Königsberg: Universitäts-buchhand-
lung/Leipzig: Müller, 1825);

Kritische Blätter nebst geografischen Abhandlungen,
2 volumes (Stuttgart: Metzler, 1828);

Sämmtliche poetische Werke, edited by Abraham Voß
(Leipzig: Müller, 1835);

*Johann Heinrich Voß (lithograph by W. Unger, 1826, after a
painting by Wilhelm Tischbein)*

*Anmerkungen und Randglossen zu Griechen und Rö-
mern,* edited by Abraham Voß (Leipzig: Müller, 1838);

Oden und Lieder (Düsseldorf: Voß, 1851);

Poetische Werke, 2 volumes (Berlin: Hempel,
1867-1869).

OTHER: J. L. d'Alembert, *Versuch über den Um-
gang der Gelehrten und Großen, über den
Ruhm, die Mäcenen und die Belohnungen der
Wissenschaften,* translated by Voß (Leipzig:
Weygand, 1775);

Musenalmanach MDCCLXXV: Poetische Blumenlese auf das Jahr 1775, edited by Voß (Göttingen, Gotha: Dieterich, 1775);

Thomas Blackwell, *Untersuchung über Homers Leben und Schriften,* translated by Voß (Leipzig: Weygand, 1776);

A. Galland, *Die tausend und eine Nacht, arabische Erzählungen,* translated by Voß, 6 volumes (Bremen: Cramer, 1781-1785);

Homers Odüßee übersetzt, translated by Voß (Hamburg: Privately printed, 1781);

P. W. Hensler, *Gedichte,* edited by Voß and Ph. G. Hensler (Altona: Eckard, 1782);

L. H. Ch. Hölty, *Gedichte,* edited by Voß and F. L. Graf zu Stolberg (Hamburg: Bohn, 1783);

Virgil, *Landbau,* translated by Voß (Eutin & Hamburg: Bohn, 1789);

Homer, *Werke,* translated by Voß, 4 volumes (Altona: Hammerich, 1793);

Virgil, *Vierte Ekloge,* translated by Voß (Altona: Hammerich, 1795);

Virgil, *Ländliche Gedichte,* translated by Voß, 4 volumes (Altona: Hammerich, 1797-1800);

Ovid, *Verwandlungen nach Publius Ovidius Naso,* translated by Voß, 2 volumes (Berlin: Vieweg, 1798);

Virgil, *Werke,* translated by Voß, 3 volumes (Brunswick: Vieweg, 1799);

Taschenbuch für 1801, edited by Voß, F. Gentz and Jean Paul (Brunswick: Vieweg, 1801);

Hesiod, *Hesiods Werke und Orfeus der Argonaut,* translated by Voß (Heidelberg: Mohr & Zimmer, 1806);

Horace, *Werke,* translated by Voß, 2 volumes (Heidelberg: Mohr & Zimmer, 1806);

William Shakespeare, *Othello und König Lear,* translated by Voß (Jena: Frommann, 1806);

Theocritos, Bion und Moschos, translated by Voß (Tübingen: Cotta, 1808);

Albius Tibullus und Lygdamus, translated by Voß (Tübingen: Cotta, 1810);

Shakespeare, *Schauspiele,* translated with notes by Voß, Abraham Voß, and Heinrich Voß, 9 volumes (Stuttgart: Metzler, 1818-1829);

Aristophanes, *Werke,* translated by Voß, 3 volumes (Brunswick: Vieweg, 1821);

Des Aratos Sternerscheinungen und Wetterzeichen, translated by Voß (Heidelberg: Winter, 1824);

Hymne an Demeter, translated by Voß (Heidelberg: Winter, 1826);

Aeschylus, *Werke,* translated by Heinrich Voß; completed by Voß (Heidelberg: Winter, 1826);

Sextus Propertius, *Werke,* translated by Voß (Brunswick: Vieweg, 1830).

Johann Heinrich Voß is an indispensable link in the chain of those who brought about a regeneration of German intellectual life in the last quarter of the eighteenth century. He was not a first-rate poet, but his poetic talent combined with his vast knowledge of philology made him a first-rate translator of the literature of antiquity. He established the model for other translators to follow, made Homer a "German" poet, and ushered in a new era of appreciation of Greek Classicism. He remained in constant touch with the poetic life of the Germanies, even when he lived in remote places, because of his twenty-five years as editor of the *Göttinger Musenalmanach.* Toward the end of his life he became something of an anachronism because he retained the convictions of his youth almost unchanged; he was firmly rooted in the Enlightenment and the humanism of antiquity and scorned any notions of fatherland and Romanticism. His last years were spent in tireless defense of his ideas, without any appreciation for the ferment of the age.

Voß's family tree can be traced back only to his paternal grandfather, a freed serf, whose son Johann Heinrich Voß was the first in the family to escape the monotony of Mecklenburg farm life, to acquire some school learning, and to travel to Lübeck and Hamburg. His first marriage ended with the death of his wife. He married her best friend, Catharine Dorothee Carstens, after the birth of their son, Johann Heinrich, on 20 February 1751 in Sommersdorf. The elder Voß bought a house and an inn at Penzlin, a small town about twelve miles southwest of Neubrandenburg. The local intelligentsia frequented the inn, and the young Johann Heinrich Voß was exposed early to conversations about the ideas of rationalism which were then beginning to circulate in Penzlin. There is no indication that the boy received particular religious instructions other than those of a pious Protestant home.

Voß excelled in grade school, especially in memorization and rhythmics; he learned to play the piano well enough to find solace with this instrument in later years. From 1759 to 1765 he attended the city school of Penzlin where he was instructed in Latin, and then the Lateinschule (high school) in Neubrandenburg from 1766 to 1769 at a great cost to his family, plunged into poverty by the Seven Years War. Although Mecklenburg had not been directly involved in this war, it had suffered from the encroachments of Frederick II and the effects of his worthless money. Before Voß left for Neubrandenburg, all savings, including his own earnings from calligraphy work, were scraped together, free meals from volunteer families were secured, and young Voß prepared himself in Greek and Hebraic studies. The school in Neubrandenburg emphasized Latin; less attention was paid to logic, geography, history, very little to mathematics, so that Voß taught himself in areas that the institution slighted. He founded a secret society with fellow students for the study and reading of German and Greek literature. His poetic heroes were recent German writers, Karl Wilhelm Ramler (whose odes he copied and memorized), Friedrich von Hagedorn, Albrecht von Haller, Johann Peter Uz, and Salomon Geßner. They inspired him to try his hand at composing odes and songs, even idylls in hexameter. He later burned these early attempts.

At the end of his Lateinschule studies the way to the university was closed to him because of his family's poverty, but it was too late for him to turn back; he had been in too much contact with scholarship to be satisfied with a trade. In 1769 one of his teachers succeeded in recommending him for the position of tutor to three children of a noble family in Ankershagen, about a mile from Penzlin, quite an honor for an eighteen-year-old without a university education. He hoped to save enough money to pave his way to the university at Halle and to support his parents, but he was paid very little and was treated like a servant; the humiliations he had to endure served to reinforce his earlier antagonism toward the nobility for as long as he lived.

Near Ankershagen he found his first friendship for life in the pastor of Groß-Vielen, Ernst Theodor Brückner (1746-1805), who introduced the young man to Shakespeare and rationalism and encouraged him to write poetry. Seven poems date from this period. At Easter 1771 an opportunity for financial help toward university studies appeared to open up, on the strength of which he quit his detested position; his successor arrived, but no money came. Just then he happened to read the *Göttinger Musenalmanach* of 1771, edited by Heinrich Christian Boie, compared his own poetry with the Anacreontic poems published therein, and decided to send three poems to Boie. Boie detected genius–the magic concept of the day–in Voß's work, accepted one poem, "Die Rückkehr" (The Return),

for publication in the *Musenalmanach* of 1772, and lent him a helping hand to come to Göttingen.

Voß's years in Göttingen shaped the rest of his life: he abandoned the study of theology–then considered the surest means to secure a position–in favor of philological studies, he pursued his poetry, he became a member of the group of poets known as the Dichterbund (Poet's League) or Göttinger Hain (Göttingen Grove), and he won the love of Boie's sister Ernestine, a source of blessing for his entire life. Philology, the study of antiquity, languages, and literature, was not yet an autonomous field, but Voß pursued it nevertheless. His teacher was Christian Gottlob Heyne with whom he read the *Iliad,* Pindar, Horace, and Virgil. Voß was to deny later, in *Mythologische Briefe* (Mythological Letters, 1794), that Heyne had had any influence on him, but in Göttingen he appreciated Heyne's recognition of philology as a branch of knowledge and his reestablishment of Greek studies in Germany although his innate sense as a budding poet made him realize that Heyne had "studied" tastes, not natural ones, and little feel for the German language.

Homer became the nucleus of Voß's interests, and he began the habit of forming into German verse what he was reading in order to deepen his understanding. The first translations he wrote down, however, were of Hesiod, Horace, and Pindar; his first Homeric lines in German appeared in his 1776 translation of Thomas Blackwell's *Enquiry Into the Life and Writings of Homer,* in which he rendered the quotations in German hexameters. For the purpose of enhancing his own poetry he began an intensive study of the German language. He was in a sense bilingual–Low German was spoken at home–and quite naturally interested in comparisons. Luther's German directed him toward the archaic, the strong, the expressive. He wanted to enrich modern German, which he considered insipid, with older usage, and was encouraged in this endeavor by the recent unearthing of medieval poetry; he even engaged Brückner's help to collect Low German items for him to use along with selected words from other dialects. Here began his dream of a general dictionary of German to contain all words, obsolete and modern, with derivations and earliest sources, comparison with their cognates in other languages, a dream he was to abandon only late in life when he realized the infinity and futility of the task at a time when no sci-

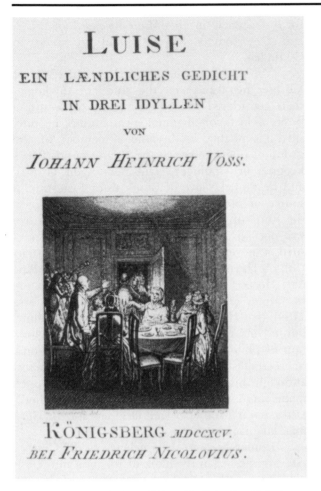

LUISE

EIN LÆNDLICHES GEDICHT

IN DREI IDYLLEN

VON

IOHANN HEINRICH VOSS.

KÖNIGSBERG MDCCXCV.

BEI FRIEDRICH NICOLOVIUS.

Title page of the first edition of Voß's Luise *(1795)*

ence of linguistics existed.

When Voß first came to Göttinge he found a circle of student-poets grouped around Boie and the *Musenalmanach;* he joined. The *Almanach* was to be a forum for every poet in Germany; every voice–including Wieland, Friedrich Gottlob Klopstock, Gleim, Herder, and aspiring poets– should be heard. Contributing members of Boie's group were Ludwig Christian Hölty, Johann Martin Miller, and Johann Friedrich Hahn. Gottfried August Bürger had just left the university. Noncontributing members were J. T. L. Wehrs, C. H. Esmarch, and G. D. Miller, a cousin of Johann Martin Miller. Voß felt closely akin to Hahn because of Hahn's antagonism toward the French and his patriotic republicanism. The formation of the Dichterbund, or Göttinger Hain, was not planned. On 12 September 1772 six of the friends (Voß, Hölty, the two Millers, Hahn, and Wehrs) went on an outing to the village Weende, walked to an oak grove, and under an oak tree swore eternal friendship on the spur of the mo-

ment. Election made Voß the Elder, or leader, which he remained to the end of his Göttingen days in 1774, in effect the end of the Bund. They referred to their union as Göttinger Hain to place the grove at the center of German poetry in analogy with and contrast to the Greek Mount Parnassus. They met weekly, took in new members–Boie, the counts Christian and Friedrich Leopold von Stolberg–and made Klopstock their ideal. A veritable Klopstock cult developed. On his birthday, 2 July 1773, Wieland was banned, the French spirit was banned, freedom above all was proclaimed, and the pen was declared a weapon.

Voß had corresponded with Boie's sister Ernestine in Flensburg for some time, and in April 1774 he traveled, not without stopping in Hamburg to see Klopstock, to meet her. She became his muse, but there were insurmountable obstacles to their marriage: he had neither position nor money. Then Boie handed him the editorship of the *Musenalmanach,* and Voß settled in the Hamburg suburb Wandsbeck, near the writer Matthias Claudius, whose friendship he won. He visited the theater in Hamburg, met Gotthold Ephraim Lessing, visited Klopstock and worked: on Socrates, Pindar, Sophocles, and on his German *Odyssey* which he took with him everywhere, on lonely walks, to the kitchen table of his bride-to-be, and on his wedding trip to Mecklenburg in 1777. Voß and his new wife lived modestly in Wandsbeck until he was offered the position of director of the *Lateinschule* in Otterndorf near Stade where they lived a "Froschleben" (frog's life) in the damp climate from 1778 to 1782. Two sons were added to the one born in Wandsbeck, and by 1785 they had five sons. In September 1781 F. L. von Stolberg was able to secure a position as school director in Eutin for his Dichterbund brother. In 1782 began the main station of Voß's life, and his happiest.

As school director in Eutin he fought against the dependence of the school on the church, against the supremacy of Latin in the curriculum, and for the study of German and Greek. He founded the school library. His teaching extended beyond the classroom to groups gathering around him, often at his house. He continued to edit the *Musenalmanach* until 1800; he continued to translate Horace–fifty-eight odes by 1798; he completed the translations of Virgil and of parts of Ovid's *Metamorphoses,* and began the commentaries. As his own poetic powers were on the wane, his interest in metric perfection increased.

Voß had no interest in politics until the French Revolution; he had no firm footing anywhere, not even in Meckleburg, least of all in Prussia. The Revolution brought all his antinobility sentiments to the surface. And when F. L. von Stolberg, who had been in favor of the Revolution to begin with but changed after the abolition of feudal privileges, converted to Catholicism–a betrayal, in Voß's mind–Eutin lost its attractiveness as well. In 1802 he asked for and was granted dismissal with a pension and set out to find a place where he could live only for his studies. He chose Jena as a stopover and stayed for three years, longer than he intended. There he made contact with Goethe and Schiller. Goethe and Voß had not much more in common than their interest in metrics–Voß was too much a one-sided pedant for Goethe–but Goethe engaged Voß's services to write review essays for his new *Literaturzeitung*. The work for Goethe marked the first time Voß used this genre, which he was to exploit later as a vehicle for his various controversies. Goethe wanted to keep Voß in Jena, and as a favor to him wrote a diplomatic review of Voß's poems in 1804. Voß, however, felt tied down, obligated, without the freedom he had sought. He traveled through southern Germany in search of a permanent home, but when he returned, Goethe tried even harder to chain him to Jena with the promise of a new house and other benefits. But then Heidelberg invited Voß to work there, to lend prestige to the then-not-so-famous university.

The years in Heidelberg, 1805 to 1826, brought Voß fulfillment of his dreams: unhampered leisure for continued translations, no financial worries, good health, a home and garden. Voß spent much time during these years fighting for his eighteenth-century ideals against the new currents as if he had to protect the old against the new. He engaged in controversies which he conducted without judgment or fairness; he knew only either-or, black or white.

Voß detested Romanticism for its lack of rules and principles, for its rapture and ecstasy. It seemed like an attack on everything he believed in. He hated the moral as well as the poetic license, the doctrine that genius is always right when he could detect no real genius in the group. He saw his beloved old poets and the Enlightenment misjudged, the Nibelungs set above Homer, the Minnelied above Pindar and Horace.

He could not understand Romanticism as a movement but saw it as a system and method of the aristocracy designed to downgrade and destroy the achievements of the eighteenth century. Most disturbing were Catholic tendencies of the Romantics. Voß had considered the wars of liberation to be only an interlude after which the Enlightenment would reign again; when this did not come to pass he pinpointed the cause as a conspiracy concocted in Rome.

Voß waged his war against Romanticism and Catholicism by means of reviews, against the former in his *Antisymbolik* (1824-1826), a two-volume response to Friedrich Creuzer's *Symbolik und Mythologie der alten Völker* (Symbolism and Mythology of Ancient Peoples, 1810-1812); against Catholicism in two works directed against his former friend F. L. von Stolberg, one on Stolberg's "Über den Zeitgeist" (On the Spirit of the Age) and *Die Geschichte der Religion Jesu Christi* (The History of the Religion of Jesus Christ) in "Wie ward F. L. Stolberg ein Unfreier?" (How did F. L. Stolberg Become a Slave?) and the other titled "Bestätigung der Stolbergschen Umtriebe" (Confirmation of Stolberg's Intrigues), both published in 1818. Voß accused Creuzer, the philologist in Heidelberg since 1804, of inexact methodology. Voß's attacks on Stolberg were of a personal nature without regard for the friendship and kindness Stolberg had shown him in the past. In his endeavor to reestablish the ideals of the Enlightenment Voß had no sensitivity toward anyone who did not agree with him.

Voß's earliest extant poetry dates from his days at Ankershagen. He continued to write odes, songs, poems, and idylls in Göttingen, Wandsbeck, Otterndorf, and Eutin. Most of his poems from 1782 to 1802 were written for the *Musenalmanach*. He published his first volume of poetry in 1785, his second in 1795. In the latter Schiller could not find one poem with any significance, but the volume did not include Voß's masterpiece, the idyll *Luise* (1795)(. The poet Voß is best in the idyll, not continuing the ideal world of Salomon Geßner's idylls but writing in the tradition of the idylls of Theocritus. Theocritus had described the lives of shepherds which, Voß realized, were not an integral part of the idyll as a genre but of Sicilian reality: simple folk against the background of their natural environment. This concept transferred to the northern German landscape dictated that Voß depict German country folk in their daily activities. Voß hoped to enhance and elevate everyday life of the working people with poems such as "Die Bleicherin" (The Bleacher Woman) and the Low German "De Winterawend" (Winter Evening), but then he abandoned the description of country labor in favor of that of bourgeois country life, the manse, the schoolhouse, to which he could contribute his own memories. The idyll does not demand much clever poetic invention, but it does require painstaking description. Homer's influence is undeniable, not only in the form–hexameter– but also in method: the stopping of action for the sake of careful delineation. Significant idylls, and those in which Voß plants a message, include "Die Leibeigenschaft" (Serfdom), a bitter complaint about the curse of serfdom; "Der Ährenkranz" (The Wreath of Grain), an expression of gratitude by a young couple for having received freedom; and "Die Erleichterten" (The Relieved Ones) showing a lord's reflections on how to ease the burdens of his subjects and finally his announcement of freedom. In "Der Bettler" (The Beggar), an old man goes begging not for himself but for a poverty-stricken pastor who had been dismissed for preaching the true word of God instead of its human distortions. "Das Ständchen" (The Serenade) ridicules the nobility and the nobleman's lust for young country girls; "Der Abendschmaus" (The Evening Meal) shows a simple peasant scorning the sumptuous meal he has taken with his lord, and his contempt for those who enjoyed it. One of the most successful idylls is the brief "Der siebzigste Geburtstag" (The Seventieth Birthday), a description of the joyful preparation for the arrival of an old couple's son and his new bride for a birthday celebration. Voß's longest idyll is *Luise*, portions of which appeared in the *Musenalmanach* in 1783 and 1784. Part 1, "Das Fest im Walde" (The Party in the Forest), takes place on Luise's eighteenth birthday and describes the walk of Luise and her beloved Walter through the forest to a picnic spot, while the parents arrive by boat. Luise's father, pastor of Grünau, reminisces and is given an opportunity to express Voß's religious tolerance. The second part, "Der Besuch" (The Visitor), relates the arrival at the manse of the bridegroom and other events of the morning and afternoon before the wedding day. On the evening of the same day in part 3, "Der Brautabend" (Wedding Eve), Luise tries on her bridal gown her fiancé shows her off to the family and guests, and the pastor decides to marry the couple on the spot. The story line is thin; much of the idyll is taken up by descriptions of nature, people, work, food, the qualities

of country folk and their activities. Voß's characters are educated, financially secure people with virtues and, occasionally, senses of humor. However cumbersome with didacticisms the idyll is, Goethe was fond of it and chose it for readings to his friends. He found in it an impulse for his epic poem *Hermann und Dorothea* (1797).

Voß's other poetry spans a wide variety of topics, from the benefits the potato brought to mankind to the evils of feudalism. August Wilhelm Schlegel reviewed Voß's poetry published in the *Musenalmanach* in 1796 and 1797, and his pronouncements on those poems can be applied to the others as well. Schlegel divides the poems into two main categories: those of philosophical or religious contemplation, and those of social intercourse. In the former he finds cosmopolitanism, cordiality, and tender masculinity but no charm, levity, or wit, and too often wooden expression. The latter, poems of nature, home, and friends, Schlegel finds a bit slanted toward the materialistic; much eating and drinking is detailed: "It is good that the household is taken care of, but that is not really the task of the muses."

Voß's translations began a new era of insight into Greek and Roman antiquity because he understood and interpreted Homer and Virgil "als wären sie nur in Raum von uns entfernte Zeitgenossen" (as if they were our contemporaries removed from us only in space). After earning praise for the translation he did at Göttingen of poems by Horace and Pindar, he proceeded to the *Odyssey*. His first version appeared in 1781. It was not the first translation into German of the *Odyssey*, but it was the first popular one. Unhampered by theory and by the exigencies of Voß's later stricter method, this version made evident his gifts for combining what poetic talent he had with his vast philological knowledge. He had sensitivity not only for the meaning of the words but also for tone and nuance. The number of lines agrees with the original. He enriched the German vocabulary with archaic and dialectic forms, neologisms, and composita in order to make Homer live for the Germans. The revision of the *Odyssey*, undertaken after he had schooled himself with Virgil's *Georgics* and published with his translation of the *Iliad* in 1793, reveals several peculiarities for the sake of meter; the flowing language, harmony, simplicity, and spontaneity have given way to pedantic exactness, stiffness, and complexity. The translator had become a virtuoso. In *Zeitmessung der deutschen Sprache* (Metrics in German, 1802) he explains the principles applied to his translations as well as his prosodic theory.

Translation of Virgil occupied Voß from 1789 to 1799, and he also translated Ovid in 1789; Horace and Hesiod in 1806; Theocritus, Bion, and Moschus in 1808; Tibullus in 1810; Propertius in 1820; and Aristophanes in 1821. That he undertook to translate Aristophanes shows that he had energy in his old age, but being the pedant he was, he could not render the poet's tone and color, his quick change from high seriousness to the lowest joke. Voß's sons Heinrich and Abraham persuaded him to translate Shakespeare; in all he did ten volumes (1806, 1818-1829). This was not a fortunate undertaking because there was, after Schlegel, no need, and drama was alien to Voß.

Translation was only part of Voß's ambition to make antiquity live for the Germans. He wrote voluminous commetaries consisting of interpretations of individual passages, remarks on geographical problems, customs, and institutions, and questions on mythological and political properties. Voß's investigations were so thorough that he, for example, sought the advice of a Captain Müller in Stade about the construction of a raft such as Odysseus'. Much of his quarrel with Heyne and Creuzer was that they were not thorough and arrived at conclusions without proof. In *Antisymbolik* Voß insists that, if one wants to establish the origin and significance of a given custom, for example, one must ask under what circumstances and by whom this custom was first maintained, what the concepts of the world and the divine were at the time, and whether the name of the custom had retained its meaning as a lexical item over the centuries. It is this kind of inquiry that distinguishes Voß's research from that of his adversaries; his was a line of research according to strict critical principles, and for this he will be remembered.

On 26 February 1826 Voß suffered a sudden fainting spell, and after a brief period of recovery experienced a second. In the midst of talking about what the Greeks imagined happened to the soul after death, he died in Heidelberg, on 29 March 1826 shortly before 6:00 P.M.

Letters:
Briefe von Johann Heinrich Voß nebst erläuternden Beilagen, edited by Heinrich Voß, 3 volumes (Halberstadt: Bruggemann, 1829-1832).

Biographies:
Wilhelm Herbst, *Johann Heinrich Voß*, 3 volumes (Leipzig: Teubner, 1876; republished, Bern: Lang, 1970);

Gerhard Kamin, *Johann Heinrich Voß: Ein Leben im Dienst des Menschlichen. Ein Beitrag zur Kulturgeschichte Eutins* (Eutin: Struve, 1957).

References:
Lotte Engel-Lanz, "Voßens 'Luise': Interpretation," Ph.D. dissertation, Zurich University, 1959;

Hartmut Fröschle, "Johann Heinrich Voß als Kritiker der Romantik," *Carleton German Papers*, 8 (1980): 1-23;

Gerhard Hämmerling, *Die Idyllen von Geßner bis Voß: Theorie, Kritik, und allgemeine geschichtliche Bedeutung* (Frankfurt am Main & Bern: Lang, 1981);

Günther Häntzschel, "Johann Heinrich Voß' 'Der siebzigste Geburtstag': Biedermeierliche Enge oder kritischer Impetus?," in his *Gedichte und Interpretationen* (Stuttgart: Reclam, 1982);

Häntzschel, *Johann Heinrich Voß: Seine Homerübersetzung als sprachschöpferische Leistung* (Munich: Beck, 1977);

Gerhard Hay, *Die Beiträger des Voß'schen Musenalmanachs* (Hildesheim & New York: Georg Olms Verlag, 1975);

A. Kelletat, ed., *Der Göttinger Hain* (Stuttgart: Reclam, 1967);

Ernst Metelmann, "E. Th. J. Brückner und der Göttinger Dichterbund," *Euphorion*, 33 (1932): 341-420;

York-Gothart Mix, "Systematische Auswahl arbeitsorientierter Lektüre: Die Privatbibliothek des Dichters und Philologen Johann Heinrich Voß," *Wolfenbütteler Notizen zur Buchgeschichte*, 6 (1981): 308-320;

Karl Preissendanz, "Voßiana," *Euphorion*, 20 (1913): 402-404;

Karl Reinhardt, "Homer und die Telemachie: Zu einer Ausgabe der Voßischen Übersetzung," *Tradition und Geist* (1960): 37-46;

Helmut Jürgen Eduard Schneider, "Bürgerliche Idylle: Studien zu einer literarischen Gattung des 18. Jahrhunderts am Beispiel von Johann Heinrich Voß," Ph.D. dissertation, Bonn University, 1975;

A. Schröter, *Geschichte der deutschen Homerübersetzung* (Jena, 1882);

A. Schulze, "J. H. Voß' Auseinandersetzung mit F. L. Stolberg und Vertretern der jüngeren

Romantik," Ph.D. dissertation, University of Potsdam, 1956;

Manfred Stosch, "Johann Heinrich Voß und seine Bibliothek," *Archiv für Geschichte des Buchwesens*, 21 (1980): 719-748.

Wilhelm Heinrich Wackenroder
(13 July 1773-13 February 1798)

Wolfgang Nehring
University of California, Los Angeles

BOOKS: *Herzensergießungen eines kunstliebenden Klosterbruders*, anonymous, by Wackenroder and Ludwig Tieck (Berlin: Unger, 1796 [dated 1797]); Wackenroder's contributions translated by Mary Hurst Schubert as "Confessions from the Heart of an Art-Loving Friar," in *Confessions and Fantasies* (University Park & London: Pennsylvania State University Press, 1971), pp. 79-160;

Phantasien über die Kunst, für Freunde der Kunst, anonymous, by Wackenroder and Tieck, edited by Tieck (Hamburg: Perthes, 1799); Wackenroder's contributions translated by Schubert as "Fantasies on Art for Friends of Art," in *Confessions and Fantasies*), pp. 161-197;

Phantasien über die Kunst, von einem kunstliebenden Klosterbruder, edited by Tieck (Berlin: Realschulbuchhandlung, 1814);

Werke und Briefe, edited by F. von der Leyen, 2 volumes (Jena: Diederichs, 1910);

Werke und Briefe (Berlin: Schneider, 1938; revised, Heidelberg: Schneider, 1967);

Werke und Briefe, edited by Gerda Heinrich (Munich & Vienna: Hanser, 1984).

OTHER: *Das Kloster Netley: Eine Geschichte aus dem Mittelalter*, translated anonymously by Wackenroder (Berlin & Leipzig: Nicolai, 1796).

Wilhelm Heinrich Wackenroder is little known in literary history. He died too young to make a name for himself, and his achievements were often attributed to his friend Ludwig Tieck, who edited his writings and propagated his ideas.

But Wackenroder's work marks the beginning of German Romanticism, its liberation from the restrictions of Enlightenment, and its transformation of related elements originating in Sentimentalism. Major tendencies and motives of the Romantic movement–the rediscovery of medieval and Renaissance art, the inclination toward the colorful religiosity of Catholicism, the yearning for a golden age, and the attempt to rejuvenate reality through the arts–appear as early as 1796 in a work Wackenroder coauthored with Tieck, *Herzensergießungen eines kunstliebenden Klosterbruders* (translated as "Confessions from the Heart of an Art-Loving Friar," 1971). His most significant contribution consists of a new appreciation of art, and more specifically, the recognition of the effect of art on the soul. This concept had profound reverberations during the Romantic movement and in the nineteenth century, and it continues to exert an influence. Yet the same writer who advocates a new distinction for art was the first to call his own idea into question. Anticipating objections to the aesthetic values of authors who would write three generations later, his ideas provide the basis for a century of discussions about art.

Wackenroder's life and work were influenced by three major factors: his father, his friend Tieck, and his exposure to art and culture in Southern Germany. The author was born in Berlin on 13 July 1773, the only child of Christoph B. Wackenroder and Christiane D. Wackenroder, née Grundmann. His father was a high-ranking official in the Prussian judicial administration and an advocate of Enlightenment

*Marble medallion of Wackenroder by Friedrich Tieck (courtesy of the
Bildarchiv der Österreichischen Nationalbibliothek, Vienna)*

who provided his son with an excellent education through a combination of school and private teachers. Wackenroder studied music with C. F. Fasch and art and aesthetics with Karl Philipp Moritz while attending the renowned Friedrichwerdersche Gymnasium in Berlin, but there was no question that he would have to study law at the university to enter civil service. The young man's love, however, belonged to the world of music, fine arts, and literature. In his schoolmate Tieck he found an ally with whom he could practice or discuss his preferences: reading, acting, writing, playing music. With him he frequented the house of the composer and writer J. F. Reichardt and became part of the modern cultural scene. After their graduation in 1792 Tieck attended universities in Halle and Göttingen while Wackenroder prepared at home for his study of law. Their correspondence during that year is one of the most important documents of a Romantic friendship and an invaluable record of the literary and cultural environment of that time.

In 1793 Tieck and Wackenroder spent a semester at the University of Erlangen. They took several trips to the neighboring city of Nurem-

berg, the home of the sixteenth-century artists Albrecht Dürer and Hans Sachs; to Bamberg, an old Catholic center of the baroque period; and to the castle of Pommersfelden with its famous art gallery, where they admired the "Pommersfelder Madonna," considered to be a work by Raphael.

In Berlin Wackenroder had studied old German literature and culture with the literary historian Erduin J. Koch. In Nuremberg, and later in Göttingen and Cassel, he collected bibliographical data and other information for his teacher from libraries and private collections. At the same time his own works started to germinate. Descriptions and impressions of the "Raphael" Madonna, works by Dürer, and a Catholic service in the Bamberg cathedral would be reflected in *Herzensergießungen eines kunstliebenden Klosterbruders* and in *Phantasien über die Kunst, für Freunde der Kunst* (1799; translated as "Fantasies on Art for Friends of Art," 1971). The friends spent the following two semesters in Göttingen, where they listened to the art historian Fiorillo, whose lectures influenced Wackenroder's own reflections on art. After Wackenroder returned to Berlin in 1794 to work as a legal clerk, he condensed his memories and ideas into short essays

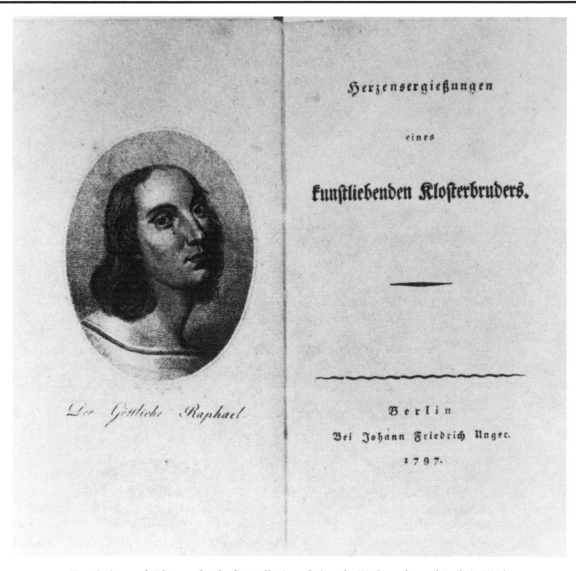

Frontispiece and title page for the first collection of pieces by Wackenroder and Ludwig Tieck

and stories which he showed to Tieck, who was so impressed with these writings that he made attempts in the same style. He added a few pieces and published the whole work as *Herzensergießungen eines kunstliebenden Klosterbruders,* which appeared late in 1796 with the publishing date of 1797. In the subsequent collection, *Phantasien über die Kunst, für Freunde der Kunst,* which appeared after Wackenroder's death, the majority of contributions are by Tieck.

Herzensergießungen eines kunstliebenden Klosterbruders is a collection of seventeen essays and narratives, two of them in verse, with an introduction in which the Klosterbruder (the fictitious author of the work) professes his enthusiasm for the arts and challenges contemporary art criticism. Sixteen of the essays deal with the fine arts,

with historic or imaginary painters, and with paintings. The centerpiece is "Ehrengedächtnis unsers ehrwürdigen Ahnherrn Albrecht Dürers" (Memorial to our Venerable Ancestor Albrecht Dürer). Other historic names include Leonardo da Vinci, Michelangelo, and particularly Raphael, whose art seems to be the model for the new ideal. Only the final text, "Das merkwürdige musikalische Leben des Tonkünstlers Joseph Berglinger" (The Remarkable Musical Life of the Composer J. B.), discusses music. However, Berglinger's fictitious biography, which tells of a contemporary Romantic artist in all his splendor and misery, is certainly the most important piece in the collection. *Phantasien über die Kunst, für Freunde der Kunst* contains ten pieces on the fine arts (partly involving the same artists as

Herzensergießungen eines kunstliebenden Klosterbruders) and nine on music, which are introduced as the posthumous papers of Joseph Berglinger. A verse allegory, "Der Traum" (The Dream), concludes the book.

In *Herzensergießungen eines kunstliebenden Klosterbruders* only the introduction and two minor pieces are incontestably Tieck's work. Two further contributions, "Brief eines jungen deutschen Malers in Rom an seinen Frend in Nürnberg" (Letter of a Young German Painter in Rome to His Friend in N.) and "Die Bildnisse der Maler" (The Portraits of the Painters), were claimed by Tieck in 1798, but were republished by him as Wackenroder's works in 1814. Most scholars tend to rely on the original testimony, but there is also some evidence for Wackenroder's authorship, and one must consider the possibility that the two friends worked together on these texts. In *Phantasien über die Kunst, für Freunde der Kunst* only two essays of the fine arts section and the first six of the musical texts seem to belong to Wackenroder although the authorship of the sixth musical contribution, "Ein Brief Joseph Berglingers" (A Letter by J. B.), is not undisputed since Tieck's account is, again, contradictory.

What, then, is so innovative about Wackenroder's conception of art? The Klosterbruder is opposed to all professional art criticism. Even his language differs from that of other critics. He eschews technical terminology and uses, instead, a simple naive language. He believes that any cold rational approach to art, all comparing and measuring of artists, is not only wrong but almost a sacrilege: art speaks to the soul, and the great painters are "Kunstheilige" (Saints of Art) who should be revered with love and enthusiasm, with devotion and piety. Particularly Raphael appears as a superior being who is a painter not because of his artistic skill but, rather, on account of divine inspiration.

In the Berglinger story, the young musician despises all mechanical aspects of his art. Music is not an acoustic or aesthetic phenomenon but, rather, a psychological effect which stimulates the fantasies and feelings of the sensitive listener. The composer's main concern is to express his emotions in sounds so that they can be understood by his audience. Music, above all, instrumental music, the symphony, appears as the highest art form because it is the most remote from everyday life and the best suited to arouse feelings. Music and art liberate man from his worldly

plight and serve as a form of religion. It is a religion without doctrine, without rite and dogma, a religion of radical subjectivity, but like a spirit from above, it elevates the soul "zum lichten Himmel" (to heaven) and makes it "reiner und edler" (purer and nobler).

This idea constitutes a radical break with the traditional role of art in society. Berglinger suffers a great deal in his life because, with the highest esteem for his deity in his heart, he must confront first the bourgeois prejudice which condemns art as useless idleness, then the aristocratic practice which belittles art as a casual pastime for insensitive people. The lot of art and the artist in the world stands in sharp contrast to the dignity Wackenroder claims for it.

But the challenge to the divine character of art comes not only from superficial and unreceptive worldliness, as in most Romantic works, but also from problems intrinsic in art itself. In his "Ein wunderbares morgenländisches Märchen von einem nackten Heiligen" (Wondrous Oriental Tale of a Naked Saint), Wackenroder has his "holy man," who suffers from a nihilistic dread of the clockwork of time, redeemed by the sound of an ethereal music which transforms him into a lofty genius. On the other hand, Berglinger, who has overcome all obstacles to his youthful desire to become a great composer, who has seemingly reached "die höchste Stufe des Glücks, die er je hatte erwünschen" (the highest level of good fortune to which he had ever been able to aspire), must realize that while pursuing his divine art he has neglected his social and family obligations. His life is torn apart by the two worlds and he cannot survive the extreme tension of this division. In "Ein Brief Joseph Berglingers" it is the artist himself who questions the high opinion of his art when he looks at the active living world of the "andern, bessern Menschen" (the other, better human beings). In his depressed mood, he doubts if his goddess might not be a vain idol and his devotion to her a deceptive superstition.

Thus, Wackenroder's conception of art is a rather complex idea. Art, once emancipated from its traditional role as aristocratic amusement and from its bourgeois denouncement as a useless waste of time, appears as the highest possibility of the human soul and as divine power. There is a direct connection between this concept and the art cult in the nineteenth century, the tradition that is highlighted by the writings of E. T. A. Hoffmann and Arthur Schopenhauer, culminating in the music of Richard Wagner. On the other hand, there are new objections against art as self-gratifying aestheticism that link Wackenroder to the aesthetic criticism of Thomas Mann, Hugo von Hofmannsthal, and Heinrich Mann at the turn of the century.

Wackenroder's inconspicuous and modest writings certainly deserve the fullest attention of literary and cultural historians. It is impossible to know what would have become of him if he had lived longer: whether he would have concentrated on poetry, on music, on aesthetic criticism, or on philology. His untimely death of a "Nervenfieber" (nervous fever) in Berlin on 13 February 1798–Tieck once said that he died because of fear of his law exams–abruptly ended one of the most promising aesthetic careers of his period.

Bibliography:
Martin Bollacher, *Wackenroder und die Kunstauffassung der frühen Romantik* (Darmstadt: Wissenschaftliche Buchgesellschaft, 1983), pp. 141-152.

References:
Richard Alewyn, "Wackenroders Anteil," *Germanic Review*, 19 (1944): 48-58;
Richard Benz, Introduction to Wackenroder and Ludwig Tieck's *Herzensergießungen eines kunstliebenden Klosterbruders* (Stuttgart: Reclam, 1979), pp. 127-138;
Martin Bollacher, "Wilhelm Heinrich Wackenroder, *Herzensergießungen eines kunstliebenden Klosterbruders*," in *Romane und Erzählungen der deutschen Romantik. Neue Interpretationen*, edited by Paul M. Lützeler (Stuttgart: Reclam, 1981), pp. 34-57;
Elmar Hertrich, *Joseph Berglinger: Eine Studie zu Wackenroders Musiker-Dichtung* (Berlin: De Gruyter, 1969);
Paul Klussmann, "Andachtsbilder: Wackenroders ästhetische Glaubenserfahrung und die Be-
stimmung des Künstlertums," in *Festschrift für Friedrich Kienecker*, edited by Gerd Michels (Heidelberg: Groos, 1980), pp. 69-95;
Werner Kohlschmidt, "Der junge Tieck und Wackenroder," in *Die deutsche Romantik: Poetik, Formen und Motive*, edited by Hans Steffen (Göttingen: Vandenhoeck & Ruprecht, 1967), pp. 30-44;
Rudolf Köpke, *Ludwig Tieck: Erinnerungen aus dem Leben des Dichters nach dessen mündlichen und schriftlichen Mitteilungen* (Leipzig: Brockhaus, 1855);
Heinz Lippuner, *Wackenroder, Tieck und die bildende Kunst: Grundlegung der Romantischen Aesthetik* (Zurich: Juris, 1965);
Richard Littlejohns, *Wackenroder-Studien: Gesammelte Aufsätze zur Biographie und Rezeption des Romantikers* (Frankfurt am Main & Bern: Lang, 1987);
Wolfgang Nehring, Introduction to Wackenroder and Ludwig Tieck's *Phantasien über die Kunst* (Stuttgart: Reclam, 1983), pp. 142-158;
Roger Paulin, *Ludwig Tieck: A Literary Biography* (Oxford: Clarendon Press, 1985);
Hans Joachim Schrimpf, "W. H. Wackenroder und K. Ph. Moritz: Ein Beitrag zur frühromantischen Selbstkritik," *Zeitschrift für deutsche Philologie*, 83, no. 4 (1964): 385-409;
Friedrich Strack, "Die 'göttliche' Kunst und ihre Sprache: Zum Kunst- und Religionsbegriff bei Wackenroder, Tieck und Novalis," in *Romantik in Deutschland, Ein interdisziplinäres Symposion*, edited by Richard Brinkmann (Stuttgart: Metzler, 1978), pp. 369-391.

Papers:
There is no collection of Wackenroder's posthumous papers. Individual documents (mostly letters and philological notations) can be found in libraries and archives in Düsseldorf; Frankfurt; Göttingen; Hannover; Kiel; Kraków, Poland; Marbach; Munich; Nuremberg; Weimar; and Zürich.

Wilhelm Waiblinger

(21 November 1804-17 January 1830)

E. F. Hoffmann
City University of New York

BOOKS: *Lieder der Griechen* (Stuttgart: Franckh, 1823; reprinted, Tübingen: Schwäbische Verlagsgesellschaft, 1979);

Phaëton: Zwey Theile (Stuttgart: Franckh, 1823; reprinted, Tübingen: Schwäbische Verlagsgesellschaft, 1979);

Vier Erzählungen aus der Geschichte des jetzigen Griechenlands (Ludwigsburg: Nast, 1826, actually 1825);

Drei Tage in der Unterwelt: Ein Schriftchen das Vielen ein Anstoß seyn wird, und besser anonym herauskäme. Mit dem Motto: Nichts für ungut! (Stuttgart: Franckh, 1826);

Blüthen der Muse aus Rom: 1827 (Berlin: Reimer, 1829);

Anna Bullen, Königin von England: Trauerspiel in fünf Aufzügen (Berlin: Reimer, 1829);

Gesammelte Werke: Mit des Dichters Leben. Rechtmäßige Ausgabe letzter Hand, edited by H. von Canitz, 9 volumes (Hamburg: Heubel, 1839-1840; revised, 1842);

Gedichte, edited by Eduard Mörike (Hamburg: Heubel, 1844);

Liebe und Haß: Ungedrucktes Trauerspiel. Nach dem Manuskript, edited by André Fauconnet (Berlin: Behr, 1914; reprinted, Nendeln, Liechtenstein: Kraus, 1968);

Friedrich Hölderlins Leben, Dichtung und Wahnsinn (Hamburg: Ellermann, 1947);

Wandertage des jungen Waiblinger: Unveröffentlichte Landschaftsschilderungen des Dichters, edited and with an introduction by Herbert Meyer (Tübingen: Heckenhauer, 1948);

Die Tagebücher: 1821-1826, edited by Meyer and Erwin Breitmeyer (Stuttgart: Klett, 1956);

Mein flüchtiges Glück: Eine Auswahl, edited by Wolfgang Hartwig (Berlin: Rütten & Loening, 1974);

Werke und Briefe: Textkritische und kommentierte Ausgabe in fünf Bänden, edited by Hans Königer, 6 volumes to date (Stuttgart: Cotta, 1980-1989).

Wilhelm Waiblinger (self-portrait; by permission of the Schiller-Nationalmuseum, Marbach)

OTHER: *Taschenbuch aus Italien und Griechenland auf das Jahr 1829 (1830),* edited and largely written by Waiblinger, 2 volumes (Berlin: Reimer, n.d.)–comprises volume 1, *Rom;* volume 2, *Neapel und Rom.*

Wilhelm Waiblinger is one of the less-known Swabian poets of the early nineteenth century. He began to write and publish early and remained a prolific writer throughout his short life. When he died at age twenty-five he had written lyric and narrative poetry, drama, fiction, criticism, travel reports, and autobiographical accounts; much of his work was done for periodicals. His talent is unquestionable; but his work is of uneven quality, and its reception has ranged from quick dismissal or omission in literary histories to serious scholarly studies and praise for specific achievements. An oversimplified public image as a wild, arrogant, and finally failed genius probably hindered evaluation of his work.

Waiblinger is also noteworthy for his acquaintance with several literary figures. Before he was eighteen he met Gustav Schwab, Friedrich von Matthisson, and Ludwig Uhland; Eduard Mörike was a close friend for a while. Waiblinger sought out Friedrich Hölderlin in Tübingen and repeatedly visited the mentally ill poet. In Italy he met August von Platen. He was evidently able to make contacts quickly; he was, however, unable to maintain friendships for long.

Friedrich Wilhelm Waiblinger was born on 21 November 1804 in Heilbronn, the son of a petty official of limited means. An intense youth, unwilling to accept limits, he soon knew that he had a special gift for writing and desperately sought fame. His first chance at making himself known came when he attended the Obere Gymnasium (upper-level secondary school) in Stuttgart from 1820 to 1822; Schwab was one of his teachers. He met and impressed several of the city's prominent literary and intellectual figures, and his first poem was published when he was barely seventeen. In the course of the following year he finished a five-act tragedy and a two-part novel in letters. At the same time he was presumably preparing himself for the Protestant Theological Seminary in Tübingen, the famous "Stift," where Hölderlin, Friedrich Wilhelm Joseph Schelling, and Georg Wilhelm Friedrich Hegel had studied.

The tragedy, *Liebe und Haß* (Love and Hate), presents, largely in blank verse, the story of an Italian couple who love each other contrary to the will of the girl's father. It ends with the father killing the hero and the daughter committing suicide. The play was not performed and remained unpublished until André Fauconnet's edition of 1914. It provides an example of Waiblinger's early formal talent and his ability to make productive use of his reading–above all Shakespeare, Schiller, and Goethe.

The epistolary novel, *Phaëton* (1823), was written after Waiblinger had first seen the mentally ill Hölderlin and had read his *Hyperion* (1797-1799). It strongly reflects that influence and, to a lesser extent, that of Goethe's *Die Leiden des jungen Werthers* (The Sorrows of Young

Illustration by Joseph Führich for Waiblinger's "Das Märchen von der blauen Grotte"

Werther, 1787). Phaëton, a sculptor and an ardent admirer of classical Greece, falls in love with a girl who turns out to be the daughter of an exiled Greek freedom fighter. After a period of harmony Phaëton has to leave. During his absence he becomes mentally deranged and, soon after, fully insane when his beloved dies. In the early part of the novel the hero largely shows Waiblinger's attitudes and personality; the description of Phaëton's illness, however, is based on Hölderlin's case. Waiblinger probably used papers written by Hölderlin as the basis for passages that exemplify Phaëton's writing in his insane state.

Waiblinger was admitted to the "Stift" in October 1822. He devoted most of his time there to his literary endeavors and was not a good student. During his first few months in Tübingen he wrote a group of eleven poems inspired by the Greek national struggle against Turkey; *Lieder der Griechen* (Songs of the Greeks) came out in January 1823 and became his first published book, for *Phaëton* appeared somewhat later that year. Two more novels that he wrote during his years in Tübingen, "Feodor" and "Lord Lilly," were not published, and their manuscripts are lost. During vacations he made extended journeys, mostly on foot. He visited Switzerland and Northern Italy in the fall of 1823, recording his impressions in many poems, and Venice and Trieste the following year. In 1824 his life was complicated by an intense love affair which he was forced to break off and which involved him in a minor local scandal. He later often mentioned and deplored this unfortunate relationship in his writings. His conduct apparently became quite eccentric; he was warned repeatedly to improve his performance and behavior at school, and in the fall of 1826 he was expelled. But his real aim had not been to become a Protestant pastor or theologian; he wanted to be a famous poet.

His next book, a collection of narrative poems written between 1823 and 1825, titled *Vier Erzählungen aus der Geschichte des jetzigen Griechenlands* (Four Tales from Present-day Greece), appeared in 1825. The poems are mostly about love and its difficulties and tell of heroic men and beautiful women at the mercy of often ruthless Turks. None has a happy ending. While his earlier philhellenic works mainly showed Hölderlin's influence, the impact of Byron becomes evident in this book. In 1825 he wrote another full-length tragedy, *Anna Bullen, Königin von England* (Anne Boleyn, Queen of England); it is reminiscent enough of Schiller's *Maria Stuart* (1801) to invite comparison but falls far short of that model drama. Waiblinger repeatedly tried to have it produced; he published it in 1829 after making some revisions.

During his last year in Tübingen he turned to literary satire, finishing two more manuscripts. *Drei Tage in der Unterwelt* (Three Days in Hades) appeared in July 1826, just a few months after it was written. In it the author visits a literary netherworld, meets departed writers as well as literary creations (including his own *Phaëton*), and voices his opinions about them. Noteworthy is his negative attitude toward what he considers Romanticism. The other satire, the short quasi-novel "Olura," was published in volume 3 of Hans Königer's critical edition of Waiblinger's *Werke und Briefe* (Works and Letters, 1986). Here he makes fun of the Romantic interest in hypnosis by introducing a talking cat as a medium who discusses literature and a talking flea as her friend and former magnetizer. "Olura" also con-

tains references to Waiblinger's ill-fated love affair. The manuscript included a series of thirty poems, "Lieder der Verirrung" (Songs of Aberration), which show how upset he was about the affair at the time; the poems have been published in volume 1 of *Werke und Briefe*.

Although he failed to secure full financial backing from the Stuttgart publisher Cotta for a stay in Italy, Waiblinger left Tübingen in October 1826 and arrived in Rome on 20 November. In 1827 he suffered a period of great poverty but eventually secured work as a free-lance writer and journalist. His reports on people, places, and events in Rome and elsewhere in Italy appeared primarily in the *Abend-Zeitung* in Dresden but also in other publications in Germany. In 1827, in spite of his poverty, he took trips to the Alban and Sabine mountains near Rome; in the following years he went to the Abruzzi, Naples, Pompeii, and Capri, and made a lengthy journey through Sicily in August and September 1829. Unlike better funded and less outgoing tourists he came into close contact with the local people, which makes his generally lively reports especially interesting for the present-day reader. He also used his earlier German experiences as subject matter for journalistic contributions, writing an essay on Hölderlin as well as autobiographical reminiscences from his childhood.

In 1828 and 1829 Waiblinger's financial situation improved when Reimer in Berlin agreed to publish his *Taschenbuch aus Italien und Griechenland* (Pocketbook from Italy and Greece), a kind of literary yearbook. The texts in the two volumes for 1829 and 1830 are, with one exception, Waiblinger's own work. They consist mostly of stories and poems as well as explanations of the plates in the books. In spite of the title, neither volume deals with Greece. The stories he wrote for them combine realistic Italian background descriptions with often rather contrived plots. "Die heilige Woche" (Holy Week) is an account of the events of Holy Week in Rome as experienced by a fictional German hero. "Das Blumenfest" (The Flower Festival), set in Genzano in the Alban mountains, tells of a beautiful sixteenth-century country girl and her various suitors, one of them a prince. It is a rather hackneyed tale of love, intrigue, and abduction, but it also reflects Waiblinger's first-hand knowledge of jealousy and violence in the countryside. The satirical "Die Briten in Rom" (The British in Rome) seems to have been prompted by

Waiblinger's resentment of British tourists who had the money he lacked but lacked his sensitivity. His longest tale, "Francesco Spina," has another unlikely, complex plot, but it also provides good descriptions of Rome and of other places Waiblinger knew well, such as Tivoli. "Das Märchen von der blauen Grotte" (Fairy Tale of the Blue Grotto) uses Capri as the locale for a fairy tale set in the middle ages.

Waiblinger's most serious and ambitious literary effort in Italy was probably his lyric poetry. It is informed by his love for Italy and the Italians and by his lively appreciation of the monuments and reminders of past greatness there. Quite a few of his poems are written in demanding classical meters such as the Sapphic and Alcaic, and his success in handling these meters in German confirms his considerable formal talent. Among his Italian poems are epigrams commenting mostly on past and contemporary literature, art, and artists; some quite biting ones criticize German artists then living in Rome, such as the Nazarenes, and attest to the tensions which had developed between Waiblinger and these compatriots. More than two hundred epigrams are included, together with other poems from his first years in Italy, in the collection *Blüthen der Muse aus Rom: 1827* (Blooms of the Muse from Rome: 1827, 1829); the lyric work of 1828 and 1829 appeared mostly in his own and other literary yearbooks. Some of his most accomplished verse can be found in the cycles from his later trips, such as the "Bilder aus Neapel" (Pictures from Naples) and the "Sizilianische Lieder" (Sicilian Songs), which present observations and reflections in elegiac meter.

Waiblinger's health had not been stable for some time, and he fell seriously ill in Rome in November 1829. He died there on 17 January 1830.

Since his death there have been efforts to make unpublished material available in print and to republish parts of his previously published work. The latter was attempted in the nine-volume *Gesammelte Werke* (Collected Works) edited by H. von Canitz in 1839-1840, but the edition is neither complete nor trustworthy as a textual source. The critical edition begun by Königer in 1980 provides dependable texts and a wealth of information about them and their author, including the history of individual works and data about first printings.

Biography:
Karl Frey, *Wilhelm Waiblinger: Sein Leben und seine Werke* (Aarau: Sauerländer, 1904).

Bibliographies:
Lampros Mygdales, *Wilhelm-Waiblinger-Bibliographie* (Heilbronn: Stadtarchiv Heilbronn, 1976);

Hans Königer, "Zur Waiblinger-Ausgabe der deutschen Schillergesellschaft: Die Überlieferung der Werke und Briefe," *Jahrbuch der deutschen Schillergesellschaft*, 26 (1982): 527-554.

References:
Gerhard Hagenmeyer, *Wilhelm Waiblingers Gedichte aus Italien: Ein Beitrag zur Literaturgeschichte der Restaurationszeit und zur Geschichte der deutschen Italiendichtung* (Berlin: Ebering, 1930; reprinted, Nendeln, Liechtenstein: Kraus, 1967);

Georg Schwarz, "Wilhelm Waiblinger," *Sinn und Form*, 6 (1954): 741-757;

Gerhard Storz, *Schwäbische Romantik: Dichter und Dichterkreise im alten Württemberg* (Stuttgart: Kohlhammer, 1967), pp. 99-120, 122-124;

Lawrence S. Thompson, *Wilhelm Waiblinger in Italy* (Chapel Hill: University of North Carolina Press, 1953).

Papers:
The largest collection of Wilhelm Waiblinger's manuscripts is at the Schiller-Nationalmuseum/ Deutsches Literaturarchiv, Marbach, West Germany.

Friedrich Gottlob Wetzel

(14 September 1779-29 July 1819)

Joachim J. Scholz
Washington College

BOOKS: *Kleon, der letzte Grieche, oder Der Bund der Mainotten* (Zwickau: Schumann, 1802);

Gedichte: Erster Band. Strophen (Leipzig: Märker, 1803);

Die Nachtwachen des Bonaventura, attributed to Wetzel (Penig: Dienemann, 1804 [dated 1805]); translated by Gerald Gillespie as *The Night Watches of Bonaventura* (Austin: University of Texas Press, 1971);

Magischer Spiegel, darin zu schauen die Zukunft Deutschlands und aller umliegenden Lande (N.p., 1806); revised and edited by Kristian Klaus as *Magischer Spiegel; von der Herrlichkeit unseres Reiches edler deutscher Nation* (Leipzig: Kreisel, 1939);

Sieben Briefe des Mannes im Monde an mich (N.p., 1808);

Fischers Reise von Leipzig nach Heidelberg im Herbst 1805 (Görlitz, 1808);

Rhinoceros: Ein lyrisch-didaktisches Gedicht in einem Gesange, anonymous (Nuremberg: Stein, 1810);

Schriftproben: Mythen, Romanzen, lyrische Gedichte, 2 volumes (Bamberg: Kunz, 1814-1818);

Aus dem Kriegs- und Siegesjahre Achtzehnhundert Dreyzehn: Vierzig Lieder nebst Anhang (Altenburg: Brockhaus, 1815);

Prolog zum Großen Magen (Leipzig & Altenburg: Brockhaus, 1815);

Jeanne d'Arc: Trauerspiel in fünf Aufzügen (Leipzig & Altenburg: Brockhaus, 1817);

Hermannfried, letzter König von Thüringen: Trauerspiel in fünf Aufzügen (Berlin: Realschulbuchhandlung, 1818);

Gesammelte Gedichte und Nachlaß, edited by Karl Friedrich Kunz as Z. Funck (Leipzig: Brockhaus, 1838);

Gesammelte Werke, edited by Kurt Riedel, 14 volumes (Dresden: Riedel, 1941-1943).

Were it not for the possibility that Friedrich Gottlob Wetzel might be the author of German Romanticism's most pessimistic vision, *Nachtwachen* (1804; translated as *The Night Watches of Bonaventura*, 1971), his name would no longer occupy even a modest place in the history of German literature. In any case, Wetzel assumed this place only ninety years after his death, when the painstaking detective work of Franz Schultz's *Der Verfasser der Nachtwachen des Bonaventura* (The Author of the Night Watches of Bonaventura, 1909) arrived at the startling conclusion that the almost totally unknown Wetzel had to be the man behind the not uncommon pseudonym "Bonaventura." For over one hundred years *Nachtwachen* was suspected to be an early work of the philosopher Friedrich Wilhelm Joseph von Schelling. An intense search for more plausible alternatives during the first two decades of the twentieth century also suggested Schelling's wife, Caroline Schlegel-Schelling, as well as the famous Romantic writers Clemens Brentano and E. T. A. Hoffmann as possibilities. Only Schultz's thesis of Wetzel's authorship still enjoys broad, if not always enthusiastic, support among scholars. In more recent years such secondary figures as Ernst Eugen Klingemann, Johann B. Erhard, and Jens Baggesen have been introduced into the debate but have not replaced Wetzel as the candidate of consensus.

The second child of an impecunious clothier, Wetzel was born on 14 September 1779 and attended school in his hometown of Bautzen, in eastern Saxony. A modest scholarship allowed him to enroll at the University of Leipzig as a student of medicine. Two years later, he decided to transfer to the University of Jena, where Schelling's new philosophy of nature had begun to exert its influence. Unable to pay the fees for his doctorate, Wetzel was forced to leave Jena in 1803. He then embarked on years of restless wanderings, making a pitiful living by anonymous or pseudonymous writings. It was during these years of his frustrating fight for a place in life and society that according to Schultz, he composed *Nachtwachen*.

The sixteen vigils of *Nachtwachen* contain some of the most rigorous negations of God, world, man, and art ever composed in literature. A first-person narrator uses the recounting of his bizarre life to expose the cruel senselessness of all existence. The fictional autobiography starts at the end, with Bonaventura's present despair, and winds through a thicket of seemingly discontinuous digressions and diatribes to his beginnings, a grotesquely maculate conception by the power of the devil. The once hopeful idealist, having been disabused of all notions of human happiness, becomes a cynical misanthrope who supports himself as a night watchman. In this role, which he pursues with gleeful masochism, Bonaventura explores forms of human despair while making a conscious mockery of the many lies of appeasement by which human beings shield themselves from the brutality of truth: love, religion, art, reason, justice, and the worship of nature. Only the twentieth century has fully grasped the frightening radicality of Bonaventura's phantasmagoria and has decided that *Nachtwachen*, for better or for worse, belongs to its permanent literary canon.

In 1805 Wetzel was finally awarded his doctorate. The following year he married Johanna Heuäcker. Though he gained no firm employment as a physician, his wife's dowry allowed Wetzel to direct his life into less turbulent channels. He published several medical tracts but in the end decided on a career in journalism. The *Dresdner Abendzeitung* and Heinrich von Kleist's *Phöbus* and *Berliner Abendblätter* published his contributions. In 1809 Wetzel moved to Bamberg to become editor of the *Fränkischer Merkur*, a position he held until his untimely death. During all these years there is nothing in Wetzel's literary productivity that can compare to *Nachtwachen*, a fact made more palatable only by the recognition that this is equally true of the more recent competitors for the authorship of the orphaned masterpiece. He comes closest to the mood of *Nachtwachen* in his satires: *Sieben Briefe des Mannes im Monde an mich* (Seven Letters of the Man in the Moon to Me, 1808), *Fischers Reise von Leipzig nach Heidelberg im Herbst 1805* (Fischer's Journey from Leipzig to Heidelberg in the Fall of 1805, 1808), *Rhinoceros* (1810), and *Prolog zum Großen*

Magen (Prologue to The Great Stomach, 1815). These works have never been reprinted and are extremely rare. It is one of the many curiosities surrounding Wetzel's belated fame that no effort has ever been made to assess these forgotten works in the context of Wetzel's greatest, yet also least certain accomplishment.

Biographies:

Karl Friedrich Kunz as Z. Funck, *Erinnerungen aus meinem Leben in biographischen Denksteinen und anderen Mitteilungen*, volume 1 of *Aus dem Leben zweier Dichter: Ernst Theodor Wilhelm Hoffmann's und Friedrich Gottlob Wetzel's* (Leipzig: Brockhaus, 1836);

Hans Trube, *Friedrich Gottlob Wetzels Leben und Werk* (Berlin: Ebering, 1928).

Bibliography:

Franz Schultz, *Der Verfasser des Nachtwachen des Bonaventura* (Berlin: Weidmann, 1909), pp. 222-230.

References:

Richard Brinkmann, "*Nachtwachen von Bonaventura*. Kehrseite der Frühromantik?" in *Die deutsche Romantik*, edited by Hans Steffen (Göttingen: Vandenhoeck and Ruprecht, 1967), pp. 134-158;

Ellis Finger, "Bonaventura through Kreuzgang: *Nachtwachen* as Autobiography," *German Quarterly*, 53 (May 1980): 282-297;

Gerald Gillespie, "Bonaventura's Romantic Agony: Prevision of an Art of Existential Despair," *Modern Language Notes*, 85 (October 1970): 697-726;

Wolfgang Paulsen, "Bonaventura's *Nachtwachen* im literarischen Raum, Sprache und Struktur," *Jahrbuch der deutschen Schillergesellschaft*, 9 (1965): 447-510;

Jeffrey Sammons, *"Die Nachtwachen von Bonaventura." A Structural Interpretation* (The Hague: Mouton, 1965);

Dorothee Sölle-Nipperdey, *Untersuchungen zur Struktur der Nachtwachen von Bonaventura* (Göttingen: Vanderhoeck & Ruprecht, 1959).

Books for Further Reading

Behler, Diana. *The Theory of the Novel in Early German Romanticism*. Berne: Peter Lang, 1978.

Bennett, Edwin K. *A History of the German Novelle*, 2nd edition, revised by H. M. Waidson. Cambridge: Cambridge University Press, 1961.

Blackall, Eric A. *Goethe and the Novel*. Ithaca: Cornell University Press, 1976.

Blackall. *The Novels of the German Romantics*. Ithaca: Cornell University Press, 1983.

Borcherdt, Hans Heinrich. *Der Roman der Goethezeit*. Urach & Stuttgart: Port, 1949.

Closs, August. *Genius of the German Lyric; An Historical Survey of its Formal and Metaphysical Values*, revised & enlarged edition. London: Cresset, 1962.

Cowen, Roy C. *Das deutsche Drama im 19. Jahrhundert*. Stuttgart: Metzler, 1988.

Furst, Lilian R. *Romanticism*, 2nd edition. London: Methuen, 1976.

Hatfield, Henry. *Goethe: A Critical Introduction*. Cambridge: Harvard University Press, 1964.

Hoffmeister, Gerhart. *Deutsche und europäische Romantik*. Stuttgart: Metzler, 1978.

Huch, Ricarda. *Die Romantik*, 5th edition. Tübingen: Wunderlich, 1979.

Hughes, Glyn Tegai. *Romantic German Literature*. London: Arnold, 1979.

Jacobs, Jürgen. *Wilhelm Meister und seine Brüder: Untersuchungen zum deutschen Bildungsroman*. Munich: Fink, 1972.

Kohlschmidt, Werner. *Geschichte der deutschen Literatur von der Romantik bis zum späten Goethe*, volume 3 of *Geschichte der deutschen Literatur von den Anfängen bis zur Gegenwart*. Stuttgart: Reclam, 1974.

Kunz, Josef. *Die deutsche Novelle zwischen Klassik und Romantik*. Berlin: Schmidt, 1966.

Lange, Victor, ed. *Goethe: A Collection of Critical Essays*. Englewood Cliffs, N.J.: Prentice-Hall, 1968.

Lewes, George Henry. *The Life of Goethe*. New York: Ungar, 1965.

MacLeod, Norman. *German Lyric Poetry*. New York: AMS Press, 1971.

Mahoney, Dennis. *Der Roman der Goethezeit (1774-1829)*. Stuttgart: Metzler, 1988.

Menhennet, Alan. *The Romantic Movement*. London: Croom Helm/Totowa, N.J.: Barnes & Noble, 1981.

Paulin, Roger. *The Brief Compass: The Nineteenth-Century German Novelle*. Oxford: Clarendon, 1985.

Prawer, Siegbert. *German Lyric Poetry: A Critical Analysis of Selected Poems from Klopstock to Rilke.* New York: Barnes & Noble, 1952.

Prawer, ed. *The Romantic Period in Germany: Essays by Members of the London University Institute of Germanic Studies.* New York: Schocken, 1970.

Robertson, John George. *A History of German Literature,* 6th edition, edited by Dorothy Reich. Edinburgh & London: Blackwood, 1970.

Selbmann, Rolf. *Der deutsche Bildungsroman.* Stuttgart: Metzler, 1984.

Stahl, Ernest L. and W. E. Yuill, *German Literature of the Eighteenth and Nineteenth Centuries.* New York: Barnes & Noble, 1970.

Storz, Gerhard. *Klassik und Romantik: Eine stilgeschichtliche Darstellung.* Mannheim: Bibliographisches Institut, 1972.

Tismar, Jens. *Kunstmärchen.* Stuttgart: Metzler, 1977.

Tymms, Ralph. *German Romantic Literature.* London: Methuen, 1955.

Wellek, René. *The Romantic Age,* volume 2 of *A History of Modern Criticism 1750-1950.* New Haven: Yale University Press, 1955.

Wiese, Benno von, ed. *Deutsche Dichter der Romantik: Ihr Leben und Werk,* 2nd revised and enlarged edition. Berlin: Schmidt, 1983.

Wiese, ed. *Deutsche Dichter des 19. Jahrhunderts: Ihr Leben und Werk,* 2nd edition. Berlin: Schmidt, 1979.

Wiese, ed. *Das deutsche Drama vom Barock bis zur Gegenwart,* 2 volumes. Düsseldorf: Bagel, 1958.

Wiese, ed. *Die deutsche Lyrik: Form und Geschichte,* 2 volumes. Düsseldorf: Bagel, 1970.

Wiese, ed. *Die deutsche Novelle von Goethe bis Kafka Interpretationen,* 2 volumes. Düsseldorf: Bagel, 1962.

Willoughby, Leonard A. *The Romantic Movement in Germany.* New York: Russell & Russell, 1930.

Contributors

Edward M. Batley ....*University of London Goldsmiths' College*
Jeannine Blackwell ....*University of Kentucky*
Ruth B. Bottigheimer ....*State University of New York at Stoney Brook*
Donald H. Crosby...*University of Connecticut*
Liselotte M. Davis...*Yale University*
Martin Donougho...*University of South Carolina*
Charlotte B. Evans..*Central Michigan University*
John Francis Fetzer ....*University of California, Davis*
Bernd Fischer ....*Ohio State University*
Doris Starr Guilloton ....*New York University*
James Hardin ....*University of South Carolina*
John L. Hibberd...*University of Bristol*
Roland Hoermann ....*University of California, Davis*
Erich P. Hofacker, Jr...*University of Michigan*
E. F. Hoffmann ....*City University of New York*
Robert C. Holub...*University of California, Berkeley*
Lee B. Jennings ....*University of Illinois at Chicago*
Otto W. Johnston ....*University of Florida*
Gerda Jordan...*University of South Carolina*
Edward T. Larkin ....*University of New Hampshire*
Richard Littlejohns...*University of Birmingham*
Mark R. McCulloh...*Davidson College*
James M. McGlathery ....*University of Illinois at Urbana-Champaign*
Andreas Mielke ....*Skidmore College*
Wolfgang Nehring.......................................*University of California, Los Angeles*
William Arctander O'Brien ....*University of California, San Diego*
Klaus Peter.......................................*University of Massachusetts–Amherst*
T. H. Pickett...*University of Alabama*
Helene M. Kastinger Riley..*Clemson University*
Lawrence Ryan ....*University of Massachusetts–Amherst*
Jeffrey L. Sammons ....*Yale University*
Steven Paul Scher..*Dartmouth College*
Jürgen E. Schlunk ....*West Virginia University*
Joachim J. Scholz...*Washington College*
Clinton Shaffer....................................*University of North Carolina at Chapel Hill*
H. M. Waidson...*University of Wales, Swansea*

365

Cumulative Index

Dictionary of Literary Biography, Volumes 1-90
Dictionary of Literary Biography Yearbook, 1980-1988
Dictionary of Literary Biography Documentary Series, Volumes 1-6

Cumulative Index

DLB before number: *Dictionary of Literary Biography,* Volumes 1-90
Y before number: *Dictionary of Literary Biography Yearbook,* 1980-1988
DS before number: *Dictionary of Literary Biography Documentary Series,* Volumes 1-6

A

Cumulative Index

E

Cumulative Index

I

L

P

Y

Z